DATA ANALYTICS AND VISUALIZATION

GAGAN RAJ GUPTA
Associate Professor, Department of Computer Science and Engineering, Indian Institute of Technology (IIT), Bhilai

NARESH KUMAR NAGWANI
Professor, Department of Computer Science and Engineering
National Institute of Technology, Raipur

PHI Learning Private Limited
Delhi-110092
2026

In fond memory of ***Shri Asoke K. Ghosh*** *(October 1942 – February 2024), Founder Chairman and Managing Director of PHI Learning, whose vision endlessly inspires.*

The Legacy Continues....

Published by Pushpita Ghosh, PHI Learning Private Limited, Rimjhim House, 111, Patparganj Industrial Estate, Delhi-110092 and Gopsons Printers Pvt. Ltd., A-14, Sector-60, Noida, Gautambudh Nagar, Noida, Uttar Pradesh-201301.

₹995.00

DATA ANALYTICS AND VISUALIZATION
Gagan Raj Gupta and Naresh Kumar Nagwani

ISBN-978-93-5443-931-5 (Print Book)
ISBN-978-93-5443-934-6 (e-Book)

Contents

Part II
Data Visualization

Part III
Model Building

Case Study 1: Titanic Survival Prediction

Case Study 2: House Price Prediction

Case Study 3: Sentiment Analysis of Airline Review

Part IV
Advanced Data Analysis and Visualization

Preface

Data analysis is a classic subject which forms the basis of scientific theories. In today's world, it has become much easier to collect data, but it is very complex and difficult to understand. The purpose of this book is to introduce students to various algorithms and techniques for data analysis and visualization. The insights obtained from data can help people in diverse areas make effective decisions: healthcare, industry, governments, and science. Real-world data has errors of various types (missing data, incorrect data, etc.). Often, it is incomplete and is hard to clean (e.g., user reviews/ratings, distorted images). Data Visualization is critical to help us engage more diverse audience in the process of analytical thinking.

This book, "**Data Analytics and Visualization**" consists of **21** chapters ranging from basic concepts to various advanced topics. There are four major parts of the book. The first part "**Introduction and Mathematical Foundations**", comprises of 5 chapters. The foundations of mathematical concepts and data analytics is covered in this part. It helps us develop intuition and quantify correlations in the data before we begin to model it. We need to be aware of the assumptions involved in mathematical modelling of data in order to interpret and validate the results.

The second part of the book is, "**Data Visualization**" and there are two chapters in it. Chapter 6 and Chapter 7 of this part deals with the design principles of visualization and visualization of tabular data.

The third part of the book is, "**Model Building**". In this part, there are total 8 chapters. This part deals with the model development in data analysis tasks. Techniques such as, classification models, clustering models, regression, neural networks, recommendation systems are covered in this part of the book. Chapter 15 provides case studies of data analysis for better understanding of various data analysis technologies.

The fourth part of the book is, "**Advanced Data Analysis and Visualization**". In this part, there are 6 chapters dealing with the advanced techniques for data analysis and visualization. Topics such as deep neural networks, time series analysis, graph data, stream data, and natural language processing are covered in this part. Chapter 21 provides special attention to advanced data visualization techniques.

The book is primarily designed for the following groups of peoples:

(a) **Undergraduate and MCA students:** The primary purpose of the book is to provide a comprehensive overview of data science and visualization techniques to the students at the university in the undergraduate courses such as B.Tech., B.Sc. (Computer Science), and BCA, & postgraduate courses like MCA, and M.Sc. (Computer Science).

(b) **Preparation for GATE examination:** GATE (Graduate Aptitude Test in Engineering) examination has started conducting the separate examination in the stream of Data Science and Artificial Intelligence. This stream is consisting of seven subjects, out of which three subjects are covered in this book. The GATE subjects namely, Linear Algebra, Calculus and Optimization, and Machine Learning are covered in various chapters of this book.

(c) **Advanced topics for M.Tech. students:** The book also covers some of the important advanced topics in the domain of data science. Chapter 14 to chapter 20 covers the advanced topics in the domain of data science. The topics covered are Recommender Systems, Time Series Analysis, Deep Neural Networks, Graph Data Mining, Text Data Mining, and Stream Data Mining.

(d) **Skill development in the domain of data science:** The book is also suitable for the professionals working in the domain of data science, and machine learning.

The book covers numerous numerical problems along with the exercises in the different topics in data science. The MCQs are also given topic-wise for the readers wishing to appear in the competitive examinations having data science, and machine learning as one of the components. For most of the topics, real world case studies are also covered for better explanation and practical suitability of the various data science technologies. We hope that the readers will like the content and flow of the book.

Readers can report any mistake or errors at the following email address:

- Dr. Gagan Raj Gupta (gagan@iitbhilai.ac.in)
- Dr. Naresh Kumar Nagwani (nknagwani.cs@nitrr.ac.in)

Wishing all the readers a very happy learning!!!

Dr. Gagan Raj Gupta
Dr. Naresh Kumar Nagwani

Acknowledgments

The content of this book 'Data Analytics and Visualization' is designed and planned by both the authors after conducting a number of meetings and considering their valuable feedback to enhance the coverage and utility of the literature. Both authors have taught the subjects in the domain of *Data Analytics and Data Visualization* in the past many years, and both planned to document their understanding and teaching methodologies in a book format.

Dr. Gupta would like to thank his student, Mr. Naman Agarwal for helping with design of the chapters on data visualization and case studies. His students, Mr. Santosh Singh, Mr. Kartik Pandey and Mr. Vikrant Sahu helped with illustrations and content. Mrs. Arati Gupta helped with proof-reading and creating MCQs of some chapters.

Dr. Nagwani wanted to thank his Ph.D. Scholars Dr. Rama Ranjan Panda, and Dr. Deepak Suresh Asudani for providing feedback and inputs for some of the chapters. Dr. Nagwani would also like to thank Mr. Shani Verma, Mr. Saptarsi Panda, and Mr. Raunak Kumar Nagwani for providing support and contribution towards visual arts related to some chapters. Dr. Nagwani also wanted to thank the students, staffs, and institute management of NIT Raipur for providing all kind of support in writing this book.

Authors also wanted to thank PHI Learning for providing necessary support and facilities to get this book published and reachable to the audience. At last, we also wanted to thank the readers for choosing this book towards learning and developing the skillset in the domain of data science and visualization.

Dr. Gagan Raj Gupta and
Dr. Naresh Kumar Nagwani

Part I

Introduction and Mathematical Foundations

1 Data Science Process

Data science is a broad field that brings together the processes, theories, concepts, tools and technologies that enable us to review, visualize, analyze and extract valuable knowledge and information from raw data. These have been developed in various disciplines and sub-disciplines (Figure 1.1) such as statistics, machine learning, data management, human computer interaction (HCI) and business intelligence systems.

While databases were traditionally used to store structured data and query efficiently, data science tools aim at deriving insights and predictions even from unstructured, noisy and complex datasets. The applications of data science are wide ranging and expanding to include businesses, governance, scientific studies, politics, environment and so on.

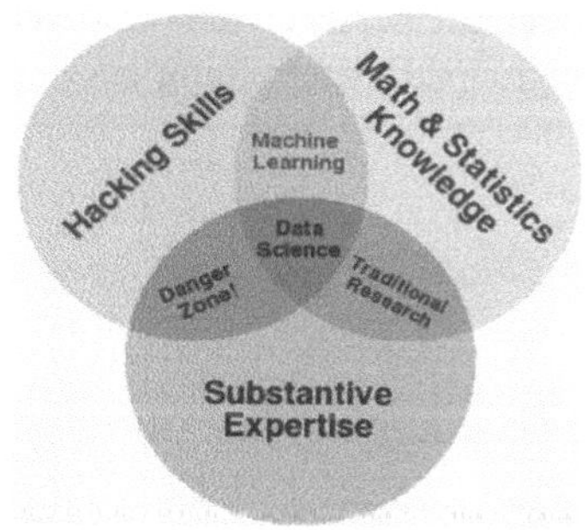

FIGURE 1.1 "Drew Conway's Venn Diagram of Data Science" along with the image source.

Introduction

Data Analysis study is consistent with the scientific discovery process. It begins with an interesting question that we are seeking to answer and the type of analysis we would like to perform. As we know from the history of science, asking the right question involves a lot of ingenuity. We then *gather data* in the form of facts, measurements, transaction histories, images, videos, articles, graphs etc. pertinent to the question. We then *explore* the data by performing descriptive analysis where we compute aggregate measures of data such as its mean, variance etc. We also explore relationships between different variables in our data. At this stage, *visual descriptions* of data are very useful in the form of distribution plots, scatter plots, heatmaps etc. We then attempt to *model* the data to perform various kinds of analysis: predictive, causal, inferential etc. Finally, we *communicate* the findings of the study, report the results, and generate recommendations accompanied with various visualizations.

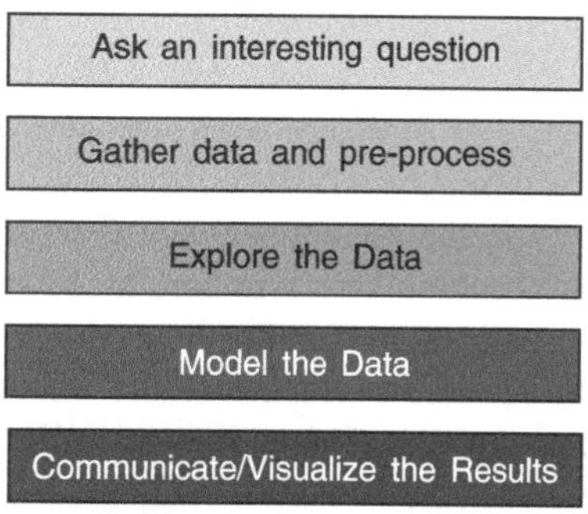

FIGURE 1.2 Data Science Process.

1.1 STAGES OF DATA ANALYSIS PROCESS

In this part, we will dive deeper into each of the stages of data analysis process Figure 1.3. In the first segment of the Part I, we will discuss techniques of data collection, data cleaning, data wrangling[1], normalization and exploration. Nowadays, public and private enterprises and NGOs have an ever-increasing amount of structured and unstructured data from which useful insights can be obtained to improve their efficiency. Data often has errors of various types (invalid types, spelling mistakes, incorrect entries etc.), is incomplete and is hard to clean. For example, consider the case of product ratings and reviews on an e-commerce website like Amazon.com. The review and the rating may be inconsistent, some reviews may even be fake etc. Such errors are hard to correct because we don't have enough information. Similarly, using a clipped image or distorted image, it is difficult to generate the original image. Even though getting data is becoming easier day by day, it is still very complex and difficult for people to understand. Thus, before delving into a detailed modeling study, it is important to do these pre-processing steps.

We have also included some foundational mathematical concepts along with their applications in data analysis. We will learn to view data from a probabilistic or statistical perspective as well as from an algebraic and geometric perspective. In the statistical perspective, we are concerned about the distribution of data which helps us in estimating the probability of various outcomes. The geometric perspective is also very helpful in visualization of data, determining how data is organized or grouped, determining curve fits, decision boundaries, reducing dimensionality etc.

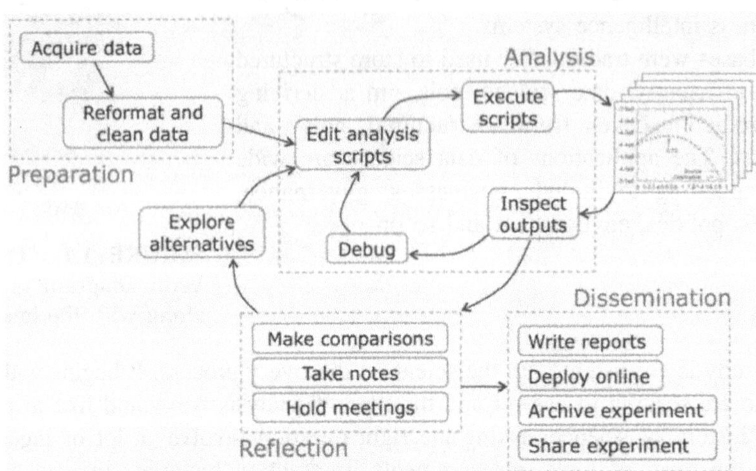

FIGURE 1.3 Data Science Process.

(*Source:* The figure is taken from: https://cacm.acm.org/blogcacm/data-science-workflow-overview-and-challenges/The plot is blurred. [Reference 2]

In the second segment (Part II), we will discuss various techniques of data visualization which are becoming very important. In addition to the standard plots for two-dimensional data, we discuss visualization of multi-dimensional data. Since datasets are often very large and sometimes dynamic in nature, we emphasize the importance of adding interactive visualizations to engage the users in the process of data analysis. Often, there is a need to produce a new type of visualization for a given type of analysis (Figure 1.4) and we provide some examples in the form of case studies.

[1] Data wrangling is the process of combining complex datasets and cleaning them to make them easier to analyze.

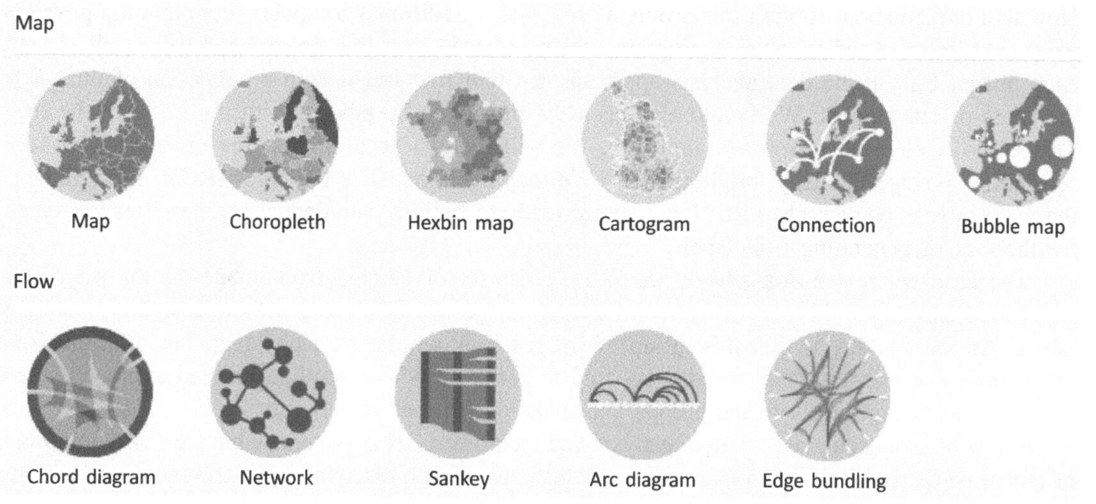

FIGURE 1.4 Visualizations supported in D3.js.

The third segment (Part III) is devoted to building models of various types. The reader might be familiar with the process of curve fitting, where we draw a curve or a line that passes through some points. This is an example of a regression model where the model is simply the equation of the curve. Our aim here is to minimize errors while keeping the model simple. Simple models generalize well to unseen examples. The reason is that the underlying data used to fit the curve itself may have some noise and trying to fit it perfectly will make the model overly complex. This is called overfitting. On the other hand, when the model is too simple, it will make too many mistakes and not be able to capture the pattern in the data. Thus, an optimal model complexity is sought. When the curve is a line, it is referred to as a linear regression model. This can also be generalized to a polynomial regression problem where the output variable is a polynomial in the input variables. Figure 1.5 gives an example of a regression model.

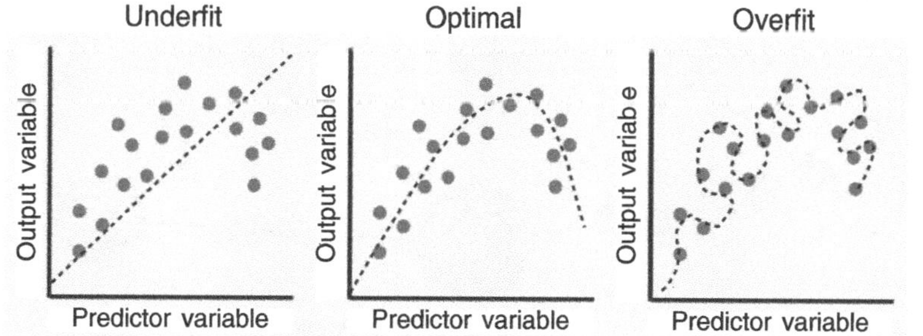

FIGURE 1.5 Curve-fitting data with optimal model: minimize errors while keeping the model simple.

Another familiar model is one which groups or classifies data into different groups by assigning them labels. For example, one may be given a dataset containing images of different fruits and asked to label them. For the sake of simplicity, let us assume that each image contains only a single fruit.

How will one go about solving this problem? If it was a traditional computer programming problem, we would be expected to write a program which is based on some pre-defined rules will classify each image. But, in the data analysis approach, we will first begin with a collection of images of the fruits of our interest. We would also need the images to be labeled with the name of the fruit. This is also called the supervised approach. We will then try to normalize the images to the same resolution, average intensity, brightness etc. We may even visualize the color (RGB) histograms of the pixel intensities of each fruit. Now, we are ready to build a data-dependent classification model for the task of generating fruit labels.

The case where we don't have access to a dataset of labeled fruit images is known as unsupervised learning and here, we can build clusters or groups of images without assigning them any labels. All we can say is that this group of images look similar to each other, but different from other groups of images. This can also be used to come up with a semi-supervised approach where a human can assign labels to the groups and make corrections if necessary.

We will also discuss association analysis and recommendation systems which are very important of e-commerce applications. In association analysis, we aim to discover those commodities or items, which are very likely to be bought together. For example, shampoo and conditioners are likely to be bought together. So, in a physical store, these items may be placed together. In an online shopping website, a customer buying shampoo may be recommended to buy conditioner (possibly with some discount) and vice-versa.

Finally, in the fourth segment we discuss some of the advanced techniques used in data analysis and visualization. In many applications, data may have complex correlations and may be non-i.i.d. (independent and identically distributed). To address these, special techniques are necessary. For example, these datasets may be modeled using graphs. Common examples of these are social networks (Figure 1.6), drug-protein interactions, transportation networks, knowledge graphs etc. Such correlation

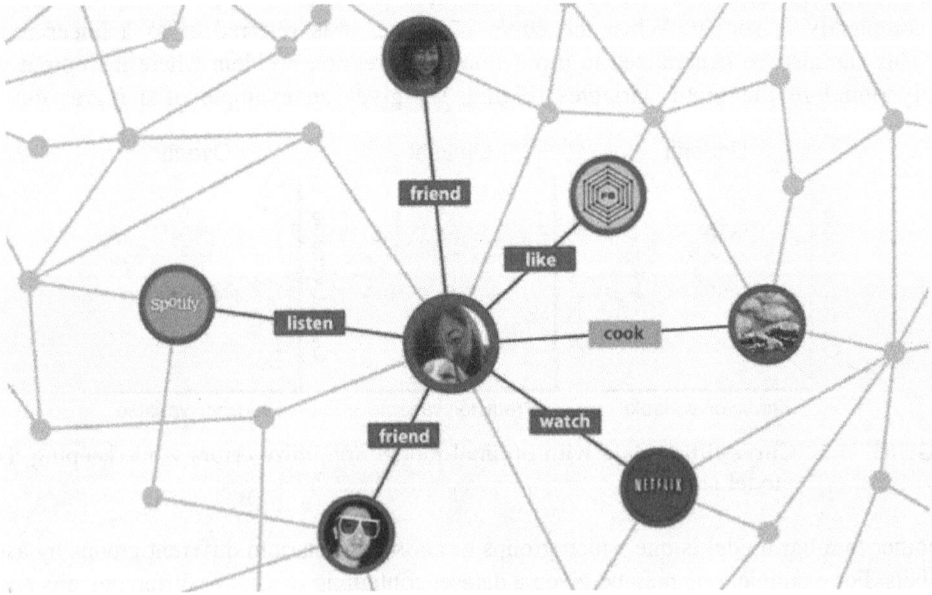

FIGURE 1.6 A social network.

also commonly occurs in time-series data, which is very important in economic data analysis, industrial application, weather forecasting, environmental impact analysis, medical data etc. One of the types of analysis which is important here is anomaly detection where some observation deviates from the general trend.

Another important type of data analysis technique which is gaining importance nowadays is streaming data where data needs to be analyzed within a short time of being generated. For example, companies like Google need to analyze the trends of queries to optimize the results for subsequent queries. An airline company may change its pricing depending on the demand from the users. A power generation company may optimize its processes based on the rapidly changing demands. In some cases, the data volume may be very high, and it may not be possible to store it for a longer time. It is seen only once and processed only once. Yet, it can be used efficiently to make decisions.

1.2 UNDERSTANDING DATA

Let us now discuss the different types of data and develop a deeper understanding of how to model the data itself. A dataset is a collection of data points or objects. Each data object has various attributes or fields. Data could be classified as follows:

(a) **Structured:** In structured data, every data point or object has a well-defined format of fields, their types, valid values, size etc. For example, a table in SQL database or a table in a spreadsheet is structured. In the case of SQL database, the columns of the table need to be pre-defined before the data may be loaded into the table. It is easy to parse the data and looking up a particular field or attribute or column is efficient.

(b) **Unstructured:** In unstructured data, different data points consist of different number of fields and often heterogeneous formats even for the same fields. Thus, it is difficult to search and query. Common examples are emails, blogs, audio clips, video clips, messages and posts from social media. For example, different emails differ in the length of the text, language and characters used, number of attachments, size of attachments, type of files attached etc. On a social media post, one may find images, text, video, tables, emojis. It may be commented upon, liked etc. by various people. These complexities and variations in the structure of each data point make it difficult to store and analyze them using traditional SQL databases. In many cases, one may not even know what to expect in the data before actually collecting and organizing it.

(c) **Semi-structured:** This type of data falls in the middle in terms of complexity, with certain fields being structured and others being unstructured. Several formats such as JSON, XML, Html etc. have been developed to store and organize this type of data. For example, one may have to store the details of all the members of a household as a data object. Clearly, each household may have a variable number of members. Furthermore, certain fields like education and employment history may be highly variable. This can be handled efficiently, for example, by using a nested JSON format.

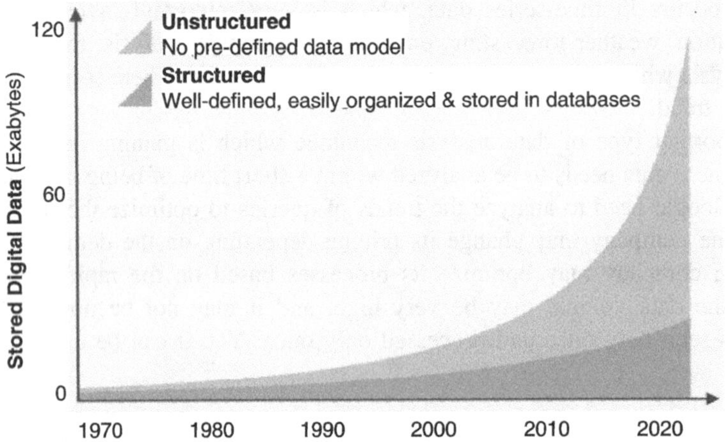

FIGURE 1.7 Growth of unstructured data.

EXAMPLE 1.1: JSON stands for JavaScript Object Notation. Here, each data object is organized as key-value pairs separated by commas. The key is the attribute name. The number of key-values pairs may be different for different objects as shown below. However, it is possible to parse and organize them because the name of attribute is specified.

```
{
"student 1": {"name": "Rishit", "age":20, "city": "Raipur"}
}
{
"student 2": {"name": "Vaibhav", "city": "Ambala"}
}
{
"student 3": {"name": "Madhur", "city": "Surat"}
}
```

Attributes can also be of multiple types. When performing a data analysis study, the type of attributes can play a significant role. This will be essential in collection, storage, organization and subsequent tasks. For example, the age of a person can be modeled as either integer in terms of number of years or number of days since birth. Another approach is to use a floating-point number for age. In some applications, for the sake of simplicity, one may just need to classify the person as an infant, child, youth, middle-aged or old.

(a) **Quantitative:** These attributes have numerical values, like height and weight. They can be incorporated directly into algebraic formulas or displayed in conventional graphs and charts. This is also known as ratio attributes.

(b) **Nominal or Categorical:** These attributes are like labels describing properties of objects, e.g., gender, color, occupation, employee id, aadhaar number etc. A special case is **binary attribute** where only 2 classes 0/1 are present. There is no ordering of classes here.

(c) **Ordinal:** The values of these attributes can be ordered or arranged in an ascending or descending manner. However, mapping to a numerical value may or may not exist. For example, the level of customer satisfaction can be expressed as a star rating. Another example is the grade one gets in a subject.

(d) **Interval:** An attribute takes numerical values such that the difference between values is meaningful, but there is no true zero point.

(e) **Complex:** These are attributes of an unstructured dataset and are represented as Blobs (binary large objects). For example, video clips, audio clips etc. are files encoded in different formats and cannot be understood by opening in a text editor. Parsing and analyzing them requires special software.

The following table summarizes the important attribute types:

Attribute Type	Brief Description	Key Characteristics	Examples
Nominal	Categorical data with no intrinsic order or ranking.	Categories are mutually exclusive, no meaningful order, can only count or classify.	Gender (Male, Female), Marital status (Single, Married)
Ordinal	Categorical data with a meaningful order, but no fixed intervals between values.	Ordered categories, differences between categories are not measurable. Can rank, but not quantify.	Education level (High school, Bachelor's, Master's), Customer satisfaction (Poor, Fair, Good)
Interval	Numeric data with meaningful intervals but no true zero point.	Equal intervals between values, Addition and subtraction are meaningful, Ratios are not meaningful.	Temperature (Celsius, Fahrenheit), Dates (Year 2000, Year 2020), IQ scores
Quantitative (Ratio)	Numeric data with both meaningful intervals and a true zero point.	True zero (zero indicates the absence of the quantity). Can compare differences and ratios. All mathematical operations are meaningful (addition, subtraction, multiplication, division).	Weight, Height, Income, Age, Distance
Binary	Nominal attribute with only two categories (usually 0 and 1).	Two categories, often used to represent presence/absence or true/false. Can be coded as 0/1 or True/False.	Yes/No, Male/Female, Pass/Fail, On/Off

Another type of classification of attributes is based on the number of values the attributes can take:

(a) **Discrete:** These attributes have only a finite or countably infinite set of values. Examples include pin codes, counts, or the set of words in a collection of documents. These are often represented as integer variables. Note that binary attributes are a special case of discrete attributes.

(b) **Continuous:** These attributes have real numbers as attribute values. Examples include temperature, height, or weight. Practically, real values can only be measured and represented using a finite number of digits. Continuous attributes are typically represented as floating-point numbers in a computer.

(c) **Asymmetric:** These attributes have two states where one state is more important than the other. For example, in a medical dataset the presence or absence of a disease. Clearly, the presence of a disease is very significant, even though most people may not have the disease. In a text processing application, one may model the presence or absence of a word in the corpus of documents. In an e-commerce dataset, one may model the presence or absence of an item in customer transactions.

1.3 DATA COLLECTION

The first and most important step in any data analysis study is collection of data itself. "*Data is the new oil.*" In any real-life data analysis project, data has to be collected and curated with great effort. It is a painstaking process that requires great care. The government of India conducts census every 10 years and it is a huge undertaking involving thousands of people to collect the data from a population of more than a billion. The budget allocated to carry it out is more than rupees 37 billion! This gives an estimate of its importance. Government of India has an Open Government Data platform: https://data.gov.in/

There are vast academic datasets containing economic, medical, demographic, historical and scientific data. Their references can be found in research publications in relevant fields.

There are companies that are collecting data about us based on our activity on the phone, internet, websites etc. They use our activities, likes, dislikes, location history and other information about us to send advertisements and promotions to sell products. To do this, they need an identifier for each customer which can be their Gmail id, phone number, device id etc. Using some special techniques (fingerprinting), this may be done even if they don't have access to the above. For example, they can determine information about the device one is using, such as its operating system, its browser, the software installed on the device, time zone of the user, language settings, screen resolution and color depth, browser extensions, and even more granular technical specifications about the graphics card, drivers, and more. But this data would typically be restricted to only the employees of that company. Even then, they may have internal data access polices which restrict the employees for using it only for certain purposes.

Many companies release certain data, typically by rate-limited application program interfaces (APIs). This allows customers and third parties with data that can increase sales. Such datasets are called *secondary datasets* because they contain information that has already been collected, compiled, and published by someone else. So, we must first look for public APIs and above sources before trying to build the dataset ourselves using secondary data for a cost-effective, time and resource saving overview. Next, one must collect *primary data* for validation, gathering specific information, overcoming bias, obtaining up-to-date information and improving overall data quality.

1.3.1 How does One Go about Collecting Data?

As we mentioned before, in most real-life scenarios, one has to collect and curate *primary data*. In some cases, they are pre-formatted as .csv files, text files, pdf files etc. The end of the chapter lists some public data sources. Usually, these can be easily extracted using standard python libraries. We have added some example python code in the GitHub repo accompanying the book. Many times, we get the information we need but only as an image or embedded in a PDF (portable document format) as an image. Instead of trying OCR and cleaning up the values, it might be just easier to manually type them.

One may also scrape data from websites. However, this is more complex and error prone. Text in a natural language has no tags, no delimiters, and no data types, but may be a rich source of information. We may want to know if (and how often) certain words are used in the text (word and sentence tokenization), what kind of text it is (text classification), whether it conveys a positive or negative message (sentiment analysis), who or what is mentioned in the text (entity extraction), and so on. We can read and process a text or two with our own eyes, but massive text analysis calls for automated natural language processing (NLP). A lot of NLP functionality is implemented in the Python module nltk[2] (Natural Language Toolkit). The module is organized around corpora (collections of words and expressions), functions, and algorithms.

You may also have participated in surveys or given your feedback about some service or product. Designing survey questions requires a lot of thought and careful planning. A properly designed survey questionnaire should be clear, concise and interesting. We must think of the analysis we are going to perform after the data collection and design the questions accordingly.

For example, we must give an exhaustive list of options for each question. Rather than forcing some response and making them guess, we must provide options that are as exhaustive as possible. This will ensure the respondent can find an option which best suits his answer. To allow other possible options, we can include an "Other: please specify ________" category as one of the options. When assessing factual knowledge, it is important to include "Don't know" as one of the responses as not all respondents may know the answer to the question.

The order of the questions should be logical, starting with simple questions before moving to more complex questions. We must avoid asking two things in one question. This will lead to difficulty in interpreting the responses when analyzing the data. In questions which solicit opinions, a scale with a range of responses is preferred to a yes/no answer. Likert scale (usually 5-point or 7-point) is a commonly used method.

1.4 DATA ANALYTICS EXAMPLES

Let us now discuss some examples of data analysis studies to illustrate the high-level approach discussed in the previous section. Hopefully, the reader will be able to appreciate that there is a common pattern of steps involved in every data analysis study. Some of these will also serve as running examples that we will discuss repeatedly in the book to explain and illustrate various data analysis approaches. We will also provide a list of example projects that one can carry out to gain experience, skill and confidence.

1.4.1 Predicting Child's Height at Adulthood

As a first example, let us begin with a question of predicting the height of a child when he or she becomes an adult. To answer this question, one would collect several types of data regarding the child. Here the height of the child is an outcome (dependent) variable, that depends on several factors known as predictor variables. Let's jot down some that first come to mind.

(i) H_{mother}: Height of mother
(ii) H_{father}: Height of father
(iii) Indicator variables for gender: $I_{gender} = 1$ if male else -1 if female
(iv) Income: Income of family
(v) BirthPlace: Place of birth.

Among these, i, ii and iv are quantitative, continuous attributes and can be stored as an integer or float type. iii is a binary categorical variable which we have encoded as two integer values. v is also a categorical variable with millions of possible values. We could reduce it to only the countries in the world or specific geographical regions.

How do we collect all this information? Suppose we choose to survey a group of people; it is important to determine which questions we should ask them. We also need to specify units, for example, of height in inches or cm. We need to have some checks to ensure that the answers are

[2] https://www.nltk.org/

valid. For example, height can't be negative and will also be in a certain range. We don't know of anyone in recent history who is taller than 120 inches. Now, at first, we may not know exactly which of these are more important than others. What can we do if someone doesn't know the exact values of the height of their parents?

Once we have collected this data, we would explore the data for any missing values, invalid entries etc. We would also do distribution plots for the various predictor variables. Then, we will build correlation metrics etc. and identify which variables should be used in building the model. For example, the income of the family and place of birth may not be correlated with height.

We now need to have data from adults whose height is known and attempt to build a model (function) which estimates the height from other predictor variables. This model (function) can then be used to predict the value of height of children when other predictor variables are known.

An example of such model may look like:

$$H_{\text{child}} = \frac{H_{\text{father}} + H_{\text{mother}} + 5I_{\text{gender}}}{2}$$

where the heights are in inches.

The above model is an example of linear regression where the outcome variable H_{child} is continuous and is linear in the predictor variables (H_{father}, H_{mother}, I_{gender}). Notice that some of the potential predictor variables were not used in the model. This simple model may not be perfect in predicting the heights as in some cases children may be much taller than their parents or vice-versa.

1.4.2 Screening Loan Applications

Assume that a bank has thousands of applications for loan every year and it wants to have an automated way to screen loan applications. A loan application will be forwarded to the loan officer only if it satisfies certain criterion. How can we come up with the criterion? Note that the prediction would be binary {Yes, No}. Such type of models where the outcome variable takes discrete values are called classification models.

Let us try to think which type of predictor variables we could use to do perform this task:

(i) Age
(ii) Job
(iii) Marital Status
(iv) Education
(v) Balance
(vi) Category of Loan
(vii) Defaulted on a loan before?

Try to think, what is the type of each of these attributes and how you would represent them efficiently. How can the bank collect this data? Can we trust the answer provided by the customer applying for the loan? Can we also write a formula to make the prediction?

We will consider the answers to these questions and the techniques to build classification models in Chapter 10.

1.4.3 Identifying Groups and Faces in Image Datasets

With the growth of internet, digital cameras, mobile phones, etc. there is a huge increase in the amount of number of images that are publically available. Even a single household may have a collection of thousands of photos that they have taken from different cameras and devices. Can we organize these photos by grouping them? Can we identify faces in the images automatically? Can we search for images where a particular friend of ours is present and make a collage for his or her birthday?

Each one of us has a lot of personal data and can apply machine learning algorithms to solve our own problems.

EXERCISES

1. Study the price of smartphones using e-commerce product catalogs and write down some important predictor variables which determine their prices. Build your own dataset and a simple model to do so.
2. You have applied for a job at a company, and you got an offer with salary and other details. How can you make a decision to accept it or not? Think of important predictor variables (such as skill set, education, experience) which might help you in estimating the right salary and benefits. You can look for internet resources or conduct a survey to build your dataset.
3. Investigate how to build a project to predict the next word that someone is going to type on their mobile keyboard based on their past history?
4. Collect data about an environmental problem in your neighborhood/area. Use it to bring awareness to people and take some positive steps in correcting them.
5. Collect data about prices of gold historically and plot its trends. What is the right time of the year to buy gold? Why?

MULTIPLE CHOICE QUESTIONS

1. Which of the following datasets is an example of structured data?
   (a) Messages sent on WhatsApp
   (b) A table in a relational database like Oracle DB
   (c) Blog posts on a travel website
   (d) Audio files.
2. Which of the following statement is true about unstructured data?
   (a) It is always organized into rows and columns.
   (b) It is easily searchable using relational database tools.
   (c) It can only be stored in relational databases.
   (d) It includes data like emails, videos, and social media posts.
3. Why is data formatting important in the data science process?
   (a) To ensure that the data is consistent and ready for analysis
   (b) To visualize datasets effectively
   (c) To reduce the size of datasets
   (d) To make data collection process easier.
4. Which of the following file formats is commonly used for storing structured data?
   (a) JSON (b) CSV
   (c) MP4 (d) PDF.
5. Which of the following is NOT a common task during data cleaning?
   (a) Removing duplicate entries
   (b) Filling in missing values
   (c) Correcting data types
   (d) Forecasting using data trends and patterns.

6. Which of the following is an effective method for handling missing data?
   (a) Ignoring missing data
   (b) Removing all rows with missing values
   (c) Using mean or median imputation
   (d) Adding new random values.
7. Which of the following is an example of a categorical attribute?
   (a) Age of a person
   (b) Salary in rupees
   (c) Hair color
   (d) Temperature in Fahrenheit.
8. An attribute takes numerical values and the difference between values is meaningful, but there is no true zero point. What is its type?
   (a) Nominal (b) Ordinal
   (c) Interval (d) Quantitative.
9. Which of the following is a method for collecting primary data?
   (a) Purchasing data from third-party companies
   (b) Conducting surveys and asking people to respond to questionnaires
   (c) Using data from public databases
   (d) Web scraping from government websites.
10. Which of the following is an example of a secondary data source?
   (a) A company's internal sales data
   (b) Logs of customer behaviors (purchases, returns, reviews, feedback etc.) in a store
   (c) Conducting customer interviews
   (d) A government census dataset.
11. In the JSON format, which of the following is TRUE about the structure?
   (a) JSON format can directly include functions as data types.
   (b) JSON format only supports string data types.
   (c) JSON format supports key-value pairs, where keys are strings and values can be of different types.
   (d) JSON format cannot be nested, i.e., it doesn't support objects within objects.
12. Which of the following is NOT a valid JSON format?
   (a) {name: "Alice", age: 25}
   (b) {"name": "Alice", "age": 25}
   (c) {"employees": ["John", "Doe", "Smith"]}
   (d) {"isActive": true, "grades": null}.
13. Given the following JSON structure, which of the following Python snippets would correctly extract the value of "city"?

```
{
  "person": {
    "name": "John",
    "address": {
      "city": "New York",
      "postalCode": 10001
    }
  }
}
```

   (a) data["address"]["city"]
   (b) data["person"]["address"]["city"]
   (c) data["city"]
   (d) data.get("city").

REFERENCES

[1] Techopedia
[2] CACM: Data Science Process
[3] Link: Fang et al. (2014). From Captions to Visual Concepts and Back. [Online] arXiv: 1411.4952. Available: https://arxiv.org/abs/1411.4952v3 (2015 version).
[4] Visualizations supported in D3.js
[5] https://www.mayoclinic.org/healthy-lifestyle/childrens-health/expert-answers/child-growth/faq-20057990
[6] Khamis HJ, Roche AF, "Predicting adult stature without using skeletal age: the Khamis-Roche method", Pediatrics, 1994
[7] https://www.ncbi.nlm.nih.gov/pmc/articles/PMC4797036/ by Ng Chirk jenn

ANSWER KEY

1. (b) **2.** (d) **3.** (a) **4.** (b) **5.** (d) **6.** (c) **7.** (c) **8.** (c) **9.** (b) **10.** (d)
11. (c) **12.** (a) (Explanation: JSON keys must always be enclosed in double quotes.) **13.** (b)

2 Data Exploration and Wrangling

Introduction

In this chapter, we will learn about some techniques which help us with understanding our data and bringing it to a form such that it can be easily analyzed. We will begin with techniques for exploration of tabular data which is simplest to deal with. We will also discuss the time-series briefly. Details on more complex data types such as images, video, texts and graphs will be considered in Chapters 16–20.

2.1 TABULAR DATA

Tabular data comprises of data organized in the form of tables. The table has multiple rows and columns. Generally, each row corresponds to a different record or data-point or data object. The columns represent different attributes. Each attribute has its own type, as we have already discussed in Chapter 1. We will first focus on some descriptive statistics to summarize numerical attributes and then to summarize categorical attributes. Descriptive statistics provide ways to capture the properties of a given dataset/sample.

2.1.1 Extremes and Middle Value

Perhaps the most important values are the two extremes, maximum and minimum and the middle value. The middle value can be computed as the mean or median. These are also known as measures of central tendency.

$$\text{Mean} = \bar{x} = \frac{\sum_{i=1}^{n} x_i}{n}; \text{ where } x_i \text{ is the value of the attribute } x \text{ in } i^{\text{th}} \text{ row}$$

To obtain the median, we first sort the data (arrange in ascending or descending order) and use the following rule.

$$\text{Median} = \begin{cases} \text{single middle value, if } n \text{ is odd} \\ \text{Mean of two middle values if } n \text{ is even} \end{cases}$$

EXAMPLE 2.1: Suppose we have the data for the heights (in cm) of 20 students in an engineering class as follows: 170, 171, 173, 165, 163, 162, 168, 172, 173, 172, 165, 168, 169, 172, 163, 164, 165, 168, 172, 178. Here, height, is the only attribute given to us.

The max and min for height, *h,* are 178 and 162 cm respectively.

The mean, $\overline{h}$ is 168.65 cm.

As $n = 20$ is even, the median is the mean of two middle values, 168 and 169. So, the median is 168.5 cm. In this data, mean and median are quite close to each other.

Mean is meaningful for symmetric distributions without outliers or extreme values. Even a few or a single extreme value can corrupt the mean. Calculate, what would be the mean height if there was one student in the above example whose height was 20000 cm! We will see that on the other hand, the median works better even when there are outliers or skews in the data distribution.

***Note*:** A related notion of central tendency is the mode or the most frequent value in the data. In the above example, 4 students have a height of 172 cm and hence it is the mode. It is not affected by extreme values. There could be multiple modes in our data. It is commonly used for categorical data where the mean and median can't be computed.

2.1.2 5-Number Summaries

So far, we have 3 numbers to summarize the data. Let us now add two more numbers. For this, we will divide our data into two halves and then compute the 3 numbers again for each half. The first half are the numbers below the median position and second half are the numbers above the median position. This gives two additional numbers which are the medians of the two halves. They are also known as the 25-percentile (first quartile or Q1 or lower hinge) and 75-th percentile (3rd quartile or Q3 or upper hinge) of the data respectively.

EXAMPLE 2.2: Let us illustrate this on the data in Example 2.1 above:

1st half:	162	163	163	164	165	165	165	168	168	168
2nd half:	169	170	171	172	172	172	172	173	173	178

Again, there are 10 values in each half.

The first half is summarized as: Min = 162, Median = 165, Max = 168.

The second half is summarized as: Min= 169, Median = 172, Max = 178.

The five number summary of the entire data is: Min = 162, Hinge 1 = 165, Median = 168.5, Hinge 2 = 172, Max = 178.

2.1.3 Box-and-whisker Plots

The 5-number summary obtained above is represented efficiently in the form of a box-and-whisker plot. The "box" contains the middle portion of data, and the "whiskers" show the spread of data. The lower end of the box is Hinge 1 and the upper end of the box is Hinge 2. The line in the center of the box is the median and the cross mark is the average. The two bars in the extreme are called the whiskers and represent the minimum and maximum. At times, we may want to label interesting points or see how they are distributed. The small circles are the individual measurements.

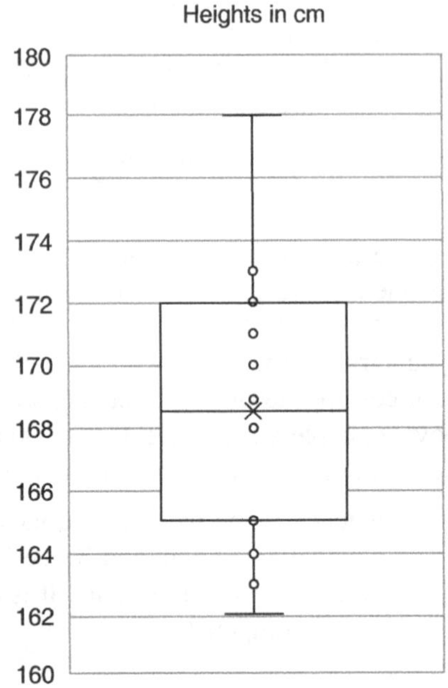

FIGURE 2.1 Box and Whiskers plot of student heights Ex 2.1.

If we obtain a wide box and long whiskers, the data is spread out. If the box is small and the whiskers are short, then the data has a small spread. If the box is small and the whiskers are long, it indicates the presence of "outliers" or extreme values. If the box is big and the whiskers are small, it indicates presence of multiple sub-groups in the data as we will see in the next example.

This is an extremely useful summary of the data. We can prepare the box-and-whisker plot for every attribute in the data and also plot them together.

EXAMPLE 2.3: This example is based on Lord Rayleigh's discovery of Argon, a new gaseous element in 1893–94. Lord Rayleigh was investigating the density of nitrogen from various sources. He had previously found discrepancy between the densities of nitrogen produced by removing the oxygen from air and nitrogen produced by decomposition of a chemical compound. This led him to investigate further the composition of air, chemically freed of oxygen and led to the discovery of Argon.

Figure 2.2 summarizes his measurements in a box-and-whisker plot. Notice that the whiskers are too close to the hinges. This shows that there are two pattens in the data. Some data points are concentrated around the value 2.31 and others are around 2.3. Could this be due to the present of another substance in air? Let's divide the measurements into two groups: those obtained from air and those from other sources. We see a clear distinction as shown in Figure 2.3.

Weight of a standard volume of "nitrogen" obtained from different sources.

Origin	NO	NO	NO	NO	Air	Air	Air	Air
Weight	2.30143	2.29816	2.30182	2.2989	2.31017	2.30986	2.31017	2.3101

Origin	N_2O	N_2O	NH_4NO_2	NH_4NO_2	Air	Air	Air
Weight	2.31001	2.29889	2.2994	2.29849	2.31024	2.3103	2.31028

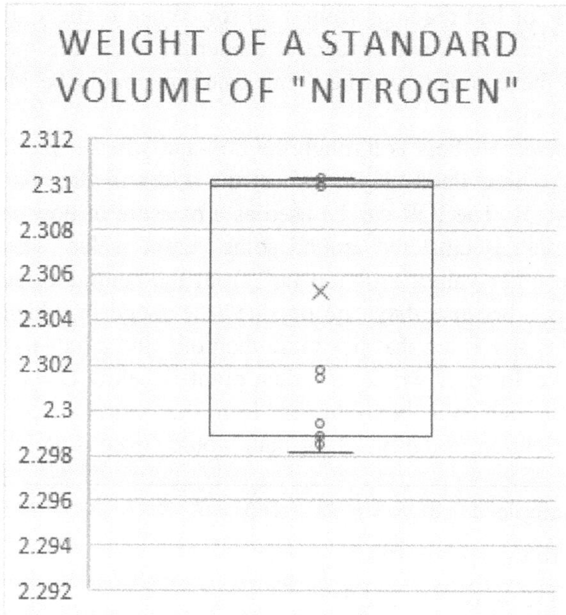

FIGURE 2.2 Box and whiskers plot of entire data in Ex 2.3.

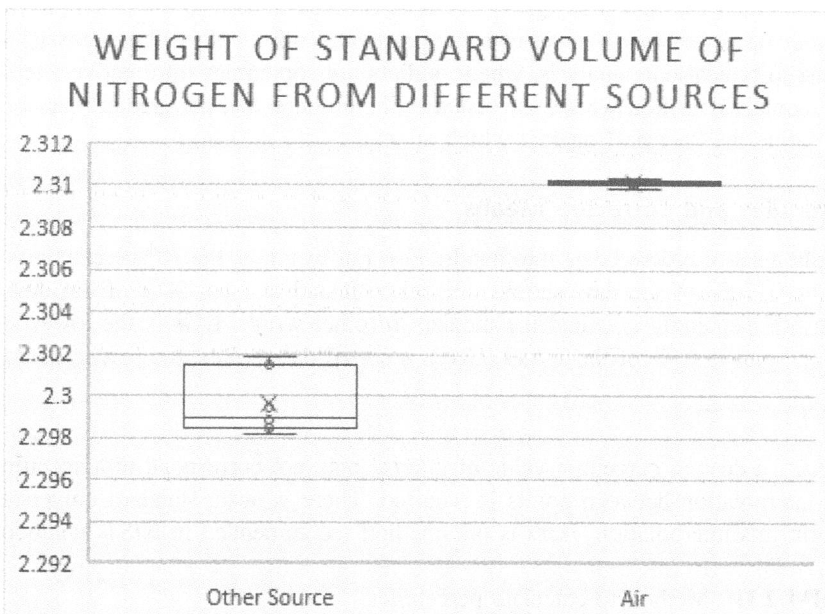

FIGURE 2.3 Box and whiskers plot showing the distribution of data by source

2.1.4 Detecting Outliers and Extremes

Let's move on to detecting outliers and extreme values in data. These require special investigation. Outliers and extremes are often the result of data errors such as mixing data of different units (kilometers versus meters) or bad readings from a sensor. When outliers are the result of bad data, the mean will result in a poor estimate of central tendency, while the median will still be valid. In other cases, they may be completely valid. Thus, outliers should be identified and are usually worthy of further investigation.

One simple way to detect outliers is through the box-and-whisker plot as we mentioned above. The "interquartile range", abbreviated "IQR", is just the width of the box in the box-and-whisker plot. That is, IQR = Q3 – Q1. The IQR can be used as a measure of how spread-out the values are.

In many cases, the data is clustered around some central value. The IQR can also be used to tell when some of the other values are "too far" from the central value. These "too far away" points are called "outliers", because they "lie outside" the range in which we expect them. As a rule of thumb, an outlier is any value that lies more than one and a half times the length of the box from either end of the box. In other words, if a data point is below L = Q1 – 1.5 × IQR or above U = Q3 + 1.5 × IQR, it is viewed as being too far from the central values to be reasonable. For a Normal or Gaussian distribution, roughly 1% of data would be considered outlier.

EXAMPLE 2.4: In example 2.2, IQR = 172 – 165 = 7.

L = Q1 – 1.5 × IQR = 165 – 10.5 = 154.5.

U = Q3 + 1.5 × IQR = 172 + 10.5 = 182.5.

We find that there is no data beyond these limits and hence there is no outlier in the data.

The values which are less than Q1 – 3 × IQR or greater than Q3 + 3 × IQR can be called *extremes*, as they have very low chances of being present even for a Normal or Gaussian distribution.

In contrast to typical data analysis, where outliers are sometimes informative and sometimes a nuisance, in anomaly detection we are interested in the outliers, and the greater mass of data serves primarily to define the "normal" against which anomalies are measured.

2.1.5 Percentiles and Corrected Means

Percentiles split a set of ordered data into hundredths. For example, the 70th percentile is the number such that at most 70% of the data should fall below it and at most 30% of the data should fall above it. The 50th percentile is called the median. In other words, 65% is the lowest score that is greater than or equal to 65% of the scores. Given n sorted data points, the percentile corresponding to the ith point is $\frac{i}{n+1}$.

Many times, a desired percentile value of interest may not correspond to a specific data point. In this case, interpolation between points is required. There is not a standard universally accepted way to perform this interpolation. Here is one method recommended in NIST handbook:

ALGORITHM 2.1: Method to calculate percentiles.

---

1. Arrange n number of data points in ascending order: $x_1, x_2, x_3, ..., x_n$
2. Calculate the rank r for the percentile p you want to find: $r = \frac{p}{100}(n-1)+1$
3. If r is an integer, then the data value at location r, x_r, is the percentile p: $p = x_r$.
4. If r is not an integer, p is interpolated using r_i, the integer part of r, and r_f, the fractional part of r: $p = x_{r_i} + r_f(x_{r_{i+1}} - x_{r_i})$

We discussed earlier how the mean may get corrupted or badly influenced by extreme values. A *trimmed mean* is calculated by dropping a fixed number of sorted values at each end and then taking an average of the remaining values. 5% trimmed mean excludes the 5% largest and 5% smallest values from the sample (other trimmed means are possible: 10%, 20% etc.) The *mid-mean* is computed using data between 25th and 75th percentiles, which is the center of the box in the box-and-whisker plot.

5% trimmed mean: $\overline{x} = \frac{\Sigma_{j_5}^{j_{95}} x_i}{1 + j_{95} - j_5}$; where j_5 and j_{95} are the indices of the 5th and 95th percentile values.

For example, in international diving the highest and lowest scores from five judges are dropped, and the final score is the average of the three remaining judges. This makes it difficult for a single judge to manipulate the score, perhaps to favor his country's contestant. Trimmed means are widely used, and in many cases, are preferable to use instead of the ordinary mean.

EXAMPLE 2.5: For the data in example 2.1

5th percentile is calculated as follows:

1 = 0.05(19) + 1 = 1.95, which is not an integer.

Hence, $p_5 = x_1 + 0.95(x_2 - x_1) = 162 + 0.95 = 162.95$.

Similarly, 95th percentile can be calculated as 173.25.

5% trimmed mean can be calculated as: 168.5.

Mid mean is: 168.8.

2.1.6 Weighted Means

Another type of mean is a weighted mean, which is calculated by multiplying each data value by a weight and dividing the sum by the sum of the weights. The formula for a weighted mean is:

$$\text{Weighted Mean} - \overline{x}_w = \frac{\Sigma_{i=1}^{n} w_i x_i}{\Sigma_{i=1}^{n} w_i}$$

There are two main motivations for using a weighted mean are:

1. Some values are intrinsically more variable than others, and highly variable observations are given a lower weight. For example, if we are taking the average from multiple sensors and one of the sensors is less accurate, then we might down-weight the data from that sensor.
2. The data collected does not equally represent the different groups that we are interested in measuring. For example, because of the way an online experiment was conducted, we may not have a set of data that accurately reflects all groups in the user base. To correct that, we can give a higher weight to the values from the groups that were underrepresented.

2.1.7 Frequency Tables and Histograms

Another important way, we can understand data is by plotting the frequency tables and histograms of each attribute. Suppose the attribute is categorical, for example color. We can count how many data objects are of each color and build a frequency table. For a numerical attribute, if there are many distinct values, we can first divide the range into several contiguous, non-overlapping intervals and count the number of data points in each interval. This is called a histogram. The size of intervals is dependent on the data. Increasing the number of intervals gives us a more detailed understanding of the data. Usually, it suffices to have 10–15 intervals, and we don't want to have more than 100 intervals. We can have very large intervals at the two ends to count the number of extreme values.

EXAMPLE 2.6: The Palmerpenguins dataset contains data for 344 penguins. There are 3 different species of penguins in this dataset, collected from 3 islands in the Palmer Archipelago, Antarctica. It contains the measurements of their bill length, bill depth, flipper (wing) length, body mass, sex and the island in which they were found. Let us explore this dataset using the techniques we have learnt.

FIGURE 2.4 3 species of penguins in Ex 2.6.

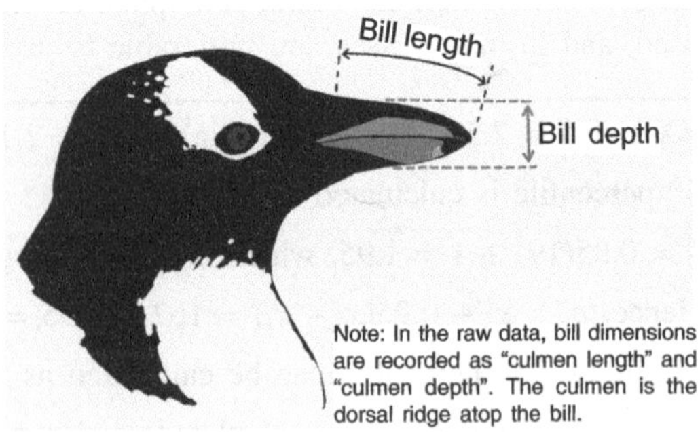

FIGURE 2.5 Explanation of attributes in Ex 2.6.

Here is a sample of the data:

	Species	Island	Bill_length_ mm	Bill_depth_ mm	Flipper_ length_mm	Body_ mass_g	Sex
0	Adelie	Torgersen	39.1	18.7	181.0	3750.0	Male
1	Adelie	Torgersen	39.5	17.4	186.0	3800.0	Female
2	Adelie	Torgersen	40.3	18.0	195.0	3250.0	Female
3	Adelie	Torgersen	Nan	Nan	Nan	Nan	Nan
4	Adelie	Torgersen	36.7	19.3	193.0	3450.0	Female

The name of the species is a categorical variable. We first count the number of penguins in each of the 3 species. In the dataset, Chinstrap penguins are fewest in numbers (around 65) while more than 145 Adelie penguins have been measured. Thus, we have an imbalance. Similarly, we can count the number of penguins of each island.

We now plot the histogram of flipper length (mm). We have made the histogram with 30 bins and can see that the data distribution appears to be bi-modal, i.e., it has 2 peaks (first around 190 mm and another around 215 mm). Could the different species have different sized flippers? Indeed, each of them have a distinct distribution of flipper lengths.

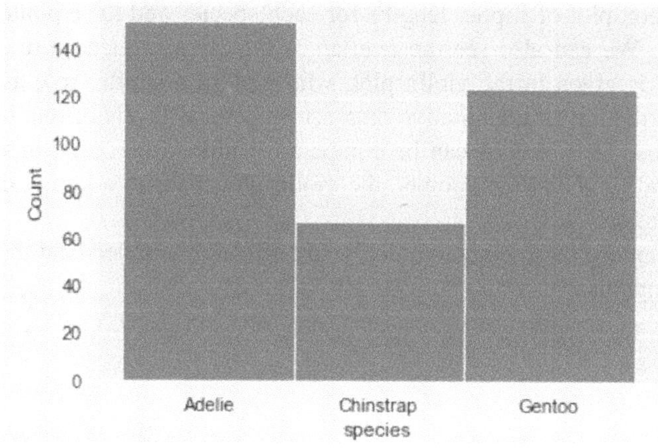

FIGURE 2.6 Frequency table.

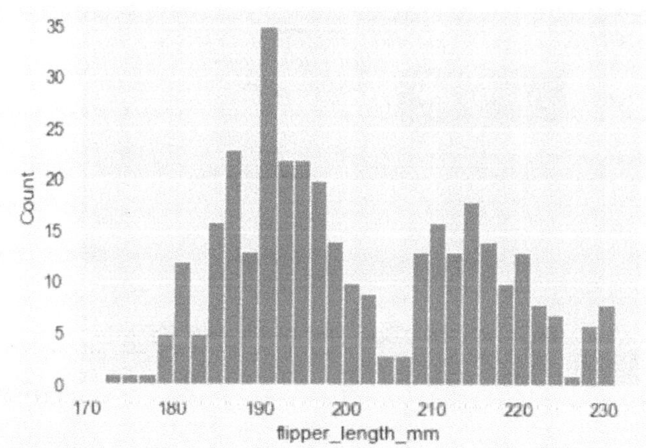

FIGURE 2.7 Histogram of Flipper Length.

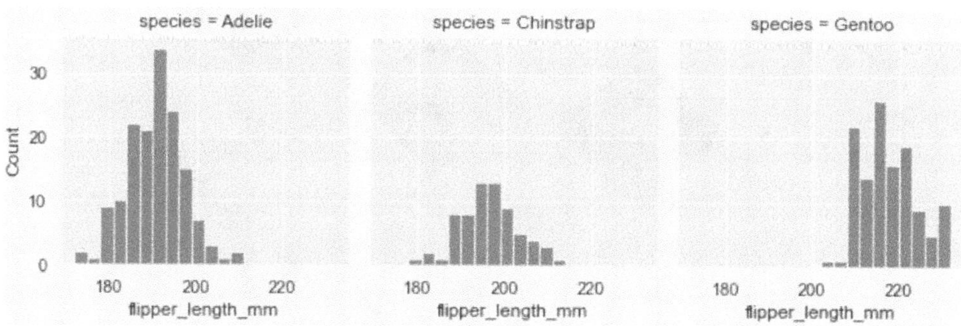

FIGURE 2.8 Histograms of Flipper Lengths by Species

Gentoo penguins have flippers longer than 202 mm while Adelie penguins usually have flippers shorter than 202 mm. Chinstrap penguins are somewhere in the middle. Let us draw a box plots to make another comparison.

Here, we have a box plot of flipper lengths for each species and have plotted them side by side for easier comparison. We can also see the overlap in the ranges much more clearly.

Yet another view is given in the violin plot, which plays a similar role as a box and whisker plot. It shows the distribution of quantitative data across several levels of one (or more) categorical variables such that those distributions can be compared. Unlike a box plot, in which all of the plot components correspond to actual data points, the violin plot features a kernel density estimation of the underlying distribution.

To wrap up, we can use these plots to quickly and effectively understand the difference between various species of penguins.

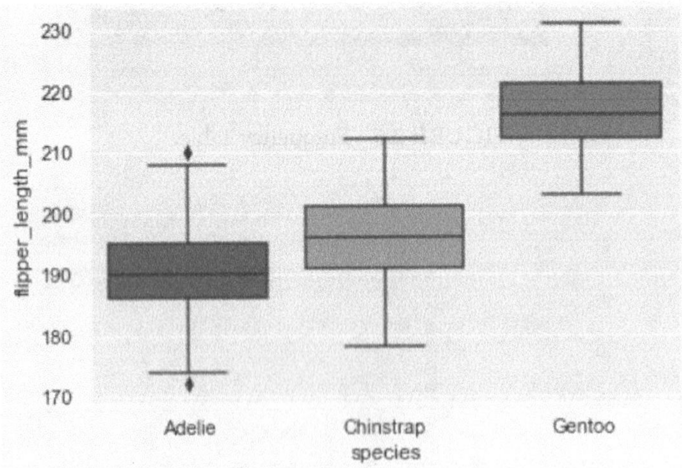

FIGURE 2.9 Box Plot of Flipper Lengths.

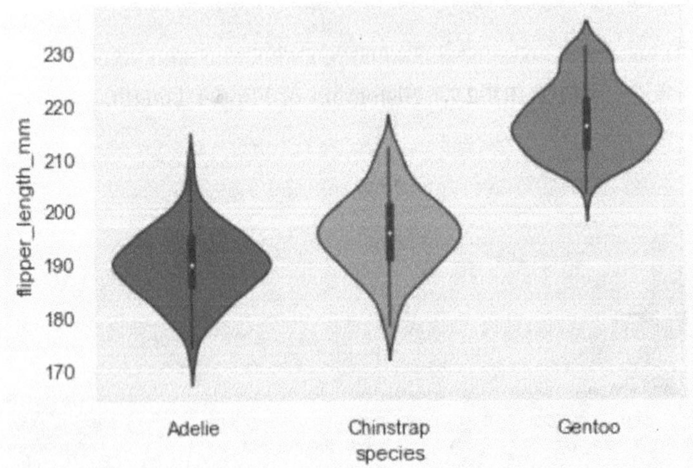

FIGURE 2.10 Violin Plots of Flipper Lengths.

2.1.8 Correlation between Attributes

Correlation helps us to study the relationships between two numerical attributes. In particular, the *Pearson correlation* studies the linear relationship between them. Suppose we are given two attributes (variables) x and y, represented by a set of values (x_i, y_i), for $1 \le i \le n$. We say that x and y are *correlated* when we can estimate the values of y based on the values of x.

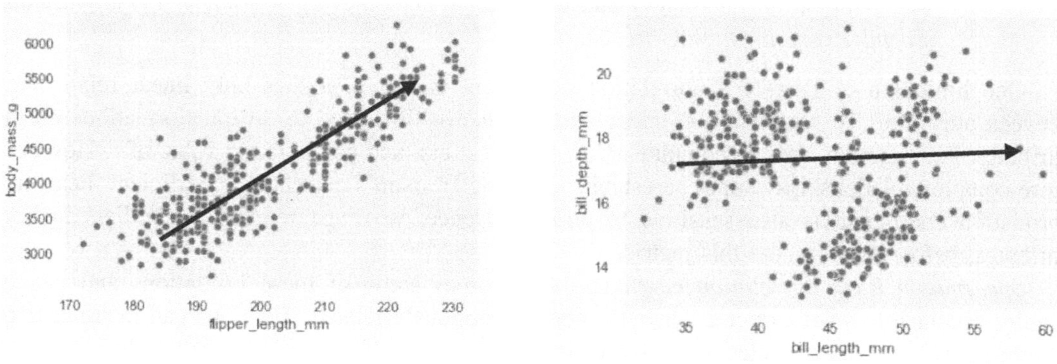

Positive Correlation **No Correlation**

FIGURE 2.11 Scatter Plots to study Correlation between Attributes in the Penguin Dataset.

Value of correlation coefficient varies between -1 to 1. A correlation coefficient close to 1 means that for every positive increase in one variable, there is a positive increase of a fixed proportion in the other. For example, in the Penguin Dataset, the body mass of penguins goes up with their flipper length.

A correlation coefficient close to -1 means that for every increase in one variable, there is a decrease of a fixed proportion in the other. Correlations around 0 are useless for prediction. The two just aren't related. We observe that bill depth and bill length are not correlated in the penguin dataset.

The formula for Pearson correlation is given as:

$$r = \frac{\Sigma_{i=1}^{n}\left(X_i - \overline{X}\right)\left(Y_i - \overline{Y}\right)}{\sqrt{\Sigma_{i=1}^{n}\left(X_i - \overline{X}\right)^2}\sqrt{\Sigma_{i=1}^{n}\left(Y_i - \overline{Y}\right)^2}} = \frac{Cov(X, Y)}{\sigma(X)\sigma(Y)}$$

Here $\overline{X}$ is the mean of X and $\overline{Y}$ is the mean of Y. $\sigma(X)$, $\sigma(Y)$ are the standard deviations of X and Y respectively.

There is another way to compute Pearson correlation called the moments form, which doesn't require the computation of means.

$$r = \frac{n\,\Sigma_{i=1}^{n}\left(X_iY_i\right) - (\Sigma_{i=1}^{n} X_i)\left(\Sigma_{i=1}^{n} Y_i\right)}{\sqrt{n(\Sigma_{i=1}^{n} X_i^2) - (\Sigma_{i=1}^{n} X_i)^2}\sqrt{n(\Sigma_{i=1}^{n} Y_i^2) - (\Sigma_{i=1}^{n} Y_i)^2}}$$

Suppose X and Y have a highly positive correlation. Then if X_i is greater than the mean $\overline{X}$, we would expect that Y_i would also be greater than the mean $\overline{Y}$.

Some example of studies involving correlation are as follows:

(a) Smoking increases the mortality rate. The observed correlation is $r = 0.76$ [Lai et al. Impact of smoking cessation duration on lung cancer mortality: A systematic review and meta-analysis, Critical Reviews in Oncology/Hematology]

(b) Taller people are likely to remain lean. The observed correlation between height and body mass index (BMI) is $r = -0.711$ [Sperrin et al. Body mass index relates weight to height differently in women and older adults: serial cross-sectional surveys in England (1992-2011). J Public Health (Oxf). 2016 Sep;38(3):607-613.]

(c) Violent video games increase aggressive behavior. There is a weak but significant correlation with $r = 0.19$ ["Video Games and Aggressive Thoughts, Feelings, and Behavior in the Laboratory and in Life," Anderson et al. *Journal of Personality and Social Psychology*, Vol. 78, No. 4.]

One limitation of Pearson's correlation coefficient is that it studies only linear relationship between attributes. To establish non-linear correlation, we first need to do transformations on the attributes. For example, we can compute x^2, x^3, $\log(x)$, e^x etc. and compute the value of r. However, more complex relationships cannot be established using Pearson's correlation coefficient. Pearson's correlation coefficient is also sensitive to outliers. Hence, we must remove all outliers in both attributes, before we compute this metric.

Spearman's Rank correlation coefficient, overcomes some of these limitations and can be used to establish to what extent 2 attributes are monotonously related. Thus, we can measure if by increasing x, y is also expected to increase. It doesn't matter if that relationship is linear or not. It is also a number between –1 and +1. This metric is also very useful when we are dealing with ordinal variables, for which we cannot compute *Pearson's correlation coefficient.* It is also not sensitive to outliers.

To compute it, we compute rank(x), the rank position of X_i in sorted order among all X_i. Similarly, rank(Y_i), the rank position of Y_i in sorted order among all Y_i. Spearman's rank correlation metric measures the correlation between the rank(X_i) and rank(Y_i).

It is given as $\rho = 1 - \frac{6\Sigma d_i^2}{n(n^2 - 1)}$; where d_i = rank(X_i) – rank(Y_i)

The next example illustrates correlation between categorical variables. (Ref: https://www.spss-tutorials.com/chi-square-independence-test/).

Assume, we have collected a random sample of data regarding the marital status and level of education of people according to a survey conducted in the US. The observed frequencies are tabulated below.

Marital Status by Education (n = 300 samples)

	Middle school or lower	High school	Bachelor's	Master's	PhD or higher	Total
Never married	18	36	21	9	6	90
Married	12	36	45	36	21	150
Divorced	6	9	9	3	3	30
Widowed	3	9	9	6	3	30
Total	39	90	84	54	33	300

This table shows four categories of marital status: Never married, Married, Divorced and Widowed.

It shows five categories of education. We can calculate the percentage of different marital levels in each education category and obtain the following table.

Marital Status by Education (n = 300 samples)

	Middle school or lower	High school	Bachelor's	Master's	PhD or higher	Total
Never married	46%	40%	25%	17%	18%	30%
Married	31%	40%	54%	67%	64%	50%
Divorced	15%	10%	11%	6%	9%	10%

(Contd.)

	Middle school or lower	High school	Bachelor's	Master's	PhD or higher	Total
Widowed	8%	10%	11%	11%	9%	10%
Total	100%	100%	100%	100%	100%	100%

We observe that more highly educated respondents have a higher chance of being married. This can be shown visually using a stacked bar chart. Clearly, the portion of bars occupied by the category "married" increased with education level and that of "Never married" decreases with education level.

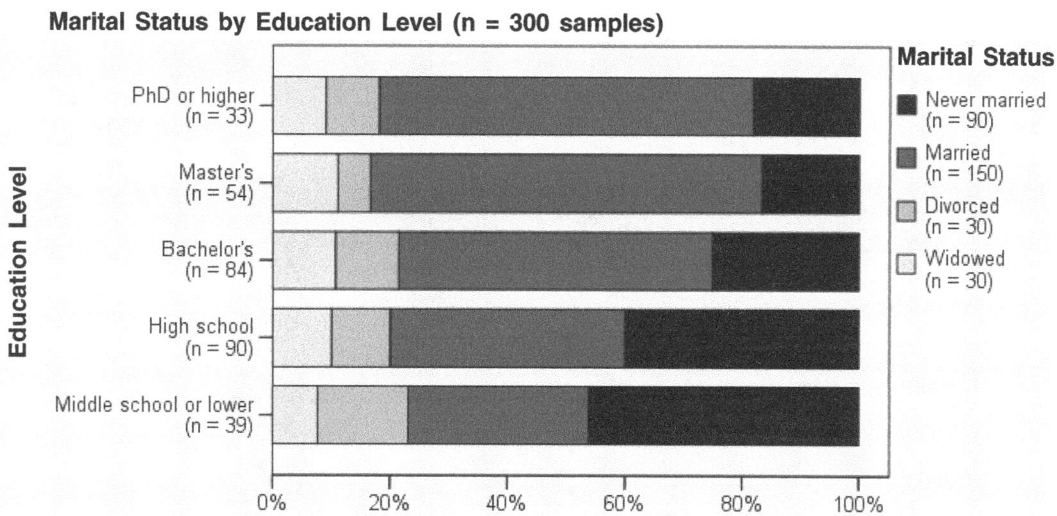

FIGURE 2.12 "Normalized Horizontal Stack bar chart of Marital Status by Education".

The mathematical way to test if two categorical variables are correlated or independent is the *Chi-squared independence test.* We will describe the details of how to perform that test in Chapter 4.

2.1.9 Combining Multiple Views of Data

Often, we need to look at data from different angles to get a better understanding of the distributions and correlations. Pairplot is a very useful tool that combines joint and marginal views of numerical attributes. It visualizes every pairwise combination of variables simultaneously. Here is an example on the Penguins dataset.

On the diagonal, we have the probability distribution functions of each attribute color coded by the species.

If we go through each row, we can observe scatter plots of the particular attribute with remaining numerical attributes. We also find that correlations between the pairs differs by species.

2.2 TIME SERIES DATA

Time series data is any type of information presented as an ordered sequence. It can be defined as a collection of observations for a single subject assembled over different, generally equally spaced, time intervals. Time is the central attribute that distinguishes time series from other types of data.

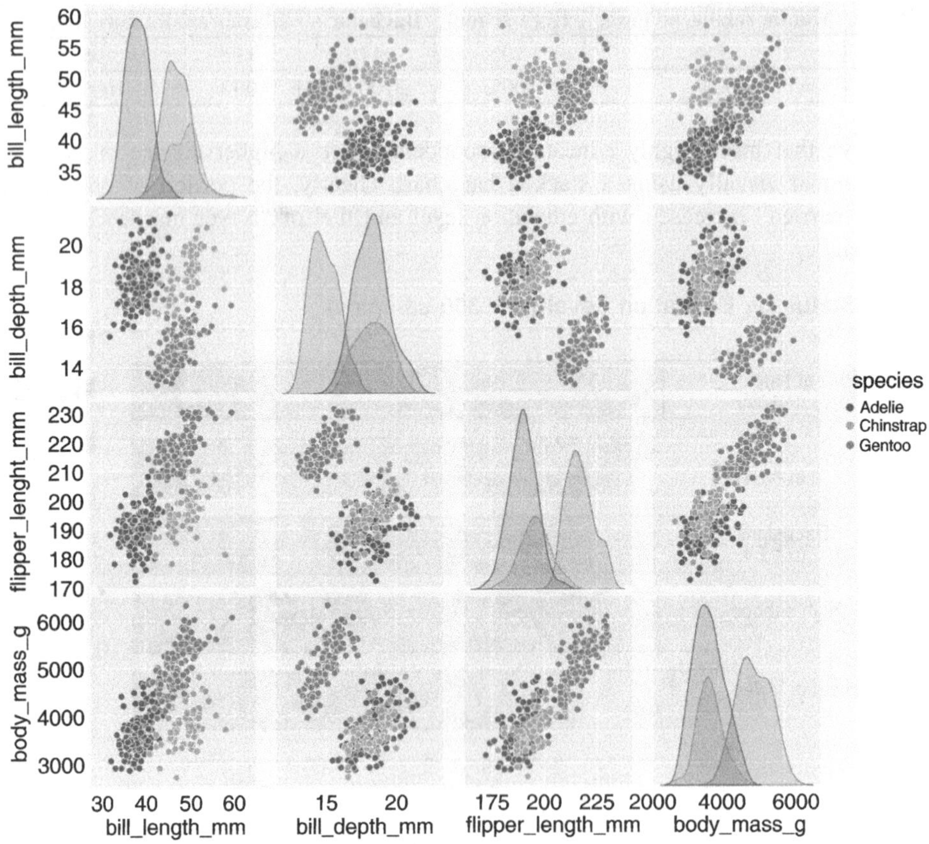

FIGURE 2.13 Pairplot of Penguin Dataset" (*See colour figure at the end of the book*).

The time intervals applied to assemble the collected data in a chronological order are called the time series frequency. So having time as one of the main axes would be the main indicator that a given dataset is a time series.

The three main characteristics that allow us to easily identify such datasets:

(a) Data arrives in time order
(b) Time is a primary axis
(c) Newly collected data is recorded as a new entry

Time series datasets are widely used across various industries, from finance and economics to sciences, healthcare, weather forecasting and engineering. Here are some examples illustrating its use:

(i) **Financial industry:** Majority of financial applications today collect, store and analyze time series data for multiple purposes, such as security, support, improvement of services, and income maximization. Stock market traders use algorithms based on real time data to optimize performance.
(ii) **Consumer electronics:** Smart home systems, for example, have access to multiple kinds of time series data, which they analyze in order to identify humans and animals, adjust temperature, detect intruders, etc. Autonomous vehicles and robotic devices of various kinds also use time series data as an essential component that allows them to move in space and avoid collisions.

(iii) **Industrial companies:** Digitalization of manufacturing, production plants and related industries produces an increasing amount of time series data. This data comes from an increasing number of sensors which are being used. Examples of sensors and data includes pressure, levels, temperature, pH and velocity used as part of industrial automation. Video streams collected from cameras in various industrial applications for process monitoring, surveillance etc.

(iv) **Healthcare:** Heart rate monitoring (ECG) and brain monitoring (EEG) are two crucial procedures that rely on time series data. Time series data helps to save lives by allowing healthcare and government institutions to quickly react upon information regarding epidemics etc. COVID-19 pandemic is one such example where global and local trends and projections were extensively used for planning.

(v) **Retail industry:** Enterprises monitor their supply and delivery chains with previously unseen efficiency. The data about moving of various goods enables retail enterprises to optimize stock/inventory and provide consumers with discounts or services such as same-day delivery.

As we can see above, the most important plot for analyzing time-series data is the line plot. We can plot multiple time series together to draw comparisons. We can also identify trends, periodicity (seasonality), anomalies in data etc., simply by careful study of the plots. In Figure 2.14, even though there are many ups and downs, a clear upward trend is observed indicating that the value of INR is decreasing as compared to USD. In Figure 2.15, we observe a periodic behavior of the EEG signal. An anomaly in time-series data can be an extreme value or a sudden change (increase or decrease) in the value.

FIGURE 2.14 Time series plot of USD to INR rates during Jul 2012 to Jul 2022.

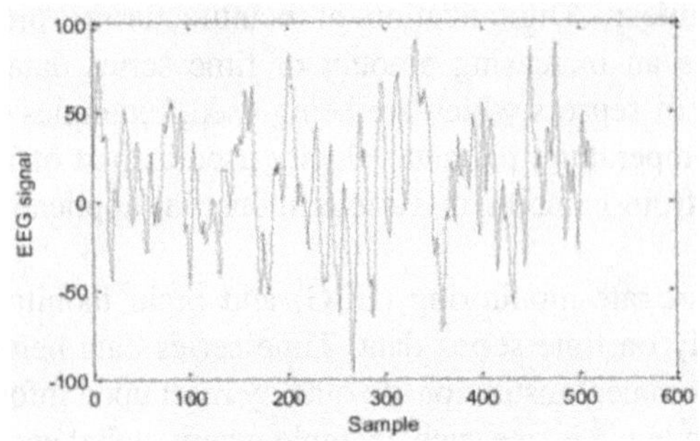

FIGURE 2.15 EEG Plot.

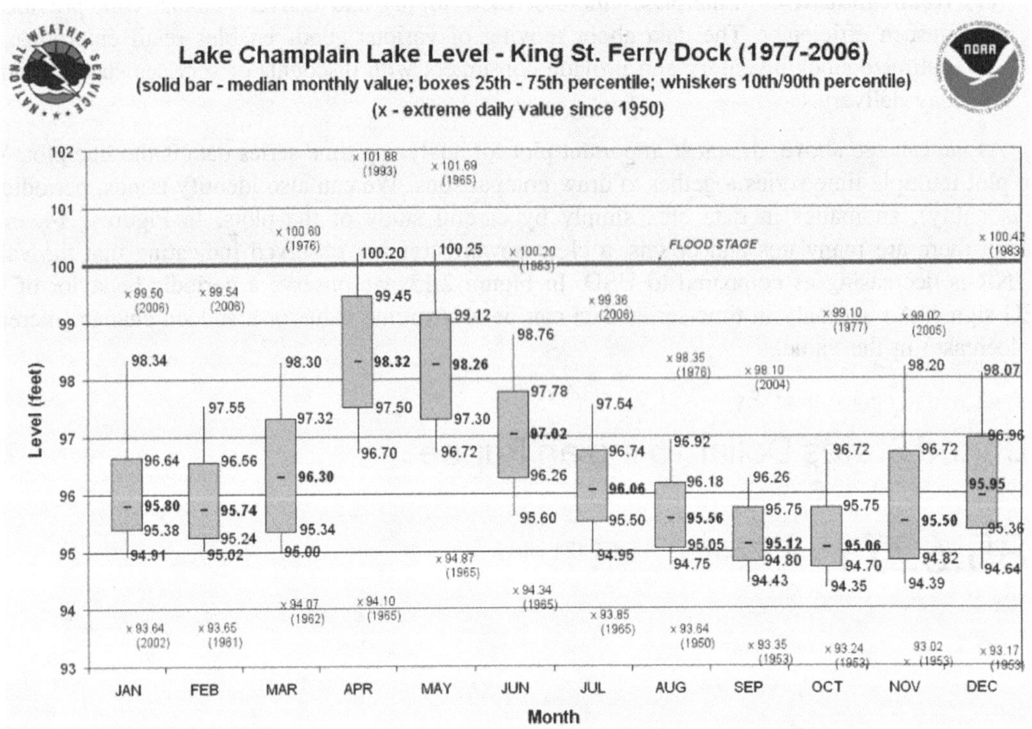

FIGURE 2.16 Box and whisker plot of monthly Lake Champlain Lake Level, based on daily readings at the King Street Ferry Dock in Burlington, Vermont.

An excellent example of the use of Box and Whiskers plot to summarize time-series data is presented by Banacos, Peter Charles [2]. The lake water level measurements (in feet) were collected daily from King St. Ferry Dock in Lake Champlain, USA from 1977 to 2006. This data shows high lake water level (mean) in the months of April and May. This is associated with the "spring melt" in April and May. We also observe large dispersion (the size of the box is larger) in March, April and May which could be associated with the variable timing of the seasonal snow melt, amount of snowpack in the basin, and precipitation.

From April to October, we observe a gradual decrease in lake level occurs throughout the months of summer. The minimum is attained in October and the IQR is also smaller (less variation in the lake water level). A secondary maximum in lake water level is also evident around December which could be associated with more frequent rain in the region and lesser evaporation rates associated with cooler air temperatures.

The Lake Champlain flood stage of 100 feet has been added to the plot. The flood stage has only been exceeded in March, April, May, June, and December (shown with x marks). The highest level of 101.88 feet occurred on a day in April 1993 and the lowest level of 93.02 feet occurred on a day in November 1953.

2.3 DATA CLEANING

"Garbage in Garbage out" is the fundamental principle of data analysis. Our analysis depends heavily on the quality of the data. Bad data can lead to wrong inferences. For example, incorrect measurements of a sensor (such as CO sensor) can be seen as an alarm. Sometimes, a false alarm may be acceptable, but we don't want to miss a catastrophic event such as a poisonous gas leakage. In another instance, a classification model was developed for detecting people who are loan risks using poor data and led to wrong inferences. Some credit-worthy candidates were denied loans, and more loans were given to individuals that default.

Our goal here is to *pre-process* the data before we do data analysis to make sure that *bad data* doesn't affect it. *Bad data* could be due to measurement *errors* or data collection *errors* (omitting an attribute, data object etc.) or both. These errors may be systematic or random. In some cases, such errors can be handled at the time of data entry, e.g., age of a human being can't be negative, neither too large such as 1000 years. We may have also missing values or duplicate data. At other times, we may have *fake data*, especially in websites, blogs, chat messages, tweets, or unmoderated content.

In the case of audio clips, there might be *artifacts* such as a loud fan or a machine. Artifacts can also be introduced by data processing errors, lossy compression, bias etc.

Errors vs. Artifacts

Errors: Information that is lost during acquisition and can never be recovered, e.g., power outage, crashed servers.

Artifacts: Systematic problems that arise from the processing of raw data. These problems can be corrected but we must first discover them.

2.3.1 Detection of Bad Data

The first step is to *detect* such errors or missing data by *visual inspection* or *data exploration.* However, for large datasets, we can't visually inspect all cases at once. We may want to plot or analyze one attribute at a time by studying its range, distribution, invalid values, missing values etc.

Once we have knowledge about the data and build a model, we can also perform *model-based detection* to detect values which are not explained by the model. This helps us identify more complex cases where the values of individual attributes are correct, but their combination is invalid. For example, it is not possible for a person of height 170 cm to have a weight of 3 kg. Humans don't produce very high pitch sounds while speaking English.

2.3.2 Fixing Bad Data

It is important to understand the cause of bad data. Is it an error or an artifact? We must ask the question, how have we collected the data? What could we have done better?

An important aspect of data cleaning is properly representing missing data. We may encounter questions such as the following:

(a) What is the year of death of a living person?
(b) A field is left blank or filled with some very large value.
(c) A small sample shows many events which are too rare to see.

Setting such values to zero is generally wrong, because we won't know whether these values should be interpreted as data or not. If the salary of a person is zero in the data, is he unemployed or he didn't answer that question? Using a *nan* or –1 in that place also doesn't solve the problem because they will lead to problems when we build models using the data. Here are some options to choose from:

(i) **Amputation:** When we have enough training data, we might drop all records with missing values.
(ii) **Imputation:** Often it is better to estimate or impute missing values instead of leaving them blank. There are several forms of imputation:
   (a) *Heuristic based:* We can use domain knowledge to make a reasonable guess for the value of certain fields. For example, one may guess the life span of an average person in India to be 65 years.
   (b) *Mean value imputation:* Using the mean value of a variable doesn't affect the mean. But it doesn't address the situation when there is a systematic reason for missing data. If we are collecting data about the salary of computer engineers in different countries, it may not be correct to impute the values of salary in one country with the mean of salaries across all the countries.
   (c) *Imputation by interpolation:* We can use linear regression to predict missing values well if few fields are missing per record. This method also works well in time series data, where we can impute missing values by interpolating known values of the closest neighbors.
   (d) *Imputation by nearest neighbors:* If the known fields match closely with a data object where all fields are known, we can impute the missing field by using the fields from its nearest neighbors.
   (e) *Random value imputation:* Instead of imputing with a single value, we can choose an estimated value as described above plus a random value. Repeatedly selecting the random values permits statistical evaluation of the impact of imputation. If we compute the model multiple times and get very different results, then there is something wrong with our methodology.

***Note*:** We must maintain both the raw data and the cleaned version. Because there might be multiple ways to fix bad data, we may want to test which approach works the best. It is also a good idea to maintain an additional column for every attribute that we fix, which has a 1 if we have imputed it and a 0 if it is untouched.

Apart from these, we may also need to perform *data de-duplication*. A common example is the names of people. For example, Ajay Rathore can be written as A. Rathore, Ajay Rathore or sometimes misspelled as Ajay Rathour etc. Suppose we are calculating the total income of Ajay Rathore from different sources, we have to sum all the values where his name has been written in any of these ways. What makes it more complex is that there might be many people with the same name or similar names. This is why a unique identifier such as Aadhaar ID or PAN is very useful.

Many times, data is collected from multiple sources and is combined together. It is especially important to review the meaning of each of the fields in any dataset we work with. We must make sure that the units are kept the same. We can stick to one system of measurement, for example the metric system. Thus, we will not mix height in inches with height in cm. In many datasets, the unit is also included in the name of attribute to avoid confusion. When merging records from diverse datasets, it is a good practice to create a "source" field to identify where each record came from.

Time stamps are used to infer relative order of events and group them. Collecting and merging event data from multiple sources requires careful cleaning to ensure meaningful results. Precise synchronization of clocks is in itself a big challenge! Time series alignment is also complex due to nature of business calendar. Financial markets are closed on weekends and holidays. Similar issues arise due to different number of days in a month. There are also many time-zones in which data could have been collected. The best practice therefore is to align all time measurements to Coordinated Universal Time (UTC). A related standard is UNIX time, which measures the number of seconds elapsed since 00:00:00 UTC on Thursday, January 1, 1970. Languages like Python contain extensive libraries to deal with time series in general and financial time series in particular.

2.4 DATA PRE-PROCESSING

Some other forms of data pre-processing involve aggregation, sampling, dimensionality reduction, feature engineering (creation, selection and transformation of attributes). We will describe them briefly now.

1. **Aggregation:** We have already seen how summarization of data helps in data exploration and visualization. Aggregation also helps remove the effects of random noise. It helps in faster processing, less memory consumption and stable behavior of attributes. However, we may lose interesting details and patterns.
2. **Sampling:** It helps us reduce the size of the dataset and speed up the model building process. We can perform random sampling with or without replacement. In stratified sampling, we sample from each representative sub-group. Sampling can also be done progressively. We can start small, measure accuracy of the generated model and increase the sample size, till it stabilizes to desired level.
3. **Dimensionality reduction:** It refers to the reduction in the number of attributes. Typically, we would like to consider only the important and useful attributes while building the model. High dimensionality makes the data very sparse in the space it occupies and makes it very hard to build good models. We can use linear algebra techniques such as PCA and SVD to reduce the dimensionality of data.
4. **Feature engineering:** It refers to the task of creating useful features for building accurate models. In typical images, there are millions of pixels, but do we need to use all of them?

EXERCISES

1. Table 2.1 contains the expenditure made by a company from May 1, 2017 to May 20, 2017. Prepare the 5-number summaries, box-and-whiskers plot and percentiles. Also prepare a histogram. Are there any outliers in this data?

TABLE 2.1 Daily Expenses of a Company

Date	Expense
5/1/2017	1199436
5/2/2017	1045515
5/3/2017	586111
5/4/2017	856601
5/5/2017	793775
5/6/2017	606535

(Contd.)

Date	Expense
5/7/2017	1112763
5/8/2017	1121218
5/9/2017	813844
5/10/2017	903343
5/11/2017	863465
5/12/2017	639224
5/13/2017	1030389
5/14/2017	1132645
5/15/2017	1018672
5/16/2017	1726870
5/17/2017	1378430
5/18/2017	532950
5/19/2017	828238
5/20/2017	823948

2. What types of outliers might be expected to occur in the following data sets:
   (a) GDP of countries
   (b) Production of wheat in every district of India
   (c) Rainfall (in mm) per district in India in the July 2022
3. An oximeter produces a stream of measurements of oxygen levels and pulse rate. Describe a technique you could use to check if the measurements from the oximeter are correct?
4. How do you find outliers in data and what should you do if you find them?
5. Why does data cleaning play an important role in data analysis?
6. During data analysis, how do you treat missing values?
7. What are the pros and cons of imputing a field with its mean?
8. Please complete the following data exploration and cleaning exercises on Kaggle datasets below:
   (a) https://www.kaggle.com/competitions/titanic/data
   (b) https://www.kaggle.com/datasets/borismarjanovic/price-volume-data-for-all-us-stocks-etfs
   (c) https://www.kaggle.com/datasets/berkeleyearth/climate-change-earth-surface-temperature-data
   (d) https://www.kaggle.com/datasets/allen-institute-for-ai/CORD-19-research-challenge
   (e) https://www.kaggle.com/datasets/benhamner/sf-bay-area-bike-share
   (f) https://www.kaggle.com/datasets/ashydv/housing-dataset
   (g) https://www.kaggle.com/competitions/sf-crime
   (h) Lakes water level data
   (i) Weather data

MULTIPLE CHOICE QUESTIONS

1. In a box plot, which of the following is used to represent the spread of the middle 50% of the data?
   (a) The whiskers (b) The median
   (c) The interquartile range (IQR) (d) The outliers.
2. Which of the following statements is TRUE regarding a box plot?
   (a) Outliers are always included within the whiskers.
   (b) The length of the box represents the standard deviation.
   (c) The whiskers extend to the minimum and maximum values of the data.
   (d) The line inside the box represents the median of the data.

3. If the Pearson's correlation coefficient between two attributes is –0.85, what does this imply?
   (a) The two attributes are weakly positively correlated.
   (b) The two attributes are strongly negatively correlated.
   (c) There is no linear relationship between the two attributes.
   (d) The two attributes are perfectly negatively correlated.
4. Which of the following does NOT affect the value of Pearson's correlation coefficient?
   (a) Non-linear relationships between attributes.
   (b) The scale of measurement used for the attributes.
   (c) The presence of outliers.
   (d) The variance of the attributes.
5. Which of the following methods would most effectively identify outliers in a dataset?
   (a) Calculating the standard deviation and finding values that deviate by more than 1.5 units.
   (b) Checking values outside 1st and 3rd quartiles.
   (c) Using the IQR method, where outliers are those values falling 1.5 times the IQR above the 3rd quartile or below the 1st quartile.
   (d) Finding values that lie between the 2nd and 3rd quartiles.
6. Outliers can have a significant effect on certain statistical measures. Which of the following is LEAST affected by the presence of outliers?
   (a) Mean (b) Standard deviation
   (c) Median (d) Correlation coefficient
7. Which of the following is typically NOT considered part of the data wrangling process?
   (a) Merging multiple datasets into a single unified dataset.
   (b) Identifying and handling missing data.
   (c) Building predictive models.
   (d) Removing duplicates in the dataset.
8. During data wrangling, you find a dataset where multiple rows represent the same entity but have slight variations due to human error. What is the BEST technique to resolve this issue?
   (a) Dropping all duplicate rows from the dataset.
   (b) Manually fixing the inconsistencies in each row.
   (c) Using fuzzy matching techniques to merge similar rows.
   (d) Applying log transformations to the data to handle the duplicates.
9. Which of the following statements is TRUE regarding histograms?
   (a) The area of each bar in a histogram represents the frequency of data in that range.
   (b) The width of each bar represents the standard deviation of the data.
   (c) Histograms are suitable for displaying categorical data.
   (d) The height of each bar represents the cumulative frequency of the data.
10. Suppose, there is an attribute with right-skewed distribution and you plot its histogram. What can you expect about the relationship between the mean, median, and mode?
    (a) mean < median.
    (b) The mean, median, and mode will be approximately equal.
    (c) mean > median > mode
    (d) median > mean.
11. In a dataset with many outliers and skewed distributions, which of the following would be the most appropriate way to analyze the relationship between two numeric variables?
    (a) Calculate Pearson's correlation coefficient.
    (b) First, use a log transformation to normalize the data, then calculate Pearson's correlation coefficient.
    (c) Plot a box plot for both variables and calculate the mean difference.
    (d) Ignore the outliers and directly calculate the correlation.
12. In a dataset where the majority of the rows have missing values for a certain attribute, which of the following is the BEST approach for cleaning the data?
    (a) Remove all rows with missing values for that attribute.
    (b) Fill missing values with the mean of the attribute.

(c) Drop the attribute altogether if it's irrelevant for the analysis.
(d) Replace missing values with random numbers.

13. Suppose you have a dataset with highly skewed numerical values. Which data cleaning technique would you most likely apply before building a predictive model?
(a) Normalize the data to have a mean of 0 and standard deviation of 1.
(b) Log-transform the skewed variables.
(c) Replace outliers with the median.
(d) Standardize categorical values into numerical format.

14. Which of the following would be considered a potential danger of data imputation during data cleaning step?
(a) It introduces new missing values.
(b) It increases data variance.
(c) It can distort the underlying distribution of the data.
(d) It slows down the data analysis process.

15. During the data cleaning process, you observe that some categorical features have high cardinality (a large number of unique values). What is a common way to address this issue?
(a) Group the least frequent categories into a single "Other" category.
(b) Replace all unique values with random numbers.
(c) Apply one-hot encoding to convert all categories to binary variables.
(d) Remove all rows where the categorical value appears infrequently.

16. When performing data cleaning, how would you handle inconsistent data entry in a column like "State," where "Chhattisgarh," "CG," and "Chattisgarh" are used interchangeably?
(a) Replace all entries with the mode value.
(b) Standardize the entries to a consistent format (e.g., "CG" for all).
(c) Remove all rows where inconsistent entries are found.
(d) Leave the entries as they are since they represent the same entity.

APPENDIX: DATA SOURCES

https://en.wikipedia.org/wiki/Weighted_median
https://en.wikipedia.org/wiki/Percentile
https://data.world/uscensusbureau/acs-2015-5-e-maritalstatus/
https://www.spss-tutorials.com/chi-square-independence-test/
The data science design manual, Steven S. Skiena, Springer 2017.

REFERENCES

[1] Penguin Dataset: Gorman KB, Williams TD, Fraser WR (2014), Ecological Sexual Dimorphism and Environmental Variability within a Community of Antarctic Penguins (Genus Pygoscelis), PLoS ONE 9(3): e90081. doi:10.1371/journal.pone.0090081
https://github.com/mwaskom/seaborn-data/blob/master/penguins.csv

[2] Lake dataset: Banacos, Peter. (2011), Box and Whisker Plots for Local Climate Datasets: Interpretation and Creation using Excel 2007/2010.

ANSWER KEY

1. (c)	**2.** (d)	**3.** (b)	**4.** (b)	**5.** (c)	**6.** (c)	**7.** (c)	**8.** (c)	**9.** (a)	**10.** (c)
11. (b)	**12.** (c)	**13.** (b)	**14.** (c)	**15.** (a)	**16.** (b)				

Linear Algebra and Applications

Introduction

One of the primary techniques in data analysis is to represent data as vectors in an n-dimensional vector space. This immediately helps us compute similarity and distances between data objects. We can also interpret them geometrically and compute class boundaries, separating hyperplanes etc. It also helps in data summarization and dimensionality reduction. In this Chapter, we will learn to use linear algebra for data analysis applications.

3.1 VECTOR SPACES AND SUBSPACES

We begin with some important definitions. A vector space is a set $\mathcal{V} = (V, +, .)$ with two operations:

Vector addition $+ : V \times V \to V$ and

Scalar multiplication $. : \mathbb{R} \times V \to V$

With regards to addition, V satisfies the properties of

(i) Closure: $\forall\, \boldsymbol{x}, \boldsymbol{y} \in V : \boldsymbol{x} + \boldsymbol{y} \in V$

(ii) Commutativity, $\forall\, \boldsymbol{x}, \boldsymbol{y} \in V : \boldsymbol{x} + \boldsymbol{y} = \boldsymbol{y} + \boldsymbol{x}$

(iii) Associativity, $\forall\, \boldsymbol{x}, \boldsymbol{y}, \boldsymbol{z} \in V : (\boldsymbol{x} + \boldsymbol{y}) + \boldsymbol{z} = \boldsymbol{x} + (\boldsymbol{y} + \boldsymbol{z})$

(iv) Neutral element (zero vector), $\forall\, \boldsymbol{x} \in V : (\boldsymbol{x} + O) = \boldsymbol{x}$

(v) Inverse element (negative of the vector is its inverse with respect to +) $\forall\, \boldsymbol{x} \in V : \boldsymbol{x}^{-1} = -\boldsymbol{x}$

Furthermore, it satisfies the properties of:

Distributivity: $\forall \lambda \in \mathbb{R},\, \boldsymbol{x}, \boldsymbol{y} \in V : \lambda.(\boldsymbol{x} + \boldsymbol{y}) = \lambda.\boldsymbol{x} + \lambda.\boldsymbol{y}$

$\forall \lambda, \beta \in \mathbb{R},\, \boldsymbol{x} \in V : (\lambda + \beta).\boldsymbol{x} = \lambda.\boldsymbol{x} + \beta.\boldsymbol{x}$

Associativity: $\forall \lambda, \beta \in \mathbb{R},\, \boldsymbol{x} \in V : \lambda.(\beta.\boldsymbol{x}) = (\lambda\beta).\,\boldsymbol{x}$

Neutral element with respect to the outer operation: $\forall \boldsymbol{x} \in V : 1.\boldsymbol{x} = \boldsymbol{x}$

Vector subspace: Intuitively, vector subspaces are subsets of the original vector spaces, such that when we perform operations (+, .) on its vectors, the resultant vectors are also contained in the same subset. This is the notion of "Closure". Formally,

Let $\mathcal{V} = (V, +, .)$ be a vector space and $U \subseteq V$ Then $\mathcal{U} = (U, +, .)$ is called a vector subspace of $\mathcal{V}$ if $\mathcal{U}$ is a vector space with vector space operations + and restricted to $U \times U$ and $R \times U$. We write $\mathcal{U} \subseteq \mathcal{V}$ to denote that $\mathcal{U}$ is a subspace of $\mathcal{V}$. For $\mathcal{U}$ to be a subspace of V, we need to ensure:

(a) $U \neq \phi$ in particular $0 \in U$

(b) Closure of U with respect to addition, $\forall \boldsymbol{x}, \boldsymbol{y} \in U : \boldsymbol{x} + \boldsymbol{y} \in \boldsymbol{U}$ and

scalar multiplication, $\forall \boldsymbol{x} \in \boldsymbol{U}, \lambda \in \mathbb{R} : \lambda \boldsymbol{x} \in \boldsymbol{U}$

In Chapter 8, we will learn the application of vector subspaces in dimensionality reduction. Let us look at some examples.

(a) For every vector space V, V and $\{0\}$ are its subspaces.

(b) The solution set of a homogenous system of linear equations $Ax = \mathbf{0}$ with n unknowns $x = \{x_1, ..., x_n\}$ is a subspace of $\mathbb{R}^n$. We will study more about these shortly.

(c) The intersection of arbitrarily many subspaces is a subspace itself.

For datasets where all attributes are numerical, it is straight-forward to represent data objects as vectors. When an attribute is categorical, we can convert the label into a vector encoding, for example, one-hot encoding. Some of the fundamental advances in NLP have become possible by improving the techniques to embed or map words to vectors in n-dimensional space. This has allowed demonstrating word analogies in terms of vector operations.

3.2 VECTORS AND MATRICES

Vector $\boldsymbol{a} = \begin{bmatrix} a_1 & a_2 & \cdots & a_d \end{bmatrix}$ is equivalent to a point in $\mathbb{R}^d$. Generally, we write a vector as a column vector, $\boldsymbol{a} = \begin{pmatrix} a_1 \\ a_2 \\ \cdot \\ \cdot \\ \cdot \\ a_d \end{pmatrix}$. In some cases, we may write the vector as a row.

If we have a collection of n data points, each with d attributes (dimension d), we represent that as a data matrix of dimensions $n \times d$ with a data vector in every row. SQL databases usually store tabular data in this way where each data vector is a record, and columns contain the attributes.

$$\mathbf{A} = \begin{bmatrix} \boldsymbol{a}_1; \boldsymbol{a}_2; \ldots; \boldsymbol{a}_n \end{bmatrix} = \begin{bmatrix} - \boldsymbol{a}_1 - \\ - \boldsymbol{a}_2 - \\ \cdot \\ \cdot \\ \cdot \\ - \boldsymbol{a}_n - \end{bmatrix} = \begin{bmatrix} \boldsymbol{a}_{1,1} & \boldsymbol{a}_{1,2} & \cdots & \boldsymbol{a}_{1,d} \\ \boldsymbol{a}_{2,1} & \boldsymbol{a}_{2,2} & \cdots & \boldsymbol{a}_{2,d} \\ \cdot & \cdot & \cdot & \cdot \\ \boldsymbol{a}_{n,1} & \boldsymbol{a}_{n,2} & \cdots & \boldsymbol{a}_{n,d} \end{bmatrix}$$

Where vector $a_i = \begin{bmatrix} a_{i,1} & a_{i,2} & \cdots & a_{i,d} \end{bmatrix}$ and $a_{i,j}$ is the element in the ith row and j^{th} column. We can write $A \in \mathbb{R}^{n\times d}$ when it is defined on the reals.

3.2.1 Geometry of Vectors and Matrices

We can think of d-dimensional vectors as points in $\mathbb{R}^d$ and the matrix with each of its columns as a point in $\mathbb{R}^d$. The "vector" can be drawn as an arrow from the origin, 0 = (0, 0,..., 0) to that point.

EXAMPLE 3.1: A collection of 3 data points in 2 dimensions can be represented geometrically as follows:

$$\text{Where } A = \begin{bmatrix} 1 & 2 \\ -1 & 2 \\ 2 & 1 \end{bmatrix}$$

A transpose operation reverses the roles of columns and rows.

$$A^T = \begin{bmatrix} | & | & & | \\ a_1 & a_2 & \cdots & a_n \\ | & | & & | \end{bmatrix} = \begin{bmatrix} a_{1,1} & a_{1,2} & \cdots & a_{n,1} \\ a_{1,2} & a_{2,2} & \cdots & a_{n,2} \\ . & . & . & . \\ a_{1,d} & a_{n,2} & \cdots & a_{n,d} \end{bmatrix}$$

In the above form, data is organized as columns.

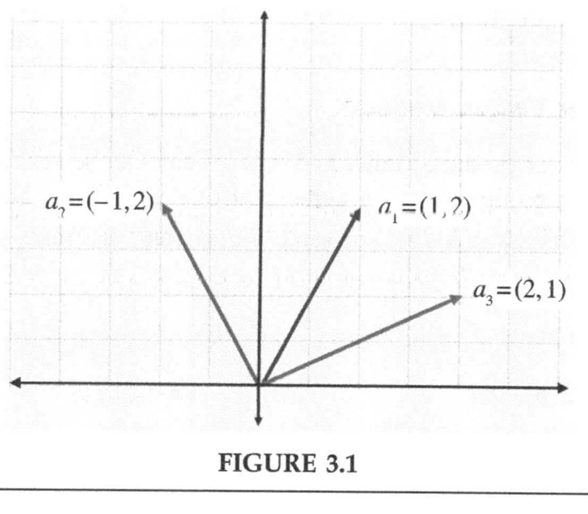

FIGURE 3.1

3.2.2 Representing Ordinal and Categorical Variables in Matrix Format

Matrices can only store numerical data. To represent ordinal and categorical attributes, we need to convert them to a numerical format. If an ordinal attribute takes three values, we can represent each of them as a number. For example, ratings of {*Very Poor, Poor, Average, Good, Excellent*} can be represented as {1, 2, 3, 4, 5}. While this representation preserves the order, it may not accurately reflect whether the difference between *Poor* and *Average* is the same as the difference between *Good* and *Excellent*. These number representations can be chosen according to the needs of your problem.

Categorical attributes can't be represented in the same way as ordinal attributes. For example, it is not meaningful to represent the colors {Green, Red, Blue} as {1,2,3}. Instead, a one-hot-encoding (a type of binary code) is used. For example, Green can be encoded as [1,0,0]; Red as [0,1,0] and Blue as [0,0,1]. In this example, one attribute color is replaced by 3 attributes: color_1, color_2, color_3; each having a 0 or 1.

3.2.3 Matrix Multiplication

Matrix Multiplication requires alignment along one dimension. For two matrices $\boldsymbol{A} \in \mathbb{R}^{n \times d}$ and $\boldsymbol{B} \in \mathbb{R}^{d \times m}$, we can obtain a new matrix $C = AB \in \mathbb{R}^{n \times m}$ where $C_{i,j}$, the element in the ith row and j^{th} column of $\boldsymbol{C}$ is defined as: $C_{i,j} = \Sigma_{k=1}^{d} A_{i,k} B_{k,j}$.

As an example, $c_{3,2}$ is produced by multiplying the 3rd row of $\boldsymbol{A}$ with 2nd column of $\boldsymbol{B}$.

$$\begin{bmatrix} . & . & . \\ . & . & . \\ a_{3,1} & a_{3,2} & a_{3,3} \end{bmatrix} \begin{bmatrix} . & b_{1,2} & . \\ . & b_{2,2} & . \\ . & b_{3,2} & . \end{bmatrix} = \begin{bmatrix} . & . & . \\ . & . & . \\ . & c_{3,2} & . \end{bmatrix}$$

This requires that to multiply $\boldsymbol{A}$ times $\boldsymbol{B}$, we require that the dimension d of each row of $\boldsymbol{A}$ matches with the dimension of each column of $\boldsymbol{B}$. Remember the following rules:

- Matrix multiplication is *associative:* $(\boldsymbol{AB})\boldsymbol{C} = \boldsymbol{A}(\boldsymbol{BC})$
- Matrix multiplication is *distributive:* $(\boldsymbol{A} + \boldsymbol{B})\boldsymbol{C} = \boldsymbol{AC} + \boldsymbol{BC}$
- Matrix multiplication is not *commutative*: $\boldsymbol{AB} \neq \boldsymbol{BA}$

If $n \neq m$ we *cannot* multiply $\boldsymbol{BA}$.

3.2.4 Inner and Outer Vector Products

There are two types of vector products: inner and outer. They can be seen as special cases of matrix multiplication with similar requirements on agreement of dimensions.

Given two column vectors $\boldsymbol{a}, \boldsymbol{b} \in \mathbb{R}^d$ of same dimensions, the inner product or dot product is written as:

$$\boldsymbol{a}^T \boldsymbol{b} = \boldsymbol{a}.\boldsymbol{b} = \langle \boldsymbol{a}, \boldsymbol{b} \rangle = \begin{bmatrix} a_1 & a_2 & . & . & . & a_d \end{bmatrix} \begin{bmatrix} b_1 \\ b_2 \\ . \\ . \\ . \\ b_d \end{bmatrix} = \Sigma_{i=1}^{d} a_i b_i$$

Note that the result is a single scalar value. It has the following properties:

- Dot product is *distributive:* $\langle \boldsymbol{a} + \boldsymbol{b}, \boldsymbol{c} \rangle = \langle \boldsymbol{a}, \boldsymbol{c} \rangle + \langle \boldsymbol{b}, \boldsymbol{c} \rangle$
- Dot product is *commutative*: $\langle \boldsymbol{a}, \boldsymbol{b} \rangle = \langle \boldsymbol{b}, \boldsymbol{a} \rangle$
- Dot product is *associative with respect to scalar multiplication:*
  $\langle \boldsymbol{a}, \boldsymbol{b} \rangle c = \langle \boldsymbol{a}, \boldsymbol{b}.c \rangle = \langle \boldsymbol{a}.c, \boldsymbol{b} \rangle = c \langle \boldsymbol{a}, \boldsymbol{b} \rangle$; where c is a scalar

Outer product

For two column vectors, $\boldsymbol{a} \in \mathbb{R}^n$ and $\boldsymbol{b} \in \mathbb{R}^d$, the *outer product* is a matrix, written as:

$$\boldsymbol{ab}^T = \begin{bmatrix} a_1 \\ a_2 \\ \cdot \\ \cdot \\ \cdot \\ a_n \end{bmatrix} \begin{bmatrix} b_1 & b_2 & . & . & . & b_d \end{bmatrix} = \begin{bmatrix} a_1b_1 & a_1b_2 & . & . & . & a_1b_d \\ a_2b_1 & a_2b_2 & . & . & . & a_2b_d \\ \cdot & \cdot & \cdot & \cdot & \cdot & \cdot \\ a_nb_1 & a_nb_2 & . & . & . & a_nb_d \end{bmatrix} \in \mathbb{R}^{n\times d}$$

The dimensions of $\boldsymbol{a}$ and $\boldsymbol{b}$ don't need to match.

3.2.5 Vector Norms

The norm of a nonzero vector $\boldsymbol{x}$ is a positive number $\|\boldsymbol{x}\|$. That number measures the "length" of the vector. There are many useful measures of length, but all of them must satisfy the following properties:

Rescaling: $\| c\boldsymbol{x} \| = |c| \|\boldsymbol{x}\|$, where c is a constant and $|c|$ is the absolute value of c.

Triangle Inequality: $\| \boldsymbol{y} + \boldsymbol{x} \| \le \| \boldsymbol{y} \| + \| \boldsymbol{x} \|$

Three most important norms are l^2, l^1 and l^∞ which are defined as follows for a vector $\boldsymbol{x} = (x_1, x_2, \ldots, x_d) \in \mathbb{R}^d$

l^2 *norm*: $\| \boldsymbol{x} \|_2 = \sqrt{\Sigma_{i=1}^d x_i^2} = \sqrt{\langle \boldsymbol{x}, \boldsymbol{x} \rangle}$ This is the same as Euclidean norm.

l^1 *norm*: $\| \boldsymbol{x} \|_1 = |x_1| + |x_2| + \ldots + |x_d|$ This is also called the 1-norm.

l^∞ *norm*: $\| \boldsymbol{x}_\infty \| = \max\{|x_1|, |x_2|, \ldots, |x_d|\}$ This is also called the max norm.

Cauchy-Schwarz inequality: Given two vectors $\boldsymbol{x}, \boldsymbol{y}$ of same dimensions,

$$|\boldsymbol{x}^T \boldsymbol{y}| \le \| \boldsymbol{x} \| \| \boldsymbol{y} \|$$

3.2.6 Matrix Norms

The norm of a matrix $\|\boldsymbol{A}\|$ must follow the following three rules:

Non-Negative: $\| \boldsymbol{A} \| > 0$ if $\boldsymbol{A}$ is not the zero matrix.

Rescaling: $\| c\boldsymbol{A} \| = |c| \| \boldsymbol{A} \|$ where c is a constant and $|c|$ is the absolute value of c.

Triangle Inequality: $\| \boldsymbol{A} + \boldsymbol{B} \| \le \| \boldsymbol{A} \| + \| \boldsymbol{B} \|$

Product Inequality: $\| \boldsymbol{AB} \| \le \| \boldsymbol{A} \| \| \boldsymbol{B} \|$

Frobenius Norm of a matrix

Square of the Frobenius Norm of $\boldsymbol{A} \in \mathbb{R}^{n\times d}$ $= \| \boldsymbol{A} \|_F^2$

$$= |a_{11}|^2 + |a_{12}|^2 + \ldots + |a_{1d}|^2 + \ldots + |a_{nd}|^2$$

Which is the sum of square of every element in the matrix.

EXAMPLE 3.2: Let us compute the above norms for v = [–2, 3, 4, 1] and matrix $A = \begin{bmatrix} 1 & 2 \\ -1 & 2 \\ 2 & 1 \end{bmatrix}$

$\| v \|_2 = \sqrt{4+9+16+1} = \sqrt{30} = 5.48$

$\|v_1\| = 2 + 3 + 4 + 1 = 10$

$\|v\|_\infty = 4$

$\|A\|_F = \sqrt{1+4+1+4+4+1} = \sqrt{15}$

3.3 LINEAR INDEPENDENCE, SPAN AND BASIS

Consider a set of n vectors $a_1, a_2, \ldots, a_n \in \mathbb{R}^d$ and a set of n scalars $\lambda_1, \lambda_2 \ldots \lambda_n \in \mathbb{R}$ we can write a new vector, $z \in \mathbb{R}^d$ as a linear combination of the n vectors:

$$z = \Sigma_{i=1}^n \lambda_i a_i$$

For the set of vectors $S = \{a_1, a_2, \ldots, a_n\}$, we say that z is *linearly dependent* on S if there exists a set of scalars $\lambda_1, \lambda_2 \ldots \lambda_n \in \mathbb{R}$, such that we can express it as the linear combination of vectors in S. If z cannot be expressed as a linear combination of vectors in S, then it is said to be *linearly independent* of S. All vectors $z \in \mathbb{R}^d$ which are linearly dependent on S are said to be in its *span*. Thus, $span(S) = \{z | z = \Sigma_{i=1}^n \lambda_i a_i, \lambda_i \in \mathbb{R}\}$

A set of vectors $S = \{a_1, a_2, \ldots, a_n\}$ is *linearly independent* if there is no way to write any vector $a_i \in S$ with as a linear combination of remaining vectors in the set.

In other words, there are no scalars $\{\lambda_1, \lambda_2 \ldots, \lambda_{i-1}, \lambda_{i+1}, \ldots, \lambda_n\} \in \mathbb{R}$ such that $a_i = \Sigma_{\substack{j=1 \\ j \neq i}}^n \lambda_j a_j$

Equivalently, if $\Sigma_{i=1}^n \lambda_i a_i = 0$ then $\lambda_1 = \lambda_2 = \ldots = \lambda_n = 0$

A *basis* of a vector space, V, e.g. $\mathbb{R}^d$, is a linearly independent subset of V that spans V. Thus, to span $\mathbb{R}^d$, we require d linearly independent vectors in $\mathbb{R}^d$.

EXAMPLE 3.3: Consider the vectors in S as $\begin{bmatrix} 2 \\ 2 \\ 1 \end{bmatrix}, \begin{bmatrix} 1 \\ -2 \\ 2 \end{bmatrix}, \begin{bmatrix} 4 \\ -2 \\ 5 \end{bmatrix}$. They are not linearly independent, since $\begin{bmatrix} 4 \\ -2 \\ 5 \end{bmatrix} = \begin{bmatrix} 2 \\ 2 \\ 1 \end{bmatrix} + 2\begin{bmatrix} 1 \\ -2 \\ 2 \end{bmatrix}$.

Since $\begin{bmatrix} 2 \\ 2 \\ 1 \end{bmatrix}$ and $\begin{bmatrix} 1 \\ -2 \\ 2 \end{bmatrix}$ are linearly independent, they form a basis that spans a plane in $\mathbb{R}^3$.

3.3.1 Rank

The *rank* of a set of vectors $X = \{x_1, x_2, \ldots, x_n\}$ is the largest subset $X \subset X$ which is linearly independent. Rank of a matrix A is the rank of the columns of the matrix which is also equal to the rank of its rows.

If $A \in \mathbb{R}^{n \times d}$ then rank(*A*) $\leq \min\{n, d\}$ because it has *n* rows and *d* columns.

If rank(*A*) $= \min\{n, d\}$, then it is called a *full rank* matrix.

A matrix is said to be a square matrix if it has an equal number of rows and columns.

EXAMPLE 3.4: The rank of $A = \begin{bmatrix} 1 & 8 & 3 \\ 1 & 6 & 2 \\ 0 & 2 & 1 \end{bmatrix}$ is 2, because the first and third columns are independent, and the second column can be represented as a linear combination of other two columns.

Nullity and Null Space

$N(A) \stackrel{\text{def}}{=} \{x : Ax = 0\}$. Null Space consists of vectors which when multiplied by *A*, lead to the zero vector. The dimension of *N*(*A*) is the called the nullity of *A*.

The rank-nullity theorem states that rank(*A*) + nullity (*A*) = *n*, the number of columns of *A*.

3.3.2 Inverse

A square matrix $A \in \mathbb{R}^{n \times n}$ may have an *inverse* denoted by A^{-1}. If it exists, it is a unique matrix which satisfies, $A^{-1}A = I = AA^{-1}$ where *I* is the $n \times n$ identity matrix, which has 1 as its diagonal elements and all other elements are 0. Only square, full rank matrices are *invertible*, i.e., they have a unique inverse. If a matrix is not square, its inverse is not defined.

EXAMPLE 3.5: $A = \begin{bmatrix} 1 & 0 & 1 \\ 1 & 1 & 0 \\ 0 & 1 & 1 \end{bmatrix}$ is invertible because the columns are independent.

Its inverse is $A^{-1} = \frac{1}{2}\begin{bmatrix} 1 & 1 & -1 \\ -1 & 1 & 1 \\ 1 & -1 & 1 \end{bmatrix}$

We can check that $\boldsymbol{AA^{-1}} = \boldsymbol{I} = \boldsymbol{A^{-1}A}$

Soon we will present the detailed method to compute inverse using elimination.

3.3.3 Column Space

To motivate this topic, let us consider a system of $n = 3$ equations in $d = 2$ variables.

$$\begin{aligned} 3x_1 + 2x_2 &= 7 \\ 2x_1 - x_2 &= 0 \\ x_1 + 2x_2 &= 5 \end{aligned}$$

We can represent them in the form of matrices as: $\boldsymbol{Ax} = \boldsymbol{b}$, where

$$\boldsymbol{A} = \begin{bmatrix} 3 & 2 \\ 2 & -1 \\ 1 & 2 \end{bmatrix}, \quad \boldsymbol{x} = \begin{bmatrix} x_1 \\ x_2 \end{bmatrix} \text{ and } \boldsymbol{b} = \begin{bmatrix} 7 \\ 0 \\ 5 \end{bmatrix}$$

One way to think about this is that $\boldsymbol{Ax}$ is a linear combination of the columns of $\boldsymbol{A}$. This is known as the column space of $\boldsymbol{A}$, represented as $C(A)$. In our example, $\boldsymbol{Ax}$ is a vector in 3-dimensional space for every value of $\boldsymbol{x}$ where x_1 and x_2 are real numbers. This 3-*d* space is called $\mathbb{R}^3$.

We first check that $\boldsymbol{a}_1 = \begin{bmatrix} 3 \\ 2 \\ 1 \end{bmatrix}$ and $\boldsymbol{a}_2 = \begin{bmatrix} 2 \\ -1 \\ 2 \end{bmatrix}$ are linearly independent because we cannot express $\boldsymbol{a}_2$ in the form $\lambda\boldsymbol{a}_1$ for any $\lambda \in \mathbb{R}$. In other words, $\boldsymbol{a}_2$ cannot be obtained by scaling $\boldsymbol{a}_1$.

Linear combinations of two independent vectors can only span a plane. Since, $\boldsymbol{a}_1$ and $\boldsymbol{a}_2$ are 3-*d* vectors, they span a plane in $\mathbb{R}^3$. The system of equations above has a solution only when $\boldsymbol{b}$ lies on that plane, or in other words, $\boldsymbol{b} \in C(A)$.

EXAMPLE 3.6: In our example above, $\boldsymbol{a}_1 + 2\boldsymbol{a}_2 = \boldsymbol{b}$, showing that $\boldsymbol{b} \in C(A)$. and $\boldsymbol{x} = \begin{bmatrix} 1 \\ 2 \end{bmatrix}$ is a solution to the above system of equations.

3.3.4 Solving Systems of Linear Equations

We have already introduced the fundamental problem in linear algebra, solving $\boldsymbol{Ax} = \boldsymbol{b}$, where $\boldsymbol{A}$ is a n-by-n matrix and $\boldsymbol{b}$ is a n-by-1 column vector. The goal is to compute the solution $\boldsymbol{x}$ which is a n-by-1 column vector, thus having n unknowns. You may have some questions at this stage. Is it necessary that this system of equations will have a solution? Will it be a unique solution? Can there be multiple solutions?

A linear system $Ax = b$ is called **homogeneous** if $b = 0$ otherwise, it is called **inhomogeneous**. If the columns of A are independent, then the only solution to $Ax = 0$ is the zero vector, $\boldsymbol{x} = \boldsymbol{0}$. In other words, independence means that only combination that adds to the zero vector has 0 times every column. In this scenario, there will be a unique solution to $Ax = b$. Since the columns of A are independent, they span $\mathbb{R}^n$. It means that every vector in $\mathbb{R}^n$ can be represented by a unique linear combination of the columns of A.

The method of Gaussian elimination converts the system of linear equations into a simple form, where the solution becomes very easy to compute.

Elementary transformations and LU factorization

These transformations simplify the system while keeping the same solution set. They include:

(a) Exchange of two equations (rows in the matrix representing the system of equations)
(b) Multiplication of an equation (row) with a constant $\lambda \in \mathbb{R}\backslash\{0\}$
(c) Addition of two equations (rows).

Assume that we have re-arranged the equations such that the top left corner of A, i.e. a_{11} is non-zero. The element a_{11} is called the pivot. We will begin with the first equation and use it to create all zeros below it. This can be done by multiplying row 1 by the numbers l_{21}, l_{31}, l_{41} ... and subtracting from rows $j = 2, 3, 4 \ldots$ where $l_{j1} = \frac{a_{j1}}{a_{11}}$.

Example: Let us begin with a 4 × 4 matrix, $\boldsymbol{A} = \begin{bmatrix} 2 & 4 & -1 & -2 \\ 3 & 2 & 1 & 2 \\ 2 & 3 & 1 & 3 \\ 1 & 2 & -1 & 1 \end{bmatrix}$. Pivot element is **2** in the first row. After elimination we get a reduced 3 × 3 matrix.

$$\boldsymbol{A} = \begin{bmatrix} 1 \\ \frac{3}{2} \\ 1 \\ \frac{1}{2} \end{bmatrix} \begin{bmatrix} 2 & 4 & -1 & -2 \end{bmatrix} + \begin{bmatrix} 0 & 0 & 0 & 0 \\ 0 & -4 & \frac{5}{2} & 5 \\ 0 & -1 & 2 & 5 \\ 0 & 0 & -\frac{1}{2} & 2 \end{bmatrix}$$

The first matrix is a rank 1 matrix $l_1 u_1^T$. Next step is to use the new row 2 (second pivot row). The pivot element is a_{22}. We multiply row 2 by l_{32} and l_{42} and subtract from rows 3 and 4 to get zeros in the second column below the pivot.

$$\boldsymbol{A} = \begin{bmatrix} 1 \\ \frac{3}{2} \\ 1 \\ \frac{1}{2} \end{bmatrix} \begin{bmatrix} 2 & 4 & -1 & -2 \end{bmatrix} + \begin{bmatrix} 0 \\ 1 \\ \frac{1}{4} \\ 0 \end{bmatrix} \begin{bmatrix} 0 & -4 & \frac{5}{2} & 5 \end{bmatrix} + \begin{bmatrix} 0 & 0 & 0 & 0 \\ 0 & 0 & 0 & 0 \\ 0 & 0 & \frac{11}{8} & \frac{15}{4} \\ 0 & 0 & -\frac{1}{2} & 2 \end{bmatrix}$$

Next step is to use the new row 3. Pivot element is a_{33}. We multiply row 3 by l_{43} and subtract from row 4 to get zeros in the third column below the pivot.

$$\mathbf{A} = \begin{bmatrix} 1 \\ \frac{3}{2} \\ 1 \\ \frac{1}{2} \end{bmatrix} \begin{bmatrix} 2 & 4 & -1 & -2 \end{bmatrix} + \begin{bmatrix} 0 \\ 1 \\ \frac{1}{4} \\ 0 \end{bmatrix} \begin{bmatrix} 0 & -4 & \frac{5}{2} & 5 \end{bmatrix} + \begin{bmatrix} 0 \\ 0 \\ 1 \\ -\frac{4}{11} \end{bmatrix} \begin{bmatrix} 0 & 0 & \frac{11}{8} & \frac{15}{4} \end{bmatrix} + \begin{bmatrix} 0 & 0 & 0 & 0 \\ 0 & 0 & 0 & 0 \\ 0 & 0 & 0 & 0 \\ 0 & 0 & 0 & \frac{37}{11} \end{bmatrix}$$

$$\mathbf{A} = \begin{bmatrix} 1 & 0 & 0 & 0 \\ \frac{3}{2} & 1 & 0 & 0 \\ 1 & \frac{1}{4} & 1 & 0 \\ \frac{1}{2} & 0 & -\frac{4}{11} & 1 \end{bmatrix} \begin{bmatrix} 2 & 4 & -1 & -2 \\ 0 & -4 & \frac{5}{2} & 5 \\ 0 & 0 & \frac{11}{8} & \frac{15}{4} \\ 0 & 0 & 0 & \frac{37}{11} \end{bmatrix} = \begin{bmatrix} 2 & 4 & -1 & -2 \\ 3 & 2 & 1 & 2 \\ 2 & 3 & 1 & 3 \\ 1 & 2 & -1 & 1 \end{bmatrix}$$

The above form is known as *LU* factorization. We have factored A into a lower triangular matrix (L) time an upper triangular matrix (*U*). This form is very useful to solve $Ax = b$ and to compute matrix inverse.

We now include b as an additional column and work with the matrix $[A\ b]$ which is same as $[LU\ b]$. Elimination will produce the matrix $\left[U L^{-1} b\right] = \left[U c\right]$.

In other words, the system of equations $Ax = b$ has been simplified to the system of equations $Ux = c$, while preserving the solution set. Since U is upper-triangular, it is easy to compute the solution by back substitution.

Example: Consider the system of equations:

$$\begin{matrix} 3x + 2y = 7 \\ 2x + 4y = 6 \end{matrix} \Rightarrow \begin{bmatrix} 3 & 2 & 7 \\ 2 & 4 & 6 \end{bmatrix} \Rightarrow \begin{bmatrix} 3 & 2 & 7 \\ 0 & \frac{8}{3} & \frac{4}{3} \end{bmatrix} = [\boldsymbol{U}\ \boldsymbol{c}]$$

Now we have $\frac{8}{3}y = \frac{4}{3}$ which gives $y = \frac{1}{2}$ and then $x = 2$.

General solution to *Ax* = *b*

The general solution to $Ax = b$, has the structure $x = x_c + x_p$, where x_p is the particular solution and x_c is the solution of $Ax = 0$. In other words, $x_c \in N(A)$, x_c belongs to the null space of A.

Computing matrix inverse

When A is a n-by-n square matrix and is full rank, i.e. rank(A) = n, we can compute its inverse by first writing the augmented matrix $[A\ I]$ where I is an n-by-n identity matrix. By applying elimination, we obtain $[UL^{-1}]$. Then by further back-substitution in the reverse order, we obtain $[I\ L^{-1}U^{-1}] = [I\ A^{-1}]$. An example will make it clear.

Example. Compute the inverse of the matrix $\boldsymbol{A} = \begin{bmatrix} 1 & 0 & 2 & 0 \\ 1 & 1 & 0 & 0 \\ 1 & 2 & 0 & 1 \\ 1 & 1 & 1 & 1 \end{bmatrix}$

We first write the augmented form.

$$\left[\begin{array}{cccc|cccc} 1 & 0 & 2 & 1 & 1 & 0 & 0 & 0 \\ 1 & 1 & 0 & 0 & 0 & 1 & 0 & 0 \\ 1 & 2 & 0 & 1 & 0 & 0 & 1 & 0 \\ 1 & 1 & 1 & 1 & 0 & 0 & 0 & 1 \end{array}\right]$$

Taking pivot in row 1, and applying elimination, we obtain.

$$\left[\begin{array}{cccc|cccc} 1 & 0 & 2 & 0 & 1 & 0 & 0 & 0 \\ 0 & 1 & -2 & 0 & -1 & 1 & 0 & 0 \\ 0 & 2 & -2 & 1 & -1 & 0 & 1 & 0 \\ 0 & 1 & -1 & 1 & -1 & 0 & 0 & 1 \end{array}\right]$$

Continuing with row 2 and 3, we obtain:

$$\left[\begin{array}{cccc|cccc} 1 & 0 & 2 & 0 & 1 & 0 & 0 & 0 \\ 0 & 1 & -2 & 0 & -1 & 1 & 0 & 0 \\ 0 & 0 & 2 & 1 & 1 & -2 & 1 & 0 \\ 0 & 0 & 1 & 1 & 0 & -1 & 0 & 1 \end{array}\right] \textbf{ and finally, } \left[\begin{array}{cccc|cccc} 1 & 0 & 2 & 0 & 1 & 0 & 0 & 0 \\ 0 & 1 & -2 & 0 & -1 & 1 & 0 & 0 \\ 0 & 0 & 2 & 1 & 1 & -2 & 1 & 0 \\ 0 & 0 & 0 & 1 & -1 & 0 & -1 & 2 \end{array}\right]$$

Notice that we have obtained an Upper Triangular matrix, U on the left side. Now we have to work backwards and make it into an identity matrix by applying row transformations.

$$\left[\begin{array}{cccc|cccc} 1 & 0 & 2 & 0 & 1 & 0 & 0 & 0 \\ 0 & 1 & -2 & 0 & -1 & 1 & 0 & 0 \\ 0 & 0 & 2 & 0 & 2 & -2 & 2 & -2 \\ 0 & 0 & 0 & 1 & -1 & 0 & -1 & 2 \end{array}\right]$$

Dividing row 3 by the number 2, we get,

$$\left[\begin{array}{cccc|cccc} 1 & 0 & 2 & 0 & 1 & 0 & 0 & 0 \\ 0 & 1 & -2 & 0 & -1 & 1 & 0 & 0 \\ 0 & 0 & 1 & 0 & 1 & -1 & 1 & -1 \\ 0 & 0 & 0 & 1 & -1 & 0 & -1 & 2 \end{array}\right]$$

Continuing like this, we obtain

$$\left[\begin{array}{cccc|cccc} 1 & 0 & 2 & 0 & 1 & 0 & 0 & 0 \\ 0 & 1 & 0 & 0 & 1 & -1 & 2 & -2 \\ 0 & 0 & 1 & 0 & 1 & -1 & 1 & -1 \\ 0 & 0 & 0 & 1 & -1 & 0 & -1 & 2 \end{array}\right]$$

And finally,

$$\left[\begin{array}{cccc|cccc} 1 & 0 & 0 & 0 & -1 & 2 & -2 & 2 \\ 0 & 1 & 0 & 0 & 1 & -1 & 2 & -2 \\ 0 & 0 & 1 & 0 & 1 & -1 & 1 & -1 \\ 0 & 0 & 0 & 1 & -1 & 0 & -1 & 2 \end{array}\right]$$

We can verify that the $A^{-1} = \begin{bmatrix} -1 & 2 & -2 & 2 \\ 1 & -1 & 2 & -2 \\ 1 & -1 & 1 & -1 \\ -1 & 0 & -1 & 2 \end{bmatrix}$

Determinant

A determinant is used in the analysis and solution of systems of linear equations. Determinants are only defined for square matrices. It is denoted by $|A|$. Determinant is a function that maps A onto a real number. A is invertible only if its determinant is non-zero. The determinant is the signed volume of the parallelepiped formed by the columns of matrix A. Its sign determines the orientation of the spanning vectors.

There are some basic rules to compute the determinant.

1. $\left|\begin{pmatrix} a & b \\ c & d \end{pmatrix}\right| = ad - bc$

2. For a diagonal matrix, the determinant is the product of diagonal elements.

   $|diag(a_1, a_2, \ldots, a_n)| = \prod_{i=1}^{n} a_i$

3. $|AB| = |A||B|$

4. $\left|\begin{pmatrix} A & B \\ 0 & C \end{pmatrix}\right| = |A||C|$

5. Laplace Expansion: $|A| = \sum_i a_{ij} A_{ij}$ where the cofactor $A_{ij} = (-1)^{i+j} |M_{ij}|$ and M_{ij} is the matrix obtained by deleting the ith row and j^{th} column from A.

   Example: Compute the determinant of the matrix $A = \begin{bmatrix} 1 & 2 & -3 \\ 3 & 1 & 2 \\ 0 & 0 & 1 \end{bmatrix}$

   Applying Laplace expansion along the first row of A,

   $|A| = (-1)^{1+1}.1. \begin{vmatrix} 1 & 2 \\ 0 & 1 \end{vmatrix} + (-1)^{1+2}.2. \begin{vmatrix} 3 & 2 \\ 0 & 1 \end{vmatrix} + (-1)^{1+3}.(-3). \begin{vmatrix} 3 & 1 \\ 0 & 0 \end{vmatrix}$

   $|A| = (1 - 0) - 2(3) - 3(0) = -5$

Special matrices

We now briefly consider some special matrixes which are important in linear algebra.

Idempotent Matrix: An idempotent matrix which, when multiplied by itself, yields itself. That is, the matrix A is idempotent if and only if $A \times A = A$. This must necessarily be a square matrix.

Example: $A_1 = \begin{bmatrix} 2 & -2 & -4 \\ -1 & 3 & 4 \\ 1 & -2 & -3 \end{bmatrix}$ is idempotent matrix since $A_1 \times A_1 = A_1$.

Projection matrix: Let V be a vector space and $U \subset V$ a subspace of V. A Projection matrix, P maps the vectors in V to U such that $P \times Pv = Pv \ \forall v \in V$

For two vectors $\boldsymbol{x}$ and $\boldsymbol{y}$, the projection of $\boldsymbol{y}$ onto $\boldsymbol{x}$ is $\frac{\boldsymbol{x}^T \boldsymbol{y}}{\boldsymbol{x}^T \boldsymbol{x}} \boldsymbol{x}$, which can be written as Py where $P = \frac{xx^T}{x^T x}$

Projection matrix will be very useful in solving normal equations.

3.3.5 Orthogonality

Two vectors $x, y \in \mathbb{R}^d$ are orthogonal if $x^T y = \langle x, y \rangle = 0$. This means that the vectors are perpendicular to each other. Orthogonal vectors have zero projection onto each other.

EXAMPLE 3.7: Given the vectors below, test which are orthogonal to each other.

$\boldsymbol{a}$ = (2, 3, 1, –2, 1), $\boldsymbol{b}$ = (1, –2, 2, 1, 4) and $\boldsymbol{c}$ = (2, 1, –4, 2, 1.5)

We find that $<\boldsymbol{a}, \boldsymbol{b}>$ = 2 – 6 + 2 – 2 + 4 = 0 and hence they are orthogonal to each other.

$<\boldsymbol{a}, \boldsymbol{c}>$ = 4 + 3 – 4 – 4 + 1.5 = 0.5 and hence they are not orthogonal.

$<\boldsymbol{b}, \boldsymbol{c}>$ = 2 – 2 – 8 + 2 + 6 = 0 and hence they are orthogonal.

Orthogonal basis: A set of basis vectors $V = \{\boldsymbol{v}_1, \boldsymbol{v}_2, \ldots v_n\}$ is an orthogonal basis if every pair of basis vectors is orthogonal, i.e. $\boldsymbol{v}_i^T \boldsymbol{v}_j = 0; i \neq j$

Orthonormal basis: An orthogonal set of basis vectors $V = \{\boldsymbol{v}_1, \boldsymbol{v}_2, \ldots v_n\}$ is an orthonormal basis if every vector is of unit length, i.e. $\boldsymbol{v}_i^T \boldsymbol{v}_i = 1$

Orthogonal matrices: A square matrix $\boldsymbol{A} \in \mathbb{R}^{n \times n}$ that has all orthonormal columns and orthonormal rows is an orthogonal matrix. $\boldsymbol{A}^T \boldsymbol{A} = \boldsymbol{I}_{n \times n} = \boldsymbol{A}\boldsymbol{A}^T$ and it follows that $\boldsymbol{A}^T = \boldsymbol{A}^{-1}$

This is because the element $p_{i,j}$ of the product is given by $\boldsymbol{a}_i^T \boldsymbol{a}_j = \langle \boldsymbol{a}_i, \boldsymbol{a}_j \rangle = \begin{cases} 0 \text{ if } i \neq j \\ 1 \text{ if } i = j \end{cases}$

The columns of orthogonal matrices are an orthonormal basis for $\mathbb{R}^n$

The rows of orthogonal matrices are also (possibly different) orthonormal basis for $\mathbb{R}^n$

***Note*:** For rectangular matrices $V \in \mathbb{R}^{n \times d}, n \neq d$ that have orthonormal columns,

$$V^T V = I_{d \times d} \text{ but } VV^T \text{ may not be } I.$$

One property of orthogonal matrices is that when we multiply a vector $x \in \mathbb{R}^n$ with an orthogonal matrix $V \in \mathbb{R}^{n \times n}$ the result, Vx has the same length as x. Thus, $\|x\| = \|V_x\|$.

Any vector $x \in \mathbb{R}^n$ can be expressed as a linear combination of the columns of an orthogonal matrix, $V \in \mathbb{R}^{n \times n}$. Thus $x = \Sigma_{i=1}^n \alpha_i v_i$ where $\Sigma_{i=1}^n \alpha_i^2 = \| x \|^2$ because v_i are unit vectors.

In other words, v_i form an orthogonal basis for $\mathbb{R}^n$

***Note*:** Every subspace of $\mathbb{R}^n$ has an orthogonal basis.

Orthogonal subspaces: A subspace U is orthogonal to another subspace V, if every vector $u \in U$ is orthogonal to every vector $v \in V$

One example of this are the row space (subspace spanned by the row vectors) and null space of a matrix (set of all vectors $\boldsymbol{x}$, such that $\boldsymbol{Ax} = \boldsymbol{0}$. This is because, $\boldsymbol{Ax} = \boldsymbol{0} \rightarrow \boldsymbol{a}_i\boldsymbol{x} = \boldsymbol{0}$ for every row vector $\boldsymbol{a}_i$ of $\boldsymbol{A}$. Since every vector in the row space is a linear combination of row vectors, it follows that it is orthogonal to every vector in the null space.

3.3.6 Block Matrix or Partitioned Matrix

When dimensions of a matrix are large, it may be beneficial to view a matrix as combined from smaller submatrices. A **block matrix** or a **partitioned matrix** is a matrix that is interpreted as having been broken into sections called blocks or submatrices. If we simultaneously partition adjacent rows and adjacent columns of a matrix into groups, this partitions the matrix into submatrices or blocks, resulting in a representation of the matrix as a partitioned or block matrix.

If matrices $\boldsymbol{A}$ and $\boldsymbol{B}$ are the same size and are partitioned in exactly the same way, then it is natural to make the same partition of the ordinary matrix sum $\boldsymbol{A} + \boldsymbol{B}$, and sum corresponding blocks. Similarly, one can subtract the partitioned matrices. Multiplication of a partitioned matrix by a scalar is also computed block by block.

Product of two block matrices

Suppose that we are given two matrices $A_{m \times p}$ and $A_{p \times n}$ that are partitioned as follows:

$$A_{m\times p} = \begin{bmatrix} E_{r\times k} & F_{r\times p-k} \\ G_{m-r\times k} & H_{m-r\times p-k} \end{bmatrix} \text{ and } B_{p\times n} = \begin{bmatrix} P_{k\times l} & Q_{k\times n-l} \\ R_{p-k\times l} & S_{p-k\times n-l} \end{bmatrix}$$

Then their product is $AB = \begin{bmatrix} (EP+FR)_{r\times l} & (\mathrm{EQ}+\mathrm{FS})_{r\times n-l} \\ (GP+HR)_{m-r\times l} & (GQ+HS)_{m-r\times n-l} \end{bmatrix}$

3.4 DERIVING NORMAL EQUATION FOR LINEAR REGRESSION

Let us use the above knowledge to solve linear regression problems. Suppose we have n observations (training data) of the form $(\boldsymbol{x}_i, y_i)$ where $\boldsymbol{x}_i$ is a d-dimensional vector of attributes (features) which will be used to predict y_i.

$$y_i = \boldsymbol{w}^T \boldsymbol{x}_i$$
$$y_i = w_0 + w_1 x_{i1} + w_2 x_{i2} + \ldots + w_d x_{id}$$

In this problem, our goal is to estimate the best set of parameters $\boldsymbol{w}$ that minimize the sum of squares error (also called Loss) across all observations, which is given as, $\boldsymbol{L} = \Sigma_{i=1}^{n} (y_i - \boldsymbol{w}^T \boldsymbol{x}_i)^2$. This solution is called the *Least Squares* solution.

This system of equations can be written in matrix form as follows:

$$\boldsymbol{y} = \begin{bmatrix} y_1 \\ y_2 \\ \cdot \\ \cdot \\ \cdot \\ y_n \end{bmatrix} = \begin{bmatrix} w_0 & w_1x_{11} & w_2x_{12} & \cdot & \cdot & \cdot & w_dx_{1d} \\ w_0 & w_1x_{21} & w_2x_{22} & \cdot & \cdot & \cdot & w_dx_{2d} \\ \cdot & \cdot & \cdot & \cdot & \cdot & \cdot & \cdot \\ \cdot & \cdot & \cdot & \cdot & \cdot & \cdot & \cdot \\ \cdot & \cdot & \cdot & \cdot & \cdot & \cdot & \cdot \\ w_0 & w_1x_{n1} & w_2x_{n2} & \cdot & \cdot & \cdot & w_dx_{nd} \end{bmatrix} = \begin{bmatrix} 1 & x_{11} & x_{12} & \cdot & \cdot & \cdot & x_{1d} \\ 1 & x_{21} & x_{22} & \cdot & \cdot & \cdot & x_{2d} \\ \cdot & \cdot & \cdot & \cdot & \cdot & \cdot & \cdot \\ \cdot & \cdot & \cdot & \cdot & \cdot & \cdot & \cdot \\ \cdot & \cdot & \cdot & \cdot & \cdot & \cdot & \cdot \\ 1 & w_0 & x_{n1} & \cdot & \cdot & \cdot & x_{nd} \end{bmatrix} \begin{bmatrix} w_0 \\ w_1 \\ \cdot \\ \cdot \\ \cdot \\ w_d \end{bmatrix} = \boldsymbol{Aw}$$

Here, $\boldsymbol{y}$ and $\boldsymbol{A}$ are known and we have to solve for $\boldsymbol{w}$.

Now, $\boldsymbol{Aw}$ is a vector which is in the column space of $\boldsymbol{A}$. If $y \in \boldsymbol{C}(\boldsymbol{A})$, then we have a perfect solution, where the error is 0. However, in most practical situations, this would not be the case.

Let us assume that $\hat{\boldsymbol{w}}$ is the optimal solution to the above problem and $\boldsymbol{A}\hat{\boldsymbol{w}} = \hat{\boldsymbol{y}}$. Then the error vector $(\boldsymbol{y} - \hat{\boldsymbol{y}})$, must be orthogonal to $\boldsymbol{C}(\boldsymbol{A})$ so that its length is minimized.

In other words, $\forall \boldsymbol{w}, (\boldsymbol{Aw})^T (\boldsymbol{y} - \hat{\boldsymbol{y}}) = 0 \Rightarrow \boldsymbol{w}^T \boldsymbol{A}^T (\boldsymbol{y} - \boldsymbol{A}\hat{\boldsymbol{w}}) = 0 \Rightarrow \boldsymbol{w}^T \left[\boldsymbol{A}^T \boldsymbol{y} - \boldsymbol{A}^T \boldsymbol{A}\hat{\boldsymbol{w}}\right] = 0$

This is only possible when $\boldsymbol{A}^T \boldsymbol{y} - \boldsymbol{A}^T \boldsymbol{A}\hat{\boldsymbol{w}} = 0 \Rightarrow \boldsymbol{A}^T \boldsymbol{A}\hat{\boldsymbol{w}} = \boldsymbol{A}^T \boldsymbol{y} \Rightarrow \boxed{\hat{\boldsymbol{w}} = \left(\boldsymbol{A}^T \boldsymbol{A}\right)^{-1} \boldsymbol{A}^T \boldsymbol{y}}$

The inverse of A^TA exists only when A has independent columns. In case A doesn't have independent columns, we can remove the dependent columns (or redundant attributes) and construct A' which can be used to solve for the regression equations.

***Note*:** The matrix $P = A(A^T A)^{-1} A^T$ is a projection matrix.

In Chapter 7, we will see other efficient methods of solving this problem which can be used when A is large (number of attributes, number of observations).

EXAMPLE 3.8: We asked students in a course to report their heights and weights. However, 2 students didn't report their weights. Can you help us estimate them?

Height (inch)	Weight (kg)
65	72
69	73
60	68
70	64
65	65
61	62
74	70
73	69
75	74
67	70
68	?
72	?

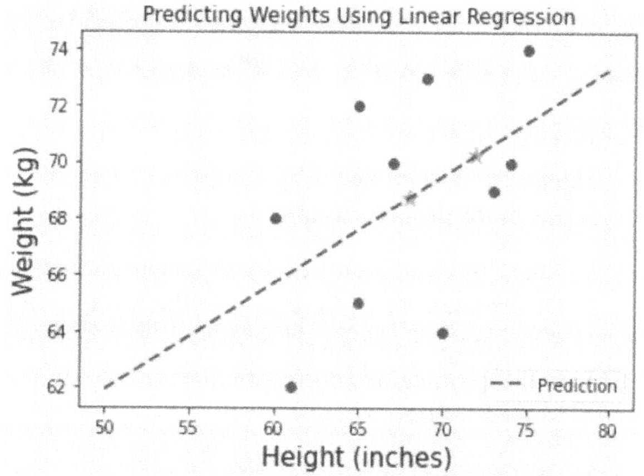

Using the above method, we get and $A^T A = \begin{bmatrix} 10 & 679 \\ 679 & 46351 \end{bmatrix}$ and $A^T y = \begin{bmatrix} 687 \\ 46741 \end{bmatrix}$ and solving for the optimal parameters, we can estimate that Weight = 42.93 + 0.38* Height. Thus, the weight of the student with height 68 inches is estimated to be 68.7 kg and the one with height 72 inches is estimated to be 70.3 kg.

***Note*:** The model may not generalize very well (for children) because the training data is limited and only covers students of heights and weights in a limited range.

3.5 EIGENVECTORS AND EIGENVALUES

An *eigenvector* of a square matrix A is a vector x such that there is some scalar λ which satisfies,

$$Ax = \lambda x$$

Thus, multiplying A with x results in a scaling x by λ, and doesn't change its direction. When x is a unit vector, i.e., it has norm 1, then the associated scalar λ is called the eigenvalue.

EXAMPLE 3.9: $A=\begin{bmatrix}2 & 1\\ 1 & 2\end{bmatrix}$ has eigenvectors $\begin{bmatrix}1\\ 1\end{bmatrix}$ and $\begin{bmatrix}1\\ -1\end{bmatrix}$ with eigenvalues 3 and 1 respectively.

The detailed method to compute eigenvalues and eigenvectors can be found in linear algebra books []. Sometime, even real matrices have complex eigenvalues!

Properties of eigenvectors

Eigenvectors and Eigenvalues have many applications, because they contain a lot of important information about the matrix. Most square matrices, $A \in \mathbb{R}^{n\times n}$ have n independent eigenvectors $x_1, x_2, \ldots x_n$ with n different eigenvalues $\lambda_1, \lambda_2 \ldots \lambda_n$. In that case, every n-dimensional vector v will be a combination of the eigenvectors.

$$v = c_1 x_1 + c_2 x_2 + \ldots + c_n x_n$$

$$Av = c_1 Ax_1 + c_2 Ax_2 + \ldots + c_n AX_n = c_1 \lambda_1 x_1 + c_2 \lambda_2 x_2 + \ldots + c_n \lambda_n X_n$$

$$A^k v = c_1 A^k x_1 + c_2 A^k x_2 + \ldots + c_n A^k X_n = c_1 \lambda_1^k x_1 + c_2 \lambda_2^k x_2 + \ldots + c_n \lambda_n^k X_n$$

We usually order the eigenvalues in decreasing order of magnitudes: $|\lambda_1| \geq |\lambda_2| \ldots \geq |\lambda_n|$

Thus, $A^k v$ is dominated by the principal eigenvector. In Example 3.7, A^k will grow like 3^k. Some more properties are:

1. Trace of A, i.e. sum of its diagonal elements, equals the sum of eigenvalues.
2. Determinant of A, (a notion of the volume of the matrix), equals the product of eigenvalues.
3. Symmetric Matrices $A^T = A$ have real eigenvalues.
4. If the eigenvalues corresponding to two eigenvectors are not equal, then they are orthogonal to each other.
5. $A^{-1}x = \frac{1}{\lambda}x$, provided $\lambda \neq 0$.
6. Eigenvalues of any triangular matrix are its diagonal entries.

3.5.1 Similar Matrices

For every invertible matrix A, the eigenvalues of AXA^{-1} are the same as the eigenvalues of X. The eigenvectors, x, of X are multiplied by A to give eigenvectors Ax of AXA^{-1}.

This can be shown as follows: Suppose x is an eigenvector of X, and $Xx = \lambda x$.

Then $(AXA^{-1})(Ax) = AXx = A\lambda x = \lambda(Ax)$.

Thus, for every invertible matrix A, the matrices AXA^{-1} are similar to X; i.e., they have same eigenvalues. This is used in computation of eigenvalues of matrices.

3.5.2 Eigen Decomposition

We can compute an Eigen decomposition for those square matrices, $A \in \mathbb{R}^{n\times n}$ which have n independent eigenvectors. For example, symmetric matrices, $S = S^T \in \mathbb{R}^{n\times n}$ have n real eigenvalues and n independent eigenvectors.

Suppose $x_1, x_2 \ldots x_n$ are the n independent eigenvectors of A. Then let us construct a matrix X, whose columns are given by these eigenvectors. Since this is a full rank matrix, it is also invertible. Let us calculate the product of A and X.

$$AX = A[x_1 \ \ x_2 \ \ \dots \ \ x_n] = [Ax_1 \ \ Ax_2 \ \ \dots \ \ Ax_n] = [\lambda_1 x_1 \ \ \lambda_2 x_2 \ \ \dots \ \ \lambda_n x_n]$$

$$= [x_1 \ \ x_2 \ \ \dots \ \ x_n]\begin{bmatrix} \lambda_1 & & \\ & \lambda_2 & \\ & & \lambda_n \end{bmatrix} = X\Lambda$$

Thus, $A = X\Lambda X^{-1}$ which is known and the *eigen decomposition* of $\boldsymbol{A}$.

The spectral theorem states that every real symmetric matrix, $\boldsymbol{S} = \boldsymbol{Q}\Lambda\boldsymbol{Q}^T$ where $\boldsymbol{Q}$ is an orthogonal matrix of its eigenvectors.

EXAMPLE 3.10: $A = \begin{bmatrix} 8 & 3 \\ 2 & 7 \end{bmatrix}$ has two eigenvalues 10 and 5 and corresponding eigenvectors $\begin{bmatrix} 3 \\ 2 \end{bmatrix}$ and $\begin{bmatrix} 1 \\ -1 \end{bmatrix}$ respectively.

Thus, $X = \begin{bmatrix} 3 & 1 \\ 2 & -1 \end{bmatrix}$ and $X^{-1} = \begin{bmatrix} \frac{1}{5} & \frac{1}{5} \\ \frac{2}{5} & -\frac{3}{5} \end{bmatrix}$ and $A = \begin{bmatrix} 8 & 3 \\ 2 & 7 \end{bmatrix} = \begin{bmatrix} 3 & 1 \\ 2 & -1 \end{bmatrix}\begin{bmatrix} 10 & 0 \\ 0 & 5 \end{bmatrix}\begin{bmatrix} \frac{1}{5} & \frac{1}{5} \\ \frac{2}{5} & -\frac{3}{5} \end{bmatrix}$

One of the utilities of this form is that it makes it much simpler to compute powers of A.

Thus, $A^k = X\Lambda^k X^{-1}$ and powers of the diagonal matrix Λ are easy to compute.

3.5.3 Positive Definite Matrices

Positive definite matrices have some special properties which make them very important for data analysis. Let us begin with some definitions and tests of positive definite matrices.

1. $\boldsymbol{A}$ is a positive definite matrix, if $\boldsymbol{x}^T \boldsymbol{A}\boldsymbol{x} > 0$, $\forall \boldsymbol{x} \neq 0$
2. A positive definite matrix has all positive eigenvalues.
   ***Note*:** Most linear algebra books assume that positive definite matrices are symmetric.
3. **Cholesky Factorization:** A positive definite matrix $\boldsymbol{S}$ can be written as $\boldsymbol{A}^T\boldsymbol{A}$, for some matrix $\boldsymbol{A}$ with independent columns.
4. All the leading determinants D_1, D_2, ..., D_n of a positive definite matrix $\boldsymbol{S}$ are positive.

EXAMPLE 3.11: $\boldsymbol{S} = \begin{bmatrix} 2 & 4 \\ 4 & 9 \end{bmatrix}$ is positive definite because.

$$\boldsymbol{x}^T \boldsymbol{S}\boldsymbol{x} = [x_1 \ \ x_2]\begin{bmatrix} 2 & 4 \\ 4 & 11 \end{bmatrix}\begin{bmatrix} x_1 \\ x_2 \end{bmatrix} = 2x_1^2 + 8x_1x_2 + 11x_2^2 = 2(x_1 + 2x_2)^2 + 3x_2^2 > 0 \, \forall \, (x_1, x_2)$$

Many machine learning problems can be expressed as optimization problems where we search for parameters which minimize a loss function, L. One of the most important applications of positive definite matrices is to test the minima of the Loss function, L. At the minima, the following conditions hold:

(a) The partial derivatives of L, i.e., $\frac{\partial L}{\partial x_i} = 0$ at x^*.

(b) The matrix S of second derivatives, $\frac{\partial^2 L}{\partial x_i \partial x_j}$ is positive definite.

If S is positive definite at all points x, then the function $L(x)$ is convex and will have a unique minimum, and gradient descent is guaranteed to find it.

3.6 MATRIX FACTORIZATION

We have already learnt to express data as a matrix, where all the data points are collected together in rows. In general, these matrices are not square matrices and not invertible. Matrix factorization is useful for solving certain computational problems in data analysis. For example, QR factorization is used to speed up solution to regression problems. Singular Value Decomposition (SVD) is used in dimensionality reduction, regression problems etc. We will discuss some basic results here.

3.6.1 QR Factorization

The goal in QR factorization is to express the matrix A in terms of product of two matrices, Q, an orthogonal matrix and R, an upper triangular matrix. If A has d independent columns $(a_1, a_2 ..., a_d)$, then Q will also have d independent, orthonormal columns $(q_1, q_2 ..., q_d)$. The process of computing Q and R is also known as the Gram-Schmidt method.

The Gram-Schmidt method proceeds as a sequence of orthogonalization, and normalization steps as follows:

$q_1 = \frac{a_1}{\| a_1 \|}$. Thus, q_1 is a unit vector in the same direction as a_1

To compute q_2, we subtract the component of q_1 from a_2 and normalize it.

Orthogonalization Step: $A_2 = a_2 - (a_2^T q_1) q_1$

Normalization Step: $q_2 = \frac{A_2}{\| A_2 \|}$

Thus, to compute q_i at the ith step,

Orthogonalization Step: $A_i = a_i - \Sigma_{j=1}^{i-1} (a_i^T q_j) q_j$

Normalization Step: $q_i = \frac{A_i}{\| A_i \|}$

To compute R, we can simply use the equation $R = Q^T A$, or in other words,

$$r_{ij} = \begin{cases} q_i^T a_j & \text{if } i \leq j \\ 0 & \text{otherwise} \end{cases}$$

Solving linear regression using QR decomposition

Since $A = QR$, $R = Q^T A$

And $A^T A = R^T Q^T Q R = R^T R$

Hence, the least squares solution to the linear regression equation $Aw = y$, is given by

$$\hat{w} = (A^T A)^{-1} A^T y = (R^T R)^{-1} R^T Q^T y = R^{-1}(R^T)^{-1} R^T Q^T y = R^{-1} Q^T y$$

3.6.2 SVD Decomposition

The SVD takes a general matrix $A \in \mathbb{R}^{(n \times d)}$ and expresses it as a product of three matrices, $U \in \mathbb{R}^{(n \times n)}$. $\Sigma \in \mathbb{R}^{(n \times d)}$ and $V^T \in \mathbb{R}^{(d \times d)}$. Singular vectors are natural extensions of eigenvectors for non-square matrices. For every matrix, we have two sets of singular vectors, the $u's \in \mathbb{R}^n$ and the $v's \in \mathbb{R}^d$ These vectors satisfy the property that, $Av_1 = \sigma_1 u_1 \ldots Av_r = \sigma_r u_r$ where r is the rank of the matrix A. For remaining vectors, $Av_{r+1} = 0 \ldots Av_d = 0$. For a matrix of rank r, there are r non-zero singular values, arranged in descending order. $\sigma_1 \geq \sigma_2 \geq \sigma_3 \ldots \geq \sigma_r > 0$. The last $(d-r)v's$ are in the null space of A, and the last $(n-r)u's$ are in the null space of A^T.

In the matrix form,

$$AV = U\Sigma,\ A\begin{bmatrix} v_1 & \ldots & v_r & \ldots & v_d \end{bmatrix} = \begin{bmatrix} u_1 & \ldots & u_r & \ldots & u_n \end{bmatrix} \begin{bmatrix} \begin{pmatrix} \sigma_1 & \cdots & 0 \\ \vdots & \ddots & \vdots \\ 0 & \cdots & \sigma_r \end{pmatrix} & \Big| 0 \\ 0 & \\ 0 & \end{bmatrix}$$

V and U are orthogonal matrices and $V^{-1} = V^T$ thus $A = U\Sigma V^T$

In the outer product form, we can express $A = \sigma_1 u_1 v_1^T + \sigma_2 u_2 v_2^T + \ldots + \sigma_r u_r v_r^T$

Geometry of SVD

Let us understand how a matrix $A = U\Sigma V^T$ acts on a vector $x \in \mathbb{R}^d$ when we multiply A with x. The figure above illustrates a 2-D case. First x is rotated by V^T to obtain $p = V^T x \in \mathbb{R}^d$. Note that

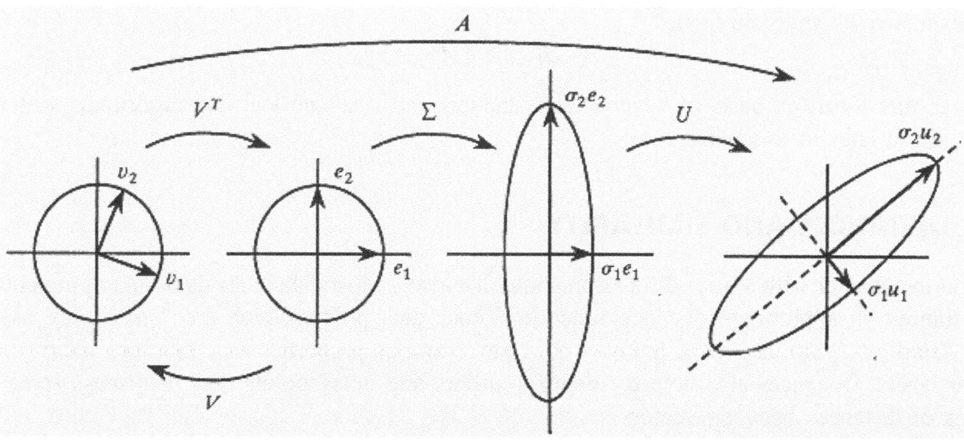

FIGURE 3.2 Geometry of the SVD (Linear Algebra and Learning from Data, Gilbert Strang).

V^T is an orthogonal matrix and doesn't change the norm of the vector. It simply performs a rotation operation. We can also interpret this as a change of basis to the right singular vectors.

Then, we multiply $\boldsymbol{p}$ with $\boldsymbol{\Sigma}$ to obtain $\boldsymbol{q} \in \mathbb{R}^n$. This is a scaling by the singular values of $\boldsymbol{A}$. We know that only r singular values are non-zero. The remaining $(n\text{-}r)$ dimensions of $\boldsymbol{q}$ are zero.

Finally, we obtain the vector $\boldsymbol{y} = \boldsymbol{Ax}$ by multiplying $\mathbf{Uq}$. This again is a rotation operation which changes the basis to align with the left singular vectors.

Connection to frobenius norm

We recall that when $\boldsymbol{Q}$ is an orthogonal matrix, $\|\boldsymbol{Qx}\|_2 = \|\boldsymbol{x}\|_2$

Similarly, when an orthogonal matrix multiplies another matrix, Frobenius norm is preserved.

$$\|\boldsymbol{QX}\|_F = \|\boldsymbol{X}\|_F$$

Since $\boldsymbol{U}$ and V^T are orthogonal matrices, we can express the Frobenius norm of A as follows:

$$\| \boldsymbol{A} \|_F = \| U\Sigma V^T \|_F = \| \Sigma V^T \|_F = \| \Sigma \|_F = \sqrt{\sigma_1^2 + \sigma_2^2 + \ldots + \sigma_r^2}$$

Pseudo-inverse and least squares solution using SVD

One of the uses of SVD in solving regression problems is the computation of the pseudo-inverse. Recall that we want to minimize the least squares error in the problem: $\boldsymbol{Aw} = \boldsymbol{y}$

Using the pseudo-inverse, we obtain the solution that $\boldsymbol{w} = \boldsymbol{A}^{+}\boldsymbol{y}$ where $\boldsymbol{A}^{+} = \boldsymbol{V\Sigma}^{+}\boldsymbol{U}^T$

Here $\boldsymbol{A} = \boldsymbol{U\Sigma V}^T$ and Σ^{+} is a $\mathbb{R}^{(d \times n)}$ matrix with entries, $s_{i,j} = \begin{cases} \dfrac{1}{\sigma_i}, & i \le r \text{ and } i = j \\ 0, & \text{otherwise} \end{cases}$

Thus, once the SVD is known, the computation of pseudo inverse and solution of the regression problem is straight-forward.

Best-K rank approximation

Suppose we want to project the data vectors in a low dimensional subspace. This can be done for noise removal, visualization of data and efficiently solving machine learning problems. The SVD decomposition gives us a principled method to construct the best k-rank approximation to A.

Let $A_k = \sigma_1 u_1 v_1^T + \sigma_2 u_2 v_2^T + \ldots + \sigma_k u_k v_k^T$, where σ_i, u_i, v_i are the singular values and singular vectors respectively. It can be shown that for any k-rank matrix $\boldsymbol{B}$ (a matrix with k linearly independent rows and columns),

$$\| \boldsymbol{A} - \boldsymbol{B}_F \| \ge \| \boldsymbol{A} - \boldsymbol{A}_k \|_F$$

These results form the basis of several data analysis and machine learning algorithms which will be discussed later in this book.

3.7 DISTANCES AND SIMILARITY

We end the chapter with a brief discussion about distances. Most data analysis tasks require choosing or designing an appropriate distance function. Those data points which are "*close*", are assumed to be "*similar*". "Similar" data points would have similar properties and thus are likely to have similar labels. Distances also help us identify outliers and noisy points. Let us discuss some basic notions of distances between vectors.

Metrics

There are certain conditions that a distance function $(d: X \times X \rightarrow \mathbb{R}^+)$ needs to satisfy to be called a metric:

1. Non-negative: $d(x, y) \geq 0$
2. Identity: $d(x, y) = 0$ if $x = y$
3. Symmetry: $d(x, y) = d(y, x)$
4. Triangle Inequality: $d(x, y) \leq d(x, z) + d(z, y)$

L^p distances

L^p or L_p distances are used to calculate distance between two vectors.

Let $x, y \in \mathbb{R}^d$ then $d_p(x, y) = \left(\Sigma_{i=1}^{d} \left(|x_i - y_i|^p\right)\right)^{\frac{1}{p}}$

Most commonly used is the L_2 distance, also called the Euclidean distance, the straight-line distance between the vectors. It does not change even when we rotate the coordinate system.

$$d_2(x, y) = \|x - y\|_2 = \sqrt{\Sigma_{i=1}^{d} (x_i - y_i)^2}$$

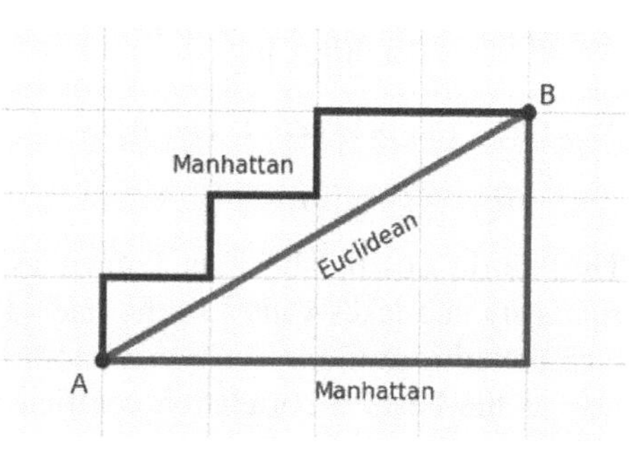

Another commonly used distance is the L_1 distance which measures the sum of lengths on each coordinate axis. This is also called the Manhattan distance; because the streets in Manhattan are perpendicular to each other and one can only go either in the x or in the y direction at a time.

$$d_1(x, y) = \|x - y\|_1 = \Sigma_{i=1}^{d} |x_i - y_i|$$

Another commonly used distance is the L_0 distance which counts the number of coordinates in which the two vectors are different. This is also called the Hamming distance and is used in Communication systems for error detection and correction (coding theory).

$$d_0(x, y) = \|x - y\|_0 = d - \Sigma_{i=1}^{d} I(x_i = y_i), \text{ where } I(x_i - y_i) = \begin{cases} 1 & \text{if } x_i = y_i \\ 0 & \text{if } x_i \neq y_i \end{cases}$$

Finally, L_∞ distance is used to measure the maximum difference along any one coordinate.

$$d_\infty(x, y) = \|x - y\|_\infty = \max_{i=1..d} |x_i - y_i|$$

This figure explains the geometry of L_p distances. All points on the green curve are at a unit distance from the origin, for their respective L_p distances. L_1 produces a diamond shape, L_2 a circle, and L_∞ a square.

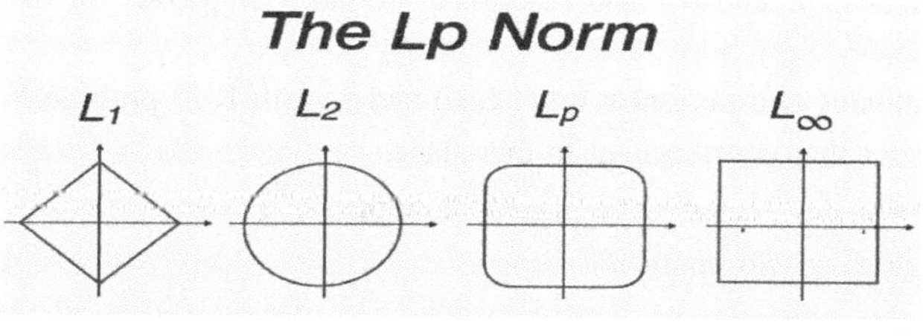

Mahalanobis distance

Sometimes, we need to weigh the difference in along some dimensions more than the others. An extension to the Euclidean distance, called the Mahalanobis distance which is defined for two vectors $\boldsymbol{x}, \boldsymbol{y} \in \mathbb{R}^d$ and symmetric positive definite matrix $M \in \mathbb{R}^{d \times d}$

$$d_M(\boldsymbol{x}, \boldsymbol{y}) = \sqrt{(\boldsymbol{x} - \boldsymbol{y})^T \boldsymbol{M}(\boldsymbol{x} - \boldsymbol{y})}$$

Cosine distance

We can use the dot product to compute the angle θ between $\boldsymbol{a}$ and $\boldsymbol{b}$ as:

$$\cos(\theta) = \frac{\langle \boldsymbol{a}, \boldsymbol{b} \rangle}{\sqrt{\langle \boldsymbol{a}, \boldsymbol{a} \rangle \langle \boldsymbol{b}, \boldsymbol{b} \rangle}} = \frac{\langle \boldsymbol{a}, \boldsymbol{b} \rangle}{\| \boldsymbol{a} \| \| \boldsymbol{b} \|},$$ where $\|\boldsymbol{a}\|$ is the norm or length of $\boldsymbol{a}$ computed as $\sqrt{\langle \boldsymbol{a}, \boldsymbol{a} \rangle}$

EXAMPLE 3.12: Here, the angle between vectors $\boldsymbol{a}_1$ and $\boldsymbol{a}_3$ can be computed as

$$\theta_{1,3} = \cos^{-1}\left(\frac{\langle \boldsymbol{a}_1, \boldsymbol{a}_3 \rangle}{\| \boldsymbol{a}_1 \| \| \boldsymbol{a}_3 \|}\right) = \cos^{-1}\left(\frac{4}{5}\right) \sim 37^\circ$$

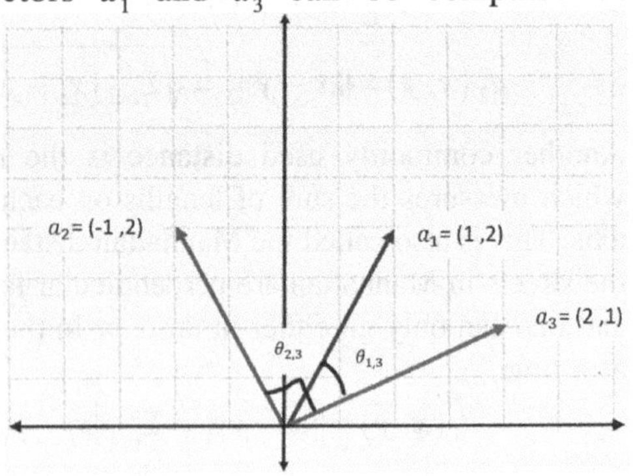

And the angle between $\boldsymbol{a}_1$ and $\boldsymbol{a}_3$

$$\theta_{2,3} = \cos^{-1}(0) = 90^\circ$$

The metric $\cos(\theta)$ above is known as the *cosine similarity* and takes values in the interval [–1, 1]. It measures the similarity of two vectors in the same way as the Pearson correlation coefficient.

EXERCISES

1. Find the number of independent columns (rank) of the following matrices:

   (a) $A = \begin{bmatrix} 1 & 3 & 10 \\ 1 & 2 & 7 \\ 0 & 1 & 3 \end{bmatrix}$ (b) $\boldsymbol{B} = \begin{bmatrix} 1 & 4 & -7 \\ 2 & 5 & -8 \\ 3 & 6 & -9 \end{bmatrix}$

   (c) $\boldsymbol{C} = \begin{bmatrix} 2 & 6 & 4 \\ 1 & 3 & 2 \\ 3 & 9 & 6 \\ 2 & 6 & -4 \end{bmatrix}$ (d) $\boldsymbol{D} = \begin{bmatrix} 1 & 2 & 6 \\ 0 & 1 & 2 \end{bmatrix}$

2. Using the matrices in Exercise 1 and determine the pairwise product of the matrices wherever it is defined.
3. Linear combination of two vectors $\boldsymbol{x}$ = (1, 2, 0) and $\boldsymbol{y}$ = (0, 1, 2) produce a plane in $\mathbb{R}^3$
   (a) Find a vector $\boldsymbol{z}$ that is orthogonal to this plane.
   (b) Find a vector $\boldsymbol{u}$ that is not in the plane. Show that $\boldsymbol{u}^T \boldsymbol{z} \neq 0$
4. Consider the following two matrices:

(a) $A = \begin{bmatrix} 4 & -1 & 3 \\ 0 & -1 & 4 \\ 2 & -2 & 6 \end{bmatrix}$ (b) $B = \begin{bmatrix} 2 & 3 & -1 \\ 5 & 3 & 5 \\ -2 & -2 & 1 \end{bmatrix}$

Calculate the following:

(i) $A^T B$
(ii) AB
(iii) BA
(iv) $B + A$
(v) $\|A - B\|_F$
(vi) If the matrices are invertible, compute the inverse.

5. Solve the system of equations $Ax = b$ where

(i) $A = \begin{bmatrix} 1 & 3 & -1 \\ 2 & 7 & 9 \\ 1 & 5 & 21 \end{bmatrix} b = \begin{bmatrix} 4 \\ 11 \\ 10 \end{bmatrix}$ (ii) $A = \begin{bmatrix} 2 & -1 & 1 & 4 \\ 1 & -1 & 2 & 3 \\ 1 & -2 & 5 & 5 \end{bmatrix} b = \begin{bmatrix} 5 \\ 6 \\ 13 \end{bmatrix}$

6. $\boldsymbol{P} = \begin{bmatrix} 0 & 0 & 1 & 0 \\ 0 & 1 & 0 & 0 \\ 1 & 0 & 0 & 0 \\ 0 & 0 & 0 & 1 \end{bmatrix}$ has orthonormal columns. Compute $\boldsymbol{P}^T\boldsymbol{P}$ and $\boldsymbol{P}^{-1}$.

7. $\boldsymbol{W} = \begin{bmatrix} 1 & 1 & 1 & 0 \\ 1 & 1 & -1 & 0 \\ 1 & -1 & 0 & 1 \\ 1 & -1 & 0 & -1 \end{bmatrix}$ Compute $\boldsymbol{W}^T\boldsymbol{W}$ and $\boldsymbol{W}^{-1}$.

8. Find the eigenvalues and eigenvectors for $\boldsymbol{A} = \begin{bmatrix} 0.8 & 0.3 \\ 0.2 & 0.7 \end{bmatrix}$. As k increases, what will be the value of $\boldsymbol{A}^k$?

9. Explain why the eigenvalues of $\boldsymbol{A}$ equal the eigenvalues of $\boldsymbol{A}^T$.

10. Factor these two matrices into $A = \boldsymbol{X\Lambda X}^{-1}$

$A = \begin{bmatrix} 5 & 4 \\ 4 & 5 \end{bmatrix}$ $A = \begin{bmatrix} 2 & -1 \\ -1 & 2 \end{bmatrix}$

Now compute $\boldsymbol{A}^k$

11. For what numbers e and f, are the matrices A and B positive definite?

$A = \begin{bmatrix} 1 & 1 & 1 \\ 1 & e & 1 \\ 1 & 1 & e \end{bmatrix}$ $\boldsymbol{B} = \begin{bmatrix} 1 & 2 & 3 \\ 1 & f & 2 \\ 2 & 1 & 3 \end{bmatrix}$

12. Without multiplying $\boldsymbol{X} = \begin{bmatrix} \cos\theta & \sin\theta \\ -\sin\theta & \cos\theta \end{bmatrix} \begin{bmatrix} 1 & 0 \\ 0 & 2 \end{bmatrix} \begin{bmatrix} \cos\theta & -\sin\theta \\ \sin\theta & \cos\theta \end{bmatrix}$ answer the following:

(a) What is the determinant of $\boldsymbol{X}$?
(b) What are the eigenvalues of $\boldsymbol{X}$?
(c) What are the eigenvectors of $\boldsymbol{X}$?
(d) Is $\boldsymbol{X}$, symmetric positive definite?

13. Suppose S is a $n \times n$ symmetric matrix, i.e., $S = S^T$ with eigenvalues $\lambda_1 \geq \lambda_2 \ldots \geq \lambda_n$ and orthonormal eigenvectors $v_1 \ldots v_n$.

Then show that the maximum value of $R(x) = \dfrac{x^T Sx}{x^T x} = \lambda_1$

14. Images are commonly used in medical diagnosis. A doctor is using 4 reference images to classify a disease. Using a suitable distance function, classify the test images below.

Reference Images

Normal

2	1	2
1	2	1
2	1	1

A

4	3	2
3	3	1
2	1	1

B

2	1	2
1	2	3
2	3	4

C

2	3	4
1	3	3
2	1	1

Test

1	2	2
1	2	1
1	1	1

1	4	4
1	3	4
2	2	1

15. Let A be a square $n \times n$ matrix whose rows are orthonormal. Prove that the columns of A are orthonormal.

16. Suppose A is square, but not necessarily invertible and has SVD $A = \Sigma_{i=1}^{r} \sigma_i u_i v_i^T$ and $B = \Sigma_{i=1}^{r} \dfrac{1}{\sigma_i} v_i u_i^T$.

Show that $BA\, \boldsymbol{x} = \boldsymbol{x}$ for all x in the span of right singular vectors of A. For this reason, B is sometimes called the pseudo inverse of A and can play the role of A^{-1} in many applications.

MULTIPLE CHOICE QUESTIONS

1. If vectors u and v are orthogonal, which of the following statements is TRUE about their dot product?
(a) The dot product of u and v is equal to the product of their magnitudes.
(b) The dot product of u and v is always positive.
(c) The dot product of u and v is equal to zero.
(d) The dot product of u and v is the angle between them.

2. Which of the following is TRUE for a square matrix A if its determinant is zero?
(a) A is invertible.
(b) A has linearly independent columns.
(c) The matrix A is singular.
(d) The matrix A has full rank.

3. Given a 2×2 matrix $A = \begin{pmatrix} a & b \\ c & d \end{pmatrix}$ which of the following is the correct formula for the determinant of A?
(a) $ad + bc$ (b) $ab - cd$
(c) $ad - bc$ (d) $bc - ad$.

4. For a matrix $\boldsymbol{A}$, if $\boldsymbol{v}$ is an eigenvector with eigenvalue λ, which of the following is TRUE?
(a) $\boldsymbol{A}v = \lambda v$ (b) $\boldsymbol{A}v = v/\lambda$
(c) $\boldsymbol{A}v = v + \lambda$ (d) $\boldsymbol{A}v = \lambda + \boldsymbol{v}$

5. Which of the following is TRUE about the eigenvalues of a diagonalizable matrix **A**?
   (a) All eigenvalues of **A** must be distinct.
   (b) **A** must be symmetric to have real eigenvalues.
   (c) **A** can be diagonalized if and only if it has a full set of linearly independent eigenvectors.
   (d) The determinant of **A** is the sum of its eigenvalues.
6. Let A be an $m \times n$ matrix. The rank-nullity theorem states that:
   (a) Rank(A) + Nullity(A) = m (b) Rank(A) × Nullity(A) = n
   (c) Rank(A) + Nullity(A) = n (d) Rank(A) = Nullity(A)
7. A system of linear equations has a unique solution if and only if:
   (a) The coefficient matrix, A, is singular.
   (b) The determinant of the coefficient matrix, A, is zero.
   (c) The coefficient matrix, A, is invertible.
   (d) The rank of the coefficient matrix, A, is less than the number of variables.
8. A set of vectors S in a vector space V is linearly dependent if:
   (a) Every vector in S can be written as a linear combination of the others.
   (b) At least one vector in S is the zero vector.
   (c) The dot product of any two vectors in S is zero.
   (d) The dimension of the span of S is equal to the number of vectors in S.
9. The dimension of a vector space is defined as:
   (a) The number of vectors in any basis for the space.
   (b) The number of linearly dependent vectors in the space.
   (c) The total number of vectors in the space.
   (d) The number of vectors that span the space.
10. For a 3 × 3 matrix A, if one row of A is multiplied by a scalar k, what happens to the determinant of A?
   (a) The determinant of A remains unchanged.
   (b) The determinant of A is multiplied by k.
   (c) The determinant of A is divided by k.
   (d) The determinant of A becomes zero.
11. If matrix A is an $n \times n$ matrix and its determinant is non-zero, which of the following is TRUE?
   (a) A has no inverse (b) A is not diagonalizable.
   (c) A is singular. (d) A has full rank.
12. What is the rank of the matrix $A = \begin{pmatrix} 0 & 0 & 0 & 0 \\ 4 & 2 & 3 & 0 \\ 1 & 0 & 0 & 0 \\ 4 & 0 & 3 & 0 \end{pmatrix}$
   (a) 0 (b) 1
   (c) 2 (d) 3
13. If Rank(A) = 3 and Rank(B) = 4 then Rank(AB) is
   (a) 3 (b) 4
   (c) 12 (d) 7

APPENDIX: DATA SOURCES

UCI: https://archive.ics.uci.edu/ml/index.php
Kaggle: https://www.kaggle.com/data
World Bank, WHO etc.
IPL, Elections, Weather, Politics etc.
National Power Portal: https://npp.gov.in/publishedReports
Air Quality: https://archive.ics.uci.edu/ml/datasets/Air+Quality
New York Taxi: https://www1.nyc.gov/site/tlc/about/tlc-trip-record-data.page
Open images dataset: https://storage.googleapis.com/openimages/web/index.html
Bengali speech transcription: https://research.google/tools/datasets/bengali-asr/
ReligiousTexts: https://archive.ics.uci.edu/ml/datasets/A+study+of++Asian+Religious+and+Biblical+Texts
Indian Economy: https://dbie.rbi.org.in/DBIE/dbie.rbi?site=statistics
Linked Open Datasets: https://lod-cloud.net/

REFERENCES

[1] Gilbert Strang, Linear Algebra and Learning from Data, Wellesley Cambridge Press (US) and Wellesley Publishers (India).
[2] Jeff Philips, Mathematical Foundations of data analysis, Springer.
[3] A. Faisal, C.S. Ong, M.P. Deisenroth, Mathematics for Machine Learning.

ANSWER KEY

1. (c) **2.** (c) **3.** (c) **4.** (a) **5.** (c) **6.** (c) **7.** (c) **8.** (a) **9.** (a) **10.** (b)
11. (d) **12.** (d) **13.** (a)

4 Optimization

Introduction

In this Chapter we look at the general optimization framework used to find optimal solutions to problems. The optimality is defined with respect to some objective function which is typically minimized under constraints on the parameters of the model. We express several data analysis problems as optimization problems. Then we describe conditions under which the optimal solution exists and techniques to find that efficiently. We also discuss some methods which are used when there is no guarantee of obtaining an optimal solution.

4.1 FUNCTIONS

A function f relates two quantities. It has an input $x \in R^n$ and targets $f(x)$. Here R^n is the domain of the function and the function values $f(x)$ are the image or codomain of f. Functions are often written as $f: R^n \rightarrow R$ and $x \rightarrow f(x)$. A function assigns exactly one value $f(x)$ to every input x.

4.1.1 Optimization Framework

In this book, we discuss optimization with a focus on minimization of a function with one or more variables. The problems will be of the form: Minimize $F(x) = F(x_1, x_2, \ldots, x_n)$

There may often be constraints on vector x. There are several types of constraints:

Linear Constraints of the form: $Ax = b$
Integer Constraints of the form: Each x_i is either 0 or 1. (Binary)
Inequality: $x \geq 0$
Argmin $F(x)$ are the values of x where F reaches its minimum.

A function may have many local maxima and minima. A function f has a local maximum at a point y if the values $f(x)$ 'near' y are all less than $f(y)$. Thus, the graph of f near y has a peak at y as shown in the Figure 4.1. A function f has a local minimum at a point z if the values $f(x)$ 'near' z are all greater than $f(z)$. Global maxima are the point(s) where the function reaches its maximum value in the domain. Similarly, global minima are the point(s) where the function reaches its minimum value in the domain.

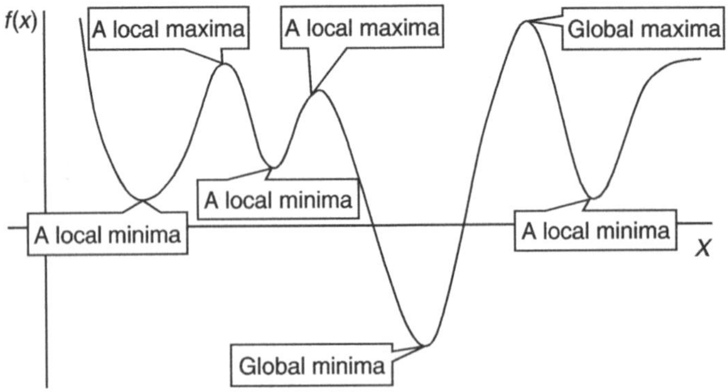

FIGURE 4.1 Local and Global optima of a function.

Limits: The limit L of a $f(x)$ as x approaches (but does not equal) a (from both sides of a) is written as $\lim_{x \to a} f(x) = L$ where a and L are both real numbers and where the values of $f(x)$ approach L.

The limit of L as x approaches a does not exist if:

(a) As x approaches a from both sides $f(x)$ approaches either positive or negative infinity.

(b) $\lim_{x \to a^-} f(x) = L$ and $\lim_{x \to a^+} f(x) = M$, where $L \neq M$

Continuity: Intuitively, A function is continuous if its graph can be drawn without lifting the pencil from paper. A function $f(x)$ is continuous at $x = c$ if

1. $f(c)$ is defined
2. $\lim_{x \to c} f(x)$ exists
3. $\lim_{x \to c} f(c) = f(c)$

If $f(x)$ is not continuous, it is discontinuous. A function is continuous on an open interval (a, b) if it is continuous on every x in the interval. A function is continuous on a closed interval $[a, b]$ if it is continuous on every x in the open interval (a, b) and right continuous at $x = a$ and left continuous at $x = b$.

Differentiability

Magnitude of derivative at a point is the rate of change of the function at that point $\frac{df(x)}{dx}$ = $\lim_{\Delta x \to 0} \frac{\Delta f(x)}{\Delta x} = \lim_{\Delta x \to 0} \frac{f(x + \Delta x) - f(x)}{\Delta x}$. This is the slope of the tangent to the function at x. The derivative points in the direction of steepest ascent of f. Positive derivative means f is increasing at x if we increase the value of x by a very small amount; negative derivative means it is decreasing. Understanding how f changes its value as we change x is helpful to understand optimization (minimization/maximization) algorithms.

Derivative becomes zero at stationary points (optima or saddle points). The function becomes "flat" ($\Delta f(x) = 0$) if we change x by a small amount at such points. These are the points where the function has its maxima/minima (unless they are saddles). Saddle points are those where the derivative is zero, but it is neither a maxima or minima, because the function increases in one direction and decreases in the other.

EXAMPLE 4.1: Derivative of a polynomial:

Let us compute the derivative of $f(x) = x^n$, $n \in N$ from first principles.

$$\frac{df}{dx} = \lim_{\Delta x \to 0} \frac{f(x+\Delta x) - f(x)}{\Delta x} = \lim_{\Delta x \to 0} \frac{(x+\Delta x)^n - (x)^n}{\Delta x}$$

We use the binomial expansion of $(x+\Delta x)^n$ to obtain.

$$= \lim_{\Delta x \to 0} \frac{\left(\sum_{k=0}^{n} \binom{n}{k} \Delta x^k x^{n-k}\right) - (x)^n}{\Delta x}$$

The first term of binomial expansion is x^n. Hence the limit simplifies to:

$$= \lim_{\Delta x \to 0} \frac{\left(\sum_{k=1}^{n} \binom{n}{k} \Delta x^k x^{n-k}\right)}{\Delta x} = \lim_{\Delta x \to 0} \left(\binom{n}{1} x^{n-1} + \sum_{k=2}^{n} \binom{n}{k} \Delta x^{k-1} x^{n-k}\right) = nx^{n-1}$$

All the terms in the summation (for $k = 2$ to n) vanish as $\Delta x \to 0$.

4.2 TAYLOR SERIES

Often, we want to approximate the values of functions to compute them efficiently. The Taylor series is a representation of a function f as the sum of (infinite number of) terms determined using the derivatives of f evaluated at a point x_0.

Taylor Polynomial of degree n of $f: R \to R$ at a is defined as:

$$T_n(x) = \sum_{k=0}^{n} \frac{f^{(k)}(a)}{k!}(x-a)^k$$

Where $f^{(k)}(a)$ is the kth derivative of f at a (assuming it exists) and $\frac{f^{(k)}(a)}{k!}$ are the coefficients of the polynomial.

Def 4.1: $f \in C^\infty$ means that f is continuously differentiable infinitely many times.

For a smooth function, $f \in C^\infty, f: R \to R,$ the **Taylor series** of f at a is defined as:

$$T_\infty(x) = \sum_{k=0}^{\infty} \frac{f^{(k)}(a)}{k!}(x-a)^k$$

If $f(x) = T_\infty(x)$, then f is called analytic function. Maclaurin series is a special case of Taylor series for $a = 0$.

EXAMPLE 4.2: Let us approximate the value of $\sqrt{2}$ using Taylor series.

First, we have to select an appropriate value of a. A useful choice of a requires: $a > 0$ so that the Taylor series exists; a is close to $x = 2$, making $|x - a|$ small so the series converges quickly; and $f(a) = \sqrt{a}$ is easy to compute so we can find the coefficients.

Convergence means that the value of the running sum, doesn't change much by adding more terms.

A value satisfying all three conditions is: $a = \frac{9}{4}$.

We tabulate the terms as follows:

k	0	1	2	3	4
$f^k(x)$	$x^{\frac{1}{2}}$	$\frac{1}{2}x^{-\frac{1}{2}}$	$-\frac{1}{2}\cdot\frac{1}{2}x^{-\frac{3}{2}}$	$\frac{1}{2}\cdot\frac{1}{2}\cdot\frac{3}{2}x^{-\frac{5}{2}}$	$\frac{1}{2}\cdot\frac{1}{2}\cdot\frac{3}{2}\cdot\frac{5}{2}x^{-\frac{7}{2}}$
$f^{(k)}\left(\frac{9}{4}\right)$	$\frac{3}{2}$	$\frac{1}{3}$	$-\frac{2}{27}$	$\frac{4}{87}$	$-\frac{40}{729}$
$\frac{f^{(k)}\left(\frac{9}{4}\right)}{k!}$	$\frac{3}{2}$	$\frac{1}{3}$	$-\frac{1}{27}$	$\frac{2}{243}$	$-\frac{5}{2187}$
$\frac{f^{(k)}\left(\frac{9}{4}\right)}{k!}\left(x-\frac{9}{4}\right)^k$	$\frac{3}{2}$	$\frac{1}{3}\left(-\frac{1}{4}\right)$	$-\frac{1}{27}\left(-\frac{1}{4}\right)^2$	$\frac{2}{243}\left(-\frac{1}{4}\right)^3$	$-\frac{5}{2187}\left(-\frac{1}{4}\right)^4$

Adding up the terms in the last row of the above table, we get $\sqrt{2} \approx 1.4142143$, which is correct to 5 places of decimal.

4.3 RULES OF DIFFERENTIATION

We state some of the important rules of differentiation.

Sum rule: $(f(x) + g(x))' = f'(x) + g'(x)$

Product rule: $(f(x)g(x))' = f'(x)g(x) + f(x)g'(x)$

Quotient rule: $\left(\frac{f(x)}{g(x)}\right)' = \frac{f'(x)g(x) - f(x)g'(x)}{(g(x))^2}$

Chain rule: $(g(f(x))' = g'(f(x))f'(x)$

EXAMPLE 4.3: Compute the derivative of $h(x) = e^{-\frac{(x-\mu)^2}{2\sigma^2}}$ where μ, σ are constants.

Let us apply the chain rule with $g(f) = e^f$ and $f(x) = -\frac{(x-\mu)^2}{2\sigma^2}$

$$f'(x) = -\frac{2(x-\mu)}{2\sigma^2} = -\frac{x-\mu}{\sigma^2} \text{ and } g'(f) = e^f$$

Thus, $h'(x) = e^f\left(-\frac{x-\mu}{\sigma^2}\right) = -\frac{x-\mu}{\sigma^2}e^{-\frac{(x-\mu)^2}{2\sigma^2}}$

This shows that the derivative at $x = \mu$ is 0.

4.4 USING DERIVATIVES TO FIND THE OPTIMA

How the derivative itself changes tells us about the function's optima. We also use the second derivative, that is the derivative of the derivative, denoted by $f''(x)$.

Maxima: $f'(x) = 0$ at x, $f'(x) > 0$ just before x and $f'(x) < 0$ just after x. $f''(x) < 0$

Minima: $f'(x) = 0$ at x, $f'(x) < 0$ just before x and $f'(x) > 0$ just after x. $f''(x) > 0$

Please refer to Figure 4.1 and observe the shape of the function carefully. Near the optima, the slope of the curve becomes 0, i.e., $f'(x) = 0$. $f''(x)$ denotes the curvature. Positive values indicate convex (bend upward) and negative values indicate concave shape (bend downward).

4.5 PARTIAL DIFFERENTIATION AND GRADIENTS

In machine learning, we mostly deal with functions of many variables. For example, the loss function for linear regression with D parameters is a multi-variate function. $L(\mathbf{w}): \mathbb{R}^D \to \mathbb{R}$.

The graph of Loss function is a surface in $D + 1$ dimensional space. The general form of derivative for functions of many variables is called gradient. The gradient of f with respect to x is calculated by *varying one variable at a time* and keeping others constant. The gradient is then, the collection of these *partial derivatives.*

We can approximate a multi-variate function as follows:

$$f(x+\Delta x) \approx f(x) + (\Delta x)^T \nabla f + \frac{1}{2}(\Delta x)^T H(\Delta x)$$

Where ∇f is the **gradient** of f, a column vector of n partial derivatives of f, $\frac{\partial f}{\partial x_1}$ to $\frac{\partial f}{\partial x_n}$. The matrix H is the Hessian matrix. H is a symmetric matrix of second derivatives where $H_{ij} = \frac{\partial^2 f}{\partial x_i \partial x_j}$.

The Hessian gives information about the curvature of the function at point x. The Hessian matrix can be used to assess the optima of the function.

- $\nabla f(x) = 0$ and $\nabla^2 f(x)$ is a positive semi-definite (PSD) matrix then x is a minima
- $\nabla f(x) = 0$, and $\nabla^2 f(x)$ is a negative semi-definite (NSD) matrix then x is a maxima

Example: The gradient of $f(x_1, x_2) = 2x_1^2 x_2 + x_1 x_2^2 \in R$, with respect to x_1, x_2 is:

$$\nabla f = \begin{bmatrix} \frac{\partial f(x_1, x_2)}{\partial x_1} \\ \frac{\partial f(x_1, x_2)}{\partial x_2} \end{bmatrix} = \begin{bmatrix} 4x_1 x_2 + x_2^2 \\ 2x_1^2 + 2x_1 x_2 \end{bmatrix}$$

Basic rules of partial differentiation

Sum rule: $\frac{\partial}{\partial x}\left(f(x)+g(x)\right)=\frac{\partial f(x)}{\partial x}+\frac{\partial g(x)}{\partial x}$

Product rule: $\frac{\partial}{\partial x}\left(f(x)g(x)\right)=\frac{\partial f(x)}{\partial x}g(x)+f(x)\frac{\partial g(x)}{\partial x}$

Chain rule: $\frac{\partial}{\partial x}g(f(x))=\frac{\partial g}{\partial f}\frac{\partial f}{\partial x}$

Example: In the graph of a two-variable function, a saddle point occurs at a point where the surface curves upward in one direction (like a valley) and downward in a perpendicular direction (like a hill).

A classic example of a saddle point is the function $f(x, y)=x^2-y^2$, which has a saddle point at (0,0). In the x direction, f has a minimum at 0 (since $f(0, y)=-y^2$). But in the y-direction, it has a maximum (since $f(x, 0) = x^2$).

For a function $f(x, y)$, the point (x_0, y_0) is a saddle point if:

- $\nabla f(x_0, y_0) = 0$ (the gradient is zero, i.e., the point is stationary),
- but (x_0, y_0) is not a local extremum (not a local maximum or minimum).

Gradient of least-squares loss in a linear model

The loss function is the sum of squares of errors in the prediction. For each data point (x_n, y_n), the predicted value of y is $w^T x_n$, while the actual value is y_n. Thus, the error is $y_n - w^T x_n$.

$$L(\boldsymbol{w}) = \arg\min_{\boldsymbol{w}} \sum_{n=1}^{N}\left(y_n - \boldsymbol{w}^T \boldsymbol{x}_n\right)^2$$

We would like to compute $\frac{\partial L(w)}{\partial w}$. Let us compute it term by term. Since x and w are both D dimensional, the gradient of Loss function with respect to w will also be D dimensional.

$$\frac{\partial(y_n - w^T x_n)}{\partial w} = \begin{pmatrix} \frac{\partial\left(y_n - \sum_{i=1}^{D} w_i x_i\right)^2}{\partial w_1} \\ \frac{\partial\left(y_n - \sum_{i=1}^{D} w_i x_i\right)^2}{\partial w_2} \\ \cdots \\ \cdots \\ \frac{\partial\left(y_n - \sum_{i=1}^{D} w_i x_i\right)^2}{\partial w_D} \end{pmatrix} = \begin{pmatrix} 2\left(y_n - \sum_{i=1}^{D} w_i x_i\right)(-x_1) \\ 2\left(y_n - \sum_{i=1}^{D} w_i x_i\right)(-x2) \\ \cdots \\ \cdots \\ 2\left(y_n - \sum_{i=1}^{D} w_i x_i\right)(-x_D) \end{pmatrix}$$

$$2\left(y_n - \sum_{i=1}^{D} w_i x_i\right)\begin{pmatrix}(-x_1)\\(-x_2)\\ \cdots \\ \cdots \\ (-x_D)\end{pmatrix} = -2\left(y_n - \sum_{i=1}^{D} w_i x_i\right)x\_i = 2\left(y_n - w^T x_n\right)x\_n$$

Now adding all the terms, we get

$$\boldsymbol{g} = -\sum_{n=1}^{N} 2(y_n - \boldsymbol{w}^T \boldsymbol{x}_n)\boldsymbol{x}_n$$

Prediction error of current model $\boldsymbol{w}^{(t)}$ on the nth training example is given by $(y_n - \boldsymbol{w}^T \boldsymbol{x}_n)$. We observe that the (training) examples on which the current model's error is large, contribute more to the gradient and hence will have more influence on the parameter update in the gradient descent method.

4.6 DATA ANALYSIS AS OPTIMIZATION PROBLEM

Many algorithms in data science and machine learning optimize an objective function $L(w)$ with respect to a set of model parameters (w). The general form of such problem is:

$w_{opt} = \arg\min_{w \in C} L(\boldsymbol{w})$, where C is the constraint set that the solution w_{opt} must belong to.

Finding good parameters can be formulated as an optimization problem. Examples include:

(i) Linear regression where we look for optimal parameters that minimize the Mean square error of the curve fit.
(ii) Neural networks where we look for the optimal parameters that minimize the loss function.
(iii) SVMs which attempts to compute the boundary that maximizes the distance between two classes.

4.6.1 Convex Functions and Optimality Conditions

Optimization problems can be structured or unstructured.

Unstructured: Minimize $f(x)$ for vectors x in a subset S of R^n

Structured: Consider the examples below:

Minimize a linear cost function $f(x) = c^T x$ under the constraint that $Ax = b$ and $x \geq 0$

Minimize a quadratic cost function $f(x) = \frac{1}{2} x^T S x$ under the constraint that $Ax = b$

Convex Set: A set C is a convex set if for any $x, y \in C$ and for any scalar λ with $0 \leq \lambda \leq 1$, we have

$$\lambda x + (1 - \lambda) y \in C$$

In other words, all the points lying on the line joining x and y are in C.

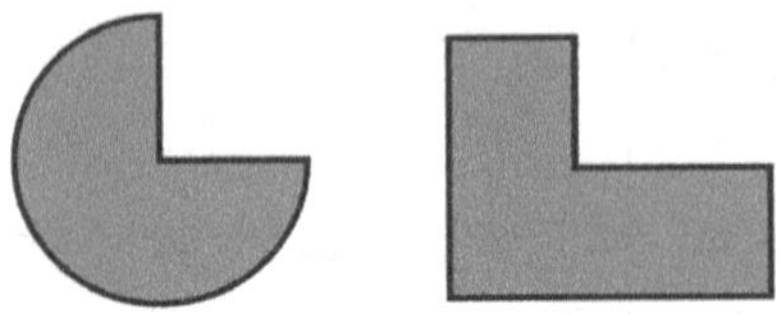

FIGURE 4.2 Example of non-convex set.

Convex function: A function such that a straight line between any two points of the function lie above the function.

Let $f: R^D \to R$ be a function whose domain is a convex set. The function f is a convex function if for all x, y in the domain of f and for any scalar λ with $0 \leq \lambda \leq 1$, we have

$$f(\lambda x + (1-\lambda)y) \leq \lambda f(x) + (1-\lambda) f(y)$$

For strictly convex function, the above inequality is strict. Then the graph of f is strictly below the chord that connects the point $(x, f(x))$ to $(y, f(y))$.

Visual test of convex function: The plot of the function stays above the tangent and below the chord.

EXAMPLE 4.4: Examples of convex functions:

(a) $x \log x$ (b) $ax + c$ (c) x^2

Convex optimization problem

When the objective function, $f(x)$ is a convex function and when the constraint sets are also convex sets, the optimization problem is called a convex optimization problem. In such cases, global optimality is guaranteed.

Standard form of a convex optimization problem:

$$\min_x f(x)$$

Subject to

$$g_i(x) \leq 0 \quad \forall i = 1, 2, \ldots, m$$
$$h_j(x) = 0 \quad \forall j = 1, 2, \ldots, n$$

Where all functions $f(x)$ and $g_i(x)$ are convex functions and $h_j(x) = 0$ are convex sets.

Special cases

(a) Linear Programming: In a linear program, both the objective function and the constraints are linear. Consider the following linear program with d variables and m linear constraints.

$$\min_{x \in R^d} c^T x$$

Subject to $Ax \leq b$

Where $A \in R^{m \times d}$ and $b \in R^m$ and $c \in R^d$

The region where $Ax \leq b$ is satisfied, is the feasible region. It is a convex polygon.

EXAMPLE 4.5: Mr. Singh has a diet chart which gives calories, protein, carbohydrate and fat content for 4 food items. He wants a diet with minimum cost. The diet chart is as follows:

	Item 1	Item 2	Item 3	Item 4	Requirement
Calories	400	200	150	400	500
Proteins	10	5	1	0	20
Carbohydrates	2	5	5	10	20
Fat	1	1	5	5	4
Cost	100	200	250	150	

Formulation:

Let x_i be the quantity of each item to be bought.

Objective function: $100x_1 + 200x_2 + 250x_3 + 150x_4$

Constraints: For meeting calories, proteins, carbohydrates and fat requirements:

$$400x_1 + 200x_2 + 150x_3 + 400x_4 \geq 500$$

$$10x_1 + 5x_2 + 1x_3 \geq 20$$

$$2x_1 + 5x_2 + 5x_3 + 10x_4 \geq 20$$

$$1x_1 + 1x_2 + 5x_3 + 5x_4 \geq 4$$

Furthermore, each of the $x_i \geq 0$.

The above program can be solved using Python or *LP* solvers.

(b) Quadratic Programming: A quadratic program has a quadratic objective function with affine constraints.

$$\min_{x \in R^d} \frac{1}{2} x^T Qx + c^T x$$

$$\text{Subject to } Ax \leq b$$

Where $A \in R^{m \times d}$ and $b \in R^m$ and $c \in R^d$. Q must be square symmetric positive definite matrix, thus making the objective function convex. It has d variables and m constraints.

4.7 SOLVING OPTIMIZATION PROBLEMS

Some optimization problems have a closed form solution, and some can be solved numerically. Convex optimization problems have a global optimum and there are algorithms which are guaranteed to converge to the optimal solution. When the optimization problem is non-convex, obtaining optimal solutions becomes difficult. We may be able to obtain only local optima, which may be far from the global optima. We will discuss a few important approaches for solving optimization problems.

4.7.1 Closed Form Solutions

Sometimes we are lucky to have closed form solutions for optimization problems. PCA and Linear regression are two such examples. The approach works only for very simple problems where the objective is convex and there are no constraints on the values $\boldsymbol{w}$ can take. This is known as the first order optimality condition, i.e. the gradient $\boldsymbol{g} = \dfrac{\partial L(w)}{\partial w}$ must be equal to zero at the optima.

In some cases, when we set $\mathbf{g} = \mathbf{0}$ and solve for $\mathbf{w}$, we obtain a closed form solution. For linear regression, we can write the loss function in vector notation as follows: Where Y are the observations and X are the input features.

The error in predictions can be expressed as a vector: $e(w) = y - Xw$

The loss function is the 2 norm of the error vector: $L(e) = \|e\|^2 = (y - Xw)^T (y - Xw)$

To minimize the loss function, we compute the gradient: $\dfrac{\partial L(w)}{\partial w} = \dfrac{\partial L(e)}{\partial e}\dfrac{\partial e(w)}{\partial w}$

$$\frac{\partial L(e)}{\partial e} = 2e^T \text{ and } \frac{\partial e(w)}{\partial w} = -X \text{ and hence } \frac{\partial L(w)}{\partial w} = -2e^T X = -2(y - Xw)^T X$$

Thus, at the optima, $\dfrac{\partial L(w)}{\partial w} = 0$

$$(y - Xw)^T X = 0 \rightarrow X^T(y - Xw) = 0 \rightarrow X^T y = X^T Xw \rightarrow w = (X^T X)^{-1} X^T y$$

Thus, we have obtained the same closed form solution as we saw in chapter 3 using normal equations.

4.7.2 Gradient Descent

This is the general method for solving optimization problems. We know that when f is smooth, all the first derivatives of function are zero the at the minima. The gradient descent approach uses the gradient of the function to update the parameters so as to minimize the value of the function. We initialize the parameters randomly (usual practice is to initialize with Normal distribution random variable). Then we iteratively update the parameters such the loss function decreases and approaches the minima. This is summarized below.

- Initialize $\mathbf{w}$ as $\mathbf{w}^{(0)}$
- For iteration t = 0, 1, 2, ... (or until convergence)
  - Calculate the gradient $\mathbf{g}^{(t)}$ using the current iterates $\mathbf{w}^{(t)}$
  - Set the learning rate η_t
  - Move in the opposite direction of gradient
  - $\mathbf{w}^{(t+1)} = \mathbf{w}^{(t)} - \text{h}_t\mathbf{g}^{(t)}$

We can test convergence by measuring the change in the value of the function. When the change in function value becomes smaller than a pre-defined threshold, we stop the update process and select the current value of parameters to be the best (optimal) value.

The learning rate very important to set. It should be set carefully (fixed or chosen adaptively). If the learning rate is too low, the convergence will be slow. If the learning is too high, there might be rapid fluctuations in the value of the function and it may oscillate around the minima and never converge.

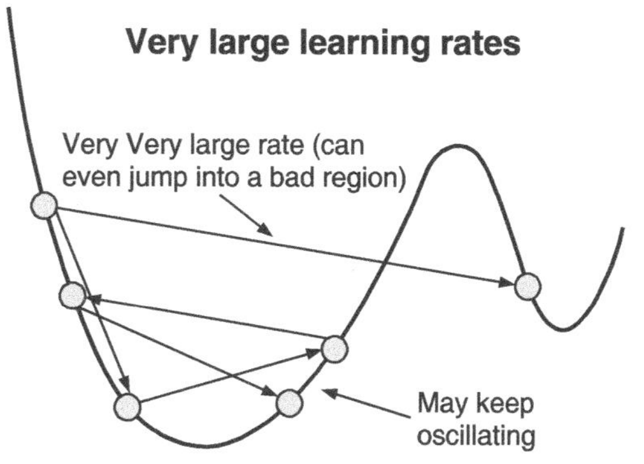

FIGURE 4.3 Impact of learning rate.

EXAMPLE 4.6: For linear regression, the update equation is as follows:

$$w^{(t+1)} = w^{(t)} + \eta_t \sum_{n=1}^{N} 2\left(y_n - w^{(t)T} x_n\right) x_n$$

Stochastic gradient descent

This is an efficient way to perform gradient descent on large datasets. Consider a loss function of the form $L(w) = \frac{1}{N}\sum_{n=1}^{N} \ell_n(w)$.

The gradient is an average of N terms: $g = \nabla_w L(w) = \nabla_w [\frac{1}{N}\sum_{n=1}^{N} \ell_n(w)] = \frac{1}{N}\sum_{n=1}^{N} g_n$

Stochastic Gradient Descent (SGD) approximates g using a randomly selected training example and approximating it $g \approx g_i - \nabla_w \ell_i(w)$. Such gradients are noisier but are much faster to compute and hence may speed up convergence.

Mini-batch SGD helps in reducing the variance in the estimate of g by averaging the gradients on a random batch of training examples. $g \approx \frac{1}{B}\sum_{i=1}^{B} g_i$

This method is usually used for training neural networks.

We will study more about the applications of Optimization in the later chapters for training various types of machine learning models.

EXERCISES

1. Suppose $y = \frac{1}{1 + e^{-(wx+b)}}$. Both w and b are scalars. Please compute $\frac{\partial y}{\partial w}$ and $\frac{\partial y}{\partial b}$.
2. Show that the following functions are convex:

   (a) $-x \log x$ (b) $\log (e^x + e^z)$

   (c) $\left(|x_1|^p + |x_2|^p\right)^{\frac{1}{p}}$

3. Please find the stationary points of the function $f(x) = x^4 + 6x^3 - 3x^2 - 5x$, and tell whether they are maxima, minima or saddle points.

MULTIPLE CHOICE QUESTIONS

1. For a function $f(x)$, if $f'(x) = 0$ and $f''(x) > 0$ at some point $x = a$, what can be said about the point a?
   (a) a is a local maximum.
   (b) a is a global maximum.
   (c) a is a local minimum.
   (d) a is an inflection point.
2. For the function $f(x) = e^{2x} - x^2$, what is the behaviour of $f(x)$ as $x \to \infty$?
   (a) $f(x) \to 0$
   (b) $f(x) \to \infty$
   (c) $f(x) \to -\infty$
   (d) $f(x) \to -2x$
3. The range of function $f(x) = \sin(x)$
   (a) $[-1, 1]$ (b) $(-\infty, \infty)$
   (c) $(0, \infty)$ (d) $[-2, 2]$
4. Limit $\lim_{x \to a} \frac{x^n - a^n}{x - a}$ given $a > 0$.
   (a) ∞ (b) 1
   (c) a^{n-1} (d) na^{n-1}
5. Let $f(x) = \sin^2 x + \log x$ then the domain of $f(x)$ is:
   (a) $[0, \infty)$ (b) $[-\infty, \infty)$
   (c) $(0, \infty)$ (d) $(-1, \infty)$
6. What would be the domain of function $f(x) = 1/x$ for it to be defined everywhere on the domain?
   (a) $(2, \infty)$ (b) $(-\infty, \infty) - \{0\}$
   (c) $[0, \infty)$ (d) None of the mentioned
7. Consider the function $f(x) = x^3 - 6x^2 + 9x + 5$. What are the critical points of $f(x)$?
   (a) $x = 0$ (b) $x = 1$ and $x = 3$
   (c) $x = 2$ and $x = 4$ (d) $x = 0$ and $x = 3$.
8. If a function $f(x)$ is concave down at $x = a$ and $f'(a) = 0$, what can be said about the point a?
   (a) a is a local minimum
   (b) a is a local maximum
   (c) a is an inflection point
   (d) a is neither a maximum nor a minimum
9. Let $f(x) = x^4 - 4x^3$. Find the points where $f(x)$ has local minima.
   (a) $x = 3$ (b) $x = 0$ and $x = 3$
   (c) $x = 1$ and $x = 3$ (d) $x = 0$ and $x = 1$
10. For a continuous function $f(x)$ defined on a closed interval $[a, b]$, which of the following is TRUE?
   (a) The global maximum occurs at a critical point within the interval.
   (b) The global maximum always occurs at an endpoint.
   (c) The global extrema can occur either at critical points or endpoints.
   (d) The global minimum is equal to the global maximum for all continuous functions.

11. For the function $f(x) = 2x^3 - 3x^2 - 12x + 5$, which of the following points is a global minimum on the interval [–2, 2]?

(a) $x = -2$ (b) $x = 0$
(c) $x = 2$ (d) $x = -1$

12. The Taylor series of e^x around $x = 0$ is given by:

(a) $e^x = 1 + x + \frac{x^2}{2} + \frac{x^3}{3} +$ (b) $e^x = 1 + x + \frac{x^2}{2!} + \frac{x^3}{3!} +$

(c) $e^x = x + \frac{x^2}{2} + \frac{x^3}{3} +$ (d) $e^x = x + \frac{x^2}{2!} + \frac{x^3}{3!} +$

13. Which of the following is TRUE about the remainder term $R_n(x)$ in a Taylor series expansion?

(a) The remainder term always tends to zero as $n \to \infty$.
(b) The remainder term can be ignored if x is small.
(c) The remainder term measures the error in approximating the function by the Taylor polynomial.
(d) The remainder term is only non-zero for polynomials.

14. What is the second derivative of $f(x) = e^{3x}$?

(a) $3e^{3x}$ (b) $6e^{3x}$
(c) $9e^{3x}$ (d) e^{3x}

15. For the function $f(x, y) = x^2y + 3xy^2$ what is the gradient ∇f?

(a) $(2xy + 3y^2, x^2 + 6xy)$ (b) $(2x^2y + 3xy^2, x^2 + 6xy)$

(c) $(5xy, 7xy)$ (d) $(xy + 3y^2, xy^2 + 6xy)$

16. The gradient of $f(x, y, z) = x^2 + y^2 + z^2$ at the point (1, –2, 3) is:

(a) $(2x, 2y, 2z)$ (b) (1, –2, 3)
(c) (2, –4, 6) (d) (2, 2, 2)

17. For a scalar function $f(x_1, x_2, \ldots, x_n)$, what does the ∇f represent geometrically?

(a) The direction of the steepest ascent of f.
(b) The magnitude of the second derivative of f.
(c) The Hessian matrix of f.
(d) The tangent plane to the level set of f.

18. In a standard linear programming problem, what is the condition for an optimal solution to exist at a vertex of the feasible region?

(a) The objective function must be linear.
(b) The problem must be unbounded.
(c) The feasible region must be a convex polyhedron.
(d) There must be no constraints.

19. In gradient descent, if the learning rate η is too large, what is most likely to happen?

(a) The algorithm will converge more quickly.
(b) The algorithm may overshoot the minimum and fail to converge.
(c) The algorithm will get stuck at a local minimum.
(d) The algorithm will compute gradients inaccurately

20. The primary difference between stochastic gradient descent (SGD) and batch gradient descent is:

(a) SGD uses a subset of data at each step, while batch gradient descent uses the entire dataset.
(b) SGD is always faster than batch gradient descent.
(c) SGD guarantees better accuracy than batch gradient descent.
(d) SGD cannot handle non-convex problems, unlike batch gradient descent.

21. In stochastic gradient descent, why does using mini-batches often result in faster convergence than using individual data points?
    (a) It provides a better estimate of the true gradient than individual samples.
    (b) It reduces the number of iterations required to reach a local minimum.
    (c) It prevents overfitting.
    (d) It increases the variance of gradient estimates.

REFERENCES

[1] Gilbert Strang, Linear Algebra and Learning from Data, Cambridge University press.
[2] Jeff Philips, Mathematical Foundations of data analysis, Springer.
[3] A. Faisal, C.S. Ong, M.P. Deisenroth, Mathematics for Machine Learning.

ANSWER KEY

1. (c) **2.** (c) **3.** (a) **4.** (b) **5.** (c) **6.** (b) **7.** (b) **8.** (b) **9.** (d) **10.** (c)
11. (d) **12.** (b) **13.** (c) **14.** (c) **15.** (a) **16.** (c) **17.** (a) **18.** (c) **19.** (b) **20.** (a)
21. (a)

5 Probability and Statistics for Data Science

Introduction

Probability theory and statistics study random phenomena, mostly in the form of random samples such as random numbers and random categorical variables. Probability theory concerns itself with the origin and production of random samples. We draw random samples from appropriate probability distributions and use them to simulate raw data for model testing, split raw data into testing and training sets etc. Probability is used to measure uncertainty: in data, in models learnt from data and in the predictions made by the models.

On the other hand, statistics is more about studying properties of already collected random samples. Experimental raw data almost always has an element of uncertainty and unpredictability. We'll use various statistical measures to describe the observations of a dependent variable and possible interactions between dependent and independent variables. Statistics help us analyze data, answer questions about the data (hypothesis testing), develop models, figure out the underlying process that explains observations and helps us make predictions. Thus, it is critical to understand its fundamental concepts of probability and statistics to perform data analysis. In Chapter 2, we have already seen the role of descriptive statistics for data exploration and the use of correlation analysis to discover the associations or relationships between the attributes in data.

In this Chapter, we review some important concepts regarding probability, and study distributions such as the Power Law and Multivariate-Gaussian in some detail. We will also learn about Hypothesis testing, Parameter Estimation and Sampling techniques.

5.1 PROBABILITY AND RANDOM VARIABLES

We start with a *sample space* Ω, the set of all outcomes. For example, $\Omega = \{H, T\}$ when we study coin-tossing. When we study heights of people, which must be positive, $\Omega = (0, \infty)$. One may say that the height must at least be 4 inches and cannot be more than 120 inches and restrict it: $\Omega = [4,120]$.

We are usually interested in the *probability* of observing an event $A \in \Omega$. The probability of an event $P(A)$, satisfies the following properties (also known as the *axioms of probability*):

(a) $0 \le P(A) \le 1$, for any A,

(b) $P(\Omega) = 1$, and

(c) Probability of disjoint events $(A_i \cap A_j = \phi)$ is equivalent to sum of their individual probabilities.

$$P\left(\bigcup_{i=1} A_i\right) = \sum_{i=1} P(A_i)$$

A *random variable* is a function that maps possible outcomes in a sample space to another *measurable* space, often the real numbers. In other words, it is a real valued function of the outcome of an experiment involving a random process.

Now consider two events A and B. They are *independent* if $P(A \cap B) = P(A).P(B)$

Independence means that there is no special relationship between A and B. The occurrence of A doesn't influence occurrence of B or vice versa.

In probability theory, two events are said to be *mutually exclusive events* if they cannot occur at the same time or simultaneously. In other words, mutually exclusive events are called disjoint events. Further, if two events are considered disjoint events, then the probability of both events occurring at the same time will be zero. $P(A \cap B) = 0$. When you toss a coin, you either get heads or tails, but there is no other way you could get both results. This is an example of mutually exclusive events.

To study more than one random variable at a time, we use *joint distributions*, where the probability is determined jointly by all the variables involved.

EXAMPLE 5.1: Assume we have a random variable X, that counts the number of heads (H) when we toss a coin two times. There are four possible outcomes and X maps them to 3 distinct values $\{0,1,2\}$.

$$X(H, H) = 2$$
$$X(T, H) = X(H, T) = 1$$
$$X(T, T) = 0$$

If the coin is fair, $P(H) = P(T) = 0.5$ and the tosses are independent, we obtain:

$$P(X=2) = P(H,H) = 0.5 \times 0.5 = 0.25$$
$$P(X=1) = P((T,H) \cup (H,T)) = P(T,H) + P(H,T) = 0.5 \times 0.5 + 0.5 \times 0.5 = 0.5$$
$$P(X=0) = P(T,T) = 0.5 \times 0.5 = 0.25$$

If the coin is biased and $P(H) = 0.7$ and $P(T) = 0.3$ and the tosses are independent, we obtain:

$$P(X=2) = P(H,H) = 0.7 \times 0.7 = 0.49$$
$$P(X=1) = P((T,H) \cup (H,T)) = P(T,H) + P(H,T) = 0.3 \times 0.7 + 0.7 \times 0.3 = 0.42$$
$$P(X=0) = P(T,T) = 0.3 \times 0.3 = 0.09$$

Given a joint distribution, over random variables X and Y, we can talk about the *marginal distribution* of X or that of Y. The marginal distribution refers to the probability distribution of a random variable on its own. To find out the marginal distribution of a random variable, we *sum out* all the other random variables from the distribution. Formally, we mean $P(X) = \sum_y P(X, Y)$.

The name of marginal distribution comes from the fact that if we add up all the entries of a row (or a column) of a joint distribution, and write the answer at the end (i.e., margin) of it, this will be the probability of the random variable taking on that value. Of course, thinking in this way only helps when the joint distribution involves two variables.

In many situations, one event influences another and we model it using *conditional probabilities.* The conditional probability of event A given that B is true is written as $P(A|B)$. When $P(B) > 0$, we can write $P(A|B) = \dfrac{P(A \cap B)}{P(B)}$.

EXAMPLE 5.2: Consider two random variables O and D. O is 1 if someone is overweight and 0 otherwise. D is 1 if someone has diabetes and 0 otherwise. Suppose we collect data from N = 100 patients and prepare the following table:

	D = 1 (Diabetes)	**D = 0 (No Diabetes)**
O = 1 (Overweight)	20	10
O = 0 (Not overweight)	15	55

The joint probabilities can be calculated by dividing each cell by N.

	D = 1 (Diabetes)	**D = 0 (No Diabetes)**
O = 1 (Overweight)	0.2	0.1
O = 0 (Not overweight)	0.15	0.55

Note that the sum of the cells is 1. Conditional probability of having diabetes, given the person is overweight is given as $P(D=1|O=1) = \dfrac{P(D \cap O)}{P(O)} = \dfrac{0.2}{0.2+0.1} = 0.666.$

If we don't know anything about the weight of the person, the probability of having diabetes is $P(D = 1) = 0.2 + 0.15 = 0.35$. Since, $P(D=1|O=1) \neq P(D=1)$, being diabetic (D = 1) and being overweight (O = 1) are not independent events. In other words, an overweight person is more likely to be diabetic.

5.2 PROBABILITY DISTRIBUTIONS

We often speak about the *distribution* of a variable. This formally refers to the probability of a random variable taking on certain values. A random variable may take discrete values as in examples 4.1 and 4.2 or may take continuous values such as weight or height.

For discrete random variables, the p.m.f. the **probability mass function (p),** or the **frequency function** is used to determine the probabilities of various values of the random variable X. If those values are denoted by $x_1, x_2, \ldots,$ then $p(x_i) = P(X = x_i)$ and $\Sigma_i p(x_i) = 1$.

The **cumulative density function (CDF)** of a random variable is defined as:

$$F(x) = P(X \leq x), \; -\infty \leq x \leq \infty$$

For a continuous random variable, the role of the frequency function is taken by a **probability density function (pdf), $f(x)$**, which has the properties that $f(x) \geq 0$, f is piecewise continuous, and

$\int_{-\infty}^{\infty} f(x) = 1$. If X is a random variable with a density function f, then for any $a < b$, the probability that X falls in the interval (a, b) is the area under the density function between a and b:

$$P(a < X < b) = \int_a^b f(x)$$

One consequence of this definition is that the probability that a continuous random variable X takes on any particular value is 0: $P(X = c) = \int_c^c f(x) = 0$.

5.3 EXPECTATION

Expected value is the mean of the random variable, X and is denoted by μ_X. The concept of the expected value of a random variable is similar to taking weighted averages. The possible values of the random variable are weighted with the probability of their occurrence.

Definition: If X is a discrete random variable with frequency function, $p(x)$, the expected value of X, denoted as $E[X]$, is:

$$E[X] = \Sigma_i x_i \, p(x_i)$$

When X is a continuous random variable, with probability density function, $f(x)$, its expected value is given by the following integral:

$$E[X] = \int_{-\infty}^{\infty} x f(x)$$

In both these cases, if the summation or integral diverges, then the expectation is undefined.

Variance

The variance of a random variable is the expectation of the square deviations from the mean. It is denoted by $V[X]$ and calculated as follows:

$$V[X] = E[X^2] - E[X]^2 = E\left[(X - \mu_X)^2\right]$$

5.4 IMPORTANT DISTRIBUTIONS

Let us now study some classical distributions which teach us what patterns to look for in the shapes of the histograms and distribution functions which we encounter in practice.

(a) **Uniform Distribution:** The uniform distribution is a distribution whereby all outcomes are equally possible. Uniform distributions are often used to represent numeric random variables when all that is known is the range of possible values.

$$P(X = k) = \frac{1}{n} \text{ where } k \in \{a, a+1, \ldots, b-1, b\} \text{ and } n = b - a + 1$$

(b) **Binomial Distribution:** Measures the number of *successes* in n successive trials and each trial results in a *success* with probability p and a failure with probability $1 - p$.

$$P(X=k)=\binom{n}{k}p^k(1-p)^{n-k}$$

The above formula can be derived by considering different sequences of successes and failures of length n. There are $\binom{n}{k}$ such sequences with k successes and n-k failures. The probability of each sequence is $p^k(1-p)^{n-k}$ because every trial is independent.

(c) **Geometric Distribution:** Here we measure the probability of achieving first *success* at the kth trial. There is exactly one sequence that satisfies the condition and hence the probability is:

$$P(X=k)=(1-p)^{k-1}p$$

(d) **Negative Binomial Distribution:** Here we measure probability of achieving r *successes* at the kth trial. This can also be thought of the sum of r independent Geometric random variables.

$$P(X=k)=\binom{k-1}{r-1}p^r(1-p)^{k-r}p$$

(e) **Poisson Distribution:** Poisson p.m.f. can be used to approximate binomial probabilities for large n and small p with $\lambda = np$. In other words, the probability of success is very small, but the number of trials is very large. Thus, the expected number of successes is $\lambda = np$. The Poisson frequency function uses this $\lambda, (\lambda > 0)$, as the success rate parameter and the p.m.f. is given as:

$$P(X=k)=\frac{\lambda^k}{k!}e^{-\lambda},\ k=0,1,2....$$

The Poisson distribution is of fundamental theoretical and practical importance and has been used in analysis of telephone systems, computer networks, call centers, data centers, queueing systems etc. to model the number of requests coming in during a unit of time. One important assumption to note is that the incoming requests must be independent of each other for the Poisson model to work. Thus, bursts of requests, heavy traffic scenarios can't be modeled as Poisson.

(f) **Power Law Distributions:** Many data distributions exhibit a long-tail phenomenon: as X grows large, the probability doesn't decay fast. The populations of cities, countries, income of people, profit of companies, visitors on internet sites, words frequencies in literature. A few entities dominate the rest of the population. You may have heard "rich are becoming richer." This is a manifestation of power law. The power law distribution is given by:

$$P(X=x)=cx^{-k}$$

where we have two constants: exponent k and normalization constant c.

A power-law has a well-defined mean over $x \in [1, \infty)$ only if $k > 2$ and it has a finite variance only if $k > 3$. It is interesting to note that most of the identified power laws in nature have exponents such that the mean is well-defined, but the variance is not. Thus, one has to be careful while applying traditional statistics that are based on variance and standard deviation (such as regression analysis). The median does exist, however: for a power law x^{-k}, with exponent $k > 1$, it takes the value $2^{\frac{1}{k-1}} x_{min}$, where $x_{\min}$ is the minimum value for which the power law holds.

EXAMPLES 5.3:

(a) Type 1 Diabetes is considered to be genetically inherited. If a man has type 1 diabetes, the odds of his child developing diabetes are 1 in 17. A man has four children, what is the p.m.f for the number of children who will have the disease?

We can use the **binomial distribution** to model this problem. $p(k) = \binom{4}{k}\frac{1}{17}^{k}\left(1-\frac{1}{17}\right)^{n-k}$

(b) Communication channels (e.g., wireless) are often noisy. If a single bit (0 or 1) is transmitted over a noisy communications channel, it has probability p of being incorrectly transmitted. To improve the reliability of the transmission, the bit is transmitted n times, where n is odd. *A* majority decoder at the receiving end, decides that the correct message is that carried by a majority of the received bits. Assume a simple noise model, where each bit is independently subject to being corrupted with the same probability p. The number of bits that is in error, X, is thus a **binomial random variable** with n trials and probability p of error. Suppose, for example, that $n = 5$ and $p = .1$. The probability that the message is correctly received is the probability of two or fewer errors, which is

$$\sum_{k=0}^{2}\binom{n}{k}p^{k}(1-p)^{n-k} = 0.9914$$

(c) The **Poisson distribution** has been used in the analysis of telephone systems. The number of calls coming into an exchange during a unit of time might be modeled as a Poisson variable if the exchange services a large number of customers who act more or less independently. One of the earliest uses of the Poisson distribution was to model the number of alpha particles emitted from a radioactive source during a given period of time. The Poisson distribution has also been used by traffic engineers as a model for light traffic. The number of vehicles that pass a marker on a roadway during a unit of time can be counted. If traffic is light, the individual vehicles act independently of each other. In heavy traffic, however, one vehicle's movement may influence another's, so the approximation might not be good.

It would be a good exercise to derive the mean and variance of each of the above distributions in terms of their parameters. We have summarized them in the table here.

Distribution	Binomial	Geometric	– ve Binomial	Poisson	Power Law
Mean	np	$\frac{1}{p}$	$\frac{r}{p}$	λ	Finite only if $k > 2$
Variance	$np(1-p)$	$\frac{1-p}{p^2}$	$\frac{r(1-p)}{p^2}$	λ	Finite only if $k > 3$

Let us now study some important continuous random variables characterized by their probability density functions.

(a) **Uniform:** Uniform random variable X on the interval $[a, b]$ is a model for what is meant when we say "choose a number at random between a and b. Any real number in the interval is a possible outcome and the probability of X lying in a sub-interval should be proportional to the length of the sub-interval.
The density function is given by

$$f(x) = \begin{cases} \frac{1}{b-a}, & a \le x \le b \\ 0 & x < a \text{ or } x > b \end{cases}$$

(b) **Exponential:** Exponential distributions are characterized by a rate parameter, λ. It can be used to model the probability distribution of time between events in a Poisson process. The pdf is given as:

$$f(x, \lambda) = \begin{cases} \lambda e^{-\lambda x} & x \ge 0 \\ 0 & x < 0 \end{cases}$$

Clearly, the pdf is non-zero only for non-negative values of x.

$$E[X] = \frac{1}{\lambda} \quad \text{and} \quad Var[X] = \frac{1}{\lambda^2}$$

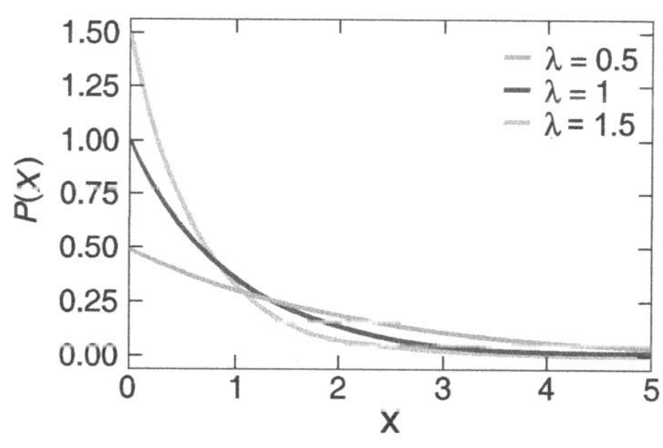

FIGURE 5.1 Characteristics Curve.

(c) **Normal:** The *Gaussian distribution*, also known as the *normal distribution*, is one of the most commonly used distributions in probability theory. For example, it can be used to approximate the binomial distribution when the number of experiments is large, or the Poisson distribution when the average arrival rate is high. For many problems, we will also often assume that the noise in the system is Gaussian distributed. It is characterized by two parameters, μ (mean) and σ (standard deviation). Its probability density function is given as:

$$f(x) = \frac{1}{\sqrt{2\pi\sigma}} \exp\left(-\frac{(x-\mu)^2}{2\sigma^2}\right)$$

To get a better sense of how the distribution changes with respect to the mean and the variance, we have plotted three different Gaussian distributions in Figure 5.2. We notice

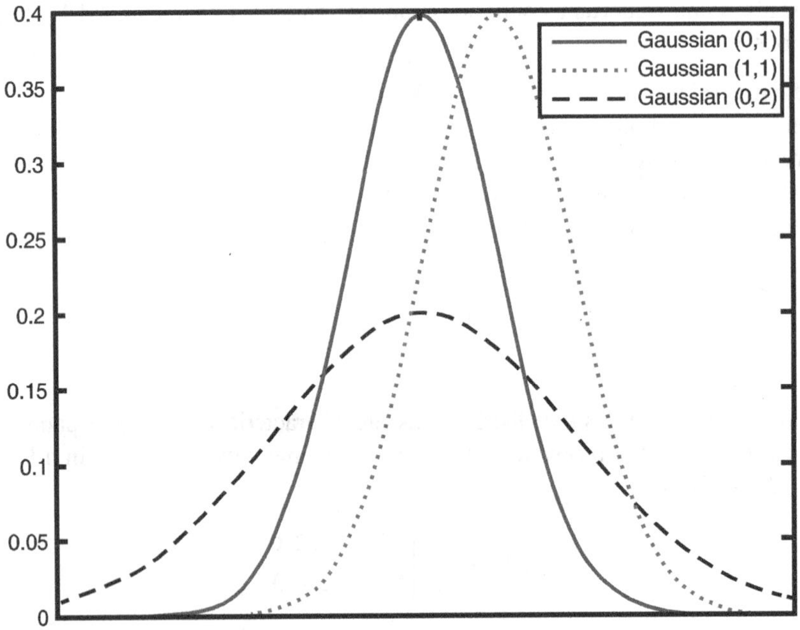

FIGURE 5.2 Gaussian Distribution.

that the probability density is the highest around the mean and decays rapidly as x goes away from the mean. The density function is symmetric around the mean producing a characteristic bell shape. If σ is high, the curve is spread out and if σ is low, the curve is concentrated.

(d) **Standard normal:** The standard normal distribution is a special case of the Gaussian distribution with mean 0 and variance 1.

(e) **Chi-squared distribution:** If Z is a standard normal random variable, the distribution of $U = Z^2$ is called the chi-square distribution with 1 degree of freedom. The chi-squared distribution with 1 degree of freedom is denoted as χ_1^2. It is useful to note that if $X \sim N(\mu, \sigma^2)$, then $\frac{X-\mu}{\sigma} \sim N(0,1)$ and therefore $\left[\frac{X-\mu}{\sigma}\right]^2 \sim \chi_1^2$.

If $U_1, U_2 \ldots U_n$ are independent chi-square random variables with 1 degree of freedom, the distribution of $V = U_1 + U_2 + \ldots + U_n$ is called the chi-square distribution with n degrees of freedom and is denoted by χ_n^2. It can be shown that $E[V] = n$ and $V_{ar}(V) = 2n$.

It is interesting to note that if U and V are independent and $U \sim \chi_n^2$ and $U \sim \chi_m^2$ then $U + V \sim \chi_{m+n}^2$.

(f) **T-distribution:** If $Z \sim N(0, 1)$ and $U \sim \chi_n^2$ and Z and U are independent, then the distribution of $\frac{Z}{\sqrt{\frac{U}{n}}}$ is called the t-distribution with n degrees of freedom.

The t-distribution is symmetric about 0. Thus, $f(t) = f(-t)$. As the number of degrees of freedom approach infinity, the t-distribution tends to the standard normal distribution.

EXAMPLES 5.4:

(a) **Current flows in muscle and nerve cells:** Muscle and nerve cell membranes contain large numbers of channels through which selected ions can pass when the channels are open. Using sophisticated experimental techniques, neurophysiologists can measure the resulting current that flows through a single channel. Experimental records often indicate that a channel opens and closes at seemingly random times. In some cases, simple kinetic models predict that the duration of the open time should be *exponentially distributed.*

(b) **Acoustic recordings made in the arctic ocean:** They contain substantial background noise. To detect sonar signals of interest, it is useful to characterize this noise as accurately as possible. In the Arctic, much of the background noise is produced by the cracking and straining of ice. Scientists have studied recordings of Arctic undersea noise and characterized the noise as a mixture of a *Gaussian distribution* and occasional large-amplitude bursts.

(c) **Turbulent air flow:** It is sometimes modeled as a random process. Since the velocity of the flow at any point is subject to the influence of a large number of random eddies in the neighborhood of that point, one might expect from the central limit theorem that the velocity would be *normally distributed.*

(d) **IQ Scores:** Scores on a certain standardized test, IQ scores, are approximately normally distributed with mean μ = 100 and standard deviation σ = 15. Here we are referring to the distribution of scores over a very large population, and we approximate that discrete cumulative distribution function by a *normal continuous cumulative distribution* function.

5.5 CONDITIONAL DISTRIBUTIONS

If X and Y are jointly distributed discrete random variables, the conditional probability that $X = x_i$ given that $Y = y_j$ is, if $P(Y = y_j) > 0$,

$$P(X = x_i | Y = y_j) = \frac{P(X - x_i, Y - y_j)}{P(Y = y_j)} = \frac{p_{XY}(x_i, y_j)}{p_Y(y_j)}$$

This probability is defined to be 0 if $p_Y(y_j) = 0$. We will denote this conditional probability by $p_{X|Y}(x \mid y)$. Note that $p_{X|Y}(x|y) = p_X(x)$ if X and Y are independent.

EXAMPLE 5.5

	Y				
X	0	1	2	3	4
0	1/10	2/10	2/10	1/10	0
1	0	1/10	2/10	0	1/10

The conditional frequency of X given $Y = 1$ is:

$$p_{X|Y}(0|1) = \frac{\frac{2}{10}}{\frac{1}{10} + \frac{2}{10}} = \frac{2}{3}$$

$$p_{X|Y}(1|1) = \frac{\frac{1}{10}}{\frac{1}{10} + \frac{2}{10}} = \frac{1}{3}$$

A nice relationship between joint and conditional frequency distributions can be given as:

$$p_{XY}(x_i, y_j) = p_{X|Y}(x|y)\, p_Y(y_j)$$

Summing both sides over all the values of *y*, we obtain,

$$p_X(x) = \sum_y p_{X|Y}(x|y)\, p_Y(y_j)$$

In analogy with the definition for discrete case, if *X* and *Y* are jointly continuous random variables, the conditional density of *Y* given *X* is defined to be:

$$f_{Y|X}(y|x) = \frac{f_{XY}(x,y)}{f_X(x)} \text{ if } 0 < f_X(x) < \infty, \text{ and 0 otherwise.}$$

The joint density can be expressed in terms of marginal and conditional densities as follows:

$$f_{XY}(x, y) = f_{X|Y}(x|y)\, f_Y(y)$$

Integrating both sides over *y* will give us the marginal density of *X* expressed as:

$$f_X(x) = \int_{-\infty}^{\infty} f_{X|Y}(x|y)\, f_Y(y)\, dy$$

EXAMPLE 5.6: Bivariate Normal Density:

Bivariate Normal density models the relationship between two random variables. One of the earliest uses of this was to model the joint distribution of the heights of fathers and sons. The density is given by:

$$f(x, y) = \frac{1}{2\pi\sigma_X\sigma_Y\sqrt{1-\rho^2}} \exp\left(-\frac{1}{2(1-\rho^2)}\left[\frac{(x-\mu_X)^2}{\sigma_X^2} + \frac{(y-\mu_Y)^2}{\sigma_Y^2} - \frac{2\rho(x-\mu_X)(y-\mu_Y)}{\sigma_X\sigma_Y}\right]\right)$$

This depends on five parameters:

$-\infty < \mu_X < \infty$: The mean of *X*

$-\infty < \mu_Y < \infty$: The mean of *Y*

$\sigma_X > 0$: The standard deviation of *X*

$\sigma_Y > 0$: The standard deviation of *Y*

$-1 < \rho < 1$: The coefficient of correlation between *X* and *Y*

We will see a general form of this density function for n random variables in terms of the correlation matrix between the random variables.

The marginal distributions of *X* and *Y* are $N(\mu_X, \sigma_X^2)$ and $N(\mu_Y, \sigma_Y^2)$, respectively. The marginal density of *X* is

$$f_X(x) = \int_{-\infty}^{\infty} f_{XY}(x, y)\, dy$$

Making change of variables $a = \frac{x - \mu_X}{\sigma_X}$ and $b = \frac{y - \mu_Y}{\sigma_Y}$, we get

$$f_X(x) = \frac{1}{2\pi\sigma_X\sqrt{1-\rho^2}} \int_{-\infty}^{\infty} \exp\left(-\frac{1}{2(1-\rho^2)}\left[a^2 + b^2 - 2\rho ab\right]\right) db$$

We note that $a^2 + b^2 - 2\rho ab = (b - \rho a)^2 + a^2(1-\rho^2)$

Substituting, we get

$$f_X(x) = \frac{1}{2\pi\sigma_X\sqrt{1-\rho^2}} \int_{-\infty}^{\infty} \exp\left(-\frac{1}{2(1-\rho^2)}\left[(b-\rho a)^2 + a^2(1-\rho^2)\right]\right) db$$

$$= \frac{1}{2\pi\,\sigma_X\sqrt{1-\rho^2}} e^{-\frac{a^2}{2}} \int_{-\infty}^{\infty} \exp\left(-\frac{1}{2(1-\rho^2)}(b-\rho a)^2\right) db$$

This is the normal density with mean ρa and variance $(1-\rho^2)$ and hence will integrate to 1.

Thus, $f_X(x) = \frac{1}{2\pi\sigma_X} e^{-\frac{(x-\mu_X)^2}{2\sigma_X^2}}$

The conditional density of Y given X is the ratio of the bivariate normal density to a univariate normal density.

$$f_{Y|X}(y|x) = \frac{1}{\sigma_Y\sqrt{2\pi(1-\rho^2)}} \exp\left(-\frac{\frac{1}{2}\left(y - \mu_Y - \frac{\rho\sigma_Y}{\sigma_X}(x - \mu_X)\right)^2}{\sigma_Y^2(1-\rho^2)}\right)$$

This is a normal density with mean $\mu_Y + \frac{\rho(x-\mu_X)\sigma_Y}{\sigma_X}$ and variance $\sigma_Y^2(1-\rho^2)$. Thus, the conditional distribution of Y given X is a univariate normal distribution.

5.6 BAYES RULE

Bayes rule describes the probability of an event based on the prior knowledge of conditions that might be related to the event. We can use conditional probabilities to derive the statement of the Bayes rule. We know that $P(A \cap B) - P(A|B) * P(B)$ and $P(A \cap B) - P(B|A) * P(A)$. Combining the two, we get,

$$P(A|B)*P(B) = P(B|A)*P(A) \Rightarrow P(A|B) = \frac{P(B|A)*P(A)}{P(B)}$$

This gives us a way to invert the direction of conditioning of the events (random variables) and doesn't require the events (random variables) to be independent. Here, $P(B|A)$ is called the *likelihood ratio, P(A)* is called the *prior,* and $P(A|B)$ is called the *posterior.*

One of the major applications of the Bayes Rule is in evaluating models of data. We ask the following question, "Given some data, which model is most probable?" A *maximum a posteriori* (or MAP) estimate is the model M that maximizes $P(M|D)$. Using Bayes Rule, we can compute this as follows:

$$P(M|D) = \frac{P(D|M)*P(M)}{P(D)}$$

Observe that data, D is fixed and has the same probability for all possible models. Thus, we have to maximize the term: $P(D|M)*P(M)$. Now we may have two cases:

(a) If we assume all models are equally probable, we just have to maximize $P(D|M)$. This is the model that maximizes the likelihood of the data and is called the *maximum likelihood estimate.*

(b) If some models are more likely than others, we can assign different *prior probabilities* $P(M)$ to them.

Example: We are given a set of salaries of individuals at a small company and asked whether they came from a uniform distribution or an exponential distribution.

Here, S is the Salary data of 8 employees (in Lakhs of rupees per year): 4.8, 5.1, 5.4, 5.5, 6, 6.3, 8.1, 15.

We have to tell whether M_1 (exponential) or M_2 (uniform) distribution, models the data better. In other words, which of these is more probable to have generated this data?

The mean salary is: 7.025 lakhs

For exponential distribution, $\lambda = \frac{1}{7.025} = 0.142$. The distribution $p(s) = 0.142 * e^{-0.142(s-4.8)}$, where s is the salary of any individual.

For the uniform distribution, $p(s) = \frac{1}{15-4.8} = 0.098$

We have tabulated the probabilities of individual salaries, $p(s_i|M_1)$ and $p(s_i|M_2)$

ID	Salary	Uniform P (M_2)	Exp P (M_1)
1	4.8	0.098	0.142
2	5.1	0.098	0.136
3	5.4	0.098	0.131
4	5.5	0.098	0.129
5	6	0.098	0.120
6	6.3	0.098	0.115
7	8.1	0.098	0.089
8	15	0.098	0.033

$$P(S|M_1) = \prod_{i=1}^{8} p(s_i \mid M_1) = 1.3 * 10^{-8}$$

$$P(S|M_2) = \prod_{i=1}^{8} p(s_i \mid M_2) = 0.85 * 10^{-8}$$

Clearly, exponential distribution explains the salary data with higher probability.

5.7 CENTRAL LIMIT THEOREM

This theorem states that the if X_1, X_2, ... X_n are i.i.d random variables with finite mean μ and finite variance σ^2, then their average $\overline{X_n} = \frac{1}{n}(X_1 + X_2 + \ldots + X_n)$ has a limiting distribution that is a Gaussian with mean μ and variance $\frac{\sigma^2}{n}$.

This is very significant because the original distribution of $X_i^{'}s$ may be very general. In simple terms, the sampling distribution of the sample mean is approximately Gaussian. This approximation can be used to quantify the error committed in estimating the population mean by the sample mean, thus giving us a good understanding of the accuracy of estimates produced by a simple random sample.

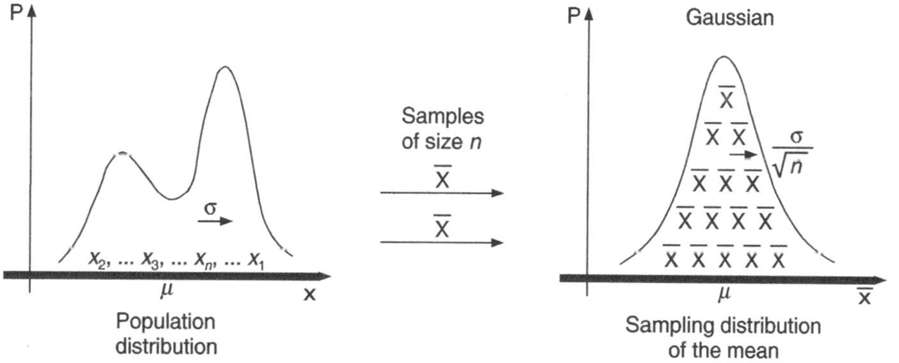

FIGURE 5.3 Central Limit Theorem.

Confidence interval: The above theorem helps us derive a confidence interval for the population mean, μ. A confidence interval for a population parameter, θ, is a random interval, calculated from the sample, that contains θ with some specified probability. For example, a 95% confidence interval for μ is a random interval that contains μ with probability .95.

If we take many random samples and form a confidence interval from each one, about 95% of these intervals would contain μ. If the coverage probability is $1 - \alpha$, the interval is called a $100(1 - \alpha)\%$ confidence interval. Confidence intervals are frequently used in conjunction with point estimates to convey information about the uncertainty of the estimates.

Z-score: For $0 \leq \alpha \leq 1$, let $z(\alpha)$ be that number such that the area under the standard normal density function to the right of $z(\alpha)$ is α. Note that the symmetry of the standard normal density function about zero implies that $z(1 - \alpha) = -z(\alpha)$.

5.8 INFERENCE

Inference is a branch of statistics that deals with forming inferences and predictions about a population based on a sample of data.

Point estimation is concerned with the use of sample data to measure a single value which serves as an approximate value or the best estimate of an unknown population parameter. For example, *sample mean,* $\bar{x}$, (mean of the values in the sample) is an estimate of the mean of the population, μ. The CLT assures us that the sample mean will be very close to the population mean as the sample size becomes large.

There are several methods used for inference:

(a) **Method of Moments:** Estimates are found out by equating the first K sample moments to the corresponding K population moments.
(b) **Maximum Likelihood:** A parameterized model is used, and the parameters are chosen to maximize a likelihood function for the given sample.
(c) **Bayes' Estimators:** They minimize the average risk which is defined in terms of an expectation of random variables.
(d) **Best Unbiased Estimator:** A parameter is approximated by optimizing a certain criterion.

Interval estimation is concerned with estimating a range of values in which an unknown population parameter lies. *Confidence interval* is the measure of the confidence that the interval estimate contains the parameter, e.g., population mean, μ. For example, if $P(a<\theta<b)=1-\alpha$, then the interval, (a, b) is called a $100(1-\alpha)\%$ confidence interval of θ. The quantity $(1-\alpha)$ is called the confidence level of the interval and α is known as the *significance level.*

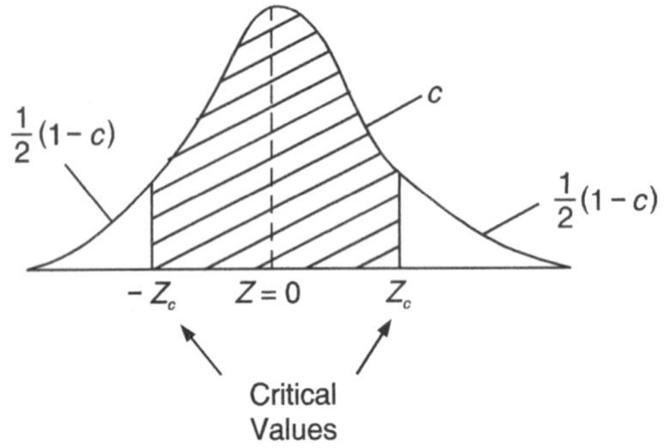

FIGURE 5.4 Critical Values.

The difference between the point estimate and the actual population parameter values is called sampling error. When μ is estimated, the sampling error is the $A_i - B_i$. The margin of error, E, for a given level of confidence is the greatest possible distance between the point estimate and the value of the parameter that is being estimated.

$E = z_c \frac{\sigma}{\sqrt{n}}$, where z_c is the critical value of confidence interval and n is the sample size.

The level of confidence, c, is the area beneath the normal curve between the critical values, z_c. Corresponding z score can be calculated using the standard normal table. For example, a confidence of 90% corresponds to a z-score of 1.645.

EXAMPLE 5.7: A random sample price of 100 textbook prices is taken from a local college bookstore. The sample mean is $\bar{x} = ₹\,275$ and the sample standard deviation is $s = 50$. Use a 95% confidence level ($z_c = 1.96$) and find the margin of error for the mean price of all textbooks in the bookstore.

Solution: Margin of error $= E = z_c \cdot \dfrac{\sigma}{\sqrt{n}} = 1.96 * \dfrac{50}{\sqrt{(100)}} = ₹\,9.8$

EXAMPLE 5.8: A sample of 25 circuits from a large normal population has a mean resistance of 5 ohms. We know from past testing that the population std. deviation is 0.2 ohms. Determine a 95% confidence interval for the true mean of the population.

Solution: Here, $n = 25$, $\bar{x} = 5$, $\sigma = 0.2$ and Confidence level, $(1-\alpha) = 0.95 \Rightarrow \alpha = 0.05$

Thus, confidence interval is $\bar{x} \pm z_{0.95}\dfrac{\sigma}{\sqrt{n}} = 5 \pm 1.96 * \dfrac{0.2}{5} = 5 \pm 0.08$

In other words, we are 95% confident that the average resistance of circuits lies between 4.92 to 5.08 ohms. 5% of times, this may not be the true mean.

5.9 MULTI-VARIATE NORMAL

Multi-variate normal is an extension of normal distribution to multivariate (d-dimensional) random variables. It is characterized by a d-dimensional mean vector μ and a co-variance matrix Σ of dimensions $d \times d$. The probability density function is given as:

$$p(x \mid \mu, \Sigma) = (2\pi)^{-\frac{d}{2}} \mid \Sigma \mid^{-\frac{1}{2}} e^{-\frac{1}{2}(x-\mu)^T \Sigma^{-1}(x-\mu)}$$

The eigen-decomposition of Σ is given as $\Sigma u_i = \lambda_i u_i$ where $\lambda_1 \geq \lambda_2 \geq \ldots \geq \lambda_d \geq 0$ are the eigenvalues and u_i the corresponding eigenvectors.

The covariance matrix can be compactly written as $\Sigma = U \Lambda U^T$ where

$$\Lambda = \begin{pmatrix} \lambda_1 & 0 & \cdots & 0 \\ 0 & \lambda_2 & \cdots & 0 \\ \vdots & \vdots & \ddots & \vdots \\ 0 & 0 & \cdots & \lambda_d \end{pmatrix} \qquad \mathrm{U} = \begin{pmatrix} | & | & & | \\ u_1 & u_2 & \cdots & u_d \\ | & | & & | \end{pmatrix}$$

The eigenvectors represent the new basis vectors, with the covariance matrix given by Λ (all covariances become zero). Since the trace of a square matrix is invariant to similarity transformation, such as a change of basis, we have

$$\text{var}(D) = tr(\Sigma) = \sum_{i=1}^{d} \sigma_i^2 = \sum_{i=1}^{d} \lambda_i = tr(\Lambda)$$

5.10 SAMPLING FROM DISTRIBUTIONS

In simulation experiments and statistical analysis, it is often necessary to generate sample data from a known distribution.

Inverse transform sampling can be used to sample from any arbitrary distribution, using its CDF (C). We first use a uniform random number generator to select a value p in the interval [0, 1]. Now, p is used as an index on the CDF. We find a point x such that $C(x) = p$. Thus, $x = C^{-1}(p)$, where C^{-1} is the (left) inverse of C. These points x that are generated using the process, satisfy the distribution.

Left inverse of a function $F_X^{-1}(u) = \inf x : F_X(x) \geq u.$

$$F_X\left(F_X^{-1}(u)\right) = u.$$

EXAMPLE 5.9: Generating points with exponential distribution using the inverse transform method. The PDF of an exponential distribution with rate parameter λ is given as:

$$f(x, \lambda) = \begin{cases} \lambda e^{-\ddot{e}x} & x \geq 0 \\ 0 & x < 0 \end{cases}$$

By integrating, its CDF is given as:

$$F(x, \lambda) = \begin{cases} 1 - e^{-\ddot{e}x} & x \geq 0 \\ 0 & x < 0 \end{cases}$$

Let u be a uniformly distributed random variable. We then set $u = F(x, \lambda)$ and solve for x to get

$$x = F^{-1}(u) = -\frac{1}{\lambda}\ln(1 - u)$$

The random variable $-\frac{1}{\lambda}\ln(1 - u)$ has an exponential distribution.

5.11 REJECTION METHOD

There are cases when we either do not know the CDF or can't invert it. An alternate method can be used in such situations, if we know the p.d.f. $f_A(x)$ of the random variable A, that we are trying to generate. We also need to know how to generate another random variable B, where A and B take the same set of values (range space). In other words, $f_A(x) > 0 \leftrightarrow f_B(x) > 0.$

We will generate samples from B, and either accept or reject them in a way that the accepted samples appear to be generated from A. For doing this, we first compute the smallest constant c, such that $\frac{f_A(x)}{f_B(x)} \leq c, \forall x, s.t. f_A(x) > 0$.

Now, we begin sampling from B. Let us say, that the value sampled is x. We will accept this sample with probability $\frac{f_A(x)}{cf_B(x)}$, else we will reject it and continue generating new samples with the same process.

In most cases, the candidates generated from B fall within the range of A. If they come from a region where B has a higher p.d.f. Than A, we simply reject a portion of them so that we get the right proportions. It can be shown that the expected number of iterations needed to generate one sample of A is c. In order to generate n samples from A, on an average, we need to generate $c \times n$ samples of B, out of which n samples will be accepted and $(c - 1) \times n$ samples will be rejected.

For example, we can use this method to generate normal random variable (A) from the exponential random variable (B). Since exponential distribution generates only positive values, we can multiply the values by -1 with probability 0.5 to cover $\mathbb{R}$.

5.12 ESTIMATION OF PARAMETERS OF A DISTRIBUTION

Maximum Likelihood estimation

Maximum Likelihood Estimation (MLE) aims at finding a model that fits the data well. We compute the conditional probability $p(y|x)$. We assume the conditional distribution to be some appropriate distribution and treat the weights w as learnable parameters of the model. It may not be a linear model. For probabilistic linear regression, with observations $(x_1, y_1),\ldots,(x_n, y_n)$; one may use the following function:

$$p(y|x, w) = \mathcal{N}(y \mid w^T x, \beta^{-1})$$

Where w are the parameters of the linear model and β^{-1} is the variance. In other words, the conditional distribution is assumed to be Gaussian. For a fixed value of $\mathbf{w}$, $\mathbf{x}$, it provides us the likelihood of observing y.

We assume that the set of observations $(x_1, y_1),\ldots,(x_n, y_n)$; are i.i.d. (independent and identically distributed). Thus, the likelihood of the entire dataset can be factorized into a product of the likelihoods of each individual observation.

$$p(Y|X, \mathbf{w}) = \prod_{i=1}^{n} p(y_i \mid x_i, \mathbf{w})$$

Let us know define negative log-likelihood as the objective function that we seek to minimize:

$$L(\mathbf{w}) = -\log(p(Y| X, w) = -\sum_{i=1}^{n} \log p(y_i \mid x_i, \mathbf{w})$$

Since (x_i, y_i) are known, the negative log-likelihood is a function of $\mathbf{w}$

$$p(y_i \mid \mathbf{w}, \mathbf{x}_i) = \mathcal{N}\left(y_i \mid \mathbf{w}^T \mathbf{x}_i, \beta^{-1}\right) = \sqrt{\frac{\beta}{2\pi}} \exp\left[-\frac{\beta}{2}\left(y_i - \mathbf{w}^T \mathbf{x}_i\right)^2\right]$$

Therefore, $L(\mathbf{w}) = \frac{\beta}{2} \sum_{i=1}^{n} \left(y_i - \mathbf{w}^T \mathbf{x}_i\right)^2 - \sum_{i=1}^{n} \log\left(\sqrt{\frac{\beta}{2\pi}}\right)$

As β is a constant, minimizing $L(w)$ corresponds to solving the least squares problem that we have familiar with.

5.13 HYPOTHESIS TESTING

Statisticians use hypothesis testing to formally check whether the hypothesis is accepted or rejected. Hypothesis testing is conducted in the following manner:

(a) Hypothesis formulation and statement of *Null and Alternate Hypothesis*
(b) Formulating a plan for analyzing the hypothesis and determining the *test statistic,* a value that we compute using the sample
(c) Analysis of the sample data, calculation and interpretation of *test statistic*
(d) Applying the decision rule and interpretation of the results.

Null Hypothesis (H_o) states that the result is no different from the assumption.
Alternate Hypothesis (H_a) states that the result disproves the assumption.
Significance of the test is a threshold α that is specified according to the domain. It tells us the probability of making Type-I error.
These describe two approaches for hypothesis testing.

(a) P-value: This is the probability (computed using the test statistics) that measures the support provided by the sample for the null hypothesis, H_o. If p-value is high, it supports the null hypothesis and if $p -$ value $\leq a$, we reject the null hypothesis.
(b) Critical Value approach: This uses a critical value of the test statistic beyond which the null hypothesis is rejected.

Let us demonstrate these with the help of some examples.

EXAMPLE 5.10: Delhi Food delivery service claims that they deliver food in less than 30 minutes. The population std. deviation is believed to be 10 minutes. The mean response time for a random sample of 30 deliveries was found to be 32 minutes. The food delivery service wants to perform a hypothesis test with α = 0.05 level of significance to determine whether their service goal of 30 minutes or less is being achieved on average.

Solution: Sample: mean, $\overline{x} = 32$ min , n = 30

Population:

Step 1: Develop the hypothesis. Since both overfilling and underfilling are problems, we go for a two-tailed test. $H_o : \mu \leq 30$ and $H_a : \mu > 30$

Step 2: Specify the level of significance, α = 0.05

Step 3: Compute the test statistics: $z = \dfrac{\overline{x} - \mu}{\dfrac{\sigma}{\sqrt{n}}} = \dfrac{32 - 30}{\dfrac{10}{\sqrt{30}}} = 1.095$

Step 4: Determine whether to reject H_o

EXAMPLE 5.11: A dairy packs 1000 ml. milk in glass bottles. A sample of 30 bottles was taken and the sample mean was found to be 1005 ml. The population std. dev. is believed to be 10 ml. Perform a hypothesis test at the 0.03 level of significance, population mean 1000 ml. and help determine whether the filling process should continue operation or be stopped and corrected.

Solution: Sample: mean, $\bar{x} = 1005$ ml., $n = 30$

Population: $\sigma = 10$ ml., $\mu = 1000$ ml., $\alpha = 0.03$

Step 1: Develop the hypothesis. Since both overfilling and underfilling are problems, we go for a two-tailed test. $H_o : \mu = 1000$ ml and $H_a : \mu \neq 1000$ ml.

Step 2: Specify the level of significance, $\alpha = 0.03$

Step 3: Compute the test statistics: $z = \dfrac{\bar{x} - \mu}{\frac{\sigma}{\sqrt{n}}} = \dfrac{1005 - 1000}{\frac{10}{\sqrt{30}}} = 2.74$

Step 4: Determine whether to reject H_o

5.14 *T*-TEST

The *t*-test evaluates whether the population means of two samples are different. This problem commonly arises in comparing two groups for *AB* testing. The *t*-test can be applied in multiple ways and we need to consider whether the groups being compared come from a single population or two different populations, and whether we want to test the difference in a specific direction.

If the groups come from a single population (e.g., measuring before and after an experimental treatment), then we perform a **paired *t*-test**.

If the groups come from two different populations (e.g., two different species, or people from two separate cities), we perform a **two-sample *t*-test** (a.k.a. independent *t*-test).

If there is one group being compared against a standard value (e.g., comparing the acidity of a liquid to a neutral pH of 7), we perform a one-sample *t*-test.

If we only care whether the two populations are different from one another, we perform a two-tailed *t*-test. If we want to know whether one population mean is greater than or less than the other, we perform a one-tailed *t*-test.

The *t*-test is a parametric test of difference, meaning that it makes the following assumptions:

(a) are independent
(b) are (approximately) normally distributed
(c) have a similar amount of variance within each group being compared (a.k.a. homogeneity of variance)

If the data does not fit these assumptions, a nonparametric test, such as the Wilcoxon Signed-Rank test for data with unequal variances.

The *t*-statistic is given by: $t = \dfrac{\overline{\mu_1} - \overline{\mu_2}}{\sqrt{\dfrac{\sigma_1^2}{n_1} + \dfrac{\sigma_2^2}{n_2}}}$, where μ_i, σ_i and n_i are the mean, standard deviation and population size of sample *i* respectively. By paying close attention to the test statistic, we can observe that it is high if the two means differ significantly or when the standard deviations are small or when the number of samples is very high. To perform the test, the test-statistic is looked up in an appropriate table for a desired significance level α.

EXAMPLE 5.12: Suppose we find two different species of irises growing in a garden and measure 25 petals of each species. Now, we want to know whether the mean petal length of iris flowers differs according to their species. We can test the difference between these two groups using a *t* test and null and alternative hypotheses.

The **null hypothesis** (H_0) is that the true difference between these group means is zero.

The **alternate hypothesis** (H_a) is that the true difference is different from zero.

In this example, our observations come from two separate populations (separate species), so you perform **a-two-sample *t*-test**. We don't care about the direction of the difference, only whether there is a difference, so we must choose to use a **two-tailed *t*-test.**

We now calculate the *t*-statistic. A larger value shows that the difference between group means is greater than the pooled standard error, indicating a more significant difference between the groups.

We can compare the calculated *t-value* against the values in a critical value chart (e.g., Student's *t*-table) to determine if *t-value* is greater than what would be expected by chance. If so, you can reject the null hypothesis and conclude that the two groups are in fact different.

Final statement: The difference in petal length between iris species 1 (M = 1.46; SD = 0.206) and iris species 2 (M = 5.54; SD = 0.569) was significant ($t(30) = -33.7190$; $p < 2.2e\text{-}16$).

5.15 CHI-SQUARE TEST OF INDEPENDENCE

A chi-square (X_2) test of independence is a nonparametric hypothesis test. You can use it to test whether two categorical variables are related to each other.

EXAMPLE 5.13: Suhas teaches ML and wants to encourage all his students to come to class on time.

He decides to test an intervention: sending a personal email or having a personal conversation. He randomly assigns them to email, conversation or control group (no intervention). He will use the results of the experiment to decide which intervention to use in his future courses.

Suhas plans to use a chi-square test of independence to test whether attendance level differs between the interventions. If two variables are related, the probability of one variable having a certain value is dependent on the value of the other variable. The chi-square test of independence calculations is based on the observed frequencies, which are the numbers of observations in each combined group. The test compares the observed frequencies to the frequencies you would expect if the two variables are unrelated. When the variables are unrelated, the observed and expected frequencies will be similar.

Like all hypothesis tests, the chi-square test of independence evaluates a null and alternative hypothesis. The hypotheses are two competing answers to the question "Are variable 1 and variable 2 related?"

Null hypothesis (H_0): Whether a student comes late to class and the type of intervention they receive are **not related** in the population; The proportions of students who come late to class are the same for all interventions.

Alternative hypothesis (H_a): Whether a student comes late to class and the type of intervention they receive are **related** in the population; The proportions of students who come late to class are not the same for all interventions.

5.16 CONTINGENCY TABLES

We begin with organizing data in a frequency distribution table called a contingency table. A contingency table, also known as a cross tabulation or crosstab, shows the number of observations in each combination of groups. It also usually includes row and column totals.

Intervention	Attend Class on Time	Late Attendance	Row Total
Email	38	8	46
Personal Conversation	42	2	44
Control	30	15	45
Column Total	110	25	N = 135

Expected Frequencies can be calculated by assuming that proportion of late attendance is same for all interventions. Expected frequency for row r and column c is: $\frac{\text{Row } r \text{ total} \times \text{Column c total}}{N}$

Test Statistic

Pearson's chi-square (X^2) is the test statistic for the chi-square test of independence:

$$X^2 = \Sigma \frac{(O-E)^2}{E}$$

Where O is the observed frequency and E is the expected frequency. The chi-square test statistic measures how much the observed frequencies differ from the expected frequencies if the two variables are unrelated. It is large when there's a big difference between the observed and expected frequencies ($O - E$ in the equation).

Expected frequencies for the above example are calculated as follows:

Intervention	Attend Class on Time	Late Attendance	Row Total
Email	(46 × 110)/135 = 37.48	(46 × 25)/135 = 8.51	46
Personal Conversation	(44 × 110)/135 = 35.85	(44 × 25)/135 = 8.14	44
Control	(45 × 110)/135 = 36.66	(45 × 25)/135 = 8.33	45
Column Total	110	25	135

The test statistic (X^2) is calculated as:

$$\frac{(38-37.48)^2}{37.48} + \frac{(8-8.51)^2}{8.51} + \frac{(42-35.85)^2}{35.85} + \frac{(2-8.14)^2}{8.14} + \frac{(30-36.66)^2}{36.66} + \frac{(15-8.33)^2}{8.33}$$

$$= 0.007 + 0.03 + 1.055 + 4.63 + 1.209 + 5.34 = 12.271.$$

We can find the critical value in a chi-square critical value table or using statistical software. We need to know two numbers to find the critical value:

The degrees of freedom (*df*): For a chi-square test of independence, the *df* is (number of variable 1 groups – 1) × (number of variable 2 groups – 1). Since there are three intervention groups (email, personal conversation, and control) and two outcome groups (on time attendance and late attendance) there are (3 – 1) × (2 – 1) = 2 degrees of freedom.

By convention, we take the Significance level (α) = 0.05

For a test of significance at $\alpha = .05$ and $df = 2$, the X^2 critical value is 5.99 based on the table.

The test statistic X^2 is greater than the critical value. Therefore, Suhas rejects the null hypothesis. Suhas concludes that their interventions have an effect on whether students come on time OR late to classes!

5.17 KS TEST

This is a non-parametric test that compares the CDF of two given distributions to assess how similar they are. Very often, we find a situation where we wish to compare the distribution of an attribute with another attribute, or even the same attribute in another time period. We want to know if the model is being used on a data distribution that is different from the one used for training. The Kolmogorov-Smirnov (KS) test is a non-parametric statistical test that can be used to compare distributions, *A* and *B* to see if they are different.

The KS test statistic is defined as the maximum value of the difference between *A* and *B*'s cumulative distribution functions (CDF). Typically, we use empirical CDF which is defined as:

$$\widehat{F_A}(t) = \frac{\text{number of elements in the sample} \leq t}{N}, \text{ where } N \text{ is the size of the sample.}$$

$$\text{KS test statistic } (D) = \sup_x \left| \widehat{F_A}(x) - \widehat{F_B}(x) \right|$$

The hypothesis regarding *A* and *B* having same distribution is rejected if the test statistic, *D*, is greater than the critical value obtained from a table.

5.18 USING VISUALIZATION FOR STUDY OF DISTRIBUTIONS

Quantiles are essential to visualize distributions. The *f* quantile *q(f)* of a dataset is a value along the measurement scale of the data with the property that approximately a fraction *f* of the data are less than or equal to *q(f)*. Two distributions are similar if their *q(f)* is similar for every value of *f*.

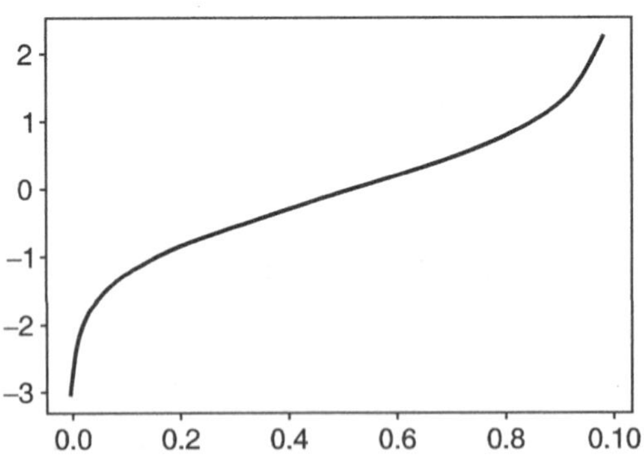

FIGURE 5.5 Quantile Plot for normal distribution.

Let $x_{(i)}$ for $i = 1$ to n, be the data ordered from smallest to largest; thus $x_{(1)}$ is the smallest observation and $x_{(n)}$ is the largest. On a quantile plot, $x_{(i)}$ is plotted against f_i. Plotting univariate measurements on a quantile plot is a simple and effective way to have a first look at their distribution. First the values of all the data are displayed and we can assess both overall behavior and unusual occurrences.

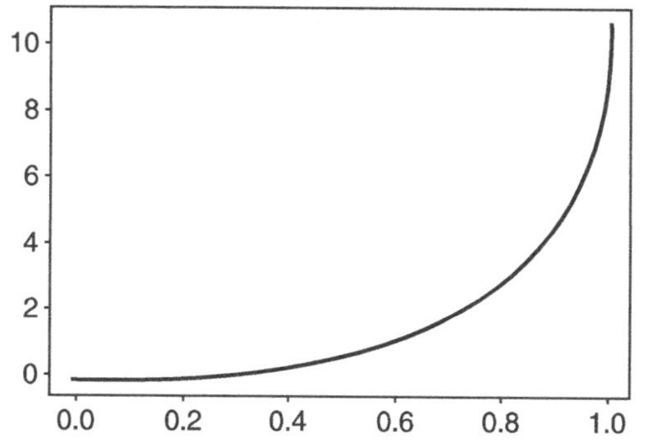

FIGURE 5.6 Quantile plot for lognormal distribution.

QQ Plots

Quantile-quantile plot is a powerful visualization method for comparing the distributions of two or more sets of univariate measurements. When distributions are compared, our goal is to understand how the distributions shift from one dataset to another. The key idea is to plot the quantiles of one distribution against the corresponding quantiles of the other.

If the distributions of two random variables A and B are the same, then QQ plot will be close to the line $A = B$.

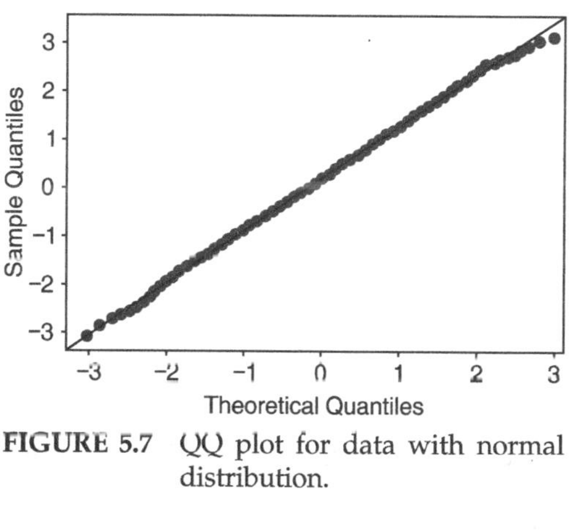

FIGURE 5.7 QQ plot for data with normal distribution.

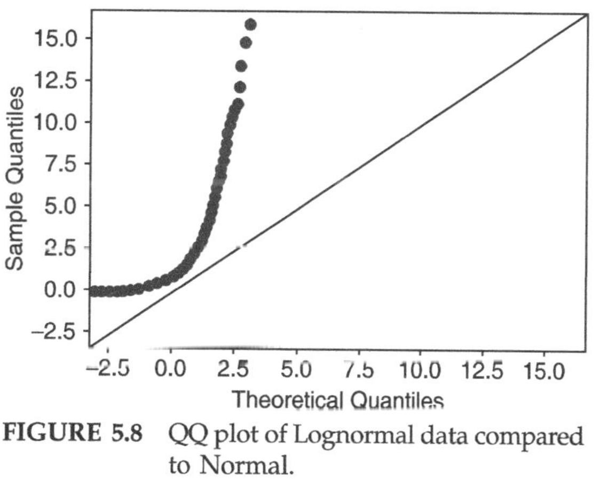

FIGURE 5.8 QQ plot of Lognormal data compared to Normal.

The Tukey mean difference plot is a plot derived from the QQ plot where the difference $A_i - B_i$ are plotted against the means $\frac{A_i + B_i}{2}$. The line $A = B$ becomes the zero line and a shift is assessed by judging deviations from the zero line and makes it easier.

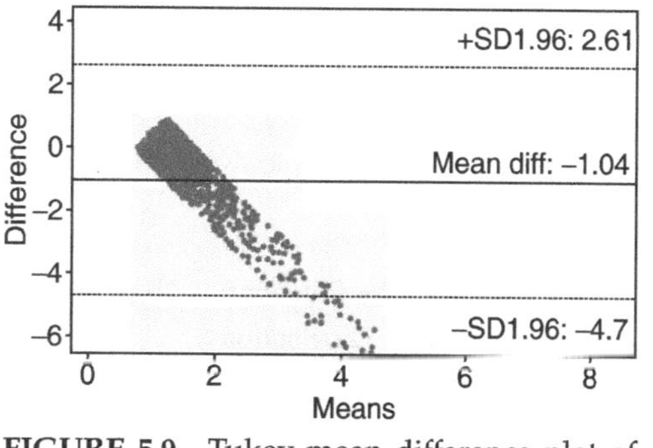

FIGURE 5.9 Tukey mean difference plot of normal and lognormal data.

EXERCISES

1. Let X be a random variable counting the number on a dice throw and Y is an indicator variable that takes on value 1 if we get a Head and 0 if we get a tail. If both the dice and the coin are fair, please write the joint p.d.f.
2. Consider two independent binary random variables, X and Y, where $P(X = 0) = p$ and $P(Y = 0) = q$. What is $P(X + Y \geq 1)$?
3. How many tosses of a fair coin are expected until two consecutive heads appear for the first time?
4. A fair coin is flipped twice, and it is given that at least one tail has been observed. Compute the probability of getting two tails.
5. Given n particles and m ($> n$) boxes, we place each particle in one of the boxes uniformly at random. What is the probability that no box receives more than one particle?
6. A total of 28 percent of males living in India like to eat Gulab Jamuns, 56 percent like Rasagullas, and 20 percent like to eat both of them. What percentage of males like neither of them?
7. Ms. Pintu estimates that there is a 30 percent chance that her company will set up a branch office in IIT Bhilai Research Park. If it does, she is 60 percent certain that she will be made manager of this new operation. What is the probability that Ms. Pintu will be a branch office manager at IIT Bhilai Research Park?
8. Suppose you are appearing in a GATE entrance test comprising 20 multiple-choice questions, each with 4 options. You are certain about the answers to 10 questions, but for the remaining 10, you guess by random selection. Your exam score denoted as X corresponds to the total number of correct answers. Determine the Probability $P(X \geq 15)$.
9. If two dice are thrown simultaneously, what is the probability of getting a multiple of 2 on one dice and multiple of 3 on the other dice?
10. The mean of the observations of the first 50 observations of a process is 10 and variance is 1. If the 51st observation is 100, then, the mean of the first 51 observations of the process, rounded off to two decimal places is ....and the variance is ....
11. Given n particles and m ($> n$) boxes, we place each particle in one of the boxes uniformly at random. What is the probability that no box receives more than one particle?
12. X is a random variable with expectation $E[X] = 100$ and variance $V[X] = 20$. Find
    (a) $E[(X - 2)(X + 2)]$
    (b) $E[-X]$
    (c) $V[-X]$

MULTIPLE CHOICE QUESTIONS

1. Two independent events A and B have probabilities $P(A) = 0.9$ and $P(B) = 0.5$. What is $P(A \cap B)$, the probability that both events occur?
   (a) 0.20 (b) 0.45
   (c) 0.10 (d) 0.90
2. If X is a random variable with $P(X = 2) = 0.4$ and $P(X = 4) = 0.7$, what is the expected value $E(X)$?
   (a) 3.6 (b) 2.8
   (c) 3.5 (d) 4.5
3. Which of the following is **NOT** a discrete probability distribution?
   (a) Poisson Distribution (b) Binomial Distribution
   (c) Exponential Distribution (d) Geometric Distribution

4. Which distribution is appropriate for modeling the number of events occurring in a fixed interval of time or space when these events happen independently and at a constant rate?

(a) Normal Distribution
(b) Binomial Distribution
(c) Poisson Distribution
(d) Exponential Distribution

5. The probability density function (PDF) of a continuous random variable X is given by $\frac{1}{2\pi}e^{-\frac{x^2}{2}}$. This represents the:

(a) Uniform Distribution
(b) Exponential Distribution
(c) Normal Distribution
(d) Gamma Distribution

6. In a normal distribution, approximately what percentage of data lies within one standard deviation of the mean?

(a) 95%
(b) 68%
(c) 50%
(d) 99.7%

7. In a simple random sample, what is the probability that a specific data point is chosen from a population of 500 if the sample size is 50?

(a) $\frac{1}{500}$
(b) $\frac{50}{500}$
(c) $\frac{1}{50}$
(d) None of the above

8. A researcher wants to estimate the average height of students in a university. To minimize bias and ensure representation, they divide students into groups based on their academic year and select samples from each group. This method is known as:

(a) Systematic Sampling
(b) Cluster Sampling
(c) Stratified Sampling
(d) Simple Random Sampling

9. If the Pearson correlation coefficient between two variables X and Y is -0.88, which of the following statements is TRUE?

(a) X and Y have a weak positive linear relationship.
(b) X and Y have a strong positive linear relationship.
(c) X and Y have a weak negative linear relationship.
(d) X and Y have a strong negative linear relationship.

10. A correlation coefficient of 0 between two variables implies that:

(a) There is no linear relationship between the variables.
(b) The variables are independent.
(c) The variables are uncorrelated in any way.
(d) There is a perfect linear relationship between the variables.

11. Which of the following best describes **multicollinearity** in a regression model?

(a) A situation where the predictor variables are highly correlated with each other.
(b) A situation where the response variable is highly correlated with one predictor variable.
(c) A violation of the assumption of homoscedasticity.
(d) A situation where the data have high variance.

12. In hypothesis testing, a **Type I error** occurs when:

(a) The null hypothesis is rejected when it is true.
(b) The null hypothesis is not rejected when it is false.
(c) The alternative hypothesis is accepted when it is false.
(d) The p-value is larger than the significance level.

13. A researcher conducts a two-tailed hypothesis test at a 5% significance level. The p-value for the test is 0.03. What conclusion should the researcher make?
    (a) Fail to reject the null hypothesis.
    (b) Reject the null hypothesis.
    (c) Increase the significance level to 10%.
    (d) The result is inconclusive.
14. In hypothesis testing, if the significance level α is increased, what happens to the probability of committing a Type II error?
    (a) Increases (b) Decreases
    (c) Stays the same (d) Becomes zero
15. In a hypothesis test for a population mean, if the sample size increases while keeping all other factors constant, the standard error:
    (a) Increases (b) Decreases
    (c) Remains unchanged (d) Becomes zero
16. Which of the following tests is commonly used to check whether a dataset follows a normal distribution?
    (a) Chi-square Test (b) Kolmogorov-Smirnov Test
    (c) Wilcoxon Test (d) Mann-Whitney U Test

REFERENCES

[1] Gilbert Strang, Linear Algebra and Learning from Data, Cambridge University press.
[2] Jeff Philips, Mathematical Foundations of data analysis, Springer.
[3] A. Faisal, C.S. Ong, M.P. Deisenroth, Mathematics for Machine Learning.
[4] John A. Rice Mathematical statistics and Data analysis.

ANSWER KEY

1. (b) **2.** (a) **3.** (c) **4.** (c) **5.** (c) **6.** (b) **7.** (b) **8.** (c) **9.** (d) **10.** (a)
11. (a) **12.** (a) **13.** (b) **14.** (b) **15.** (b) **16.** (b)

Part II

Data Visualization

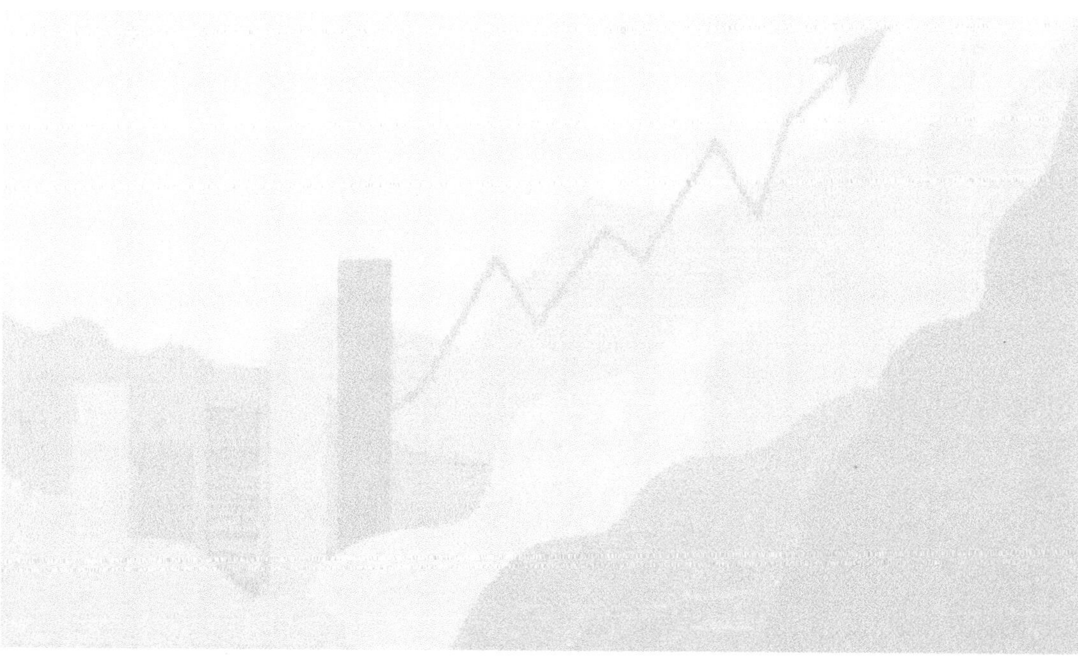

6 Visualization Design Principles

Introduction

We have discussed the importance of data visualization during the data exploration phase in Chapter 2. In this chapter, we will begin with the basics of visualization design and learn how to design and/or choose effective data visualizations. We must understand the needs of our users, show them the information that is necessary for them to perform their tasks, and show it in a way that the user can interpret it accurately and efficiently. We must think of the questions our visualization should help readers answer easily, without reading too much.

Data visualization helps people perform their tasks such as analysis, search, comparing trends, discovering patterns more effectively. In many cases, the exact questions are not known in advance and visualization helps in defining the objectives of data analysis. Visualization also helps debug and refine the models. It helps end users to verify and build trust in the models.

Sometimes, summaries lose information, and it may be necessary to have the details in order to confirm expected and discover unexpected patterns. In most applications, users engage with visualizations in real time and thus, they should be fast and interactive.

6.1 EXAMPLE OF ANSCOMBE'S QUARTET

In the example below, 4 different datasets with identical summary statistics are shown. Each of them has the same values of mean and variance of x and y and the Pearson's correlation coefficient between x and y. Yet each of the datasets is very different. This shows that the summaries often lose information.

One of the main challenges of data visualization is that the displays are limited by the number of pixels available. **Information density** is the ratio of space used to encode information divided by the unused whitespace. There is a tradeoff between dense visualization (packing too much information) versus wasting space. Some of the computational challenges of data visualization include computation time and system memory limits. Apart from that, there are human limits such as human time, human memory, and human attention. We have to address all these challenges.

Anscombe's Quartet

Identical statistics	
x mean	9
x variance	10
y mean	7.5
y variance	3.75
x/y correlation	0.816

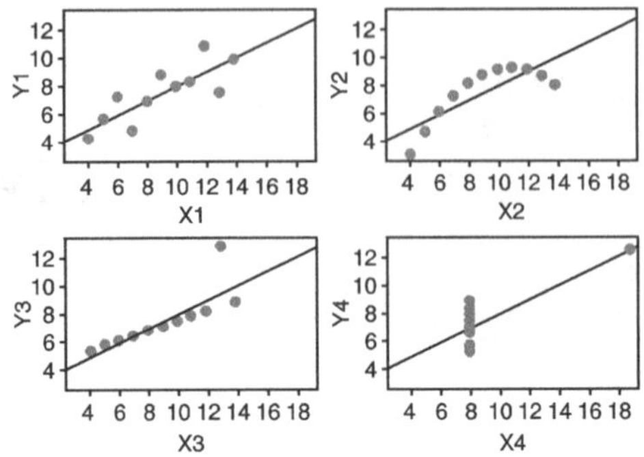

FIGURE 6.1 Summary statistics of 4 example datasets: data is different, but summaries are exactly same.

In order to design effective visualizations, the designer must ask three fundamental questions: **What** data to show, **Why** the user will use the visualization, and **How** to visually encode and interact with the data?

The time-series plot in Figure 6.2 gives an example of important features of good data visualization which has the following properties.

- **Clear and concise title:** "Sales Over Time"
- **Appropriate chart type:** Line chart to show trends over time
- **Legible axis labels:** Both axes are labeled with units of measure
- **Proper use of color:** Colors distinguish different data series without causing confusion
- **Data points are clear:** Data points are distinct and easy to follow
- **Minimal clutter:** Only necessary grid lines and labels are included

On the other hand, the pie-chart in Figure 6.2 illustrates what is not desirable.

- **Unclear title:** "Data"
- **Inappropriate chart type:** Pie-chart used for time series data
- **No axis labels:** Axes are not labeled, making it hard to interpret
- **Poor color choices:** Colors are too similar or distracting
- **Overlapping data points:** Data points are cluttered and overlap
- **Excessive clutter:** Too many grid lines, unnecessary decorations

Now, we discuss the What, Why and How of data visualization in more detail and lay out some fundamental principles to guide the design.

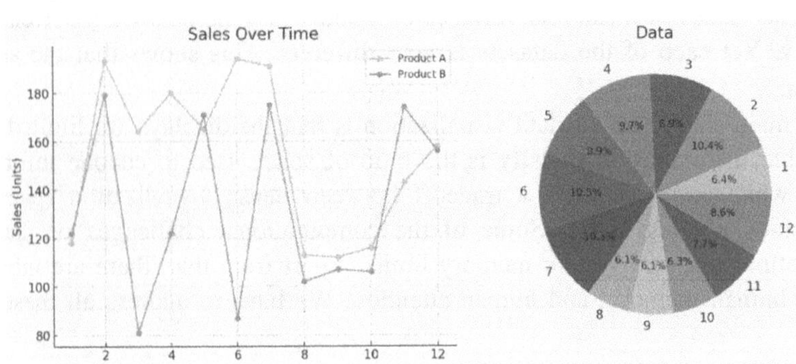

FIGURE 6.2 Comparison of Good and Bad Visualization.

6.2 DATA ABSTRACTION

Data abstraction deals with the "**what**" of data visualization. What do we want to visualize? Often, we don't just draw what is given. We transform the data to a new form. We have already discussed structured, unstructured and semi-structured data and various types of attributes. Data may also be represented by graphs. A graph has a set of nodes (entities) and edges (relations among entities). Datasets can be static or dynamic in the form of streams. Temporal datasets have time as an attribute. Additional information may also be present in the form of metadata.

It is important for us to understand the semantics (meaning of the data). Data may have key attributes, that act as an index to retrieve data value (other attributes). For example, in a school dataset, the roll number of a student is a key attribute that can be used to retrieve the name, address, age, height, weight, class, attendance, marks, etc., of the student. We can then use it to calculate the BMI of the students and measure its trend to determine the effectiveness of a mid-day meal program.

We must first identify the dataset type(s) and types of attributes. We must identify the cardinality, i.e., number of levels for categorical data and the range for quantitative data. We must consider whether or not to transform data guided by an understanding of the tasks.

For example, suppose we have temperature measurements in degree C. Now, for different applications, we may transform those measurements differently. Let's take 3 different cases:

(a) Task is weather forecasting: In this case, we would like to model temperature as a continuous quantitative attribute with 2 significant Figure. For example 15°C, 14°C, 35°C. (see Figure 6.3.a)

(b) Deciding if the milk is ready to drink: In this case, we can use an ordinal attribute for milk temperature with 3 levels hot, warm and cold (e.g., see Figure 6.3.b).

(c) Deciding if we can go outside our house during summer: In this case, we may simply use a categorical attribute: safe to go, too hot.

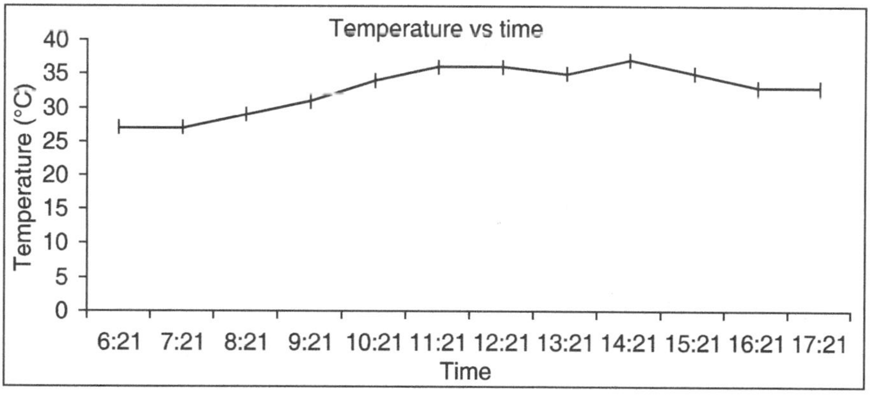

FIGURE 6.3 (a) Line chart representing the change in temperature over time.

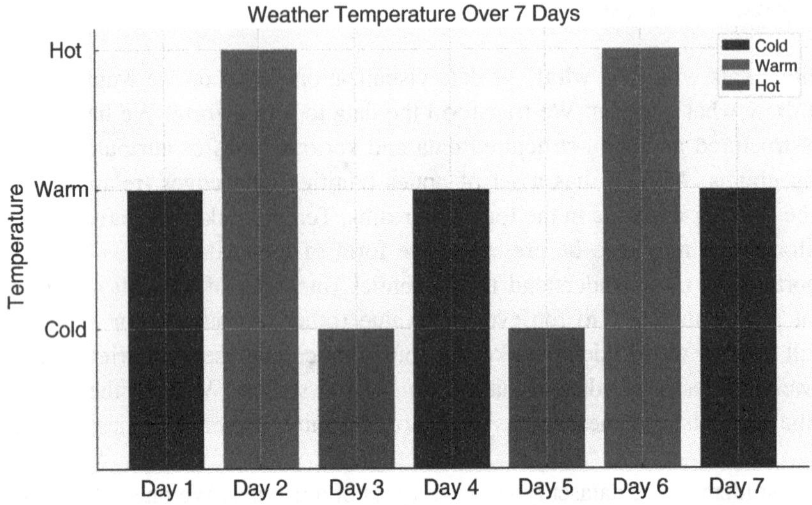

FIGURE 6.3 (b) Here's the bar chart visualization of the weather temperature throughout the week. Each bar represents the temperature on a specific day, with different colors indicating the temperature levels: blue for cold, red for warm, and green for hot.

6.2.1 Deriving Attributes

We can change the type, acquire additional data or compute a complex transformation to make the visualization easy to understand.

Suppose we want to understand the profit/loss of a company:

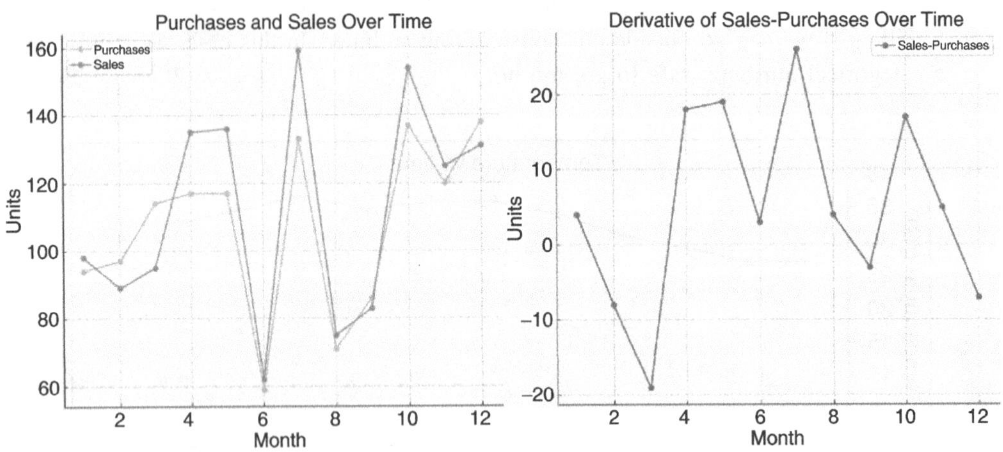

FIGURE 6.4 Analysis of the data trends and their derivatives.

Purchases and Sales Over Time: This plot shows the trends for purchases and sales over a period of 12 months.

Sales-Purchases Over Time: This plot shows the difference (derivative) between sales and purchases over the same period._The red line represents the trend of the difference, indicating whether sales were higher or lower than purchases each month.

6.2.2 Task Abstraction

Task abstraction deals with the **"why"** of data visualization? We must have an understanding of the reason the user is looking at data. Some of the important use cases for data visualization are as follows:

(a) **Analysis:** It is common for the user to discover patterns in the data and present them to others. They may be interested in understanding data distribution, correlations or similarities between multiple attributes. They may also enrich the data by adding annotations, labels, recording important elements such as persistent artifacts (e.g., screenshots) and deriving new data elements based on existing data.

(b) **Search:** The user may want to search for interesting elements within the visualization. For example, one may "lookup" the GDP of India in a visualization of the GDPs of all countries in the world. Sometimes the user may want to identify items that match a certain criterion, such as the growth rate of GDP must be greater than 5%. Another common use case is identification of outliers, anomalous spikes in time-series or unexpected patterns.

(c) **Query:** Another goal of a user might be to identify, compare or summarize relevant information. For example, one may identify election results for Delhi, compare the election results of Delhi with Uttar Pradesh, or summarize the election results across all states in India to determine how many favored one political party or the other. The goal of summarization or providing an overview is extremely common.

6.3 VISUALIZATION IDIOMS

Idioms deal with **"how"** to arrange (encode) data within a view. There are two aspects: visual encoding idiom that specifies how to draw and interaction idiom that specifies how to manipulate data.

Marks and channels: A mark is a basic graphical element in an image. Some examples of marks are points, lines and areas. A visual channel is a way to control the appearance of marks. Some important visual channels are aligned or unaligned spatial position, depth, and spatial region. Others pertain to color, which has three aspects: hue, saturation and luminance. Angle or tilt, curvature and shapes are also visual channels.

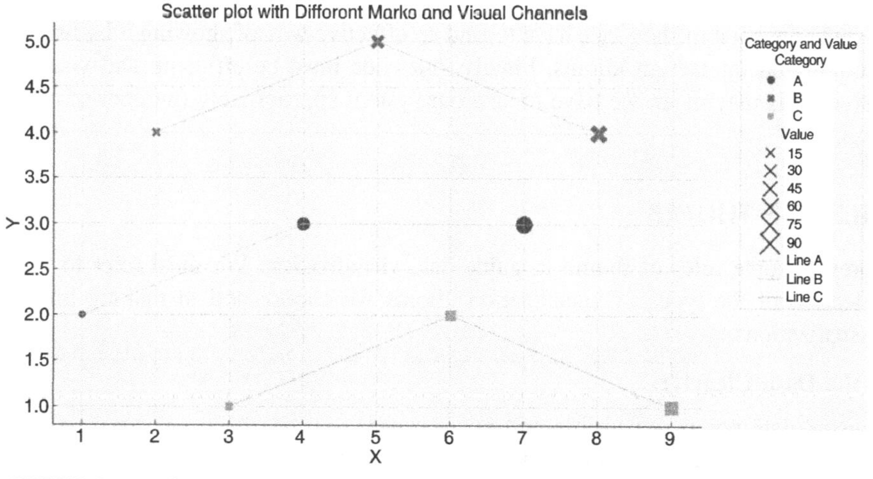

FIGURE 6.5 Scatter plot demonstrating different marks and visual channels.

Points: Different shapes represent different categories, **Lines:** Dashed lines connect points within the same category, **Color:** Different colors represent different categories, **Size:** The size of each point represents the value associated with it.

We must strive to use visual channels that are expressive and effective. **Expressiveness** means that visual encoding should express all the information in the dataset, but not imply relationships or patterns that don't exist. For example, if data is unordered, it shouldn't be shown in a way that implies order. A visualization is **effective** if the most important attributes are encoded with the most effective channels so that they are easily noticeable.

Choice of visual channels for ordered attributes: Based on a study by Cleveland and McGill, the most effective channel for encoding ordinal or quantitative attributes is aligned spatial position followed by unaligned spatial position. Then comes length, then angle/tilt, then area and then depth. Finally, luminance and saturation are almost equivalent in their effectiveness.

Choice of visual channels for categorical attributes: The most effective channel for encoding categorical attributes is spatial region, followed by color hue and finally shape.

The following criteria can be applied to judge the effectiveness of channels:

(a) Accuracy: Ensuring that the human perception is close to what we want to depict.
(b) Ability to distinguish differences between items. Each visual channel provides a different number of options (bins). For example, linewidth can be used to encode the magnitude, but is effective only for depicting 3-4 distinct values of the attribute.
(c) Making a distinct item stand out from others immediately. For this one can use tilt, size, shape, proximity and shadow direction.
(d) Ability to provide groupings

6.4 DESIGNING AND VALIDATING A DATA VISUALIZATION

A designer has to work closely with his target audience to understand their requirements. We must understand what is their domain of interest, their questions, and their data. To do this one may conduct interviews with the users and observe them interacting with the data with existing tools.

Once the needs of the user are understood, one performs data and task abstraction. This maps the domain specific requirements to generic requirements. Here, we do data pre-processing, data transformation and identify the tasks the user wants to perform.

Once we know what to show, we have to find an effective way of showing it by using appropriate visual encoding and interaction idioms. Finally, our code must be efficient, and visualization must be responsive. This may mean we have to size our system appropriately (number of cores, memory, storage etc.).

6.5 RULES OF THUMB

We now present some rules of thumb to guide data visualization. We must refer to these points in making selection of the types of visualization idioms we choose and in making improvements to existing visualizations.

(1) Show the Data-Clearly:

(a) Ensure data points are visible and not obscured.
(b) Label titles and axes clearly and accurately.
(c) Maintain constant measurement scales and avoid distortions.

(2) Use Simplicity in Design:

(a) Strive for a clean, uncluttered look.
(b) Avoid unnecessary elements like shading, 3D effects, and excessive color.

(3) Use Alignment on a Common Scale:

(a) Allow accurate estimation by using a single linear scale.
(b) Add gridlines to assist with comparison and estimation.

(4) Keep Visual Encoding Transparent:

(a) Make decoding easy with astute design choices.
(b) Consider element ordering, use meaningful color and shading, and solve detection problems with appropriate symbols.

(5) Proper Use of Axes:

(a) Pay attention to units of measure, range, number of tick marks, breaks in the axis, and the size of the axis.
(b) Ensure axes are well-labeled and appropriately scaled.

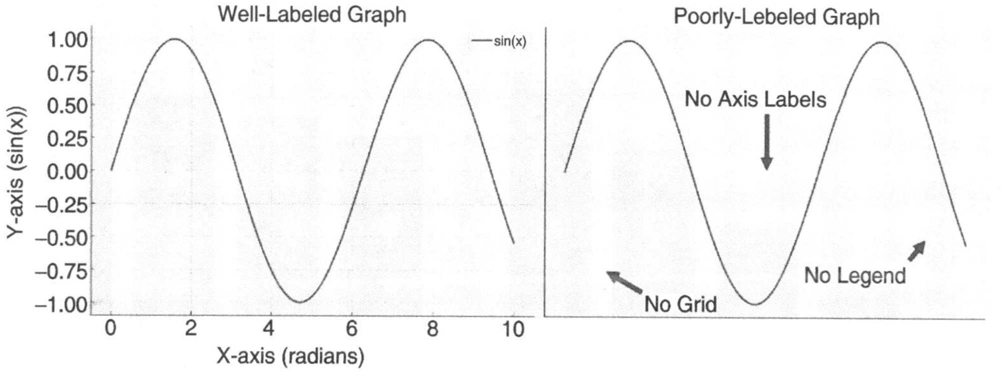

FIGURE 6.6 Comparison between a well-labeled graph and a poorly labeled graph.

(6) Proper Use of Color:

(a) Use color to encode categorical data or quantitative values in a meaningful way.
(b) Avoid using color for decoration.

(7) Choose Distinguishable Symbols:

(a) Use symbols that are easily distinguishable from one another.

(8) Maximize Data Density:

(a) Show as much data as possible without cluttering the visualization.
(b) Draw attention to the data, not the design elements.

(9) Maximize Data-Ink Ratio:

(a) The proportion of ink used to present actual data should be high.
(b) Erase non-data-ink and redundant data-ink.

(10) Minimize Chart-junk:

(a) Avoid unnecessary decorative elements that do not convey information.

(11) Use Visually Prominent Elements:

(a) Highlight the data with graphical elements that stand out.

(12) Keep Interior of Scale-Line Rectangle Clear:

(a) Avoid cluttering the interior with legends, labels, and lines.
(b) Use reference lines sparingly and appropriately.

(13) Aspect Ratios:

(a) Use appropriate aspect ratios, such as the golden ratio, to ensure the accurate representation of data.

(14) Lie Factor:

(a) Lie Factor is *"the size of an effect shown in a graphic divided by the actual size of the effect in the data"*.

- Integrity of a graphic: Lie Factor should be between 0.95 and 1.05
- If the Lie Factor > 1: "Overstating"
- If it less than 1, the graphic is "Understating"

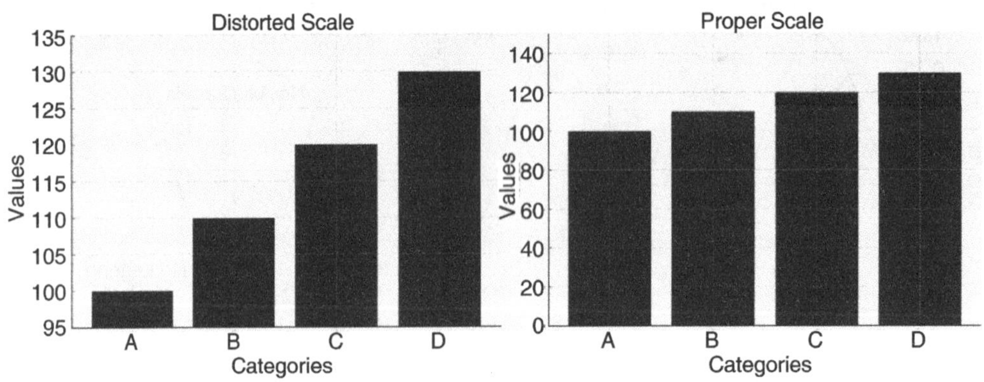

FIGURE 6.7 Comparison of Overstating and Understating Effects.

By following these principles, you can create clear, accurate, and effective visualizations that accurately represent the underlying data and facilitate easy understanding and analysis.

(15) Revise and Edit:

(a) Continuously refine graphs to best tell the data's story.
(b) Ensure the visualization's integrity by checking the Lie Factor, aiming for it to be between 0.95 and 1.05.

These principles will guide the design and improvement of your visualizations of data. We must always validate our designs with the users and incorporate their feedback for improvement. In the next chapter, we will learn some techniques to visualize multi-dimensional data. Chapter 8 will teach us about dimensionality reduction, which is important, both for data visualization and model development for high dimensional datasets. We will also practice visualization in Chapter 15, where we perform some case studies. Finally, some advanced techniques for data visualization are presented in Chapter 21 of the book.

EXERCISES

1. Himanshu is a sports teacher. He wants to group 150 students according to their heights and weights for determining suitability for various sports: basketball, weight-lifting, athletics. How will you collect and visualize the data? Please answer with reference to the What, Why and How questions.
2. Naman is a school teacher. He wants to teach the concept of angles using shadows of trees and buildings around their school at different times of the data. Design a data visualization approach for Naman.
3. Kesav has prepared the following pie-chart to illustrate where his time is spent during the day. Can you suggest some improvements or alternate visualizations to Kesav?

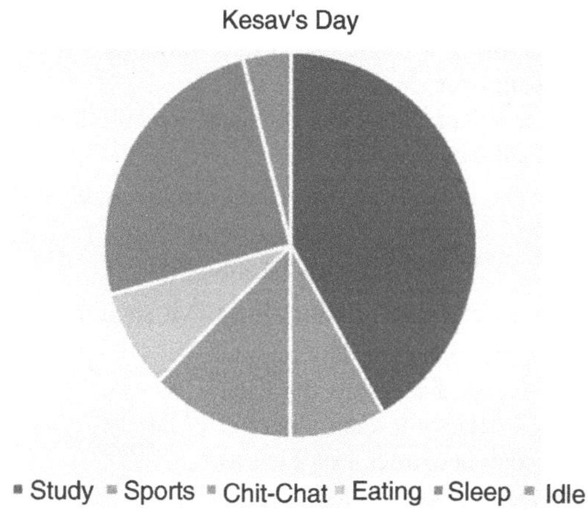

4. Raghav is a young data scientist. He has been tracking his walking activity (number of steps walked each hour) for 6 months. Please design a visualization so that he can become more regular.
5. Amir is a data scientist working in telecommunications industry. He wants to find the time it takes to load Google.com from different web-browsers over different devices: phones, laptops, tablets with different operating systems. Please design a visualization so he can compare the performance with different technologies.

MULTIPLE CHOICE QUESTIONS

1. Which of the following best describes **"data-ink ratio"** in visualization design?
   (a) The amount of ink used in a chart relative to the number of data points.
   (b) The proportion of a chart's ink that is dedicated to displaying the data.
   (c) The size of the chart in proportion to the amount of data being visualized.
   (d) The ratio of visual elements that improve readability to those that don't.
2. Which principle should be followed when designing a chart to ensure clarity and avoid misleading the audience?
   (a) Use a 3D perspective to make charts more visually appealing.
   (b) Always normalize data to improve readability.
   (c) Use consistent scales on axes, especially in time series plots.
   (d) Incorporate as many colors as possible to distinguish data points.
3. In a line chart, if the x-axis is not continuous but categorical, which type of chart would be more appropriate to show trends over categories?
   (a) Scatter plot (b) Histogram
   (c) Bar chart (d) Pie-chart

4. Which of the following visualization idioms is most appropriate for showing **proportions** of a whole?
   (a) Line chart
   (b) Scatter plot
   (c) Pie-chart
   (d) Heatmap
5. A **scatter plot** is best suited for visualizing:
   (a) The distribution of a single continuous variable.
   (b) The relationship between two continuous variables.
   (c) The frequency of categorical data.
   (d) Proportions of a whole in a dataset.
6. A **heatmap** is primarily used for:
   (a) Displaying the distribution of a single categorical variable.
   (b) Showing changes in data over time.
   (c) Visualizing a matrix of values with color intensity representing magnitude.
   (d) Representing hierarchical data.
7. Which of the following is the best idiom for visualizing hierarchical data?
   (a) Bar chart
   (b) Box plot
   (c) Tree map
   (d) Histogram
8. Which of the following is an example of **chart-junk** that should be avoided?
   (a) Gridlines that help viewers compare data points.
   (b) Excessive use of 3D effects that distort the data.
   (c) Annotations that provide clarity to data points.
   (d) Color coding to represent categories in a pie-chart.
9. In data visualization, **chart-junk** refers to:
   (a) Redundant or non-informative visual elements that distract from the data.
   (b) Any non-data ink that is added to improve aesthetics.
   (c) Low-quality charts that are hard to interpret.
   (d) Misleading data representations due to incorrect scaling.
10. To reduce **chart-junk**, which of the following practices is recommended?
    (a) Use detailed textures and shading on bars in bar charts.
    (b) Add background images to make the chart more visually appealing.
    (c) Remove unnecessary gridlines, tick marks, and decorative elements.
    (d) Use as many fonts as possible to emphasize different parts of the chart.
11. What is one way to improve the **clarity** of a visualization while minimizing chart-junk?
    (a) Use multiple fonts and bright colors for better readability.
    (b) Add data labels only where necessary and remove redundant legends.
    (c) Include 3D visual effects to make charts more engaging.
    (d) Always use a dark background to highlight data points.
12. When designing a visualization, **color** should be used to:
    (a) Represent data categories and emphasize specific patterns.
    (b) Fill the entire chart background for aesthetic purposes.
    (c) Make the chart more complex and visually appealing.
    (d) Distract the user from less important data points.
13. Which of the following **color schemes** is appropriate for showing **sequential data** in a heatmap?
    (a) A diverging color scale with two distinct hues.
    (b) A rainbow color scale with a variety of hues.
    (c) A single-hue gradient, from light to dark.
    (d) A random assignment of colors to each data point.

14. Which of the following is an **effective strategy** when trying to visualize a **large dataset**?
    (a) Use a pie-chart to summarize all data points.
    (b) Aggregate the data and use a bar or line chart to show trends.
    (c) Use a complex 3D chart for better visualization.
    (d) Avoid visualizing large datasets; use tables instead.

15. When using a **bar chart**, how can you ensure that it communicates data accurately and effectively?
    (a) Adjust the baseline of the y-axis to emphasize differences between categories.
    (b) Keep the baseline at zero to prevent misinterpretation of relative sizes.
    (c) Use random colors for each bar to make the chart more engaging.
    (d) Add gridlines with varying line thickness to highlight differences.

16. This is a heatmap plot of passengers who took flights during 1949 to 1960. Identify the busiest month in this whole period.

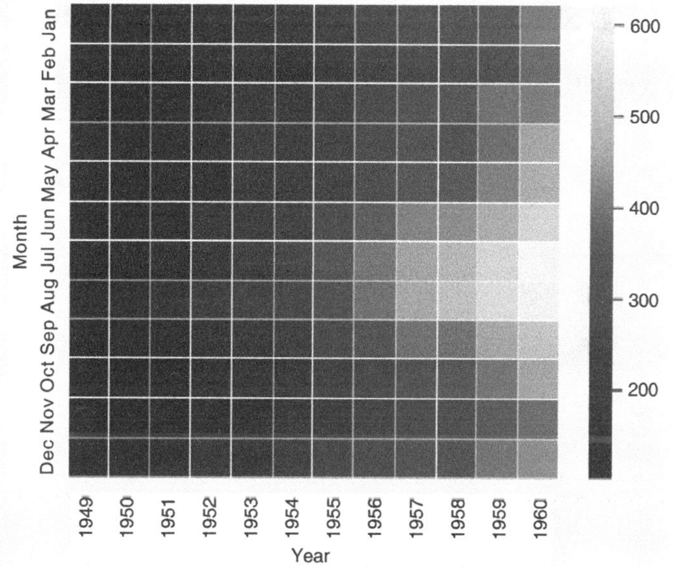

(a) Dec | (b) Jan
(c) July | (d) May

17. This is a normalized stacked bar chart using data which contains crop yields over different regions and different years in the 1930s. Which site has the least production of No. 475 variety?

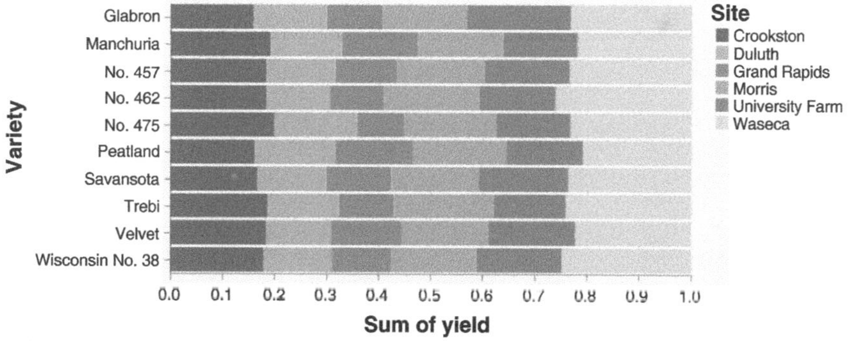

(a) Duluth | (b) Grand Rapids
(c) Waseca | (d) Crookston

REFERENCES

[1] Tamara Munzner, Visualization Analysis and Design, A.K. Peters Visualization Series, CRC Press, 2014.
[2] Colin Ware, Information Visualization: Perception for Design.
[3] William S. Cleveland, The Elements of Graphing Data.
[4] Edward R. Tufte, The Visual Display of Quantitative Data.
[5] Will Schroeder and Ken Martin and Bill Lorensen, The Visualization Toolkit: An Object-Oriented Approach to 3D Graphics.
[6] Edward R. Tufte, Visual Explanations.
[7] Interactive Visual Data Analysis, Christian Tominski and Heidrun Schumann, A.K. Peters Visualization Series, CRC Press.

ANSWER KEY

1. (b) **2.** (c) **3.** (c) **4.** (c) **5.** (b) **6.** (c) **7.** (c) **8.** (b) **9.** (a) **10.** (c)
11. (b) **12.** (a) **13.** (c) **14.** (b) **15.** (b) **16.** (c) **17.** (b)

7 Visualization of Tabular Data

A common way to collect and organize data is in the form of tables. Simple tables consist of columns and rows. More complex tables may have groups which are further divided into sub-columns and rows. An important discussion is whether we should present the data in form of tables or plot them as charts. Before designing a chart, consider if a table might be the clearer choice. Sometimes, a well-made table is the best solution.

Tables are ideal when the users need specific data, like information about their company, or when precise value comparisons are important. They are better than charts and maps when there is no clear visual or spatial pattern. Some important principles while designing tables are as follows:

1. Highlight column headers on the top, so that they stand out above the data.
2. Group and sort data to highlight meaningful patterns.
3. Labels can be placed in the first row of the group and repetition may be avoided.

Group	Food	Color	Calories per serving
Fruits	Apple	Red	52
	Banana	Yellow	90
	Mango	Ycllow	60
Vegetables	Carrot	Orange	41
	Cucumber	Green	16

The above table shows us the calories per serving (100 gm) of different fruits and vegetables. In each group, the column food is alphabetically sorted. It is easy to look up any food item by name (which is unique) or by colour (which is not unique). We note that cucumbers have the lowest calories per serving among all the food items presented in the table.

We must organize data presentation to focus the attention of the reader on the most important elements, to help them focus on the key points. We must visualize the important patterns. We must remove any clutter that can be distracting. Images such as the slope of a line chart, or clustering of dots on a scatter chart, can communicate your evidence to readers' eyes more effectively than text or tables.

Creating meaningful charts that draw our attention to key insights in your data requires clear thinking about design choices. Decisions about chart types are based on two main factors: the format of your data, and the kind of story you wish to tell. For example, line charts work best to show a series of continuous data points (such as change over time), while range charts are better suited to emphasize the distance between data categories (such as inequality gaps). We now discuss some important chart/plot types, their pros and cons and their scalability considerations.

7.1 HISTOGRAMS

A histogram represents the distribution of a numerical dataset. It groups data into intervals, called bins, and represents the frequency (count) of data points within each bin using bars. The height of each bar represents the number of data points (frequency) that fall into that bin. Bars are adjacent, with no gaps, emphasizing the continuous nature of the data. The width of the bins affects the appearance of the histogram.

Histograms are used to visualize distribution, understand the spread, shape and measures of central tendency. They are used to identify patterns such as skewness, peaks, gaps and outliers in the data.

Figure 7.1 shows that the distribution of flipper lengths of penguins is bi-modal indicating that the data contains multiple species.

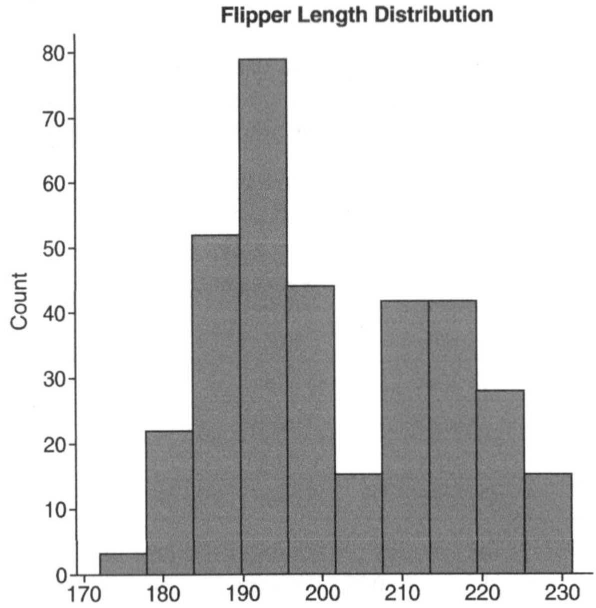

FIGURE 7.1 Distribution of flipper length for penguins dataset introduced in Ch-2.

By using different colors for each species, we can re-plot the data and produce this Figure 7.2. We can observe that the flipper lengths of "Gentoo" species of penguins is larger than those of "Adelie". These correspond to the two peaks in the overall flipper length histogram in Figure 7.1.

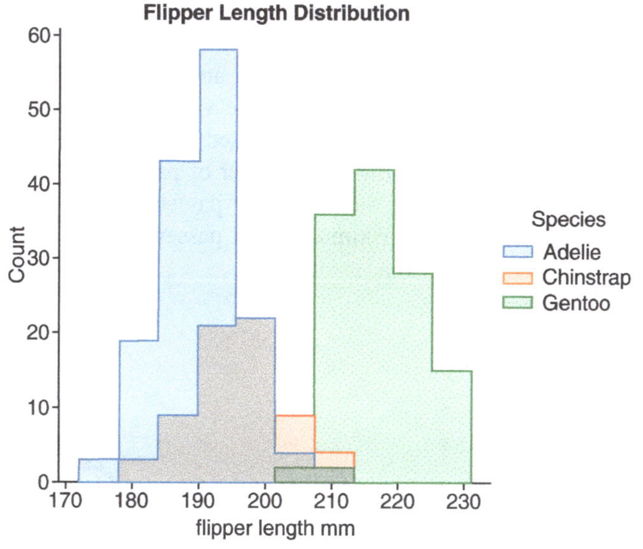

FIGURE 7.2 Histogram plot with categories.

7.2 VIOLIN PLOT

This combines a box plot (discussed in chapter 2) with a kernel density plot to show data distribution. Figure 7.3 shows the distribution of sepal lengths of iris flowers for three different species. The sepal length of "setosa" iris flowers has a median (white marker) of 5 mm while that of virginica is around 6.5 mm. The spread of "virginica" is more than that of "setosa".

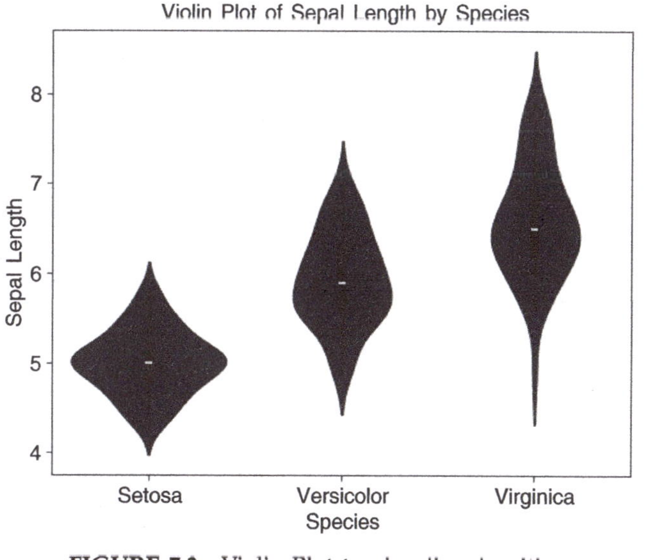

FIGURE 7.3 Violin Plot to visualize densities.

7.3 LINE CHARTS

Line charts encode 2 quantitative attributes with one key and one value. The marks are connected with line. The lengths are aligned to express quantitative values. They are separated and ordered by key attributes into horizontal regions. These can be used to find trends and are very commonly used to plot time-series data. Figure 7.4 shows the number of passengers taking flights in the USA in each month of the year. We observe that the number of passengers has an increasing trend. Also, the months of July and August have the maximum flight passengers.

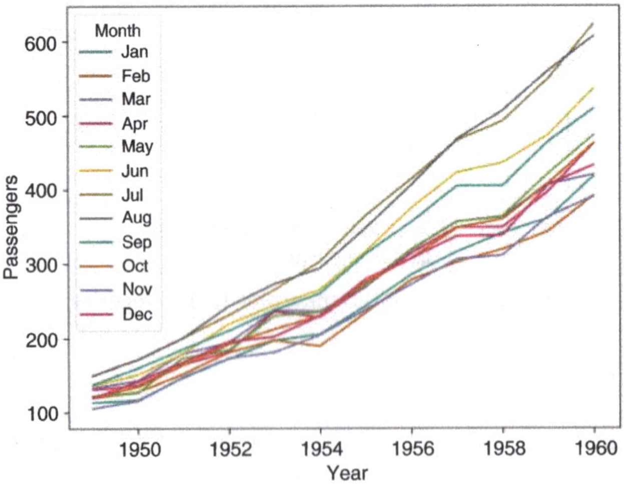

FIGURE 7.4 Line chart to depict number of passengers taking flights per month.

7.4 AREA CHARTS

An area chart is a variant of the line chart where the area around the line is shaded with a color. These charts can be used to represent accumulated totals, confidence intervals, etc. In Figure 7.5,

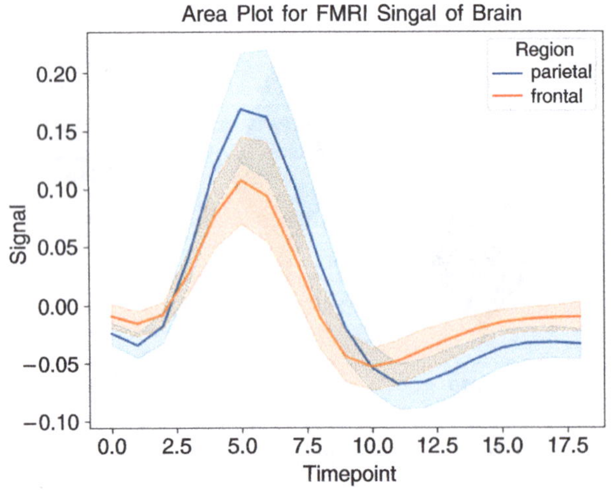

FIGURE 7.5 Confidence intervals with area charts.

FMRI signals from "parietal" and "frontal" regions of the brain are collected from many patients and 95% confidence interval (area) around the mean is shaded. The solid line is a line plot of the mean values.

7.5 BAR AND COLUMN CHARTS

In bar charts, we can show data points with one categorical and one quantitative attribute. The marks are lines with some thickness (rectangles to be more precise) and the length is used to express the quantitative values. The categories are separated horizontally and aligned vertically for easy comparison. We can also look up values. It can be scaled to hundreds of levels and tens of categories.

We can order the bars by either names of categories (alphabetic order) or the values in order for easy lookup and/or comparisons. In Figure 7.6, we have plotted the number of men, women and children of each class who boarded titanic.

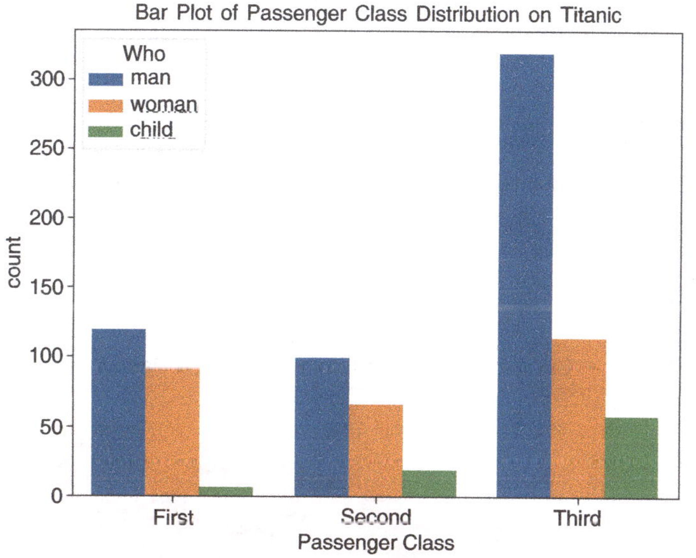

FIGURE 7.6 Passengers on titanic.

7.6 STACKED BAR CHARTS

These are used when we have 2 categorical attributes and one quantitative attribute in the data. A vertical stack of line marks (rectangles) is used to represent the data. The length is used to encode the quantitative value and the colour is used for encoding categories. This is useful to understand part-to-whole relationship.

Figure 7.7 depicts the number of customers visiting a restaurant in the morning and evening. We can see that most customers come on Friday and Friday evenings are busier than Friday mornings.

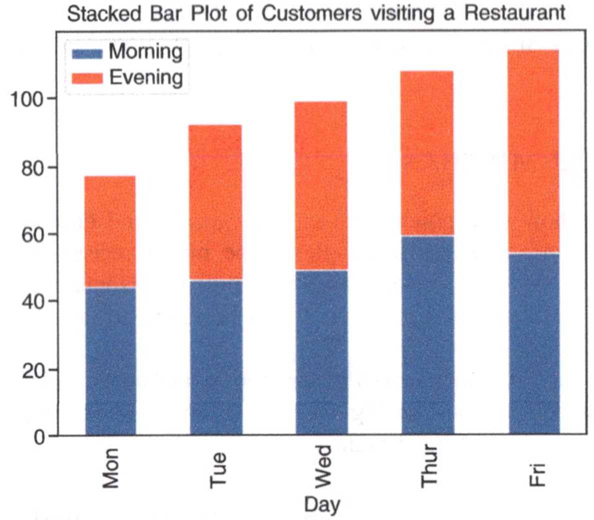

FIGURE 7.7 Customers visiting a restaurant.

7.7 STREAMGRAPH

Streamgraphs emphasize horizontal continuity. They have a categorical key attribute, one ordered key attribute (generally time) and 1 quantitative value attribute. Here the thickness of the layer encodes the quantity. It is scalable to hundreds of time keys and tens of categories.

Figure 7.8 presents the same data as Figure 7.7, but as a continuous flow making the trend easier to follow.

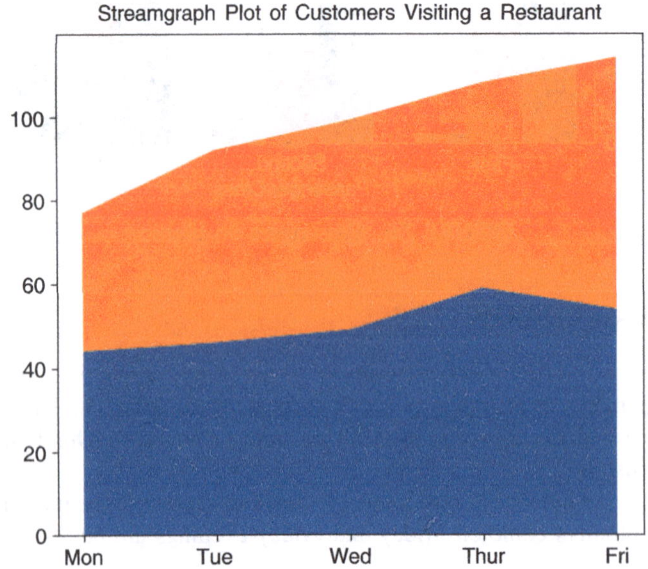

FIGURE 7.8 Customers visiting a restaurant.

7.8 SANKEY DIAGRAM

A Sankey diagram illustrates flow or connections between entities, useful for process or resource analysis.

Figure 7.9 shows the flow of passengers from India and USA to different countries. The thickness of the lines encodes the number of passengers. We can observe that total number of passengers from USA is much more than that from India. Also, there are more travellers from USA to Germany than to Spain.

FIGURE 7.9 Travellers from USA vs. India.

7.9 SLOPE GRAPH

Slope graph is useful to study change in values. In Figure 7.10, per capita GDP (in USD) is plotted for each continent. We have values from 2002 and 2007. We find that all continents have an increase

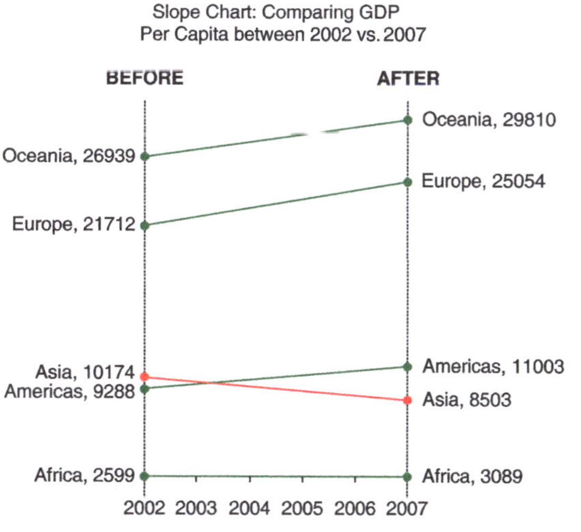

FIGURE 7.10 Using slope graph to spot an error in the GDP data.

in per capita GDP, which is indicated by a positive slope line (colored green). However, we notice that per-capita GDP of Asia has decreased from 10174 in 2002 to 8503 in 2007. This appears to be an anomaly and could be due to a data collection error. Thus, slope graph can be used to analyze change, highlight anomalies, etc.

7.10 PARALLEL COORDINATES

Parallel coordinates is a visualization technique used to explore multi-dimensional data. Each variable is represented as a vertical axis, and data points are plotted as lines that connect their corresponding values across the axes. This allows for the detection of patterns, relationships, clusters, and outliers in high-dimensional datasets. The order of the axes can impact insights, and adding colors or transparency helps in distinguishing groups and reducing clutter. It is widely used in data analysis, machine learning, and decision-making scenarios.

From Figure 7.11, we can notice a positive correlation between age and height in the data. This means that when age increases, height also increases. We also notice a positive correlation between height and weight. This means that for the individuals studied in the dataset, the weight increases with height. Due to the specific ordering of attributes, we can't easily find a relationship between age and weight, because there are no connecting lines between them.

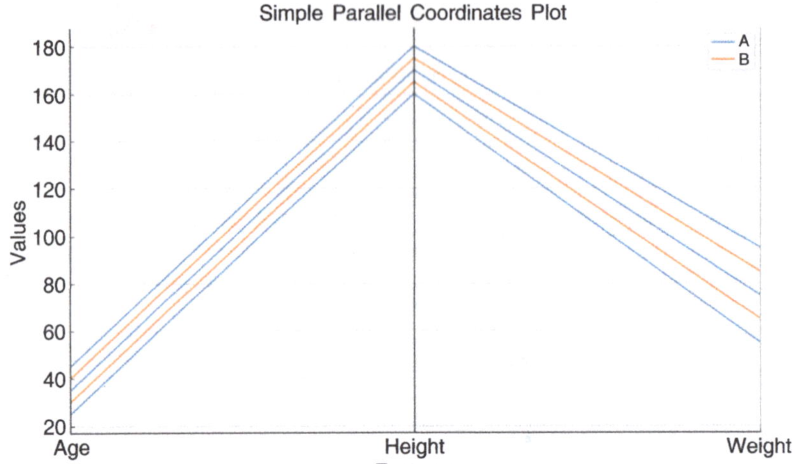

FIGURE 7.11 Parallel Coordinated plot.

7.11 PIE CHART

A pie chart is a circular statistical graphic divided into slices, where each slice represents a proportion of the whole. It is widely used to visualize percentage or proportional data. Each slice's size corresponds to its value relative to the sum of all values, making it easy to compare parts of a dataset.

Pie charts are best suited for datasets with a few categories to avoid clutter. They are commonly used in business reports, surveys, and demographic studies to show distribution. While visually intuitive, pie charts can become less effective when dealing with many categories or similar-sized proportions, where bar charts might offer better clarity.

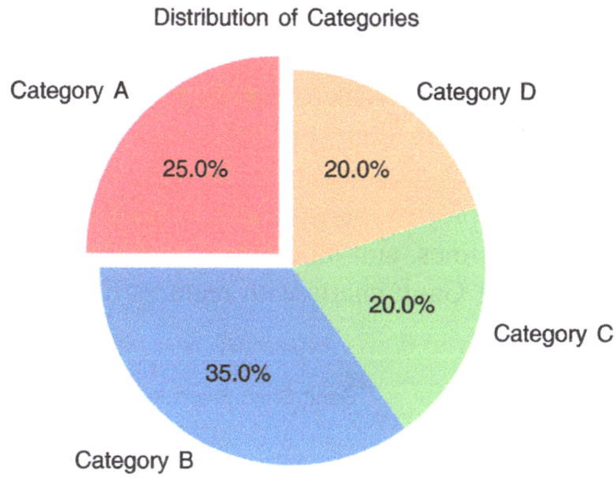

FIGURE 7.12 Pie chart showing distribution.

7.12 HEATMAP

Uses color intensity to show the relationship between two variables.

The heatmap in Figure 7.13 visualizes ranking of per-capita COVID cases for each state. Red shades correspond to higher values (low rank), while blue shades indicate lower values (high rank).

Heatmaps are ideal for identifying patterns, correlations, or clusters in data. Labels and annotations enhance readability and make it easy to interpret the relationships.

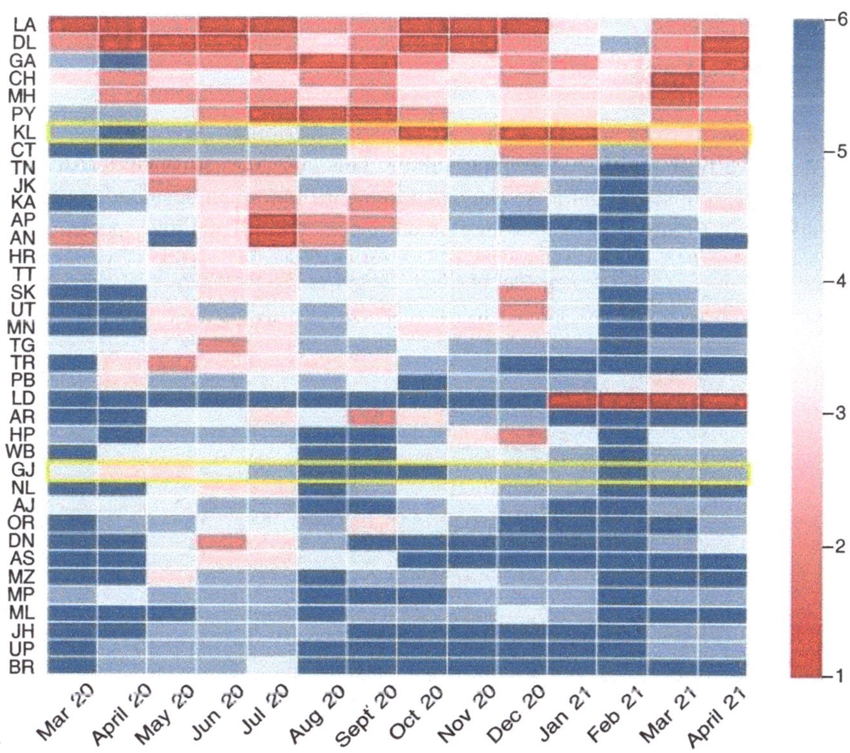

FIGURE 7.13 Number of COVID cases per month for each state.

7.13 GANTT CHARTS

A Gantt chart is a type of bar chart used to visualize project schedules. It displays tasks or activities along the vertical axis and time intervals along the horizontal axis. Each task is represented by a horizontal bar, with its position and length indicating the start date, end date, and duration.

Gantt charts are widely used in project management to plan, track, and coordinate tasks. They help identify task dependencies, timelines, and milestones, providing a clear overview of a project's progress. Modern tools often enhance Gantt charts with features like color coding, progress tracking, and resource allocation.

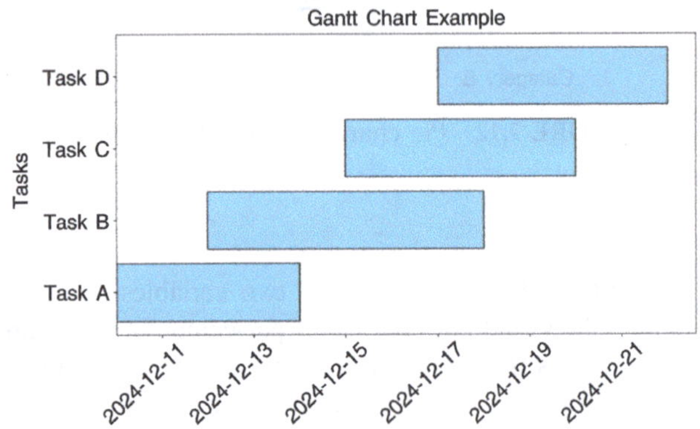

FIGURE 7.14 Gantt Chart for scheduling tasks.

7.14 SCATTER CHARTS

A scatter plot is used to express data with 2 quantitative attributes. We use points as marks and use horizontal and vertical position to encode values. This can be used to find distribution, trends, correlation, clusters (groups) and outliers. The categorical attributes can be encoded with color, shape or size of markers. In Figure 7.15, sepal lengths and sepal widths of three species of Iris flowers

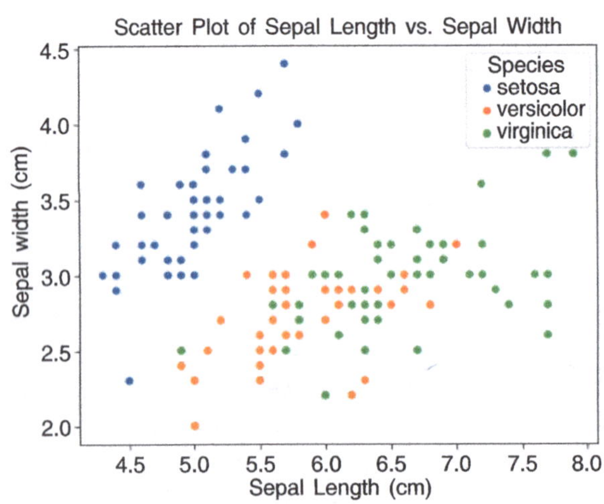

FIGURE 7.15 Sepal length vs. Sepal width for IRIS flower dataset.

are depicted. We can notice that the species setosa has lower sepal lengths but higher sepal widths and tend to cluster in the top left region of the plot.

Scatter plots can scale to hundreds of data points. As the number of points increase, there is overlapping problem. By adding transparency in points, we can differentiate between regions with higher and lower density.

In Figure 7.16, we have plotted thousands of data points from diamonds dataset which show a positive correlation between weight of diamonds in carats and their prices. There is a lot of variation in prices, which is explained by other attributes such as color, clarity, etc. which are not depicted in the plot.

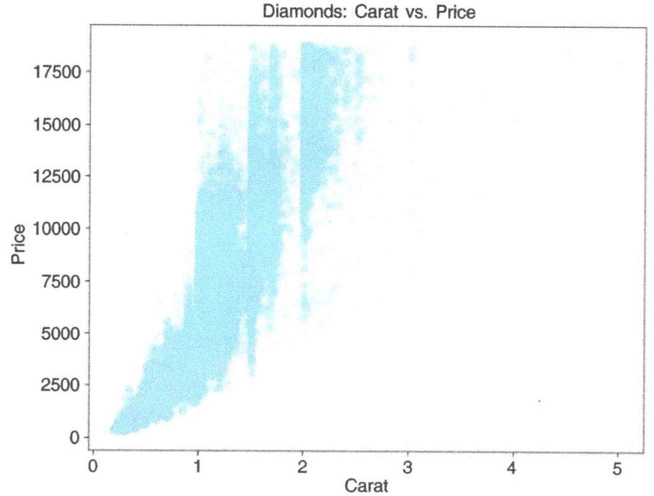

FIGURE 7.16 Scatter Plot of diamonds dataset.

Figure 7.17 gives more insights into the impact of clarity of the diamond on its price.

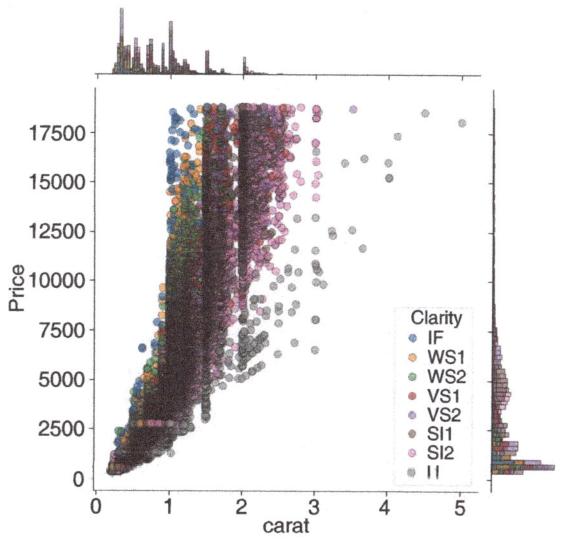

FIGURE 7.17 Scatter Plot of Diamond Price (*See colour figure at the end of the book*).

We can observe a separation of the data points with different clarity. The slopes are different. The clarity type I1 (with flaws) are lowest in price per carat and have least slope. On the other hand, clarity type "IF" (internally flawless) diamonds are very highly priced per carat.

7.15 BUBBLE CHART

In a scatter plot, the size of each point represents an additional variable. Figure 7.18 shows the life expectancy of different countries by GDP per capita. The size of the bubbles encode the population of the country.

We notice that life expectancy tends to increase with the per-capita GDP.

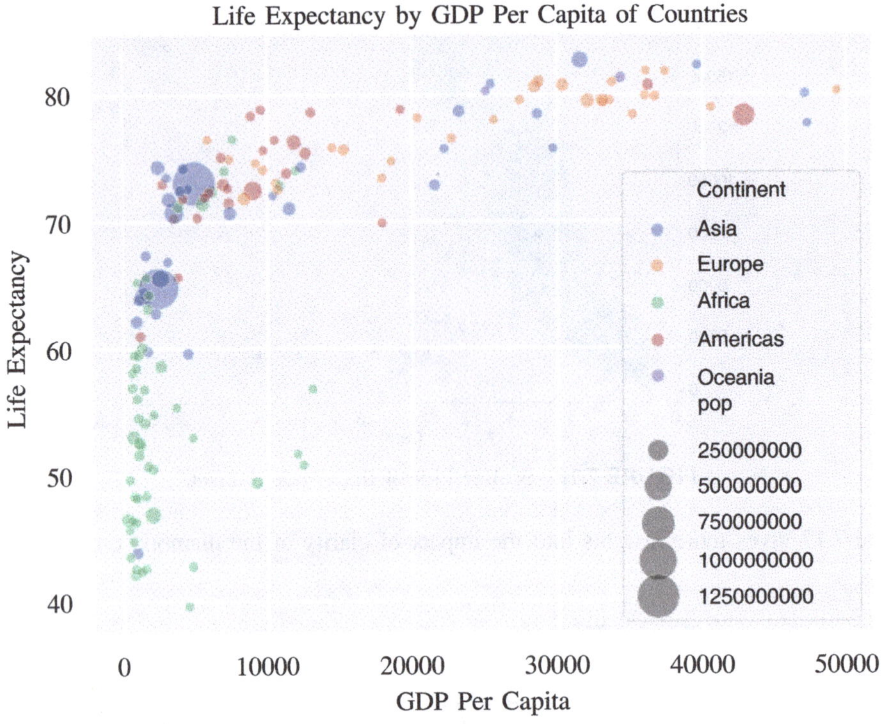

FIGURE 7.18 Life Expectancy by GDP.

7.16 CARTOGRAPHY

It is important to visualize spatial relationships using maps. For example, it allows us to see where resources are concentrated, where environmental changes are occurring, or how infrastructure is distributed across a region. In the example below, we present the information of fatal car accidents in New York City area. The data is color coded. Red color shows the region with highest intensity while the blue colored regions have lower intensity. We can also observe the main landmarks and highways. This information can be used by the traffic police to enforce stricter speed limit and warning signs in those regions to reduce accidents.

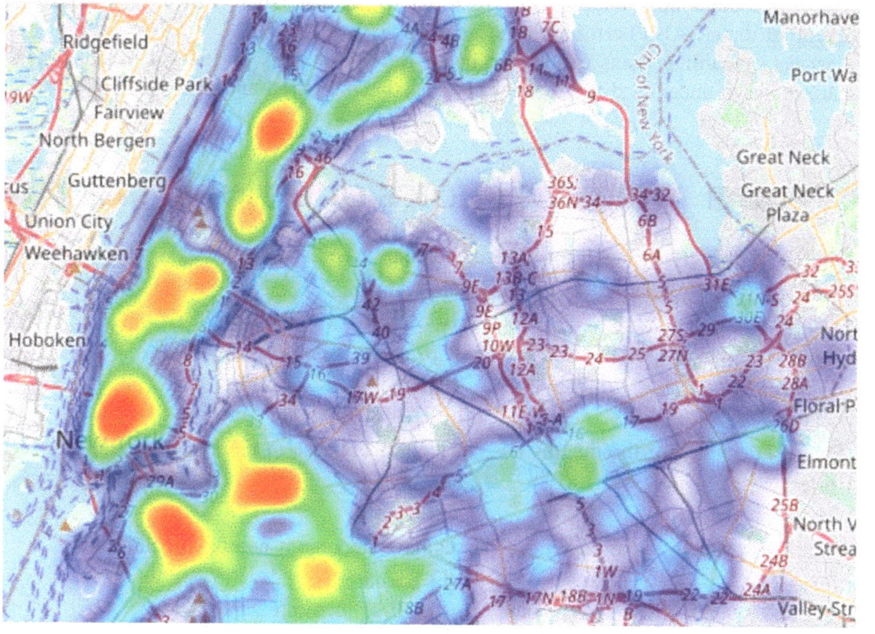

FIGURE 7.19 An example of Cartography showing information of fatal car accidents in New York City area (*See colour figure at the end of the book*).

Cartography is an old science and has been used extensively to **explore, represent, and understand the world** for centuries. It has been extensively used for documenting geographic discoveries, supporting navigation and trade, establishing political boundaries, aiding military strategy, promoting cultural exchange, facilitating scientific exploration and urban planning, expressing cultural worldviews, managing the environment, and shaping geopolitics.

Cartography helps condense large, complex datasets into easy-to-understand visuals. Through the use of maps, geographic data can be presented in a way that reveals patterns, trends, and relationships that might otherwise be difficult to discern.

With modern digital cartography, users can interact with maps by zooming, panning, or filtering data layers. This interactivity adds depth to the visualization and allows users to explore data in a dynamic way, revealing additional insights through different perspectives. Cartography allows for the representation of multiple variables on a single map, enabling the analysis of how different factors (such as climate, population, and infrastructure) are interconnected across geographical space.

EXERCISES

1. The finance team of a company has to present the profit and loss account to senior management. It includes the sales, revenue, expenses of various types and profit calculations. What would be more suitable: tables or charts? If they have to present the trends over last 5 years, what would be more suitable? Please justify.
2. In this chapter, we saw several examples of mixture of distributions, species of penguins, flowers etc. Suppose the class labels are not present. How will you separate the samples into classes?
3. Please calculate the mean, median and mode using the histogram in Figure 7.1.

4. Explore the "diamonds" dataset and create charts to understand distributions and correlations of different attributes. Also perform cluster analysis.
5. Collect data regarding trains connecting major railway stations in your state and design appropriate visualizations to understand the flow of passengers, congestion and delay of trains.

MULTIPLE CHOICE QUESTIONS

1. In Figure 7.2, which species has the highest count?
   (a) Adelie (b) Chinstrap
   (c) Gentoo (d) All of them are same
2. In Figure 7.3, which species has the highest peak in its density?
   (a) Versicolor (b) Virginica
   (c) Setosa (d) All of them are same
3. In Figure 7.4, which of the months has the highest increase in number of passengers each year?
   (a) July (b) January
   (c) March (d) October
4. In Figure 7.6, which of the passenger classes have maximum number of children?
   (a) First (b) Second
   (c) Third (d) All of them are same
5. Sankey plot typically used to represent:
   (a) Spatial data (b) Flow of quantities between categories
   (c) Statistical distributions (d) Hierarchical data
6. In a Sankey diagram, flows typically move:
   (a) From left to right (b) From right to left
   (c) From top to bottom (d) In any direction depending on design
7. In a slope graph, the lines connecting points represent:
   (a) Changes or trends between two variables
   (b) Hierarchical relationships
   (c) Flow of data between nodes
   (d) Clusters of data points
8. Which of the following is NOT a common use case for slope graphs?
   (a) Comparing changes between two points in time
   (b) Showing trends in hierarchical data
   (c) Visualizing before-and-after scenarios
   (d) Highlighting rank shifts
9. Which design element is most important in making a slope graph effective?
   (a) Use of color to differentiate categories
   (b) Adding flow elements to the graph
   (c) Including more data points for accuracy
   (d) Representing data with thick lines
10. Which of the following tools can be used to create heat maps?
    (a) Python (Seaborn, Matplotlib) (b) Excel
    (c) Tableau (d) All of the above
11. What does a heat map primarily use to represent data values?
    (a) Line thickness (b) Symbols and icons
    (c) Colors or shades (d) Text labels

12. In a heat map, darker or more saturated colors typically indicate:
(a) Lower values (b) Higher values
(c) Constant values (d) Categorical data

13. What does a scatter plot typically represent?
(a) Distribution of categorical data
(b) Flow of data between nodes
(c) Changes over time
(d) Relationships between two variables

14. How is a bubble plot different from a scatter plot?
(a) A bubble plot uses bars instead of points
(b) A bubble plot adds a third variable represented by the size of the bubbles
(c) A bubble plot is only used for time-series data
(d) A bubble plot uses categories instead of numerical data

15. In a Sankey plot, the width of the flow (or the link) represents:
(a) The category name
(b) The magnitude of the flow or quantity
(c) The distance between nodes
(d) The number of nodes

16. In a scatter plot, what do the points on the graph represent?
(a) Individual data points
(b) Categories
(c) Aggregate data values
(d) Continuous trends

17. Which of the following datasets is ideal for a bubble plot?
(a) Sales revenue, profit margin, and number of products sold across regions
(b) Monthly rainfall over 10 years
(c) A comparison of test scores between two groups
(d) Daily temperatures in a single city

18. What is the primary advantage of using a scatter or bubble plot?
(a) Highlighting correlations or clusters in the data
(b) Displaying hierarchical relationships
(c) Visualizing trends over time
(d) Representing data flow

REFERENCES

[1] https://help.tableau.com/
[2] https://github.com/mwaskom/seaborn-data
[3] https://colab.research.google.com/drive/1Z5QAUMBNSKXzWJYGAHEFukfEk3ExltFN?usp=sharing

ANSWER KEY

1. (a) **2.** (c) **3.** (a) **4.** (c) **5.** (b) **6.** (d) **7.** (a) **8.** (b) **9.** (a) **10.** (d)
11. (c) **12.** (b) **13.** (d) **14.** (b) **15.** (b) **16.** (a) **17.** (a) **18.** (a)

Part III

Model Building

8 Dimensionality Reduction and Feature Selection

Introduction

High dimensional datasets are commonplace in applications such as bioinformatics, financial technology, industry 4.0 and computer vision. When the number of dimensions in data is high, several data analysis algorithms become slow, unstable or yield poor quality results. This is known as the curse of dimensionality.

Dimensionality reduction aims at reducing the number of dimensions (attributes) in the data for facilitating its analysis and visualization. This may be accomplished by selecting important attributes (feature selection), by discovering hidden (latent) attributes or by learning projection functions that preserve the structure in the data.

Formally, we can state dimensionality reduction problem as determining a function F that maps the data in R_n to R_m, where $m << n$ while preserving important structure in the data. For example, we may want to preserve the pair-wise distances (similarity) among points or their neighbourhoods, etc.

In this chapter, we will study some of the important techniques for data pre-processing, dimensionality reduction, and feature selection based on the applications.

8.1 DATA PRE-PROCESSING

Data pre-processing is an important activity in knowledge discovery in databases. Dimensionality reduction and feature selection techniques comes under the umbrella of data pre-processing. There are numerous techniques for both dimensionality reduction and feature selection. In this chapter, some of the commonly used techniques for dimensionality reduction and feature selection are discussed, and some of the other common data pre-processing techniques are also discussed in brief.

A brief overview of data cleaning techniques like noisy data handling, missing value analysis, along with the data transformation techniques and data summarization techniques like sampling techniques and data summarization using visual techniques is presented.

Data cleaning techniques are broadly categorized in two parts, missing value analysis and noisy data and outliers.

Missing value analysis: Data can have missing values. One of the simplest techniques in handling missing values is replacing the missing values by average values. For example, in a given dataset of customers, "Age" is an attribute then for missing values of Age, it can be replaced by average value of Age of all the customers in the database.

Noisy data and outliers: Noisy data in a dataset may be present due to many reasons like faulty instruments, data entry errors, etc., outliers are the abnormalities in the dataset which is not following the characteristics of the normal data. Noisy data or outliers should be identified in the dataset and removed from the dataset for analysis. Outlier detection techniques and clustering techniques can be used to identify the outliers in dataset. The outliers are the data points which does not belong to any of the cluster, so clustering techniques can identify the outliers easily by identifying the data points not belonging to any of the clusters.

8.1.1 Data Transformation

Data transformation techniques are essential data pre-processing techniques in which original data is transformed to some other format. For example, suppose Amazon, an online e-commerce platform wanted to analyse the profit made in selling of electronic goods worldwide, then profit data should be collected and converted to the uniform current format before analysing. In this way, depending on the particular analysis task the data transformation activity is performed. Data normalization is a popular technique of data transformation. Two popular data transformation techniques are z-score normalization and min-max normalization techniques.

Standard deviation or z-score normalization: The z-score normalization is measured in terms of distance of a data point from mean in terms of standard deviation. The z-score normalization is calculated using the below equation.

$$A^T = \frac{A - \mu_A}{\sigma_A}$$

Where A is the value of a particular attribute, μ_A and σ_A are the mean and standard deviation of the attribute A, and A^T is the transformed value of the attribute A.

Example: Suppose the following data set is given, and z-score calculation is required to be calculated for each data point in the data set, then,

$$D = \{10, 11, 12, 13, 14\}$$

The mean of the attribute D, is $\mu_D = 12$ and standard deviation is $\sigma_D = 1.414$, so value 10 is transformed to $\frac{10-12}{1.414} = -1.41$. So the transformed dataset is:

$$D^T = \{-1.41, -0.71, 0, 0.71, 1.41\}$$

Min-max normalization: The min-max normalization technique is used for transforming the data into a new range (with new minimum and new maximum) from the old range. The min-max normalization is calculated by the following equation.

$$A^T = (A - m) \times \frac{(M^T - m^T)}{(M - m)} + (m^T)$$

Where A^T is the transformed value after normalization for the given value A. M^T is the new maximum value, m^T is the new minimum value and M and m are the maximum and minimum values in the existing old range.

Example: Suppose the following data set is given, and min-max normalization is required to be calculated for each data point in the data set. The data needs to convert to a new range of [1...100] then,

$$D = \{10, 11, 12, 13, 14\}$$

The existing minimum value is 10 and maximum value is 14, the new minimum value given is 1 and new maximum value given is 100 then by applying the equation of min-max normalization data is transformed, e.g. the value 10 is transformed as:

$$(10 - 10) \times \frac{(100 - 1)}{(14 - 10)} + 1 = 1$$

And 12 is transformed as:

$$(12 - 10) \times \frac{(100 - 1)}{(14 - 10)} + 1 = 50.5$$

The transformed dataset is $D^T = \{1, 25.75, 50.5, 75.25, 100\}$.

8.1.2 Sampling Techniques

Sampling is one of the very popular techniques by which samples from the original data are selected for analysis and machine learning models are developed. Random sampling is the most popular technique for sampling from the large collection of data. Random sampling has two variants, in one technique the selected samples is not re-selected again (Random Sampling without Replacement), whereas in the other, selected samples may be repeated again (Random Sampling with Replacement). Cluster sampling is another special type of sampling technique in which the samples are selected from the clusters of the original data, which minimizes the biasing towards selection of the samples from a specific group of data.

8.1.3 Data Summarization and Visual Representation

Data summarization is another useful tool for data pre-processing. It helps in reducing the amount of original data by providing a compact representation of the data which is sufficient for a particular analysis task. Various visualizations can also help in summarizing the data. Three commonly used visualization techniques for data summarization are covered here in brief.

Histograms

Histograms are very commonly used plots to visualize the data and its corresponding frequencies. The highest frequencies indicate the dominating data in the dataset. Histograms help in understanding the basic nature of data like central tendencies, distribution of data, etc.

Example: The histogram for the given dataset B is shown in Figure 8.1.

$$B = \{11, 13, 12, 11, 13, 15, 18, 20, 25, 22, 15, 17, 18, 22, 24, 28, 18, 19, 20, 11\}$$

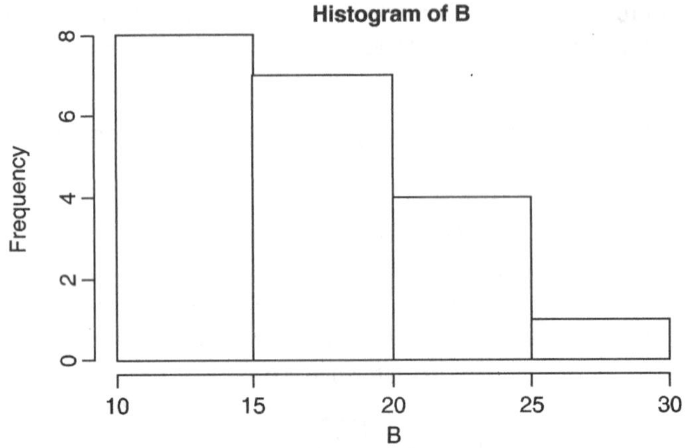

FIGURE 8.1 Histogram for the sample dataset.

Boxplots

Boxplot is very popular technique for data summarization and comparing two datasets. A boxplot is consisting of five points, {minimum, first quartile, median, third quartile, maximum} so it is also called as the five points summaries of the datasets.

Example: The boxplot (five-point summary) for the following dataset D is shown below along with the graphical representation.

$$D = \{11, 13, 12, 11, 13, 15, 18, 20, 25, 22, 15, 17, 18, 22, 24, 28, 18, 19, 20, 11\}$$

The corresponding five-point summary is, $\text{Boxplot} = \{11.0, 13.0, 18.0, 20.5, 28.0\}$.

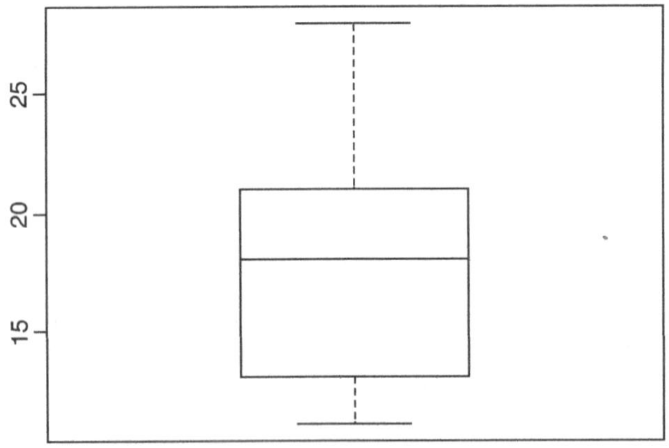

FIGURE 8.2 Boxplot for the sample dataset.

Stem and leaf plots

A Stem-and-Leaf plot is used to represent the dataset in compact form and thus can be utilized as an effective way of data compression. The Stem-and-Leaf plot is a useful technique for presenting numerical data. The Stem-and-Leaf plot has two components stem and leaf. The stem indicates the higher places of digits (like tens, hundred, etc.) and leaf plot indicates the lower places of numbers (like unit places, etc.). Suppose stem-and-leaf plot for the following data is to be created:

$$D = \{11, 13, 12, 11, 13, 15, 18, 20, 25, 22, 15, 17, 18, 22, 24, 28, 18, 19, 20, 11\}$$

Then the output of the stem-and-leaf plot is:

1 | 1 1 1 2 3 3 5 8 8 9
2 | 0 0 2 2 4 8

FIGURE 8.3 Stem-and-leaf plot for the sample dataset.

Stem is presented before the pipe sign (|) and leaf is presented after the pipe sign. In this way, a compact representation of the original data is presented in a summarized way.

8.2 UNDERSTANDING DIMENSIONALITY REDUCTION

Curse of dimensionality is a challenging issue in data science. The graphical summary of curse of dimensionality is presented in Figure 8.4. Theoretically, it is assumed that more features can lead to improvements of performance of data analysis work, but practically adding more features can confuse the machine learning models and can lead to degradation of performance as shown in figure. It is therefore necessary to identify and select relevant features from the data for any data analysis work. Dimensionality reduction will not only be minimizing the volume of data for data analysis but also it will make the machine learning process faster (as lesser amount of data is processed). The performance of any machine learning system also depends on the optimized number of features selected for the data analysis work.

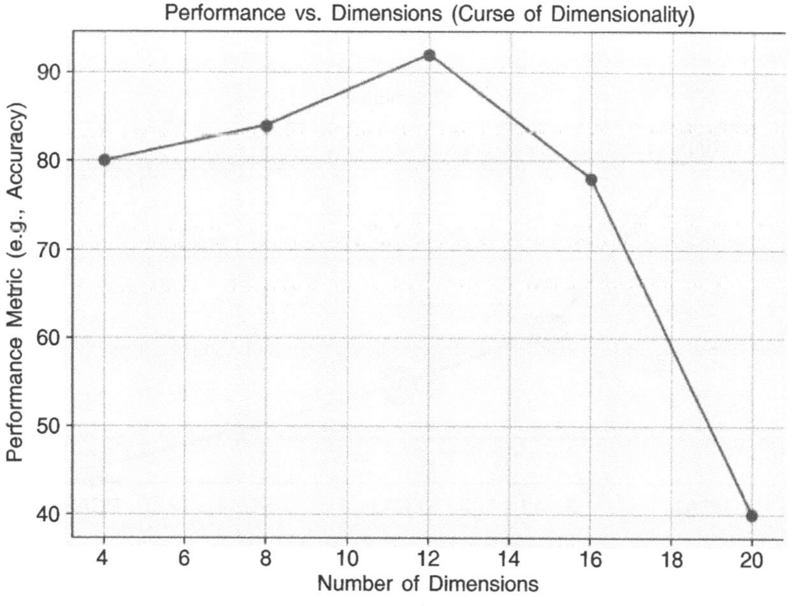

FIGURE 8.4 Curse of dimensionality.

Feature selection is the process of selection of most relevant features for the data analysis, whereas feature extraction is the process of deriving and generating more additional features logically from the data for better analysis of the data. The problem of dimensionality reduction deals with both of these types of feature handling. Sometimes feature extraction generates the additional information which replaces the existing information from the original data and helps in dimensionality reduction.

The dimensionality reduction techniques are broadly categorized into two major categories namely, linear and non-linear techniques. In linear techniques, the relationship between the original data and the reduced data is assumed to be linear, examples of such techniques are Principal Component Analysis (PCA), and Linear Discriminant Analysis (LDA). Whereas in non-linear dimensionality reduction techniques, the relationship between the original data and the reduced data is assumed to be complex and non-linear, example of such techniques are, *T*-distributed Stochastic Neighbour Embedding (*t*-SNE), Isomaps, and Locally Linear Embedding (LLE).

8.2.1 Principal Component Analysis (PCA)

The principal component analysis (PCA) is a very popular and widely used dimensionality reduction technique in the domain of data science. The PCA technique works on the concept of principal components which are derived from the eigenvalues of the data matrix generated from the original data. These principal components help in determining directions with highest variance. This corresponds to the highest information content in the data. The original data is transformed in the direction of principal components and transformed data is generated with lesser dimensions preserving the statistical features from the original dataset.

The PCA algorithm is applied in five major steps. In the first step data is standardized, then in the second step, compute covariance matrix for the data generated in the first step. In the third step, eigenvalues and eigenvectors are calculated for the covariance matrix. Then in the fourth step, principal components are selected. Then in the last step, project the data onto the principal components.

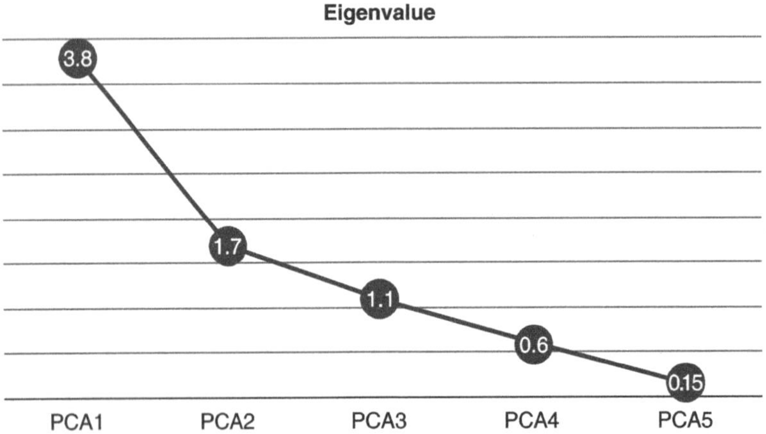

FIGURE 8.5 Scree plot for PCA.

The PCA technique generates a number of principal components and deciding the appropriate number of principal components is a key problem. This problem can be solved with the help of a special visualization technique called as scree plot. A sample scree plot is shown in Figure 8.5. In the scree plot, in x-axis, principal components are shown and in y-axis, eigenvalues of some other statistical measures such as variance, etc. is shown for a respective principal component. The number of principal components is selected using the selection criteria. The Kaiser's rule (Kaiser-Guttman criterion) is selected where PCA are selected till the variance exceeds a given threshold value. For example, first k-component account for a percentage of total variation greater than threshold (e.g., 75%). The criteria may be modified to consider top-k principal components based on the eigenvalues of the principal components.

8.2.2 Singular Value Decomposition (SVD)

Singular Value Decomposition (SVD) is another type of dimensionality reduction technique. The Principal Component Analysis (PCA) is a special type of SVD technique. The PCA technique is developed based on the eigenvector's values, whereas the SVD is developed based on the singular values and the singular values represent the square roots of the eigenvalues. The SVD decomposition is consisting of three components, i.e., left singular values, diagonal matrix, and right singular values. Both PCA, and SVD are orthogonal transformation techniques.

The SVD decomposition for a given matrix A is given by the following equation:

$$A = U\,\Sigma V^T$$

The SVD decomposition for a given matrix is calculated as follows. In the first step the matrix is multiplied by its transpose, i.e. AA^T is computed. Then in the second step, eigenvalues, and eigenvectors are calculated for this matrix AA^T. The singular values are derived from the eigenvalues by taking the square root of the non-zero eigenvalues. Then the three components U, V, and Σ are derived from these singular values.

The SVD for dimensionality reduction is used as follows. Calculate the singular values from the matrix and then select the top k singular values from the matrix Σ. From the selected top singular values, the original data is transformed into lower dimensional data.

A simple numerical example of calculating SVD decomposition is presented here for better explanation. Suppose SVD decomposition for a matrix A is required to be calculated. The stepwise calculations are presented as follow.

Given matrix $A = \begin{bmatrix} 1 & 0 & 2 \\ 3 & 2 & 5 \\ 2 & 1 & 0 \end{bmatrix}$

The transpose of the matrix is calculated as shown below.

$$A^T = \begin{bmatrix} 1 & 3 & 2 \\ 0 & 2 & 1 \\ 2 & 5 & 0 \end{bmatrix}$$

The product of matrix with its transpose is calculated next.

$$W = AA^T = \begin{bmatrix} 1 & 0 & 2 \\ 3 & 2 & 5 \\ 2 & 1 & 0 \end{bmatrix}\begin{bmatrix} 1 & 3 & 2 \\ 0 & 2 & 1 \\ 2 & 5 & 0 \end{bmatrix} = \begin{bmatrix} 5 & 13 & 2 \\ 13 & 38 & 8 \\ 2 & 8 & 5 \end{bmatrix}$$

Find eigenvalues and eigenvectors of W.

The eigenvalues are 0.32, 3.45, and 44.23

The eigenvectors are $\begin{bmatrix} 3.92 \\ -1.57 \\ 1 \end{bmatrix}$, $\begin{bmatrix} -0.30 \\ -0.12 \\ 1 \end{bmatrix}$, and $\begin{bmatrix} 1.55 \\ 4.51 \\ 1 \end{bmatrix}$

Find the square root of the non-zero eigenvalues σ_i

$$\sigma_1 = 0.57,\ \sigma_2 = 1.86,\ \text{and}\ \sigma_3 = 6.65$$

The Σ matrix is a zero matrix with σ_i on its diagonal.

$$\Sigma = \begin{bmatrix} 0.57 & 0 & 0 \\ 0 & 1.86 & 0 \\ 0 & 0 & 6.65 \end{bmatrix}$$

The elements of matrix U are the normalized (unit) vectors:

$$U = \begin{bmatrix} 0.90 & -0.28 & 0.32 \\ -0.36 & -0.11 & 0.93 \\ 0.23 & 0.95 & 0.21 \end{bmatrix}$$

For matrix V, each column v_i is calculated as $v_i = \dfrac{1}{\sigma_i} A^T u_i$

e.g. $v_1 = \dfrac{1}{\sigma_1} A^T u_1 = \dfrac{1}{0.57} \begin{bmatrix} 1 & 3 & 2 \\ 0 & 2 & 1 \\ 2 & 5 & 0 \end{bmatrix} \begin{bmatrix} 0.90 \\ -0.36 \\ 0.23 \end{bmatrix} = \begin{bmatrix} 0.50 \\ -0.87 \\ 0.007 \end{bmatrix}$

so,

$$V = \begin{bmatrix} 0.50 & 0.69 & 0.53 \\ -0.86 & 0.39 & 0.31 \\ 0.007 & -0.61 & 0.79 \end{bmatrix}$$

So, the SVD decomposition for the given matrix is:

$$\begin{bmatrix} 1 & 0 & 2 \\ 3 & 2 & 5 \\ 2 & 1 & 0 \end{bmatrix} \cong \begin{bmatrix} 0.90 & -0.28 & 0.32 \\ -0.36 & -0.11 & 0.93 \\ 0.23 & 0.95 & 0.21 \end{bmatrix} \begin{bmatrix} 0.57 & 0 & 0 \\ 0 & 1.86 & 0 \\ 0 & 0 & 6.65 \end{bmatrix} \begin{bmatrix} 0.50 & -0.87 & 0.007 \\ 0.69 & 0.39 & -0.61 \\ 0.53 & 0.31 & 0.79 \end{bmatrix}$$

8.2.3 Other Linear Techniques

Linear discriminant analysis (LDA)

The LDA technique maximizes ratio of between-class variance to within-class variance. The LDA dimensionality reduction technique is applied in the five major steps. The steps are as follows: in the first step, mean vectors for each class are computed, then in the second step, two matrices namely, within-class scatter matrices and between-class scatter matrices are calculated. In the third step, eigenvalues and eigenvectors of both of the matrices are calculated. In the fourth step, eigenvectors are sorted in the decreasing order of eigenvalues. Finally, in the last step, the original data is transformed onto the new subspace with low dimensional using the selected eigenvectors. In this way the high dimensional data is transformed into the low dimensional data.

Factor analysis (FA)

Factor Analysis is a dimensionality reduction technique where individual factors are extracted from the original dataset and extracted factors are rotated for getting best interpretation of the original dataset, and the best interpretation is selected with minimum factors for dimensionality reduction. The factor analysis method of dimensionality reduction is applied in four steps. In the first step, correlation matrix from the original dataset is calculated, then in the second step, factors are extracted from the correlation matrix. In the third step, factors are rotated for better interpretation of the data and finally in the fourth step, best interpretation is selected for dimensionality reduction.

While computing the correlation matrix, Bartlett's test of sphericity is performed to check whether the sample in the dataset has equal variance. The Kaiser-Meyer-Olkin (KMO) measure is also calculated for finding correlation and partial correlation between the variables and suitability of the variables for the factors. Factor extractions are performed using some of the standard techniques like PCA or other methods such as maximum likelihood method, principal axis factoring, alpha method, unweighted least square method, generalized least square method, image factoring, and scree plot techniques. Factors are rotated to make the factors more meaningful and easier to interpret. Most popular methods of rotation are variance rotation. Other rotation methods are quartimax (orthogonal) rotation, equimax rotation, and promax rotation techniques. Factor rotation with most interpretability (or best interpretability) is selected as the lower dimensional data.

Independent component analysis (ICA)

The primary use of Independent Component Analysis (ICA) is to extract the independent (individual) components from the mixture of the non-Gaussian mixture of data. The component extraction method is utilized for the feature extraction model also and in this way, ICA is utilized as a feature selection technique.

The primary difference between the PCA and IACA techniques are, the PCA works on Gaussian models and applied to orthogonal vectors, whereas the ICA technique works on non-Gaussian models and applied to non-orthogonal vectors.

One of the samples in a non-Gaussian mixture of data is presented in the following equation:

$$X_i = a_{i1}s_1 + a_{i2}s_2 + \ldots + a_{in}s_n$$

Where a_{ik} is the mixing weights for the kth component, and s_k is the kth independent component.

The ICA techniques work in two steps. In the first step, data is cantered (by removing the mean) and then in the second step, whitening process is applied to eliminate uncorrelated data and scale the data variance to unit for extracting the independent components.

The ICA technique helps in extracting the independent component out of this non-Gaussian mixture of data. The central limit theorem of probability distribution help in extracting the independent components from a non-Gaussian mixture. The central limit theorem says that, if many non-Gaussian independent components will be mixed together then the mixed state will tend to become a Gaussian distribution. The primary limitation of ICA technique is, it cannot determine the variation of independent components and cannot determine the order of independent components.

8.2.4 Non-linear Dimensionality Reduction Techniques

T-distributed stochastic neighbor embedding (*t*-SNE)

The *t*-SNE method is used for representing of high dimensional data into low dimensional data by retaining the information from the original data by clustering the high dimensional data. The *t*-SNE uses perplexity parameter. Perplexity is the expected density of the clusters based on high similarity. The *t*-SNE uses *t*-distribution based on unscaled similarity scores.

Geodesic distance through Haversine formula is calculated as given below.

$$d = 2r \times arcsin\left(\sqrt{\sin^2\left(\frac{\Delta lat}{2}\right) + \cos(lat_1) \times \cos(lat_2) \times \sin^2\left(\frac{\Delta lan}{2}\right)}\right)$$

Where r is the radius of earth, lat_1, lat_2 are the latitude of the two points, Δlat is the difference between the two latitudes, Δlan is the difference between two longitudes. The *arcsin* is the inverse sine function to calculate the angle for the given value.

Isomap

It is a non-linear dimensionality reduction technique and is the extension of kernel-PCA technique. It preserves the geometric structures on the underlying manifold structure.

Manifold structure: Manifold structure handles the problem of unreliable distances between the scattered high-dimensional data. The manifold structure focuses on the two factors, i.e., intrinsic dimensionality and data locality.

The Isomap dimensionality reduction technique is applied in four steps. In the first step, a nearest neighbour graph is created for the original dataset. In the second step, the shortest path distance in the nearest neighbour graph is calculated using the Geodesic distances. In the third step, embedding of the shortest path is performed using the multidimensional scaling (MDS) technique. And finally, in the last step, dimensionality reduction is carried out using the embeddings.

RandomMaps

RandomMaps is a wrapper-based dimensionality reduction technique based on the random projections. The random projections are created by multiplying the original high-dimensional data with the random matrix. Once the random projections are created, then by preserving the approximate similarity between the original data points dimensionality is reduced from the original high-dimensional data. RandomMaps technique a fast and computationally simple technique of dimensionality reduction. RandomMaps are popularly used for dimensionality reduction in clustering and information retrieval tasks.

UMAP

The UMAP (Universal Manifold Approximation and Projection) is another standard technique of dimensionality reduction. It is a faster algorithm for dimensionality reduction. It converts the high dimensional data into the low dimensional data using similarity score. The UMAP technique is applied typically with three or higher dimensional data and produces the low-dimensional graph as output. In the output graph, data clusters are formed based on the similarity on the data points. The UMAP technique produces a lower-dimensional graph for a given higher-dimensional data and preserves the clustering features and relationship of original data. The lower-dimensional graph is updated till the clustering features of higher-dimensional data is preserved. In this way the dimensionality reduction is carried out by preserving the characteristics of the original data. For preserving the characteristics of original data, UMAP first measures the distances between the pair of high-dimensional data. The clustering is performed using the distances calculated and based on nearest neighbour's concept. The UMAP is similar to *t*-SNE technique but there are some differences between UMAP and *t*-SNE techniques. The first difference between *t*-SNE starts with the random initialization where UMAP starts with spectral embedding for initialization of low-dimensional data. The other difference is, *t*-SNE updates on a single data point, whereas the UMAP moves or updates a small subset of data points.

Locally linear embedding (LLE)

The LLE technique works in the following steps. In the first step, nearest neighbours are identified. In the second step, local reconstruction is performed by the linear combination of *k* nearest neighbours. In the third step, dimensionality reduction is performed based on the effectiveness of nonlinear manifolds which preserves local structures. The primary disadvantage of LLE technique is, computational cost is high, and choice of suitable value of *k* is complicated (for nearest neighbours). Mostly LLE models are used for visualizing anomaly detection, and pattern recognition tasks.

Locality sensitive hashing (LSH)

Locality Sensitive Hashing (LSH) is the nearest neighbour-based dimensionality reduction technique. LSH uses hashing functions to put similar data items on the same bucket. A hashing function is chosen in such a manner that more collision may occur during the hashing process. More collision indicates more similarity of data points and helps in achieving dimensionality reduction in a better way. Multiple functions are deployed for the hashing operations in LSH. Groups of similar data points are created in the buckets by hashing functions. By performing the query search operation on the buckets relevant dimensions for data analysis are selected and dimensionality reduction is achieved, in this way LSH provides a trade-off between the search space and improved computation (as the search space is limited to buckets only instead of original data points). The primary application of LSH dimensionality reduction technique is in anomaly detection, and development of efficient recommended systems.

8.2.5 Evaluation of Dimensionality Reduction Techniques

The evaluation of dimensionality reduction techniques can be performed in several ways. Three popular ways of evaluating dimensionality reduction techniques are based on some performance matrices, cross-validation and model selection techniques, and visualization techniques.

Mean Square Error: The most common parameter for evaluating the dimensionality reduction technique is the error measures. Mean Square Error (MSE) parameter help in identifying the best dimensionality reduction technique. The good technique should have minimum MSE.

Variance explained: The amount of variance preserved in the lower dimensional data with respect to the variance present in the original data.

Cluster quality: Cluster indicates the group of similar data. When dimensionality reduction technique is applied it creates the groups of data at the lower levels, technically that can be seen as the clusters of related data. Clustering performance parameters like Silhouette, Dunn, and DB-index can be utilized for identifying the best dimensionality reduction techniques using these parameters.

Visual separation: Visualization techniques help in visualizing the low dimensional data to understand the broader view of the transformed original data. There are a number of visualization techniques suitable for understanding and interpretation of the transformed data.

Computational cost: The complexity of the dimensionality reduction technique is one of the important factors by which the dimensionality reduction techniques can be compared. The good dimensionality reduction technique should be simple and should utilize minimum computation time.

Interpretability: Interpretability refers to the measure by which one can understand and interpret the low dimensional data generated from the original data.

8.2.6 Cross-validation and Model Selection

Validation techniques such as cross validation technique is also used for selecting the appropriate machine learning model by evaluating several dimensionality reduction techniques. Different approaches and its combinations are experimented in the cross-validation techniques to achieve the desired performance of the machine learning models and the best configuration is selected for further activities and data analysis tasks.

8.3 FEATURE SELECTION METHODS

Dimensionality reduction and feature selection, both techniques are used for reducing the number of features and selecting most relevant and suitable features from the large original data set. The primary difference between these techniques is, in dimensionality reduction technique the original high dimensional features are transformed to low dimensional features by preserving the characteristics of the original data (basic statistical property of the original data) whereas the feature selection technique filters the most relevant features from the original data based on some criteria (or some measures) without transforming the original data set.

8.3.1 Filtering-based Approaches

Filtering-based approaches for feature selection is developed by ranking the features based on some scores. There are various techniques for calculating the scores for a particular feature. Some of the commonly used techniques for calculating scores are chi-square test, mutual information measure, correlation-based measures, information gain or entropy of the features and many more. The choice of selecting the appropriate technique for calculating score depends on various factors including the type of variables, for example, the chi-square test is most suitable for the categorial variables. On the other hand, Relief technique can be used for feature weighting scheme and, feature importance can be measured from tree-based models also by identifying the attributes or features for the tree splitting criteria.

Information gain

Information gain for an attribute is calculated in terms of entropy. The minimum entropy indicates the higher information gain for an attribute. The attribute (or variable) with higher information gain is more relevant for the data analysis.

$$E(A) = -\sum_{i=1}^{m} p_i \log_2 p_i$$

Chi-square test

The statistical significance between two categorical (or nominal) variables is tested with the help of Chi-square test method. Features which are significantly correlated with each other are selected for the data analysis task. The significance of two variables is calculated using the following equation:

$$\chi^2 = \Sigma \frac{(O - E)^2}{E}$$

Where O is the observed and E is the expected outcome. The pairs of variables are kept as observed and target variables and the chi-square value are calculated and tested against the significant threshold value as per the contingency table, if values are above the threshold value then variables are correlated.

Correlation-based test

In correlation-based test techniques, features or dimensions are selected as per their correlation values. More correlated values are filtered together and selected for data analysis task whereas the least correlated values are not selected for data analysis task.

8.3.2 Wrapper-based Methods

The filtering-based techniques selects the independent suitable feature in the feature selection process whereas wrapper-based methods focus on the selection of relevant subsets of the features from the original feature sets for feature selection. The wrapper-based methods include the tasks of subsets-generation, model evaluation, and feature subset selection and validation. These tasks are performed in iterations to get the desired relevant subsets of the features.

The primary advantage of wrapper-based methods is that the performance of the selected machine learning models is assessed over the iterations to get the desired feature subset. So, the selected feature subset is most appropriate for the machine learning model. The disadvantages of wrapper-based method are two-fold. First, it is computationally expensive technique as the feature subset selection is carried out in iterations and second, sometimes the wrapper-based methods tend to be overfitting (suitable for small training data but does not perform well for the unseen testing data).

Some of the commonly used wrapper-based methods are: Recursive Feature Elimination (RFE), Sequential Feature Selection (SFS), and Genetic Algorithm (GA).

Recursive feature elimination (RFE)

Recursive Feature Elimination (RFE) is one of the wrapper methods of feature selection. It recursively eliminates features till the group of desired subsets of features are selected at the required level of feature selection. The RFE works in the following steps.

In the first step, identify a suitable model for the machine learning for training. In the second step, rank the features as per the importance of the features. The ranking is done using some criteria like, how a particular feature is selected frequently as one of the splitting attributes in the decision tree. In the third step, non-relevant features are eliminated (low rank features are eliminated). In the fourth step, the model is evaluated for the selected subset of the features. The third and fourth steps are repeated till the termination condition (i.e., the desired level of features are selected in the feature selection process). In this way an optimal subset of features is selected.

RFE is a computationally expensive technique particularly for the high dimensional datasets. But the major advantage of RFE is, the selected subset is directly linked to the performance of the machine learning model as the primary criteria for feature selection is linked with feature importance for a machine learning model performance.

Forward/backward selection

In forward selection technique, one dimension is selected at a time as per the relevance of the data analysis and then another dimension is selected till the desired level of dimensions are selected to achieve the goal of data analysis. The backward elimination technique is opposite to forward selection technique in which initially all the dimensions are selected and then one irrelevant dimension is eliminated at a time till the desired level of dimensionality reduction is achieved.

Visualization techniques

Visualization techniques help in understanding the dimensions and features of the datasets. It also represents the correlation between the features of a dataset. There are a number of standard plots which can demonstrate the characteristics of the features and correlations for deciding about the importance of a particular feature. Some commonly used visualization techniques are discussed here in brief.

Scatter plots (2D): The scatter plots represent the correlation between the features of a dataset. A sample scatter plot is shown in Figure 8.6.

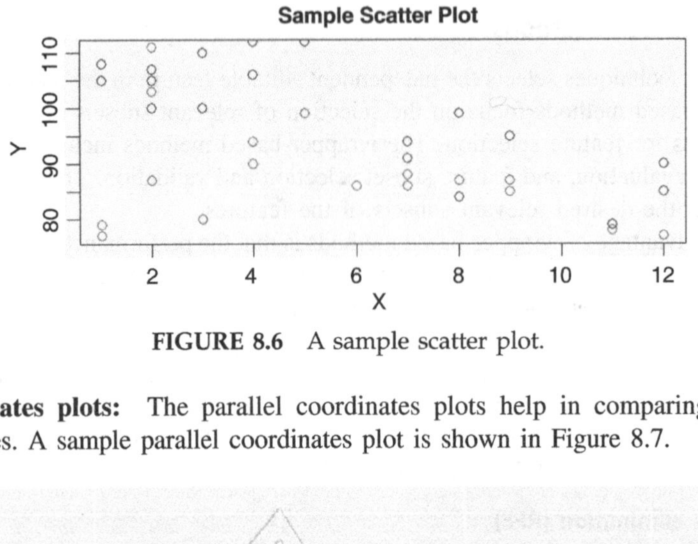

FIGURE 8.6 A sample scatter plot.

Parallel coordinates plots: The parallel coordinates plots help in comparing features of the individual samples. A sample parallel coordinates plot is shown in Figure 8.7.

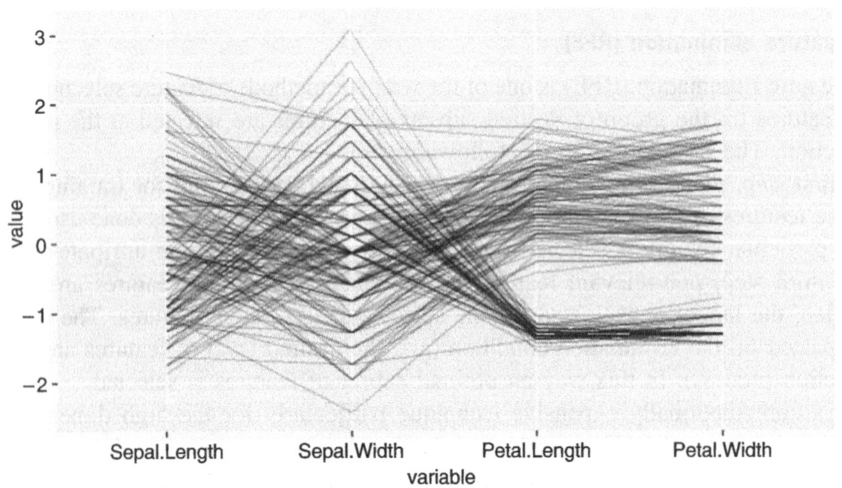

FIGURE 8.7 A sample parallel coordinates plot.

Pairplots: The relationship between each pair of variables is presented with the help of pairplots. A sample pairplot for 3 variables is presented in Figure 8.8.

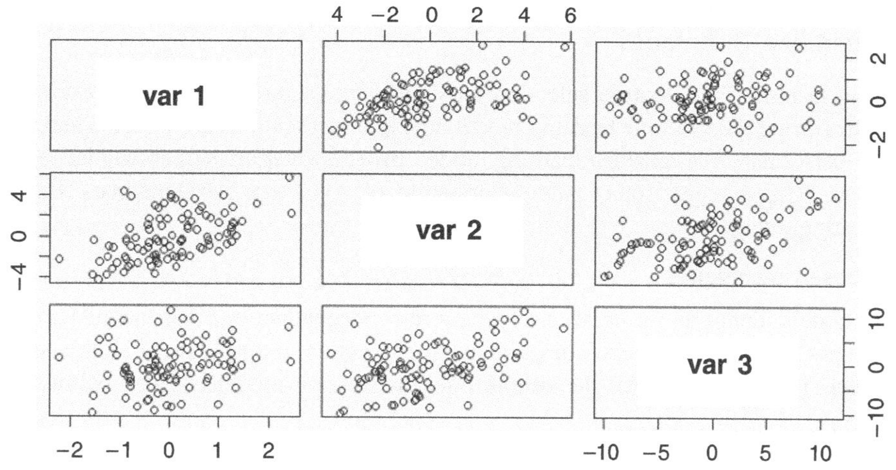

FIGURE 8.8 A sample pairplot.

Heatmaps: Heatmaps visualize the proximity/similarity between the data points. A sample heatmap is presented in Figure 8.9.

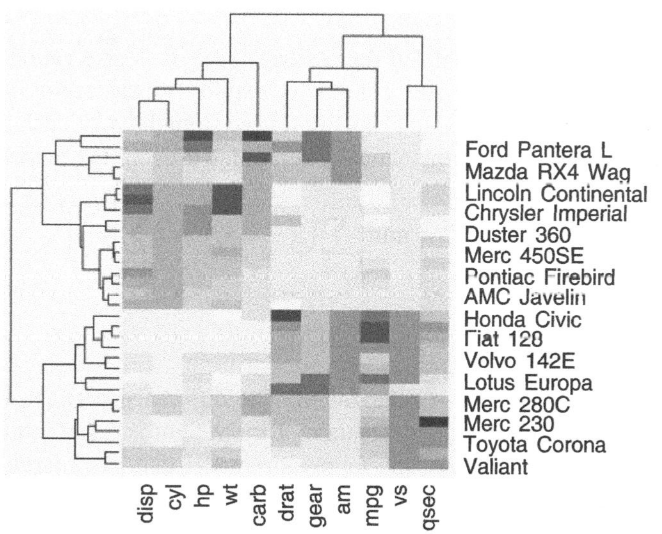

FIGURE 8.9 A sample heatmap.

Scree plot: The scree plot was shown for the PCA technique, it is an elbow technique which help users to select appropriate number of principal components up to a desired level of dimensionality reduction.

3D and Interactive Visualization Techniques: Apart from the above-mentioned plots and visualization techniques, most of the programming languages for data science provides several advanced visualization techniques to plot 3D and interactive plots for better understanding of correlations between features.

8.3.3 Embedding Techniques

In embedding techniques of feature selection most relevant features are selected during the model training itself. During the machine learning model development features are selected and incorporated for tuning of performance of machine learning model. Broader categories of embedded techniques are regression-based (Lasso regression of L1-regularization, etc.) and tree-based methods (RandomForest, GradientBoosting, etc.)

Regression-based techniques

Regression models identifies the relationship between independent and dependent variables. There are several types of regression techniques like linear regression, multiple regression, and polynomial regression, etc. The expression for the simple linear regression model is given below.

$$Y = w_0 + w_1x_1 + w_2x_2 + \ldots + w_nx_n$$

Where Y is the derived variable (or dependent variable) and x_i is the ith independent variable with w_i is the weight associated with it. The regularization techniques provide a way to assign more weights to the relevant features and less weights to the irrelevant features. These techniques are covered in brief here.

Lasso regression (L1-regularization)

Lasso regression is also called as penalized regression model. It is also called as L1-regularization technique. In Lasso regularization, some penalty is applied to the regression relation to avoid overfitting. The irrelevant variables (features) are eliminated from the relationship in Lasso regression. The Lasso regression technique is mathematically represented using the below equation.

$$L_{LASSO}(X,Y) = \min\left(\sum_{i=1}^{n}(y_i - w_ix_i)^2 + \lambda\sum_{i=1}^{n}|w_i|\right)$$

λ is called the penalty term.

Ridge regression (L2-regularization)

Ridge regression is also called as L2-regularization. The difference between the Lasso and Ridge regression is, in Ridge regression technique, square of the weight is taken in the penalty term. The Ridge regression reduces the variance of the regression model that has a large number of variables (or features). The Ridge regression is mathematically represented as the below equation.

$$L_{RIDGE}(X,Y) = \min\left(\sum_{i=1}^{n}(y_i - w_ix_i)^2 + \lambda\sum_{i=1}^{n}w_i^2\right)$$

ElasticNet regression

The Lasso regression model uses the more correlated variables as features for the regression, whereas the Ridge regression model uses the reduced features for the correlated variables. The ElasticNet regression model combines both the Lasso and Ridge techniques and take advantage of both techniques. It minimizes the parameters for the correlated variables and at the same time eliminates the non-relevant features in the regression model. The ElasticNet regression model is mathematically represented as shown below.

$$L_{ElasticNet}(X, Y) = \min\left(\sum_{i=1}^{n}(y_i - w_i x_i)^2 + \lambda_1 \sum_{i=1}^{n}|w_i| + \lambda_2 \sum_{i=1}^{n} w_i^2\right)$$

Where λ_1 and λ_2 are the penalty terms for Lasso and Ridge regressions respectively.

Tree-based techniques

In tree-based techniques, attributes selected as splitting nodes in decision-trees or RandomForest techniques are selected as the most relevant features for the data analysis and the attributes which are not selected as the splitting attributes are discarded as the irrelevant attributes. During the decision tree construction, the splitting nodes are selected using some criteria, so the selected attributes are most relevant for making decisions from the datasets.

8.3.4 Hybrid Approaches

Feature selection and dimensionality reduction both are combinedly applied in a dataset as per the requirements of data analysis. These combined approaches are called the hybrid approaches. The choice of feature selection and dimensionality reduction techniques depends on specific analysis tasks and requirements of the algorithm.

8.4 APPLICATIONS

Dimensionality reduction and feature selection techniques are very important activities in knowledge discovery process particularly with the high volume of data. Both of these techniques do not only help in filtering the subset of most relevant data for analysis but also help in optimizing the computing complexity of machine learning algorithms with the best desired performance. There are plenty of applications of both of these technologies in machine learning domain involving large data. Dimensionality reduction and feature selection techniques are widely used in text mining, natural language processing, social media analysis, financial data analysis, bioinformatics, and genomics.

EXERCISES

1. Normalize the following two-dimensional data:
   $D = \{(2, 3), (2, 4), (2, 7), (3, 1), (3, 5), (5, 3), (7, 4), (8, 6), (9, 2), (9, 5)\}$
   (a) Using z-score normalization
   (b) Use min-max normalization and normalize the two-dimensional data in the range of 0...1 for both dimensions.
2. Create the Boxplot and Stem-and-Leaf plot for the following data:
   $D = \{11, 15, 17, 21, 29, 33, 46, 58, 71, 89, 93, 95, 97, 98\}$
3. Calculate the singular value decomposition (SVD) for the following given matrix:

$$A = \begin{bmatrix} 1 & 0 & 0 \\ 1 & 0 & 0 \\ 0 & 0 & 1 \end{bmatrix}$$

4. List out the cases where you feel that which of the visualization technique out of parallel coordinate plots, heatmaps, and pairplot is best suited to dataset you are working with for the following cases: (also justify your answer)
   (a) For analysing feature correlations
   (b) For comparing the higher number of features available in the dataset
   (c) For comparing the smaller number of features available in the dataset
5. Differentiate between the Lasso and Ridge regression techniques? How to select one of the techniques for improving regression?

MULTIPLE CHOICE QUESTIONS

1. After applying the z-score normalization what is the value of 5 in the given dataset $D = \{3, 5, 11, 17, 19, 21\}$?
   (a) – 0.24 (b) – 1.11
   (c) – 1.41 (d) 0.92
2. After applying the z-score normalization for which input value the transformed value is 0.63 for the given dataset $D = \{3, 5, 11, 17, 19, 21\}$?
   (a) 5 (b) 11
   (c) 17 (d) 19
3. Apply the Min-Max normalization and transform the value 17 for the given dataset $D = \{3, 5, 11, 17, 19, 21\}$: into the new range of the values [1..5]. The calculated value is:
   (a) 4.56 (b) 2.78
   (c) 1.44 (d) 4.11
4. For which value the Min-Max normalization will give the transformed value of 1.44 for the given dataset $D = \{3, 5, 11, 17, 19, 21\}$: into the new range of the values [1..5]?
   (a) 17 (b) 5
   (c) 19 (d) 11
5. The Five-Point summary for the given dataset $D = \{3, 5, 11, 17, 19, 21\}$: will be:
   (a) [3, 5, 14, 19, 21] (b) [3, 5, 11, 17, 21]
   (c) [3, 5, 11, 19, 21] (d) [3, 5, 11, 17, 19]
6. What is the purpose of stem-and-leaf plot?
   (a) To provide the frequency of the numerical data
   (b) To provide the categorical data representation
   (c) To provide the representation of noise in the data
   (d) To provide the numerical data compression representation
7. Which is true about the phenomena of curse of dimensionality?
   (a) Adding more features can confuse the machine learning models and can lead to degradation of performance.
   (b) Adding more features can improve the machine learning models and can lead to improving of performance.
   (c) Adding more features can improve the training of machine learning models but lead to degradation of performance.
   (d) Reducing the number features can improve the performance of machine learning models.
8. What is the primary difference between the linear and non-linear dimensionality reduction techniques?
   (a) The reduced features are reduced in linear proportions in linear models whereas it is reduced in non-linear proportions in non-linear models.
   (b) The relationship between the original data and the reduced data is linear in linear models and non-linear in non-linear dimensionality reduction models.

(c) The time complexity of the linear and non-linear dimensionality reduction models is polynomial and non-polynomial respectively.
(d) All of the above.

9. What is the purpose of scree plot in principle component analysis?
(a) It is supporting plot to PCA model for better understanding.
(b) It uses Kaiser's rule to decide the appropriate number of components.
(c) It helps in determining the appropriate number of principle components in PCA model.
(d) All of the above.

10. Which parameter is used for the optimizing the number of clusters in *t*-SNE algorithm of dimensionality reduction?
(a) Perplexity (b) Nearest Neighbours
(c) Radius (d) Noise

11. What is the primary purpose of manifold structure in Isomap algorithm?
(a) Manifold structure normalizes the data for better analysis.
(b) Manifold structure handles the problem of unreliable distances between the scattered high-dimensional data.
(c) Manifold structure identifies noise in the data.
(d) Manifold structure is a complex data structure to filter the irrelevant data.

12. What is true about UMAP and *t*-SNE algorithms?
(a) The *t*-SNE updates on a single data point, whereas the UMAP moves or updates a small subset of data points.
(b) Both UMAP and *t*-SNE algorithms are used for dimensionality reduction.
(c) The *t*-SNE starts with the random initialization whereas UMAP starts with spectral embedding for initialization of low-dimensional data.
(d) All of the above.

13. Which is true about the Locality Sensitive Hashing (LSH) algorithm?
(a) It uses a unique hash function to map the local data into the same bucket.
(b) It eliminates noise automatically.
(c) It uses multiple hash functions.
(d) None of the above.

14. What is the primary difference between the filtering based and wrapper-based feature selection techniques?
(a) Both transforms the data into the lower dimensional data for dimensionality reduction.
(b) The filtering-based techniques selects the independent suitable features whereas wrapper-based methods focus on the selection of relevant subsets.
(c) The filtering-based techniques transforms the original features whereas wrapper-based methods focus on the filtering the features based on some criteria.
(d) None of the these.

15. Chi-square test is useful for which particular type of attributes?
(a) Numerical (b) Ordinal
(c) Categorical (d) Hybrid

16. What is the key benefit of the Recursive Feature Elimination (RFE) technique?
(a) RFE technique is computationally simple.
(b) RFE technique select the subset which is directly linked to the performance of the machine learning model.
(c) RFE technique can handle the high dimensional data efficiently.
(d) RFE technique handles overfitting of the model.

17. How embedding techniques of feature selection are different from the other techniques?
(a) The embedding techniques are computationally simpler than other techniques.
(b) The embedding techniques combines multiple techniques of feature selection.

(c) The embedding techniques selects the most relevant features during the model training.
(d) None of these.

18. Which is true about the Lasso and ridge regression techniques?
(a) The Lasso regression model adds penalty for avoiding overfitting whereas Ridge regression does not.
(b) Both Lasso and Ridge regression models improves the performance of regression.
(c) Both Lasso and Ridge regression models can not handle the unseen data.
(d) The Lasso regression model uses the more correlated variables as features for the regression, whereas the Ridge regression model uses reduces the features for the correlated variables.

19. Apart from the data reduction what is the other benefit of dimensionality reduction techniques?
(a) There is no need of applying validation techniques for the machine learning model.
(b) It improves the performance of machine learning model.
(c) Data pre-processing is not required.
(d) None of these.

20. What are the disadvantages of wrapper-based feature selection techniques?
(a) It is computationally expensive technique.
(b) It tends to overfitting.
(c) Scalability is a challenge for wrapper-based feature selection techniques,
(d) All of the above.

REFERENCES

[1] Saeys, Y., Inza, I., & Larranaga, P. (2007), A review of feature selection techniques in bioinformatics, *Bioinformatics*, 23(19), pp. 2507–2517.
[2] Chandrashekar, G., & Sahin, F. (2014), A survey on feature selection methods, *Computers & electrical engineering*, 40(1), pp. 16–28.
[3] Miao, J., & Niu, L. (2016), A survey on feature selection, *Procedia computer science*, 91, pp. 919–926.

ANSWER KEY

1. (b)	**2.** (c)	**3.** (d)	**4.** (b)	**5.** (a)	**6.** (d)	**7.** (a)	**8.** (b)	**9.** (d)	**10.** (a)
11. (b)	**12.** (d)	**13.** (c)	**14.** (b)	**15.** (c)	**16.** (b)	**17.** (c)	**18.** (d)	**19.** (b)	**20.** (d)

9 Regression Models

Introduction

Regression models help us predict continuous variables as a function of some predictor attributes. We have already seen regressions models for predicting height in Chapter 1, derivation of normal equations in Chapter 3, optimization techniques to solve regression problems in Chapter 4 and the maximum likelihood formulation of regression in Chapter 5. In this chapter, we will learn more complex regression models, estimate the accuracy of regression models and discuss how to generalize them on unseen data.

We will assume that the response variable, Y, relates to the predictors, X, through some unknown function 'f' expressed generally as:

$$Y = f(X) + \varepsilon$$

Here, f is the unknown function expressing an underlying rule for relating Y to X, ε (with mean 0) is the random amount (unrelated/independent to X) that Y differs from the rule $f(X)$.

In essence, statistical learning refers to a set of approaches for estimating f. In this chapter we outline some of the key theoretical concepts that arise in estimating f, as well as tools for evaluating the estimates obtained. A *statistical model* is any algorithm that estimates f. We denote the estimated function as $\hat{f}$ and prediction of Y as $\hat{Y}$. There are two main reasons that we may wish to estimate f: prediction and inference. We discuss each in turn.

Prediction task: We are only interested in the correct output "Y". The model may be black-box, we may not know the relationships between X and Y and which attributes influence Y in what way, etc. The accuracy of $\hat{Y}$ as a prediction for Y depends on two types of errors: reducible error and irreducible error. *Reducible errors* can be minimized by choosing better learning algorithms. But since Y also depends on ε, which cannot be predicted using X, there will always be some *irreducible error.* The quantity ε may contain unmeasured variables that are useful in predicting Y or even some unmeasurable variations.

Square of expected prediction error: $$E\left(Y-\hat{Y}\right)^2 = E\left[f(X)+\varepsilon-\hat{f}(X)\right]^2 = E\left[f(X)-\hat{f}(X)\right]^2 + Var(\varepsilon).$$

Where the first term is reducible error and the second term is irreducible error.

Inference task: We are more interested in the relationships of the attributes ($X_1, X_2, ..., X_p$) with Y. We want to know which attributes are more important, how they influence Y, is the relationship linear or non-linear, etc.

9.1 CURVE FITTING APPROACHES

We are familiar with curve-fitting. We have performed experiments and collected observations and readings. Often, we are interested in understanding relationships of a quantity/variable on other attributes. We draw a curve that passes through the observed points and write its equation. How to draw the correct curve? Should the curve pass exactly through each point? Or we should choose a **simpler** curve which may not pass exactly through each point, but is close to every point?

Model complexity vs. training accuracy is a fundamental trade-off that we will encounter repeatedly in machine learning (ML). We don't want to **overfit the curve** (model) to the training data. Overfitting means that the model doesn't generalize well to unseen data (test data). In other words, we want to have a balance between model complexity and the training error.

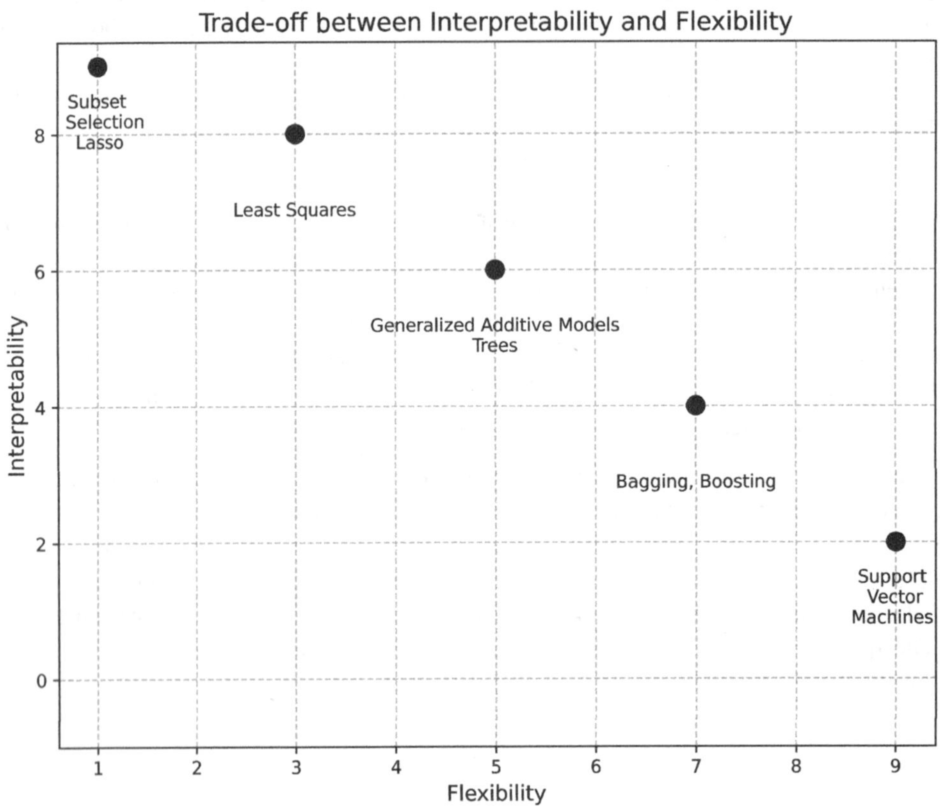

FIGURE 9.1 Trade-off between Model Interpretability and Flexibility.

There are many methods of regression (that estimate *f*). Some are less flexible but more interpretable. These are useful for inference problems where we want to study the relationships between predictor variables. For example, linear models allow for relatively simple and interpretable inference, but may not yield as accurate predictions as some other approaches. Highly non-linear approaches can potentially provide quite accurate predictions for *Y*, but may be difficult to interpret and may also be prone to overfitting! Depending on whether our ultimate goal is prediction, inference, or a combination of the two, different methods for estimating *f* may be appropriate.

ML algorithms have the objective of generalization, i.e. models must perform well on data that they have not seen during training/optimization of their parameters. There are many ML techniques and ML models have several parameters. How to choose the best one? This is also known as **model selection.** Let us now discuss the general approach used in training machine learning models. During the process of training, we determine the optimal parameters (and hyperparameters) of the model.

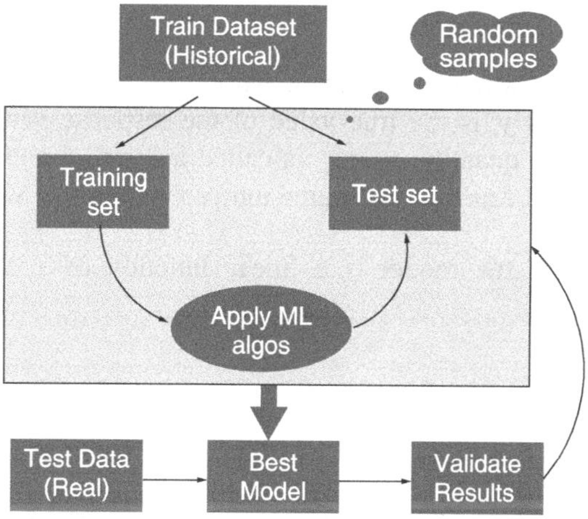

FIGURE 9.2 General Approach used in Training Machine Learning Models.

9.2 ML MODEL TRAINING PROCESS

The Machine Learning process consists of three steps:

(a) Model Training or Parameter estimation
(b) Hyperparameter tuning and model selection
(c) Prediction or Inference.

To begin with, the input dataset is divided into random train/validation/test splits, e.g. (80/10/10) or (70/10/20) to be used for training, validation and testing respectively. If "test data" is provided separately, we may divide the training data only into train and validation sets.

Test data is considered unknown and cannot be used for training or hyperparameter tuning. The validation set is a subset of the available training data that we keep aside for hyperparameter tuning and model selection. A practical issue with this approach is that the amount of labeled data is usually limited, and ideally, we would like to use as much of the data available to train the model. This would require us to keep our validation set *V* small, which then would lead to a noisy estimate (with high variance) of the predictive performance. One solution to these contradictory objectives (large training set, large validation set) is to use *cross-validation.*

K-fold cross-validation effectively partitions the data into *K* chunks, *K*-1 of which form the training set *R*, and the last chunk serves as the validation set *V* (similar to the idea outlined previously). Cross-validation iterates through (ideally) all combinations of assignments of chunks to R and V. This procedure is repeated for all K choices for the validation set, and the performance of the model from the K runs is averaged. For each split, model is generated and tested for accuracy. This is repeated 5 times or 10 times and average error is computed. The best model is selected and used in real world scenario.

When the dataset size is small, we may use a special technique called leave one out cross-validation (LOOCV). In this approach, each observation is considered as the validation set and the rest (N-1) observations are considered as the training set. Thus, a new model is trained N times and used to predict a value for the observation that was left out during training. This is a special case of K-fold cross-validation in which the number of folds is the same as the number of observations ($K = N$). This method helps to reduce bias and prevents over fitting.

9.2.1 Metrics for Model Evaluation

In order to quantify how well a model performs, we define a *loss* or *error function.* Suppose x_i is the vector of predictors and y_i is the true value of the response variable. $\hat{y}_i$ is the prediction of the model based on x_i. The quantity $y_i - \hat{y}_i$ is called a *residual* and measures the error at the i-th prediction. A common loss function for regression problem is the Mean Squared Error (MSE): $L = MSE = \Sigma_{i=1}^{n} \frac{(y_i - \hat{y}_i)^2}{n}$. If the model is a linear function of x_i then $\hat{y}_i = w^T x_i$ and MSE $= \Sigma_{i=1}^{n} \frac{(y_i - w^T x_i)^2}{n}$.

The quality of the model can be assessed by computing the R^2 metric. $R^2 = 1 - \frac{\Sigma(y_i - \hat{y}_i)^2}{\Sigma(y_i - \bar{y})^2}$

Where $\bar{y}$ is the mean of y_i; i.e. average value of response. If our model is as good as the mean value, $\bar{y}$, then $R^2 = 0$. If our model is perfect then $R^2 = 1$. R^2 can be negative if the model is worse than the average. This can happen when we evaluate the model in the real-life test set.

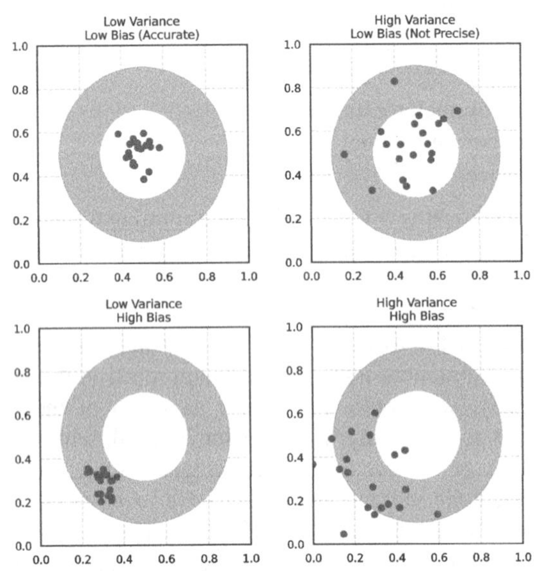

FIGURE 9.3 Scatter Plots of Y vs. Y˜ to understand Model Bias and variance.

9.2.2 Bias-Variance Tradeoff

Bias is error from erroneous assumptions in the model, like making it linear/simplistic. This is known as underfitting. Bias is how much off we are from the target. There are various kinds of bias: sampling bias, model bias.

Variance is error from sensitivity to small fluctuations in the training set, indicating it will not work in real world. This is known as overfitting. Variance is the spread in our predictions.

The total error of a regression model can be expressed as follows:

Total Error = Bias^2 + Variance + Irreducible Error.

Bias is the average distance of estimate $\hat{f}$ from the true mean of $f(x)$. Variance is the sq. dev (squared deviation) of the estimate $\hat{f}$ around its mean.

As shown in the figure, first-principle models are likely to suffer from bias, with data-driven models in greater danger of overfitting.

Occam's razor: This philosophical principle states that "the simplest explanation is best".

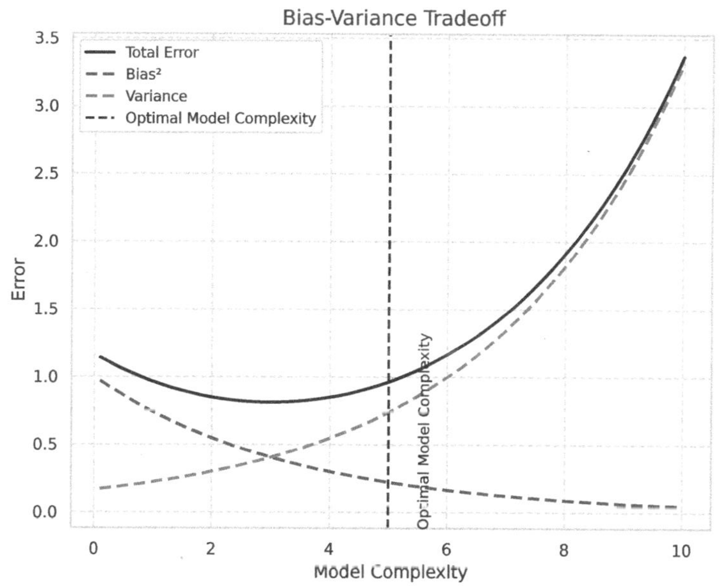

FIGURE 9.4 Bias-Variance Tradeoff.

9.3 K-NEAREST NEIGHBOR

The *k-Nearest Neighbor (kNN) model* is an intuitive way to predict a quantitative response variable: "*to predict a response for a set of observed predictor values, we use the responses of other observations most similar to it.*" This strategy can also be applied in classification to predict a categorical variable. For a fixed value of k, the predicted response for the i-th observation is the average of the observed response of the k-closest observations. If $\{x_{n1},..., x_{nk}\}$ are the k observations most similar to x_i (*similar* refers to a notion of distance between predictors). The response $(\hat{y}_n)$ can be written as follows:

$$\hat{f}(x) = \hat{y}_n = \frac{1}{k}\sum_{i=1}^{k} y_{n_i}$$

Usually, Euclidean distance is chosen (sqrt of squared coordinate differences). Very few assumptions are made here about the nature of '*f*'. We assign equal weights for the values of *y*, regardless of their distance from *x*. This method is non-parametric, as we don't have any parameters except for '*k*', the number of neighbors. This method is easy to implement and works very well in several problem settings.

There are two limitations of this method:

1. As dimensionality of data increases, it becomes hard to find neighbors (of x_i) close by and *f* may change significantly. Thus, the estimate may not be very good in quality.
2. Discontinuity: The neighborhood set changes discontinuously/abruptly, causing $\hat{f}(x)$ to be discontinuous.

A generalization of KNN method is as follows. If we took all the points, not just the k nearest points, and introduce a weighting function that weights by distance (so that we weight the value of closer points more) $\hat{y}^* = \dfrac{\sum_n K(x^*, x_n)y_n}{\sum_n K(x^*, x_n)}$.

This method can be used to produce a smooth approximation of the function. The traditional kNN method can be seen as a 0/1 weighting model with the closest *K* points getting a weight of 1 and the other points weight 0. Examples of other kernels include the Epanechnikov quadratic Kernel, Tri-cube Kernel, and Gaussian Kernel whose formulae are given below:

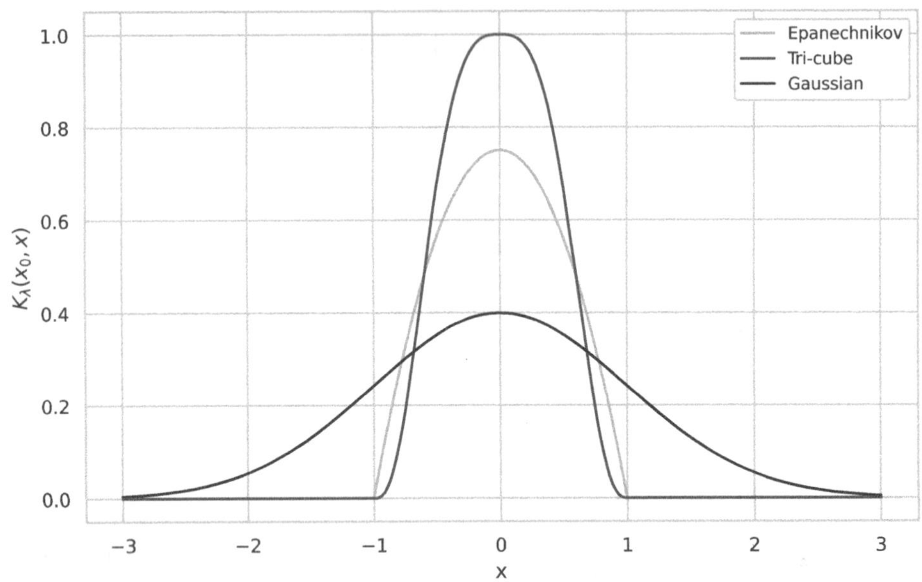

FIGURE 9.5 Comparative Assessment of different Kernel Functions.

Epanechnikov Quadratic kernel: $$K(x^*, x_n) = \begin{cases} \frac{3}{4}\left(1 - \frac{|x^* - x_n|}{\lambda}\right)^2 & if \frac{|x^* - x_n|}{\lambda} < 1 \\ 0 & \text{otherwise} \end{cases}$$

In this case, the weight of the neighbors that are at a distance λ or more is 0. For those neighbors whose distance is less than λ, the weight increases gradually as shown in the above figure.

Tri-cube kernel: $K\left(x^*, x_n\right) = \begin{cases} \frac{3}{4}\left(1 - \frac{\left|x^* - x_n\right|^3}{\lambda^3}\right)^3 & if \frac{\left|x^* - x_n\right|}{\lambda} < 1 \\ 0 & \text{otherwise} \end{cases}$

This is similar to the Epanechnikov kernel, with the additional property of being differentiable at the boundary.

Gaussian Kernel: $K\left(x^*, x_n\right) = \frac{1}{\sqrt{2\pi}} e^{-\frac{\left|x^* - x_n\right|^2}{\lambda^2}}$

Notice that every point will now have a non-zero weight. λ now acts as a standard deviation.

The kernel-width, λ, is a hyperparameter of the above kernel based KNN model that needs to be optimized/estimated by data. If the kernel-width, λ, is small, there will be larger variance in predictions, $\hat{f}(x)$, as the average is computed over fewer neighboring points. At the same time, it would have a smaller bias, as closer instances are used. Thus, there is a risk of bumps in the plot of $\hat{f}(x)$.

If the kernel-width, λ, is large, the variance in predictions, $\hat{f}(x)$, will be small, as the average is computed over a greater number of neighboring points. The bias would be larger bias, as instances further apart are used. Thus, there is a risk of the model being too rigid (inflexible) and over-smoothed. In other words, it won't be able to capture the minute variations that may be needed.

9.4 LINEAR REGRESSION

We now move on to parametric approaches for linear regression which involve computation of the optimal parameters that minimize the MSE. We have already seen optimal solution to the problem using Normal equations, Optimization technique, etc. The optimal solution is given as:

$$\hat{w} = \left(A^T A\right)^{-1} A^T y$$

Where $A = \begin{bmatrix} 1 & x_{11} & x_{12} & . & . & . & x_{1d} \\ 1 & x_{21} & x_{22} & . & . & . & x_{2d} \\ . & . & . & . & . & . & . \\ . & . & . & . & . & . & . \\ . & . & . & . & . & . & . \\ 1 & w_0 & x_{n1} & . & . & . & x_{nd} \end{bmatrix}$ and $y = \begin{bmatrix} y_1 \\ y_2 \\ . \\ . \\ . \\ y_n \end{bmatrix}$

Now we will discuss important topics such as: avoiding overfitting by regularization, selection of predictor variables, confidence interval on parameters and predictions, etc.

9.4.1 Accuracy of the Parameter Estimates

Consider a simple linear regression problem: $y = w_0 + w_1 x + \varepsilon$

Here w_0 is the intercept, w_1 is the slope and ε is the error term that is independent of x. We estimate the values of w_0, w_1 using the observations $(x_1, y_1)....(x_n, y_n)$. Now if the observations change, the estimate of w_0, w_1 will also change. Thus, we would like to estimate the error in the value of these parameters obtained as a solution to linear regression.

Using the least squares approach, we can show that the parameters can be estimated as follows:

$$\hat{w}_1 = \frac{\Sigma_{i=1}^{n}\left(x_i - \bar{x}\right)\left(y_i - \bar{y}\right)}{\Sigma_{i=1}^{n}\left(x_i - \bar{x}\right)^2} \text{ and } \hat{w}_0 = \bar{y} - \hat{w}_1\bar{x} \qquad \text{where } \bar{x} = \frac{\Sigma_{i=1}^{n} x_i}{n} \text{ and } \bar{y} = \frac{\Sigma_{i=1}^{n} y_i}{n}$$

Intuitively, we would expect that the error in parameter estimates would be higher if $Var(\varepsilon)$ is higher. Also note that as the number of observations increase, we would expect that these estimates will converge to their true value. The standard errors associated with the estimates, $\hat{w}_0$ and $\hat{w}_1$ can be calculated as follows:

$$SE\left(\hat{w}_0\right)^2 = \sigma^2\left[\frac{1}{n} + \frac{\bar{x}^2}{\Sigma_{i=1}^{n}\left(x_i - \bar{x}\right)^2}\right] \text{ and } SE\left(\hat{w}_1\right)^2 = \frac{\sigma^2}{\Sigma_{i=1}^{n}\left(x_i - \bar{x}\right)^2} \text{ where } \sigma^2 = Var(\varepsilon)$$

In case, the variance of noise/errors $Var(\varepsilon)$ is not known, it can be estimates as the Residual Standard error (RSE) given by $RSE = \sqrt{\frac{MSE}{n-2}} = \sqrt{\frac{\Sigma_{i=1}^{n}\left(\hat{y}_i - y_i\right)^2}{n-2}}$

The 95% confidence intervals for $\hat{w}_1$ is given by [$\hat{w}_1$ – 2 SE($\hat{w}_1$), $\hat{w}_1$ + 2 SE($\hat{w}_1$)]. In other words, there is a 95% chance that the true value of w_1 lies in the above interval. Similarly, the 95% confidence interval for $\hat{w}_0$ is given by [$\hat{w}_0$ – 2 SE($\hat{w}_0$), $\hat{w}_0$ + 2 SE($\hat{w}_0$)].

9.4.2 Hypothesis Testing of Relationship between Response and Predictors

Standard errors can also be used to perform hypothesis tests on the parameters. The most common hypothesis to test is whether a predictor variable/attribute is even related to the response? We first discuss the case of simple linear regressions where we have only 1 predictor variable.
The null hypothesis can be written as follows:

H_0: There is no relationship between x and y

And the alternative hypothesis is as follows:

H_a: There is some relationship between x and y

This corresponds to testing $H_0 : w_1 = 0$ vs. $H_a : w_1 \neq 0$; since if $w_1 = 0$, then the model reduces to $y = w_0 + \varepsilon$ and x is not associated with y. To test the null hypothesis, we need to determine whether $\hat{w}_1$, our estimate for w_1, is sufficiently far from zero that we can be confident that w_1 is non-zero.

Intuitively, if w_1 is large and SE ($\hat{w}_1$) is small, we can be fairly confident that there is a relationship between x and y. In practice, we compute a t-statistic, given by $t = \frac{\hat{w}_1 - 0}{SE(\hat{w}_1)}$ which measures the number of standard deviations that w_1 is away from 0.

If x is not related to y, then the t-statistic will have $n - 2$ degrees of freedom and for $n > 30$, it converges to the standard normal distribution. Now we compute the probability of observing $\hat{w}_1$ equal to $|t|$ or larger in absolute value, assuming $w_1 = 0$. This probability is called the *p-value*. A small p-value indicates that it is unlikely to observe such a substantial association between the predictor and the response due to chance. If we see a small p-value, then we can infer that there is an association between the predictor and the response. We *reject the null hypothesis*—that is, we declare a relationship to exist between x and y. Typical p-value cutoffs for rejecting the null hypothesis are 5% or 1%.

We now move on to the case of multiple linear regression, where we have multiple (d) attributes or predictors. The following questions are important:

1. Is at least one of the predictors, $x_1, x_2, ..., x_d$ useful in predicting the response?
2. Is every predictor important, or only a subset?
3. Given the predictor values, what is the confidence interval for the response?

We now discuss each of these.

1. The null hypothesis in this case can be written as follows:

   $$H_0 : \text{There is no relationship between } x_1, x_2, ..., x_d \text{ and } y.$$

   And the alternative hypothesis is as follows:

   H_a : There is some relationship between at least one of predictors $x_1, x_2, ..., x_d$ and y

   This corresponds to testing $H_0 : w_1 = w_2 ... = w_d = 0$ vs. $H_a : \exists i, w_i \neq 0$

   We compute a F-statistic, given by $F = \dfrac{\left[\Sigma(y_i - \bar{y})^2 - \Sigma(y_i - \hat{y_i})^2\right]/d}{\Sigma(y_i - \hat{y_i})^2 / (n-d-1)}$

   It can be shown that when there is no relationship between predictors and response, the value of F statistic would be close to 1. The corresponding p-value is computed and if it is close to zero, we reject the null hypothesis.
2. Let us assume we want to test that a particular subset of q of the parameters are zero. The null hypothesis in this case can be written as follows:

   $$H_0 : w_1 = w_2 ... = w_q = 0$$

   The appropriate statistic is a F-statistic, computed as follows: $F = \dfrac{\left[\Sigma(y_i - \bar{y})^2 - \Sigma(y_i - \hat{y_i})^2\right]/q}{\Sigma(y_i - \hat{y_i})^2 / (n-d-1)}$

   and the corresponding p-value is computed and if it is close to zero, we reject the null hypothesis.

9.4.3 Feature Selection

It is possible that all of the d-predictors are associated with the response, but it is more often the case that the response is only associated with a subset of the predictors. The task of determining which predictors are associated with the response, in order to fit a single model involving only those predictors, is referred to as *attribute selection or feature selection*. We discuss some approaches briefly:

(a) **Forward selection:** In this approach, we begin will a null set, S. We perform d linear regressions, each with exactly one variable. We add the variable that results in lowest Cross-validation error to the set, S. We again, perform d-1 linear regressions with 2 variables. We add the variable that results in lowest Cross-validation error to the set, S. We continue until some stopping criteria is reached. For example, the cross-validation error is not decreasing.

(b) **Backward selection:** It begins with all the variables and removes the variable with highest p-value at successive steps. We continue until some stopping criteria is reached. For example, the cross-validation error is not increasing much.

(c) **Mixed selection:** It is similar to Forward Selection, but it may also remove a variable if it doesn't yield any improvement to the model.

Given the predictor values, what is the confidence interval for the response?

Once we have fit the multiple regression model, it is straightforward to apply the linear model to predict the response y on the basis of a set of values for the predictors $x_1, x_2 \ldots, x_d$. However, there are three sources of uncertainty associated with this prediction.

(a) Uncertainty in the parameters $\hat{w}_i$ of the model, which are estimates of the true parameters w_i. This is related to the reducible errors discussed before. By collecting more samples, we may be able to improve the parameter estimates and reduce this uncertainty.

(b) Model bias: We are assuming a linear model for $f(x)$ which is an approximation of the true function and is an additional source of *reducible errors.*

(c) Finally, we have the irreducible errors which are caused due to random errors ε.

We use *prediction intervals* to estimate the response y given x. Prediction intervals are always wider than confidence intervals, because they incorporate both the error in the estimate for $f(x)$ (the reducible error) and the uncertainty as to how much an individual point will differ from ideal regression model (the irreducible error).

9.4.4 Overfitting and Regularization

Regularization is a term that we add to the loss function to prevent the model from becoming too complex. We use optimization techniques to solve for the best parameters that minimize the loss function. We have seen the basics of matrix algebra to solve the least squares problem in Chapter 3. Our goal is now to reduce overfitting of data by adding a new term $R(w)$, a regularization loss term that is also a function of w, the parameters of the model. This loss reduces the degrees of freedom and encourages selection of simpler models by the optimization algorithm.

$$L_{reg}(w) = L(w) + \lambda R(w)$$

For a linear model, regularization is typically achieved by constraining the weights of the model where λ is a scalar that gives the weight (or importance) of the regularization term. Fitting the model using the modified loss function L_{reg} would result in model parameters with desirable properties (specified by R).

We now discuss three important types of Regularization Loss functions that have been studied in the context of linear regression.

(1) Ridge regression: We choose a regularization term that penalizes the squares of the parameter magnitudes. Then, our regularized loss function is

$$L_{Ridge}(w) = \frac{1}{n} \Sigma_{i=1}^{n} \left| y_i - w^T x_i \right|^2 + \lambda \Sigma_{j=1}^{D} w_j^2$$

Note that $\Sigma_{j=1}^{D} w_j^2 = \|\boldsymbol{w}\|_2^2$ is the square of the l_2 norm of $\boldsymbol{w}$.

This works best when the least-square estimates have high variance. As λ increases the flexibility of the model decreases, because of which the variance in the estimate and predictions decrease although the bias increases slightly. Ridge regression reduces the parameter values but doesn't force them to go to zero. Thus, if our goal is to simplify the model by reducing the number of predictor variables or attributes needed for the model, we use another related technique known as Lasso.

(2) LASSO regression: In LASSO regression, the l_1 norm of $\boldsymbol{w}$ is used as the loss function.

$$L_{LASSO}(w) = \frac{1}{n}\Sigma_{i=1}^{n}\left|y_i - w^T x_i\right|^2 + \lambda\Sigma_{j=1}^{D}\left|w_j\right|$$

In both ridge and LASSO regression, we see that the larger our choice of the **regularization parameter** λ, the more heavily we penalize large values in $\boldsymbol{w}$**.** If λ is close to zero, we recover the MSE, i.e. ridge and LASSO regression is just ordinary regression. If λ is sufficiently large, the MSE term in the regularized loss function will be insignificant and the regularization term will force w_{ridge} and w_{LASSO} to be close to zero. To avoid ad-hoc choices, we should select λ using cross-validation. Once the model is trained, we use the unregularized performance measure to evaluate the model's performance.

(3) Elastic Net: In Elastic Net, the regularization term is a simple weighted combination mix with L_2 and L_1 loss with a parameter '*r*'. Elastic Net has better convergence features over LASSO.

$$L_{Elastic\_Net}(w) = \frac{1}{n}\Sigma_{i=1}^{n}\left|y_i - w^T x_i\right|^2 + \lambda(1-r)\Sigma_{j=1}^{D}\mathrm{w}_\mathrm{j}^2 + \lambda r\Sigma_{j=1}^{D}\left|w_j\right|$$

9.4.5 Handling Qualitative Predictors

If a qualitative predictor/attribute only has two possible values, then incorporating it into a regression model is very simple. We simply create an indicator or *dummy variable* that takes on two possible numerical values 0 and 1 which may be used to indicate the absence or presence.

When a qualitative predictor has more than two levels, a single dummy variable cannot represent all possible values. In this situation, we can create additional dummy variables and combine them to represent multiple levels. Another option is to use one-hot-encoding as discussed in Chapter 2.

9.4.6 Non-linear Regression

So far, we have made the assumption that the function is linear in the predictor attributes. But that is a very strong "bias" as it limits our ability to model complex phenomenon. For example, the gravitational force between two masses obeys an inverse square law. It is a non-linear function.

$$\text{Gravitation Force } F_G = f(m_1, m_2, r)$$

We need to add non-linear features, e.g. $m_1 m_2$, $\frac{1}{r}$, m_1 by applying transformations to the input attributes/variables. These act as new features and we are able to understand the dependency of the target variable on the input variables.

9.4.7 Generalized Linear Models

In the above example, we can try to model the logarithm of gravitation force $\log(F_G) = f(m_1, m_2, r)$ which turns out to be a linear function of $\log(m_1)$, $\log(m_2)$, $\log(r)$. We now need to learn the optimal constants from the experimental data.

9.5 RESIDUAL ANALYSIS

We now discuss an important graphical/visualization tool for improving and debugging regression models. We first compute residuals, $r_i = y_i - \hat{y}_i$ for each data point (x_i, y_i). The residuals are the same as errors. When we estimated the variance of ε, we assumed that the residuals $r_i = y_i - \hat{y}_i$ were uncorrelated and normally distributed with mean 0 and fixed variance. These assumptions need to be verified using the data. In residual analysis, we typically create two types of plots:

1. a plot of r_i with respect to x_i or $\hat{y}_i$. This allows us to compare the distribution of the noise at different values of x_i.
2. a histogram of r_i. This allows us to explore the distribution of the noise independent of x_i or $\hat{y}_i$.

Residuals are easier to interpret than the model which may involve multiple attributes. We plot r_i with y_i, so the graph is always 2-D.

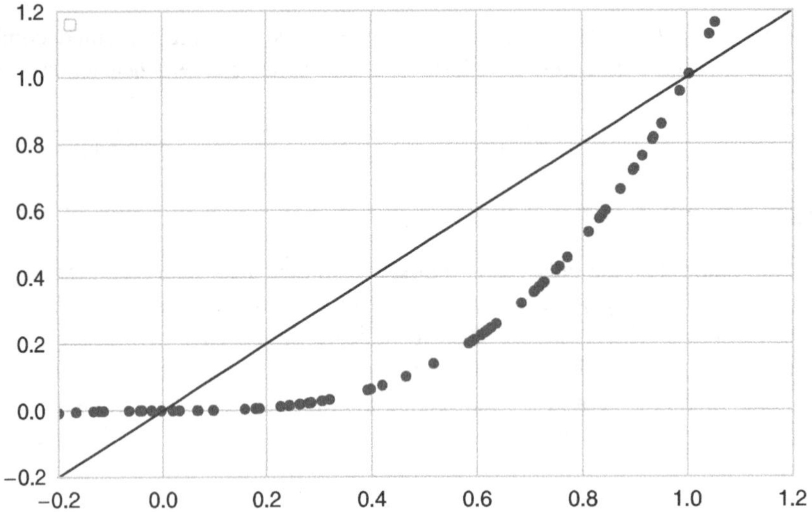

FIGURE 9.6 Residuals Analysis.

9.6 POTENTIAL PROBLEMS OF LINEAR MODELS

Now, we discuss some of the common problems of linear models along with the standard solution approaches to address them.

(a) **Non-linearity:** The linear regression model assumes that there is a straight-line relationship between the predictors and the response. If the true relationship is highly non-linear, then almost all of the conclusions that we draw from the model may be misleading. In addition, the prediction accuracy of the model can be significantly reduced.

Residual plots are a useful graphical tool for identifying non-linearity. To address this problem, we can use polynomial linear regression or design better features. We will also study techniques to learn non-linear regression models such as decision trees, random forest, SVMs, Neural Networks, etc., later in the book.

(b) **Outliers:** An *outlier* is a point for which y_i is far from the value predicted by the model. Outliers can arise for a variety of reasons, such as incorrect recording of an observation during data collection. Outliers may affect the parameters of the model because of the quadratic penalty (loss). They may increase the size of confidence interval. Thus, removal of outliers can improve the quality of prediction and our confidence in the model. We need

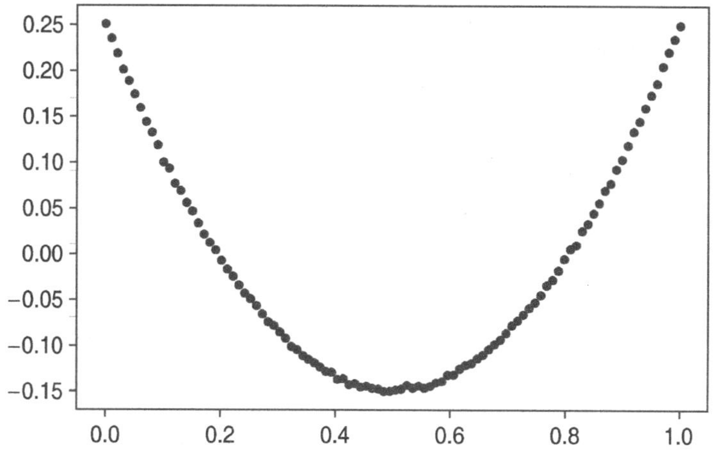

FIGURE 9.7 Nonlinearity in Linear Regression Model.

to discard outliers carefully through EDA, box-plots on attributes, residual plots, inspecting points with high errors, etc. However, care should be taken, since an outlier may instead indicate a deficiency with the model, such as a missing predictor.

(c) **High-leverage points:** High leverage points are outliers in the predictor variables. Just as outliers are observations for which the response y_i is unusual given the predictor x_i, observations with *high leverage* have an unusual value for x_i. High leverage observations tend to have a sizable impact on the estimated regression line. It is cause for concern if the least squares line is heavily affected by just a couple of observations, because any problems with these points may invalidate the entire fit. For this reason, it is important to identify high leverage observations and discard them, for example, using box-plots.

In a simple linear regression, high leverage observations are fairly easy to identify, since we can simply look for observations for which the predictor value is outside of the normal range of the observations. But in a multiple linear regression with many predictors, it is possible to have an observation that is well within the range of each individual predictor's values, but that is unusual in terms of the full set of predictors. This problem is more pronounced in multiple regression settings with more than two predictors, because then there is no simple way to plot all dimensions of the data simultaneously. In order to quantify an observation's leverage, we compute the *leverage statistic*. This statistic is calculated as follows:

$$\text{We know that } \hat{w} = \left(A^T A\right)^{-1} A^T y \text{ and thus, } \hat{y} = A\left(A^T A\right)^{-1} A^T y$$

The **H matrix,** also known as the Hat Matrix is defined as, $H = A\left(A^T A\right)^{-1} A^T$ and $\hat{y} = Hy$.

In other words, the predicted response $(\hat{y})$ can be expressed as a linear combination of the observed responses (y). The diagonal elements of this H matrix, h_{ii}, are called the leverage of the x_i. The larger the value of h_{ii}, the larger the influence of this single data point x_i is on the response.

If there are d predictor variables and n observations, i^{th} observation is flagged as having high leverage if $h_{ii} > 3\left(\dfrac{d}{n}\right)$.

(d) **Collinearity (2 or more predictor variables have high correlation):** *Collinearity* refers to the situation in which two or more predictor variables are closely related to one another. For example, we can find some relation between height and weight, Area of house and number of rooms, experience and income and so on. The presence of collinearity can pose problems in the regression context, since it can be difficult to separate out the individual effects of collinear variables on the response and may lead to errors in estimating the parameters. When the accuracy of model parameters drops, we cannot tell the actual relation between response and predictor and hence, model accuracy also decreases.

There are two possible solutions to the problem:

(i) Drop one or more predictor variables: Collinearity implies that the information provided by one variable in the presence of other variables, is redundant. Hence, we can drop the variable without much impact on the model quality.

(ii) Combining the variable: We can combine highly correlated predictor variables to form a new variable. These techniques are called feature engineering. For example, merge weight and height to get BMI (Body mass index).

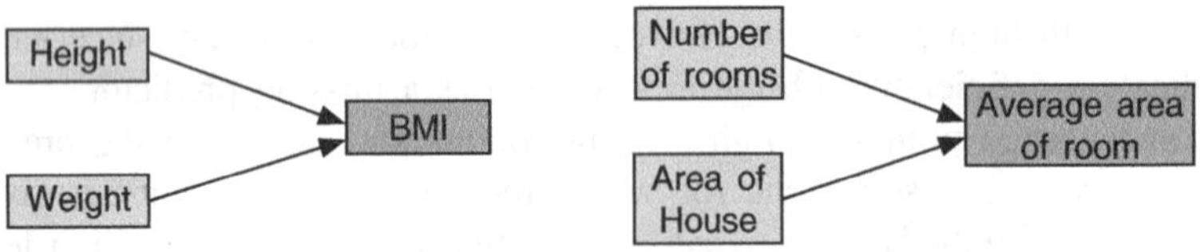

FIGURE 9.8 Combining variables which are correlated into single variable.

It is possible for collinearity to exist between three or more predictor variables even if no pair of variables has a particularly high correlation. We call this situation *multicollinearity*. One way to detect multicollinearity is to build a regression model for predicting one of the predictor variables (e.g. weight) based on remaining variables (e.g. age, height). If this regression model has high R^2, we can drop this variable without affecting the quality of the original regression model.

(e) **Correlation of error terms:** An important assumption of the linear regression model is that the error terms (residuals), $r_1, r_2, ..., r_n$ are uncorrelated. It means that if r_i is positive, it provides little or no information about the sign of r_{i+1}. The standard errors that are computed for the estimated regression coefficients or the fitted values are based on the assumption of uncorrelated error terms. If there is correlation among the error terms, then the estimated standard errors will tend to underestimate the true standard errors. As a result, confidence and prediction intervals will be narrower than they should be and we will falsely have more confidence in our model.

Correlation among error terms is frequently found in time series data (eg. readings from sensors). In many cases, observations that are obtained at adjacent time points will have positively correlated errors. In order to determine if this is the case for a given data set, we can plot the residuals from our model as a function of time. If the errors are uncorrelated, then there should be no discernible pattern. On the other hand, if the error terms are positively correlated, then we may see *tracking* in the residuals—that is, adjacent residuals may have similar values.

In general, the assumption of uncorrelated errors is extremely important for linear regression as well as for other statistical methods, and good experimental design is crucial in order to mitigate the risk of such correlations.

(f) **Non-constant variance of error terms:** The standard errors, confidence intervals, and hypothesis tests associated with the linear model rely upon the assumption that error terms have a constant variance. Often, the variances of the error terms are non-constant. For instance, the variances of the error terms may increase with the value of the response. One can identify non-constant variances in the errors, or *heteroscedasticity*, from the presence of a *funnel shape* in the residual plot.

We observe that the magnitude of the residuals tends to increase with the fitted values. When faced with this problem, one possible solution is to transform the response Y using a concave function such as log Y. Such a transformation results in a greater amount of shrinkage of the larger responses, leading to a reduction in heteroscedasticity.

To conclude, we have seen several problems that may affect linear regression models, their identification and solutions based on residual plots, data transformations, feature engineering, etc.

In the next chapter, we will discuss support vector machines (SVM), Decision trees and Random Forests for building classification models. These can be used for regression as well. So instead of discussing them in detail in this chapter, we just give a brief intuition here and provide more details in next chapter.

SVM regression uses the concept that the there should be no penalty in the loss function for small errors ($< \varepsilon$). This makes the model more robust against overfitting. The fit can thus be a channel of width (2ε) instead of a line. The goal is to fit as many data points as possible on the channel while limiting the points that are far from the channel. Adding more training data points within the channel doesn't change the loss function and hence the model parameter remain the same. This loss function is also called ε insensitive loss.

$$V_{\varepsilon}(r) = \begin{cases} 0 & if\,|r| < \varepsilon \\ |r| - \varepsilon, & \text{otherwise} \end{cases}$$

The SVM regression problem can be solved using optimization techniques with ε as a hyperparameter. In other words, we have to determine the value of ε based on validation accuracy.

Decision trees partition the attribute space in to non-overlapping axis-aligned regions. These are hyper-rectangles. In each of these regions, y is a very simple function, usually constant. **Random forests** are collection of decision trees trained on independent subsets of data. They reduce the overfitting in the model and can be thought of as a form of ensemble learning.

EXERCISES

1. Engineers from American Motors (AMC) are working on a new car (AMX). They are analysing how the mileage of this car matches up with their other cars and the competition. It is common knowledge that the mileage of a car is dependent on its Engine's displacement or size of the engine in CC and the Weight, W. They develop an equation to predict mileage as miles per gallon (mpg) using the following regression model where CC is measured in units of 100cc and W in tonne.

$$P = w_0 + w_1 CC + w_2 W$$

Car Name	CC_i	W_i	Actual Mpg (M_i)	Predicted P_i	Error ($E_i = P_i - M_i$)
Ford pinto	1	2	36		
AMC gremlin	2.3	2.6	19		
AMC hornet sportabout (sw)	2.6	3	18		
Ford torino 500	2.5	3.3	19		
Ford galaxie 500	3.5	4.2	14		

Write the information in a matrix form, write Normal Equations for solving regression problem and obtain the least squares fit for the data. You may use a calculator, but don't use a computer to solve this problem.

2. The salaries of Froogle Engineers were scraped from social media and the following table was prepared.

Role	# of Years Experience (Y)	Salary ($K/year)
SDE	3.5	128
SDE	4.5	133
SDE	1	97
SDE	2.5	118
SDE	10	164
SDE	6	145
Data Scientist	2	118
Data Scientist	3	142
Data Scientist	1	100
Data Scientist	2.5	130

(a) Please use matrix methods (or any other technique you like) to determine the regression line for predicting the salary of Data Scientists working at Froogle.

Salary of Data Scientist = ... + Y* ....

Please fill the table below using the above equation.

Role	Y	Salary ($K/year)	Comments
Data Scientist	3		
Data Scientist	7		
Data Scientist	0		

(b) Using 3 nearest neighbors, predict the salary of following employees. You are free to choose the weights you want to give to the neighbors.

Role	Y	Salary ($K/year)
SDE	3	
SDE	7	
SDE	0	

How did you assign weights to the neighbours?

(c) Examining the predictions above, who is more highly paid at Froogle, SDE or Data Scientists? Can you say this confidently for engineers with more than 5 years' experience?

3. This data is based on a research paper "A Data Mining Approach to Predict Forest Fires using, Meteorological Data" published in 2007. The authors attempt to predict the area of the forest burned based on meteorological data: temperature and wind speed.
We begin with the following linear regression model. $A = \alpha T + \beta W$. Where, A is the area burnt (hectares), T is the temperature (Degree Celsius) and W is the wind speed (km/hr.).

Temp	Wind	Area	Prediction	Error	Sq. Error
11	6	27			
14	9	60			
15	3	32			
18	4	39			
20	5	26			

(a) We begin with the initial values of $\alpha = 0.5$, $\beta = 5$. Please complete the above table by computing the predicted value of A, calculating Error and Squared Error.
(b) Write the expression of L = Loss (mean squared error) for this problem as a function of α, β.
(c) Write the expressions of and compute them for the current values of the parameters.
(d) Update the parameters using the value of the learning rate to be 0.01 and report the new values of α, β.
(e) [10 marks] Now re-compute the prediction and errors, using the updated parameter values. Have the errors reduced? Has the Loss reduced? Write your interpretation of this.

Temp	Wind	Area	Prediction	Error	Sq. Error
11	6	27			
14	9	60			
15	3	32			
18	4	39			
20	5	26			

MULTIPLE CHOICE QUESTIONS

1. In **LASSO regression**, which of the following is the primary effect of increasing the regularization parameter λ?
   (a) It increases model complexity by introducing more features.
   (b) It reduces overfitting by driving some feature coefficients to zero.
   (c) It minimizes the bias of the model while keeping variance unchanged.
   (d) It makes the model resistant to multicollinearity without affecting feature selection.
2. Which of the following is **NOT** a key difference between **Lasso** and **Ridge regression**?
   (a) Lasso can shrink some coefficients to zero, while Ridge cannot.
   (b) Ridge aims to minimize the sum of squared coefficients, while Lasso minimizes the sum of absolute coefficients.
   (c) Lasso tends to perform better in cases of highly correlated features.
   (d) Ridge is better suited for cases with multicollinearity than Lasso.
3. The **Elastic Net** regularization combines which two penalty terms?
   (a) l2-norm and l3-norm
   (b) l1-norm and l2-norm
   (c) Cross-validation error and model complexity
   (d) Sum of residuals and total variance

4. Which of the following methods is **most likely** to help prevent overfitting in a machine learning model?
   (a) Increasing the number of features used by the model.
   (b) Reducing the training data size to remove noise.
   (c) Increasing the regularization parameter in the model.
   (d) Using a model with higher capacity, such as a deep neural network.
5. You are training a linear regression model and observe that it performs very well on the training data but poorly on the validation data. What is the **most probable cause** of this discrepancy?
   (a) The model is underfitting the data.
   (b) The model is overfitting the data.
   (c) There is a large amount of noise in the data.
   (d) The model is suffering from multicollinearity.
6. Which of the following issues can arise in linear regression when the predictor variables are highly correlated?
   (a) The model will become more interpretable.
   (b) The model will generalize better to unseen data.
   (c) The model will suffer from multicollinearity, leading to unstable coefficients.
   (d) The variance of residuals will decrease, improving model performance.
7. Which features should be selected for modelling? (Select all that apply)
   (a) Those which are highly correlated to each other
   (b) Those which are not correlated to each other
   (c) Those which are correlated with the output variable
   (d) Those which have a large non-zero coefficient in a model
8. Why is regularization important in regression models?
   (a) It helps the model take into account each of the outlier points in the dataset
   (b) It lets the model use larger weight values, which improves the model's performance
   (c) It prevents the model from being too sensitive to random errors or outliers in the dataset
   (d) None of the above
9. What do the number of folds in a K-fold cross-validation represent?
   (a) The number of subsets of the training set used to train the model each iteration
   (b) The number of total subsets that the training set is split into
   (c) The number of subsets of the training set used to validate the model each iteration
   (d) The number of total subsets that the test set is split into
10. In **K-nearest neighbors (KNN)** regression, how is the predicted output for a query point determined?
    (a) It is the average of the target values of the k-nearest points.
    (b) It is the most common target value among the k-nearest points.
    (c) It is a weighted sum of the distances to the k-nearest points.
    (d) It is the sum of the k-nearest target values divided by their distances.
11. When using **KNN regression**, increasing the value of k tends to:
    (a) Increase the model's variance and reduce bias.
    (b) Decrease the model's variance but increase bias.
    (c) Increase both the model's bias and variance.
    (d) Decrease both the model's bias and variance.
12. One of the main drawbacks of **K-nearest neighbors** is:
    (a) It performs better with fewer training examples.
    (b) It is computationally expensive at training time.
    (c) It has a slow prediction time, especially with large datasets.
    (d) It assumes a linear relationship between features and the target.

13. **Cross-validation** is used in model training primarily to:
    (a) Minimize the training error of the model.
    (b) Reduce the computational cost of model training.
    (c) Test the model on independent subsets of the data to improve generalization.
    (d) Ensure that the training data is not biased.
14. The **learning curve** of a model helps to diagnose:
    (a) Whether the model is suffering from high bias or high variance.
    (b) Whether the model is overfitting or underfitting the training data.
    (c) Whether the optimization algorithm is converging.
    (d) The correlation between predictor variables.
15. **Early stopping** is a regularization technique used primarily in which type of models?
    (a) Support Vector Machines (b) Decision Trees
    (c) Neural Networks (d) Linear Regression
16. Which of the following metrics is used to penalize model complexity when comparing different models?
    (a) Mean Squared Error (MSE)
    (b) R2 Score
    (c) Akaike Information Criterion (AIC)
    (d) Adjusted Root Mean Squared Error (RMSE)
17. When increasing model complexity, the **bias-variance tradeoff** states that:
    (a) Bias and variance both decrease with increasing complexity.
    (b) Bias decreases, but variance increases.
    (c) Bias increases, but variance decreases.
    (d) Both bias and variance increase with complexity.
18. When fitting a linear regression model, how does adding more irrelevant features affect model performance?
    (a) It increases the model's interpretability.
    (b) It leads to overfitting and increased variance.
    (c) It reduces overfitting by increasing bias.
    (d) It improves model performance by reducing the residual sum of squares.

REFERENCES

[1] Introduction to Statistical Learning with Python, Gareth James, Daniela Witten, Trevor Hastie, Robert Tibshirani, Jonathan Taylor, Springer Publications.
[2] Learning with Data, Gilbert Strang.

ANSWER KEY

1. (b) **2.** (c) **3.** (b) **4.** (c) **5.** (b) **6.** (c) **7.** (b), (c), (d) **8.** (c) **9.** (b)
10. (a) **11.** (b) **12.** (c) **13.** (c) **14.** (b) **15.** (c) **16.** (c) **17.** (b) **18.** (b)

10 Classification Models

Introduction

Classification is the task of labeling items. The geometric approach to classification is based on determining the decision boundaries that separate the datapoints belonging to different classes. Such boundaries can be learnt based on the training examples which contain class labels. These decision boundaries can be used at the time of making prediction on unseen test data.

The probabilistic approach on the other hand, aims at trying to understand the generative process of data. Each class is assumed to be generated by a random process. We try to estimate the probability of a test example being generated from each of the random processes. The class which maximizes this probability (likelihood) for the given test example is chosen. In this chapter, we will discuss various approaches and their pros and cons.

10.1 GEOMETRIC APPROACHES TO CLASSIFICATION

The most basic approach is called "*learning by prototypes*". We first determine some prototypical examples of each class and then a test object is classified based on the prototype with least distance. This approach can be extended further by considering "*K nearest neighbors*" and taking the majority vote for the final label.

The *Perceptron* algorithm is a "*Learning from Mistakes*" approach and iteratively updates the equation of a decision boundary in case of a mistake on a training example. *Logistic regression* also works with a linear decision boundary that is updated based on the magnitude of mistakes it makes. Large errors require large updates and small errors require small updates to the parameters.

Support vector machines aim to find robust decision boundaries, which separate the classes by maximum possible distance. This makes them resistant to noise in the data and leads to better generalization.

Decision trees examine each attribute one at a time and apply simple rules at every stage to determine the final class label. We now explain each of these approaches in detail.

10.1.1 Learning by Prototypes

In this approach, we first determine a prototypical example of each class. The prototype may be given to us or can be computed as the mean of several (or all) training examples of the same class. Let us assume that we have been given a prototype of both positive and negative class in the form of vectors. If multiple examples of each class are given, then we can take their respective means to get an average prototype. Let us call them μ_+ and μ_-. The decision boundary is the set of those points which are equidistant from both the average protypes. Thus, it is the equation of the perpendicular bisector of the line joining μ_+ and μ_-. We now look at an example to make it clear.

Example: Deriving Decision Boundary for Learning with Prototypes (**LwP) Classifier**

These are some training examples of –ve class: (2,3,4); (1,1,2); (0,2,0)
These are some training examples of +ve class: (4,3,2); (2,1,1); (3,5,3)

Step 1: Compute the average feature vectors of +ve and –ve class examples.

$$\mu_- = \left(\frac{2+1+0}{3}, \frac{3+1+2}{3}, \frac{4+2+0}{3}\right) = (1, 2, 2)$$

$$\mu_+ = \left(\frac{4+2+3}{3}, \frac{3+1+5}{3}, \frac{2+1+3}{3}\right) = (3, 3, 2)$$

Step 2: Determine the vector w which joins μ_+ and μ_- : $w = \mu_+ - \mu_-$

$$w = (3, 3, 2) - (1, 2, 2) = (2, 1, 0)$$

Step 3: We know that the decision boundary passes through the mid-point of the prototypes (as it is a perpendicular bisector). Thus, w (the vector that joins μ_+ and μ_-) is normal to the decision boundary. Hence its equation is given by $w^T x + b = 0$.

Since, it passes through the mid point, it must satisfy, $w^T\left(\frac{\grave{\imath}_+ + \grave{\imath}_-}{2}\right) + b = 0$

Thus, $b = -\frac{(\mu_+ - \mu_-)^T(\mu_+ + \mu_-)}{2} = \frac{1}{2}\left(\|\mu_-\|^2 - \|\mu_+\|^2\right)$

For the given example, $b = \frac{9 \quad 22}{2} = -\frac{13}{2}$

Distance of a point $\boldsymbol{x}$ from the decision boundary $w^T x + b = 0$, is given by $d(x) = \frac{w^T x + b}{\|w\|}$.

The points with +ve distance will be classified in the +ve class, whereas the points with –ve distance will be classified in the negative class. Thus, the sign of $w^T x + b$ is enough for classification.

The classification rule can be written as

Predict an input x to be in +ve class if $w^T x + b > 0$ and in –ve class if $w^T x + b < 0$

Prediction rule therefore is: predict +1 if $w, x + b > 0$, else predict –1

Exercise: Let us now compute the distances of the training examples from the decision boundary and see if there any errors in classification using the (LwP) classifier?

We begin with the training examples of -ve class:

(a) (2, 3, 4): $\boldsymbol{w}^T \boldsymbol{x} + \boldsymbol{b} = (2, 1, 0)^T (2, 3, 4) - 6.5 = 0.5.$

Hence distance = $\frac{0.5}{\sqrt{5}}$. Predicted class: +ve. This is a *mis-classification.*

(b) (1, 1, 2): $\boldsymbol{w}^T \boldsymbol{x} + \boldsymbol{b} = (2, 1, 0)^T (1, 1, 2) - 6.5 = -3.5.$

Hence distance = $\frac{-3.5}{\sqrt{5}}$. Predicted class: $-$ve.

(c) (0,2,0): $\boldsymbol{w}^T \boldsymbol{x} + \boldsymbol{b} = (2, 1, 0)^T (0, 2, 0) - 6.5 = -4.5.$

Hence distance = $\frac{-4.5}{\sqrt{5}}$. Predicted class: –ve.

Now let us compute distances for training examples of +ve class:

(a) (2, 3, 4): $\boldsymbol{w}^T \boldsymbol{x} + \boldsymbol{b} = (2, 1, 0)^T (4, 3, 2) - 6.5 = 4.5$

Hence distance = $\frac{4.5}{\sqrt{5}}$. Predicted class: +ve.

(b) (1, 1 ,2): $\boldsymbol{w}^T \boldsymbol{x} + \boldsymbol{b} = (2, 1, 0)^T (2, 1, 1) - 6.5 = -1.5.$

Hence distance = $\frac{-1.5}{\sqrt{5}}$. Predicted class: –ve. This is a *mis-classification.*

(c) (0, 2, 0): $\boldsymbol{w}^T \boldsymbol{x} + \boldsymbol{b} = (2, 1, 0)^T (3, 5, 3) - 6.5 = 4.5.$

Hence distance = $\frac{4.5}{\sqrt{5}}$. Predicted class: + ve.

We note that the current decision boundary is not perfect. It makes two mistakes.

The learning with prototypes approach is advantageous for its simplicity and interpretability, making it suitable for small to moderate-sized datasets. However, it may struggle with large datasets and high-dimensional spaces due to scalability and computational challenges. Additionally, careful consideration is needed in prototype selection and managing the risk of overfitting.

Now, lets' look the approach of using nearest neighbours to make the predictions.

10.1.2 Perceptron Algorithm

Perceptron algorithm takes a *"learning by mistakes"* approach. We are trying to learn the equation of a hyperplane of the form $w^Tx + b = 0$. At first, we may begin with a random value of w and b. Now, we start making a pass on the training examples, predicting their class using our current equation of the hyperplane. As discussed before, the prediction is given by: $\hat{y} = \text{sign}\,(w^T x + b)$. When the model is correct, $\hat{y} = y$ and no correction is necessary, but if $\hat{y} \neq y$, the equation is updated in a way as to make the errors decrease.

Let us assume some example (x_i, y_i) which gets misclassified. In other words, $y_i(w^T x_i + b) < 0$, since their signs are opposite. Now, let's update $\boldsymbol{w}$ by adding a correction term to it.

$w^* = w + \eta y_i x_i$, where η is the learning rate (usually a small positive real number).

By making this change, we ensure that the product $y_i(w^{*T} x_i + b)$ will become more positive since a positive quantity $y_i\left(y_i\, x_i^T\, x_i\right)$, will be added to it.

$$y_i(w^* x_i + b) = y_i\left(\left(w + \eta y_i x_i\right)^T x_i + b\right) = y_i(w^T x_i + b) + \eta y_i\left(y_i x_i^T x_i\right)$$

If $y_i = +1$ and $\left(w^T x_i + b\right) < 0$, after the update $w^{*T} x_i + b$ will be less negative.

Likewise, if $y_i = -1$ and $(\mathbf{w}^T \mathbf{x}_i + b) > 0$, after the update $w^{*T} x_i + b$ will be less positive.

The process is repeated on all the training examples. Note that, after rotation, the hyperplane may misclassify a point that was previously classified correctly. But, if training data is linearly separable, the Perceptron algo will converge in a finite number of iterations.

Assuming the initial value of $w^{(0)} = 0$, it is easy to see that the final w has the form $w = \sum_{i=1}^{N} \eta \alpha_i y_i x_i$, where α_i is total number of mistakes made by the algorithm on example (x_i, y_i).

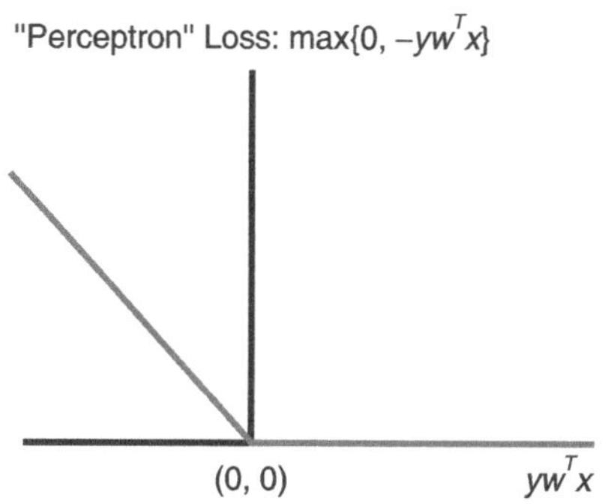

FIGURE 10.1 Perceptron Loss Function.

The above process can also be understood in terms of applying an SGD algorithm using the Perceptron loss function: $L(w) = \sum_{i-1}^{N} \max\{0, -y_i(\mathbf{w}^T \mathbf{x}_i + b)\}$. This means that when the prediction is correct, there is 0 loss, but when it is incorrect, the loss is $-y_i(w^T x_i + b)$. We can also use this method to update the value of b (which is equivalent to translation of the hyperplane). Stochastic Sub-grad descent on Perceptron loss is also known as the Perceptron algorithm.

Example: These are some training examples of –ve class: (2, 3, 4); (1, 1, 2); (0, 2, 0)
These are some training examples of +ve class: (4, 3, 2); (2, 1, 1); (3, 5, 3)

1. **Initialization:** $w_1 = 0.5,\ w_2 = 0.5,\ w_3 = 0.5,\ b = 0,\ \eta = 0.1$
2. **First Point:** (2, 3, 4) in –ve class

We first compute $w^T x_i + b = 4.5$

$$\hat{y}_1 = \text{sign}(4.5) - 1$$

This is incorrect as $y_1 = -1$ since the example belongs to –ve class. Thus, we must update the weights as follows:

$$w^* = \begin{pmatrix} 0.5 \\ 0.5 \\ 0.5 \end{pmatrix} + \eta y_1 \begin{pmatrix} 2 \\ 3 \\ 4 \end{pmatrix} = \begin{pmatrix} 0.5 \\ 0.5 \\ 0.5 \end{pmatrix} + 0.1 \times (-1) \times \begin{pmatrix} 2 \\ 3 \\ 4 \end{pmatrix} = \begin{pmatrix} 0.3 \\ 0.2 \\ 0.1 \end{pmatrix}$$

3. **Repeat for Other Points:** Let's consider the point (4, 3, 2) which belongs to +ve class.

We first compute $w^T x_i + b = \begin{pmatrix} 0.3 \\ 0.2 \\ 0.1 \end{pmatrix} . \begin{pmatrix} 4 \\ 3 \\ 2 \end{pmatrix} + 0 = 1.2 + 0.6 + 0.2 + 0 = 2$

$\hat{y}_1 = \text{sign}(4.5) = 1$ which is correct and no update is needed.

The same process is continued till we find a boundary which separates the data perfectly.

Perceptron algorithm can be used in online learning settings, where weights can be updated incrementally. It is computationally efficient for linearly separable problems, but doesn't converge when the boundaries are non-linear. The perceptron is a foundational algorithm in machine learning, but its limitations in handling non-linearity and its lack of probabilistic interpretation mean that more advanced methods are often preferred for complex tasks.

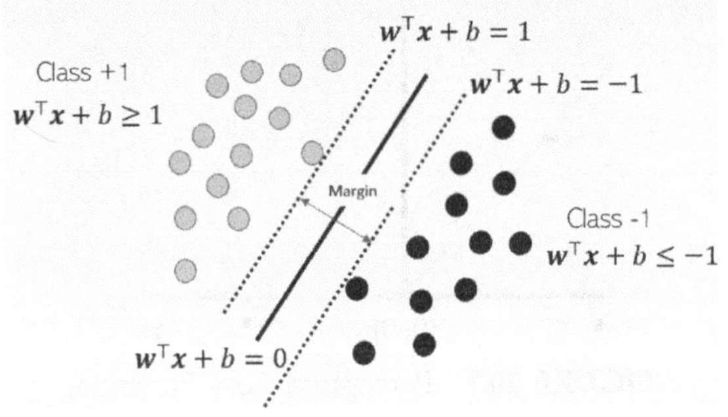

FIGURE 10.2 Learning robust decision boundaries with Support Vector Machines.

10.1.3 Support Vector Machines

As we have seen so far, LwP and Perceptron aim to find a hyperplane that separates the classes. When the data is linearly separable, there exists at least one hyperplane (decision boundary) that can perfectly separate the examples of each class. It is possible that many different hyperplanes may separate the data. In such a case, which hyperplane is the best? The goal of support vector machines is to learn an optimal separating hyperplane. An optimal separating hyperplane maximizes the margins. The margin is the distance to the nearest example from the decision boundary. SVM ensures a large margin around the hyperplane. This is beneficial as it would provide good generalization for unseen test examples, which might be close to the boundary.

We will assume a linear hyperplane to be of the form $w^T x + b = 0$. A hard margin SVM enforces the condition that every training example must fulfil margin condition $y_n(w^T x_n + b) \geq 1$. This means that there must not be any example in the margin region. Also, want to maximize margin $2\gamma = \frac{2}{w}$. This is equivalent to minimizing $||w||^2$ or $\frac{||w||^2}{2}$. This is the objective function for hard-margin SVM. The optimization problem can be written as follows:

$$\min_{w,b} f(w, b) = \frac{\|w\|^2}{2}$$

$$\text{subject to } y_n\left(w^T x_n + b\right) \geq 1, \qquad n = 1,\ldots, N$$

We will not go into the details of solving the above optimization problem, but would like to note that there are efficient algorithms for the same, provided the data is linearly separable. Using a kernel function or data transformations, it can be extended to find optimal boundaries even in the non-linear case. However, when the data is not separable, we need to relax the condition (constraints) and allow some training examples to fall within the margin region or even on the wrong side of the hyperplane. The extent of "violation" by a training input (x_n, y_n) is known as slack $\xi_n \geq 0$. $\xi_n > 1$ means totally on the wrong side.

$$w^T x_n + b \geq 1 - \xi_n \quad \textit{if} \quad y_n = +1$$

$$w^T x_n + b \leq -1 + \xi_n \quad \textit{if} \quad y_n = -1$$

$$y_n(w^T x_n + b) \geq 1 - \xi_n \quad \forall n$$

$$\min_{w,b\,\xi} f(w, b, \xi) = \frac{\|w\|^2}{2} + C\sum_{n=1}^{N} \xi_n$$

$$\text{subject to } y_n\left(w^T x_n + b\right) \geq 1 - \xi_n, \xi_n \geq 0 \quad n = 1,\ldots, N$$

The goal is to maximize the margin such that the soft-margin constraints $y_n(w^T x_n + b) \geq 1 - \xi_n$ are satisfied for all training examples. At the same time, we do not have too many margin violations (sum of slacks $\sum_{n=1}^{N} \xi_n$ should be small). Hyperparameter C controls the trade off between large margin and small training error (need to tune). A large value of C not only results in smaller training error but also small margin and hence is not a good choice. A small value of C not only results in large margin but also large training error (bad).

Some advantages of SVM are that they perform well with high-dimensional data and large feature spaces, are robust to overfitting and can handle non-linear classification through the use of various kernel functions (e.g., polynomial, RBF). However, training can be slow for large datasets, especially with complex kernels. Additionally, it requires careful tuning of parameters (e.g., C, kernel parameters) and can be sensitive to their choice.

10.1.4 Nearest Neighbors Approach

In this approach, the entire training dataset is used to make the predictions. For a given test point, we will first determine the K nearest training examples (neighbors). For determining the nearest neighbors, we can use Euclidean distance, Cosine Similarity or any other suitable distance metric. Once the K nearest neighbors have been determined, we check their labels and compute the majority label. The given test point is then classified as belong to the majority class.

This approach is very simple and can learn non-linear decision boundaries. The value of K can be chosen according to the dataset. Thus, K is the only hyperparameter of this approach. K is usually taken to be an odd number to avoid ties. Let us take an example with the same points as the previous example.

These are some training examples of –ve class: (2, 3, 4); (1, 1, 2); (0, 2, 0)

These are some training examples of +ve class: (4, 3, 2); (2, 1, 1); (3, 5, 3)

Suppose we have to predict the class of a new point (2,3,3). We first compute its distance from all the given points and select the $K = 3$ nearest neighbors. These distances are tabulated below:

Data Point	Distance from (2,3,3)	Class
(2, 3, 4)	1	–ve
(1, 1, 2)	$\sqrt{6}$	–ve
(0, 2, 0)	$\sqrt{14}$	–ve
(4, 3, 2)	$\sqrt{5}$	+ve
(2, 1, 1)	$\sqrt{8}$	+ve
(3, 5, 3)	$\sqrt{5}$	+ve

The nearest neighbors are (2, 3, 4), (2, 1, 1), (3, 5, 3). Two of them belong to +ve class while one of them is in –ve class. Thus, +ve class neighbors are in majority. Hence by KNN method, (2, 3, 3) is predicted to be in the +ve class.

10.1.5 Decision Trees

Decision trees take a divide and conquer approach to building good classifiers. At every stage, we ask one "simple" question (rule) on one attribute/feature and branch out such that the problem is divided into two simpler (independent) problems with smaller dataset and one attribute less than the previous stage. Let's study the previous example.

These are some training examples of –ve class: (2, 3, 4); (1, 1, 2); (0, 2, 0)

These are some training examples of +ve class: (4, 3, 2); (2, 1, 1); (3, 5, 3)

Let the three attributes be x_1, x_2, x_3. We notice that for negative classes the value of x_1 is less than or equal to 2 and for the positive classes, the value of x_1 is greater than or equal to 2.

So, our first decision node (rule) is:

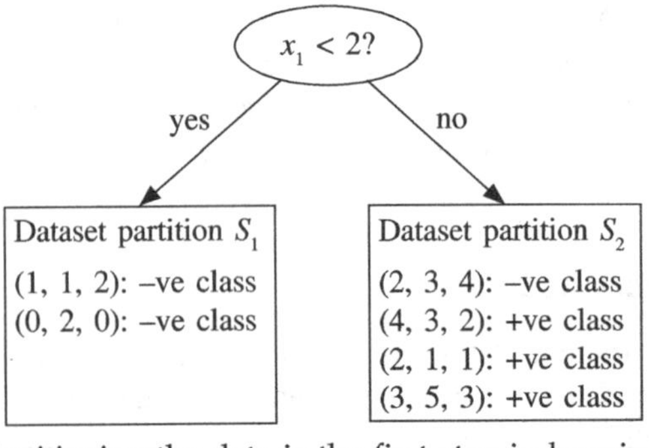

FIGURE 10.3 Partitioning the data is the first step in learning a decision tree.

We observe that in S_1, all examples belong to the same class (–ve class). Hence, we don't need to branch any further and can create a leaf node which gives the output label (–ve class). On the other hand, in S_2, there are three examples of +ve class, but only 1 example of –ve class.

Thus, we need to find an attribute and a criterion to branch further. We observe that for –ve class, x_3 is greater than 3.5 while for +ve class, x_3 is less than 3.5. The final decision tree is as follows:

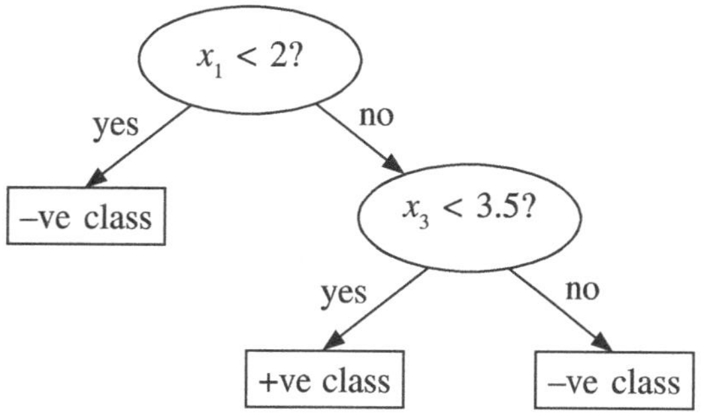

FIGURE 10.4 Final decision tree obtained.

This process of creation of decision tree can be formalized as follows: At every stage, we aim to sub-divide the dataset such that it becomes much easier to classify the resultant subsets of data. For example, if a subset contains only a single class, we can build a perfect classifier. To determine the purity (or ease of classification) of a dataset, metrics such as entropy, gini index, etc. are used. The process of creating more nodes (rules) is stopped when one of the following occurs:

- It consists of all training examples having the same label (the node becomes "pure")
- We run out of features to test along the path to that node
- The decision tree starts to overfit (can be checked by monitoring the validation set accuracy)

Assume a dataset of labelled inputs $\boldsymbol{S}$ from $\boldsymbol{C}$ classes, p_c is f the fraction of training examples of class c. The **entropy** of the set $\boldsymbol{S}$ is defined as $\mathrm{H}(\boldsymbol{S}) = -\sum_{c \in C} p_c \log p_c$. Uniform sets (all classes roughly equally present) have high entropy (randomness). On the other hand, skewed sets where examples of a particular class dominate, have low entropy.

Suppose a rule split $\boldsymbol{S}$ into two smaller disjoint sets $\boldsymbol{S}_1$ and $\boldsymbol{S}_2$. Reduction in entropy after the split is called information gain (*IG*).

$$IG = H(S) - \frac{|S_1|}{|S|} H(S_1) - \frac{|S_2|}{|S|} H(S_2)$$

We wish to select that rule which maximizes the information gain. This is illustrated in the Figure below.

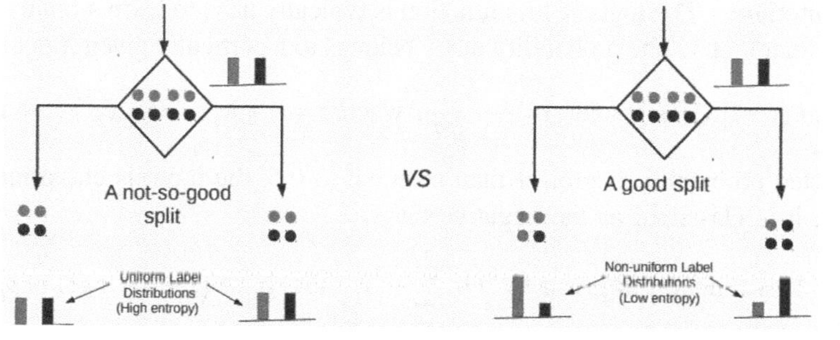

FIGURE 10.5 A Good vs Bad Split in the Decision Tree.

Gini index is similar to entropy, but is easier to compute as it doesn't involve logarithms.

$$G(t) = \sum_{c \in C} p_c (1 - p_c)$$

It is desirable that we build a decision tree that is not too big in size, yet fits the training data reasonably. An example of a very simple decision tree is a "decision-stump". A decision-stump only tests the value of a single feature (or a simple rule). It is not very powerful in itself but often used in large ensembles of decision stumps.

When features are real-valued, there can be many values to try. We can use tests based on thresholding feature values. We need to be careful with respect to the number of threshold points and how fine each range is, etc.

To summarize, decision trees are simple and easy to interpret. They can easily handle different types of features (real, categorical, etc.). They are very fast at test time. Multiple decision trees can be combined via ensemble methods: more powerful (e.g., Decision Forests). They are used in several real-world ML applications, e.g., recommender systems, gaming, etc. Learning optimal decision tree is NP-hard, or intractable. Existing algorithms are mostly greedy heuristics. It can sometimes become very complex unless some pruning is applied.

Optimization based functional approach to classification

We now discuss an optimization-based approach to classification. This involves learning a function $y = f(x)$ such that $y = +1$ for positive class and $y = -1$ for negative class examples. The function parameters are updated using a loss function and gradient calculation is updated as discussed in Chapter 4 of the book.

Assume that the expected output is $y = \pm 1$, and a classifier score is $\hat{y} = \mathbf{w}^T \mathbf{x} + b$. An ideal loss function for classification should satisfy the following properties:

(a) Loss is small or near-zero if y and sign($\hat{y}$) match. In other words, large positive $y.\hat{y}$ means that loss must be small or near-zero

(b) Loss is large if y and sign($\hat{y}$) do not match. In other words, large negative $y.\hat{y}$ means that loss must be large.

Hinge loss: For an expected output $y = \pm 1$, and a classifier score of $\hat{y}$, the hinge loss of the prediction y is defined as: $l(y) = \max(0, 1 - y.\hat{y})$. When $\hat{y}$ and y have the same sign (meaning $\hat{y}$ predicts the right class) and $y > 1$, the hinge loss is 0. When they have opposite signs, $l(y)$ increases linearly with $\hat{y}$, and similarly if $\hat{y} > 1$, there is some loss even if it has the same sign. This is because the prediction is correct, but not by enough margin. Hinge loss is often used with SVM.

Logistic Loss function: The logistic loss function is typically used to learn a binary classifier where the output $\hat{y}$ is either 0 or 1. The probability that y belongs to a particular given X is modeled using the sigmoid function: $P(y = 1|X) = \text{sigmoid}(z) = \dfrac{1}{1 + e^{-z}}$, where $z = b + w_1 x_1 + w_2 x_2 + \ldots + w_n x_n = w^T x + b$

If the predicted probability is greater than or equal to 0.5, the input is classified as the positive class; otherwise, it is classified as the negative class.

The logistic loss function is given by $l = \sum_{i=0}^{n} -\left(y_i * \log(p_i) + (1 - y_i)\log(1 - p_i)\right)$

Here n is the number of training samples. y_i is the true class for the index i, and p_i is the model prediction for the index i. Gradient descent is commonly used to find the optimal parameters (weights) that minimize the cost function. Minimizing the logistic loss is equivalent to maximizing the Log-Likelihood. **Logistic Regression** is a statistical method used in machine learning for binary classification tasks. It is used to predict the probability that a given input belongs to a certain class, typically classifying inputs into one of two categories.

10.2 PROBABILISTIC APPROACH

In the **probabilistic approach,** we estimate the probability of each class given the input features. Unlike deterministic classifiers that provide a single class label, probabilistic classifiers output probabilities that represent the likelihood of an instance belonging to each possible class. This approach is flexible, allows for better handling of uncertainty and make informed decisions.

We use the Bayes' Theorem to compute the posterior probability of class C given features X, using:

- $P(X|C)$: likelihood, the probability of observing features X given class C.
- $P(C)$: Prior probability of class C.
- $P(X)$: Evidence or marginal likelihood of features X.

$$P(C|X) = \frac{P(X|C).P(C)}{P(X)}$$

The denominator $P(X)$ is assumed to be constant across classes, so that the classification decision can be simplified to choosing the class with the highest posterior probability:

$$\hat{C} = \arg\max_{C}\left(P(C|X)\right)$$

There are various methods for estimating likelihood of features given the class. The prior probability $P(C)$ represents the initial belief about the likelihood of each class before observing the features and can also be estimated from the training data.

Example: For example, we may build a model to diagnose a disease based on several symptoms. We want to classify whether a patient has the disease (positive class) or is healthy (negative class).

1. **Calculate Prior Probabilities:** Estimate the prior probabilities of having the disease $P(\text{Disease})$ and not having it $P(\text{Healthy})$, based on historical data.
2. **Estimate Likelihoods:** Use training data to estimate the likelihoods of observing each symptom given the presence or absence of the disease. For instance, $P(\text{Symptom 1}|\text{Disease})$ and $P(\text{Symptom 1}|\text{Healthy})$.
3. **Apply Bayes' Theorem:** Compute the posterior probability of having the disease given the symptoms using Bayes' Theorem. For a patient showing symptoms X:

$$P(\text{Disease}|X) = \frac{P(X|\text{Disease}).P(\text{Disease})}{P(X)}$$

4. **Classify:** Compare the posterior probabilities for having the disease and Healthy. Classify the patient as having the disease if $P(\text{Disease}|X)$ is higher than $P(\text{Healthy}|X)$.

10.3 NAÏVE BAYES

Naïve Bayes is a family of simple yet effective probabilistic classifiers based on Bayes' Theorem. They are particularly known for their efficiency and ease of implementation in supervised learning tasks, especially for text classification problems like spam detection, sentiment analysis, and document categorization. The "Naive" aspect of the algorithm refers to the assumption that features are conditionally independent given the class label, which simplifies the computation.

Conditional Independence Assumption: Naive Bayes assumes that the presence (or absence) of a particular feature in a class is independent of the presence (or absence) of any other feature, given the class label. This assumption simplifies the computation of $P(X|C)$ to: $P(X|C) = P(x_1|C).P(x_2|C)...P(x_n|C)$, where x_1, x_2, ... x_n are the individual features.

Example (Spam Detection): Suppose we want to build a spam filter that classifies emails as "spam" or "not spam" based on the words they contain.

1. **Data Preparation:**
   - Collect a dataset of emails labeled as "spam" or "not spam."
   - Extract features from the emails, such as the presence or frequency of certain words.
2. **Model Training:**
   - Calculate the prior probabilities P(spam) and P(not spam).
   - For each word, calculate the likelihood P(word|spam) and P(word|not spam) based on word frequencies in spam and not spam emails.
3. **Prediction:**
   - For a new email, calculate the posterior probabilities P(spam|X) and P(not spam|X), where X represents the words in the email.
   - Classify the email as "spam" if P(spam|X) is greater than P(not spam|X).

Naïve Bayes algorithm works well with High-Dimensional Data and is particularly effective in text classification tasks. One of the disadvantages however is the assumption of feature independence is often unrealistic in real-world data, potentially leading to less accurate predictions. If a categorical feature value in the test set was not observed in the training set, the model might assign a zero probability to that feature. This can be mitigated using techniques like Laplace smoothing.

10.4 CLASSIFICATION METRICS

Once a model has been trained, we need to evaluate it. In this section, we will discuss some important metrics to evaluate classification models. We need to understand the needs of the applications and choose the appropriate metric. We first discuss the confusion matrix which tabulates a summary of model's performance by comparing predicted labels with actual labels. It includes information about true positives, false positives, true negatives and false negatives. These can then be used to compute various important metrics such as precision, recall, F1-score, etc. The confusion matrix is especially useful for understanding the distribution of errors and for evaluating the performance of a model in multi-class classification tasks and when dealing with imbalanced datasets.

For a binary classification problem, the confusion matrix is a 2 × 2 table with the following components:

	Predicted Positive	**Predicted Negative**
Actual Positive	True Positive (TP)	False Negative (FN)
Actual Negative	False Positive (FP)	True Negative (TN)

As we can see from the table, **True Positives (TP)** is the number of instances correctly predicted as positive. **False Positives (FP)** is the number of instances incorrectly predicted as positive (also known as Type I errors). **True Negatives (TN)** is the number of instances correctly predicted as negative. Finally, **False Negatives (FN)** is the number of instances incorrectly predicted as negative (also known as Type II errors).

Example: We have trained a model to predict whether a patient has a tumor (positive class) or not (negative class) based on the MRI scan. After testing, the results are summarized in the confusion matrix:

	Predicted Positive	**Predicted Negative**
Actual Positive	80	20
Actual Negative	10	100

10.4.1 Metrics Derived from the Confusion Matrix

From the confusion matrix, various performance metrics can be calculated:

1. **Accuracy:** Measures the overall correctness of the model.

$$A = \frac{TP + TN}{TP + TN + FP + FN}$$

In the example above, $A = \dfrac{80 + 100}{80 + 100 + 10 + 20} = \dfrac{180}{210} = 0.857$

2. **Precision:** Measures the proportion of true positive predictions among the total positive predictions.

$$P = \frac{TP}{TP + FP}$$

In the example above, $P = \dfrac{80}{80 + 10} = \dfrac{8}{9} = 0.888$

3. **Recall (Sensitivity):** Measures the proportion of actual positives correctly identified. It is also known as the true positive rate.

$$R = \frac{TP}{TP + FN}$$

In the example above, $R = \dfrac{80}{80 + 20} = \dfrac{8}{10} = 0.8$

4. **Specificity:** Measures the proportion of actual negatives correctly identified. In other words, specificity tells us how well the model identifies the absence of a condition or class. It is also known as the true negative rate.

$$S = \frac{TN}{TN + FP}$$

In the example above, $S = \dfrac{100}{100 + 10} = \dfrac{10}{11} = 0.909$

5. **F1 Score:** The harmonic mean of precision and recall, providing a balance between the two.

$$F1 = \frac{2}{\frac{1}{P} + \frac{1}{R}}$$

In the example above, F1 = $\frac{2}{\frac{1}{0.88} + \frac{1}{0.8}} = 0.838$

6. **Area Under the Curve (AUC)** is used to evaluate the quality of a binary classification model. It refers to the area under the Receiver Operating Characteristic (ROC) curve. The ROC curve plots the true positive rate (recall) against the false positive rate at various threshold settings. An AUC value of 1 indicates a perfect classifier, meaning it distinguishes perfectly between positive and negative classes. An AUC score of 0.5 means that the model has no discriminative power, equivalent to random guessing. If the AUC score is less than 0.5, its performance is worse than random guessing, indicating a problem with the model. AUC is particularly useful because it is threshold-independent, meaning it evaluates the model's performance across all possible classification thresholds. This makes it a robust metric for comparing models, especially when the classes are imbalanced.

10.5 ENSEMBLE MODELS

Ensemble models combine multiple individual machine learning models to produce a single, robust model. The core idea is that if the models are independent, then their combination can achieve better performance than any individual model on its own. It is similar to error correction. Independent models make different mistakes, and it is likely that the majority vote will have less errors than any single model. They can be used for regression, classification and other machine learning tasks.

10.5.1 Types of Ensemble Models

1. **Bagging (Bootstrap Aggregating):** Bagging involves training multiple instances of the same model on different subsets of the training data, which are obtained by random sampling with replacement. An example of this is Random Forests, which is obtained by training multiple decision trees. Each tree in a random forest is trained on a different bootstrapped subset of the data, and the final prediction is typically made by majority voting (for classification) or averaging (for regression).
2. **Boosting:** Boosting involves training a sequence of models, where each new model focuses on correcting the errors made by the previous models. Notable examples are Gradient Boosting Machines (GBM), AdaBoost, XGBoost. Each model in the sequence is trained on a weighted version of the dataset, with more emphasis placed on examples that were previously misclassified.
3. **Stacking (Stacked Generalization):** Stacking involves training multiple models (called base learners) and then combining their predictions using a meta-model (or meta-learner). A common setup might include a combination of decision trees, support vector machines, and neural networks as base learners, with a logistic regression model as the meta-learner. The base learners make predictions on the training data, and these predictions are used as input features for the meta-learner, which makes the final prediction.

4. **Voting:** Voting involves combining the predictions of multiple models by taking a majority vote (for classification) or an average (for regression). An example is a voting classifier that combines logistic regression, *k*-nearest neighbors, and decision trees. Each model casts a vote for the predicted class, and the final prediction is the class that receives the most votes.

An advantage of ensemble models is improved accuracy. By combining multiple models, ensembles can often achieve higher accuracy and generalization than individual models. Ensembles tend to be less prone to overfitting, especially when using techniques like bagging. They are more robust to noisy data and outliers. However, they are more complex and computationally expensive to train and deploy. The predictions made by ensembles can be harder to interpret compared to single models, especially in the case of complex models like stacking or boosting.

To summarize, in this chapter we presented various approaches to building classification models and their respective strengths and weakness. We also studied some important metrics. In the next chapter, we will learn about neural networks, which are being increasingly used these days owing to their high performance.

EXERCISES

1. Suppose we have three prototype images for Apple, Banana and Orange given as: x_a, x_b, x_c and a test image x_t. This question explores the connection between Cosine similarity $C(x, y)$ and Euclidean distance, $E(x, y)$ between a pair of images x and y.
Each of the image is a unit norm, N-dimensional vector; i.e., $||x_a||_2 = ||x_b||_2 = ||x_o||_2 = ||x_t||_2 = 1$

(i) Relate the Euclidean distance of the test image with a prototype to its cosine similarity to the same prototype. Derive the formula: $E(x, x_t)$

(ii) Plot $E(x, x_t)$ vs. $X(x, x_t)$

(iii) If $(x_a, x_t) = 0.5$, then $E(x_a, x_t)$

(iv) If cosine similarities of x_t with x_a, x_b, *and* x_o are 0.5, 0.45 and 0.6 respectively, which of the statement(s) are true:

(a) x_a will have the minimum Euclidean distance to x_t

(b) x_o will have the minimum Euclidean distance to x_t

(c) We can't conclude anything about minimum Euclidean distance to a prototype as it depends on the value of N

(d) x_t must be classified as an orange.

2. The following data was collected in 1994 census in the US. The age, education and hours per week are given for the employees and our task is to predict whether they earn more than 50K USD per year or NOT.
Please create a decision tree which can perfectly predict the Salary Class.

Age	Education	Hours per week	Salary Class
36	10th	40	<=50K
27	10th	40	<=50K
63	10th	40	<=50K
55	10th	45	<=50K
45	Bachelors	40	<=50K
44	Bachelors	60	>50K

(Contd.)

Age	Education	Hours per week	Salary Class
30	Bachelors	40	<=50K
47	Bachelors	40	>50K
37	Masters	40	<=50K
34	Masters	35	>50K
41	Masters	65	>50K
49	Masters	45	>50K

Using your decision tree, please classify the following test examples.

Age	Education	Hours per week	Salary Class
90	10th	40	
49	10th	99	
25	Bachelors	55	
24	Bachelors	40	
33	Masters	45	
37	Masters	50	
39	Masters	45	
39	Masters	40	

Identify where there may be a possible over-fitting in your decision tree and suggest options to regularize it.

3. A dataset for predicting low quality turbines was collected and cleaned. We have two features, A and B which can be used for binary classification into +ve (shown with +) and –ve class (indicated by circle) in the plot below.

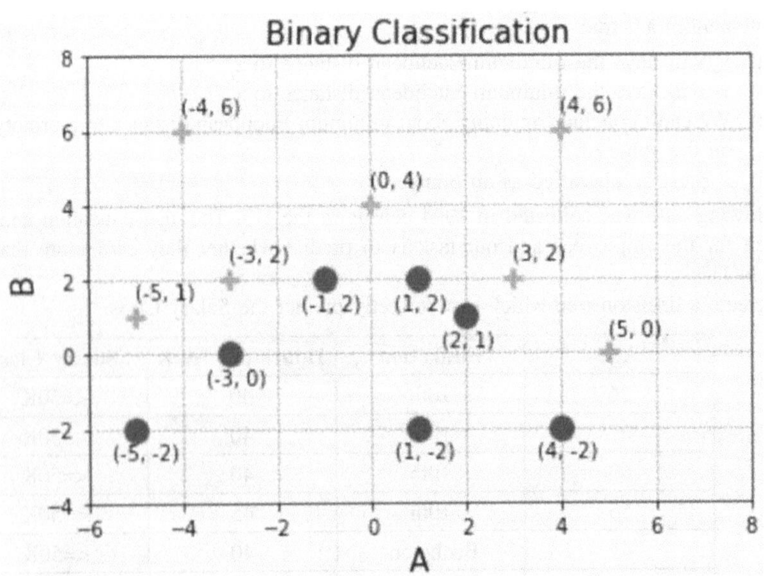

(a) Can we separate this data with a linear classifier in original features (A, B)? Why or why not?
(b) Is it possible to separate this data with a classifier that is polynomial in A and B? What is the degree of the polynomial that should suffice? Why or why not?
(c) Please write the equation of a classifier that separates this data perfectly?

Hint: You can use polynomial or piece-wise linear function. Please make sure that all points are correctly classified.

4. Glaucoma is a serious disease that is the leading cause of irreparable blindness. An AI Fundus Camera has been developed to screen patients at large for Glaucoma, based on the image of the Retina. The positive patients will be referred to expert eye doctors for further assessment.

Three different models were trained for this purpose and it turned out that each classifier had its own strengths and weaknesses. They sometimes agreed with each other on their predictions and sometimes differed. We are given the confusion matrices for each of the models on the Validation set.

Model (M1)	**Actual**	
Predicted	Yes	No
Yes	18	10
No	2	90
Model (M2)	**Actual**	
Predicted	Yes	No
Yes	16	4
No	4	96
Model (M3)	**Actual**	
Predicted	Yes	No
Yes	19	11
No	1	102

Please compute the metrics: Precision, Recall, F1 Score and Accuracy for each of the models. Which of these is best suited for Glaucoma Screening? Why?

Let us use an ensemble of the three models above in the following way. Each model will be given a weight.

Ensemble Model: Weight Function $= \ln\left(\frac{err}{1-err}\right)$

Which metric (Precision, Recall or F1 Score) would you use for determining weights? Why?

Model	**Weight**
M1	
M2	
M3	

The table below tells you the probability of Glaucoma in the eye based on its image for each model. Combine the predictions from these models using hard, soft and weighted voting strategies.

Test Example	**M1**	**M2**	**M3**	**Hard Voting**	**Soft Voting**	**Weighted Voting**
P1 Right Eye	0.4	0.4	0.8			
P1 Left Eye	0.3	0.75	0.55			

Which of these strategies you feel would work the best for this application?

5. Fill in the blanks
   (a) An ensemble of weak models (low accuracy) will become strong (high accuracy) provided that the models are ....
   (b) In a classification problem, the examples that are most difficult to classify lie .... the decision boundary.
   (c) In a binary classification problem, hard margin Support Vector Machines aim to .... the margin between the two classes.
   (d) For a soft margin SVM, in their objective function, the term $\frac{\|w\|^2}{2}$ is for .... and $C\sum_{n=1}^{N}\xi_n$ is for ....

MULTIPLE CHOICE QUESTIONS

1. In decision trees, which criterion is most commonly used to decide the best split at a node?
   (a) Sum of squared errors
   (b) Gini impurity or entropy
   (c) Euclidean distance
   (d) Bayesian probability
2. One major disadvantage of decision trees is that they:
   (a) Are prone to overfitting, especially when grown to full depth.
   (b) Require a large amount of data to perform well.
   (c) Are always computationally expensive compared to other classifiers.
   (d) Cannot handle categorical variables directly.
3. In **prototype-based learning**, the "prototype" refers to:
   (a) The set of all possible points in the feature space.
   (b) The center (or centroid) of a cluster representing the group.
   (c) The nearest neighbor to a new data point.
   (d) A decision boundary between two classes.
4. When using ***K*-means** for classification purposes, how does increasing the number of prototypes (clusters) generally affect the model?
   (a) It increases bias but decreases variance.
   (b) It decreases bias but increases variance.
   (c) It has no effect on bias or variance.
   (d) It always improves accuracy on unseen data.
5. In ***K*-Nearest Neighbors (KNN)** classification, the value of K determines:
   (a) The number of decision boundaries created.
   (b) The size of the decision regions.
   (c) The number of features used for classification.
   (d) The number of misclassified points.
6. One of the primary drawbacks of ***K*-Nearest Neighbors** is:
   (a) It is sensitive to outliers because it makes local decisions.
   (b) It requires an expensive training phase.
   (c) It assumes linear decision boundaries.
   (d) It only works for categorical data.
7. In KNN, when using **Euclidean distance**, what happens if you **normalize** the features of the dataset?
   (a) It helps all features contribute equally to the distance calculation.
   (b) It increases the impact of features with small ranges.
   (c) It decreases the algorithm's accuracy for high-dimensional data.
   (d) It forces the decision boundaries to become linear.

8. The **kernel trick** in SVM allows:
   (a) The decision boundaries to become non-linear in the original feature space.
   (b) The training data to be transformed into categorical variables.
   (c) The feature vectors to be reduced in dimensionality.
   (d) The model to handle only linear decision boundaries.
9. In an **SVM**, which of the following is true about the **support vectors**?
   (a) They are the data points closest to the decision boundary.
   (b) They are the outliers in the dataset.
   (c) They are the data points that lie farthest from the decision boundary.
   (d) They are the points that are always misclassified by the model.
10. In **SVM**, what role does the **regularization parameter CCC** play?
   (a) It controls the trade-off between maximizing the margin and minimizing classification error.
   (b) It sets the maximum number of support vectors.
   (c) It determines the number of misclassified data points.
   (d) It controls the degree of the polynomial kernel.
11. The **Naive** assumption in **Naive Bayes** refers to:
   (a) Assuming all features are independent of each other given the class.
   (b) Assuming that all classes are equally probable.
   (c) Assuming that all prior probabilities are zero.
   (d) Assuming that all data points are evenly spaced in feature space.
12. **Naive Bayes** is particularly well-suited for text classification because:
   (a) It can handle missing data more effectively than other classifiers.
   (b) It performs well when features are independent, as in bag-of-words representations.
   (c) It requires large amounts of data to train effectively.
   (d) It minimizes the variance of predictions compared to decision trees.
13. In classification, which of the following metrics is the most appropriate when class imbalance is present?
   (a) Accuracy (b) F1-Score
   (c) Root Mean Squared Error (d) Adjusted R-squared
14. **Precision** is defined as:
   (a) The proportion of true positives to the total number of positive predictions.
   (b) The proportion of true positives to the total number of actual positives.
   (c) The proportion of true positives to the total number of negative predictions.
   (d) The total number of correct predictions divided by the total number of predictions.
15. **AUC-ROC** is useful in evaluating classifiers because it:
   (a) Measures the error between the predicted and actual values.
   (b) It can be used to assess the quality of the model by plotting the true positive rate against the false positive rate.
   (c) Represents the model's performance at a specific threshold.
   (d) Computes the average precision and recall.
16. The **primary advantage** of ensemble methods such as **bagging** and **boosting** is:
   (a) They help reduce the bias of the model by averaging predictions.
   (b) They always reduce the computation time of model training.
   (c) They help improve model performance by combining weak learners.
   (d) They require less data than single models for accurate prediction.
17. In **Random Forest**, which feature of the algorithm helps reduce **overfitting**?
   (a) Using decision trees with a high depth.
   (b) Using only a random subset of features at each split.
   (c) Always choosing the feature with the largest information gain.
   (d) Restricting the maximum number of leaves in each tree.

18. Which of the following best describes **boosting**?
    (a) It builds multiple independent trees to reduce variance.
    (b) It combines weak learners by training each new model to correct errors of the previous one.
    (c) It generates multiple models and averages their predictions to minimize error.
    (d) It uses random sampling of features to reduce overfitting.
19. Increasing the depth of a **decision tree** can often lead to:
    (a) Reduced bias and increased variance.
    (b) Increased bias and decreased variance.
    (c) Reduced accuracy on the training set.
    (d) Fewer splits in the tree.
20. Which of the following techniques is commonly used to reduce overfitting in decision trees?
    (a) Pruning
    (b) Increasing the depth of the tree
    (c) Increasing the number of leaves
    (d) Adding more features to the model
21. The **bias-variance tradeoff** in classification refers to:
    (a) The balance between the accuracy on the training set and the accuracy on the test set.
    (b) The balance between the training time and the test time.
    (c) The conflict between overfitting and underfitting a model.
    (d) The balance between high-dimensional data and model complexity.
22. Which of the following is **NOT** a characteristic of **logistic regression**?
    (a) It is a linear classifier used for binary classification problems.
    (b) It outputs probabilities for each class.
    (c) It assumes that the features are normally distributed.
    (d) It uses the sigmoid function to map predictions between 0 and 1.

ANSWER KEY

1. (b)	**2.** (a)	**3.** (b)	**4.** (b)	**5.** (b)	**6.** (a)	**7.** (a)	**8.** (a)	**9.** (a)	**10.** (a)
11. (a)	**12.** (b)	**13.** (b)	**14.** (a)	**15.** (b)	**16.** (c)	**17.** (b)	**18.** (b)	**19.** (a)	**20** (a)
21. (c)	**22.** (c)								

11 Neural Networks

Introduction

Artificial Neural Networks (ANNs) is an important technology in data science. The ANN is consisting of three important keywords, i.e., "Artificial", "Neural", and "Networks". It is important to understand these three words for understanding the ANN technologies. Out of these three words, let us first understand "Neural", this word is driven from the word neuron, which is the basic element of a human brain involved in any kind of decision making. The purpose of the human brain is to perform decision making and the human brain is consisting of millions of such neurons. The third word "Network" indicates that the neurons are connected with each other for making the decisions. The information between the neurons is communicated using this network. The first word, "Artificial", indicates that the neurons networks of human brain is simulated using the computers and thus called as artificial neural networks.

The neural networks are designed with the biological inspiration and functioning of the brain. The human brain has tremendous learning potential, and the working mechanism of the brain can be simulated with the help of computers. Two important components of the brain are neurons and synapses. Neurons are the basis elements of brain. The neurons in the brain are connected with the synapses. The synapses provide the basic communication between the neurons and is responsible for signal transmission between the neurons, integration of information, and provides learning capabilities.

11.1 FUNDAMENTALS OF NEURAL NETWORKS

Development of an artificial neural network requires the representation of neurons (named as nodes in ANN), connections between the nodes, and learning mechanism using the mathematical non-linear activation function for progressive building of the learning capacity. The neural networks can be designed using a simple neuron or can be designed using thousands of neurons connected in multiple layers combined with a number of nonlinear activation functions. The architectural designing process of a neural network is a complex task and varies from problem to problem. The overview of various design aspects of neural networks is covered in this chapter.

The general architecture of the neural network is shown in Figure 11.1.

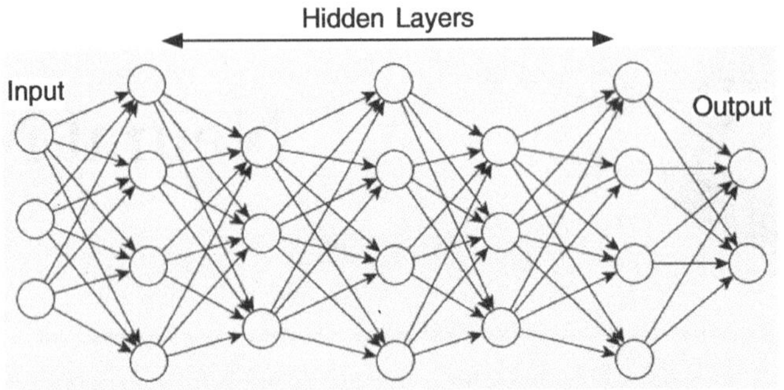

FIGURE 11.1 General Architecture of the Neural Network.

A neural network has the following major components:

Input layer: The input layer takes inputs (training data) being the first layer of the neural network.

Weight and bias: Each input is assigned some weights depending on its importance. Bias is sometimes also added in the input. The weight and bias are randomly initialized and are updated in the successive iterations.

Hidden layer: The hidden layer plays an important role in training of the artificial neural networks. The training is performed with the help of nonlinear activation functions.

Output layer: The output layer is responsible for generating outputs. In order to generate the required outputs (depending upon the problem type), an appropriate output function is used.

11.1.1 Weights and Bias

Weight and bias are the two important parameters in any neural network. Each input in the neural network is associated with some weights. Apart from the weights, some bias is also added in the input for proper training of the network.

11.1.2 Weight Initialization

One of the simple strategies is to initialize the weights randomly. Weight initialization is important because the small weight nearly zero tends to be vanishing gradient whereas large weights can lead to exploding gradient problem. Ideally the variance of weight should be proportional to size of network. Two common weight initialization techniques are Kaiming and Xavier techniques.

Kaiming technique: In Kaiming technique of weight initialization, weights are uniformly distributed, and standard deviation of weight is proportional to input size. Kaiming technique is most suitable in the cases where ReLU activation functions are used in hidden layers.

Xavier technique: Xavier technique of weight initialization is most suitable for the networks uses Sigmoid or Tanh activation functions. In Xavier technique, normal distribution is used for the weight distribution, and standard deviation is proportional to input and output size.

11.2 TYPES OF NEURAL NETWORKS

There are several ways of designing a neural network and the types of neural networks also depend on the way it is designed. The simple type of neural networks is perceptron. The perceptron may be configured in a single-layer or in multiple-layers for the complex neural networks.

11.2.1 Perceptron

A perceptron is the basis element in the artificial neural network. The input to the perceptron is $\sum_i w_i I_i$, where w_i is the weight of the ith input. If the input value $\sum_i w_i I_i$ is greater than or equal to the threshold value τ then the output value is set to 1, otherwise the output value is 0.

$$y = \begin{cases} 1 \; if \sum_i w_i I_i \geq \tau \\ 0 \quad \text{otherwise} \end{cases}$$

11.2.2 Single Layer vs. Multi-layer Perceptron

Single layer perceptron does not have any hidden layer whereas the multi-layer perceptron has multiple hidden layers. The weight update in the single-layer perceptron is simply by adjusting the delta values (differences between the desired output and the actual output), whereas in multi-layer perceptron the weight update is carried out using the backpropagation (weights are updated in consecutive layers).

Example: A multi-layer perceptron is drawn to take a decision for a person whether the person can buy a car based on the income and expenditure of the person. Suppose we are designing the multi-layer perceptron in such way that the person can buy the car if the income is greater than expenditure, the input vector to the neural network will consist of two components, income and expenditure, i.e. [x_1, x_2], where x_1 represents income and x_2 represents expenditure. For simplicity we are considering the income and expenditure as a single component, but in real world scenarios, income can have different components like salary, interest, dividend, so in the vector format the income I can be represented as [i_1, i_2, i_3...] and similarly the expenditure can have components (like grocery, and monthly bills) so the vector representation the expenditure E will be [e_1, e_2...]. And there can be bias also, remember bias can be taken negative also. Apart from this each income and expenditure component is associated with some weights, for example the salary component may be given higher weight as compared to the dividend because salary component is generally fixed whereas dividend component is variable in a particular financial year.

The input and output can be represented as shown below.

$$\begin{array}{l} [x_1, x_2] \; y \\ [3 \quad 1] \; 1 \\ [2 \quad 2] \; 0 \\ [1 \quad 2] \; 0 \\ [2 \quad 1] \; 1 \end{array}$$

The multi-layer perceptron for the given example is shown in Figure 11.2. The input along with the bias is shown on the left side, whereas the output is shown on the right side of the network.

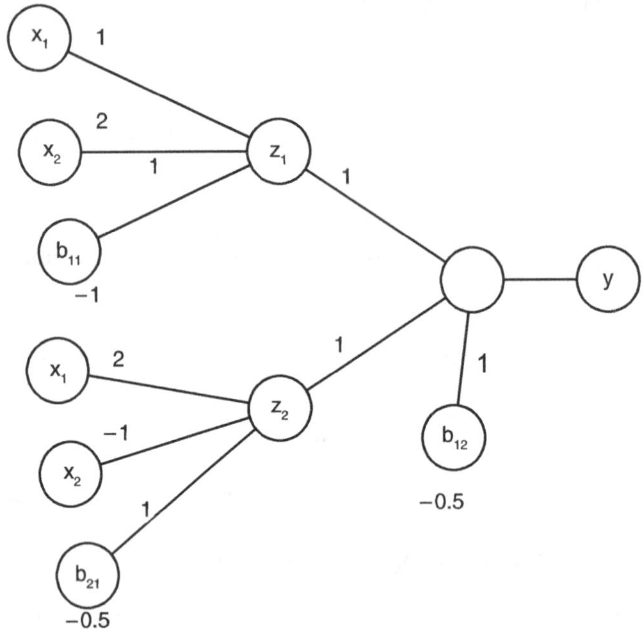

FIGURE 11.2 An Example of Multi-layer Perceptron Neural Network.

The input weight vectors are given as follows:

$$\overrightarrow{w_{11}} = [1, 2],\ b_{11} = -1$$
$$\overrightarrow{w_{21}} = [2, -1],\ b_{21} = -0.5$$
$$\overrightarrow{w_{12}} = [1, 1],\ b_{21} = -0.5$$

Each node in the network is perceptron, so the output is 1, if the input is greater than the threshold value otherwise the output is 0. Suppose the threshold value for the example is 0, i.e. for any positive value greater than 0, the output will be 1. To understand the working of this multi-layer perceptron model, let us answer the following questions.

Question	Discussion
When can Z_1 be 1?:	The output at the first layer Z_1 will be 1 when $x_1 + 2x_2 - 1 > 0$ which implies that $[x_1 > 0]$ or $[x_2 > 0]$, i.e. either x_1 or x_2 should be grater than 0.
When can Z_2 be 1?	The output Z_2 will be 1 when $2x_1 - x_2 - 1.5 > 0$.
When can y be 1?	Finally, the output of the network will be 1, when $[Z_1 > 0]$ or $[Z_2 > 0]$.

The Z_1 and Z_2 are the output generated at the middle layer or hidden layer. The hidden layer in the neural network has specific task to maximize the learning process. The purpose of hidden layer is explained with the help of an illustration.

11.2.3 A Generalized Illustration of Neural Network with one Hidden Layer

A neural network with one hidden layer can be illustrated (with internal details) as shown in Figure 11.3. The working of neural network with internal layer is summarized in the following steps:

Step 1 (Process Input): Each input x_n transformed into several pre-activations using linear models. The processed input is supplied to the model by initial weights and bias.

Step 2 (Activation Functions): Nonlinear activation applied are applied on each set of inputs to establish an approximate relationship between the inputs.

Step 3 (Model Learning): Linear model learned on the new "features" h_n. The models leans over the iterations with update weights and bias values.

Step 4 (Output Calculation): Finally, output is produced as $y = o(s_n)$, by considering all the features and weights associated with it.

Step 5 (Weight Optimization and Performance Improvement): The performance of the model is assessed using the loss function etc., and performance can be improved by updating weights $(w_1, w_2, \ldots, w_K, v)$ learned by minimizing some loss function, for example $\mathcal{L}(W, v) = \sum_{n=1}^{N} \ell(y_n, o(s_n))$ (squared, logistic, SoftMax, etc.).

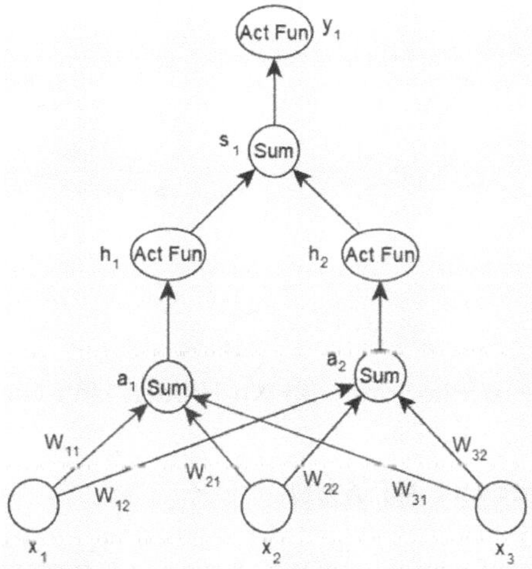

FIGURE 11.3 An Illustration of Neural Network with One Hidden Layer.

11.2.4 Multi-layer Perceptron (MLP)

A Multi-layer Perceptron (MLP) is consisting of an input layer, an output layer, and one or more hidden layers. An MLP can be seen as a composition of multiple linear models combined nonlinearly. An example of MLP architecture is shown in the Figure 11.4.

A MLP architecture with no hidden unit and one hidden unit is shown in Figure 11.5. Although computation can be performed using without hidden unit in MLP, but implementation of nonlinear functions is practically difficult in it, if implemented then accuracy will be less. On the other hand, it is proven in the earlier studies that the single layer MLP model with sufficient hidden layers can approximate any computing function. This is due to the power of nonlinear activation functions. The nonlinear activation functions can transform the input and extract the most relevant features for decision making.

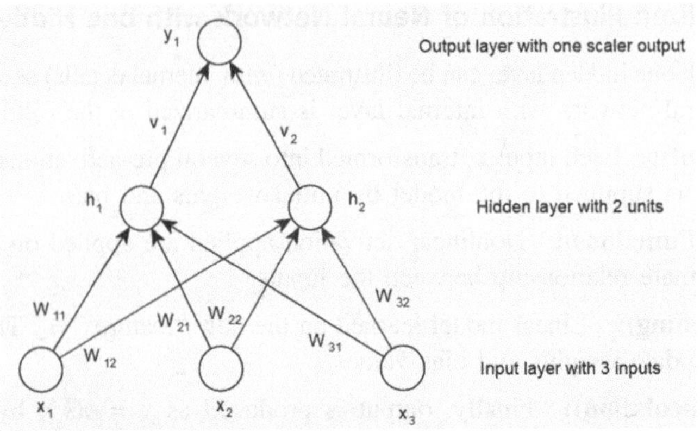

FIGURE 11.4 An Example of MLP Architecture.

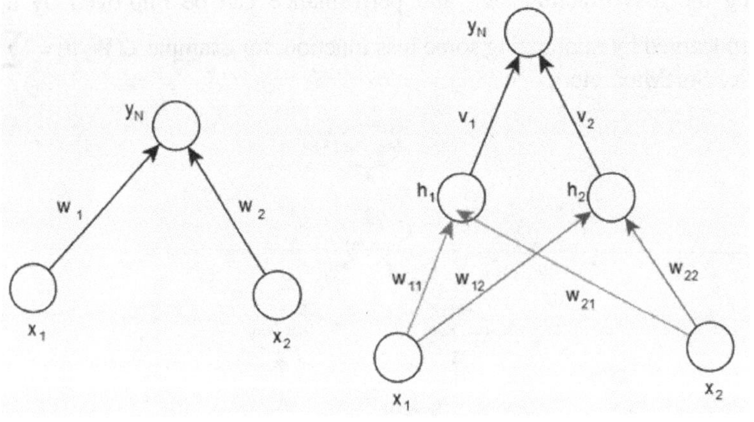

FIGURE 11.5 MLP Architecture with No Hidden Unit and One Hidden Unit.

11.3 LEARNING PROCESSES IN ANN

Learning is an important aspect of neural networks. Learning is performed with the help of nonlinear activation functions typically at the hidden layers. There are two major learning processes in artificial neural networks namely, backpropagation, and forward propagation.

Backpropagation: The primary objective of the backpropagation process is to minimize the error of learning. Backpropagation is performed in three major steps. These steps are loss computation, gradient computation, and updating the weights and biases. The loss is computed using one of the loss functions to minimize the error of neural networks. Based on the loss function, gradient is computed for updation of the weights of the inputs for improvement of the accuracy of the neural network.

Forward Propagation: The primary purpose of forward propagation is to generate the output. The forward propagation is consisting of five major components. The first component is the input to the network, the second component is weight and biases assigned to the input layer, the third components are the nonlinear activation functions, fourth component is the hidden layers, and the last component is the output layers.

11.3.1 Feedforward Neural Networks (FFNNs)

Feedforward neural networks are another important type of neural networks. The FFNNs have three major components namely, the input layer, hidden layer, and the output layer. Inputs are taken at the input layer along with the weights and bias values, then in the hidden layer activation functions are used for processing of input values, and the output is generated at the output layer. The FFNNs have two important phases. The first phase is feedforward phase, and the second phase is backpropagation phase. The feedforward phase is used for generation of the output and the backpropagation phase is used for minimizing the error of the neural network, as the error is backpropagated in the previous layers.

Architecture

The architectural design of a neural network depends on various factors. The process of neural network design along with some of the commonly used architects are discussed in this section.

Neural network design

Designing a neural network is a complex task and a lot of parameters need to be considered for effective designing of a neural network. Consider a case of neural network shown in Figure 11.6. It is a most general case, where multiple hidden layers (with same or different number of hidden nodes in each) and a scalar or vector-valued output is utilized for developing a neural network.

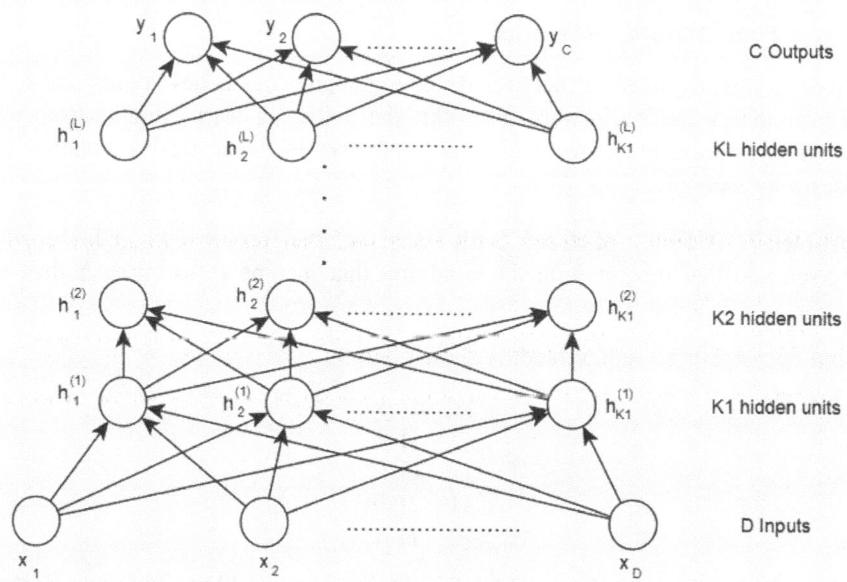

FIGURE 11.6 A general case of Neural Network Design with multiple hidden layers and scalar or vector valued output.

11.4 DESIGN ISSUES FOR NEURAL NETWORKS—SOME DESIGN ASPECTS

Designing a neural network is a complex process and requires understanding of the problem and experience. Building a neural net to solve a given problem is partially art and partially science. The design process starts with training a network by finding the weights on the inputs that serve our goals, we have to make a number of design decisions. Some of the following important points one need to consider for designing a neural network:

1. **The number of hidden layers:** It is very difficult to decide the number of hidden layers for a neural network as there is no rule of thumb for deciding this number.
2. **The number of nodes:** Just like the previous point, there is no standard for deciding the number of nodes in the hidden layer, it is problem specific and varies from case-to-case basis.
3. **Type of connection:** Nodes can be interconnected in a number of ways so deciding a suitable connection type is also a big challenge.
4. **Type of activation function:** Today, there exists a number of non-linear activation functions so deciding a suitable one for the given problem is another challenge.
5. **Type of loss or cost function:** For designing a good neural network the effective loss function (or cost function) is necessary. Devising a loss function is again a complex task. The cost function is the sum of all the loss functions.
6. **Type of optimizer function:** Selecting or customizing an optimizer for proper weight updation in the neural network is a challenging research area.

Answering the above questions is not a simple task. The answers to the above questions depend on the type of problems to be solved using neural networks, user experience, and a number of experiments for finding the optimal values of the above points.

11.4.1 Dense Feedforward Networks

One of the most common choices of network designing approaches is developing dense feedforward networks. Under the dense feedforward networks, the ability to learn weights from training data is developed. The working of dense feedforward networks in linear algebra notation is explained using the following example.

Example problem: A length of vector 2 bit-vectors of the form $x = [x_1, x_2]$, the output y is 1, when the person can buy the car with the condition that income (x_1) is greater than expenditure (x_2), i.e., $x_1 > x_2$.

The input and output can be represented as shown below.

$$\begin{array}{ll} [x_1, x_2] & y \\ [3 \quad 1] & 1 \\ [2 \quad 2] & 0 \\ [1 \quad 2] & 0 \\ [2 \quad 1] & 1 \end{array}$$

The neural network is shown in Figure 11.1 for the buys car problem. In linear algebra notation, the input weights are given as shown below.

$$w_{11} = [w_{111}, w_{112}]$$

$$w_{12} = [w_{121}, w_{122}]$$

Hidden node vector $h = [h_1 h_2]$, where $h_1 = \text{sgn}\left(w_{1i}{}^T \times + b_1\right)$, and $h_2 = \text{sgn}\left(w_{2i}{}^T \times + b_2\right)$.

i.e., $h_i = \text{sgn}\left(w_i{}^T \times + b_i\right)$ for i = 1, 2.

By organizing w_{11} and w_{12} in a 2 × 2 matrix W, where i^{th} row is w_i^T.

$$h = \text{sgn}\left(w_1 \times + b\right)$$

where sgn() function works elementwise on vectors.

$$y = \text{sgn}\left(w_2 h + c\right)$$

11.4.2 Interconnection among Nodes

Neural networks can differ in how nodes in one layer interact to the next layer (towards right direction). The most general case is the interconnection is fully connected, where all the nodes are connected with each other in the consecutive layers. The number of parameters for fully connected interconnected network are $(n_1 + 1)n_2$, where n_1 is the number of parameters for left layer, +1 indicates the bias on the left layer, and n_2 is the number of parameters for right layer. The alternation popular interconnection options are random interconnection, pooled, and convolutional interconnections.

Random: In random interconnection, for some given m nodes, pick m out of n_1 nodes and make them input ${}^{n1}C_m$ options available for interconnection between the nodes as shown in the below Figure.

Pooled: In next layer (pooling layer) there is one node for each other cluster and this node has all & only the member of its cluster as inputs. The example of pooled interconnection is shown in the Figure 11.7.

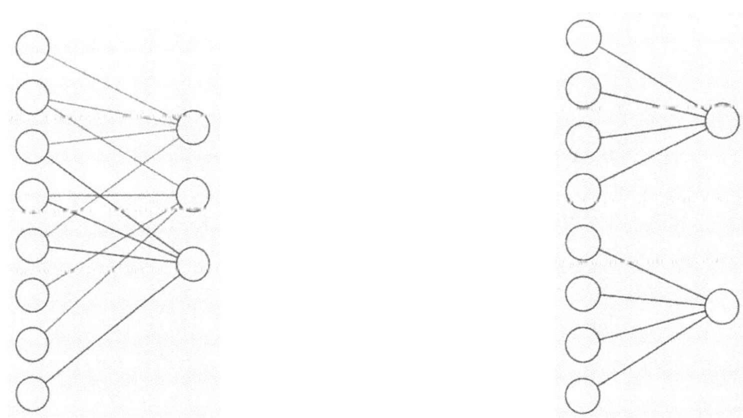

(a) Random Interconnection (b) Pooled Interconnection

FIGURE 11.7 Random and Pooled Interconnection between the Nodes in Neural Network.

Convolutional: The convolutional neural networks (CNN) networks use the convolutional interconnections where convolutional functions are used to extract meaningful features and connect it to the next layer. The CNN networks are discussed in detail in the chapter of Deep Learning.

11.4.3 Information Flow

Each layer has its own additional matrix of weights and vector of biases along with activation functions. Perceptron's uses sign functions, but other choices also exist. Since edges are directed forwarded. Information flows from left to right. Feedforward network with no cycle. Suppose there are l hidden layers and additional output layers $l + 1$. Let weight matrix for i^{th} layer be W_i and bias vector be b_i. $W_1W_2 \dots W_{l+1}$ and $b_1b_2 \dots b_{l+1}$. These are the parameters of the model.

11.5 ACTIVATION FUNCTIONS

Activation functions are very important in neural network, and deep learning models. The weights are updated using activation functions in the hidden layers. Activation functions are also used for the output layers.

Activation functions are the mathematical backbone of neural network, and deep learning models by which the weights are updated for the neural network, and deep learning models. The primary requirement for activation functions is, these functions should be non-linear in nature so that weights are properly updated in the subsequent layers. Other requirements for activation functions are, the computational complexity of the functions should be simple, and functions should be able to avoid vanishing or exploding gradient problems. The commonly used activation functions in the neural network, and deep learning are discussed in this section.

11.5.1 Sigmoid Activation Function

The range of output from the sigmoid function is in the range of [0 ... 1]. The sigmoid function is best suited to output layer for generating the outputs. The equation of sigmoid function is given below.

$$\sigma = \frac{1}{1 + e^{-x}}$$

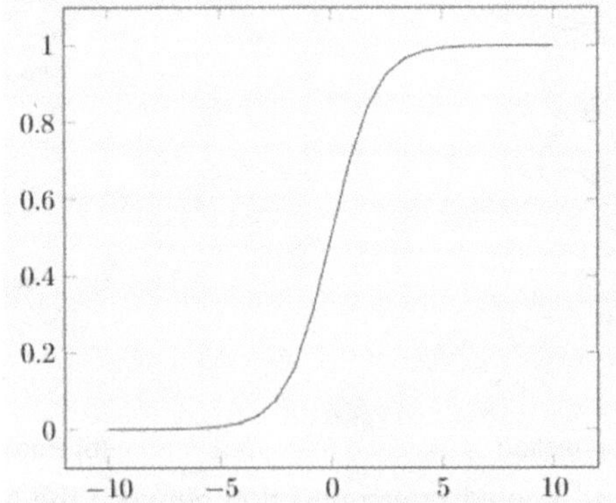

FIGURE 11.8 Characteristics curve for Sigmoid activation function.

11.5.2 Tanh Activation Function

The range of output from the tanh function is in the range of [−1 ... +1]. The tanh function is best suited for the hidden layers for updating of weights. The equation of tanh activation function is given as under:

$$\sigma = \frac{e^x - e^{-x}}{e^x + e^{-x}}$$

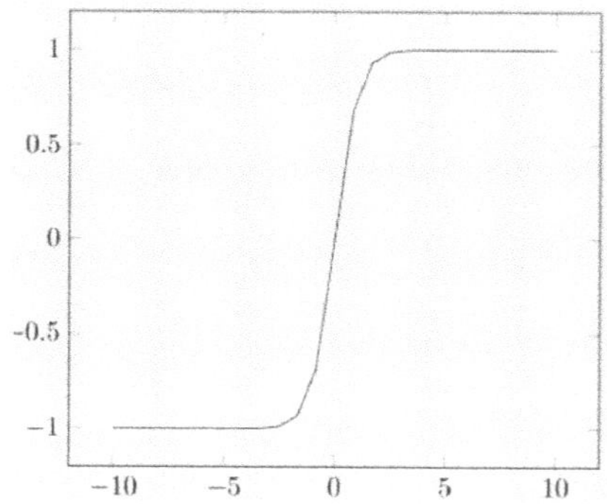

FIGURE 11.9 Characteristics curve for Tanh activation function.

11.5.3 ReLU Activation Function

The ReLU (Rectified Linear Unit) is a very popular and most widely used activation in deep learning. ReLU is most appropriate for the hidden layers and performs better than the other activation functions. The equation of ReLU activation function is given below.

$$\sigma = \max(0, x)$$

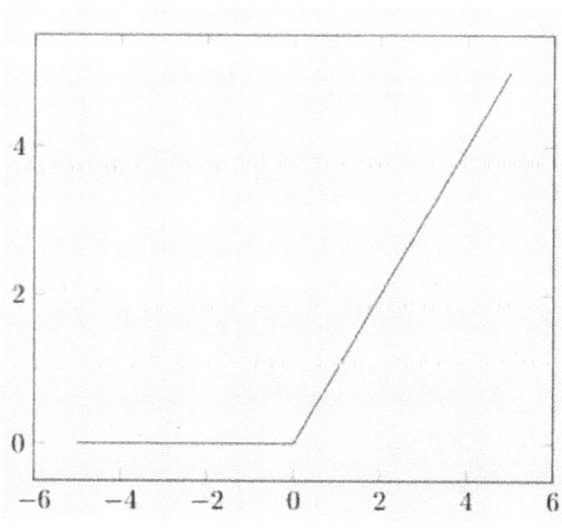

FIGURE 11.10 Characteristics curve for ReLU activation function.

11.5.4 Leaky-ReLU Activation Function

Leaky-ReLU is the extension of the ReLU activation function. It is also used for hidden layers and equation for leaky-globally activation function is given below.

$$\sigma = \begin{cases} \alpha x & for\ x < 0 \\ x & for\ x \geq 0 \end{cases}$$

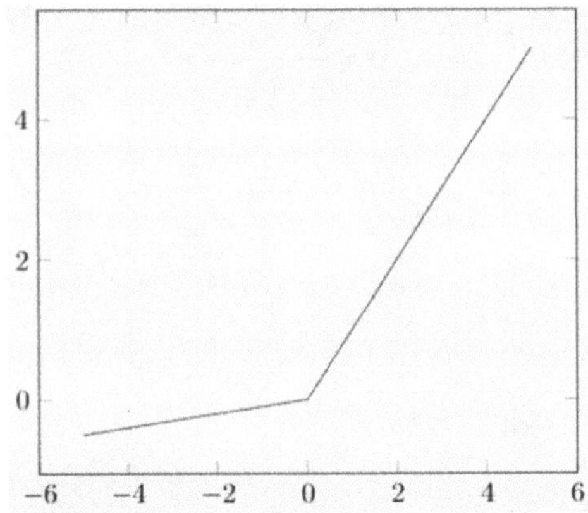

FIGURE 11.11 Characteristics curve for Leaky-ReLU activation function with $\alpha = 0.1$.

11.5.5 Swish Activation Function

Swish is the recent activation function developed by Google. Swish activation function is also used for the hidden layers for updation of the weights. The equation for Swish activation function is given below.

$$\sigma = x \times \text{sigmoid}(x) = x \times \frac{1}{1+e^{-x}} = \frac{x}{1+e^{-x}}$$

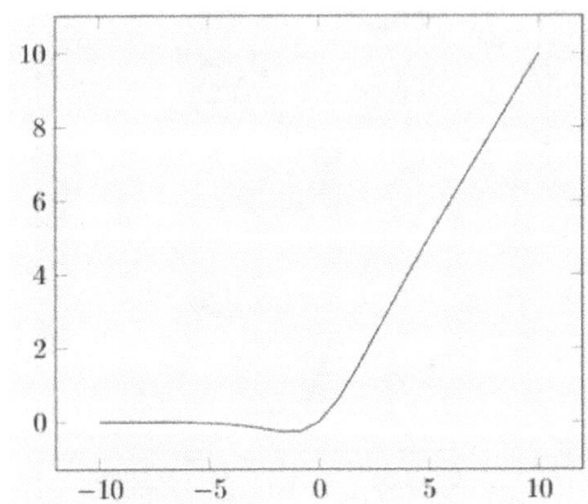

FIGURE 11.12 Characteristics curve for Swish activation function.

11.5.6 SoftMax Activation Function

This activation function is suitable for outputs from the deep learning models.

$$\sigma(z)_i = \frac{e^{z_i}}{\sum_{j=1}^{K} e^{z_j}}$$

Where Z_i is an element to the input vector z, K is the number of classes. The values are transformed in such a way that the sum of all transformed values is equal to 1, i.e. $\Sigma\sigma(z)_i = 1$.

Example: Suppose the input vector is (2, 3, 11, 12) then the SoftMax values are calculated as follows:

$$\sigma(2)=\frac{e^2}{e^2+e^3+e^{11}+e^{12}}=0.000033$$

$$\sigma(3)=\frac{e^3}{e^2+e^3+e^{11}+e^{12}}=0.00009$$

$$\sigma(11)=\frac{e^{11}}{e^2+e^3+e^{11}+e^{12}}=0.269$$

$$\sigma(12)=\frac{e^{12}}{e^2+e^3+e^{11}+e^{12}}=0.731$$

The sum of transformed values $\sigma(2)+\sigma(3)+\sigma(11)+\sigma(12)=1$

11.6 FEATURE LEARNERS/ENCODERS

An abstract representation of features learned by neural networks is shown in Figure 11.13. The Hidden layers can be seen as learning a feature representation $\phi(x_n)$ for each input x_n.

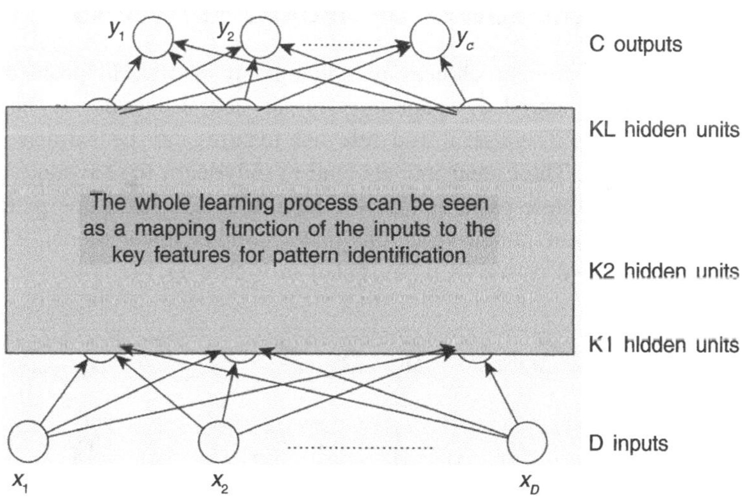

FIGURE 11.13 An abstract representation of the feature learning in a neural network.

Node values in each hidden layer tell us how much a "learned" feature is active in x_n. Hidden layer weights are like pattern/feature-detector/filter.

All the incoming weights (a vector) on this hidden node can be seen as representing a pattern/ feature-detector/filter. All the incoming weights (a vector) on this hidden node can be seen as representing a template/pattern/feature-detector.

11.7 KERNEL METHODS VS. NEURAL NETWORKS

The working mechanism of kernel methods is similar to the neural network; however, it is important to understand the difference between the kernel methods and the neural networks.

Prediction rule for a kernel method (e.g., kernel SVM) is given as under:

$$y = \sum_{n=1}^{N} \alpha_n k(x_n, x)$$

This is analogous to a single hidden layer NN with fixed/pre-defined hidden nodes $\{k(x_n, x)\}_{n=1}^{N}$ and output weights $\{\alpha_n\}_{n=1}^{N}$

The prediction rule for a deep neural network is given by

$$y = \sum_{k=1}^{K} v_k h_k$$

Here, the h_k's are learned from data (possibly after multiple layers of nonlinear transformations).

Both kernel methods and deep *NNs* can be seen as using nonlinear basis functions for making predictions. Kernel methods use fixed basis functions (defined by the kernel) whereas *NN* learns the basis functions adaptively from data.

11.8 REPRESENTATIONAL POWER OF NEURAL NETWORKS

The neural networks are the popular choices of solving any real-world problems in the recent scenario. The primary reason behind the popularity of the neural network is the representational power of the neural networks. The useful and relevant features can be extracted in an effective way from the neural networks. The Linear models tend to only learn the "average" pattern whereas the deep models can learn multiple patterns (each hidden node can learn one pattern). Thus, deep models can learn to capture more subtle variations that a simpler linear model. The illustration of representational power of neural networks is presented in Figure 11.14.

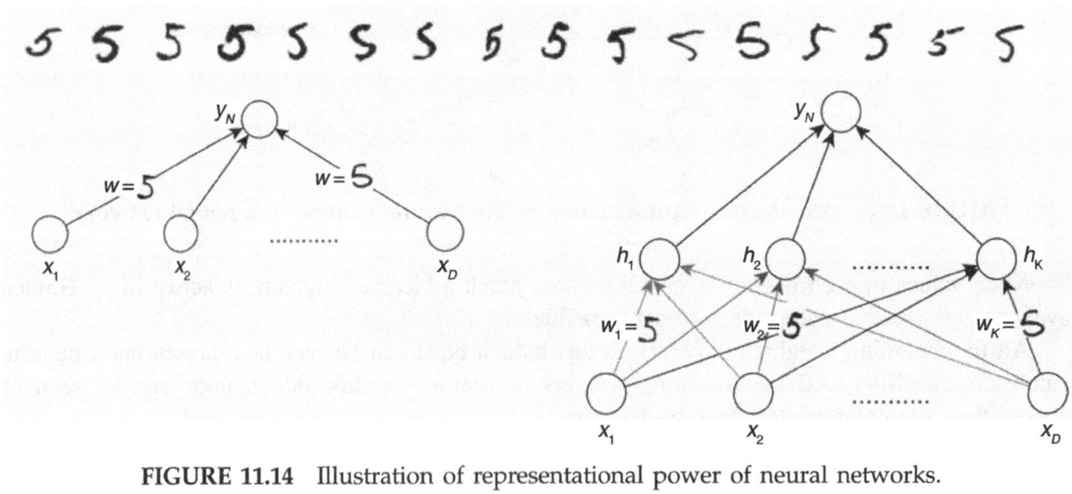

FIGURE 11.14 Illustration of representational power of neural networks.

11.9 LOSS FUNCTION

Loss function indicates errors in the neural networks. The term loss in the loss function refers to the variation between the predicted value and the actual desired values in the given neural network. The loss function is sometimes also referred to as the cost function of the neural network but there is a slight difference between the cost function and the loss function. The cost function is the sum of all the loss functions in a given neural network. Typically, when there is only one loss function involved in the network then it is equal to the cost function of the network. The most commonly used loss functions in the neural networks are Mean Square Error (MSE) loss function, and Cross Entropy Loss function. The objective of any neural network is to minimize the cost or loss function, the minimum value of loss function indicates a better performance of the given neural network. A brief description of both Mean Square Error (MSE) loss, and Cross Entropy loss is given in this section.

11.9.1 Mean Square Error (MSE) Loss

The mean square error loss function is calculated as

$$L_{MSE} = \frac{1}{n}\sum_{i}\left(\hat{y}_i - y_i\right)$$

Where $\hat{y}_i$ is the computed output and y_i is the desired i^{th} output, and h is the number of samples. The mean square error loss is always giving the positive values and it is used most frequently for the prediction related tasks such as forecasting of weather, forecasting of stock price, etc.

11.9.2 Cross Entropy Loss

Consider a multi-class classification problem with target classes C_1, C_2, C_3,..., C_n. Suppose each point in training set is of the form (x, p) where x is input and p = [1, p_2, p_3,..., p_n] is output. p_i is the probability that input x belongs to class C_i with $\sum_i p_i = 1$. If we are certain that an input belongs to a particular class, C_i then $p_i = 1$ and $p_j = 0 \ \forall j \neq i$. We can design our neural network to produce output q = [q_1, q_2, q_3,..., q_n], using SoftMax for output. Hence both input and output are probability distributions. Cross entropy loss is a popular loss function used in multi-class classification task in the neural network. It is entropy-based loss function. Recall that the entropy is calculated as $-\sum_i p_i \log p_i = H(p)$. The cross entropy is slightly different from the entropy and is calculated as follows:

$$\text{Cross entropy} = -\sum_i p_i \log q_i = H(p, q)$$

In information theory it is used to quantify sub-optimal codes. The p_i is the actual probability (ground truth), q_i is the estimated probability. In general, $H(p, q) \geq H(p)$.

The KL Divergence loss is the special type of entropy-based loss function which is sometimes also referred to as relative entropy. It measures the difference between the two probability distributions namely the distribution of the generated or predicted data and the distribution of the actual or desired data. The KL divergence is calculated as shown below.

$$\text{KL Divergence } D(pq) = H(p, q) - H(p) = \sum_i^n \log\frac{p_i}{q_i}$$

11.10 COMPUTE GRAPH

The compute graph provides an effective representation of the working of the neural network model. It helps in finding good values for parameters of the model (weights and threshold). The compute graphs are the directed acyclic graphs (DAG). The compute graph shows the operations, variables, and output of the neural networks. The nodes in the compute graphs indicates the operations including the activation functions, and the edge represents the data flow between operations and variables. For the forward pass neural networks, compute graph follows the path from input to operations, and from the operations to the output. Whereas for the backward pass compute graphs calculates the gradients of loss functions for each variable (both weights and biases) and update the variables based on the gradients. Each node has an operand or an operator (+, ×, σ, MSE). When a node has both an operand and operator, operator is written above the operand.

Example: The compute graph for the following expression is shown in the Figure 11.15 below:

$$y = (x + y)z$$

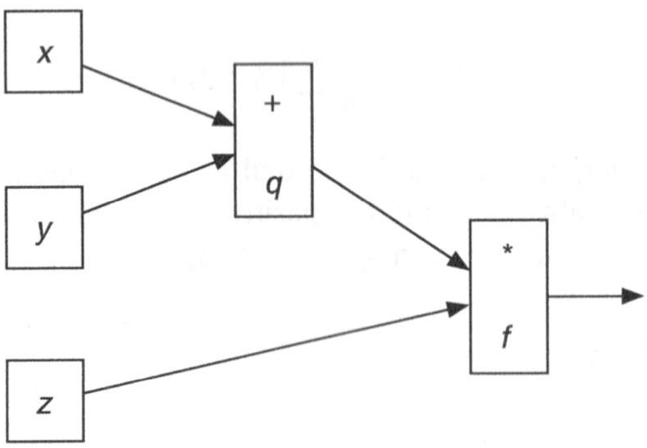

FIGURE 11.15 Compute Graph for the Given Example Function.

Example: The compute graph for the following set of operations for the neural networks is shown in the Figure 11.16.

$$y = \sigma(Wx + b)$$

$$u = Wx$$

$$v = u + b$$

$$y = \sigma(v)$$

$$L = \text{MSE}(y, \hat{y})$$

Where $\hat{y}$ is the actual (desired) output and y is the predicted output. L is the loss function, and W, and b are the weights and biases respectively.

Exercise: Draw the compute graph for the following function.

$$f(w, x) = \frac{1}{1 + e^{-(w_0 x_0 + w_1 x_1 + w_2)}}$$

Assume $w_0 = 2$, $w_1 = -3$, $x_0 = -1$, $x_1 = -2$, $w_1 = -3$ are input nodes. Now perform the forward and backpropagation to compute gradient w.r.t. each input x_i and w_i.

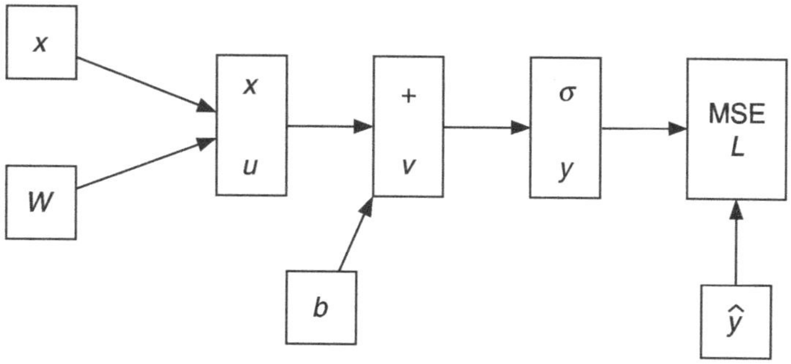

FIGURE 11.16 Compute Graph with Activation and Loss Functions.

11.11 BACKPROPAGATION

The training in the neural network is performed by derivative/derivation of the loss in each of the layer of network. The actual loss of the network is calculated at the output layer which indicates the error in the neural network. The impact of error is routed back to the previous layers as the derivative of the loss. This process is called as backpropagation. The compute graph helps in understanding the calculation of derivatives of the layer of neural network.

The backpropagation technique is used for training of the neural networks. The major steps in backpropagation are—forward pass, calculate loss function, backward pass, and weight update. In forward pass, the input weights and bias are initialized in the input layer and based on the activation function the calculated values are forwarded to the next layer. Then in the successive layers, loss function is calculated as the error in the network. Based on the error rate estimated by the loss function, the weights are updated in the previous layers of the neural networks.

Example of Backpropagation: Now let us consider the example of demonstrating the compute graph for the following function with calculations of backpropagation (i.e. computation of the gradients, etc.). The compute graph of the example is shown in the Figure 11.17.

$$f(x, y, z) = (x + y)z$$

The computation is performed in the following two steps:
Step 1: $q = x + y$
Step 2: $f = qz$

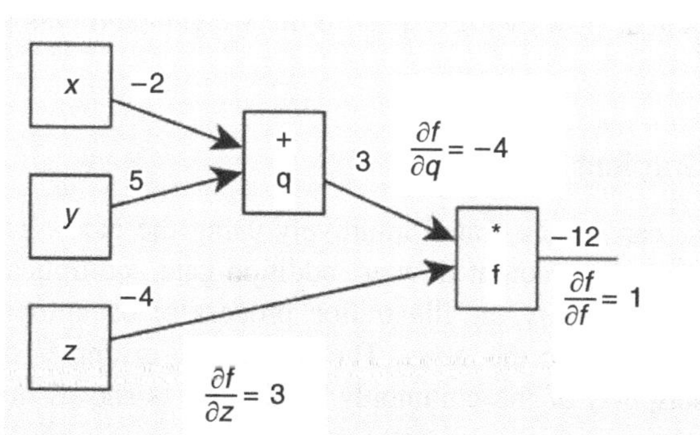

FIGURE 11.17 Compute Graph for Backpropagation.

In order to compute the backpropagation linear algebra and partial differentiation is used. For this example, we need to compute the derivatives $\frac{\partial f}{\partial x}, \frac{\partial f}{\partial y}, \frac{\partial f}{\partial z}$, i.e. derivative of the function f with respect to the variables x, y, and z.

The derivates are calculated as follows:

$$\frac{\partial q}{\partial x} = 1, \quad \frac{\partial q}{\partial y} = 1, \quad \frac{\partial f}{\partial q} = z, \quad \frac{\partial f}{\partial z} = q$$

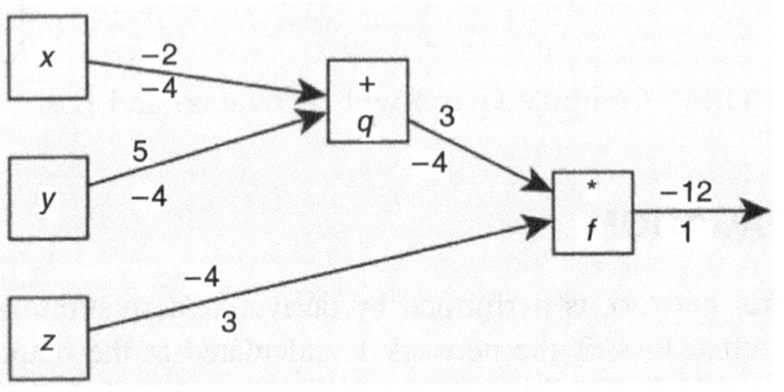

FIGURE 11.18 Calculation of Backpropagation in Compute Graph.

For example, the derivative $\frac{\partial f}{\partial y}$ is computed using the chain rule as shown below.

$$\frac{\partial f}{\partial y} = \frac{\partial f}{\partial q}\frac{\partial q}{\partial y} = -4\ .1 = -4$$

$\frac{\partial f}{\partial q}$ is the upstream gradient and $\frac{\partial q}{\partial y}$ is the local gradient.

$$\frac{\partial f}{\partial x} = \frac{\partial f}{\partial q}\frac{\partial q}{\partial x} = -4.1 = -4$$

11.11.1 Upstream and Downstream Gradients

Gradients flow in the two directions in the neural network, i.e. upstream gradients and downstream gradients. In the upstream gradients, gradients flow with respect to the output of the layer, in other words, the direction of gradient flow is from the deeper layer to the previous layers. In case of downstream layer, the gradient flows with respect to the weights and bias parameters of the current layer.

11.11.2 Patterns in Gradient Flow

The gradient flow process can be illustrated intuitively using the gates. The commonly used gates in neural networks to present the gradient flow are addition gate, multiplication gate, copy gate, and maximum gate. These gates simplify the illustration process of backpropagation as the derivative calculations are demonstrated using the gates. The illustrative examples of these gates are shown in Figure 11.19. The description of the commonly used gates is shown in the Table 11.1 below.

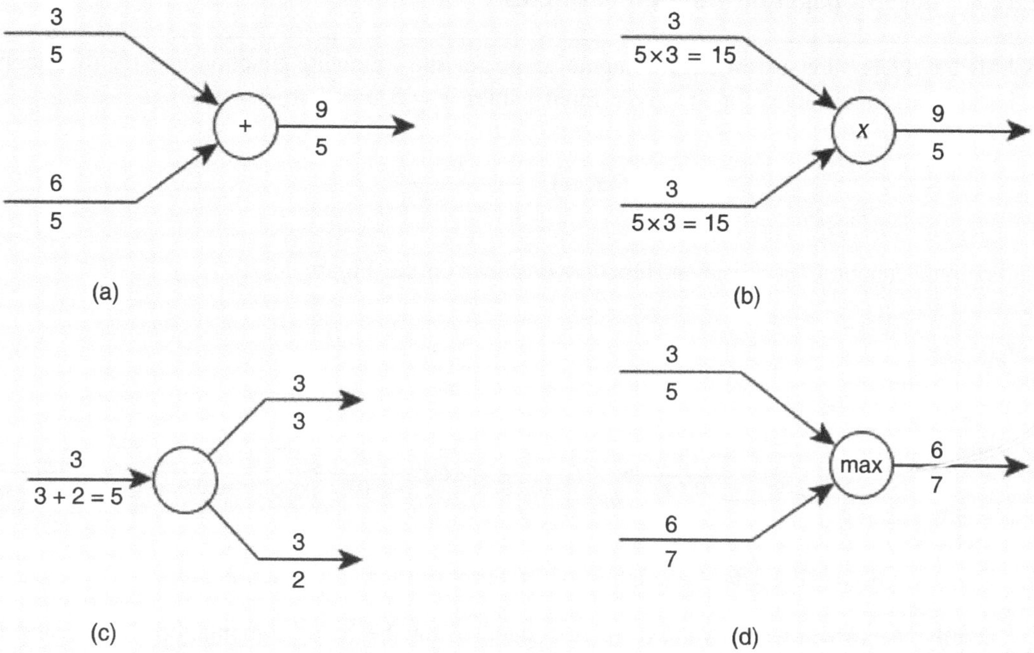

FIGURE 11.19 Illustration of Commonly Used Gates in Backpropagation.

TABLE 11.1 Commonly Used Gates in the Compute Graph

Gate	Description
Addition Gate	Equally distributes the gradient output to all its input.
Multiplication Gate	Multiplies the output gradient with inputs.
Copy Gate	Copies the gradient to the inputs.
Maximum Gate	Distributes the computed gradient to one of its inputs.

11.11.3 Backpropagation with Vectors

The process of backpropagation is not only applicable for the scaler values but also to the vector-based inputs. For the complex neural networks where input parameters (weights and biases) are represented in the vector format, the concept of backpropagation can be extended to deal with the vectored inputs.

The backpropagation in the two or higher layer networks is calculated by computing the gradient descent using chain rule of derivatives. The chain rule of derivatives is calculated using the chain rule. For example, if $y = f_1(x)$ and $x = f_2(z)$ then $\frac{\partial y}{\partial z} = \frac{\partial y}{\partial x}\frac{\partial x}{\partial z}$.

11.11.4 Backpropagation through Examples

EXAMPLE 11.1: Let us create a compute graph for the following function and try to calculate the backpropagation values for the given input values $w = 3$, $x = -1$, $b = +2$.

$$f(x, w) = \frac{1}{1 + e^{-(wx + b)}}$$

The compute function for the given function is shown in the Figure 11.20.

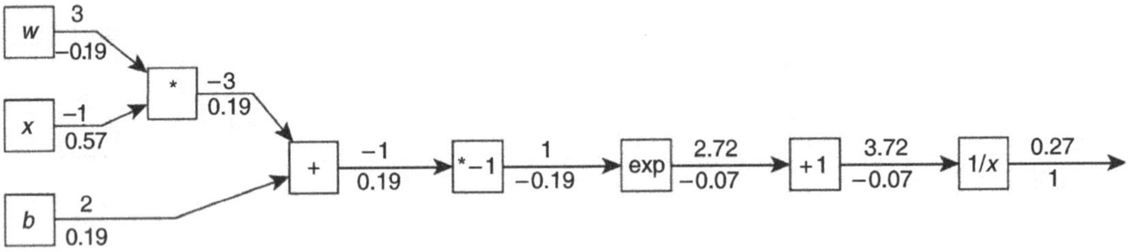

FIGURE 11.20 Calculation of Backpropagation in Compute Graph.

Initially the forward pass values are calculated using the basic computation. Now using the calculations of the derivatives backpropagated values are calculated.

Recall the following formulas for computation of derivatives for the given function:

$$\frac{de^x}{dx} = e^x, \quad \frac{d(ax)}{dx} = a, \quad \frac{d\left(\frac{1}{x}\right)}{dx} = -\frac{1}{x^2}, \text{ and } \frac{d(c + x)}{dx} = 1$$

The backpropagated values are calculated by multiplying the upstream gradient with local gradient. For example, the backpropagated value for the previous stage to the output is calculated as follows: $(1)\left(-\frac{1}{3.72^2}\right) = -0.07$. Since $\frac{d\left(\frac{1}{x}\right)}{dx} = -\frac{1}{x^2}$ is the last operation of the function. The upstream gradient (1) is multiplied with the local gradient $\left(-\frac{1}{3.72^2}\right)$. In this way the values are backpropagated in the neural networks. Then for further backpropagation of the value $\frac{d(c + x)}{dx} = 1$ is used since the previous function is $+1$, so it will give the multiplication of upstream gradient and local gradient as $(-0.07)(1) = -0.07$. Further, in the next step of backpropagation the previous function was e^x, so $\frac{de^x}{dx} = e^x$ will give the same output as e^x. The computed gradient for this stage is $(-0.07)(e^1) = -0.19$. In this way the backpropagation calculates the gradient in the backward pass.

EXAMPLE 11.2: Let us consider a neural network with two layers as shown below:

The inputs and weights in the vector representation are shown below.

$$x = [x_1, x_2]^T$$

$$W^1 = \begin{bmatrix} W_{11}^1 & W_{21}^1 \\ W_{12}^1 & W_{22}^1 \end{bmatrix}$$

$$W^2 = [W_{11}^2, W_{21}^2]$$

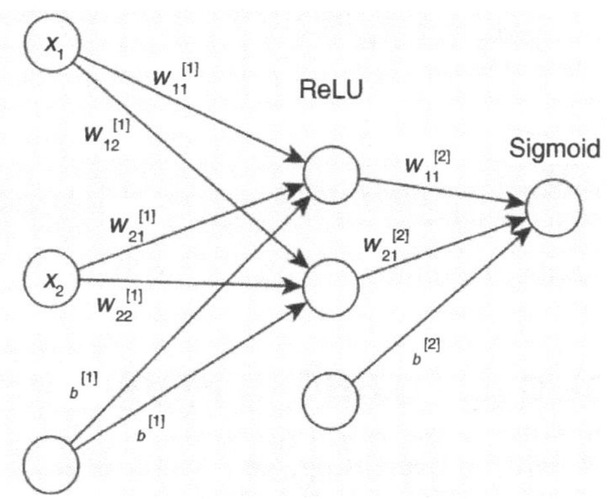

FIGURE 11.21 Compute Graph for Neural Network with Two Layers.

The operations of the neural networks are shown below.

The output at the different layers is shown below:

$$Z^{[1]} = W^{[1]}x + b^{[1]}$$

$$a^{[1]} = ReLU(Z^{[1]})$$

$$Z^{[2]} = W^{[2]}a^{[1]} + b^{[2]}$$

$$a^{[2]} = \sigma(Z^{[2]})$$

$$\hat{y} = a^{[2]}$$

The compute graph for the neural network is shown below.

In order to calculate the backpropagation, the derivatives are required to be calculated. The derivatives for the sigmoid and ReLU functions can be calculated as shown below.

$$\frac{d\sigma(z)}{dz} = \sigma(z)(1-\sigma(z)), \text{ and } \frac{d\,\text{ReLU}(z)}{dz} = \begin{cases} 0 & \text{for } z < 0 \\ 1 & \text{for } z \geq 0 \end{cases}$$

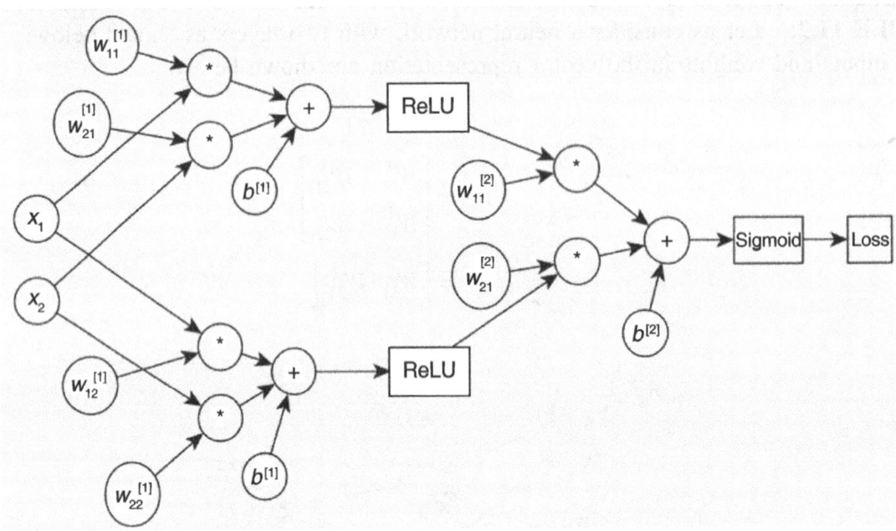

FIGURE 11.22 Detailed Compute Graph for the Two Layer Neural Network.

11.12 PREVENTION OF OVERFITTING IN NEURAL NETWORKS

Sometimes the neural network will be overfitting, i.e., outperforming with highest accuracies (very minimum loss values or error values). There could be several reasons behind the overfitting, but the primary reason is that ANN model accommodates all type of input training data including the noisy data. Such condition of overfitting is never desired by any neural network model. Some of the common strategies to avoid the overfitting of the neural networks are:

(a) **Regularization:** In regularization, some penalties are added to the training process of the network. These penalties are added to the loss functions. L1 and L2 regularization techniques are the popular regularization techniques.

(b) **Data Augmentation:** In training dataset additional data is added randomly (augmented) during the training process, the augmented data eliminates the overfitting of the data.

(c) **Early Stopping:** Stopping training earlier based on model's performance evaluation might help in avoiding overfitting of the network.

(d) **Cross-Validation:** Cross-validation techniques such as 10-fold cross-validation techniques can be utilized for handling overfitting problems of the networks. In cross-validation techniques, the training dataset is divided into the training and testing datasets and validation is performed over the iterations by swapping the training and testing datasets.

(e) **Dropout:** Under the dropout technique, intentionally the output of some of the randomly selected nodes is set to 0 (zero), thus the selected nodes are not participating in the computational process of neural networks which may cause some drop in the performance of the networks, but it helps in handling of the overfitting.

11.13 DEEP LEARNING—WIDE VS. DEEP?

A wide neural network is the neural network with a smaller number of hidden layers but each layer has a large number of nodes. Whereas a deep neural network is the network with larger number of hidden layers, but each layer has lesser number of nodes as compared to the wide neural network. An illustration of wide and deep neural networks is presented in Figure 11.23.

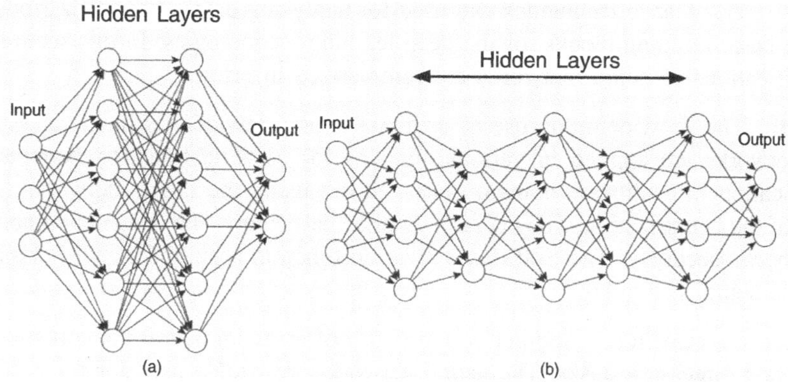

FIGURE 11.23 (a) A Wide vs. (b) A Deep Neural Network.

It is theoretically difficult to decide about which type of neural network is better, a wide neural network (a larger number of nodes in a hidden layer) or a deep neural network (a larger number of hidden layers)?

Although there is no rule of thumb behind the selection of one of these models. Few studies based on their experiences presented some key points on the basis of which some comparison can be made. The summary of these key points is presented in Table 11.2.

If the relationship between the features is simpler then wide networks are preferred whereas for complex relationships where more interactions are required between the features generally the deep networks are preferred. Computationally the wide networks are faster as compared to the deep networks. The probability of overfitting is also less for wide networks as compared to the deep networks. The interpretation of wide networks is easy as compared to the deep networks.

TABLE 11.2 A Comparison of Wide and Deep Neural Networks

Parameter	Wide NN	Deep NN
Speed	Faster	Slower
Problem type	Simple	Complex
Dataset Size	Small	Large
Probability of Overfitting	Low	High
Interpretation	Easy	Difficult

Although a comparison between the wide and deep neural network is presented in this section but the applicability of these models depends on the nature of the problem and type of datasets. As mentioned earlier it is theoretically difficult to decide whether one of the models is suitable and mostly this decision is taken based on the experience of the data scientist, and it is decided experimentally.

11.14 APPLICATIONS OF NEURAL NETWORKS

The artificial neural networks are utilized in a number of tasks. The ANNs are one of the oldest states of the art data science techniques and used for analysing data related to various domain. The ANNs are the basic building blocks for the deep learning technologies. In this section, some of the important applications of neural networks are summarized in brief.

Classification: The most common use of artificial neural networks is in the classification tasks. The neural networks are applied in various domains for classification, for example, the medical image classification in healthcare domain is carried out using the neural networks to improve the performance of the classification. The neural networks, particularly the deep neural networks classify objects with better accuracy. The SoftMax activation function is used for multi-class classification problem in the neural networks.

Regression and Forecasting: Another common use of artificial neural networks is in the domain of regression and forecasting tasks. The neural networks are widely used for forecasting tasks such as, financial data prediction, electricity load and demand forecasting. Activation functions like ReLU (Rectified Linear Unit) is widely used for regression and prediction tasks because the forecasted values are expected at the output layer.

Pattern Recognition: In general, the artificial neural networks are utilized for general pattern recognition tasks. The neural networks are most widely used in numerous tasks such as, process and quality control in different industries. Speech recognition and machine translation tasks are another popular task where neural networks are utilized widely.

EXERCISES

1. Consider a two-layer perceptron network with the following configuration. Calculate the output of each neuron at the hidden and output layer?

Input layer	2 neurons
Output layer	1 neuron with the Sigmoid function
Hidden layer	2 neurons with the Sigmoid activation function
Initial input	[1, 0.7]
Weights	
Input to First Hidden Layer	[0.25, −0.1]
First Hidden Layer to Second Hidden Layer	[0.75, 0.5]
Second Hidden Layer to Output	[0.8, 0.6]
Bias	[0.1, 0.1]

2. Calculate the output of the following activation functions for the given value of (i) $x = 0.1$ (ii) $x = 0.5$, and (iii) $x = 0.95$
   (a) Sigmoid activation function
   (b) ReLU activation function
   (c) Tanh activation function
   (d) Leaky-ReLU activation function with $\alpha = 0.1$
   (e) Swish activation function

3. What is the purpose of SoftMax activation function? For the given input vector x = [3, 4, 5, 8, 10], calculate the SoftMax values?
4. What is the primary difference between the deep vs. wide neural networks? In your opinion how to decide about deep or wide model for a given dataset? Perform a comparative analysis by implementing both of these techniques by varying the number of layers with the same activation functions for a common dataset?
5. Draw the compute graph for the following function:

$$f(w, x) = \frac{1}{1 + e^{-(w_0 x_0 + w_1 x_1 + w_2)}}$$

Assume $w_0 = 1$, $w_1 = -1$, $x_0 = -1$, $x_1 = -1$, $w_1 = -1$ are input nodes. Now perform the forward and backpropagation to compute gradient w.r.t. each input x_i and w_i.

MULTIPLE CHOICE QUESTIONS

1. The smaller weight initialization in the artificial neural network causes which of the following problems?
   (a) Exploding gradient
   (b) Vanishing gradient
   (c) Increases time complexity
   (d) Requires more activation functions
2. The backpropagation process in artificial neural network:
   (a) Optimize and update weights in different layers
   (b) Transforms the inputs
   (c) Minimize the complexity of activation functions
   (d) None of these
3. The main objective of activation function is to:
   (a) The activation function updates the weights of the inputs.
   (b) The activation function transforms the higher dimensional data into the lower dimensional data.
   (c) The activation functions lean the complicated patterns using non-linear functions.
   (d) The activation functions aggregate the input data.
4. The purpose of the perceptron in artificial neural networks is to:
   (a) The perceptron is the basic unit of artificial neural networks for binary classification.
   (b) The perceptron does not generate any output.
   (c) The perceptron takes two inputs at a time.
   (d) All the above statements are true.
5. The Sigmoid function will calculate the value of 0.5 as:
   (a) 0.52 (b) 0.62
   (c) 0.65 (d) 0.71
6. The Tanh activation function will calculate the value of 0.5 as:
   (a) 0.46 (b) 0.49
   (c) 0.56 (d) 0.59
7. The property of ReLU activation function is:
   (a) It gives the output in the range of [0...1]
   (b) It never gives the negative values.
   (c) It gives the output in the range of [–1...1]
   (d) It always gives positive value less than 1.

8. Which function is best suitable for generating output for the multi-class classification task in artificial neural networks?
   (a) Sigmoid (b) Tanh
   (c) SoftMax (d) ReLU
9. The SoftMax activation function will generate the probabilities for the generated outputs [5, 10, 20] as:
   (a) [0, 0.25, 0.75] (b) [0, 0, 1]
   (c) [0.1, 0.30, 0.60] (d) [0.1, 0.35, 0.55]
10. What is the main challenge in designing a neural network?
    (a) Deciding the number of hidden layers.
    (b) Deciding the number of nodes in each hidden layer.
    (c) The type of interconnection required between the hidden layers.
    (d) All of these.
11. What is the primary difference between the kernel functions and neural networks?
    (a) The kernel functions are more powerful than the neural networks.
    (b) The kernel functions are linear whereas the neural networks are non-linear.
    (c) The kernel functions are computationally simpler than the neural networks.
    (d) The kernel methods use fixed basis functions (defined by the kernel) whereas neural networks learn the basis functions adaptively from data.
12. What is the difference between the loss function and cost function in artificial neural networks?
    (a) Both cost function and loss function are same.
    (b) Cost function is dependent on the output, whereas the loss function is dependent on input of the artificial neural network.
    (c) The cost function is suitable for densely connected neural networks whereas the loss function is suitable for the simpler neural networks.
    (d) The cost function is the sum of all the loss function in a given artificial neural network.
13. In artificial neural networks, the cross-entropy loss function is suitable for:
    (a) Binary classification problems.
    (b) Multi-class classification problems.
    (c) Prediction problems.
    (d) None of these.
14. The primary purpose of the compute graph is to:
    (a) The compute graph is used for calculation flow in the neural network.
    (b) The process of backpropagation can be visualized and explained with the help of compute graphs.
    (c) It is used specific operands and operators for different activation functions for better explanations of neural networks.
    (d) All of these.
15. Which of the following is NOT a step in the backpropagation?
    (a) Feature selection (b) Calculate loss function
    (c) Backward pass (d) Weight update
16. Which of the following rule of linear algebra is very important in calculating the backpropagation?
    (a) Quotient rule (b) Chain rule
    (c) Product rule (d) Limit rule
17. What is the purpose of addition gate in the compute graph?
    (a) Equally distributes the gradient output to all its input.
    (b) Multiples the output gradient with inputs.
    (c) Copies the gradient to the inputs.
    (d) Distributes the computed gradient to one of its inputs.

18. What is the purpose of maximum gate in the compute graph?

(a) Equally distributes the gradient output to all its input.
(b) Multiples the output gradient with inputs.
(c) Copies the gradient to the inputs.
(d) Distributes the computed gradient to one of its inputs.

19. Which of the following techniques is NOT suitable for overfitting of the neural networks?

(a) Regularization (b) Backpropagation
(c) Early stopping (d) Cross-validation

20. Which makes an artificial neural network a deep neural network?

(a) Complex activation functions
(b) Weight initialization with higher values
(c) Higher number of outputs
(d) More number of hidden layers

REFERENCES

[1] https://faculty.cc.gatech.edu/~jarulraj/courses/8803-f19/slides/04-neural-networks.pdf
[2] http://www.cs.umd.edu/class/fall2018/cmsc470/slides/slides_8.pdf
[3] https://www.cs.cmu.edu/~aarti/Class/10315_Spring22/315S22_Rec6.pdf
[4] https://cs231n.github.io/optimization-2/
[5] https://cs.gmu.edu/~kosecka/cs747/06_backprop.pdf

ANSWER KEY

1. (b)	**2.** (a)	**3.** (c)	**4.** (a)	**5.** (b)	**6.** (a)	**7.** (b)	**8.** (c)	**9.** (b)	**10.** (d)
11. (d)	**12.** (d)	**13.** (b)	**14.** (d)	**15.** (a)	**16.** (b)	**17.** (a)	**18.** (d)	**19.** (b)	**20.** (d)

12 Clustering Models

Introduction

So far, we have seen supervised models where the labels were present in the training data and the labels for output data were predicted by the model. Many times, we have data but we don't have any labels. What can we do to understand that data? In this chapter, we will learn to organize unlabeled data into groups or clusters. These clusters could be well separated (without overlaps) or overlapping. They could have regular shape or be irregular. Clustering analysis will also help us detect anomalies and outliers in the data as they will be isolated and won't fall into groups.

Clustering is a process of organizing the dataset into groups based on ***similarity***. The similarity function gives the similarity in the range of [0…1], where 0 (minimum value) indicates that objects are most dissimilar and value 1 (maximum) indicates that objects are identical (exactly similar). If distance functions are used then minimum distance indicates the maximum similarity and maximum distance indicates the minimum similarity.

The machine learning techniques are broadly categorized into the three types namely, supervised techniques, unsupervised techniques and semi-supervised techniques. Clustering is a type of unsupervised machine learning technique as labels are not required for the training data to identifying clusters. Classification in contrast belongs to the supervised machine learning technique as it requires a labelled training dataset. The semi-supervised techniques are applied in the cases where combination of label and unlabelled data is available. Training is performed using the available labelled data and the trained model can be used to generate.

The clustering process is illustrated in Figure 12.1, where it is shown that similar types of objects are grouped together. In real-world scenario there are a few objects which do not fall under any clusters (in other words, they are not similar to the other objects) are also identified during the clustering procedure and these objects are called as **outliers**. Outlier detection also has important significance in data science and has a plenty of real-world applications.

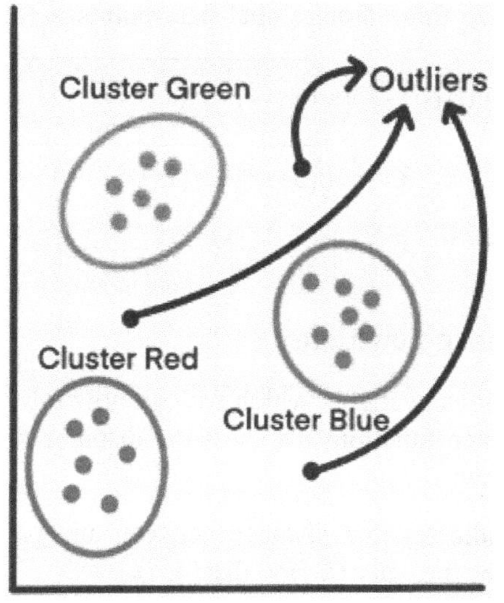

FIGURE 12.1 Clustering Illustration.

Clustering can be seen as an optimization problem where the objective is to find the clusters with maximum intra-cluster similarity (within the cluster similarity) and minimum inter-cluster similarity (in between a pair of cluster similarity).

12.1 DISTANCE AND SIMILARITY MEASURES

During clustering, groups of similar objects are created. In order to perform clustering distance (or similarity) functions are required to measure the distance (or similarity) between any pair of objects. The pair of objects are said to be similar, if distance between the pair is smaller or in other words similarity is higher. The most commonly used distance and similarity functions are described here with the help of suitable examples. Suppose X_1 and X_2 are two N dimensional data points, i.e., $X_1(X_{11}, X_{12},..., X_{1N})$ and $X_2(X_{21}, X_{22},..., X_{2N})$.

12.1.1 Distance Functions

For the numerical data the most common distance functions are Euclidean distance, Minkowski distance and Manhattan (or city-block) distance functions which are given in Eq. (12.1) to Eq. (12.3). In Minkowski distance function, parameter q is called as order of the distance. When order is one it will be Manhattan distance and when order is two it is called the Euclidean distance function.

$$\text{Euclidean}\left(X_1, X_2\right) = \sqrt{\left(X_{11} - X_{21}\right)^2 + \left(X_{12} - X_{22}\right)^2 + \ldots + \left(X_{1N} - X_{2N}\right)^2} \tag{12.1}$$

$$\text{Minkowski}\left(X_1, X_2\right) = \sqrt[q]{\left(X_{11} - X_{21}\right)^q + \left(X_{12} - X_{22}\right)^q + \ldots + \left(X_{1N} - X_{2N}\right)^q} \tag{12.2}$$

$$\text{Manhattan}\left(X_1, X_2\right) = \left|X_{11} - X_{21}\right| + \left|X_{12} - X_{22}\right| + \ldots + \left|X_{1N} - X_{2N}\right| \tag{12.3}$$

Let us assume that we have two three-dimensional data points $X_1(3, 2, 1)$ and $X_2(3, 5, 5)$ then

$$\text{Euclidean}\left(X_1, X_2\right) = \sqrt{(3-3)^2 + (2-5)^2 + (1-5)^2} = 5$$

$$\text{Minkowski}\left(X_1, X_2\right) = \sqrt[3]{(3-3)^3 + (2-5)^3 + (1-5)^3} \cong 4.49$$

$$\text{Manhattan}\left(X_1, X_2\right) = |3-3| + |2-5| + |1-5| = 7$$

12.1.2 Properties of Distance Functions

There are many distance functions available which we can utilize for the purpose of clustering, and we can develop our own distance functions also. All the distance functions should satisfy some of the basic properties given below:

Symmetry: This property indicates that distance between any pair of objects i and j should be equal irrespective of their order, i.e., dist(i, j) = dist(j, i).

Triangle inequality: Triangular property indicates that distance between i and j should be always lesser than or equal to sum of distances between i and k and distance between k and j, where k is some intermediate point between i and j. Mathematically, dist$(i, j) \leq$ dist(i, k) + dist(k, j).

Non negativity: The distance between any pair of objects should never be negative, i.e., dist$(i, j) \geq 0$.

Identity of indiscernibility: The distance between an object with itself should always be 0, i.e., dist$(i, i) = 0$.

12.1.3 Similarity Measures

Often, distance functions are used for numerical data, where minimum distance indicates that the pair of objects are similar. Apart from the distance functions, similarity techniques are also available. Some of the popular similarity techniques are described here using suitable illustrative examples. The similarity function calculates the similarity between the pair of objects and return a number in the range of [0…1] where 0 indicates that objects are dissimilar and 1 indicates that objects are identical.

Let us assume that X_1 and X_2 are two N dimensional data points, i.e., $X_1(X_{11}, X_{12},\ldots, X_{1N})$ and $X_2(X_{21}, X_{22},\ldots, X_{2N})$ then the three popular similarity functions namely Jaccard, Dice and Cosine are expressed in Eq. (12.4) to Eq. (12.6)

$$\text{Jaccard}\left(X_1, X_2\right) = \frac{|X_1 \cap X_2|}{|X_1 \cup X_2|} \tag{12.4}$$

$$\text{Dice}\left(X_1, X_2\right) = 2 \times \frac{|X_1 \cap X_2|}{|X_1| \times |X_2|} \tag{12.5}$$

$$\text{Cosine}\left(X_1, X_2\right) = \frac{X_{11} \times X_{21} + X_{12} \times X_{22} + \ldots + X_{1N} \times X_{2N}}{\sqrt{(X_{11})^2 + (X_{12})^2 + \ldots + (X_{1N})^2} \times \sqrt{(X_{21})^2 + (X_{22})^2 + \ldots + (X_{2N})^2}} \tag{12.6}$$

Let us assume that we have two three-dimensional data points $X_1(3, 2, 1)$ and $X_2(3, 5, 5)$ then

$$\text{Jaccard}(X_1, X_2) = \frac{|X_1 \cap X_2|}{|X_1 \cup X_2|} = \frac{|(3,2,1) \cap (3,5,5)|}{|(3,2,1) \cup (3,5,5)|} = \frac{|(3)|}{|(1,2,3,5)|} = \frac{1}{4} = 0.25$$

$$\text{Dice}(X_1, X_2) = 2 \times \frac{|X_1 \cap X_2|}{|X_1| \times |X_2|} = 2 \times \frac{|(3,2,1) \cap (3,5,5)|}{|(3,2,1)| \times |(3,5,5)|} = 2 \times \frac{|(3)|}{3 \times 3} = 2 \times \frac{1}{9} \cong 0.22$$

$$\text{Cosine}(X_1, X_2) = \frac{3 \times 3 + 2 \times 5 + 1 \times 5}{\sqrt{(3)^2 + (2)^2 + (1)^2} \times \sqrt{(3)^2 + (5)^2 + (5)^2}} = \frac{24}{\sqrt{14} \times \sqrt{59}} \cong 0.84$$

Distance for non-numerical data

For binary data, the similarity and distances are measured using the contingency table for the pair of objects having binary data as shown in Table 12.1. The binary data can have the two possible states (Yes or No) (1 or 0). So, combinations of 0's and 1's are first tabulated in the contingency table and then using similarity and distance functions, similarity or dissimilarity is measured for binary data.

TABLE 12.1 Contingency Table for Binary Data

Sim (X_1, X_2)		X_2: 1	X_2: 0
X_1	1	Y_{11}	Y_{10}
	0	Y_{01}	Y_{00}

$$\text{Jaccard}(X_1, X_2) = \frac{Y_{11}}{Y_{11} + Y_{10} + Y_{01}} \tag{12.7}$$

$$\text{Dice}(X_1, X_2) = \frac{2 \times Y_{11}}{2 \times Y_{11} + Y_{10} + Y_{01}} \tag{12.8}$$

Distance between X_1 and X_2 for symmetric data

$$\text{dist}(X_1, X_2) = \frac{Y_{10} + Y_{01}}{Y_{11} + Y_{10} + Y_{01} + Y_{00}} \tag{12.9}$$

Asymmetric data

$$\text{dist}(X_1, X_2) = \frac{Y_{10} + Y_{01}}{Y_{11} + Y_{10} + Y_{01}} \tag{12.10}$$

Example: Let us assume that there are two binary variable $X_1(1,0,0,0,1,0,0,0,1,1)$ and $X_2(0,0,0,1,1,0,0,0,1,0)$ then their corresponding contingency table is shown in Table 12.2.

TABLE 12.2 Contingency Table for Example Binary Data

Sim (X_1, X_2)		X_2: 1	X_2: 0
X_1	1	2	2
	0	1	5

$$\text{Jaccard}\left(X_1, X_2\right) = \frac{2}{2+2+1} = 0.4$$

$$\text{Dice}\left(X_1, X_2\right) = \frac{2 \times 2}{2 \times 2 + 2 + 1} = \frac{4}{7} \cong 0.57$$

Distance between X_1 and X_2 for symmetric data

$$\text{dist}\left(X_1, X_2\right) = \frac{2+1}{2+2+1+5} = 0.3$$

Asymmetric data

$$\text{dist}\left(X_1, X_2\right) = \frac{2+1}{2+2+1} = 0.6$$

Nominal or Categorical data

For nominal or categorical data where variables can have values from a possible set of values the similarity is measured using Eq. (12.11).

$$\text{dist}\left(X_1, X_2\right) = \frac{\text{\#Categorical Attributes} - \text{\#Matchings}}{\text{\#Categorical Attributes}} \tag{12.11}$$

Where #Categorical Attributes is the total number of attributes of the categorical or nominal type and #Matchings indicates matching values of the variables.

Example: Suppose two data points belong to one nominal (categorical) data type having the set of possible values as ["Home Loan", "Car Loan", "Personal Loan"]. Let X_1 ("Home Loan") and X_2 ("Car Loan"), then,

$$\text{dist}\left(X_1, X_2\right) = \frac{1-0}{1} = 1$$

And let if X_1 ("Home Loan") and X_2 ("Home Loan"), then,

$$\text{dist}\left(X_1, X_2\right) = \frac{1-1}{1} = 0$$

Another complex example of it is, let us assume that there are two nominal attributes as given below in Table 12.3. There are two nominal attributes namely Loan Type ["Home Loan", "Car Loan"] and Customer Rating ["Good", "Average"].

TABLE 12.3 Example dataset for the nominal or categorical attributes

Data	Loan Type	Customer Rating
P_1	Home Loan	Good
P_2	Car Loan	Average
P_3	Home Loan	Good
P_4	Home Loan	Average

Then,

$$\text{dist}(P_1, P_3) = \frac{2-2}{2} = 0$$

$$\text{dist}(P_1, P_4) = \frac{2-1}{2} = 0.5$$

12.2 CLUSTERING ALGORITHMS

Clustering algorithms are broadly categorized into three major categories namely, partitioning based, hierarchical, density-based clustering algorithms. Any algorithm which is not falling under these three algorithms is termed as mathematical model-based clustering algorithm. All these categories along with popular algorithms in it are discussed here in brief. The problem of clustering can also be seen as the optimization problem where we have to optimize two primary constraints. The first constraint is to achieve maximum intra-cluster similarity (or minimize intra-cluster distance) and the second constraint is to minimize inter-cluster similarity (or maximize inter-cluster distance).

12.2.1 Partitioning-based Algorithms

Partitioning-based clustering techniques are the simplest algorithms for clustering in which data is partitioned into different partitions and then using some logic these partitions are optimized in order to convert them into the clusters. Partitioning based clusters starts with the parameter called as initial number of partitions, denoted by the symbol *K*. Therefore, all the partitioning-based algorithms start with the prefix symbol *K* for example *K*-Means clustering algorithm, here *K* indicates the number of partitions or more technically number of clusters (as these partitions are going to become clusters).

K-Means clustering algorithm

K-Means clustering algorithm is a very popular and simple partitioning-based clustering algorithm. The working of *K*-Means cluster algorithm is given below. "*K*" indicates the number of clusters and "**Means**" indicates that using mean (or average) the cluster centers are calculated.

_K_-Means Clustering Algorithm Working

Step-1: Randomly select *K* data points as initial cluster centers.
Step-2: Calculate the distance of all the data points from the *K* initial centers.
Step-3: Identify the minimum distance for all the data points and assign the cluster label to all the data points.
Step-4: Update the clusters with the updated cluster labels.
Step-5: Calculate the mean value of all the clusters. It works as the updated cluster centers.
Step-6: Replace the cluster centers with the updated values.
Step-7: Repeat steps 2 to 6, till the cluster centers are updated. If there is no change in the cluster centers (or in other words cluster labels) then stop.

Example of *K*-Means clustering algorithm

Let us assume that there is a two-dimensional data with 9 two-dimensional data points $D((1, 4), (1, 5), (2, 6), (3, 5), (8, 2), (8, 3), (9, 1), (9, 2), (9, 3))$. Suppose we have to create two clusters

(K = 2) for the dataset D using Euclidean distance function. The data distribution for the sample dataset is shown in Figure 12.2.

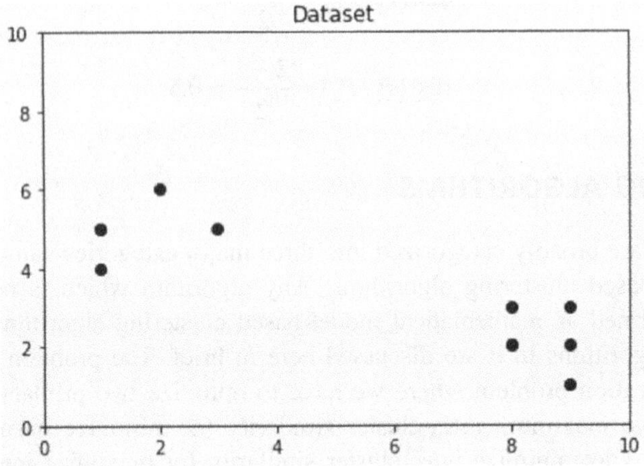

FIGURE 12.2 Data distribution for the sample dataset.

In the first step of K-Means clustering algorithm randomly we can select two data points as the cluster centers as we have to create two clusters. Suppose we have selected the two data points (2, 6) and (8, 3) as cluster centers. Now, in the second step we have to calculate the distance of all the data points from these cluster centers as shown in Table 12.4. Euclidean distance function is used for calculating distance. After calculating the distances, in step 3 we have to identify minimum distances from the centers and assign the cluster labels (minimum distance indicates the belongingness of data point to that particular cluster). The minimum distance is highlighted in blue color in Table 12.4 and cluster label is assigned in the last column of the table. This cluster labelling provides us the initial clusters as mentioned in step-4. The initial clusters are C_1((1, 4), (1, 5), (2, 6), (3, 5)) and C_2((8, 2), (8, 3), (9, 1), (9, 2), (9, 3)). The first cluster consists of 4 data points whereas the second cluster is consisting of 5 data points.

TABLE 12.4 Distance of Data Points from the Cluster Centers for the Sample Dataset

Data Point	Cluster Center–I (2,6)	Cluster Center–II (8,3)	Cluster Label
P_1(1, 4)	$\sqrt{5}$	$\sqrt{50}$	I
P_2(1, 5)	$\sqrt{2}$	$\sqrt{53}$	I
P_3(2, 6)	0	$\sqrt{45}$	I
P_4(3, 5)	$\sqrt{2}$	$\sqrt{29}$	I
P_5(8, 2)	$\sqrt{52}$	1	II
P_6(8, 3)	$\sqrt{45}$	0	II
P_7(9, 1)	$\sqrt{74}$	$\sqrt{5}$	II
P_8(9, 2)	$\sqrt{65}$	$\sqrt{2}$	II
P_9(9, 3)	$\sqrt{58}$	1	II

In step-5, we need to update the cluster centers by calculating the cluster means. The means of the clusters are calculated as shown below.

$$C_1 = \left(\frac{1+1+2+3}{4}, \frac{4+5+6+5}{4}\right) = (1.75, 5)$$

$$C_2 = \left(\frac{8+8+9+9+9}{5}, \frac{2+3+1+2+3}{5}\right) = (8.6, 2.2)$$

The calculated cluster centers are $C_1(1.75, 5)$ and $C_2(8.6, 2.2)$. This concludes the first iteration of *K*-Means clustering algorithm. Now we have to update the centers and calculate the distance again for the next iteration. The distance calculation for second iteration is shown in Table 12.5.

TABLE 12.5 Distance of Data Points from the Updated Cluster Centers

Data Point	Cluster Center–I (1.75, 5)	Cluster Center–II (8.6, 2.2)	Cluster Label
$P_1(1, 4)$	1.25	7.81	I
$P_2(1, 5)$	0.75	8.1	I
$P_3(2, 6)$	1.03	7.62	I
$P_4(3, 5)$	1.25	6.26	I
$P_5(8, 2)$	6.93	0.63	II
$P_6(8, 3)$	6.56	1	II
$P_7(9, 1)$	8.28	1.26	II
$P_8(9, 2)$	7.85	0.45	II
$P_9(9, 3)$	7.52	0.89	II

$$C_1 = \left(\frac{1+1+2+3}{4}, \frac{4+5+6+5}{4}\right) = (1.75, 5)$$

$$C_2 = \left(\frac{8+8+9+9+9}{5}, \frac{2+3+1+2+3}{5}\right) = (8.6, 2.2)$$

The final clusters are shown graphically in Figure 12.3.

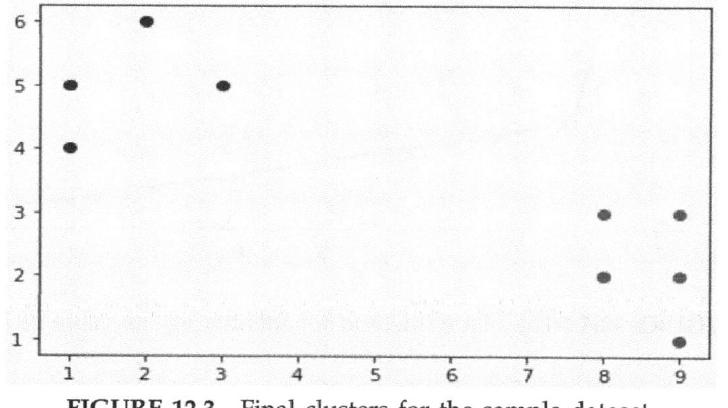

FIGURE 12.3 Final clusters for the sample dataset.

Pros and cons of *K*-Means clustering algorithm

The primary benefit of *K*-Means clustering algorithm is simple computation, as only distance calculation and mean calculation for centers is required. There are two main disadvantages of *K*-Means clustering algorithms. The first disadvantage is guessing the suitable value of *K* (number of clusters) is a tedious job and selecting inappropriate *K* can lead to bad clustering of data. And the second disadvantage is outlier detection is not possible in *K*-Means clustering algorithm. Let us assume that there is a far located data point, still it will belong to one of the clusters where the distance from the center is minimum.

There are various variations on *K*-Means clustering algorithms available in the literature. Apart from the *K*-Means algorithm, other popular partitioning-based clustering algorithms are *K*-Medians and *K*-Medoids clustering techniques. The only difference between *K*-Means and other algorithms is, in case of *K*-Medians clustering algorithm, centers are calculated using the medians (middle values) instead of mean (average) values. And in case of *K*-medoid algorithm, an actual point of cluster (most centrally located) is selected as the cluster centers instead of mean or median values of the data points in a cluster. Just like *K*-Means clustering algorithm, *K*-Medians, *K*-Medoids and other variants of partitioning-based algorithms have the same pros and cons.

Elbow method

Guessing *K* is a tedious job in partitioning-based clustering technique. It typically depends upon the choice of decision makers and application domain. However, there are a few supporting techniques which help in guessing the tentative number of clusters for partitioning-based cluster algorithms. The Elbow method is one such technique. In Elbow technique a two-dimensional graph is created, where clustering evaluation parameter is shown on Y-axis and number of clusters (*K*) is represented in the X-axis. The example illustration of working of Elbow technique is shown in Figure 12.4, here Distortion is taken as clustering performance parameter and is shown in Y-axis. Various clustering performance parameters are covered in the later section of this chapter. For good clustering distortion should be minimized. From the graph we can observe that suitable choice for *K* can be 3, 4 or 5.

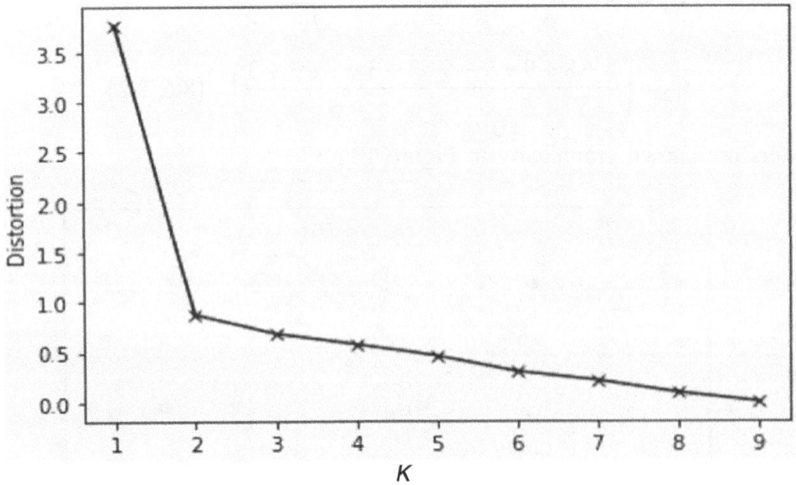

FIGURE 12.4 The Elbow Method for Identifying the value of *K*.

12.3.2 Hierarchical Clustering Algorithms

Hierarchical is another major category of the clustering techniques. It is equally popular as partitioning-based and density-based clustering techniques for clustering. The outcome of a hierarchical clustering algorithm is a special graph, namely, Dendrogram. A Dendrogram graphically represents merging of data items in a particular similarity threshold and thus represents clusters (groups of similar data items) in a particular similarity threshold set by the user. Dendrograms can be generated depending upon the kind of analysis selected in hierarchical clustering. Three major analyses in hierarchical clustering are single-link analysis, average-link analysis, and complete-link analysis.

The first step in applying hierarchical clustering is generating the distance matrix from the data. After generation of distance matrix, Dendrogram is generated using an appropriate analysis technique. Hierarchical clustering algorithm uses the concept of merging of data points. From the initial distance matrix, minimum distances are selected for merging of data points. These merged data points act as the initial clusters. After merging of the data points distance matrix is again re-computed. While calculating the distance between the merged data points (initial clustering) with the data points a suitable analysis technique such as single-link, average-link, complete-link, centroid or ward analysis method is used. This procedure is repeated till all the data points are merged as a single data point.

Working of hierarchical clustering algorithm

Step-1: Compute distance matrix.
Step-2: Select the minimum value from the distance matrix and merge the data points.
Step-3: Re-compute the distance matrix by calculating the distances between merged data points with the rest of the data points. While calculating the distance from the merged data points (initial clusters) uses one of the analysis techniques like single-link, average-link, complete-link, centroid or ward method.
Step-4: Repeat step-2 and step-3 till all the data points are merged as a single data point.
Step-5: Create Dendrogram using the data point merging information.

Single-link analysis

Single-link analysis selects the minimum distance from the all the distances of all the pairs of objects between the clusters. It selects the minimum connectivity between the two clusters. The single-link analysis distance between the two clusters C_i and C_j is calculated using Eq. (12.12).

$$D(C_i, C_j) = \min_{x_1 \in c_i, x_2 \in c_j} D(x_1, x_2) \tag{12.12}$$

Average link analysis

Average-link analysis selects the average distance from the all the distances of all the pairs of objects between the clusters. It selects the average connectivity between the two clusters. The average-link analysis distance between the two clusters C_i and C_j is calculated using Eq. (12.13). $|C_K|$ indicates the number of data points in a particular cluster C_K.

$$D(C_i, C_j) = \frac{1}{|C_i|}\frac{1}{|C_j|}\sum_{x_1 \in c_i}\sum_{x_2 \in c_j} D(x_1, x_2) \tag{12.13}$$

Complete link analysis

Complete-link analysis selects the maximum distance from the all the distances of all the pair of objects between the clusters. It selects the maximum connectivity between the two clusters. The complete-link analysis distance between the two clusters C_i and C_j is calculated using Eq. (12.14).

$$D(C_i, C_j) = \max_{x_1 \in c_i, x_2 \in c_j} D(x_1, x_2) \tag{12.14}$$

Centroid method

The centroid method computes the distance between the centers of the clusters. The centroid method computes the distance between the two clusters C_i and C_j using the Eq. (12.15).

$$D(C_i, C_j) = D\left(\left(\frac{1}{|C_1|}\sum_{x_1 \in c_i} \overrightarrow{x_1}\right), \left(\frac{1}{|C_2|}\sum_{x_2 \in c_j} \overrightarrow{x_2}\right)\right) \tag{12.15}$$

Ward method

The ward method computes the sum of all the distances between all the objects (data points) with the center of the combinedly joined together clusters. The ward method computes the distance between the two clusters C_i and C_j using the Eq. (12.16).

$$D_{C_1 \cup C_2} = \sum_{x \in C_1 \cup C_2} D\left(x, \mu_{C_1 \cup C_2}\right)^2 \tag{12.16}$$

Example: Let us assume that we have to create clusters on the given one-dimensional dataset $D = \{1, 2, 3, 7, 8, 9, 21, 23, 25\}$ using single-link analysis of hierarchical clustering algorithm. The data distribution is presented in Figure 12.5.

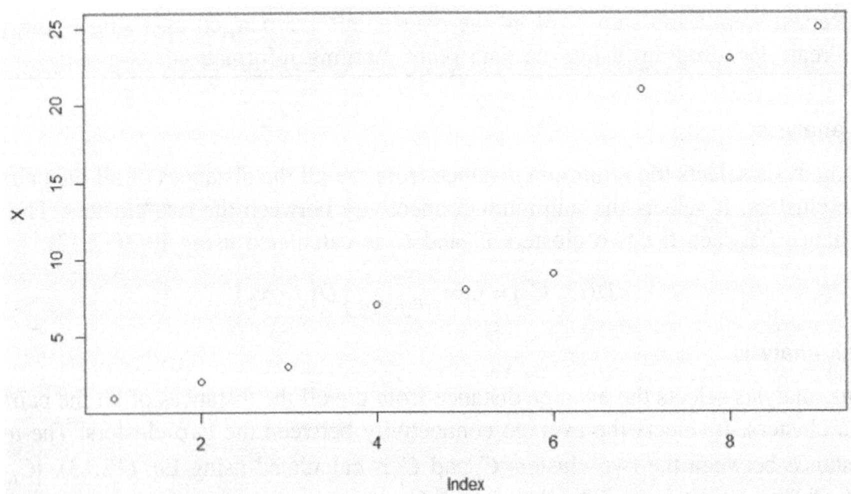

FIGURE 12.5 Data distribution of one-dimensional sample data for hierarchical clustering.

The first step in hierarchical clustering is to create the distance matrix. The distance matrix represents the distances between the ith and j^{th} object at the (i, j) cell of the distance matrix. The distance matrix representation is shown in Eq. (12.17). The distance functions follow the property of symmetricity and Identity of indiscernibility. So, all the diagonal elements in the distance matrix are 0 and value at cell (i, j) is equal to the value at cell (j, i).

$$D=\begin{bmatrix} d_{11} & d_{12} & \cdots & d_{1N} \\ d_{21} & d_{22} & & d_{2N} \\ \vdots & & \ddots & \vdots \\ d_{N1} & d_{N2} & \cdots & d_{NN} \end{bmatrix}=\begin{bmatrix} 0 & - & \cdots & - \\ d_{21} & 0 & & - \\ \vdots & & \ddots & \vdots \\ d_{N1} & d_{N2} & \cdots & 0 \end{bmatrix} \tag{12.17}$$

For the example dataset, data is one-dimensional so using Euclidean distance, the distance matrix is calculated and shown below. The minimum distance is highlighted in the distance matrix.

Data	1	2	3	7	8	9	21	23	25
1	0								
2	1	0							
3	2	1	0						
7	6	5	4	0					
8	7	6	5	1	0				
9	8	7	6	2	1	0			
21	20	19	18	14	13	12	0		
23	22	21	20	16	15	14	2	0	
25	24	23	22	18	17	16	4	2	0

The minimum value in the distance matrix is 1 and the same is highlighted at four places. It indicates that these points will be selected for merging of data points. The merging of data {1, 2} and {2, 3} will take place initially. At the same time merging of {7, 8} and {8, 9} will also take place since the distance is again 1 (minimum at the distance matrix). So, after the initial merging we will get the data points as {{1,2,3}, {7,8,9}, 21, 23, 25}. Now in step-3, distance matrix re-computation is required for merged data points with the other data points. The updated distance matrix is shown below. For updating the distance matrix, single-link analysis is used. The example of single-link distance calculation using Eq. (12.11) is given below.

$$\begin{aligned} D(\{1,2,3\},\{7,8,9\}) &= \min\{D(1,7),D(1,8),D(1,9),D(2,7),D(2,8),D(2,9),D(3,7),D(3,8),D(3,9)\} \\ &= \min\{6,7,8,5,6,7,4,5,6\} = 4 \end{aligned}$$

Another example,

$$D(21, \{1, 2, 3\}) = \min\{D(21,1), D(21,2), D(21,3)\} = \min\{20, 19, 18\} = 18$$

In this way we can update the distance matrix and identify the minimum value in the updated distance matrix.

Data	{1, 2, 3}	{7, 8, 9}	21	23	25
{1, 2, 3}	0				
{7, 8, 9}	4	0			
21	18	12	0		
23	20	14	2	0	
25	22	16	4	2	0

The minimum value is highlighted in blue color. The minimum distance (2) appears between the objects {21, 23} and {23, 25}. So, merging of data point {21, 23, 25} will take place in the second iteration. Again, the same steps are repeated, and distance matrix is updated. The updated matrix is given below.

Data	{1, 2, 3}	{7, 8, 9}	{21, 23, 25}
{1, 2, 3}	0		
{7, 8, 9}	4	0	
{21, 23, 25}	18	12	0

Further, the distance matrix is updated again, and we will get,

Data	{1, 2, 3, 7, 8, 9}	{21, 23, 25}
{1, 2, 3, 7, 8, 9}	0	
{21, 23, 25}	12	0

After all the iterations, the last step in hierarchical clustering algorithm is to create the dendrogram. The dendrogram for the example dataset is shown in Figure 12.6. Dendrogram represents

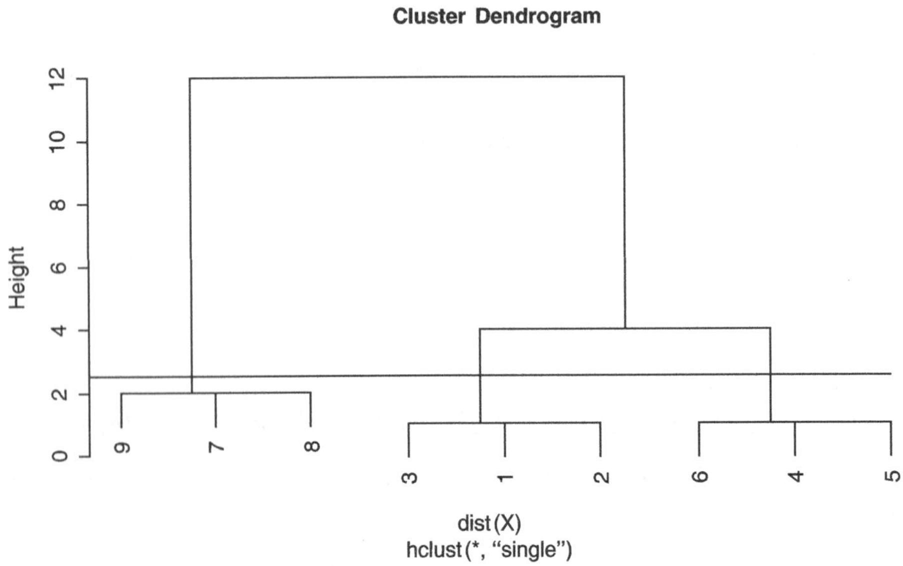

FIGURE 12.6 Dendrogram using single-link analysis for the sample dataset.

the merging of the data points at the distance levels at which merging is taking place. For example, in our example dataset, the first merging was performed for data points {1, 2, 3} and {7, 8, 9} with the minimum distance value of 1. In the vertical axis (height axis) of the dendrogram we can see that at height 1, merging of these data points is represented. So merging is represented till all the data points are merged at a single point. The last merging is done at height 12. For clustering (identification of clusters), a suitable height level is decided by the user and then below the height, all the merging indicates the clusters created by the hierarchical clustering algorithm. For example, if height is selected as 2.5 in our example dendrogram then we can see three merging of data points, which are representing three clusters {1, 2, 3}, {7, 8, 9} and {21, 23, 25}. The dendrogram is created using the *R* programming language which represented the data as indexed value for example index 1 data is 1, and index 9 data is 25. The horizontal line indicates the cutoff of height for cluster identification. If we can apply the word method instead of single-link analysis then we may get the dendrogram represented in Figure 12.7.

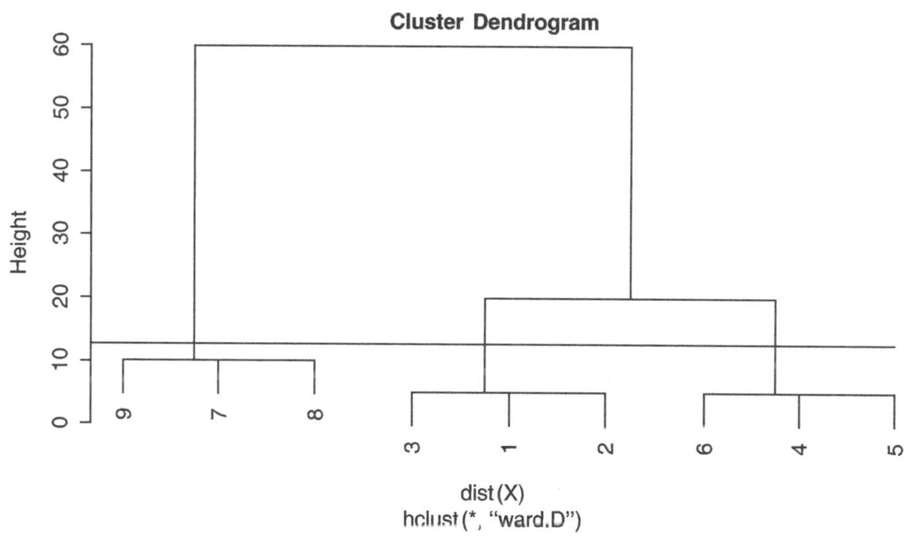

FIGURE 12.7 Dendrogram using ward method for the sample dataset.

Pros and cons of hierarchical clustering method

The advantage is hierarchical clustering is its simple calculations, as only distance matrix calculation is performed in each iteration. Another advantage is the clusters are visualized graphically as a Dendrogram, so it gives a real-world scenario of applying clustering and getting the groups of similar objects. The disadvantage of hierarchical clustering is same as *K*-Means that detection of outliers is a tedious job, however while selecting the height cutoff level of clustering one can visualize that outliers are merged at a very high level of height. Apart from this, selection of merging distance calculation technique (single-link analysis, etc.) is the choice of the user, which can lead to bad clustering sometimes.

12.3.3 Density-based Clustering Algorithms

The density-based cluster algorithms work on the basis of concepts of dense regions. The population density of data points in the nth dimensional space decides the dense regions of data points. Each dense region represents a cluster. One of the popular density-based clustering algorithms is DBSCAN (Density-Based Spatial Clustering of Applications with Noise) algorithm. The density-based clustering algorithms takes two input parameters $\boldsymbol{\varepsilon}$ and ***MinPts*** for finding out the dense regions. Parameter $\boldsymbol{\varepsilon}$ decides the reachability of a data point (radius of dense region) and ***MinPts*** decides the minimum number of data points for deciding the region as dense, i.e., a collection of data points consisting of a minimum number of ***MinPts*** is technically called a dense region. All the density-based clustering algorithms follow the principle of reachability which consists of two major properties as shown below. The working of density-based clustering is also explained and graphically presented in Figure 12.8.

Principle of Reachability

1. A data point i is reachable to another data point j if and only if the distance between i and j is less than ε.

$$i \xrightarrow{\text{reachable}} j, \text{ if } \left(\text{dist}(i, j) \leq \varepsilon\right)$$

2. If a data point i is reachable to other data point j and the data point j is reachable to data point k then the data point i is also reachable to the data point k.

$$\text{if } \left(i \xrightarrow{\text{reachable}} j\right) \text{ and } \left(j \xrightarrow{\text{reachable}} k\right) \text{ then } \left(i \xrightarrow{\text{reachable}} k\right)$$

Algorithm working

Randomly select the first data points and find all the reachable data points from this selected data point considering the principle of reachability and create a group of data points. If the total number of data points in the group are greater than or equal to *MinPts* then mark this group as a valid cluster. Then randomly select another data point and repeat this process until all the data points are covered. Any group (or single data point) consisting of numbers of data points are less than *MinPts* are marked as outliers.

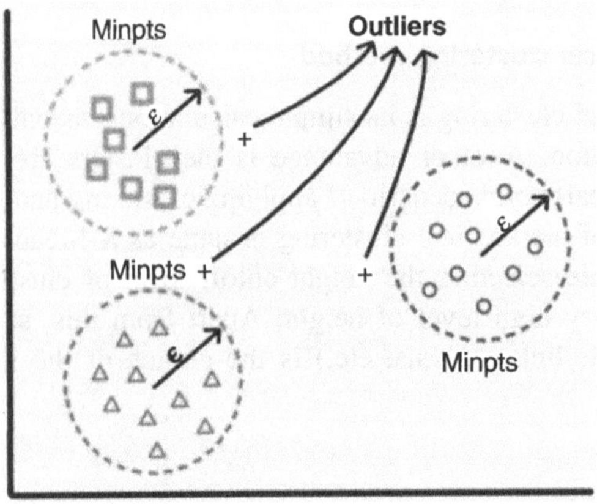

FIGURE 12.8 Working of Density Based Clustering Algorithm.

Example (Density-based clustering algorithm–1D data)

Consider the one-dimensional data point set D with 6 data point $D = \{1, 2, 3, 7, 8, 9\}$ with the input parameters $\varepsilon = 1$ and $MinPts = 3$. Find the final clusters?

For better understanding of the example, let us plot the data points in a plane shown in Figure 12.9. Please note that data points are 1-dimensional but for clear visual representation these points are shown in two-dimensional plane.

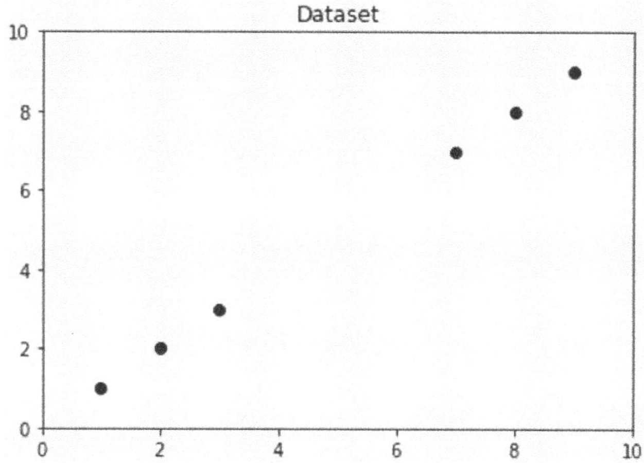

FIGURE 12.9 Data distribution for the sample dataset.

Randomly we can pick the first data point as 1 then we can find reachable data points from 1. Data point 2 is reachable to 1 as the distance between 1 and 2 is $1 (\varepsilon = 1)$. So, we will create a group consisting of $\{1, 2\}$. Now 3 is reachable to 2 as the distance between 2 and 3 is $1 (\varepsilon = 1)$, by principle of reachability 1 is also reachable to 3 (as 1 is reachable to 2 and 2 is reachable to 3). So, the group will consist of $\{1, 2, 3\}$. Now none of the other data point, i.e., 7, 8 or 9 is reachable to any of the data points in the group $\{1, 2, 3\}$ as the distance is more than ε. So, the final group is $\{1, 2, 3\}$ consisting of 3 data points which is greater than or equal to *MinPts* (3) so this group is a valid cluster. Similarly, we can get another valid cluster as $\{7, 8, 9\}$. So finally, there are two valid clusters $\{1, 2, 3\}$ and $\{7, 8, 9\}$, the dense regions are shown in the following Figure 12.10.

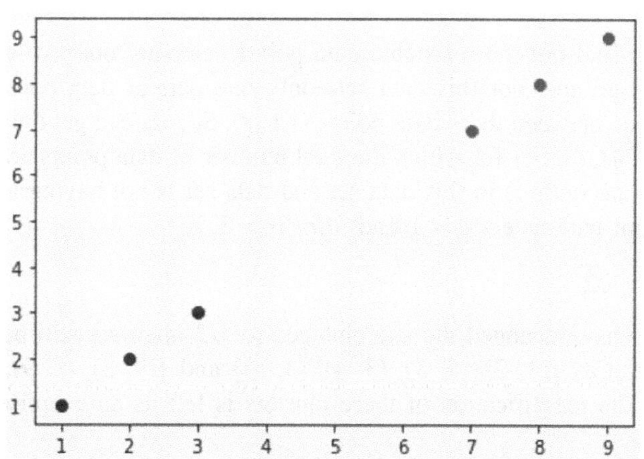

FIGURE 12.10 Clusters generated for the sample dataset.

Example (Density-based clustering algorithm–2D data)

Consider the two-dimensional data point set D with 7 data point $D = \{(1, 2), (2, 3), (3, 4), (3, 5), (7, 8), (8, 9), (9, 10)\}$ with the input parameters $\varepsilon = 1$ and $MinPts = 3$. Find the final clusters?

Now let us see the working of a density-based clustering algorithm for two-dimensional data, let us first draw the data points in a two-dimensional plane as shown in Figure 12.11.

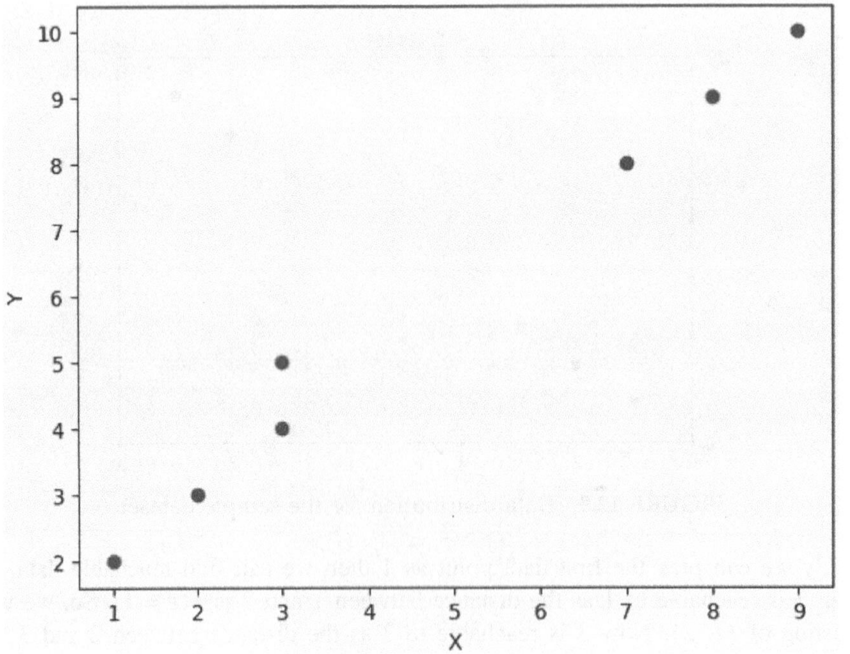

FIGURE 12.11 Visualizing two-dimensional data points of example dataset.

Let's first pick the data point (1, 2) the nearest data point is (2, 3) for which the distance is $\sqrt{2}$, which is more than ε (1). So, the first two data points are not reachable to each other.

$$\text{dist}\{(1,2),(2,3)\} = \sqrt{(1-2)^2 + (2-3)^2} = \sqrt{1+1} = \sqrt{2}$$

In this manner we can find out the reachable data points selecting one two-dimensional data point at a time and creating groups. For this data sets only one pair of data points (3, 4) and (3, 5) is reachable as the distance between these data points is 1 (ε). So, we can get only one group consisting of two data points $\{(3, 4), (3, 5)\}$ for which the total number of data points are less than $MinPts$ (3). So, all the data points are outliers in this data set and data set is not having any valid single cluster in it for the given input parameters $\varepsilon = 1$ and $MinPts = 3$.

When ε is changed to $\sqrt{2}$

Now let us assume we have changed the ε is changed to $\sqrt{2}$ then we will be getting the two valid clusters from the dataset as $\{(1, 2), (2, 3), (3, 4), (3, 5)\}$ and $\{(7, 8), (8, 9), (9, 10)\}$ as shown in the following figure. The identification of these clusters is left as an exercise for the readers.

Pros and cons of density-based clustering algorithm

The advantage of density-based clustering algorithm is outlier detection is quick and simple. Outliers do not belong to any dense regions so it can easily be identified. The drawback of the algorithm is deciding suitable values of ε and *MinPts* is complicated task and wrong selection of these values may lead to bad clustering. However, in order to eliminate this problem, there exist other supporting algorithms such as OPTICS (Ordering Points To Identify Cluster Structure). OPTICS algorithm generates a sequence of reachability distances and produces clusters so that user can be free from deciding the value of ε.

12.3.4 Expectation Maximization Clustering Algorithm

Expectation Maximization (EM) is a probability-based clustering technique. There are two major steps in it, first is expected step and second is maximization step. In expectation step, objects are assigned to the clusters based on their probabilities. In maximization step, cluster centers are readjusted for maximizing with-in cluster similarity, i.e., variation between the objects belonging to same cluster can be minimized. The flow chart of EM clustering algorithm is shown in Figure 12.12.

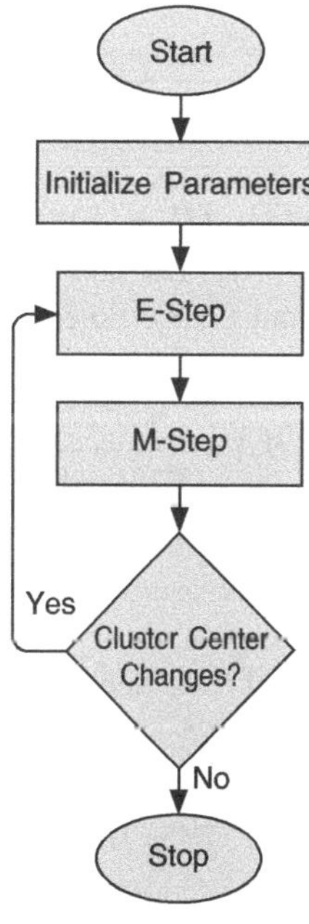

FIGURE 12.12 Working of EM Clustering Algorithm.

Working of EM Clustering Algorithm

The probability density function (Gaussian distribution) is given in Eq. (12.18) and for any n-dimensional data point $x_i(x_{i1}, x_{i2}, ..., x_{in})$ the probability for any given distribution θ is calculated using Eq. (12.19)

$$f(x) = \frac{1}{\sigma\sqrt{2\pi}} e^{-\frac{1}{2}\left(\frac{x-\mu}{\sigma}\right)^2} \quad (12.18)$$

$$P(x_i \mid \theta) = \prod_{k=1}^{n} \frac{1}{\sigma\sqrt{2\pi}} e^{-\frac{1}{2}\left(\frac{x_{ik}-\mu}{\sigma}\right)^2} \tag{12.19}$$

Step 1: Initialize the parameters w_j and σ_j with random values e.g. $w_j = 0.5$

Step 2: For each data point calculate the probability using Eq. (12.20)

$$P(z_i \mid x_i, \theta_j) = \frac{w_j P(x_i \mid \theta_j)}{\sum_{J=1}^{k} P(x_i \mid \theta_j)} \tag{12.20}$$

Step 3: Estimate (Update) the new centers using the Eq. (12.21)

$$\mu_j = \frac{\sum_{i=1}^{n} x_i \times P(x_i, \theta_j)}{\sum_{i=1}^{n} P(x_i, \theta_j)} \tag{12.21}$$

Step 4: repeat step 2 to 4 until the center changes

Working example

Suppose we have to create two clusters ($K = 2$) for the given two-dimensional dataset $X = \{(1, 1), (2, 2), (3, 4), (7, 8), (8, 9), (9, 9)\}$. Let us assume that $\sigma_1 = \sigma_2 = 0.8$ and $w_j = 0.5$. The initial cluster centers selected are (3, 4), and (7, 8). So $\mu_1(\mu_{11}, \mu_{12}) = (3, 4)$ and $\mu_2(\mu_{21}, \mu_{22}) = (7, 8)$.

$$P(x_i, \theta_j) = \frac{w_j P(x_i \mid \theta_j)}{\sum_{J=1}^{k} P(x_i \mid \theta_j)}$$

Here j can take the values 1 and 2 as there are 2 clusters. For all x_i we have to calculate the probability $P(x_i, \theta_j)$ for both clusters.

For example, the first data point $x_1(1, 1)$ we need to calculate $P(x_1, \theta_1)$ and $P(x_1, \theta_2)$.

$$P(z_1 \mid x_1, \theta_1) = \frac{w_1 \times P(x_1 \mid \theta_1)}{P(x_1 \mid \theta_1) + P(x_2 \mid \theta_2)}$$

$$P(x_1 \mid \theta_1) = \left(\frac{1}{\sigma_1\sqrt{2\pi}} e^{-\frac{1}{2}\left(\frac{x_{11}-\mu_1}{\sigma_1}\right)^2} \right) \times \left(\frac{1}{\sigma_1\sqrt{2\pi}} e^{-\frac{1}{2}\left(\frac{x_{12}-\mu_1}{\sigma_1}\right)^2} \right)$$

$$= \left(\frac{1}{0.8\times\sqrt{2\pi}} e^{-\frac{1}{2}\left(\frac{1-3}{0.8}\right)^2} \right) \times \left(\frac{1}{0.8\times\sqrt{2\pi}} e^{-\frac{1}{2}\left(\frac{1-4}{0.8}\right)^2} \right) \cong 3.2512E-12$$

$$P(x_1 \mid \theta_2) = \left(\frac{1}{\sigma_2 \sqrt{2\pi}} e^{-\frac{1}{2}\left(\frac{x_{11}-\mu_2}{\sigma_2}\right)^2} \right) \times \left(\frac{1}{\sigma_2 \sqrt{2\pi}} e^{-\frac{1}{2}\left(\frac{x_{12}-\mu_2}{\sigma_2}\right)^2} \right)$$

$$= \left(\frac{1}{0.8 \times \sqrt{2\pi}} e^{-\frac{1}{2}\left(\frac{1-7}{0.8}\right)^2} \right) \times \left(\frac{1}{0.8 \times \sqrt{2\pi}} e^{-\frac{1}{2}\left(\frac{1-8}{0.8}\right)^2} \right) \cong 9.4111E-75$$

$$P(z_1 \mid x_1, \theta_1) = \frac{w_1 \times P(x_1 \mid \theta_1)}{P(x_1 \mid \theta_1) + P(x_2 \mid \theta_2)} = \frac{0.5 \times 3.2512E-12}{0.5 \times 3.2512E-12 + 0.5 \times 9.4111E-75} \cong 1$$

$$P(z_2 \mid x_1, \theta_2) = \frac{w_1 \times P(x_1 \mid \theta_2)}{P(x_1 \mid \theta_1) + P(x_2 \mid \theta_2)} = \frac{0.5 \times 9.4111E-75}{0.5 \times 3.2512E-12 + 0.5 \times 9.4111E-75} \cong 0$$

In a similar manner we can calculate the probabilities for both clusters. The calculated values are tabulated in Table 12.6.

TABLE 12.6 Initial distribution of data points

Data	$P(z_1 \mid x_i, \theta_1)$	$P(z_2 \mid x_i, \theta_2)$	Total
(1, 1)	1	0	1
(2, 2)	1	0	1
(3, 4)	1	0	1
(7, 8)	0	1	1
(8, 9)	0	1	1
(9, 9)	0	1	1

In the next step, we need to update the cluster centers using Eq. (12.21), as shown below.

$$\mu_j = \frac{\sum_{i-1}^{n} x_i P(z_j \mid x_i, \theta_j)}{\sum_{i=1}^{n} P(z_j \mid x_i, \theta_j)}$$

$$\mu_1^{(1)} = \left(\frac{1\times1+1\times2+1\times3+0\times7+0\times8+0\times9}{1+1+1+0+0+0}, \frac{1\times1+1\times2+1\times4+0\times8+0\times9+0\times9}{1+1+1+0+0+0} \right) = (2, 2.33)$$

$$\mu_2^{(1)} = \left(\frac{0\times1+0\times2+0\times3+1\times7+1\times8+1\times9}{0+0+0+1+1+1}, \frac{0\times1+0\times2+0\times4+1\times8+1\times9+1\times9}{0+0+0+1+1+1} \right) = (8, 8.67)$$

After calculating the new center, again we need to estimate the probabilities of the clusters in next iteration. The calculated values of probabilities are shown in Table 12.7.

TABLE 12.7 Updating the probability values in second iteration

Data	$P(z_1 \mid x_i, \theta_1)$	$P(z_2 \mid x_i, \theta_2)$	Total
(1, 1)	1	0	1
(2, 2)	1	0	1
(3, 4)	1	0	1

(Contd.)

Data	$P(z_1\|x_i, \theta_1)$	$P(z_2\|x_i, \theta_2)$	Total
(7, 8)	0	1	1
(8, 9)	0	1	1
(9, 9)	0	1	1

Updating the means as per the latest probability values in second iteration.

$$\mu_1^{(2)} = \left(\frac{1\times1+1\times2+1\times3+0\times7+0\times8+0\times9}{1+1+1+0+0+0}, \frac{1\times1+1\times2+1\times4+0\times8+0\times9+0\times9}{1+1+1+0+0+0}\right) = (2, 2.33)$$

$$\mu_2^{(2)} = \left(\frac{0\times1+0\times2+0\times3+1\times7+1\times8+1\times9}{0+0+0+1+1+1}, \frac{0\times1+0\times2+0\times4+1\times8+1\times9+1\times9}{0+0+0+1+1+1}\right) = (8, 8.67)$$

Since the centers remains the same, algorithm will terminate here with the final clusters as {(1, 1), (2, 2), (3, 4)} and {(7, 8), (8, 9), (9, 9)}.

Pros and cons of EM clustering algorithm

The advantage of the EM clustering algorithm is its simplicity as only probability calculations and center updations are required. The disadvantage of this algorithm is complexity of initializing parameters and handling of high dimensional data. If dimensionality of data will increase, then probability calculations are going to be computationally expensive.

Gaussian mixture model (GMM) clustering

In real-world scenarios for multivariate data, most of the clustering algorithm does not consider the mixture of data distribution. GMM is a probability distribution-based clustering technique where it is assumed that data is distributed among the mixture of Gaussian probability distribution (each distribution indicates a probable data cluster). The most likelihood of data belonging to one of the clusters is estimated and further optimized for clustering. Expectation maximization technique is used for cluster identification, where the Gaussian distribution parameters are estimated and adjusted for finalizing the clusters.

12.3.5 Fuzzy C-means Algorithm

Clustering techniques may also be classified as two major categories namely, hard clustering and soft clustering. In hard clustering one of the data points belongs to exactly one of the clusters whereas in soft clustering techniques one data point may belong to multiple clusters with a membership degree (in the range of 0 to 1). FCM (Fuzzy C-Means) is the fuzzy version of the popular *K*-Means clustering algorithm. It is one of the popular fuzzy logic-based clustering techniques in which one data point may belong to multiple clusters with degree of membership.

Working of FCM Algorithm

Step-1: Choose initial values

Step-2: Compute mean using equation (12.22)

$$c_i = \frac{\sum_{k=1}^{N} (\mu_{ik})^m x_k}{\sum_{k=1}^{N} (\mu_{ik})^m}, 1 \le i \le c \tag{12.22}$$

Where m is called the degree of membership for fuzzy clustering. Generally, the value of m is taken in the range of 1.25 to 3.

Step-3: Computer updated membership values using (12.23)

$$\mu_{ik} = \frac{1}{\sum_{j=1}^{c}\left(\frac{d_{ik}}{d_{jk}}\right)^{\frac{2}{m-1}}}, 1 \le k \le N \text{ and } 1 \le i \le c \tag{12.23}$$

Step-4: Compare μ^{k+1} with μ^{k}, if $||\mu^{k+1} - \mu^{k}|| \le \in$ then stop else go to step-2.

Example: Let us assume that we need to create two clusters for the one-dimensional dataset $D = \{1, 2, 5, 8, 9\}$. Initially we selected data points 1 and 2 as cluster centers. Now let us calculate the membership functions for the data points to the clusters. For this purpose, distance calculation is required for all the data points with the cluster center. Let us assume that the distance function is Manhattan distance for simplicity. The distance and membership calculated for all the data points for both cluster centers is shown in the Table 12.8.

TABLE 12.8 Distance and Membership Calculations for Data Points

Data	$C_1 = 1$	$C_2 = 2$	μ_1	μ_2	$\mu_1 + \mu_2$
1	0	1	1	0	1
2	1	0	0	1	1
5	4	3	0.36	0.64	1
8	7	6	0.42	0.58	1
9	8	7	0.43	0.57	1

Let us understand the membership values calculation for the data points. For data point 1, distance from center-1 is 0 so it is clear that this data point will belong to cluster-1 with 100% membership (membership = 1), similarly data point 2 will belong to cluster-2 only with the membership value as 1. For calculating the membership value for the third data point 5, it is calculated using Eq. (12.22) for both of the clusters as, $\mu_1 = \frac{1}{\left(\frac{4}{4}\right)^2 + \left(\frac{4}{3}\right)^2} = \frac{1}{1+1.77} = 0.36,$

and, $\mu_2 = \frac{1}{\left(\frac{3}{4}\right)^2 + \left(\frac{3}{3}\right)^2} = \frac{1}{0.5625+1} = 0.64.$ Similarly, for the rest of the membership values are calculated as tabulated in Table 12.8.

Next, we need to update the cluster centers using Eq. (12.22). The updated center values are calculated as given below for the first iteration.

$$c_1 = \frac{(1)^2 \times 1 + (0)^2 \times 2 + (0.36)^2 \times 5 + (0.42)^2 \times 8 + (0.43)^2 \times 9}{(1)^2 + (0)^2 + (0.36)^2 + (0.42)^2 + (0.43)^2} = \frac{4.78}{1.50} = 3.18, \text{ similarly}$$

$$c_2 = \frac{(0)^2 \times 1 + (1)^2 \times 2 + (0.64)^2 \times 5 + (0.58)^2 \times 8 + (0.57)^2 \times 9}{(0)^2 + (1)^2 + (0.64)^2 + (0.58)^2 + (0.57)^2} = \frac{9.59}{2.06} = 4.65$$

After calculating the centers, again we need to compute the distance of all the data points from centers and update the membership values for the data points as shown in Table 12.9. Similar operations are repeated till the convergence of membership values. Repeating the same operation, after the 9th iteration are presented in Table 12.10 where the membership values are convergent and remains the same.

TABLE 12.9 Distance and membership value calculation for Iteration 1

Data	$C_1 = 3.18$	$C_2 = 4.65$	μ_1	μ_2	$\mu_1 + \mu_2$
1	2.18	3.65	0.74	0.26	1
2	1.18	2.65	0.83	0.17	1
5	1.82	0.35	0.04	0.96	1
8	4.82	3.35	0.33	0.67	1
9	5.82	4.35	0.36	0.64	1

TABLE 12.10 Distance and membership value calculation for Iteration 9

Data	$C_1 = 1.9$	$C_2 = 8.1$	μ_1	μ_2	$\mu_1 + \mu_2$
1	0.9	7.1	0.98	0.02	1
2	0.1	6.1	1	0	1
5	3.1	3.1	0.5	0.5	1
8	6.1	0.1	0	1	1
9	7.1	0.9	0.02	0.98	1

It is clearly visible from Table 12.9 that the centrally located data point 5 has membership values as 0.5 and 0.5 so this data point belongs to both clusters with equal membership.

Pros and cons of FCM clustering algorithm

The primary advantage of FCM is, it is a soft clustering technique so one data point may belong to several clusters at a time with membership function. The disadvantage of this algorithm is, sometimes convergences to the results may take many iterations that causes the computational complexity of this algorithm to be higher.

12.3.6 Spectral Clustering

Spectral clustering is a popular clustering technique particularly for graph data. Spectral clustering treats the problem of clustering as graph partitioning problem (problem of identification of similar sub-graphs). The major steps in spectral clustering are as follows:

In the first step, similarity graph is calculated using ∈-neighbourhood or KNN (*K*-Nearest Neighbors) technique. Then in the second step, dimension reduction is applied using graph Laplacian techniques and finally in the third step, clusters are identified from the transformed graph data. The process of spectral clustering is summarized in Figure 12.13.

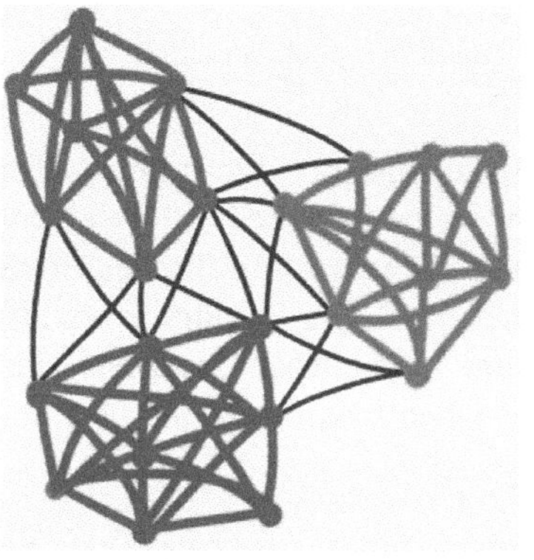

FIGURE 12.13 Spectral Clustering Process.

The spectral clustering technique uses the concept of Eigenvalues from the similarity matrix for data reduction before clustering. With fewer dimensions it identifies the clusters (subgraphs) from the graph. It is a popular clustering technique for graph clustering and has many applications where data can be represented as a graph such as social network analysis. Apart from graph-based data clustering it is also mostly used for image segmentation tasks and has a number of applications in image mining domain.

12.4 CLUSTERING PERFORMANCE EVALUATION PARAMETERS

Cluster evaluation is an important technique for measuring the quality of the clusters created by any clustering algorithm. In this section popular clustering evaluation parameters are discussed and explained with the help of numerical examples.

12.4.1 Silhouette Index, DB Index, Dunn Index and Distortion

Silhouette index

The Silhouette index is the ratio of average distances within the clusters to the average distances of data points with the other clusters. It ranges from −1 to +1, where a high value indicates that the object is well matched to its own **cluster** and poorly matched to neighboring clusters. The Silhouette index (SI) computes for each point a width depending on its membership in any cluster. This Silhouette width is then an average over all observations. Silhouette index is calculated using Eq. (12.24).

$$\text{Silhouette Index} = \frac{b-a}{\max(a, b)} \tag{12.24}$$

Where,

$$a(i) = \frac{1}{|C_I|-1} \sum_{j \in C_{I, i \neq j}} d(i, j) \tag{12.25}$$

and
$$b(i) = \min_{J \neq I} \frac{1}{|C_J|} \sum_{j \in C_J} d(i, j) \tag{12.26}$$

and symbols a and b are computed using the average values of all the $a(i)$'s and $b(i)$'s.

Davies-Bouldin (DB) index

The Davies-Bouldin index identifies clusters which are far from each other and compact. The silhouette index is normalized and a value close to 1 is always good (for this index) whatever clustering you are trying to evaluate. However, the Davies-Bouldin for instance is not normalized and it's difficult to compare 2 values of Davies-Bouldin from different data sets. Since the objective is to obtain clusters with minimum intra-cluster distances, small values for DB are interesting. Therefore, this index is minimized when looking for the best number of clusters. The DB-index is calculated using Eq. (12.27).

$$DB\text{ Index} = \frac{1}{k} \sum_{i=1}^{k} \max_{i \neq j} \left\{ \frac{\Delta(C_i) + \Delta(C_j)}{\delta(C_i, C_j)} \right\} \tag{12.27}$$

where $\delta(C_i, C_j)$ is the dissimilarity between clusters C_i and C_j and ΔC_k is the intra-cluster function (or diameter) of the Kth cluster.

Dunn index

The Dunn index (DU) identifies clusters which are well separated and compact. The goal is therefore to maximize the inter-cluster distance while minimizing the intra-cluster distance. The Dunn Index has a value between zero and infinity and should be maximized. The Dunn index for C clusters is defined by Eq. (12.28)

$$\text{Dunn Index} = \min_{1 \leq j \leq c} \left\{ \min_{1 \leq j \leq c\, j \neq i} \left\{ \frac{\delta(C_i, C_j)}{\max_{1 \leq k \leq c} (\Delta C_k)} \right\} \right\} \tag{12.28}$$

where $d(C_i, C_j)$ is the dissimilarity between clusters C_i and C_j and ΔC_k is the intra-cluster function (or diameter) of the Kth cluster. If Dunn index is large, it means that compact and well separated clusters exist. Therefore, the maximum is observed for K equal to the most probable number of clusters in the data set.

Distortion or sum of squared error (SSE)

Another useful measure for clustering evaluation is distortion or SSE (Sum of Squared Error) which is calculated using Eq. (12.29). It measures the intra-cluster variations in the clusters and should be minimized for better clustering.

$$\text{Distortion} = \sum_{k=1}^{c} \sum_{\forall x_i \in c_k} \left(x_i - \overline{c_k} \right)^2 \tag{12.29}$$

Where, K represents the number of clusters, and $\overline{c_k}$ is the center of the Kth cluster.

Example: Let us calculate the above clustering evaluation parameters with the help of a simple working example. Let we have a two-dimensional dataset D = {(1, 1), (2, 2), (3, 3), (7, 7), (8, 8), (9, 9)} with 6 two-dimensional data points, i.e., $|D| = 6$ and using any clustering algorithms like K-Means we have created two clusters from this dataset. The clusters are C_1 {(1, 1), (2, 2), (3, 3)} and C_2 {(7, 7), (8, 8), (9, 9)} consisting of 3.

Silhouette index

$$a = \frac{\frac{\sqrt{2}+\sqrt{8}}{2} + \frac{\sqrt{2}+\sqrt{2}}{2} + \frac{\sqrt{8}+\sqrt{2}}{2} + \frac{\sqrt{2}+\sqrt{8}}{2} + \frac{\sqrt{2}+\sqrt{2}}{2} + \frac{\sqrt{8}+\sqrt{2}}{2}}{6} \cong 1.89$$

$$b = \frac{\frac{\sqrt{72}+\sqrt{98}+\sqrt{128}}{3} + \frac{\sqrt{50}+\sqrt{72}+\sqrt{98}}{3} + \frac{\sqrt{32}+\sqrt{50}+\sqrt{72}}{3}}{3} \cong 8.49$$

$$\text{Silhouette Index} = \frac{8.49 - 1.89}{\max(1.89, 8.49)} \cong 0.78$$

Suppose clustering technique will create two clusters with the final clusters as C_1 {(1, 1), (2, 2), (3, 3), (7, 7)} and C_2{(8, 8), (9, 9)}.

$$a = \frac{\frac{\sqrt{2}+\sqrt{8}+\sqrt{72}}{3} + \frac{\sqrt{2}+\sqrt{2}+\sqrt{50}}{3} + \frac{\sqrt{8}+\sqrt{2}+\sqrt{32}}{3} + \frac{\sqrt{72}+\sqrt{50}+\sqrt{32}}{3} + \frac{\sqrt{2}}{1}}{5} \cong 3.86$$

$$b = \frac{\frac{\sqrt{98}+\sqrt{128}}{2} + \frac{\sqrt{72}+\sqrt{98}}{2} + \frac{\sqrt{50}+\sqrt{72}}{2} + \frac{\sqrt{2}+\sqrt{8}}{2}}{4} \cong 7.42$$

$$\text{Silhouette Index} = \frac{7.42 - 3.86}{\max(7.42, 3.86)} \cong 0.48$$

In this case the calculated Silhouette index is lesser than in the previous case. Which indicates that previous clustering is good and preferred as compared to this clustering of the sample data.

Dunn Index

$$\Delta C_1 = \sqrt{2} + \sqrt{8} + \sqrt{2} = 5.65$$

$$\Delta C_2 = \sqrt{2} + \sqrt{8} + \sqrt{2} = 5.65$$

$$\text{Dunn Index} = \frac{\sqrt{72}+\sqrt{98}+\sqrt{128}+\sqrt{50}+\sqrt{72}+\sqrt{98}+\sqrt{32}+\sqrt{50}+\sqrt{72}}{\max(5.65, 5.65)} = 13.516$$

DB Index

$$\text{DB Index} = \frac{1}{2}\left\{\frac{5.65+5.65}{\sqrt{72}+\sqrt{98}+\sqrt{128}+\sqrt{50}+\sqrt{72}+\sqrt{98}+\sqrt{32}+\sqrt{50}+\sqrt{72}}\right\} = \frac{1}{2} \times \frac{11.3}{76.41} = 0.074$$

Distortion

Cluster centers (2, 2) and (8, 8)
Distortion = 2 + 0 + 2 + 2 + 0 + 2 = 8

12.4.2 Purity

For computing purity each cluster is mapped to the class which is most frequent to that cluster. The accuracy of this mapping is measured with the number of correctly assigned clusters to the classes and it is called purity. Purity is computed using Eq. (12.30). The range of purity is between 0 and 1. Value 1 indicates the best case of purity.

$$\text{purity}\left(C, CLS\right) = \frac{1}{N}\sum_{k}\max_{j}\left|C_k \cap CLS_j\right| \tag{12.30}$$

Where C is the set of clusters and CLS is set of classes.

Cluster	A	B	C	Total
C_1	5	**25**	0	30
C_2	**45**	0	5	50
C_3	2	3	**15**	20
Total	52	28	20	**100**

$$\text{purity} = \frac{1}{100}\left(45 + 25 + 15\right) = 0.85$$

C_1 has 30 points, and its corresponding characteristics column has 28 points. The $precision_{C1} = \frac{25}{30} = 0.83$, $recall_{C1} = \frac{25}{28} = 0.89$. Similarly, $precision_{C2} = \frac{45}{50} = 0.90$, $recall_{C2} = \frac{45}{52} = 0.87$, $precision_{C3} = \frac{15}{20}$ $= 0.75$, and $recall_{C3} = \frac{15}{20} = 0.75$ are calculated. The average precision and recall are then calculated below.

$$Average\,Precision = \frac{precision_{C1} + precision_{C2} + precision_{C3}}{3} = \frac{0.83 + 0.90 + 0.75}{3} = 0.83$$

$$Average\,Recall = \frac{recall_{C1} + recall_{C2} + recall_{C3}}{3} = \frac{0.89 + 0.87 + 0.75}{3} = 0.84$$

12.4.3 Centroid, Radius and Diameter

There are three other important measures for clusters which indicate the general property of the clusters generated by a clustering algorithm. These measures are centroid, radius and diameter of the clusters. Centroid is the center of the cluster; diameter indicates the maximum distance between any pair of data points in a particular cluster and radius is the average distance of all the data points of a cluster with its center. In general, these parameters indicate the spread (scatter) of a particular cluster. When multiple clusters are created by a clustering algorithm then in order to compare these clusters these measures may be useful.

$$C_k = \frac{\sum_{i=1 \forall x_i \in c_k}^{|c_k|} x_i}{|C_k|} \tag{12.31}$$

$$R_k = \sqrt{\frac{\sum_{i=1 \forall x_i \in c_k}^{|c_k|} \left(x_i - \overline{C_k}\right)^2}{|C_k|}} \tag{12.32}$$

$$D_k = \sqrt{\frac{\sum_{i=1 \forall x_i \in c_k}^{|c_k|} \sum_{j=1 \forall x_i \in c_k}^{|c_k|} \left(x_i - x_j\right)^2}{|C_k| \times \left(|C_k| - 1\right)}} \tag{12.33}$$

Example: Let us assume that two clusters are created from the two-dimensional dataset $D = \{(1, 1), (2, 2), (3, 3), (4, 4), (5, 5), (6, 6)\}$. The clusters are $\{(1, 1), (2, 2), (3, 3)\}$ and $\{(4, 4), (5, 5), (6, 6)\}$.

The centers of the clusters are $C_1 = \left(\frac{1+2+3}{3}, \frac{1+2+3}{3}\right) = (2, 2)$ and $C_2 = \left(\frac{4+5+6}{3}, \frac{4+5+6}{3}\right)$ = (5.5). The radius and diameters of the clusters are calculated as:

$$R_1 = \sqrt{\frac{\left(\sqrt{(1-2)^2 + (1-2)^2}\right)^2 + \left(\sqrt{(2-2)^2 + (2-2)^2}\right)^2 + \left(\sqrt{(3-2)^2 + (3-2)^2}\right)^2}{3}} = \sqrt{\frac{2+0+2}{3}} = 1.15$$

$$R_2 = \sqrt{\frac{\left(\sqrt{(7-8)^2 + (7-8)^2}\right)^2 + \left(\sqrt{(8-8)^2 + (8-8)^2}\right)^2 + \left(\sqrt{(9-8)^2 + (9-8)^2}\right)^2}{3}} = \sqrt{\frac{2+0+2}{3}} = 1.15$$

$$D_1 = \sqrt{\frac{\left(\sqrt{(1-2)^2 + (1-2)^2}\right)^2 + \left(\sqrt{(1-3)^2 + (1-3)^2}\right)^2 + \left(\sqrt{(2-3)^2 + (2-3)^2}\right)^2}{3 \times 2}} = \sqrt{\frac{2+8+2}{6}} = 1.41$$

$$D_2 = \sqrt{\frac{\left(\sqrt{(7-8)^2 + (7-8)^2}\right)^2 + \left(\sqrt{(7-9)^2 + (7-9)^2}\right)^2 + \left(\sqrt{(8-9)^2 + (8-9)^2}\right)^2}{3 \times 2}} = \sqrt{\frac{2+8+2}{6}} = 1.41$$

12.5 OUTLIER DETECTION TECHNIQUES

Outlier detection can be performed in several ways. It can be done using supervised, semi-supervised and unsupervised machine learning techniques. Most of the outlier detection techniques uses the concept of statistical method, proximity-based techniques (such as KNN and distance-based) and clustering techniques (such as hierarchical and density-based techniques) for identification of outliers in real-world applications.

12.6 APPLICATIONS

Clustering has numerous applications in various domains. Some of the highlighted applications are discussed here in brief.

Market Research and Customer Profiling: Clustering has numerous applications in electronics commerce and market research. Creating a group of similar products and creating the groups of similar profile users are examples of it. Customer profiles can be generated by identifying the interest groups of the customers which can help enterprises to identify the target customers.

Recommendation Systems: Modern recommender systems utilize clustering for creating groups of similar users and identifying their potential interest in new items. Based on this, new items are recommended to the users for possible future use.

Social Network Analysis: Clustering has plenty of applications in social network analysis. A few popular applications of clustering in social network analysis are community detection and link prediction. In community detection groups of similar users are created using clustering techniques based on the profile and interest of users.

Search Engine Result Grouping: Search engines use clustering for grouping similar search results. It will help the proper organization of search results and it is easy for end users to understand the search results.

News Groups: Online news platforms use clustering to group similar kinds of news for proper management of news information. It will also help in identifying the popular and trendy news.

Medical Imaging in Healthcare Management: Clustering is also utilized in many applications of healthcare management, particularly in medical imaging technologies. Using clustering similar medical images can be grouped together which can help in identification of diagnosis of disease and other important key information related to health of the patients.

Intrusion Detection System and Fraud Management: Clustering techniques are also used for identifying outliers. Outlier detection has several applications particularly in development of intrusion detection system and fraud identification. During outlier detection, abnormalities are detected in the dataset and such abnormalities information can be utilized for development of intrusion detection system and fraud management system. Outlier detection is also utilized for fault diagnosis in many domains.

12.7 CASE STUDIES

Case Study–I: Evaluating Purity for the Clusters

The following two datasets are available in UCI machine learning repository where clustering can be applied. Clustering performance evaluation can also be analyzed by calculating various parameters like Silhouette index, DB index, Dunn index, etc. Using categories mapping purity of the cluster can also be calculated for understanding of cluster evaluation.

Water Treatment Plant Data Set from UCI machine learning repository (https://archive.ics.uci.edu/ml/datasets/Water+Treatment+Plant) consisting of 527 instances with 38 attributes. This dataset is used for classification of plant treatment dataset using clustering techniques in the earlier work.

The purpose of performing clustering was to predict faults through the state variables of the plant at each of the stages of the treatment process. A total of 13 clusters are generated from the dataset for categorizing the faults. The cluster name (represented as classes) with number of instances in each category are—Class 1: Normal situation (275), Class 2: Secondary settler problems-1 (1), Class 3: Secondary settler problems-2 (1), Class 4: Secondary settler problems-3 (1), Class 5: Normal situation with performance over the mean (116), Class 6: Solids overload-1 (3), Class 7: Secondary settler problems-4 (1), Class 8: Storm-1 (1), Class 9: Normal situation with low influent (69), Class 10: Storm-2 (1), Class 11: Normal situation (53), Class 12: Storm-3 (1), Class 13: Solids overload-2 (1).

Perform clustering on this dataset and map the clusters to these classes for computation of cluster purity.

Case Study–II: Evaluating Purity for the Clusters

Wholesale customer dataset (https://archive.ics.uci.edu/ml/datasets/Wholesale+customers) is a dataset for a clients of wholesale distributor. The dataset includes the annual spending in monetary units (mu) on diverse product categories. There is a total of 440 instances with 8 attributes.

Fresh	Milk	Grocery			
34838	5261	6045		64	0
8858	19536	27776		49	1
8001	3842	5353		327	2
	Fresh	Milk	Grocery		
High	62	1	1	64	0
Average	3	45	1	49	1
Low	4	31	292	327	2
	69	77	294	440	

Perform clustering on this dataset and then decide a suitable range of consumption for creating the classes like high consumption, average consumption, and low consumption users. Then map the clusters to these classes for calculating purity of the clusters.

Case Study–III: Cluster Sampling

Sampling is an important data pre-processing technique in which samples are selected instead of original data for optimization of computational operations. Random sampling techniques are popular techniques in sampling but the main problem with the random sampling is, selected samples can be biased from a particular distribution. Cluster sampling is an effective technique which eliminates bias as samples are selected from the clusters of the data. In cluster sampling, first, clusters are created then samples are selected from each cluster. It will ensure that the sample is selected from all the possible distribution of the original data.

Case Study– IV: Handling Missing Values

Clustering is also applied for handling of missing values in an intelligent manner. In real-world scenarios, data can have missing values and one of the simplest ways to deal with the missing values is to replace the missing value from the average value of that particular attribute. The problem with this technique is, if the range of attributes is very wide or if the distribution of values is biased then it will lead to guess inappropriate values for the missing values. Clustering provides a smart solution to this problem. Using clustering, clusters are created from the original data (by ignoring missing values) and then missing values are replaced by cluster centers. It will eliminate the biasing in replacing the missing value.

EXERCISES

1. Apply the (a) Euclidean and (b) Mankowski distance functions to calculate the distance between the two four-dimensional data points $d_1(1, 3, 4, 6)$ and $d_2(1, 5, 3, 6)$.
2. Apply the *K*-Means clustering algorithm and create two clusters ($K = 2$) for the following four-dimensional data points (using Euclidean distance):

Data Point	*w*	*x*	*y*	*z*
P_1	1	2	2	4
P_2	3	3	1	3
P_3	2	4	2	3
P_4	1	3	3	2
P_5	3	3	1	4
P_6	3	4	1	1

Also calculate the Silhouette index for the clusters.

3. Apply the AGNES Hierarchical clustering algorithm for the given dataset $D = \{1, 3, 4, 5, 6, 8, 11, 13, 17, 18, 22, 25\}$ and create the dendrogram using:
   (a) Single-link analysis
   (b) Complete link analysis
   (c) Average link analysis
4. Apply the Density-based clustering technique on the two-dimensional data points $D = \{(1, 1), (1, 2), (2, 1), (2, 3), (4, 5), (5, 5), (6, 5), (6, 7), (7, 7), (8, 8), (9, 9)\}$ and identify the clusters. Using:
   (a) $\varepsilon = 1$ and MinPts = 3
   (b) $\varepsilon = \sqrt{2}$ and MinPts = 4
5. Perform the clustering using Expectation Minimization technique. Suppose we have to create two clusters ($K = 2$) for the given two-dimensional dataset $X = \{(1, 3), (2, 4), (3, 5), (4, 3), (5, 1), (5, 3)\}$. Let us assume that $\sigma_1 = \sigma_2 = 0.6$ and $w_j = 0.3$. The initial cluster centers selected are (2, 4), and (4, 3). So $\mu_1(\mu_{11}, \mu_{12}) = (2, 4)$ and $\mu_2(\mu_{21}, \mu_{22}) = (4, 3)$.
6. Perform the clustering using Fuzzy C-Means algorithm. Suppose we have to create two clusters ($K = 2$) for the given two-dimensional dataset $Y = \{(1, 3), (2, 5), (3, 7), (4, 4), (5, 6), (5, 8), (4, 3), (3, 6), (2, 8), (1, 7)\}$.

MULTIPLE CHOICE QUESTIONS

1. Euclidean distance between the $X(1, 3, 5)$ and $Y(1, 5, 7)$ is:
   (a) 2 (b) 2.41
   (c) 2.83 (d) 4
2. Distance function property is:
   (a) Symmetry (b) Negativity
   (c) Identity of indiscernibility (d) Triangle inequality
3. The Jaccard similarity between the two data points $X(1, 3, 5, 7)$ and $Y(1, 2, 5, 8)$ is:
   (a) 0.33 (b) 0.25
   (c) 0.49 (d) 0.71

4. The Dice similarity between the two data points $X(1, 3, 5, 7)$ and $Y(1, 2, 5, 8)$ is:
   (a) 0.33 (b) 0.25
   (c) 0.49 (d) 0.71
5. The Cosine similarity between the two data points $X(1, 3, 5, 7)$ and $Y(1, 2, 5, 8)$ is:
   (a) 0.33 (b) 0.25
   (c) 0.49 (d) 0.99
6. The distance between two symmetric binary data $X(1, 1, 1, 0, 0, 0)$ and $Y(1, 0, 1, 0, 1, 0)$ is:
   (a) 0.33 (b) 0.50
   (c) 0.67 (d) 1.00
7. The distance between two asymmetric data $X(1, 1, 1, 0, 0, 0)$ and $Y(1, 0, 1, 0, 1, 0)$ is:
   (a) 0.33 (b) 0.50
   (c) 0.67 (d) 1.00
8. The output at the end of first iteration of K-Means clustering using $K = 2$ for the dataset D = [(1, 1), (1, 2), (3, 2), (5, 6), (7, 7), (7, 8), (9,9)] with the initial cluster centre as (3, 2), and (7, 8) using Euclidean distance is:
   (a) $\left[(1, 1), (1, 2), (3, 2), (5, 6)\right]$ and $\left[(7,7), (7,8), (9,9)\right]$
   (b) $\left[(1,1), (1,2), (3,2)\right]$ and $\left[(5,6), (7,7), (7,8), (9,9)\right]$
   (c) $\left[(1,1), (1,2)\right]$ and $\left[(3,2), (5,6), (7,7), (7,8), (9,9)\right]$
   (d) $\left[(1,1), (1,2), (3,2), (5,6), (7,7)\right]$ and $\left[(7,8), (9,9)\right]$
9. The complete link analysis technique
   (a) Selects the maximum distance among all the distances to group the data points.
   (b) Selects the minimum distance among all the distances to group the data points.
   (c) Selects the average distance among all the distances to group the data points.
   (d) None of the above.
10. The Ward method:
    (a) Selects the maximum of all the distances between all the objects (data points) with the centre of the combinedly joined together clusters
    (b) Computes the sum of all the distances between all the objects (data points) with the centre of the combinedly joined together clusters
    (c) Computes the average of all the distances between all the objects (data points) with the centre of the combinedly joined together clusters
    (d) Selects the minimum of all the distances between all the objects (data points) with the centre of the combinedly joined together clusters
11. The principle of reachability in density-based clustering says:
    (a) If any data point A is reachable to B, and B is reachable to C then A is not reachable to C.
    (b) If any data point A is reachable to B, and B is not reachable to C then A is reachable to C.
    (c) If any data point A is not reachable to B, and B is reachable to C then A is reachable to C.
    (d) If any data point A is reachable to B, and B is reachable to C then A is reachable to C.
12. Spectral clustering is best suited to:
    (a) Streamed data clustering
    (b) Graph data clustering
    (c) Numerical data clustering
    (d) None of these

For question number 13 to 18, let us assume that the clustering algorithm has generated two clusters C_1 = [(1, 1), (1, 2), (3, 2)] and C_2 = [(5, 6), (7, 7), (7, 8), (9, 9)] for the given dataset D = [(1, 1), (1, 2), (3, 2), (5, 6), (7, 7), (7, 8), (9, 9)].

13. The Silhouette score for the above clusters is:
    (a) 0.45 (b) 0.51
    (c) 0.67 (d) 0.90
14. The Dunn index for the above generated clusters is:
    (a) 2.41 (b) 3.67
    (c) 4.47 (d) 6.32
15. The DB-Index for the above generated clusters is:
    (a) 0.11 (b) 0.19
    (c) 0.45 (d) 0.87
16. The Distortion for both of the clusters is:
    (a) 12.32 (b) 16.34
    (c) 20.22 (d) 32.22
17. The Radius for both of the clusters is:
    (a) 3.04 and 3.67 (b) 2.22 and 2.87
    (c) 1.92 and 1.98 (d) 1.06 and 1.22
18. The Diameter for both of the clusters is:
    (a) 0.33 and 0.67 (b) 0.75 and 1.04
    (c) 1.20 and 1.44 (d) None of these.
19. The main drawback of *K*-Means clustering is:
    (a) The *K*-Means clustering algorithm generates predefined number of clusters.
    (b) The *K*-Means clustering algorithm is not able to handle outliers.
    (c) The *K*-Means clustering algorithm requires higher number of iterations.
    (d) None of these
20. The primary advantage of *K*-Means clustering algorithm is:
    (a) The *K*-Means clustering algorithm can identify the outliers easily.
    (b) The *K*-Means clustering algorithm requires less iterations to converge.
    (c) The *K*-Means clustering algorithm is computationally simple.
    (d) All of the above.
21. What is the significance of outliers in clustering algorithm?
    (a) Outliers indicate that there is some noise in data.
    (b) Outliers indicate that some data points are not nearby located to any of the clusters.
    (c) Outliers indicate that for some of the data points the characteristics is different.
    (d) All of the above.

REFERENCES

[1] Meloun, M., and Militký, J. (2011), *Statistical data analysis: A practical guide*, Woodhead Publishing Limited.
[2] https://www.geeksforgeeks.org/elbow-method-for-optimal-value-of-k-in-kmeans/
[3] Bezdek, J. C., Ehrlich, R., and Full, W. (1984), FCM: The fuzzy C-means clustering algorithm, *Computers & geosciences*, *10*(2–3), pp. 191–203.
[4] Meloun, M., and Militký, J. (2011), *Statistical data analysis: A practical guide*, Woodhead Publishing Limited.
[5] Saitta, S. Raphael, B. and Smith, I. F. C. (2007), A bounded index for cluster validity, *in* 'International Workshop on Machine Learning and Data Mining in Pattern Recognition', pp. 174–187.
[6] http://nlp.stanford.edu/IR-book/html/htmledition/evaluation-of-clustering-1.html
[7] http://en.wikipedia.org/wiki/Silhouette_%28clustering%29

Silhouette Index

```
import numpy as np
from sklearn.metrics import silhouette_score
x1 = np.array([1,2,3,7,8,9])
x2 = np.array([1,2,3,7,8,9])
X = np.array(list(zip(x1, x2))).reshape(len(x1), 2)
label = np.array([1,1,1,1,0,0])
print (silhouette_score(X, label))
```

```
> plot(hclust(dist(X), method = "single"))
> abline(h=2.5, col= "blue")
> plot(hclust(dist(X), method = "ward"))
The "ward" method has been renamed to "ward.D"; note new "ward.D2"
> plot(hclust(dist(X), method = "ward.D"))
> abline(h=5, col= "blue")
```

ANSWER KEY

1. (c) **2.** (b) **3.** (a) **4.** (b) **5.** (d) **6.** (a) **7.** (b) **8.** (b) **9.** (a) **10.** (b)
11. (d) **12.** (b) **13.** (b) **14.** (c) **15.** (a) **16.** (b) **17.** (d) **18.** (b) **19.** (b) **20.** (c)
21. (d)

13 Association Analysis

13.1 WHAT IS ASSOCIATION ANALYSIS

Association analysis or association rule mining is the study of relationship between two or more variables. It is often thought of as correlation analysis but there is a slight difference. Correlation analysis is the study of linear relationship between two variables where trend between the two variables is identified, for example, whether the variables are positive correlated (linearly increasing) or negatively correlated (linearly decreasing). There are a plenty of applications of association analysis in real-world applications such as electronic commerce sites, natural language processing, and health informatics, that makes it a popular technology in the area of data science.

13.2 ASSOCIATION RULE MINING

The outcome of association analysis is represented as association rules so generally association analysis is also referred to as association rule mining. Association Rule Mining (ARM) is an important activity in the field of data science and has numerous applications. ARM is a derived technology from market basket analysis, where the items purchased together by the same persons are identified. Some of the highlighted and popular applications are discussed here. In E-commerce platforms such as Amazon and Flipkart, activities like, "Customers who viewed this item also viewed", combo offers ("buy it with"), and "you may also like" or "Products related to this item" are driven by association rule mining. In Medical science, analysis of comorbidities (relations between the diseases) can be done efficiently with the help of association analysis.

The general Form of the Association Rule is given in Eq. (13.1)

$$(\mathrm{X}, \alpha) \rightarrow (\mathrm{X}, \beta) \text{ [support \%, confidence \%]} \tag{13.1}$$

Where α and β are the set of items associated with each other. The equation shows that if X is buying the items α then X will also buy the items β. Support and confidence are two major parameters used for indicating the quality of the association rules. Support and confidence are the parameters indicates the degree of association between the two item sets. There are several other parameters also which are discussed and explained with example in this chapter.

The simplified representation of same association rule is presented in Eq. (13.2)

$$\alpha \rightarrow \beta \text{ [support \%, confidence \%]} \quad (13.2)$$

13.3 MEASURES OF ASSOCIATION RULES

The validity of any association rule is measured by two popular parameters support and confidence. Apart from support and confidence there are few more popular parameters that are discussed and explained here. An example dataset for illustration of association rule measures is presented in Table 13.1. The dataset represents the set of items purchased together from a computer store.

TABLE 13.1 Example Dataset from a Computer Store

T_X	List of Items
T_1	Laptop, Antivirus, Pen Drive, MS Office
T_2	Pen Drive, Keyboard, Mouse
T_3	Laptop, Keyboard, Mouse, MS Office
T_4	Laptop, Antivirus, Keyboard, Mouse
T_5	Laptop, Mouse, MS Office
T_6	Keyboard, Mouse, MS Office
T_7	Antivirus, MS Office

Set of items I is {Laptop (L), Antivirus (A), Pen Drive (P), Keyboard (K), Mouse (M), MS Office (O)}, consisting of total 6 unique items I = {A, K, L, M, O, P} $|I| = 6$ and total number of transactions in the dataset are $|D| = 7$. For simplicity the items are represented as the notations given in the brackets, for example, Laptop is represented by the symbol L.

13.4 SUPPORT

The support measure of an association rule $\alpha \rightarrow \beta$ is shown in Eq. (13.3).

$$\text{Support}(\alpha \rightarrow \beta) = \frac{\text{Transactions consisting of } \alpha \text{ and } \beta}{\text{Total number of transactions}} \quad (13.3)$$

Support measure can have the value in the range of [0...1] (which is in % is [0..100]). Generally, the support and confidence parameters for association rule mining is given in %. So first of all it is necessary to convert the % support value to the minimum support count values. This conversation is presented in the Eq. (13.4).

$$\text{min\_support\_count} = \lceil \text{No. of Transactions*support \%} \rceil \quad (13.4)$$

So, if the minimum support given is 40% then the minimum support count is calculated as:

$$\left\lceil 7 \times \frac{40}{100} \right\rceil = \lceil 2.8 \rceil = 3$$

Where support % is multiplied with total number of transactions and then ceiling of the numerical value is taken for rounding off the number to the next higher integer value as the frequency of the item will be integer.

Example of calculating support from sample dataset 13.1 is, let us assume that there is an association rule $L \to O$ (association between buying MS Office software along with a new laptop), here $\alpha = \{L\}$ and $\beta = \{O\}$ in general association rule, in real world both α and β can have more than one items. Let us see the calculation of support measure for the rule $L \to O$:

$$\text{Support}(L \to O) = \frac{\text{Transactions consisting of } L \text{ and } O}{\text{Total number of transactions}} = \frac{3}{7} \times 100 \cong 43\%$$

13.5 CONFIDENCE

The confidence measure of an association rule $\alpha \to \beta$ is shown in Eq. (13.5).

$$\text{Confidence}(\alpha \to \beta) = \frac{\text{Transactions consisting of } \alpha \text{ and } \beta}{\text{Transactions consisting of } \alpha} \tag{13.5}$$

Just like support, confidence measure can have the value in the range of [0...1] (which is in % is [0..100]). Another measure related to confidence is All_confidence which is a minor variation of confidence measure and is calculated using Eq. (13.6). It satisfies downward closed closure property.

$$\text{All\_confidence}(\alpha \to \beta) = \frac{\text{support}(\alpha \cup \beta)}{\max(\text{support}(\alpha), \text{support}(\beta))} \tag{13.6}$$

Example:

$$\text{Confidence}(L \to O) = \frac{\text{Transactions consisting of } L \text{ and } O}{\text{Transactions consisting of } L} = \frac{3}{4} \times 100 = 75\%$$

$$\text{All}_{\text{confidence}}(L \to O) = \frac{\text{support}(L \cup O)}{\max(\text{support}(L), \text{support}(O))} = \frac{\frac{3}{7}}{\max\left(\frac{4}{7}, \frac{5}{7}\right)} = \frac{\frac{3}{7}}{\frac{5}{7}} = \frac{3}{5} = 60\%$$

13.6 LIFT

The lift also referred to as the interestingness measure, incorporates the prior probability of the rules consequent and thus eliminates the bias of high probability items in dataset. A lift value less than 1 indicates a negative dependence or substitute. It also indicates the expected substitution between α and β. Lift can have a value in the range of [0...∞]. Lift is calculated using Eq. (13.7).

$$\text{Lift}(\alpha \to \beta) = \frac{\text{support}(\alpha \cup \beta)}{\text{support}(\alpha) \times \text{support}(\beta)} \tag{13.7}$$

Example:

$$\text{Lift}(L \rightarrow O) = \frac{\text{support}(L \cup O)}{\text{support}(L) \times \text{support}(O)} = \frac{\frac{3}{7}}{\frac{4}{7} \times \frac{5}{7}} = 1.05$$

13.7 COSINE

Cosine measure is calculated using Eq. (13.8). Cosine value close to 1 indicates more transactions containing items also contains α item β.

$$\text{Cosine}\,(\alpha \rightarrow \beta) = \frac{\text{support}(\alpha \cup \beta)}{\sqrt{\text{support}(\alpha) \times \text{support}(\beta)}} \tag{13.8}$$

Example:

$$\text{Cosine}(L \rightarrow O) = \frac{\text{support}(L \cup O)}{\sqrt{\text{support}(L) \times \text{support}(O)}} = \frac{\frac{3}{7}}{\sqrt{\frac{4}{7} \times \frac{5}{7}}} = 0.67$$

13.8 CONVICTION

It ranges along the values [0.5…∞]. Like lift, conviction values far from 1 indicate interesting rules. It also gives a measure on whether association rule happened by chance or not. Conviction is infinite for logical implications (confidence 1) and is 1 if α and β are independent.

Conviction is calculated using Eq. (13.9).

$$\text{Conviction}(\alpha \rightarrow \beta) = \frac{1 - \text{support}(\beta)}{1 - \text{Confidence}(\alpha \rightarrow \beta)} \tag{13.9}$$

Measures the implication strength of the rule from statistical independence $\frac{P(\alpha) \times P(\bar{\beta})}{P(\alpha \cup \bar{\beta})}$, where $P(\bar{\beta})$ is the probability that the β does not appear in a transaction.

$$\text{Conviction}(L \rightarrow O) = \frac{1 - \text{support}(O)}{1 - \text{Confidence}(L \rightarrow O)} = \frac{1 - \frac{5}{7}}{1 - \frac{3}{4}} = \frac{0.286}{0.25} = 1.14$$

13.9 INTERESTINGNESS

Interestingness is calculated using the Eq. (13.10). Interestingness measures how much the association rule is surprising to the user. Apart from high frequency rules it also identified the rules comparatively less frequencies.

$$\text{Interstingness}(\alpha \rightarrow \beta) = \frac{\text{support}(\alpha \cup \beta)}{\text{support}(\alpha)} \times \frac{\text{support}(\alpha \cup \beta)}{\text{support}(\beta)} \times \left(1 - \frac{\text{support}(\alpha \cup \beta)}{|D|}\right) \quad (13.10)$$

Where $|D|$ indicates total number of transactions in the dataset D.

Example:

$$\text{Interstingness}(L \rightarrow O) = \frac{\text{support}(L \cup O)}{\text{support}(L)} \times \frac{\text{support}(L \cup O)}{\text{support}(O)} \times \left(1 - \frac{\text{support}(L \cup O)}{|D|}\right)$$

$$= \frac{3/7}{4/7} \times \frac{3/7}{5/7} \times \left(1 - \frac{3/7}{7}\right) = 0.42$$

13.10 VALID ASSOCIATION RULE

Let us assume that minimum support is 40% and minimum confidence is 70% for the given transactional dataset, then out the following two association rules

$$L \rightarrow M\left(\frac{3}{7} \times 100, \frac{3}{4} \times 100\right) \Rightarrow L \rightarrow M(43\%, 75\%) \text{ and}$$

$$M \rightarrow L\left(\frac{3}{7} \times 100, \frac{3}{5} \times 100\right) \Rightarrow M \rightarrow L(43\%, 60\%)$$

The first association rule is having support and confidence greater than minimum support and minimum confidence threshold values, so the first association rule is VALID, whereas the second rule has confidence value less that the threshold value of confidence, so it is INVALID association rule.

13.11 BINARY REPRESENTATION

The binary representation of the sample dataset shown in Table 13.1 is presented in Table 13.2. As most of the frequent itemset generation and association rule mining algorithms need counting of the items in the transactions so the binary representation assumed to be an effective representation technique for association analysis.

TABLE 13.2 Binary Representation of Example Dataset shown in Table 13.1

T_X	L	A	P	K	M	O	Total items in T_X
1	1	1	1	0	0	1	4
2	0	0	1	1	1	0	3
3	1	0	0	1	1	1	4
4	1	1	0	1	1	0	4
5	1	0	0	0	1	1	3
6	0	0	0	1	1	1	3
7	0	1	0	0	0	1	2
Item Frequency	4	3	2	4	5	5	23

13.12 FREQUENT-ITEMSET GENERATION

The association analysis or association rule identification is performed in two major steps. The first step is to identify the frequent itemsets and the second step is to generate the valid association rules from the frequent itemsets generated in the first step. Generally, the algorithms are presented for the first step, i.e., mining frequent itemsets as in the second step the combination of frequent itemsets is taken and measures are calculated to generate the valid association rules. The frequent itemsets mining algorithms is divided into two major categories. The first category is frequency-based algorithms, and the second category is tree-based algorithms. Apriori is a popular frequency-based algorithm, whereas FP-Growth (Frequent Pattern Growth) is a tree-based algorithm which uses a special tree data structure called FP-Tree (Frequent-Pattern Tree).

13.13 THE APRIORI ALGORITHM

The apriori algorithm is the most popular algorithm for generating association rules because of its simplicity. It is based on the apriori property. Apriori property states that "if any superset of items is frequent then all of its subsets are also frequent" or vice-versa "if any set of items is infrequent then none of its superset is frequent".

The working of apriori algorithm is summarized as follows:

Generation of Frequent Itemsets

Step-1: List all the unique items present in the transactions and count the frequencies of all the items throughout the dataset.

Step-2: If the frequency of the item is greater than the minimum support count then mark it as frequent otherwise mark it as infrequent.

Step-3: Apply Apriori principle to generate the combination of two items and count the frequency of two items together.

Step-4: If the frequency of the two items together is greater than the minimum support count then mark it as frequent otherwise mark it as infrequent.

Step-5: Repeat the steps 3 to 4 by combining more items (3-items, 4-items and so on) till we are getting frequent itemsets by considering apriori property.

Generation of Association Rules from the Frequent Itemsets

Step-6: Once the frequent itemsets are generated then all the possible combinations of items is selected for generation of association rules.

Step-7: Calculate the confidence % measure for all the generated association rules in the previous steps.

Step-8: Filter the association rules having support and confidence more than the minimum threshold given for support and confidence measures. The filtered association rules are VALID association rules, discard the INVALID association rules (association rules having lesser support and confidence values).

13.14 ILLUSTRATIVE EXAMPLE

The apriori algorithm is applied on the dataset shown in Table 13.1. The stepwise illustration of apriori algorithm is explained in this section. In the first step, all the unique items available in the dataset is identified and their corresponding frequencies are counted. The unique items available with its frequencies is shown in Table 13.3. Let us assume that the minimum support and confidence for this example is 40% and 70% respectively. The minimum support given is 40% then the minimum support count is calculated as $\left[7 \times \frac{40}{100}\right] = |2.8| = 3$. In the last column of Table 13.3 symbol '✓' indicates that the frequency of the item is greater than the minimum support count and hence it is marked as a frequent item in this step. The other symbol '✗' indicates that the frequency of the item is less than minimum support count and hence the item is not frequent and thus discarded in this step itself.

So from the first steps, it is visible that the individual items {A, K, L, M, O} total 5 items having frequency of occurrence greater than minimum support count (3), whereas item P is having frequency 2 which is less than minimum support count hence identified as infrequent item. This concludes step-2 of the apriori algorithm.

TABLE 13.3 Unique Items with their Frequency

Item	Count	
A	3	✓
K	4	✓
L	4	✓
M	5	✓
O	5	✓
P	2	✗

In step-3, apriori property is applied and combination of 2-items is generated. Here, in this example item P was listed as infrequent item so except item P, we can take the combination of other items and generate a list of 2-itesmsets (itemsets having 2 elements). The list of 2-itemsets along with their frequencies is shown in Table 13.4. The last column indicates whether the 2-itemsets are frequent or not. For example, the frequency of {A, K} together in the dataset is 1 which is less than minimum support count (3) so it is marked as '✗' (infrequent), whereas the frequency of itemsets {K, M} together in the dataset is 4 which is more than minimum support count (3) so it is marked as '✓' (frequent). This is end of step-4 of the apriori algorithm. The frequent itemsets having 2 items are {(K, M), (L, M), (L, O), (M, O)}.

TABLE 13.4 Combination of two items with Frequency

Item	Count	
A, K	1	✗
A, L	2	✗
A, M	1	✗
A, O	2	✗

(Contd.)

Item	Count	
K, L	2	✗
K, M	4	✓
K, O	2	✗
L, M	3	✓
L, O	3	✓
M, O	3	✓

Now further proceeding with apriori algorithm in step-5, we have to list the itemsets having 3 elements with apriori property by combining the frequent itemsets from previous step (that is by combining frequent itemsets having 2 elements). The list of 3 itemsets is shown in Table 13.5. Please note that one possible combination is {K, L, M} is not considered here as one of its subsets is {K, L} which is infrequent, so by apriori property it will be eliminated in this step. Only 1 element is qualified in this step, that is {L, M, O} as all its subset are frequent. Now we have to count the frequency of element {L, M, O} in the dataset. The frequency of {L, M, O} is 2 which is less than the minimum support count (3) hence it is marked as infrequent ('✗'). This concludes the apriori algorithm as no more combination are frequent and we cannot move further for generating higher supersets from this point.

TABLE 13.5 Combination of three items with their frequencies

Item	Count	
L, M, O	2	✗

Generation of Association Rules from the frequent itemsets

In the step-6 all the possible combinations are selected. The frequent itemsets having 2 items arc {(K, M), (L, M), (L, O), (M, O)} and there is no frequent 3 itemsets. So combinations from 2 itemsets is generated and for all these rules support and confidence % is calculated (step-7) as shown below:

$$K \to M\left(\frac{4}{7}\times 100 = 57\%, \frac{4}{4}\times 100 = 100\%\right) \quad \text{[VALID]}$$

$$M \to K\left(\frac{4}{7}\times 100 = 57\%, \frac{4}{5}\times 100 = 80\%\right) \quad \text{[VALID]}$$

$$L \to M\left(\frac{3}{7}\times 100 = 43\%, \frac{3}{4}\times 100 = 75\%\right) \quad \text{[VALID]}$$

$$M \to L\left(\frac{3}{7}\times 100 = 43\%, \frac{3}{5}\times 100 = 60\%\right) \quad \text{[INVALID]}$$

$$L \to O\left(\frac{3}{7}\times 100 = 43\%, \frac{3}{4}\times 100 = 75\%\right) \quad \text{[VALID]}$$

$$O \to L\left(\frac{3}{7}\times 100 = 43\%, \frac{3}{5}\times 100 = 60\%\right) \quad \text{[INVALID]}$$

$$M \rightarrow O\left(\frac{3}{7}\times 100 = 43\%, \frac{3}{5}\times 100 = 60\%\right) \qquad \text{[INVALID]}$$

$$O \rightarrow M\left(\frac{3}{7}\times 100 = 43\%, \frac{3}{5}\times 100 = 60\%\right) \qquad \text{[INVALID]}$$

In the last step-8, we have to filter the VALID association rules from the above rules which have support and confidence values greater than or equal to minimum support and minimum confidence threshold values.

The item set with 3 items is not frequent in our dataset. Let us assume that the frequency of this bucket, i.e., {L, M, O} is higher than the minimum support count (greater than or equal to 3) in that case this bucket will also get frequent and will be qualifying for generation of association rules consisting of three items. So, we have to consider all the combinations of three items together for association rules and identify the measures of the association rules for its validity. For this assumed case the list of association rules will be:

L ⇒ M O
M ⇒ L O
O ⇒ L M
M O ⇒ L
L O ⇒ M
L M ⇒ O

In the generalized association rule representation, it was shown that both are set of items so they can have more than one item in both sides (antecedent and descendent) of the association rule.

TABLE 13.6 Association rules with all the measures for the sample dataset of Table 13.1

Rule ID	Association Rule	Support %	Confidence %	All_Confidence %	Lift	Cosine	Conviction	Interesting-ness
1	K → M	$\frac{4}{7}\times 100$ $= 57\%$	$\frac{4}{4}\times 100$ $= 100$	$\frac{4}{\max(4,5)}\times 100$ $= 80$	$\frac{\frac{4}{7}}{\frac{4}{7}\times\frac{5}{7}}$ $= 1.4$	$\frac{\frac{4}{7}}{\sqrt{\frac{4}{7}\times\frac{5}{7}}}$ $= 0.89$	$\frac{1-\frac{5}{7}}{1-1}$ $= \infty$	0.34
2	M → K	$\frac{4}{7}\times 100$ $= 57\%$	$\frac{4}{5}\times 100$ $= 80\%$	$\frac{4}{\max(4,5)}\times 100$ $= 80$	$\frac{\frac{4}{7}}{\frac{4}{7}\times\frac{5}{7}}$ $= 1.4$	$\frac{\frac{4}{7}}{\sqrt{\frac{4}{7}\times\frac{5}{7}}}$ $= 0.89$	$\frac{1-\frac{4}{7}}{1-0.8}$ $= 2.14$	0.34
3	L → M	$\frac{3}{7}\times 100$ $= 43\%$	$\frac{3}{4}\times 100$ $= 75\%$	$\frac{3}{\max(4,5)}\times 100$ $= 60$	$\frac{\frac{3}{7}}{\frac{4}{7}\times\frac{5}{7}}$ $= 1.05$	$\frac{\frac{3}{7}}{\sqrt{\frac{4}{7}\times\frac{5}{7}}}$ $= 0.67$	$\frac{1-\frac{5}{7}}{1-0.75}$ $= 1.14$	0.26

(Contd.)

Rule ID	Association Rule	Support %	Confidence %	All_Confidence %	Lift	Cosine	Conviction	Interestingness
4	$M \rightarrow L$	$\frac{3}{7}\times 100 = 43\%$	$\frac{3}{5}\times 100 = 60\%$	$\frac{3}{\max(4,5)}\times 100 = 60$	$\frac{\frac{3}{7}}{\frac{4}{7}\times\frac{5}{7}} = 1.05$	$\frac{\frac{3}{7}}{\sqrt{\frac{4}{7}\times\frac{5}{7}}} = 0.67$	$\frac{1-\frac{4}{7}}{1-0.6} = 1.07$	0.26
5	$L \rightarrow O$	$\frac{3}{7}\times 100 = 43\%$	$\frac{3}{4}\times 100 = 75\%$	$\frac{3}{\max(4,5)}\times 100 = 60$	$\frac{\frac{3}{7}}{\frac{4}{7}\times\frac{5}{7}} = 1.05$	$\frac{\frac{3}{7}}{\sqrt{\frac{4}{7}\times\frac{5}{7}}} = 0.67$	$\frac{1-\frac{5}{7}}{1-0.75} = 1.14$	0.26
6	$O \rightarrow L$	$\frac{3}{7}\times 100 = 43\%$	$\frac{3}{5}\times 100 = 60\%$	$\frac{3}{\max(4,5)}\times 100 = 60$	$\frac{\frac{3}{7}}{\frac{4}{7}\times\frac{5}{7}} = 1.05$	$\frac{\frac{3}{7}}{\sqrt{\frac{4}{7}\times\frac{5}{7}}} = 0.67$	$\frac{1-\frac{4}{7}}{1-0.6} = 1.07$	0.26
7	$M \rightarrow O$	$\frac{3}{7}\times 100 = 43\%$	$\frac{3}{5}\times 100 = 60\%$	$\frac{3}{\max(5,5)}\times 100 = 60$	$\frac{\frac{3}{7}}{\frac{5}{7}\times\frac{5}{7}} = 0.84$	$\frac{\frac{3}{7}}{\sqrt{\frac{5}{7}\times\frac{5}{7}}} = 0.60$	$\frac{1-\frac{5}{7}}{1-0.6} = 0.71$	0.21
8	$O \rightarrow M$	$\frac{3}{7}\times 100 = 43\%$	$\frac{3}{5}\times 100 = 60\%$	$\frac{3}{\max(5,5)}\times 100 = 60$	$\frac{\frac{3}{7}}{\frac{5}{7}\times\frac{5}{7}} = 0.84$	$\frac{\frac{3}{7}}{\sqrt{\frac{5}{7}\times\frac{5}{7}}} = 0.60$	$\frac{1-\frac{5}{7}}{1-0.6} = 0.71$	0.21

13.15 ADVANTAGES AND DISADVANTAGES

The primary advantage of apriori algorithm is its simplicity. Computing is very simple as only counting of the items and filtering is required. The main drawback of the algorithm is the number of database scans are higher. In real world scenario of the size of the datasets is in GB's to TB's, so even the single scan of dataset needs several hours of time. In every step of item counting, filtering the items above minimum support and combining items need a single scan so for generating K-frequent itemsets (i.e., frequent itemsets consisting of K number of items) needs K scans of the dataset which make apriori a complex algorithm for generation of frequent itemsets.

13.16 TREE-BASED ALGORITHMS

FP-Tree (Frequent Pattern Tree)-based algorithm namely FP-Growth is one of the popular algorithms in tree-based algorithms for association rule mining. The working of FP-Growth algorithm is summarized as follows:

Construction of FP-Tree

Step-1: List all the unique items present in the transactions and count the frequencies of all the items throughout the dataset.

Step-2: Sort the items in the descending order of frequencies and discard the items having frequency less than the minimum support count. Then rearrange the datasets as per the descending order of frequencies of items.

Step-3: Start creating the FP-Tree by the root node which indicated by a null node or empty node.

Step-4: Select one transaction at a time and insert into the FP-Tree. While inserting any transaction in FP-Tree there are two possibilities:

(a) If the predecessor item is already existing in one of the branch of tree then follow the same branch till common predecessors are available and then create the new branch from the item not commonly available.

(b) No predecessors exist in the tree then create a new branch in FP-Tree. In both cases increase the item count by one while inserting the new transactions.

Step-5: Repeat the step 4 till all the transactions from the rearranged dataset is inserted into the FP-Tree.

Creation of Condition Sub-Tree for Pattern Generation

Step-6: Select one item at a time from leaf node and internal node of the FP-Tree (in the ascending order of frequencies) and identify the subtree for that item (tree branches where the selected item is available). For each selected item condition tree is created. The conditional tree list all the paths from the root node to a particular item. All the paths are listed along with their frequencies. Then common prefix paths are listed. If the cumulative frequency of the common prefix paths is greater than or equal to minimum support count, then the prefix paths items along with selected item is identified as frequent items together.

Step-7: Repeat the steps 6 till all the items are covered which are generated in step-2.

Generation of Association Rules from the Frequent Itemsets

Step-8: Once the frequent itemsets are generated then all the possible combinations of items is selected for generation of association rules.

Step-9: Calculate the confidence % measure for all the generated association rules in the previous steps.

Step-10: Filter the association rules having support and confidence more than the minimum threshold given for support and confidence measures. The filtered association rules are VALID association rules, discard the INVALID association rules (association rules having lesser support and confidence values).

13.17 ILLUSTRATIVE EXAMPLE OF FP-TREE ALGORITHM

For illustration of FP-Tree algorithm, same dataset shown in Table 13.1 is selected. In the first step of FP-Tree algorithm, all the unique items from the dataset are listed and their frequencies are counted. The outcome of this step is shown in Table 13.3, which is same as apriori algorithm.

Items having less frequency than the minimum support count are discarded. Remaining items are sorted in descending order of frequencies. The descending order of items for the sample dataset is {M, O, K, L, A}. In step-2, as per this order all the transactions are rearranged and the rearranges transactions are shown in Table 13.7.

TABLE 13.7 Rearranging the transactions as per the descending order of item frequency

Transaction	Items
T_1	O, L, A
T_2	M, K
T_3	M, O, K, L
T_4	M, K, L, A
T_5	M, O, L
T_6	M, O, K
T_7	O, A

In the nest steps (3-5) FP-Tree is created. The process of creation of FP-Tree is shown in Figure 13.1. The FP-Tree creation steps are shown in Figure 13.1 (a) to Figure 13.1 (h). Initially an empty root node is created shown in Figure 13.1(a). After creation of the root, one record at a time is inserted in the FP-Tree. All the seven records are inserted from Figure 13.1 (b) to Figure 13.1 (h).

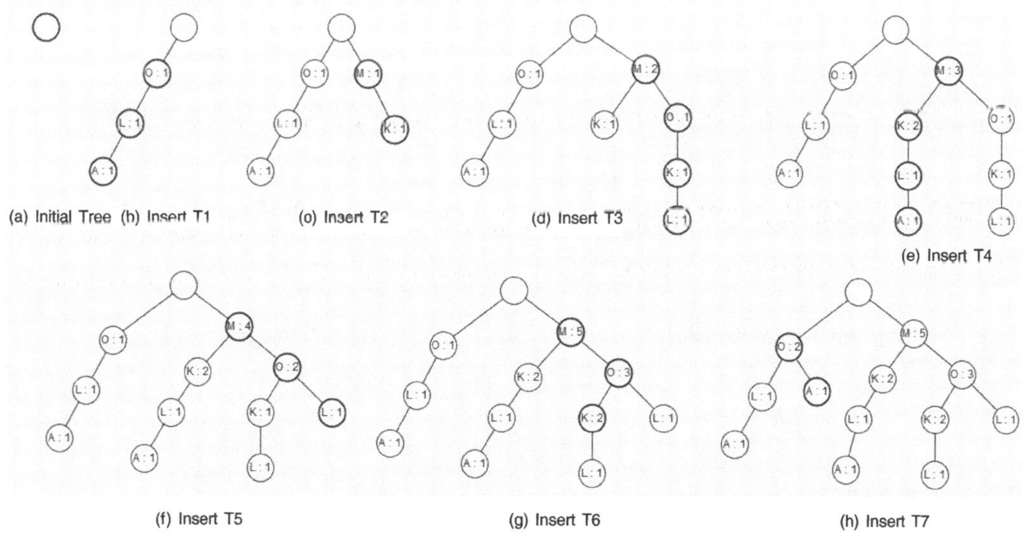

FIGURE 13.1 Creation of the FP-Tree for the sample dataset shown in Table 13.1.

In nest steps (6 and 7), conditional tree is created for all the leaf nodes and internal parent nodes of the FP-Tree as per the ascending order of frequencies of items (this is the reverse order of dataset reengagement and tree creation). The conditional tree creation process is shown in Figure 13.2. The frequent itemsets generated from each subtree is shown below:

(a) For item **A** (Subtree shown in **Figure 13.2(a)**): There are three paths available in the tree that is {O, L : 1}, {O : 1}, and {M, K, L : 1}. The only prefix path is available in the first two paths is {O : 2}, that is item O which is commonly appearing twice and is the occurring maximum with the item A, but still this cumulative frequency is less than the minimum support count (3) so none of the items is frequent with the item A.

(b) For item **L** (Subtree shown in **Figure 13.2(b)**): There are four paths for the item L. The paths are {O : 1}, {M, K : 1}, {M, O, K, : 1}, {M, O : 1}. From these four paths we can see that the common paths {M : 3} and {O : 3} is appearing greater than or equal to minimum support count (3) so both of these items individually are frequent with the item L. The combination of both M and O is not frequent with L as the cumulative frequency of common prefix paths consisting of both of these items is 2 which is less than minimum support count (3). So the frequent itemsets found on this subtree or conditional tree are **{M, L}** and **{O, L}**.

(c) For item **K** (Subtree shown in **Figure 13.2(c)**): There are two paths for the item K, which are {M : 2} and {M, O : 2}. From these two paths the common prefix paths with cumulative frequency is {M : 4}, which is greater than minimum support count (3). So the frequent itemset from this conditional tree is **{M, K}**.

(d) For item **O** (Subtree shown in **Figure 13.2(d)**): The only path for the item O along with any prefix item is {M : 3} which is greater than minimum support count (3) so **{M, O}** is a frequent itemset.

So, in summary total frequent items found from all the conditional trees are **{M, L}**, **{O, L}**, **{M, K}** and **{M, O}**. No frequent prefix elements having more than two elements.

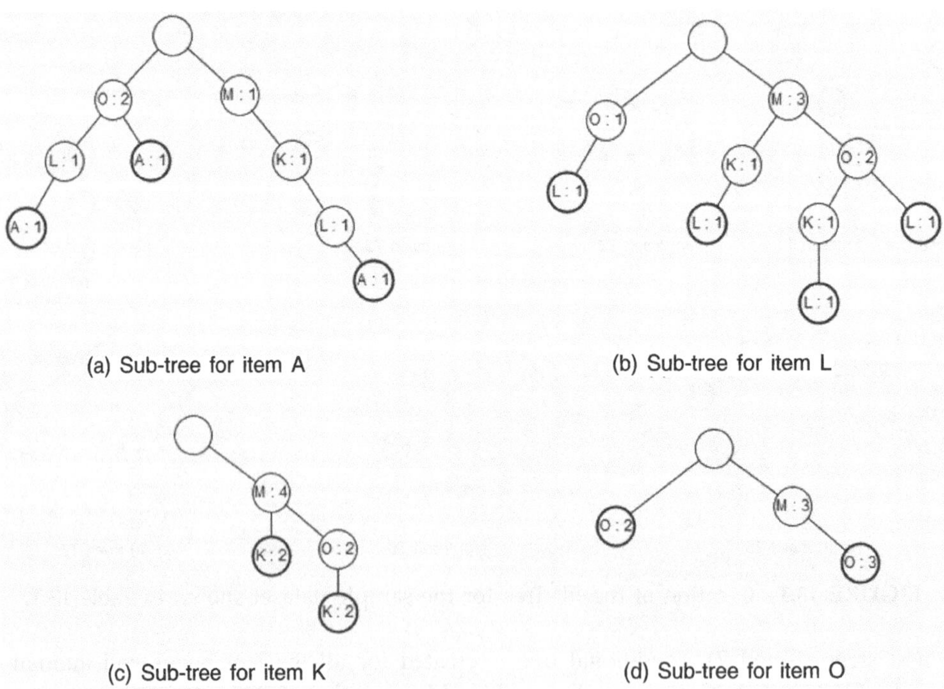

FIGURE 13.2 Creation of the subtree (condition tree) for all the items of FP-Tree.

The last steps (8-10), association rules are generated from the frequent itemsets are listed in the previous steps. From the four frequent itemsets **{M, L}**, **{O, L}**, **{M, K}** and **{M, O}**, so the there are total eight possible association rules just like the apriori algorithm. For each algorithm support and confidence measures are calculated and then VALID association rules are filtered for which the support and confidence is greater than or equal to minimum support and confidence values.

$$K \to M\left(\frac{4}{7}\times 100 = 57\%,\ \frac{4}{4}\times 100 = 100\%\right)$$

$$M \to K\left(\frac{4}{7}\times 100 = 57\%,\ \frac{4}{5}\times 100 = 80\%\right)$$

$$L \to M\left(\frac{3}{7}\times 100 = 43\%,\ \frac{3}{4}\times 100 = 75\%\right)$$

$$M \to L\left(\frac{3}{7}\times 100 = 43\%,\ \frac{3}{5}\times 100 = 60\%\right)$$

$$L \to O\left(\frac{3}{7}\times 100 = 43\%,\ \frac{3}{4}\times 100 = 75\%\right)$$

$$O \to L\left(\frac{3}{7}\times 100 = 43\%,\ \frac{3}{5}\times 100 = 60\%\right)$$

$$M \to O\left(\frac{3}{7}\times 100 = 43\%,\ \frac{3}{5}\times 100 = 60\%\right)$$

$$O \to M\left(\frac{3}{7}\times 100 = 43\%,\ \frac{3}{5}\times 100 = 60\%\right)$$

13.18 ADVANTAGES AND DISADVANTAGES

The key advantage of FP-Tree is it just need two scans of datasets for generating the frequent itemsets. The disadvantage of FP-Tree algorithm is it uses complex data structures as tree creation for large dataset and then creation of conditional trees for the larger number of items is a complex procedure.

13.19 TYPES OF ASSOCIATION RULES

There are several ways by which the association rules can be categorized. Based on the dimension of the data, association rules can be categorized as Single-dimensional rules and Multidimensional association rules. In Single-dimensional rules, associations between the itemsets are identified considering only one dimension. We have seen the example of single dimensional association rule in out transactional dataset shown in Table 13.1. The example of multidimensional association rule is given below based on the example dataset shown in Table 13.8.

TABLE 13.8 Example Dataset with Numeric Data for Multidimensional Association Rules

T_X	Age	Salary	Loan
1	26	35K	Car
2	35	80K	Home
3	37	70K	Home
4	26	50K	Car
5	38	40K	Car
6	45	95K	Home
7	28	50K	Car
8	30	40K	Car

Example of multidimensional association rule is given below. In this example "age" and "salary" of a person is considered together for finding association between the availing the "Car Loan" facility. So clearly, this association rule involves multiple dimensions for identifying the associations.

$$\text{Age}(X, \text{"26..35"}) \wedge \text{Salary}(X, \text{"35..50K"}) \wedge \text{Avail}(X, \text{"Car Loan"})$$

13.20 HANDLING NUMERIC ATTRIBUTES

In real-world scenario it is possible that the dataset can have attributes with numeric values. One example of dataset with numeric values is shown in Table 13.8. Attributes "age" and "salary" have numeric values. If we can consider each single numeric value from these attributes, then it is practically difficult to perform association analysis. So, there are several solutions to this problem. A few commonly used approaches for handing this situation are discussed here.

(a) Static discretization: Using static discretization, users can use a set of predefined ranges for creating the data intervals, usually the width of the interval is kept constant.

(b) Dynamic discretization: In dynamic discretization, based on the distribution of data and some calculations like binning, etc., dynamic width intervals are created. Intervals may have a constant width, or it may vary also depending upon the calculation logic.

(c) Distance-based association rules: The smarter way of creating the intervals is to use clustering. Using clustering, groups of similar values are created then using the diameter of the clusters (minimum and maximum value in the cluster), data intervals are created. The primary benefit of clustering or distance-based technique is, it accommodates the similar data into the same interval and keep the data having higher distance to the other interval. Thus, for real-world scenario it is the more effective technique.

Association analysis dealing with numeric values are also called as quantitative association rules. These are also called as interval information association rules sometimes as the numeric intervals are created for the numeric attributes.

13.21 CONTINGENCY TABLE REPRESENTATION

Contingency table is popular representation of dataset for interval-based numeric dataset. The contingency table representation for the dataset of Table 13.8 is shown in Table 13.9. It summarizes the data by taking combination of various discrete values specified in the interval or data range.

TABLE 13.9 Contingency Table for Example Dataset shown in Table 13.8

	income < 30K	**income 31..45K**	**income 46..95K**	**Row Total**
Home Loan	0	2	5	**7**
Car Loan	1	6	6	**13**
Column Total	**1**	**8**	**11**	**20**

The primary benefit of this representation is that it makes the calculation of support and confidence measure easier. For example, for the following two association rules, we can quickly calculate support and confidence measures.

[(X, "income 46..95K") ⇒ (X, "Home Loan") [Support = $\frac{5}{20}(25\%)$, Confidence = $\frac{5}{11}(44\%)$]

[(X, "income 31..45K") ⇒ (X, "Car Loan") [Support = $\frac{6}{20}(30\%)$, Confidence = $\frac{6}{8}(75\%)$]

13.22 HIERARCHICAL ASSOCIATION RULES

Consider the following transaction dataset for mining the association rules. If we will try to list the unique items from this table, then the frequency of individual items will be very less as brands of the items are also associated with them. For generating the frequent item sets or association rules from this type of dataset requires some addition efforts.

TABLE 13.10 Example Dataset for Hierarchical Association Rules

T_X	**List of Items**
T_1	HP Laptop, Quick Heal Antivirus, HP Pen Drive 128 GB
T_2	San Disk Pen Drive 64 GB, Logitech Keyboard, Logitech Mouse
T_3	Lenovo Laptop, Logitech Keyboard, Logitech Mouse
T_4	Dell Laptop, Norton Antivirus, HP Keyboard, HP Mouse
T_5	MacBook Air, Lenovo Mouse

Hierarchical association rules are also known as multiple level association rules mining. There are a few basic strategies for finding the multiple level association rules particularly in deciding the suitable support measures for the association rules. Two most commonly used approaches for deciding the support measure for multiple level association rules are uniform support and reducing support. In uniform support a constant value of support measure is selected for filtering of association rules in all the levels of association analysis. Whereas in the reducing support method, a variable value of support measure is selected at different levels of association analysis, in each upper level of data abstraction (upper level of concept hierarchy) the value of support is reduced for better association analysis.

13.23 REPEATING TRANSACTION REPRESENTATION

Another presentation of a transactional dataset for mining frequent items or association rules is the summarized representation or repeating representation of the dataset. An example of such representation is shown in Table 13.11. The dataset is consisting of three items namely Laptop, Antivirus software and Printer. These items are represented with their brand names, so it is also an example of multilevel association rule mining. By moving towards with upper level of concept hierarchy and representing these items with the symbols (Laptop (L), Antivirus (A) and Printer (P)) the transformed dataset is presented in the Table 13.12. Let us assume that the minimum support is 40% and minimum confidence is 80%.

TABLE 13.11 Sample Dataset for Repeating Transactions with Frequencies

T_X	Items	Frequency
T_1	Dell Laptop, Norton Antivirus	30
T_2	HP Laptop, McAfee Antivirus	40
T_3	Lenovo Laptop, HP Printer	20
T_4	MacBook Air, Cannon Printer	10
Total Transactions		100

TABLE 13.12 Symbol Representation of items after considering upper level of concept hierarchy

T_X	Items	Frequency
T_1	L, A	30
T_2	L, A	40
T_3	L, P	20
T_4	L, P	10
Total Transactions		100

Now directly we can apply the apriori algorithm on the transformed dataset shown in Table 13.12 and then discover the VALID association rules from the dataset. The minimum support count is calculated as 40 as shown below. Please note that total number of transactions are 100, which is cumulative frequencies of the items. The frequency of the individual items in the dataset is calculated and shown in Table 13.13. So only one possible association exist between {L} and {A}, so we have two possible association rules as shown below. Out of these two the association between Laptop with Antivirus software is INVALID as the calculated confidence measure is less than the minimum confidence threshold value.

$$\text{min\_support\_count} = [\text{No. of Transactions} \times \text{support }\%] = [100 \times 0.4] = 40$$

TABLE 13.13 Frequency of the individual items for the Dataset shown in Table 13.11

Item	Count	
L	100	✓
A	70	✓
P	30	×

$$L \Rightarrow A \ (70\%, 70\%) \ [\text{Invalid Association Rule}]$$
$$A \Rightarrow L \ (70\%, 100\%) \ [\text{Valid Association Rule}]$$

From the illustrative example dataset, it is clearly seen that, not all the laptop buyers are buying the antivirus software but whenever an antivirus software is sold in the dataset then there is a definite buy of the laptop.

13.24 TEMPORAL ASSOCIATION RULES

One of the special types of association rules are temporal association rules in which timing of the association between the set of items is also considered. The general for the temporal association rule is given in the Eq.

$$\alpha \rightarrow \beta \ [\text{support } \%, \text{confidence } \%, t_s, t_e]$$

Where α and β are the set of items associated with each other (frequent itemsets) with the association measures as support and confidence along with the validity period of the association rule indicated by two parameters t_s and t_e indicates the start time and end time of the association rule. The start and end time can be represented by any time unit such as day, week, month, quarter and year, etc. For generating temporal association rules it is necessary to have the transactions time available in the dataset then only one can identify the time validity of the association rules.

13.25 SPATIAL ASSOCIATION RULES

Association analysis is also applied effectively for spatial data mining (geographical/map dataset). In the domain of spatial association analysis, questions like "How many schools are located nearby gardens?", or "How many hospitals are located near to fire brigade systems?" or "How many ATMs are deployed near city centre area?" are addressed. The association between the spatial objects are represented using spatial association rule mining. The general form of spatial association rule is given below:

is_a (X, school) → close_to (X, park) (80%) ("80% of schools are close to parks")

Where, X is a spatial or non-spatial predicates, C% confidence. The above example shows that if X (a spatial object) is a school then there is 80% of the schools are located nearby parks. The is_a and close_to are the spatial relations describing the type of spatial object and proximity between the spatial objects. In spatial data mining, the spatial object relationships are described using, distance, directions and topologies.

13.26 APPLICATIONS

Although association analysis was invented from market basket analysis and have numerous applications in e-commerce systems but at in recent time it has several applications in various domain also. Some of the applications which utilize association analysis are summarized here.

(a) Entertainment: Apps like Spotify or Netflix and other OTT platforms uses association analysis for movie and music recommendations based on the historical user data. If most of the users are watching movie "Y" after watching the movie "X" then using this association information between "X" and "Y", if any user is watching anyone these movie, then system will automatically recommends the other movie for watching in future.

(b) Job recommendations: Applications like LinkedIn utilizes association analysis for recommending new jobs to the users based on their profile and expertise.

(c) Health Informatics: In health informatics association analysis is utilized for comorbidities detection and analysis. Comorbidities are chronic medical conditions that are associated with the other chronic medical conditions.

(d) Intrusion detection system-association rules are also used for making intrusion detection systems and have numerous applications in network security including in banking domain. For making intrusion detection system, rules with low support but very high lift are explored since it has high probability of threats in the systems.

(e) Text mining & NLP-association analysis is also utilized in the frequent terms and N-Gram generations. Association analysis is used for text classification and sentiment analysis. A few examples of association analysis in text analytics are "How many times the word Microsoft is appearing with the word Windows" and in medical reports "How frequently the word Blood is appearing with the word Pressure?".

13.27 CASE STUDY

Classification using Association Rule Mining: Association rule mining is also used for classification of data. For example, consider the dataset of Table 13.8 where the last column of dataset "Loan" can have two possible values "Car Loan" or "Home Loan". So, this dataset can also be seen as a dataset of binary classification, where based on the age and salary of the persons their loan type can be classified. Consider one of the example association rules for the dataset:

Age(X, "26..35") Λ Salary (X, "35..50K") Λ Avail(X, "Car Loan")

Which is indicating that person having age in the range of 26..35 and salary in the range of 35..50K has the possibility of availing the "Car Loan" from the bank. The same association rule may also be seen as a classification rule also like:

If Age = 26..35 ***and*** Salary = "35..50K" ***then*** Loan="Car Loan"

So, this act now as a classification rule also for categorization of the records. Pre-processing will be required for the dataset like individual values of age and salary needs to be converted into the suitable intervals (using discretization or clustering, etc.) then only these types of rules can be generated.

EXERCISES

Given the transactional dataset:

Transaction Id	List of Items
T_1	A B D F G
T_2	B D G
T_3	A C F
T_4	A C E F

(Contd.)

Transaction Id	List of Items
T_5	B D G
T_6	A C E
T_7	A B D E F
T_8	A C G
T_9	A B D F
T_{10}	C D
T_{11}	D F
T_{11}	B D F

1. Calculate the parameters support, confidence, lift for the association rules
   (a) A → B
   (b) B → A
   (c) F → G
2. Apply the Apriori algorithm to identify the valid association rule using
   (a) Support = 30% and confidence = 60%
   (b) Support = 40% and confidence = 80%
3. Create the FP-Tree for the transactional dataset using the FP-Growth algorithm and list all the valid association rules using
   (a) Support = 30% and confidence = 60%
   (b) Support = 40% and confidence = 80%

MULTIPLE CHOICE QUESTIONS

For questions 1 to 6, following dataset is given:

Transaction ID	Items
100	A B C
200	A C
300	A B
400	B C
500	A B

1. What is the support of the association rule A → B in the transactional dataset?
   (a) 50% (b) 60%
   (c) 75% (d) 80%
2. What is the confidence of the association rule A → C in the transactional dataset?
   (a) 50% (b) 60%
   (c) 80% (d) 100%
3. What is the lift of the association rule B → C in the transactional dataset?
   (a) 16.67% (b) 25%
   (c) 33.33% (d) 66.67%

4. What is the cosine value of the association rule A → C in the transactional dataset?
   (a) 0.30 (b) 0.42
   (c) 0.58 (d) 0.90
5. What is the conviction of the association rule A → B in the transactional dataset?
   (a) 0.5 (b) 0.9
   (c) 100 (d) ∞
6. What is the interestingness of the association rule B → C in the transactional dataset?
   (a) 0.25 (b) 0.31
   (c) 0.37 (d) 0.42
7. What is the key benefit of Apriori algorithm for association rule analysis?
   (a) It needs lesser number of scans of database.
   (b) It is computationally simple.
   (c) It automatically eliminates the infrequent items.
   (d) None of the above.
8. What is the key benefit of FP-growth algorithm for association rule analysis
   (a) It requires only one scan of database to list all the association rule
   (b) It requires only two scans of database to list all the association rule
   (c) It automatically eliminates the infrequent items.
   (d) None of the above.
9. Which technique is suitable for handling of numerical data for association rule analysis?
   (a) Static Discretization.
   (b) Dynamic Discretization.
   (c) Distance-based Association Rules.
   (d) All of the above.
10. How hierarchical association rule analysis is carried out?
    (a) The elements are move into the lower concept levels and then association rule mining algorithm is applied.
    (b) The elements are move into the upper concept levels and then association rule mining algorithm is applied.
    (c) First association rule mining algorithm is applied then hierarchy is defined.
    (d) None of these.

For questions 11 and 12 consider the following datasets:

Transaction ID	Items	Frequency
100	A B C	35
200	A C	15
300	A B	15
400	B C	25
500	A B	10

11. What is the support B → C in the repeating transactions dataset?
    (a) 35% (b) 45%
    (c) 25% (d) 95%
12. What is the confidence A → B in the repeating transactions dataset?
    (a) 75% (b) 50%
    (c) 60% (d) 45%

13. How temporal association rules are different from the ordinary association rules?
   (a) The temporal association rules are consisting of time intervals information.
   (b) How association rules changes over time.
   (c) The impact of association rules over time.
   (d) Study the behaviour of association rules over time.
14. Spatial association rules contain the information about
   (a) How the spatial objects are separated.
   (b) Correlated or collocated places of interest.
   (c) Finding characteristics of a particular spatial object.
   (d) None of these.
15. Which of the following is the example of association rule analysis?
   (a) How many times the word Microsoft appears along with the word Windows in a text document.
   (b) How many schools are located nearby parks.
   (c) How many patients having the problem of blood pressure are also having the problem of sugar.
   (d) Identifying trending videos in the YouTube.
16. The association rule analysis for the text data can be carried out using
   (a) By finding the frequency of individual words in the text document only.
   (b) By finding the frequency of co-occurring words in the text document.
   (c) By summarizing the text document.
   (d) None of these.
17. Which of the following is NOT the example of association rule analysis?
   (a) Which set of products are purchased together with.
   (b) Prediction of sales data as per the purchase history of various customers.
   (c) How many hospitals are located nearby fire stations.
   (d) What is the comorbidity of a patient.
18. Which of the following is NOT a measure of Association Rule Analysis?
   (a) Support (b) Confidence
   (c) Lift (d) Correlation

REFERENCES

[1] https://cs.ccsu.edu/~markov/ccsu_courses/DataMining-6.html
[2] Han, J., Kamber, M., and Pei J., Data Mining Concepts and Techniques (2012), ISBN-978-0-12-381479-1.
[3] https://www.sciencedirect.com/topics/computer-science/association-rules
[4] Azevedo, P. J., & Jorge, A. M. (2007, September), Comparing rule measures for predictive association rules, In *European Conference on Machine Learning* (pp. 510–517), Springer, Berlin, Heidelberg.

ANSWER KEY

1. (b) **2.** (d) **3.** (a) **4.** (c) **5.** (d) **6.** (b) **7.** (b) **8.** (b) **9.** (d) **10.** (b)
11. (c) **12.** (a) **13.** (a) **14.** (b) **15.** (d) **16.** (b) **17.** (b) **18.** (d)

14 Recommendation Systems

Introduction

Today there are plenty of applications of recommendation systems (RS) on the internet. Most of the electronic commerce systems use recommender systems to recommend new products to the users. Recommender systems have covered most of the electronic commerce domain such as books recommendation, movies recommendations, travel and tour recommendations, health system recommendation systems, educational recommendation systems and many more. The coverage of recommendation systems is from basic applications such as movie or music recommendation systems to the more specialized and advanced application domains like doctor recommendation system for patients. Recommendation system development is a popular and trending data science technology.

A general recommender system is presented in Figure 14.1. Two essential components are users and items. In general, the work of any recommender system is to recommend a new set of products or items to the users. The objective of any recommender system is two-fold, first is to maximize the profit for the organizations by marketing their products and second to suggest the new products/ items to the users to save their product searching time at the e-commerce sites.

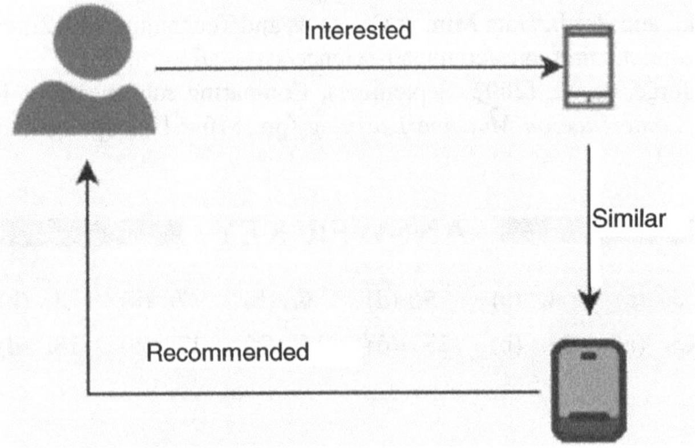

FIGURE 14.1 A General Recommender System

A recommender system can also be presented as a relation given in Eq. (14.1), where $U = \{U_1, U_2, ..., U_N\}$, is the set of users, $I = \{I_1, I_2, ..., I_M\}$, is the set of items, and $R = \{R_1, R_2, ..., R_K\}$ is the set of item ratings. The output of the recommender system is the estimated rating of the new product/item. Using the estimated rating only highly rated items are recommended to the users.

$$f : U \times I \rightarrow R \tag{14.1}$$

The user rating data is represented as a matrix of users and items where each entry represents a rating in a given scale is called utility matrix or user-item matrix shown in Table 14.1. In real-world scenarios there are a lot of missing values in the utility matrix. The task of any RS is to identify the missing values in the utility matrix.

TABLE 14.1 Utility Matrix

User/Item	I_1	I_2	...	I_M
U_1	R_{11}	R_{12}	...	R_{1M}
U_2	R_{21}	R_{22}	...	R_{2M}
⋮	⋮	⋮	⋮	⋮
U_N	R_{N1}	R_{N2}	...	R_{NM}

The categorization of recommender systems is shown in Figure 14.2. The recommender systems are broadly categorized into three categories namely, content-based recommender systems, collaborative

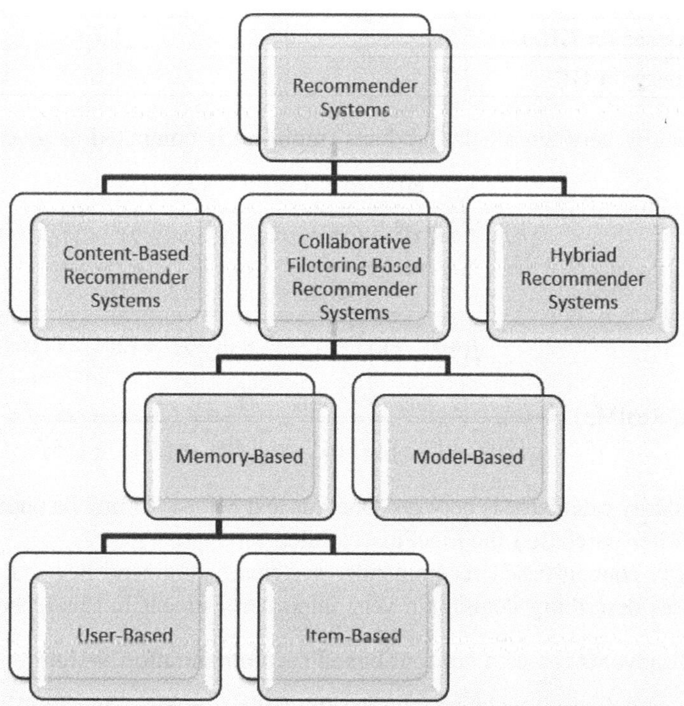

FIGURE 14.2 Types of Recommender Systems.

filtering-based recommender systems and hybrid recommender systems. The collaborative filtering recommender systems are further categorized into two types—memory-based collaborative filtering and model-based collaborative filtering recommender systems. And the memory-based recommender systems are classified as user-based and item-based recommender systems at the bottom level. All these types of recommender systems are briefly discussed and explained with the help of examples in the following sections.

14.1 CONTENT-BASED RECOMMENDER SYSTEMS

In content-based recommender systems (RS), features of the items (products) are used for developing recommender systems. Users who have purchased similar products/items earlier are recommended for possible future purchase. This technique focuses more on items attributes (features) rather than the user profiles and other user information.

Example: Let us assume that some user has purchased a OnePlus mobile phone earlier from one online e-commerce site. The important attributes (features) of mobile phones are tabulated in Table 14.2. The features considered are camera (in megapixel), processor (in GHz) and Memory (in GB) are considered in this example. Let us also assume that apart from OnePlus mobile phone the other two brands available with the same online store are MI and RealMe. The values of all the features are shown in Table 14.2.

TABLE 14.2 Features of Mobile Phone (Item)

Feature	OnePlus	MI	RealMe
Camera (in MP)	40	20	40
Processor (in GHz)	3	3.2	3.4
Memory (in GB)	32	16	16

Now, the similarity between all the products (mobiles) is computed as given below:

$$\text{Sim}(\text{OnePlus, MI}) = \frac{40 \times 20 + 3 \times 3.2 + 32 \times 16}{\sqrt{(40)^2 + (3)^2 + (32)^2} \times \sqrt{(20)^2 + (3.2)^2 + (16)^2}} = 0.99$$

$$\text{Sim}(\text{OnePlus, RealMe}) = \frac{40 \times 40 + 3 \times 3.4 + 32 \times 16}{\sqrt{(40)^2 + (3)^2 + (32)^2} \times \sqrt{(40)^2 + (3.4)^2 + (16)^2}} = 0.96$$

$$\text{Sim}(\text{MI, RealMe}) = \frac{20 \times 40 + 3.2 \times 3.4 + 16 \times 16}{\sqrt{(20)^2 + (3.2)^2 + (16)^2} \times \sqrt{(40)^2 + (3.4)^2 + (16)^2}} = 0.96$$

The maximum similarity calculated is between OnePlus and MI, so MI mobile phone is recommended to the user who earlier purchased the OnePlus mobile.

So, in summary, content-based recommender systems recommend new but similar items and item profile (features describing items) is a very important element in this technique.

Advantages and disadvantages of a content-based recommendation system

The advantage of content-based recommender system is its simple computation. The user's privacy is protected and can accommodate the problem of preference changes by the users. The problem with content-based recommender systems is, it requires detailed information about the items (all the features of items) for developing the recommender system. Sometimes all the detailed information (information about all the attributes) of items is not available in the system which can lead to inaccurate recommendations.

14.2 COLLABORATIVE FILTERING

The other popular category of recommender systems is collaborative filtering techniques. The collaborative filtering techniques are further sub-categorized as memory-based filtering techniques and model-based filtering techniques. The memory-based collaborative filtering approach utilizes the historical (past) user-ratings data to compute the similarity between users and items to recommend new items to the users. The model-based collaborative filtering technique uses machine learning models such as association rule mining, classification, clustering, fuzzy logic, and optimization techniques to develop the recommender systems.

14.2.1 Memory-based Filtering Techniques

The memory-based collaborative filtering technique utilizes historical user-rating information for recommending some items to the users. Generally, while purchasing any product users are asked to provide ratings of the product in a particular scale, for example rating is scale of [1...5] where 1 indicates the poor quality and 5 indicates the best quality of the product. This rating information is presented in a form of table, which is called as utility (user-item) matrix. The example utility matrix is shown in Table 14.3. A few entries in the utility matrix are missing. **The task of the recommender system is to predict the missing values in the utility matrix.**

TABLE 14.3 Example Utility-Matrix

User/Item	I_1	I_2	I_3	I_4	I_5
Alice	4	1	–	3	1
Bob	3	2	2	–	2
Chris	1	3	4	1	–
David	–	–	5	2	4

Normalized Utility Matrix

Sometimes the ratings are normalized by subtracting each rating by its average rating given by the user.

$$R_{ij} = R_{ij} - \overline{R_{U_i}} \tag{14.2}$$

Where, R_{ij} is the rating given by i^{th} user U_i for j^{th} item I_j and $\overline{R_U}$ is the average ratings given by the ith User U_i.

The average ratings of the users are $\overline{R_{Alice}} = \frac{4+1+3+1}{3} = 3$, $\overline{R_{Bob}} = \frac{3+2+2+2}{3} = 3$, $\overline{R_{Chris}} = \frac{1+3+4+1}{3} = 3$, and $\overline{R_{David}} = \frac{5+2+4}{3} = 3.67s$, respectively.

TABLE 14.4 Utility Matrix with Normalized Ratings

User	I_1	I_2	I_3	I_4	I_5
Alice	1	–2	–	0	–2
Bob	0	–1	–1	–	–1
Chris	–2	0	1	–2	–
David	–	–	1.33	–1.67	0.33

Using normalization of the ratings, all the below average ratings will become negatives and all the above average ratings will become positives. It will improve the similarity measurement between the users and similarity measurement between the items.

The memory-based collaborative filtering approaches are divided into two major categories namely, user-based filtering and item-based filtering. Both of the techniques use the user profile (collection of historical user preferences in terms of ratings) rating data for making new recommendations.

User-based Collaborative Filtering

The user-based collaborative filtering approach identifies the similarity between the users for making new recommendations. The basic concept behind this technique is similar users may have similar choices (for products/items), so on the basis of user similarity new products are recommended. The user-based filtering approach is summarized in Figure 14.3. The similarity between the users can be calculated using the similarity functions like cosine or Pearson coefficient.

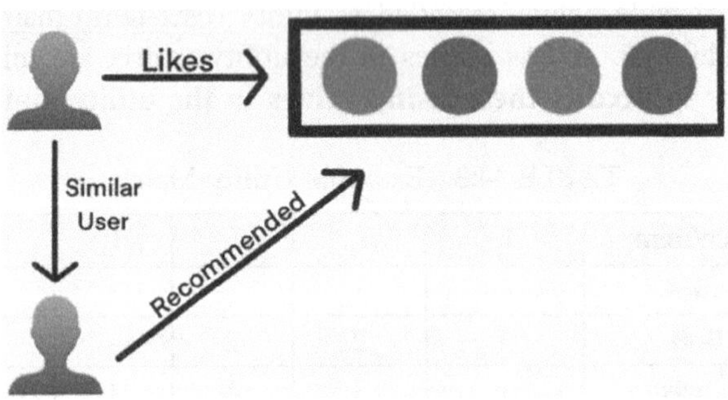

FIGURE 14.3 User-based Collaborative Filtering Approach

Under user-based collaborative filtering approach, the missing rating is estimated using Eq. (14.3).

$$R_{ij} = R(U_i, I_j) = \overline{R_{U_i}} + \frac{\sum_{k \in U} sim(U_i, U_k) \times R(U_k, I_j)}{\sum_{k \in U} sim(U_i, U_k)} \tag{14.3}$$

where, $\overline{R_{U_i}}$ is the average of ratings provided by i^{th} user, and sim(U_i, U_k) is the similarity between the ith and k^{th} user. $R(U_k, I_j)$ is the rating of jth item given by k^{th} user.

Let us understand the user-based collaborative filtering approach using a numerical example. Suppose we have been given the utility matrix of Table 14.3 and we have to estimate all the missing values in it. For example, to estimate the rating of item I_3 by the user *Alice*, first of all user similarities between Alice and all the other users rated the same item, i.e., I_3 is required. For I_3 users Bob, Chris and David have been rated. Also, average ratings provided by Alice need to be calculated as follows:

$$\text{Sim}(\text{Alice, Bob}) = \frac{4\times3+1\times2+1\times2}{\sqrt{(4)^2+(1)^2+(1)^2}\times\sqrt{(3)^2+(2)^2+(2)^2}} = 0.91$$

$$\text{Sim}(\text{Alice, Chris}) = 0.59$$

$$\text{Sim}(\text{Alice, David}) = 0.71$$

$$\overline{R_{\text{Alice}}} = \frac{4+1+3+1}{4} = 2.25$$

Then using Eq. (14.3) the rating of item I_3 for the user Alice is calculated as under:

$$R(U_{\text{Alice}}, I_3) = \overline{R_{\text{Alice}}} + \frac{\sum_{k\in U}\text{sim}(U_{\text{Alice}}, U_k)\times R(U_k, I_3)}{\sum_{k\in U}\text{sim}(U_i, U_k)} = 2.25 + \frac{0.59\times2+0.71\times4+0.81\times5}{0.59+0.71+0.81} = 6.07 \cong 6$$

Similarly, we can computer all the missing values, for the example utility matrix. The estimated missing values are shown in Table 14.5.

$$\text{Sim}(\text{Bob, Chris}) = 0.81$$

$$\text{Sim}(\text{Bob, David}) = 0.99$$

$$\text{Sim}(\text{Chris, David}) = 0.99$$

$$\overline{R_{\text{Bob}}} = \frac{3+2+2+2}{4} = 2.25$$

$$\overline{R_{\text{Chris}}} = \frac{1+3+4+1}{4} = 2.25$$

$$\overline{R_{David}} = \frac{5+2+4}{4} = 2.75$$

$$R(U_{\text{Bob}}, I_4) = \overline{R_{\text{Bob}}} + \frac{\sum_{k\in U}\text{sim}(U_{\text{Bob}}, U_k)\times R(U_k, I_4)}{\sum_{k\in U}\text{sim}(U_i, U_k)} = 2.25 + \frac{0.91\times3+0.81\times2+0.99\times1}{0.91+0.81+0.99} = 4.22 \cong 4$$

$$R(U_{\text{Chris}}, I_5) = \overline{R_{\text{Chris}}} + \frac{\sum_{k\in U}\text{sim}(U_{\text{Chris}}, U_k)\times R(U_k, I_5)}{\sum_{k\in U}\text{sim}(U_i, U_k)} = 2.25 + \frac{0.59\times1+0.81\times2+0.99\times4}{0.59+0.81+0.99} = 5.05 \cong 5$$

$$R(U_{\text{David}}, I_1) = \overline{R_{\text{David}}} + \frac{\sum_{k\in U}\text{sim}(U_{\text{David}}, U_k)\times R(U_k, I_1)}{\sum_{k\in U}\text{sim}(U_i, U_k)} = 2.75 + \frac{0.71\times4+0.99\times3+0.99\times1}{0.71+0.99+0.99} = 5.28 \cong 5$$

$$R(U_{\text{David}}, I_2) = \overline{R_{\text{David}}} + \frac{\sum_{k\in U}\text{sim}(U_{\text{David}}, U_k)\times R(U_k, I_2)}{\sum_{k\in U}\text{sim}(U_i, U_k)} = 2.75 + \frac{0.71\times1+0.99\times2+0.99\times3}{0.71+0.99+0.99} = 4.85 \cong 5$$

TABLE 14.5 Estimation of missing ratings using user-based approach

User/Item	I_1	I_2	I_3	I_4	I_5
Alice	4	1	⑥	3	1
Bob	3	2	2	④	2
Chris	1	3	4	1	⑤
David	⑤	⑤	5	2	4

Item-based filtering

The second memory-based approach is item-based collaborative filtering technique. In this technique, the similarity between the items is considered for the new recommendations. The basic principle behind this technique is that users may like to buy a similar item in future. The item-based filtering approach is summarized in Figure 14.4. Just like the user similarity, the similarity between the items can be calculated using the similarity functions like cosine or Pearson coefficient.

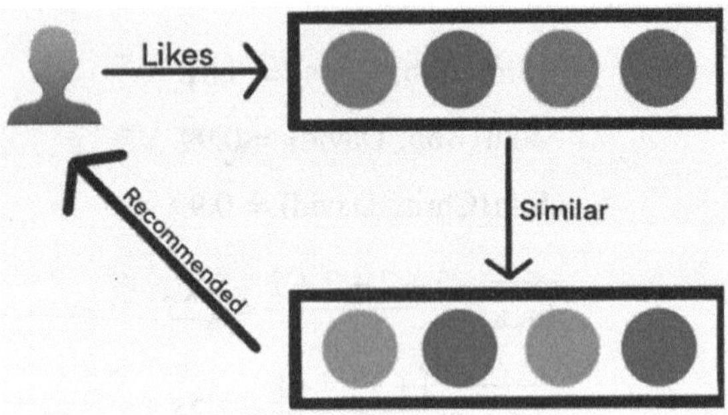

FIGURE 14.4 Item-based Collaborative Filtering Approach.

The missing values of rating using the item-based collaborative filtering approach are calculated by Eq. (14.4).

$$R(U, I_i) = \frac{\sum_j R(U, I_j) \times \text{Sim}(I_i, I_j)}{\sum_j \text{Sim}(I_i, I_j)} \tag{14.4}$$

Where, $R(U, I_j)$ is the rating of jth item provided by the user U, and $\text{Sim}(I_i, I_j)$ is the similarity between the ith and j^{th} item.

Suppose we wish to estimate the rating for the item I_2 from the user *David*, then it is estimated as given below using item-based collaborative filtering approach.

$$R(\text{David}, I_2) = \frac{\sum_j R(\text{David}, I_j) \times \text{Sim}(I_2, I_j)}{\sum_j \text{Sim}(I_2, I_j)}$$

$$= \frac{R(\text{David}, I_3) \times \text{Sim}(I_2, I_3) + R(\text{David}, I_4) \times \text{Sim}(I_2, I_4) + R(\text{David}, I_5) \times \text{Sim}(I_2, I_5)}{\text{Sim}(I_2, I_3) + \text{Sim}(I_2, I_4) + \text{Sim}(I_2, I_5)}$$

$$= \frac{5\times\left(\frac{2\times2+3\times4}{\sqrt{2^2+3^2}\times\sqrt{2^2+4^2}}\right)+2\times\left(\frac{1\times3+3\times1}{\sqrt{1^2+3^2}\times\sqrt{3^2+1^2}}\right)+4\times\left(\frac{1\times1+2\times2}{\sqrt{1^2+2^2}\times\sqrt{1^2+2^2}}\right)}{\left(\frac{2\times2+3\times4}{\sqrt{2^2+3^2}\times\sqrt{2^2+4^2}}\right)+\left(\frac{1\times3+3\times1}{\sqrt{1^2+3^2}\times\sqrt{3^2+1^2}}\right)+\left(\frac{1\times1+2\times2}{\sqrt{1^2+2^2}\times\sqrt{1^2+2^2}}\right)}$$

$$= 3.92 \cong 4$$

Similarly, we can estimate the other missing values also. The calculated values are shown in Table 14.6.

TABLE 14.6 Estimated values for the ratings using item-based approach

User/Item	I_1	I_2	I_3	I_4	I_5
Alice	4	1	②	3	1
Bob	3	2	2	②	2
Chris	1	3	4	1	②
David	④	④	5	2	4

14.2.2 Model-based Filtering

Apart from the memory-based collaborative filtering approach, the second major category under collaborative filtering approach is model-based filtering approach for developing the recommender systems. Under this category, machine learning and mathematical models are utilized for development of recommender systems. Techniques like Association Rule-based filtering, Classification (Decision Tree/SVM)-based recommender systems, clustering-based filtering, neural network-based models, and matrix-based filtering techniques are a few examples of this category. A brief overview of some of the popular techniques is discussed here.

Association Rule-based filtering

Association rule mining technique is widely used for making recommendations in electronic commerce sites because of its simplicity. An association rule indicates the relationship between the set of items purchased together frequently. For example, the following association rule indicates that whenever a user buys a laptop then he may also buy the antivirus software along with it. So, if any user has purchased a laptop earlier then antivirus software can also be recommended to the same user.

$$\text{Laptop} \rightarrow \text{Antivirus}\,[40\%, 80\%]$$

Classification (Decision Tree/SVM)-based RS

A recommender system can be seen as a classification technique of items for recommending to the users. It can be a binary classification problem with recommended or not-recommended classes. Alternatively, it can be a multi-class classification problem where class represents the rating of the products/items. Various classifiers like logistics regression, support vector machine, neural networks, and decision tree algorithms can be used for developing recommender systems. A prototype of decision tree-based recommender system is shown in Figure 14.5.

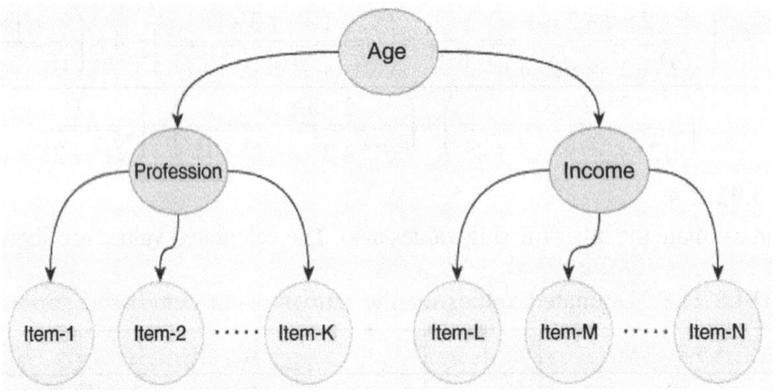

FIGURE 14.5 A Decision Tree-based Recommender System.

Clustering-based filtering

Clustering is also a widely used machine learning model for development of recommender systems. Using clustering, groups of similar users and items are created. It is assumed that similar users may like similar items. User profile data and item features are considered for creation of clusters. Then the clusters are utilized for making decisions for recommender systems.

Matrix-based filtering

Collaborative filtering uses both matrix factorization and vector decomposition techniques for making the recommendations. Matrix factorization and vector decomposition techniques help in dimension reductions of the recommender systems and handling the problem of data sparsity in utility matrix.

14.3 HYBRID FILTERING

The third major category of recommender systems is hybrid filtering techniques. As name indicates, it is a combined approach using content-based filtering and collaborative filtering approaches. It is a general cross-user or cross-item model for making recommendations to users. The combination of recommender systems can be done in many ways. Six major categories of hybrid approaches along with its description is presented in Figure 14.6.

14.4 PERFORMANCE EVALUATION OF RECOMMENDER SYSTEMS

The performance of recommender systems can be evaluated in many ways. The three major classifications of evaluation metrics for recommender systems are—error-based metrics, confusion matrix-based metrics and ranking-based metrics.

Error-based Metrics

In error-based metrics for recommender systems, errors are estimated for predicted recommendations vs. the actual recommendations. Two popular error metrics are MAE (Mean Average Error) and RMSE (Root Mean Squared Error). The MAE and RMSE are calculated using Eq. (14.5) and (14.6).

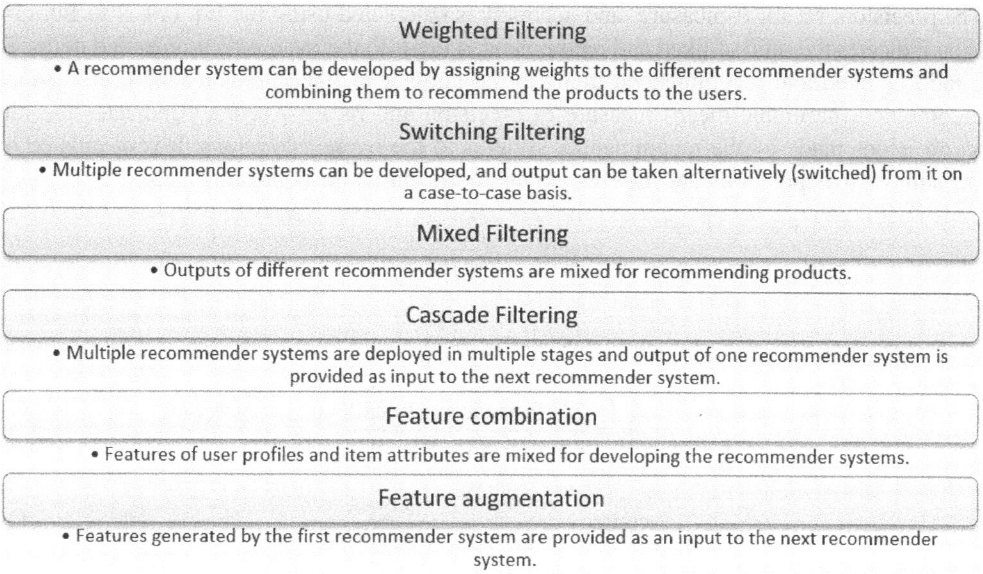

FIGURE 14.6 Hybrid Filtering Approaches for Recommender System.

$$\text{MAE} = \frac{\sum_{i=1}^{N} \left|\widehat{y_i} - y_i\right|}{N} \tag{14.5}$$

$$\text{RMSE} = \sqrt{\frac{\sum_{i=1}^{N} \left(\widehat{y_i} - y_i\right)^2}{N}} \tag{14.6}$$

where, N is the number of recommendations, $\widehat{y_i}$ are the predicted ratings and y_i are the actual ratings.

Confusion Matrix-based Metrics

In model-based recommender systems, generally machine learning techniques are utilized for developing recommender systems. Confusion matrix provides data for evaluating performance of machine learning algorithms. The confusion matrix is shown in Table 14.7. It presents the information of user likes vs recommendations made by the recommendation systems. It is having four major entries, *TP* (True Positives) indicates that user likes the items and the same is recommended, *FN* (False Negative) is user likes the items, but it is not recommended by the recommender system, *FP* (False Positive) is user do not like the items, but it is recommended, and *TN* (True Negative) is user don't like the items and it is not recommended by recommender systems also. Using these four values a number of metrics can be calculated. The most popular metrics are precision, recall, *F*-measure, and accuracy.

TABLE 14.7 Confusion Matrix

Confusion Matrix		Predicted	
		Recommended	**Not Recommended**
Actual	Likes	*TP*	*FN*
	Don't Likes	*FP*	*TN*

The precision, recall, *F*-measure, and accuracy is calculated using the Eq. (14.7) to Eq. (14.10). Precision indicates the ratio of liked and recommended items to the overall recommended items. Recall is the ratio of liked and recommended items to the number of liked items by the users. F-measure is the combined (harmonic mean) measure of precision and recall. Accuracy indicates the ratio of correct decisions made by the recommender systems to the overall decisions. It is calculated by the ratio of sum of true positions and true negatives to all entries in confusion matrix.

$$\text{Precision} = \frac{TP}{TP + FP} \tag{14.7}$$

$$\text{Recall} = \frac{TP}{TP + FN} \tag{14.8}$$

$$F = \frac{2 \times \text{Precision} \times \text{Recall}}{\text{Precision} + \text{Recall}} \tag{14.9}$$

$$\text{Accuracy} = \frac{TP + TN}{TP + FP + FN + TN} \tag{14.10}$$

Ranking-based Metrics

The last set of evaluation metrics for recommender systems are ranking-based metrics. The recommendations are ranked in an order and top *K* recommendations are chosen for the users. The important metrics are precision@*K*, recall@*K*, *F@K* (*F*-measure at *K*), and accuracy@*K*, MAP@*K* (mean average precision at *K*), and *NDCG* (normalized discounted cumulative gain). These metrics are explained using an example in this section.

Let us assume that $K = 5$, i.e., a total of 5 items, are recommended by the recommender system. Out of 5 items, 3 items are relevant to the user whereas 2 items are irrelevant. The rank of 5 recommended items is in the following sequence as shown in Table 14.8.

TABLE 14.8 Illustrative Example of Precision@*K* and Recall@*K*

Recommended	✓	×	✓	×	✓
***K* (rank)**	1	2	3	4	5
Precision@*K*	$\frac{1}{1}$	$\frac{1}{2}$	$\frac{2}{3}$	$\frac{2}{4}$	$\frac{3}{5}$
Recall@*K*	$\frac{1}{3}$	$\frac{1}{3}$	$\frac{2}{3}$	$\frac{2}{3}$	$\frac{3}{3}$
F1@*K*	$\frac{2 \times \frac{1}{1} \times \frac{1}{3}}{\frac{1}{1} + \frac{1}{3}} = 0.5$	0.4	0.67	0.57	0.75
Accuracy@*K*	$\frac{1}{5}$	$\frac{1}{5}$	$\frac{2}{5}$	$\frac{3}{5}$	$\frac{3}{5}$
rel_i	1	0	1	0	1

The calculation of precision@k, recall@K, F@K, and accuracy@K is shown in Table 14.8. K indicates the top recommendations made to the users. Precision@1 is $\frac{1}{1}$, Precision@2 is $\frac{1}{2}$, Precision@3 is $\frac{2}{3}$, Precision@4 is $\frac{2}{4}$, Precision@5 is $\frac{3}{5}$.

The average precision is $\frac{1}{3}\left(\frac{1}{1}+\frac{2}{3}+\frac{3}{5}\right) \cong 0.76$. It indicates the average of precision values for the correct recommendations.

The mean average precision (MAP) for top K recommendations is calculated using Eq. (14.11)

$$\text{MAP@}K = \frac{1}{K} \times \sum_{i=1}^{K} P(K) \times rel_K \tag{14.11}$$

rel_i is 1 if the recommended item is relevant otherwise it is 0.

For the example of Table 14.8, the MAP@5 is calculated as below.

$$\text{MAP@5} = \frac{\frac{1}{1}\times 1+\frac{1}{2}\times 0+\frac{2}{3}\times 1+\frac{2}{4}\times 0+\frac{3}{5}\times 1}{5} = 0.45$$

NDCG (Normalized Discounted Cumulative Gain)

Another measure for performance evaluation of ranking-based metrics is *NDCG* measure, which is derived from the cumulative gain and discounted cumulative gain measures. Let the relevance of items recommended by a recommender system are $r_1, r_2, \ldots, r_K$ then Cumulative Gain is calculated as sum of all the relevance, i.e., $r_1 + r_2 + \ldots + r_K$.

Discounted cumulative gain at rank K is calculated using Eq. (14.13) which is derived from general discounted cumulative gain that is calculated using Eq. (14.12).

$$DCG = r_1 + \frac{r_2}{\log_2 2} + \frac{r_3}{\log_2 3} + \ldots + \frac{r_K}{\log_2 K} \tag{14.12}$$

$$DCG_K = \sum_{i=1}^{K} \frac{2^{rel_i} - 1}{\log(1+i)} \tag{14.13}$$

where, rel_i is the relevance of ith recommendation.

Normalized discounted cumulative gain is one of the popular evaluation metrics used particularly used in web search engines recommendations.

$$NDCG_K = \frac{DCG_K}{IDCG_K} \tag{14.14}$$

where, DCG_K and $IDCG_K$ are the discounted cumulative gain at K^{th} recommendation and *IDCG* is the discounted cumulative gain for ideal case (highly relevant recommendations first) at K^{th} recommendation.

Let us understand the calculation of *NDCG* with the help of an example recommender system given in Table 14.9. A total of 5 recommendations are made and high relevance value indicates recommended item is more relevant and 0 or lesser value indicates that the recommendations made are least relevant to the user.

TABLE 14.9 Relevance of Recommended Items

Recommended	✓	×	✓	×	✓
K	1	2	3	4	5
Relevance	3	0	2	0	3

$$\text{Cumulative Gain} = \sum_{i=1}^{5} rel_i = 3 + 0 + 2 + 0 + 3 = 8$$

$$DCG_5 = \sum_{i=1}^{5} \frac{rel_i}{\log_2(i+1)} = \frac{3}{\log_2 2} + \frac{0}{\log_2 3} + \frac{2}{\log_2 4} + \frac{0}{\log_2 5} + \frac{3}{\log_2 6} = 4.67$$

$$IDCG_5 = \frac{3}{\log_2 2} + \frac{3}{\log_2 3} + \frac{2}{\log_2 4} + \frac{0}{\log_2 5} + \frac{0}{\log_2 6} = 5.89$$

$$NDCG = \frac{DCG_5}{IDCG_5} = 0.79$$

The *NDCG* score of 1 indicates that the recommended items are in perfect order and score of 0 indicates that order of recommended items is not proper.

14.5 CHALLENGES

Development of recommender system for real-world applications has several issues and challenges. A few major challenges along with their possible mitigation are discussed briefly in this section. It is discussed that recommender systems mostly utilize the user-profile and item-profile-data along with the rating information of items provided by the users (utility matrix data). In real-world scenario, these data suffer from ***changing user preferences*** (user opinion/rating changes over time) and with the problem of ***data sparsity*** (a lot of missing values). Due to this, the performance of the recommender system is sacrificed. It can lead to the ***problem of cold start***. The cold start problem is described as establishing relations between users and items is difficult due to insufficient data. The insufficient data is due to the following three major reasons:

1. New User—no detailed information about the new users.
2. New Product—no detailed information about new items.
3. New community—low interactions between users and items (also known as systematic bootstrapping).

Another major challenge in recommender systems is the ***problem of latency***. In collaborative filtering-based recommender systems, when new products are introduced in a rapid manner, then it can lead to the problem of latency. As for the newly added products, review ratings will be missing in the system, and it will cause difficulty in recommending these items. Content-based recommender system can handle the problem of latency, as, similarity of the new products will be calculated and then recommendations can be made but it will take extra computational of item similarity as well as detailed description of all the new products should be provided to the system.

Shilling attack problem in recommender system arise due to fake users provide ratings, that causes trouble in recommending the good items to users and it also eliminates trust from the user side for the recommended items. ***The synonymy problem*** arises due to similar/related items having different entries/names in the system and system get confused to make proper recommending items/ratings. Another problem in recommender systems is the ***grey sheep problem*** in which the feedback of a user does not match with neighbourhoods and hence it is difficult to find similar users/ratings for making new recommendations. ***Scalability*** is another important challenge in any recommender system which deals with the problem of accommodating increasing number of users and items in the recommender systems by maintaining the trust, novelty and performance of the recommendation systems.

Mitigation Techniques

Although a number of challenging issues exist for developing recommender systems, over the period of time a few solutions are also suggested to overcome and mitigate these challenges. The solutions are broadly categorized into three categories namely, representative approach, feature mapping and hybrid approaches. These approaches are summarized in brief below.

1. Representative approach—In this approach the representatives are selected which are closely related to users. It can help the recommender system even if it does not have detailed information about new users. Apart from this, if new users join any application, then ask a few questions or perform some minor survey for like/dislike of items or preferences, etc. so that additional information will be generated for the recommender systems for the new users.
2. Feature Mapping—In case of missing information of items techniques like matrix, factorization can be utilized for handling data sparsity. Matrix factorization helps in identifying key features from the utility (user-item) matrix even if there are missing values. Another approach of feature mapping is estimation of latent factors for missing items. For new items there is no latent factor (items linking with attributes), then by combining attribute choices latent factors may be predicted. For example, for the mobile phone attributes are camera, memory, processor speed, then by combing attribute choices latent factors (user likeness) may be derived. As although the mobile phones can be new (for which no detailed information is available to recommender system) but user might be interested in the mobile phones having good camera, high memory and processor speed, etc. so the new mobile phone can still be considered for making the new recommendations.
3. Hybrid Approach—Hybrid approach combines the solutions provided by representative approaches and feature mapping approaches. Apart from this, user information such as location, age-group, gender, etc. can also be considered to handle the cases where detailed user information or item information is missing for the development of recommender system.

Apart from these, advanced machine learning and deep learning techniques are also utilized for handling of the discussed challenges of recommendation systems.

14.6 PROPERTIES OF A RECOMMENDER SYSTEM

The recommender systems should have few desired properties. The major properties and its description are summarized in Table 14.10.

TABLE 14.10 Properties of a Recommender System

Property	Description
User Preferences	Recommendation system should be able to handle the changing of user preferences over the period of time.
Prediction Accuracy	Recommendation system should provide a good rating prediction accuracy, and good user predictions.
Coverage	Item space and user space coverage should be maximized.
Confidence	Recommendation system should provide confidence in trust in rating.
Trust	Users trust should be maximized in recommendations.
Novelty	Recommender system is supposed to recommend new items to the users.
Serendipity	Surprisingness of successful recommendations should be maximized.
Diversity	Recommendation system should cover the diversity of items and users (covers wide range of the users and items).
Utility	Value gained by the user (utility) should be maximized.
Robustness	Recommendation system should deliver secure and stable recommendations.
Privacy	Recommendation system should not reveal the private information of users.
Scalability	Recommender system should be scalable, i.e., can recommend items even if number of users or items are increased.

Ranking systems vs. Recommender systems

Ranking is simply ordering of the products in a particular order based on some criteria. Similar products can have similar ranking, but it is not necessary that the same items may be recommended by the recommender system. A recommender system should avoid recommending the duplicate product to maintain novelty for the users. The example of ranking system is search results from the search engine where the results are shown in particular order, whereas in recommender system products are recommended to the users even if they have less ranking (rating).

14.7 ADVANCED AI TECHNIQUES FOR RECOMMENDER SYSTEMS

Recently, a number of recommender systems have been developed using advanced artificial intelligence techniques. A brief overview of these technologies for development of recommender system is discussed in this section. The technologies are broadly categorized in three major categories. The first category is deep Learning based models for recommender systems. The second technique is based on advance learning techniques such as active, transfer, and reinforcement learning-based models. And the third technique is fuzzy logic and optimization-based models for recommender systems.

14.7.1 Deep Learning-based Models

Deep learning models are the advanced data science models which promise high performance for data analytics tasks. Deep learning models also help in developing the more accurate recommender systems. Deep learning-based cold-start solutions utilize the Dropout-Net and Session-based RNN (Recurrent Neural Networks) models. Various deep learning models are utilized for specific tasks, for example the MLP (Multi-Layer Perceptron) is widely used for regression and classification, AE (Autoencoder) networks are used for feature representation, CNN (Convolutional Neural Networks) are used for image processing and classification, and RNN/LSTM (Long Short-Term Memory) are used for sequence data processing. These models are used for developing recommender systems based on the type of input data and processing logic. For example, if the input data for recommender system is in image format, then CNN is the most popular model, similarly, while developing classification-based recommender systems, MLP can be a good choice.

14.7.2 Active, Transfer, and Reinforcement Learning for Recommender Systems

Recently advanced machine learning techniques are also utilized for developing recommendation systems. Active learning, transfer learning, and reinforcement learning is utilized in explored in a number of recent works for developing the recommender systems. All these learning techniques have different advantages. Active learning selects the most appropriate samples from the training dataset for better performance. Transfer learning mechanism is instead of building new models, pre-trained models are used for developing recommender systems. Reinforcement is a reward-penalty based learning model, where for good recommendations performance score is increased and for bad recommendations performance score is decreased. These learning models can be utilized individually or in combination for developing improved recommender systems.

14.7.3 Fuzzy Logic and Optimization Techniques for Recommender Systems

Optimization techniques and fuzzy logic are also used for developing the recommender systems. Optimization techniques like Particle Swarm Optimization (PSO), and Ant Colony Optimization (ACO) can be used for computational optimization during development of recommender system. Apart from this, the optimization techniques and fuzzy logic can also be used for developing the constraint-based recommender systems in which additional criteria are added during development of recommender systems.

EXERCISES

Consider the following two matrices for answer the questions.

TABLE 14.11 Feature values for the 5 different items.

Item/Features	F_1	F_2	F_3	F_4	F_5
I_1	12	1	101	23	42
I_2	10	1	100	25	49
I_3	10	3	109	21	32
I_4	11	3	105	23	54
I_5	12	2	104	23	44

TABLE 14.12 A utility matrix indicating the ratings of different items in the range of [1.5]

User/Item	I_1	I_2	I_3	I_4	I_5
U_1	5	4	2		4
U_2	1	3		3	4

(Contd.)

User/Item	I_1	I_2	I_3	I_4	I_5
U_3		3	4	3	
U_4	1		2		4
U_5	3	4		5	4

1. A user has purchased the item I_1, using the content-based recommender system recommend another item (from the set of I_1, I_2, I_3, I_4, I_5) to the same user?
2. Using the user-based filtering technique, fill in the missing ratings value of the utility matrix.
3. Using the item-based filtering technique, fill in the missing ratings value of the utility matrix.
4. A recommender system has recommended 10 items as per the following table:

Recommended	✓	✓	✓	×	✓	×	×	✓	✓	✓
K (rank)	1	2	3	4	5	6	7	8	9	10

5. Calculate Precision@K, Recall@K, and Accuracy@K for the above recommended items.

MULTIPLE CHOICE QUESTIONS

1. In content-based recommender systems:
   (a) Recommendations are made by calculating the similarities between the users.
   (b) Recommendations are made by the property or attributes of the items.
   (c) Recommendations are made by calculating the similarities between the items.
   (d) None of these.
2. In which of the following technique recommender systems are developed using mathematical modelling and machine learning techniques?
   (a) Content-based filtering (b) Collaborative filtering
   (c) Mathematical filtering (d) Model-based filtering
3. The disadvantage of content-based recommender systems is
   (a) It requires detailed information about the items.
   (b) It requires detailed information about the users.
   (c) It requires detailed information about the market space.
   (d) It is computationally very expensive.
4. In which of the following recommender systems Multiple recommender systems can be developed, and output can be taken alternatively from it on a case-to-case basis?
   (a) Mixed Filtering (b) Switching Filtering
   (c) Cascade Filtering (d) Feature Augmentation
5. In which of the following multiple recommender systems are deployed in multiple stages and output of one recommender system is provided as input to the next recommender system?
   (a) Mixed Filtering (b) Switching Filtering
   (c) Cascade Filtering (d) Feature Augmentation

For question number 6 to 9 assume that the following recommendations are generated by the recommender system:

Recommended	Yes	Yes	No	No	Yes
Rank	1	2	3	4	5

6. What is the value of precision@3?

(a) 100% (b) 66.67%
(c) 50% (d) 60%

7. What is the value of recall@4?

(a) 33.33% (b) 60%
(c) 66.67% (d) 100%

8. What is the value of Accuracy@2?

(a) 20% (b) 40%
(c) 60% (d) 80%

9. What is the value of MAP@2?

(a) 52% (b) 60%
(c) 80% (d) 100%

10. What does the NDCG (Normalized Discounted Cumulative Gain) indicates:

(a) It is a metric used to differentiate between the relevant and irrelevant recommendations.
(b) It is a ranking quality metric based on the cumulative and discounted cumulative gain.
(c) It indicates the order of the recommended items by a recommendation system.
(d) None of these.

11. The problem of cold start in recommender systems is associated with

(a) No detailed information about new users or products.
(b) No detailed information about new communities.
(c) Establishing relations between users and items is difficult due to insufficient data.
(d) All of these.

12. When new products are introduced in a rapid manner, then it can lead to

(a) Problem of Information Loss
(b) Problem of Cold Start
(c) Problem of Latency
(d) None of these.

13. Which technique can be helpful for mitigating the problem of cold start in recommender systems:

(a) Representative Approach
(b) Feature Mapping
(c) Hybrid Approach by combining (A) and (B)
(d) All of these.

14. In feature mapping technique:

(a) Matrix factorization can be utilized for handling data sparsity.
(b) Latent factors for missing items are estimated.
(c) Both (A) and (B)
(d) None of these.

15. The ***confidence*** property of recommender system is related to:

(a) Value gained by the user (utility) should be maximized.
(b) Recommendation system should provide confidence in trust in rating.
(c) Item space and user space coverage should be maximized.
(d) Surprisingness of successful recommendations should be maximized.

16. The ***serendipity*** property of recommender system is related to:

(a) Value gained by the user (utility) should be maximized.
(b) Recommendation system should provide confidence in trust in rating.
(c) Item space and user space coverage should be maximized.
(d) Surprisingness of successful recommendations should be maximized.

17. In a given content-based recommender system, a movie has the following features represented by a vector: [1, 0, 1, 1, 0] for the genres (Action, Comedy, Drama, Thriller, Romance). For another movie a feature vector is given as [0, 1, 1, 1, 1], then the Jaccard similarity between these two movies is:

(a) 0.4 (b) 0.5
(c) 0.3 (d) 0.6

18. The user-item ratings matrix for a collaborative filtering recommender system is given as:

User/Item	Item 1	Item 2	Item 3
User A	5	3	0
User B	4	0	2
User C	0	3	4

There is another user D, who is similar to user A and user C. If User D has rated Item 1 as 3 and Item 2 as 4, what would be the predicted rating for Item 3?

(a) 3.5 (b) 2.5
(c) 4.0 (d) 3.0

19. A hybrid recommender system is developed by combining two recommender systems content-based filtering and collaborative filtering. If a weight of 0.6 to content-based recommendations and 0.4 to collaborative recommendations, and it recommends an item with a content score of 8 and a collaborative score of 6, then the final score for the item is calculated as:

(a) 7.2 (b) 7.6
(c) 8.0 (d) 6.4

REFERENCES

[1] https://web.stanford.edu/class/cs276/handouts/EvaluationNew-handout-1-per.pdf
[2] https://www.geeksforgeeks.org/normalized-discounted-cumulative-gain-multilabel-ranking-metrics-ml/
[3] https://link.springer.com/chapter/10.1007/978-3-030-40037-8_8
[4] Roy, D., & Dutta, M. (2022), A systematic review and research perspective on recommender systems, *Journal of Big Data*, *9*(1), 1–36.
[5] Silveira, T., Zhang, M., Lin, X., Liu, Y., & Ma, S. (2019), How good your recommender system is? A survey on evaluations in recommendation, *International Journal of Machine Learning and Cybernetics*, *10*(5), 813–831.
[6] Zhang, Q., Lu, J., & Jin, Y. (2021), Artificial intelligence in recommender systems, *Complex & Intelligent Systems*, *7*(1), 439–457.
[7] Cold-Start Problem in Recommender Systems and its Mitigation Techniques - https://analyticsindiamag.com/cold-start-problem-in-recommender-systems-and-its-mitigation-techniques/
[8] Batmaz, Z., Yurekli, A., Bilge, A., & Kaleli, C. (2019), A review on deep learning for recommender systems: challenges and remedies, *Artificial Intelligence Review*, *52*(1), 1–37.
[9] Rajaraman, A., & Ullman, J. D. (2011), *Mining of massive datasets*, Cambridge University Press.

ANSWER KEY

1. (b) **2.** (d) **3.** (a) **4.** (b) **5.** (c) **6.** (b) **7.** (c) **8.** (b) **9.** (d) **10.** (b)
11. (d) **12.** (c) **13.** (d) **14.** (c) **15.** (b) **16.** (d) **17.** (a) **18.** (d) **19.** (b)

15 Case Studies: Data Analysis in Action

Introduction

In this chapter, we will demonstrate the application of the concepts discussed so far to real-world datasets. We will follow the five-step process discussed in chapter 1. Asking the questions, obtaining relevant data, exploring the data, modeling it and finally, communicating the insights, results and answers obtained using visualization. In our case, the datasets are public and freely available. We will discuss three case studies, which can be used as a template for your future analysis of other datasets. We have also provided code snippets and links to python notebooks which can be re-used and enhanced by the readers.

CASE STUDY 1: TITANIC SURVIVAL PREDICTION

You may have heard about the famous ship Titanic, which met with an unfortunate accident on its maiden voyage. You are asked to predict based on the details (attributes) of a passenger, whether he/she survived the disaster or not. How will you approach the problem?

Step 1 (Question for Investigation): Given the attributes of a passenger, predict whether he/she survived the disaster.
This is a **classification problem**, where the goal is to predict a categorical outcome—whether a passenger survived (1) or did not survive (0).

Step 2 (Dataset Preparation): The Titanic dataset is one of the most well-known datasets in machine learning, commonly used for classification tasks. It contains information about the passengers who were on board the Titanic, including their demographics, ticket details, and whether they survived the disaster.

Input Dataset: https://www.kaggle.com/competitions/titanic/data

The dataset includes the following attributes/features:

- PassengerId: Unique identifier for each passenger.
- Survived: Target variable indicating if the passenger survived (1) or not (0).

- Pclass: Passenger class (1st, 2nd, 3rd).
- Name: Name of the passenger.
- Sex: Gender of the passenger.
- Age: Age of the passenger.
- SibSp: Number of siblings/spouses aboard the Titanic.
- Parch: Number of parents/children aboard the Titanic.
- Ticket: Ticket number.
- Fare: Fare paid by the passenger.
- Cabin: Cabin number (often has many missing values).
- Embarked: Port of embarkation (C = Cherbourg, Q = Queenstown, S = Southampton).

2.1 PRE-PROCESSING

(a) **We will first handle missing values in the data**:
   - Features like 'Age', 'Cabin', and 'Embarked' often have missing values.
   - 'Age' can be imputed using the median age or by creating age bands.
   - 'Cabin' can be dropped or filled with a placeholder value since it has a large number of missing values.
   - 'Embarked' can be filled with the most common value.

(b) **Encoding Categorical Variables:**
   - Variables like 'Sex' and 'Embarked' need to be converted into numerical form using techniques like one-hot encoding.

(c) **Scaling Features:**
   - Features like 'Age' and 'Fare' may need to be scaled, especially if using models like SVM or KNN, which are sensitive to feature scaling.

2.2 FEATURE ENGINEERING

(a) Family Size: Create a new feature 'FamilySize' by adding 'SibSp' and 'Parch' plus one (for the passengers themselves). Larger family size have very low survival, while smaller size family (2-4), have higher survival chances.

```
# Add Fsize (Family size) by combining SibSp, Parch, and 1 (for the passenger themselves)
df['Fsize'] = df['SibSp'] + df['Parch'] + 1
```

(b) Title Extraction: Extract titles from the 'Name' feature (e.g., Mr., Mrs., Miss) and group rare titles to simplify the model.

(c) Age Bands: Group ages into bands or categories to reduce variability and capture non-linear relationships.

Step 3 (Exploratory Data Analysis (EDA)):

(a) Survival Rate by Age & Gender: Analyze how survival varies with different features like Age & Gender' Figure 15.2.

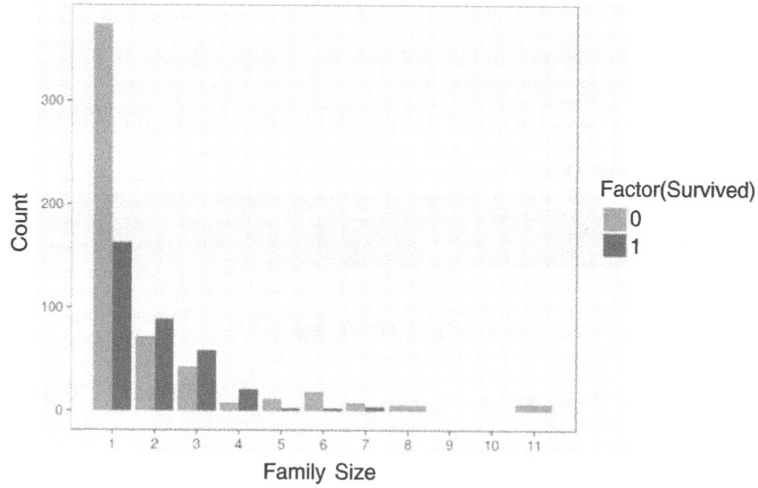

FIGURE 15.1 Bar plot showing how family size impacts survival (*See colour figure at the end of the book*).

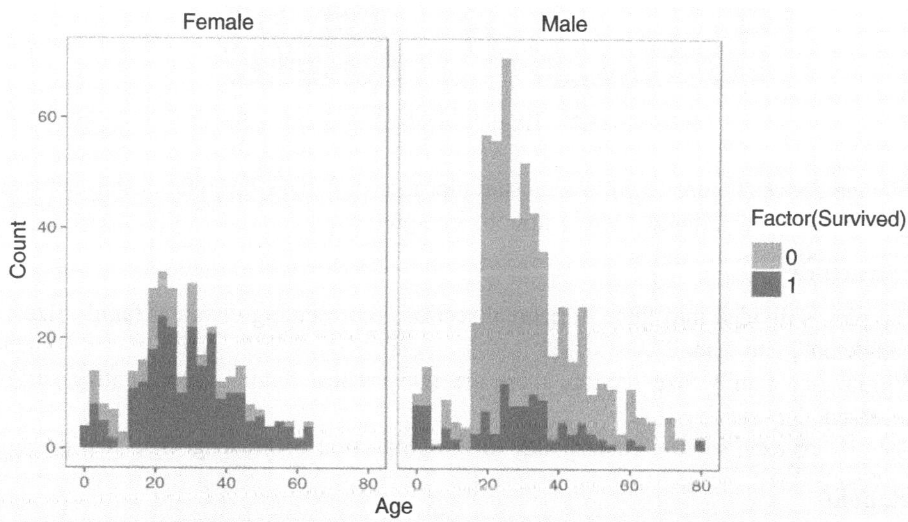

FIGURE 15.2 Titanic Survival by Gender and Age (*See colour figure at the end of the book*).

```
g=sns.histplot(data=df[:891],x='Age',hue='Survived',multiple='stack',bins=30,palette='Set1')
# Adding facets for Sex
g = sns.FacetGrid(df[:891], col='Sex', height=6, aspect=1.2)
g.map(sns.histplot, 'Age', hue='Survived', multiple='stack', bins=30, palette='Set1')
```

Figure 15.2 shows a histogram showing the distribution of age for male and female passengers on the Titanic, with different colours representing whether they survived or not.

Here are some observations from the image:

- **Age Distribution:** The age distribution for both males and females is right-skewed, meaning there were more younger passengers.

- **Survival:**
  - **Females:** A higher proportion of females survived compared to males. This is especially evident in the younger age groups.
  - **Males:** The survival rate for males is generally lower, particularly in the older age groups.

(b) Survival Rate by Family Size:

```
df['FsizeD'] = np.where(df['Fsize'] == 1, 'singleton', np.where(df['Fsize'] < 5, 'small', 'large'))
mosaic(df, ['FsizeD', 'Survived'], title='Family Size by Survival', gap=0.02, axes_label=True)
```

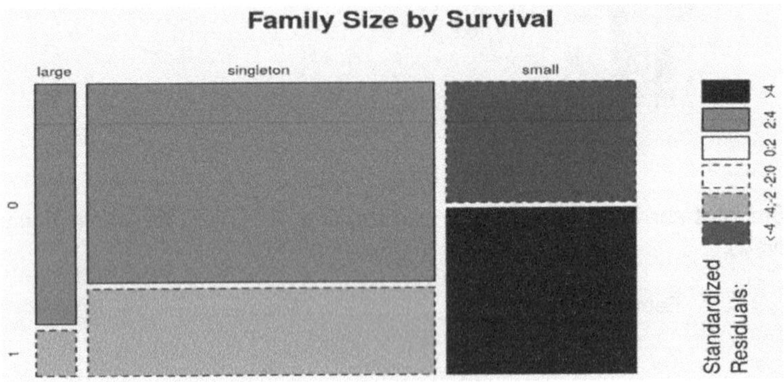

FIGURE 15.3 Titanic Survival by Family Size.

The image above (Figure 15.3) is a mosaic plot that visualizes the relationship between family size and survival on the Titanic. Here's how to interpret it:

Overall Structure:

- The plot is divided into three horizontal sections representing different family sizes: "large", "singleton", and "small".
- Within each family size section, there are two vertical sections representing survival (0 = deceased, 1 = survived).
- The size of each section corresponds to the proportion of passengers in that category.

Interpretation:

- **Large Families:** The "large" family size section has a larger area for deceased passengers (0) than for survivors (1). This suggests that individuals from large families had a lower chance of survival.
- **Singleton:** The "singleton" section (individuals traveling alone) has a larger area for survivors (1). This indicates that people travelling alone had a higher chance of survival.
- **Small Families:** The "small" family size section has a larger area for deceased passengers (0), similar to large families.

Standardized Residuals:

- The legend on the right side shows the standardized residuals for each section. These residuals represent the deviation of the observed value from the expected value, taking into account the overall proportions of survival and family size.
- Positive residuals indicate that the observed value is higher than expected, while negative residuals indicate that the observed value is lower than expected.

Inferences:

- Family size appears to be a factor influencing survival on the Titanic.
- Individuals travelling alone had a higher chance of survival compared to those travelling with large or small families.
- The standardized residuals provide additional insights into the specific patterns within each family size category. For example, the large positive residual for "singleton" survivors suggests that the observed survival rate for individuals travelling alone was significantly higher than expected.

Step 4 (Model Training and Selection):

- **Logistic Regression:** A baseline model for binary classification.
- **Random Forest:** A robust ensemble method that can handle both categorical and numerical features.
- **Support Vector Machine (SVM):** Effective for smaller datasets and can handle non-linear boundaries with kernel trick.

4.1 HYPERPARAMETER TUNING

- **GridSearchCV**: Exhaustively search through a specified parameter grid to find the best combination of hyperparameters for a model.
- **RandomizedSearchCV**: Randomly samples the parameter space, which can be faster than GridSearchCV.
- Parameters such as the number of trees in Random Forest, regularization strength in Logistic Regression, or kernel type in SVM are optimized to improve model performance.

 # Training a random-forest algorithm and visualizing the error rates in both classes

```
# Separate features and target variable
X = train[['Pclass', 'Sex', 'Age', 'SibSp', 'Parch', 'Fare', 'Embarked', 'Title', 'FsizeD', 'Child',
'Mother']]
y = train['Survlved']

# Encode categorical variables if necessary
X = pd.get_dummies(X, drop_first=True)

# Split data into training and validation sets
X_train, X_val, y_train, y_val = train_test_split(X, y, test_size=0.2, random_state=754)

# Build the Random Forest model
rf_model = RandomForestClassifier(random_state=754)
rf_model.fit(X_train, y_train)
```

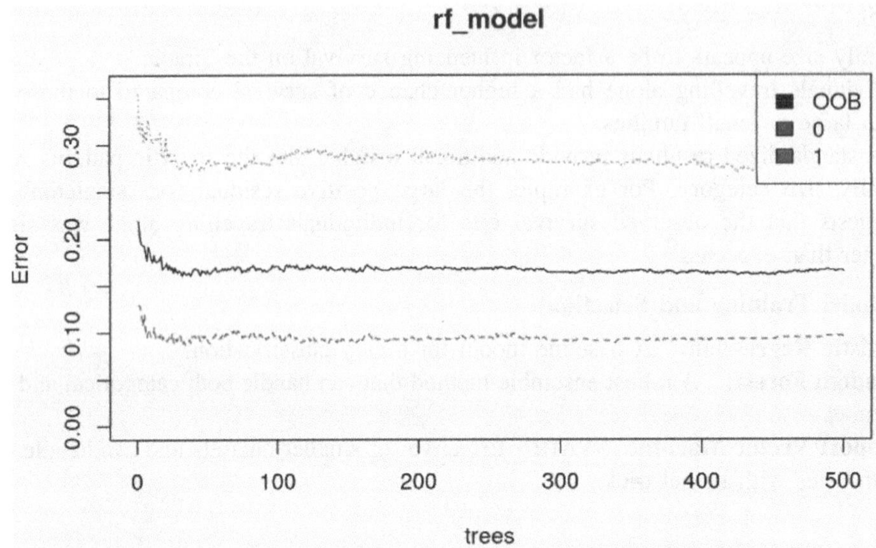

FIGURE 15.4 Error rates in Random Forest Model

The image above (Figure 15.4) is a plot showing the error rate of a random forest model as the number of trees increases. Let's break down what the plot is telling us:

Key Components:

- ***X*-axis:** Number of trees in the random forest
- ***Y*-axis:** Error rate

Lines in the Plot:

- **Black Line (OOB):** This represents the out-of-bag (OOB) error rate. The OOB error is an estimate of the model's generalization error, calculated using observations that were not used to train each individual tree in the forest.
- **Red Line (0):** This likely represents the error rate for a specific class label (e.g., class 0).
- **Green Line (1):** This likely represents the error rate for another class label (e.g., class 1).

Interpretation:

- As the number of trees increases, the OOB error rate generally decreases, reaching a plateau after a certain point. This indicates that the model's performance improves with more trees up to a certain point, beyond which adding more trees doesn't significantly reduce the error.
- The red and green lines show the error rates for the individual classes. The behaviour of these lines can vary depending on the dataset and the specific classification problem.
- If the red and green lines converge with the OOB line, it suggests that the model is performing well on both classes.
- If the red and green lines diverge from the OOB line, it might indicate that the model is overfitting to the training data.

Overall, this plot provides insights into the model's performance and the impact of increasing the number of trees. It helps assess the model's generalization ability and identify potential overfitting issues.

Step 5 (Metrics and Analysis of Results):

- **Accuracy:** The proportion of correctly predicted instances out of the total instances.
- **Precision:** The proportion of true positive predictions out of all positive predictions made by the model.
- **Recall:** The proportion of true positive predictions out of all actual positive instances in the dataset.
- **F1 Score:** The harmonic mean of precision and recall, providing a balance between the two.
- **ROC-AUC:** The area under the receiver operating characteristic curve, which measures the model's ability to distinguish between classes.

```
# Predict on validation data
y_pred = rf_model.predict(X_val)

# Calculate accuracy
accuracy = accuracy_score(y_val, y_pred)
```

Key Important Features for Random Forest:

```
# Assuming 'rf_model' is already trained and available

# Get feature importances
importances = rf_model.feature_importances_
features = X.columns

# Create a DataFrame for feature importances
importance_df = pd.DataFrame({
    'Variables': features,
    'Importance': importances
})

# Rank features based on importance
importance_df['Rank'] = importance_df['Importance'].rank(ascending=False).astype(int)
importance_df = importance_df.sort_values(by='Importance', ascending=False)
```

The image below (Figure 15.5) is a bar chart showing the importance of different variables in predicting the outcome of a model. The variables are listed on the *y*-axis, and the importance of each variable is represented by the length of the bar. The importance is measured on a scale of 0 to 60.

Here are some key observations from the chart:

- The most important variable is "Title", followed by "Sex" and "Fare".
- The least important variable is "Mother".
- The importance of the variables decreases as we move down the chart.

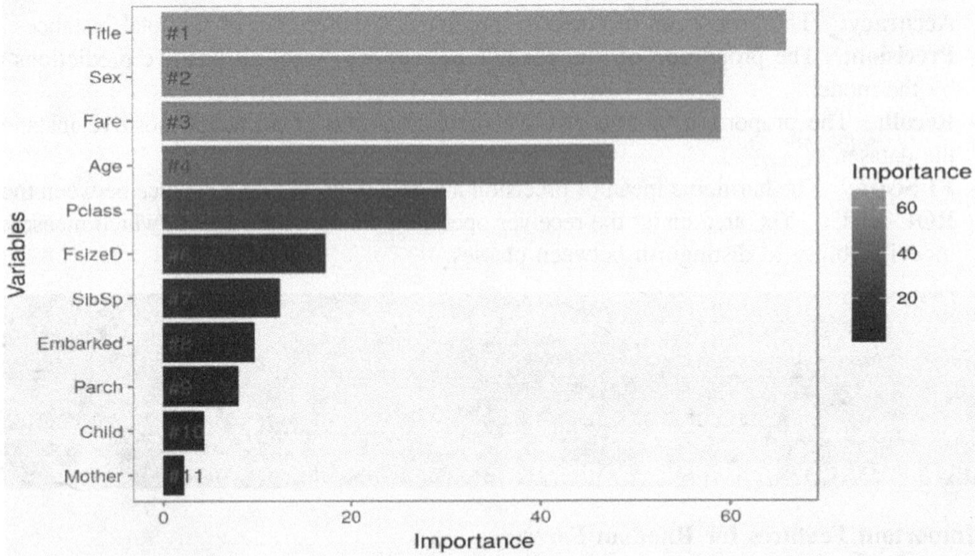

FIGURE 15.5 Important Features according to Random Forest Model.

This chart can be used to understand which variables are most important in predicting the outcome of a model. It can also be used to identify which variables are not important, and which can be removed from the model.

Each of these steps is crucial in building a robust model for predicting Titanic survival and provides a comprehensive introduction to the machine learning pipeline.

Case study 2: House Price Prediction

Your friend is going to buy a new house. He wants to know the right price for a house and negotiate with the seller. What information will you use to help him determine the correct price?

Step 1 (Question for Investigation):

This is a **regression problem**, where the objective is to predict a continuous value, which is the house price ('SalePrice').

Step 2 (Dataset Preparation):

Dataset Overview:

The House Prices dataset, often used in regression problems, contains information about various houses in Ames, Iowa, including features like the number of rooms, lot size, year built, and more. The goal is to predict the sale price of the houses based on these features.

Input dataset link: https://www.kaggle.com/competitions/house-prices-advanced-regression-techniques/data

Key Features Include:

- SalePrice: Target variable representing the price of the house.
- OverallQual: Overall material and finish quality.
- GrLivArea: Above grade (ground) living area square footage.

- GarageCars: Size of garage in car capacity.
- TotalBsmtSF: Total square feet of basement area.
- 1stFlrSF: First-floor square feet.
- YearBuilt: Original construction date.
- FullBath: Full bathrooms above grade.

2.1 PRE-PROCESSING

2.1.1 Handling Missing Data

- Identify Missing Values: Check for missing values in the dataset using functions like 'isnull()' or 'isna()' in pandas.
- Imputation: For numerical features, fill missing values using the median or mean. For categorical features, fill missing values with the mode or create a new category like "None" or "Unknown".
- Dropping Features: If a feature has a significant percentage of missing values (e.g., more than 80%), consider dropping it as it might not add value to the model.

2.1.2 Handling Outliers

- Visualization: Use boxplots or scatterplots to identify outliers in key numerical features like 'GrLivArea', 'TotalBsmtSF', and 'SalePrice'.
- Removal: If outliers are data errors or extreme values that could negatively impact the model, consider removing them.

2.1.3 Log Transformation of Skewed Data

- Check Skewness: For features that are highly skewed (like 'SalePrice'), use the 'skew()' function.
- Apply Log Transformation**:** To normalize the distribution, apply a log transformation to skewed features. For instance, 'SalePrice' can be transformed using 'np.log1p(SalePrice)'.

```
#Histogram of SalePrice before transformation
sns.histplot(train_data['SalePrice'], kde=True)
```

```
#Apply Log Transformation
train_data['LogSalePrice'] = np.log1p(train_data['SalePrice'])
sns.histplot(train_data['LogSalePrice'], kde=True)
```

The provided image contains two histograms showing the distribution of the SalePrice variable before and after applying a log transformation. Here's an explanation of the visualizations:

Left Chart: Distribution of SalePrice before Log Transformation

- The distribution is positively skewed, meaning it has a long tail on the right.
- Most values cluster around lower prices, while higher prices are less frequent.
- The skewness indicates that the variable does not follow a normal (Gaussian) distribution, which can lead to issues in statistical modeling or machine learning algorithms that assume normality.

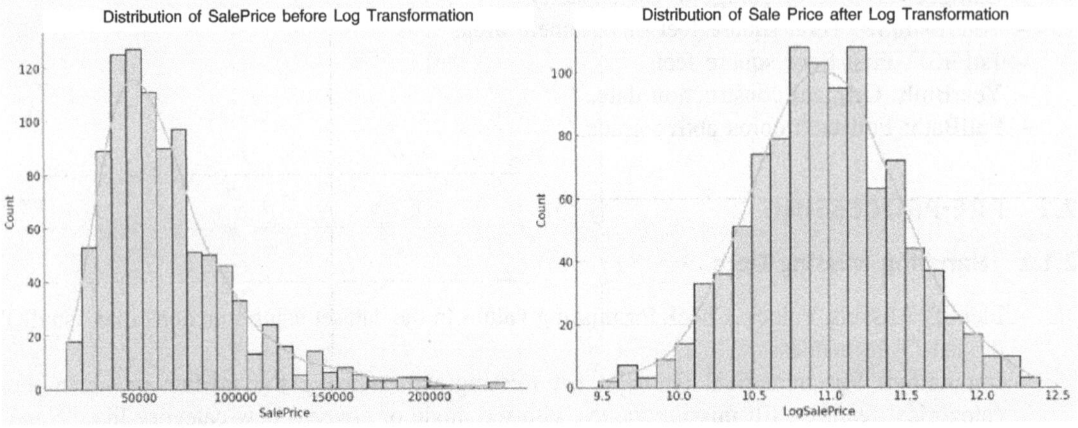

FIGURE 15.6 Before and after applying Log Transformation on SalePrice.

Right Chart: Distribution of SalePrice after Log Transformation

- After applying the log transformation (LogSalePrice), the distribution becomes more symmetric and bell-shaped, resembling a normal distribution.
- The transformation compresses the range of higher values, reducing skewness and making the data more suitable for techniques that assume normality.
- A more normal-like distribution can improve the performance of linear regression, as it stabilizes variance and satisfies assumptions of normality.

Key Interpretations:

- Purpose of Log Transformation: It is commonly used to reduce skewness and make data more normally distributed.
- Impact on Modeling: A log-transformed variable often yields better results in statistical analyses or machine learning models, especially when the original data is heavily skewed.
- Improved Symmetry: The transformation redistributes the data more evenly, enhancing the ability to capture patterns and trends.

2.2 FEATURE ENGINEERING

2.2.1 Creating Polynomial Features

- Polynomial Features: Generate new features by combining existing features in polynomial forms (e.g., square or interaction terms) to capture non-linear relationships.
- Example: Creating a new feature like 'OverallQual^2' or interaction terms like 'GrLivArea * OverallQual'.

→ Heatmap of the Correlation Matrix: Displays correlations after introducing polynomial features. It helps visualize the relationships between features like OverallQual^2, GrLivArea_OverallQual, and others.

```
#Feature Engineering
train_data['OverallQual^2'] = train_data['OverallQual'] ** 2
corr_matrix = train_data.corr()
sns.heatmap(corr_matrix, annot=True, cmap='coolwarm', fmt='.2f')
```

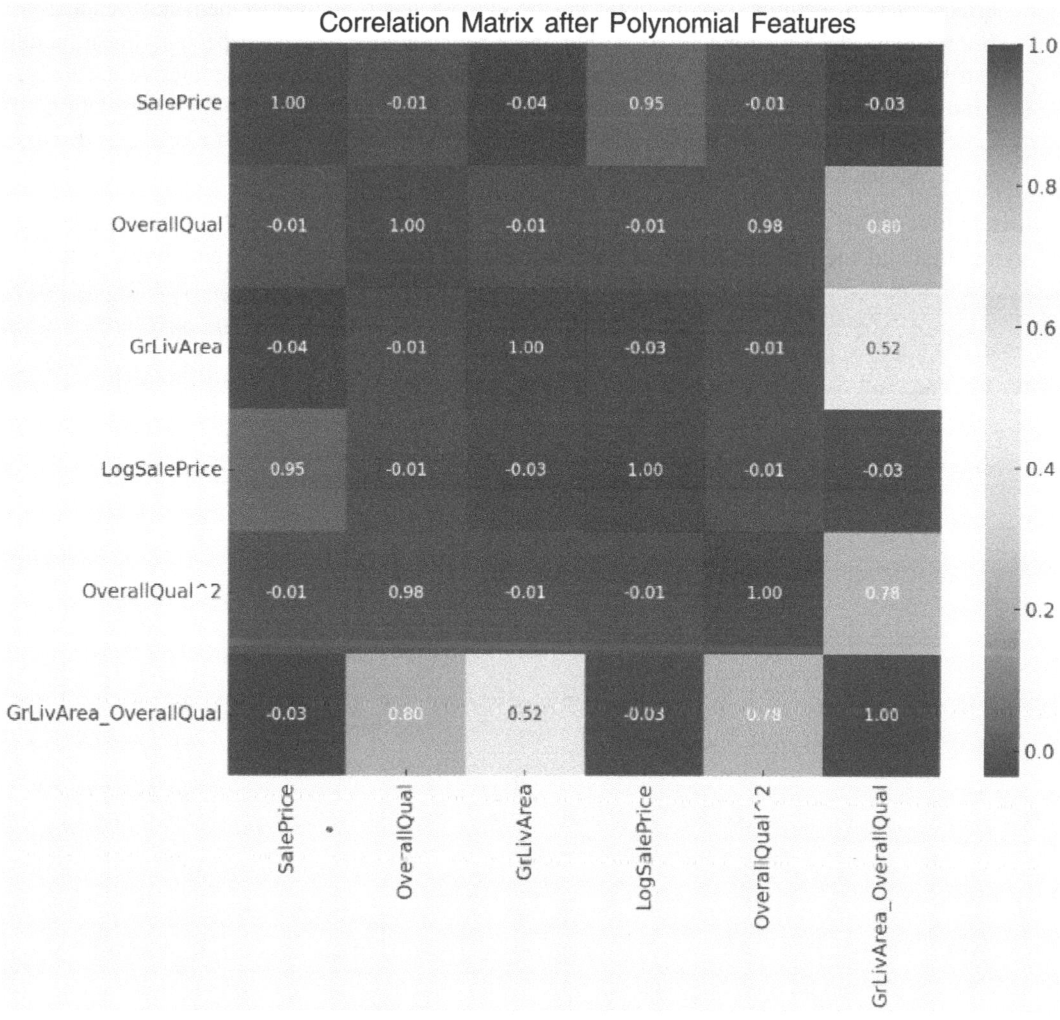

FIGURE 15.7 Correlation Matrix Highlighting Relationships after Polynomial Feature Engineering (*See colour figure at the end of the book*).

Key Insights from the Matrix:

SalePrice (Target Variable):

- Strong positive correlation with LogSalePrice (0.95). This is expected as LogSalePrice is a transformation of the original SalePrice, retaining most of its predictive power but potentially stabilizing variance and reducing skewness.
- Weak or negligible correlations with other features like OverallQual, GrLivArea, and their polynomial interactions in this specific dataset.

Benefits of Feature Engineering with Polynomial Features:

- Capture Nonlinear Relationships: Polynomial features help capture nonlinear patterns between independent variables and the target. For example, OverallQual^2 might represent the exponential effect of quality on price.
- Interaction Effects: Interaction terms like GrLivArea_OverallQual help model combined effects of two features, which might not be evident when analyzing them independently.
- Improved Model Performance: By adding these new features, models (especially linear models) can better fit complex relationships in the data, leading to improved predictive accuracy.
- Transforming Relationships: Log-transforming SalePrice (visible in the high correlation with LogSalePrice) stabilizes variance and improves the fit of regression-based models, as discussed in the earlier histogram example.

→ **Scatter plot of GrLivArea_OverallQual vs SalePrice**: This plot explores the interaction between the living area and the overall quality, revealing how the interaction term affects house prices.

```
#Use scatter plots to show interaction terms like GrLivArea * OverallQual vs SalePrice:
train_data['GrLivArea_OverallQual'] = train_data['GrLivArea'] * train_data['OverallQual']
sns.scatterplot(x='GrLivArea_OverallQual', y='SalePrice', data=train_data)
```

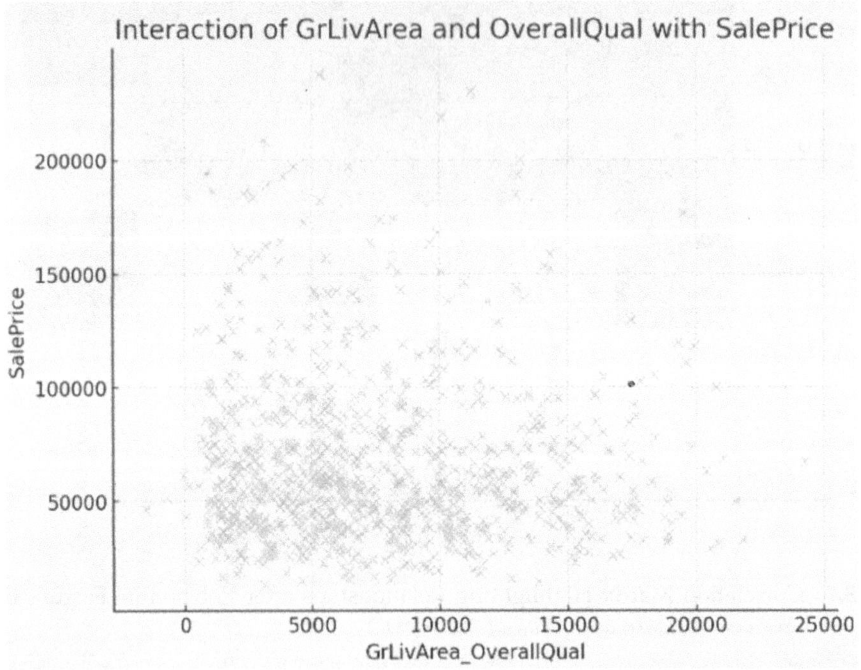

FIGURE 15.8 Impact of Interaction between Living Area and Quality on Sale Price.

This scatter plot (Figure 15.8) depicts the relationship between the interaction feature GrLivArea_OverallQual (the product of GrLivArea and OverallQual) on the x-axis and SalePrice on the y-axis. Here's the interpretation and the benefits of creating this interaction term:

Interpretation of the Plot:

- **Positive Trend:** There is a visible upward trend, indicating that as the interaction value (GrLivArea_OverallQual) increases, the SalePrice also tends to increase. This suggests that larger values of the interaction between GrLivArea (above-ground living area) and OverallQual (overall quality rating) are predictive of higher house prices.
- **Wide Dispersion:** While the trend is positive, there is some dispersion in the values. This suggests that while the interaction term is informative, other factors are also influencing the SalePrice.
- **Significance of Interaction:** The plot shows that the combination of a house's size (GrLivArea) and its quality (OverallQual) has a compounding effect on price. A house that is both large and high-quality is likely to be priced significantly higher.

Benefits of Using Interaction Terms:

- **Captures Joint Effects:** Interaction terms help capture the combined influence of two variables. In this case, it highlights how size and quality together impact house prices more effectively than considering them separately.
- **Improves Model Predictive Power:** Including interaction features like GrLivArea_OverallQual can improve the accuracy of regression or machine learning models by enabling them to learn complex relationships in the data.
- **Identifies Important Combinations:** This interaction helps uncover non-linear effects, such as how the impact of quality is amplified for larger homes or vice versa.
- **Reduces Omission of Crucial Relationships:** Ignoring interactions between variables can lead to oversimplified models that miss key insights, while including them ensures more robust modeling.
- **Enhances Interpretability:** By explicitly defining and visualizing interaction terms, analysts can better understand how two variables work together to influence the target variable.

Step 3 (Exploratory Data Analysis (EDA)):

3.1 DISTRIBUTION OF HOUSE PRICES

– Histogram/Distplot: Visualize the distribution of 'SalePrice' to understand its spread, central tendency, and skewness. This helps in deciding whether a transformation is needed (Refer Figure 1).

3.2 RELATIONSHIP BETWEEN FEATURES AND TARGET

3.2.1 Scatterplots

Plot features like 'GrLivArea', 'TotalBsmtSF', and 'OverallQual' against 'SalePrice' to identify trends and relationships (Refer Figure 15.8).

3.2.2 Box Plots

Use boxplots to see how categorical features like 'OverallQual', 'Neighborhood', and 'HouseStyle' influence 'SalePrice'.

→ **#Boxplots for categorical features like OverallQual, Neighborhood:**

```
sns.boxplot(x='OverallQual', y='SalePrice', data=train_data)
```

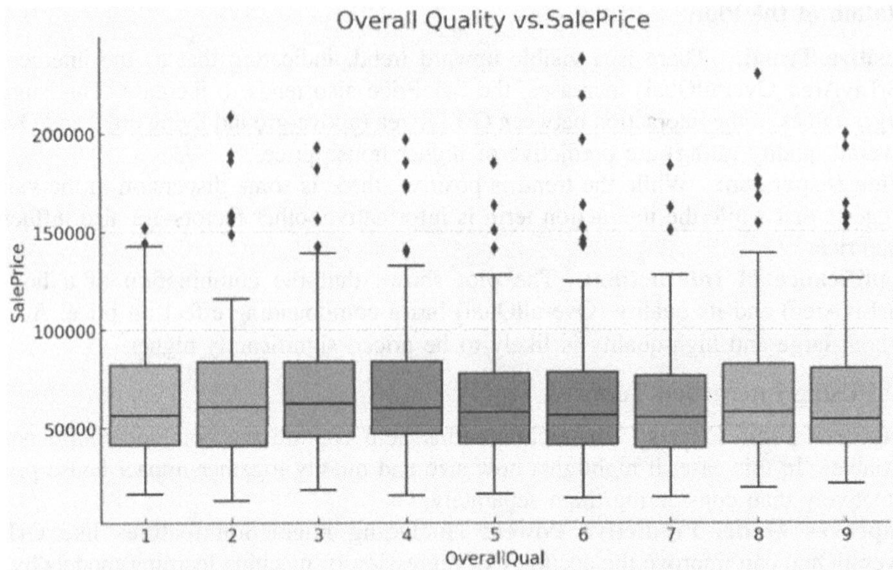

FIGURE 15.9 Box Plot for Overall Quality and SalePrice.

The image presents a box plot visualizing the relationship between Overall Quality and Sale Price of houses. Here's a breakdown of what the plot reveals:

Overall Quality: The *x*-axis represents the overall quality of houses, ranging from 1 to 9.

Sale Price: The *y*-axis shows the distribution of sale prices for houses within each quality category.

Observations:

- **Positive Correlation:** As the overall quality of a house increases, the sale price tends to increase as well. This is evident from the upward trend in the median lines and the overall spread of the boxes.
- **Spread and Outliers:** The size of the boxes indicates the variability in sale prices within each quality category. Larger boxes suggest more variability, while smaller boxes indicate less variability. Outliers, represented by individual data points outside the whiskers, can be seen in some categories, suggesting houses with exceptionally high or low prices compared to the rest of their category.

Benefits of the Box Plot:

- **Visual Representation:** The box plot provides a clear and concise visual representation of the relationship between Overall Quality and Sale Price.
- **Distribution Insights:** It shows the distribution of sale prices within each quality category, including the median, quartiles, and potential outliers.
- **Trend Identification:** The upward trend in the median lines and the overall spread of the boxes highlights the positive correlation between quality and price.
- **Outlier Detection:** Outliers can be easily identified, which might be worth investigating further to understand the reasons for their exceptional prices.

Overall, this box plot effectively communicates the relationship between Overall Quality and Sale Price, making it a valuable tool for understanding the housing market dynamics.

3.2.3 Heatmap

Generate a heatmap of the correlation matrix to visually assess the relationships between all numerical features and the target (Refer Figure 15.7).

Step 4 (Model Training and Selection):

- **Linear Regression**:
- Baseline Model: Start with a simple linear regression model to understand the linear relationship between features and the target.
- Assumptions: Ensure that the assumptions of linear regression (linearity, homoscedasticity, multicollinearity, and normality of errors) are met.

```
# Log transformation for SalePrice
data['LogSalePrice'] = np.log1p(data['SalePrice'])

# Select features for the model
selected_features = ['OverallQual', 'GrLivArea', 'TotalBsmtSF', 'GarageCars', 'YearBuilt',
'FullBath', '1stFlrSF', 'OverallQual^2', 'GrLivArea_OverallQual']
X = data[selected_features]
y = data['LogSalePrice']

# Split the data into training and testing sets
X_train, X_test, y_train, y_test = train_test_split(X, y, test_size=0.2, random_state=42)

# Scale features
scaler = StandardScaler()
X_train = scaler.fit_transform(X_train)
X_test = scaler.transform(X_test)
```

- **Ridge Regression:**
- Regularization: Ridge adds L2 regularization to penalize large coefficients, which helps in handling multicollinearity and overfitting.
- Application: Suitable when you have many features and expect that some are not very important.
- **Lasso Regression:**
- Feature Selection: Lasso adds L1 regularization, which can shrink coefficients to zero, effectively selecting a simpler model with fewer features.
- Application: Useful when you want to perform feature selection along with regression.

4.1 HYPERPARAMETER TUNING

- **Cross-Validation:**
- K-Fold Cross-Validation: Use k-fold cross-validation to ensure that the model generalizes well to unseen data. This involves dividing the data into 'k' subsets and training the model 'k' times, each time using a different subset as the validation set and the others as the training set.
- **Regularization Parameters Tuning:**
- GridSearchCV: Perform an exhaustive search over a grid of hyperparameters (e.g., alpha in Ridge and Lasso) to find the best values.

- RandomizedSearchCV: A more efficient approach that randomly samples hyperparameters from a distribution and finds the best combination.
- Example: In Ridge regression, tune the regularization parameter 'alpha' to control the trade-off between fitting the training data and keeping the coefficients small.

```
# Step 3: Model Training and Hyperparameter Tuning
# Ridge Regression
def train_ridge():
    ridge = Ridge()
    param_grid = {'alpha': [0.01, 0.1, 1, 10, 100]}
    grid_search = GridSearchCV(ridge, param_grid, cv=5, scoring='neg_mean_squared_error')
    grid_search.fit(X_train, y_train)
    return grid_search.best_estimator_, grid_search

# Lasso Regression
def train_lasso():
    lasso = Lasso()
    param_grid = {'alpha': [0.01, 0.1, 1, 10, 100]}
    grid_search = GridSearchCV(lasso, param_grid, cv=5, scoring='neg_mean_squared_error')
    grid_search.fit(X_train, y_train)
    return grid_search.best_estimator_, grid_search

ridge_model, ridge_search = train_ridge()
lasso_model, lasso_search = train_lasso()
```

Step 5 (Metrics Calculation and Results Presentation):

5.1 ROOT MEAN SQUARED ERROR (RMSE)

- Definition: RMSE is the square root of the average squared differences between the predicted and actual values. It is more sensitive to large errors than MAE.
- Interpretation: A lower RMSE indicates a better fit, but it is sensitive to outliers.

5.2 MEAN SQUARED ERROR (MSE)

- Definition: MSE is the average of the squared differences between the predicted and actual values. It gives a measure of the quality of an estimator.
- Interpretation: MSE is useful for understanding the variance of the errors, but like RMSE, it is sensitive to outliers.

5.3 R-SQUARED (R^2)

- Definition: R-squared measures the proportion of the variance in the target variable that is predictable from the features. It ranges from 0 to 1, with higher values indicating a better fit.
- Interpretation: An R^2 value close to 1 indicates that the model explains most of the variance in the target variable, while a value close to 0 indicates that the model does not explain much of the variance.

```
# Evaluate Models
def evaluate_model(model, X, y, model_name):
    predictions = model.predict(X)
    mse = mean_squared_error(y, predictions)
    rmse = np.sqrt(mse)
    r2 = r2_score(y, predictions)
    print(f"{model_name} - RMSE: {rmse:.2f}, R^2: {r2:.2f}")
    return rmse, r2

evaluate_model(ridge_model, X_test, y_test, "Ridge")
evaluate_model(lasso_model, X_test, y_test, "Lasso")
```

```
# Visualize Loss Curves for ridge
cv_results_ridge = -ridge_search.cv_results_['mean_test_score']
alphas_ridge = ridge_search.param_grid['alpha']
plt.plot(alphas_ridge, cv_results_ridge, label='Ridge', marker='o')

# Visualize Loss Curves for lasso
cv_results_lasso = -lasso_search.cv_results_['mean_test_score']
alphas_lasso = lasso_search.param_grid['alpha']
plt.plot(alphas_lasso, cv_results_lasso, label='Lasso', color='orange', marker='o')
```

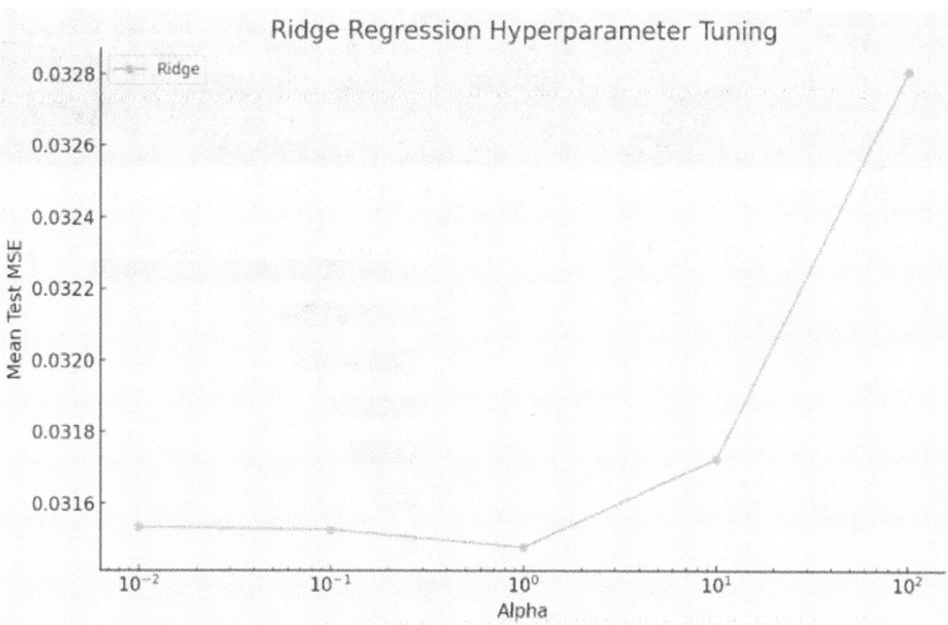

FIGURE 15.10 Ridge Regression based Hyperparameter Tuning.

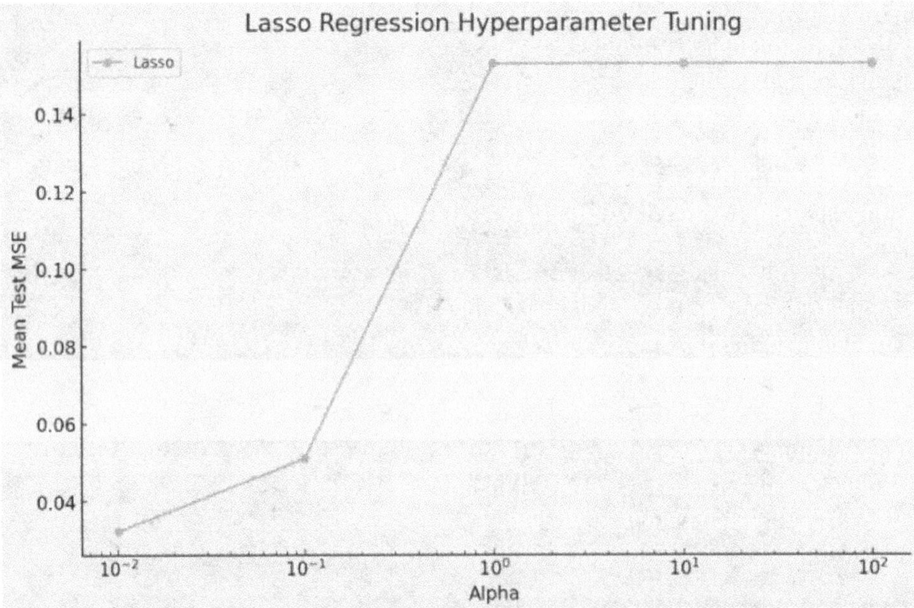

FIGURE 15.11 Lasso Regression based Hyperparameter Tuning.

```
# Feature importance for Lasso
plt.figure(figsize=(10, 6))
coef_lasso = pd.Series(lasso_model.coef_, index=selected_features).sort_values()
coef_lasso.plot(kind='barh', title='Feature Importance (Lasso)', color='orange')

# Feature importance for Ridge
plt.figure(figsize=(10, 6))
coef_ridge = pd.Series(ridge_model.coef_, index=selected_features).sort_values()
coef_ridge.plot(kind='barh', title='Feature Importance (Ridge)')
```

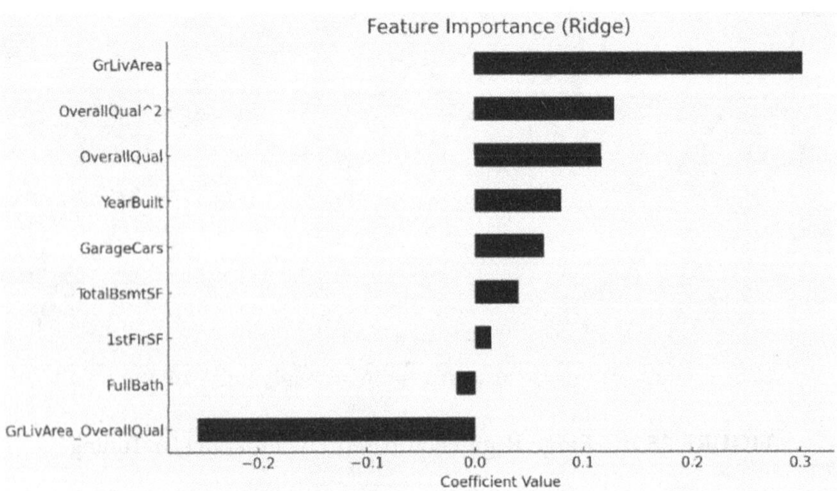

FIGURE 15.12 Feature Importance using Ridge Regression.

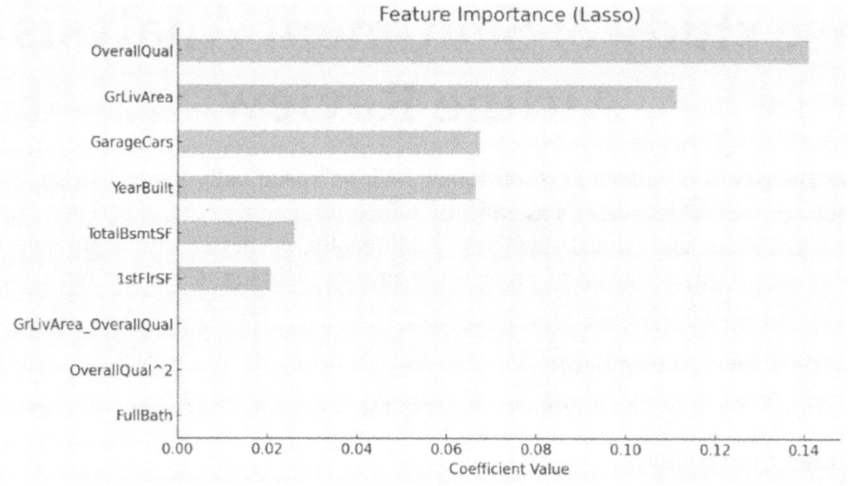

FIGURE 15.13 Feature Importance using Lasso Regression.

```
# Scatter plot to show predictions vs true values
plt.figure(figsize=(10, 6))
plt.scatter(y_test, ridge_model.predict(X_test), alpha=0.6, label="Ridge Predictions", color='blue')
plt.scatter(y_test, lasso_model.predict(X_test), alpha=0.6, label="Lasso Predictions", color='orange')
plt.plot([y_test.min(), y_test.max()], [y_test.min(), y_test.max()], '--', color='black', label="Ideal Fit")
```

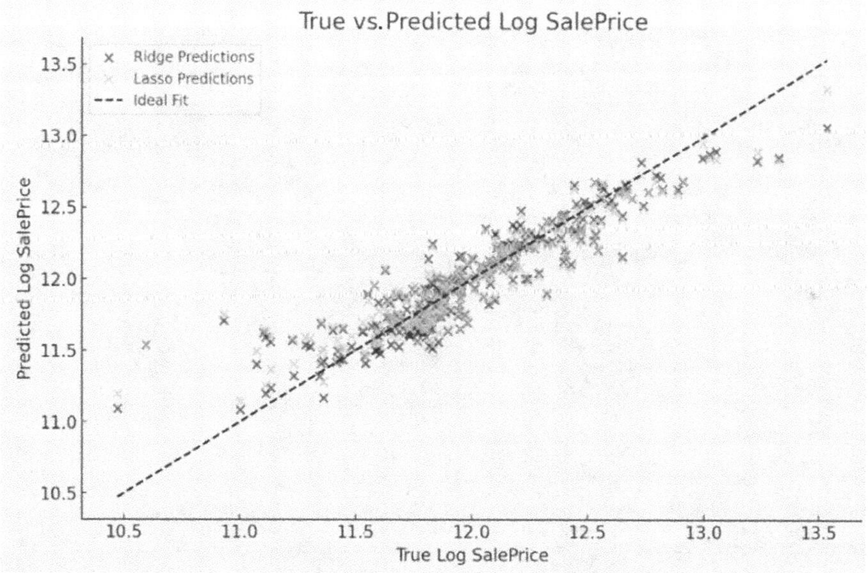

FIGURE 15.14 Actual vs Predicted Log Sale Price (*See colour figure at the end of the book*).

Each of these steps plays a critical role in building a robust predictive model for house prices, guiding you from data preparation through to model evaluation.

NOTEBOOK LINK: https://colab.research.google.com/drive/1IVXeUSIcrkp6NHkaj42QF32X65uLzWs-?usp=sharing

Case study 3: Sentiment Analysis of Airline Review

The Airline Dataset is a collection of customer reviews specifically curated to analyse feedback on Air France services. This dataset was ethically mined using apify.com, ensuring compliance with web scraping guidelines and ethical standards. Additionally, all personally identifiable information (PII) has been thoroughly removed to protect user privacy, making it safe for further analysis and application in data-driven projects.

Step 1 (Question for Investigation):

Given the review written by the customers, analyse the sentiment (e.g., positive, negative, neutral).

Step 2 (Dataset Preparation):

Input Dataset:

The dataset includes several key columns:

(a) **Review Text:** The main text of the review, capturing the customer's opinion.
(b) **Rating:** The numerical rating given by the customer, typically ranging from 1 to 5.
(c) **Review Date:** The date on which the review was posted.

2.1 PRE-PROCESSING

```
# Convert dates
data['publishedDate'] = pd.to_datetime(data['publishedDate'])

# Word Count
data['word_count'] = data['text'].apply(lambda x: len(str(x).split()))

# Sentiment Analysis
data['sentiment'] = data['text'].apply(lambda x: TextBlob(x).sentiment.polarity)

# Cleaned Text
nltk.download('stopwords')
stop = set(stopwords.words('english'))
data['cleaned_text'] = data['text'].apply(lambda x: ' '.join([word for word in x.split() if word.
lower() not in stop]))
```

The code processes text data by converting date columns, calculating word counts, performing sentiment analysis, and cleaning the text by removing stopwords. These steps help in preparing the data for further analysis or modeling. The TextBlob library to analyze the sentiment of the text, the TextBlob(x).sentiment.polarity method computes the sentiment polarity, which ranges from–1 (negative sentiment) to 1 (positive sentiment). A polarity close to 0 indicates a neutral sentiment.

Step 3 (Exploratory Data Analysis (EDA)):

(a) Distribution of Ratings:

```
sns.countplot(x='rating', data=data, palette='viridis')
```

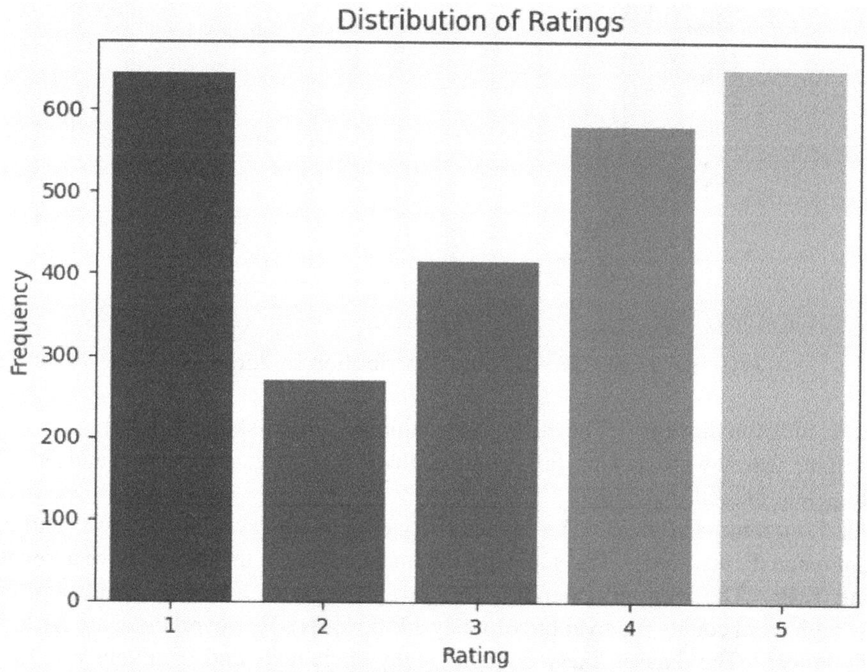

FIGURE 15.15 Distribution of Airlines Rating by Users.

The bar chart represents the distribution of ratings in a dataset. Here's a brief interpretation:

- The x-axis shows the ratings (from 1 to 5).
- The y-axis shows the frequency or count of each rating in the dataset.
- Rating 1 has the highest frequency, with over 600 occurrences, indicating that a large portion of the dataset consists of low ratings.
- Ratings 4 and 5 have higher frequencies than 2 and 3, suggesting that the ratings tend to cluster around the extremes (1 and 5), with more positive feedback compared to neutral or slightly negative feedback.
- The distribution appears somewhat skewed, with a noticeable drop in the frequency of ratings 2 and 3.

This could indicate a polarized opinion in the dataset, where people either tend to give very low or very high ratings, with fewer neutral or moderately negative responses.

(b) Word Count Distribution:

```
sns.histplot(data['word_count'], kde=True, bins=20, color='purple')
```

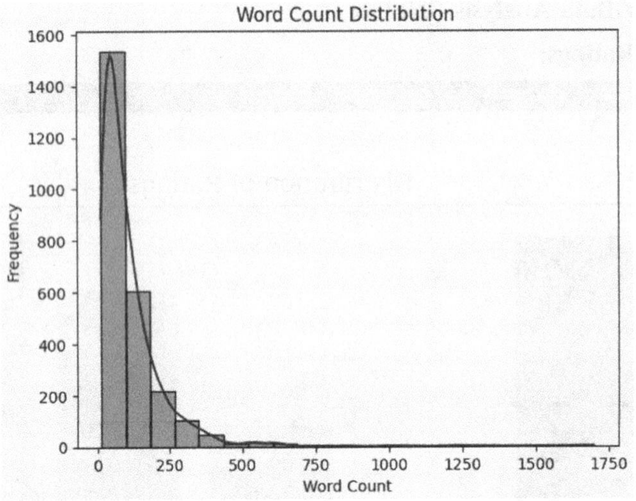

FIGURE 15.16 Word Count Distribution in Airline Dataset.

- **Shape of Distribution:** The histogram exhibits a right-skewed distribution (long tail on the right). Most word counts fall within a low range (e.g., between 0 and 90 words), and only a few exceed that range.
- **Peak Frequency (Mode):** The highest frequency is observed at the lower end of the word count range (0–90 words). This indicates that most entries in the dataset have a low word count.
- **Long Tail:** The long tail extending to the right suggests a smaller number of entries with very high word counts (up to approximately 1750 words). However, these are far less common.
- **Imbalance:** The dataset likely contains many short texts and relatively few long ones.

(c) Sentiment Polarity Distribution:

```
sns.histplot(data['sentiment'], kde=True, bins=20, color='blue')
```

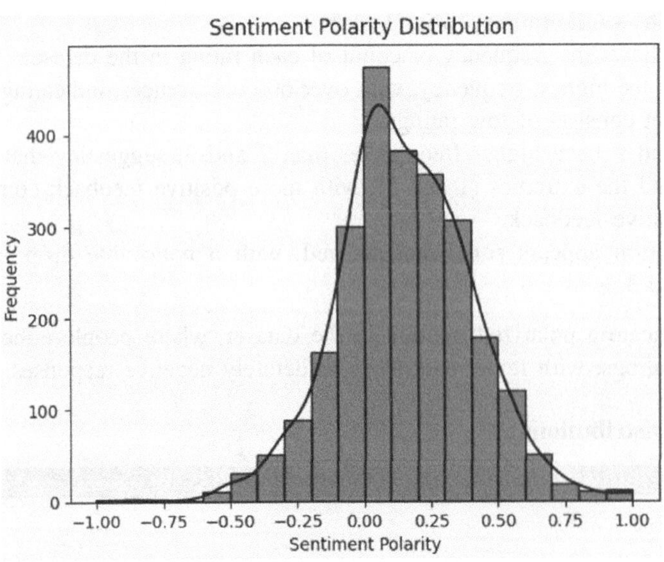

FIGURE 15.17 Sentiment Polarity Distribution of Airlines Dataset.

- **Shape of Distribution:** The distribution is approximately **normal (bell-shaped)**, centred around **0.0** (neutral sentiment). There is a higher concentration of scores around neutral, tapering off symmetrically toward both extremes (negative and positive).
- **Overlay Curve:** A smooth curve (kernel density estimate) confirms the bell-shaped distribution.

(d) Word Cloud of Reviews:

```
text = ' '.join(data['cleaned_text'])
wordcloud = WordCloud(width=800, height=400, background_color='white').generate(text)
```

FIGURE 15.18 Word Cloud of Reviews of Airlines Dataset.

This is a **word cloud** visualization titled "Word Cloud of Reviews." It represents the most frequently occurring words in a collection of text data, likely customer reviews for an airline. Here's the interpretation:

- **Prominent Words:** Larger words like **"flight," "seat," "Air France," "service," "time,"** and **"airline"** appear most frequently, indicating these are key topics discussed in the reviews. Other notable terms include **"luggage," "Paris," "staff," "plane," "business class,"** and **"airport."**
- **Sentiment Indicators:** Terms like "good," "great," and "excellent" suggest positive feedback. Words like "time," "check," and "luggage" might indicate challenges related to punctuality, check-in processes, or baggage handling.
- **Frequent Topics:** The word cloud suggests the reviews focus heavily on **flight experiences, customer service, and specific travel elements** like seating, staff, and baggage.

(e) Number of Reviews over Time:

```
data.groupby('publishedDate').size().plot(kind='line', marker='o', color='green')
```

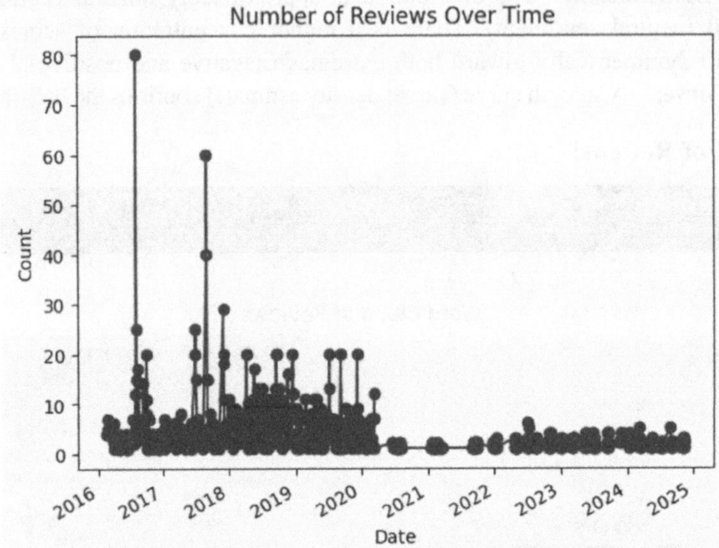

FIGURE 15.19 Number of Reviews Over Time.

- The plot shows a general downward trend in the number of reviews over time. This indicates that the frequency of reviews has been decreasing from 2016 to 2025.
- There is a sharp spike in reviews in early 2016, followed by a rapid decline. This suggests a high initial interest or activity, which quickly waned. From 2019 onwards, the trend becomes more pronounced, with a steeper decline in the number of reviews.

(f) Sentiment vs. Word Count:

```
sns.scatterplot(x='word_count', y='sentiment', hue='rating', data=data, palette='deep')
```

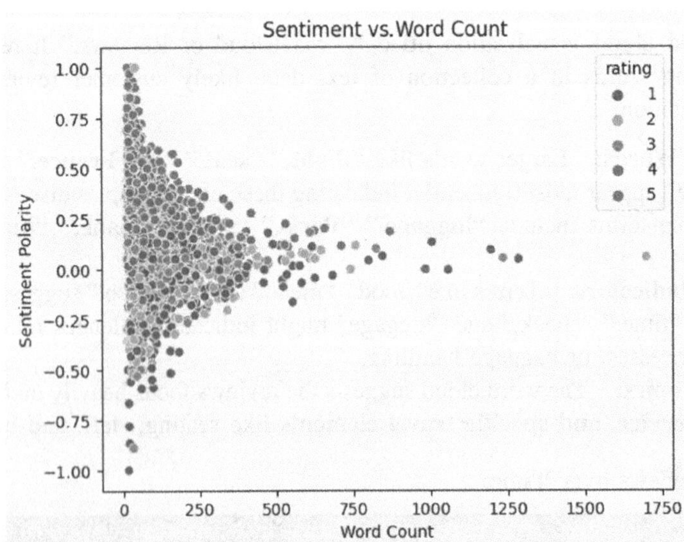

FIGURE 15.20 Sentiment Polarity vs Word Count in Airlines Dataset (*See colour figure at the end of the book*).

- The plot shows a relationship between word count and sentiment polarity, with sentiment polarity generally decreasing as word count increases. This suggests that longer reviews tend to have lower sentiment scores.

  Sentiment range by rating:

- Lower ratings (e.g., 1 and 2) tend to skew toward negative sentiment (closer to –1).
- Higher ratings (e.g., 4 and 5) often have positive sentiment (closer to +1).
- Neutral ratings (3) cluster around a sentiment polarity of 0.
- This plot helps analyse how text sentiment varies with word count and rating, providing insight into how people express feedback of different lengths. For instance, shorter reviews might show more extreme sentiments, while longer reviews may balance out.

(g) Box Plot of Sentiment by Rating:

```
sns.boxplot(x='rating', y='sentiment', data=data, palette='Set2')
```

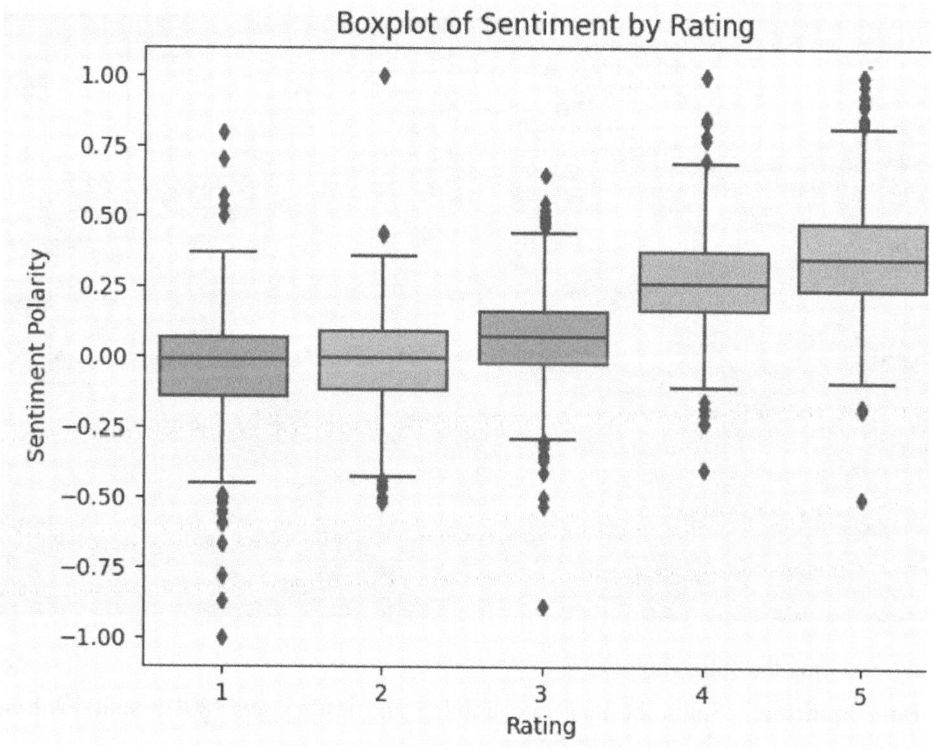

FIGURE 15.21 Boxplot of Sentiment by Rating.

General Trend:

- Lower ratings (1 and 2) have median sentiment polarity values near or below zero, indicating more negative or neutral sentiments.
- Higher ratings (4 and 5) have median sentiment values closer to + 0.25 or higher, reflecting more positive sentiments.
- The neutral rating (3) has a median sentiment polarity around 0, reflecting balanced sentiment.

Spread of Sentiment Polarity:

- Ratings 1 and 2 show broader distributions, including many outliers with very negative polarity.
- Higher ratings (4 and 5) exhibit narrower distributions skewed toward positive polarity, with fewer outliers in the negative range.

Outliers:

- All rating groups include outliers, but they are more pronounced in ratings 1 and 2, especially on the negative end.
- Ratings 4 and 5 have outliers with extreme positive sentiment.

Interquartile Range (IQR):

- The IQR (the range between the 25th and 75th percentiles) shifts upward as ratings increase, showing a clear progression from negative/neutral to positive sentiment as ratings improve.

Step 4 (Model Building):

```
# Split data into train and test
X = data['cleaned_text']
y = data['rating']
X_train, X_test, y_train, y_test = train_test_split(X, y, test_size=0.2, random_state=42,
stratify=y)

# Vectorize text using TF-IDF
tfidf = TfidfVectorizer(max_features=5000)
X_train_tfidf = tfidf.fit_transform(X_train)
X_test_tfidf = tfidf.transform(X_test)

# Train logistic regression model
model = LogisticRegression(max_iter=1000, random_state=42)
model.fit(X_train_tfidf, y_train)

# Predictions
y_pred = model.predict(X_test_tfidf)
```

This code performs the following steps:

1. **Data Splitting:** Splits the data into training and testing sets (80/20 split) with stratified sampling to maintain class distribution.
2. **TF-IDF Vectorization:** Converts the cleaned text into numerical features using TF-IDF with a maximum of 5000 features. This hyperparameter can be tuned by grid search.
3. **Logistic Regression Training:** Trains a logistic regression model on the TF-IDF-transformed training data.
4. **Prediction:** Makes predictions on the test set using the trained model.

Step 5 (Metrics and Analysis of Results):

```
# Confusion Matrix
ConfusionMatrixDisplay.from_predictions(y_test, y_pred, cmap='Blues')
```

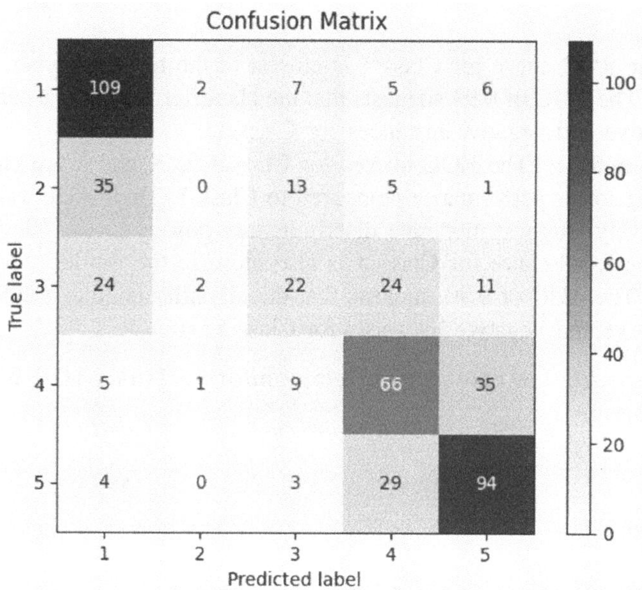

FIGURE 15.22 Confusion Matrix for Actual vs Predicted Labels.

Class-Specific Trends:

- **Rating 1:** Predicted well, with minor misclassifications to ratings 3, 4, and 5.
- **Rating 5:** Also predicted well, but some misclassifications to rating 4.
- **Ratings 2 and 3:** Poorly predicted, with most predictions scattered across other classes, indicating difficulty in distinguishing them.

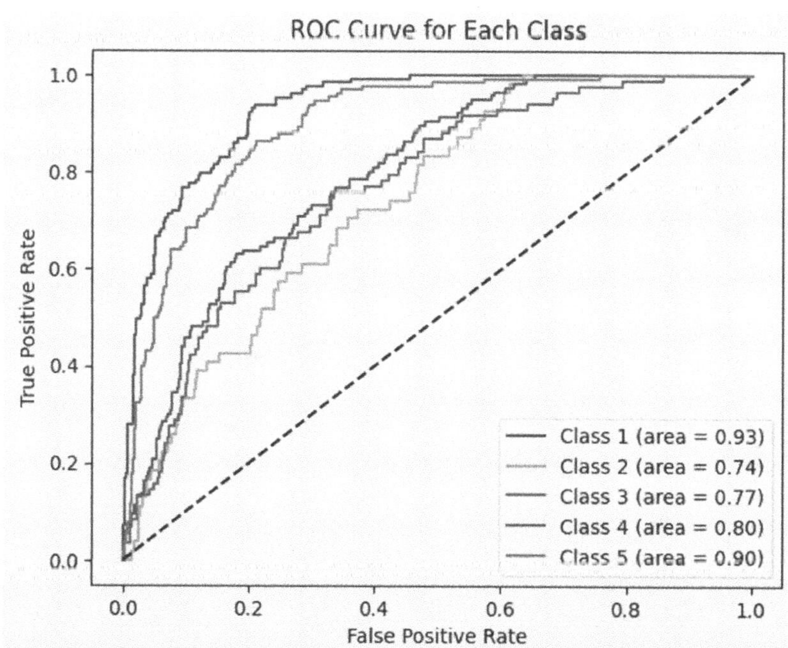

FIGURE 15.23 ROC Curve for Each Class (*See colour figure at the end of the book*).

Key Observations:

1. **Class 1:** The ROC curve for Class 1 is closest to the top-left corner, indicating excellent performance. The AUC of 0.93 suggests that the classifier is highly accurate in distinguishing between positive and negative instances for Class 1.
2. **Classes 2, 3, and 4:** The ROC curves for Classes 2, 3, and 4 are closer to the diagonal line, indicating lower performance compared to Class 1. Their AUC values (0.74, 0.77, and 0.80, respectively) suggest moderate discriminatory power.
3. **Class 5:** The ROC curve for Class 5 is also close to the top-left corner, indicating good performance. The AUC of 0.90 suggests that the classifier is quite accurate in distinguishing between positive and negative instances for Class 5.

NOTEBOOK: https://colab.research.google.com/drive/1i6Ym1OjFWwwCEwJJjO4Ic0-mctnsmU5T?usp=sharing.

Part IV

Advanced Data Analysis and Visualization

16 Deep Neural Networks

Introduction

Typically, an artificial neural network has one input layer, one hidden layer and an output layer. The learning process is mostly carried out at the hidden layer. Deep learning models are the extensions of artificial neural network models where the term Deep indicates a large number of hidden layers with a number of nodes at the hidden layers for improving the performance of machine learning models. In the recent time many deep learning models have proved that these models can carry out and automate any kind of complex task with the help of computing devices.

Deep learning models provide a number of standard architectures with the configurable hyperparameters to customise and train the models as per the requirements. The transfer learning mechanism makes the deep learning model more powerful. With the help of transfer learning the pretrained deep learning models can be directly applied to the datasets without providing a fresh training.

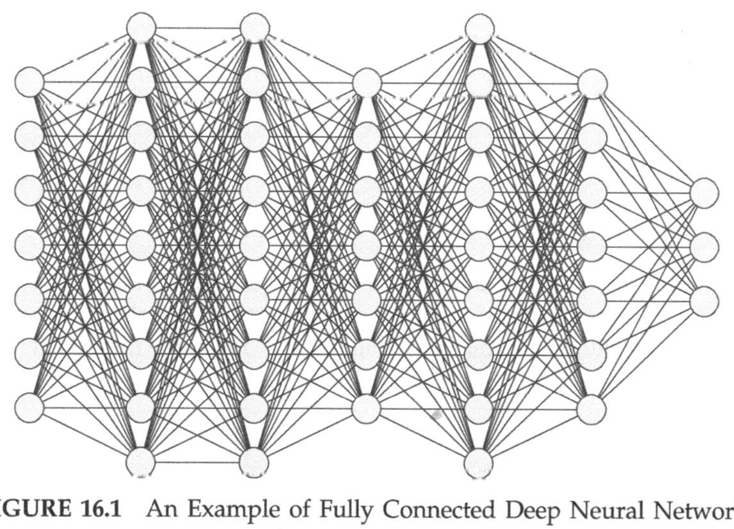

FIGURE 16.1 An Example of Fully Connected Deep Neural Network.

16.1 ACTIVATION FUNCTIONS

Activation functions are very important in deep learning models. The weights are updated using activation functions in the hidden layers. Activation functions are also used for the output layers. Activation functions are the mathematical backbone of deep learning models by which the weights are updated for the deep learning models. The primary requirement for activation functions is, these functions should be non-linear in the nature so that weights are properly updated in the subsequent layers. Other requirements for activation functions are, the computational complexity of the functions should be simple, and functions should be able to avoid vanishing or exploding gradient problems. All the popular and standard activation functions are discussed in Chapter 11.

16.2 LOSS FUNCTIONS

Loss functions are very important in the deep learning to evaluate the performance of the deep learning models. The objective of any deep learning model is to minimize the loss values. The loss value is measured in terms of the difference between the predicted value and the actual value. The loss function should be a derivative function, where the derivative value indicates the gradient (slope). The gradient helps in achieving the objective of minimizing the loss value by moving a little step (or by updating the weights across the deep learning layers) towards the minimum value of loss (towards better performance of deep learning model). The weights in the deep learning models are updated based on the loss function formulation. The generalized expression for updation of the weights is given by the following expression:

$$w_i \leftarrow w_{i-1} - \eta \times d\mathcal{L}$$

Where w_i is the weight at the ith layer, w_{i-1} is the weight at the previous layer $(i - 1)^{th}$, η is the learning rate, and $d\mathcal{L}$ is the derivative of loss function.

The two most common loss function for the general deep learning models are mean square error (MSE), and cross-entropy loss functions. The mathematical expression for both of the models is given below.

Mean Square Error (MSE) Loss Function

$$\mathcal{L} = \frac{1}{2}(\hat{y} - y)^2$$

Cross-Entropy Loss Function

$$\mathcal{L} = -\left(y \log(\hat{y}) + (1 - y)\log(1 - \hat{y})\right)$$

Where $\mathcal{L}$ is the loss function, $\hat{y}$ is the predicted output value and y is the original value.

The sum of all the loss functions for a deep learning model is called as a cost function, since the derivatives of the loss functions can be calculated and hence for the cost function also.

16.3 OPTIMIZERS

The goal of any optimizer algorithm in deep learning model is to optimize the performance of any deep learning algorithm such as it helps in minimizing the loss of any deep learning model. Optimizers help in updating the weights during the back propagation process. There are various optimizers available for deep learning algorithms. Three most popular optimizers are—stochastic gradient descent (SGD), RMSProp, and ADAM optimizers. A brief overview of these three optimizations algorithms is presented here.

16.3.1 Stochastic Gradient Descent (SGD)

During the training process, weights are updated in the hidden layer with the help of activation functions. The generalized expression for updation of weight is given as under:

$$w_i \leftarrow w_{i-1} - \eta \times d\mathcal{L}$$

Where w_i is the weight at the ith iteration, w_{i-1} is the weight at the $(i - 1)^{st}$ iteration, η is the learning rate, and $d\mathcal{L}$ is the derivative of the cost function (the cost function is the sum of the loss functions). The derivatives of cost function (or loss function) indicates gradient. The objective of any optimization function is to smooth the weight updation process and achieve the best performance (i.e., minimize the loss or cost values).

The stochastic gradient descent optimizer is designed based on gradient descent algorithm. The goal of this algorithm is to optimize the smoothness of descent and minimize the cost (or loss) values. Smoothness in SGD optimizer is achieved by weighted average of the previous values. SGD is the momentum-based optimizer. The momentum is defined as, each data point is a weighted combination of itself and previous values. The weights in the SGD optimizer is updated as given below:

$$\vartheta_t = (1-\beta)d\mathcal{J} + \beta\vartheta_{t-1}$$

$$w_t \leftarrow w_{t-1} - \eta\vartheta_t$$

Where, ϑ_t is the value at current time, ϑ_{t-1} is the value at the previous time, $d\mathcal{J}$ is the derivative of the cost function, w_t is the updated weight, w_{t-1} is the previous weight, and η is the learning rate. The value ϑ_t indicates momentum that depends on the previous value. The momentum ϑ_t is the weightage average of previous value and the cost function, where weightage average is calculated by a factor of β. SGD uses fixed learning rate. Mini-batch SGD is the special version of SGD, works on the smaller batch size.

16.3.2 RMSProp

The RMSProp (Root Mean Square Propagation) optimizer is designed on the basis of root mean square errors. The goal of RMSProp is to minimize the root mean square errors for predictions. The root mean square error value is calculated as given below:

$$rms = \sqrt{\frac{1}{n}\sum_{i=1}^{n} x_i^2}$$

$$std = \sqrt{\frac{1}{n}\sum_{i=1}^{n} (x_i - \bar{x})^2}$$

The RMSProp optimizer works exactly like SGD optimizer, but the primary difference between the SGD and RMSProp optimizer is that the RMSProp optimizer updates the learning rate based on the gradient. The values are updated on the square value of the derivative of the cost values and calculated is performed as per the given equation.

$$\vartheta_t = (1-\beta)(d\mathcal{J})^2 + \beta\vartheta_{t-1}$$

$$w_t \leftarrow w_{t-1} - \frac{\eta}{\sqrt{\vartheta_t + \varepsilon}} d\mathcal{J}$$

The w_t is the value of current weight, w_{t-1} is the value of previous weight, η is the learning rate, ϑ_t is the value similar to momentum and depends on the previous value and second derivative of cost (or loss function), ε is a very small number added to the denominator to avoid divide by zero error. ϑ_t is weighted average of previous term and second derivative of the cost (or loss function), the β is the parameter of weighted average. So, RMSProp sets the learning rate based on the gradients, for small gradients learning step learning rate is set to higher value and vice versa for higher gradients, the learning rate is set to the smaller values.

16.3.3 ADAM (Adaptive Moments)

The ADAM optimizer combines both the SGD (momentum) and RMSProp optimizers. The weights are updated in ADAM optimizer is given as per the following equation:

$$s_t = (1-\alpha_1)d\mathcal{J} + \alpha_1 s_{t-1}$$

$$r_t = (1-\alpha_2)(d\mathcal{J})^2 + \alpha_2 r_{t-1}$$

$$w_t \leftarrow w_{t-1} - \frac{\eta}{\sqrt{r_t + \varepsilon}} \tilde{s}_t$$

$$\tilde{s}_t = \frac{s_t}{1-\alpha_1}$$

In the above equation, s_t is the momentum of the cost function of SGD and r_t is the momentum of cost function of RMSProp optimizers as discussed earlier. Both s_t, and r_t are calculated using the weightage average with the weightage average coefficients associated are α_1, and α_2. The momentum (of SGD) s_t is further normalized with the scaling factor of α_1 and normalized value of momentum $\tilde{s}_t$ is used for updation of the weights in ADAM.

So, in summary ADAM combines both SGD, and RMSProp optimizers with the parameters α_1, and α_2. ADAM is one of the proven and popular optimizer for most of the modern deep learning based applications.

16.4 TRAINING DEEP MODEL

Training of a deep learning model is a complex process. To understand the training process, several key concepts need to be discussed for better understanding of the training process. In this section, some of the important concepts are discussed in brief.

16.4.1 Meta Parameters

In context to deep learning, parameters refer to the features learned by the model, whereas the meta parameters or hyperparameters refers to the user specified parameter values. Examples of meta parameters in deep learning models are—number of hidden layers, number of units per layer, activation functions selected, optimization functions, learning rate, dropout rate, loss function selected, and weight initialization techniques.

16.4.2 Vanishing and Exploding Gradient Problem

The performance of any deep learning model is typically computed using the loss function. The loss function is computed using the difference between the actual values and the predicted values. The loss function derivatives are used for calculating gradients. The objective of any deep learning model is to minimize loss or maximize accuracy for achieving the best performance.

The loss function is mathematically expressed by the following expression:

$$f(\hat{y}-y)$$

Where $\hat{y}$ is the predicted value and y is the actual value. The sum of all loss functions is called as cost function.

Learning rate is an important hyper parameter (parameter set by user) in deep learning model. Learning rate is the rate by which the weights are updated in the deep learning layers. If the learning rate is extremely small, then the weights will be updated by a little fraction as the gradient (slope of loss function) will become extremely small and network may stuck in the local minima and will never reach the desired minimum loss function value (best performance loss value). This is one of the common problems during training of deep neural network. This problem is called as vanishing gradient problem.

Another common problem with training of deep learning model is called as the exploding gradient problem. The exploding gradient problem occurs when the gradient becomes extremely large as the value of learning rate is set to a higher value. Due to the higher learning rate, the value of the loss function may skip the best optimum value and the deep learning model will never reach to the best desired value of the loss function. Hence setting of the optimum value of learning rate is a challenging problem while designing the deep learning model.

16.4.3 Regularization

Regularization penalizes from memorizing or overfitting the deep learning model. Regularization may affect the accuracy of the model and accuracy may go down by some fraction, but the model will become more generalized as overfitted is eliminated. Regularization may be applied in many ways, the three common techniques for regularization are:

1. Modify the deep learning model by some operations like Dropout, etc.
2. By applying data augmentation and batch training.
3. By applying L_1 or L_2 regularization

Out of the above three techniques dropout technique is most popular and common technique for regularization in deep learning. In dropout, randomly few nodes are removed from the deep learning model. In other words, the activations for some of the randomly selected nodes is set to zero to avoid overfitting of the deep learning model. The removal of randomly selected nodes is performed using probability of dropout. The dropout operation is shown graphically in Figure 16.2.

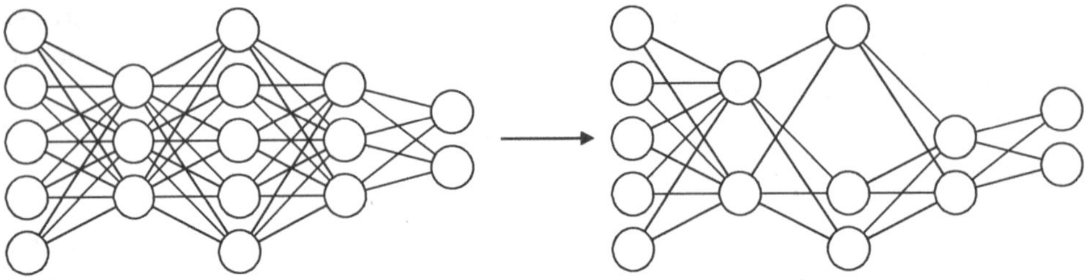

FIGURE 16.2 A Deep Neural Network before and after Dropout.

16.4.4 Batch Normalization

Some deep learning models require that input data should be normalized, but due to the complexity of the deep learning models, even though the input data is normalized it will not guarantee that in the subsequent layers the data will remain normalized. The activation functions will update the weights on the different layers and normality of data may get vanished. The batch normalization layer handles this issue by further normalizing the input data on the subsequent layers. The batch normalization layer of deep leaning controls the learning rate of the model and can also help in achieving the regularization.

16.4.5 Early Stopping

Early stopping is another simple technique of regularization in deep learning. In early stopping technique, the training for a deep learning is stopped at a certain point using some stopping criteria. The stopping criteria is decided based on the values of loss function or performance metrics such as accuracy. The point when loss increases after getting some minimum (low) value may be selected as the stopping criteria to stop the training for the deep learning network.

16.4.6 Weight Initialization

Weight initialization is an important activity in the deep learning model. One of the simple strategies is to initialize the weights randomly. Weight initialization is important because the small weight nearly zero tends to be vanishing gradient whereas large weights can lead to exploding gradient problem. Ideally the variance of weight should be proportional to size of network. Two common weight initialization techniques are Kaiming and Xavier techniques.

Kaiming technique: In Kaiming technique of weight initialization, weights are uniformly distributed, and standard deviation of weight is proportional to input size. Kaiming technique is most suitable in the cases where Relu activation functions are used in hidden layers.

Xavier technique: Xavier technique of weight initialization is most suitable for the networks uses Sigmoid or Tanh activation functions. In Xavier technique, normal distribution is used for the weight distribution, and standard deviation is proportional to input and output size.

16.5 ARCHITECTURES OF DEEP NEURAL NETWORKS

In this section, an overview of the common deep learning architectures is presented.

16.5.1 Feedforward Neural Networks (FNN)

Although the Feedforward Neural Networks (FNNs) are the general neural networks, but when for the number of hidden layers and number of nodes (height and breadth of the layer) in each layer are increased then it can become one of the simplest deep networks. A simple deep learning-based feedforward neural network is shown in Figure 16.3.

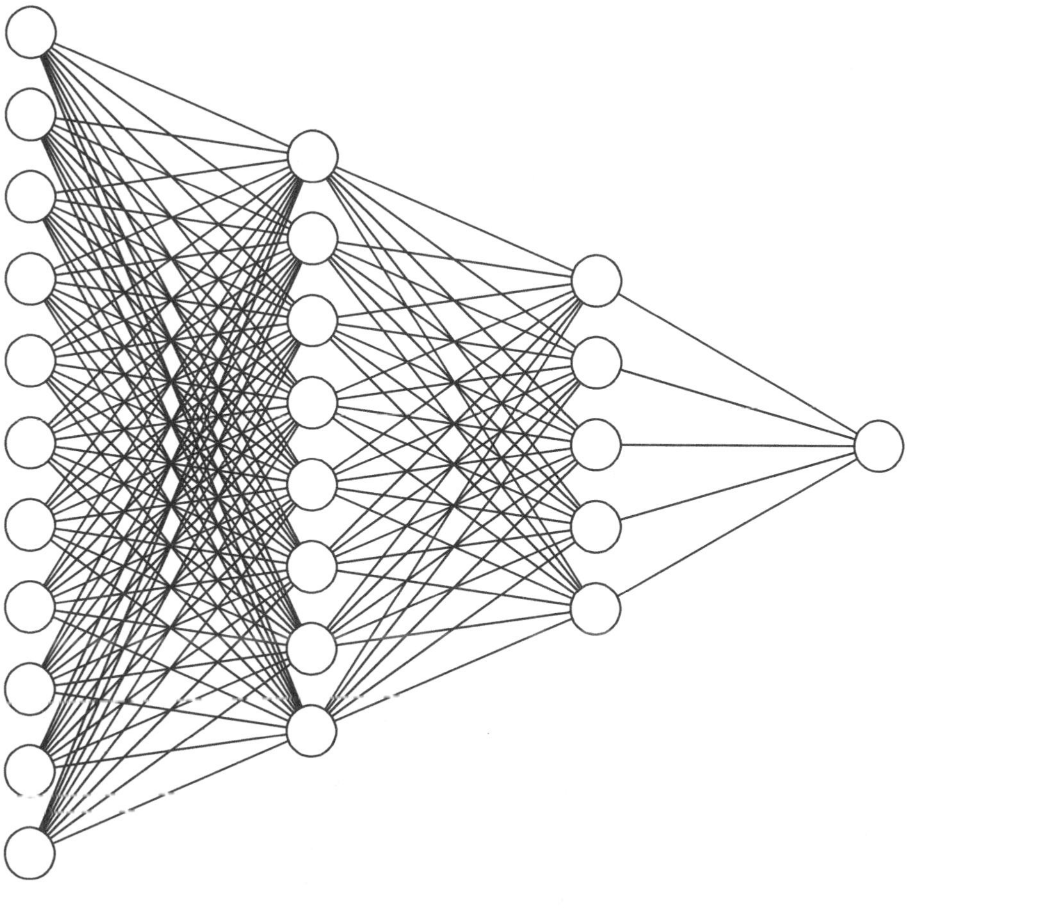

FIGURE 16.3 A Feedforward Neural Networks with mode nodes and more hidden layers.

16.5.2 Convolutional Neural Networks (CNN)

Convolutional neural networks (CNN) are the most popular networks in the deep learning. Using CNN, modern and popular applications are developed in the field of computer vision, image processing and analytics. The CNN networks are designed with the convolutional layers that perform the convolutional operation. The convolutional operation is presented in Figure 16.4. In the figure, I indicates an input matrix, K indicates a kernel matrix, and I * K indicates result of convolutional operation. The input image is given which is converted in the matrix format. The

* indicates a dot product between the input image and kernel image. The kernel function is user defined and generally it is an odd size kernel matrix (odd size is selected because the middle point is well defined for odd matrix). The kernel is applied on the image at a time and resulted convoluted matrix is computed as shown below. In the figure, the kernel is applied as shown below $-(1\times1+0\times1+0\times1)+(1\times0+1\times1+0\times0)+(1\times1+1\times0+1\times0)=3$, similarly, other values are calculated for the resultant matrix. The purpose of convolution operation is to transform the input image to the lower-dimensional space using the kernel function.

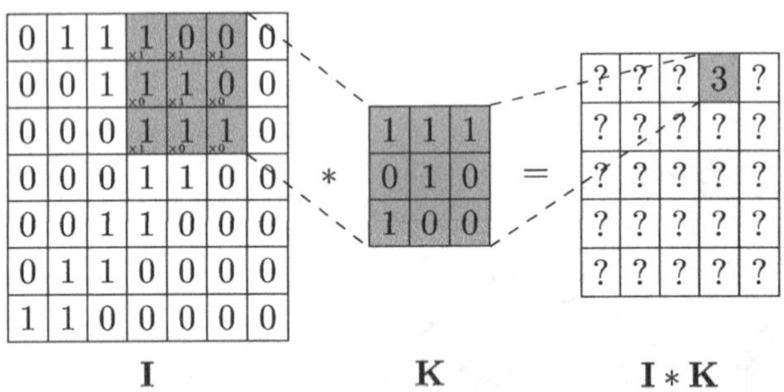

FIGURE 16.4 Graphical Representation of Convolutional Operation in CNN model.

The general architectural diagram of convolutional neural network is presented in Figure 16.5. The important layers in CNN architectures are input layer, convolutional layer, pooling layer, fully connected layer, and output layer.

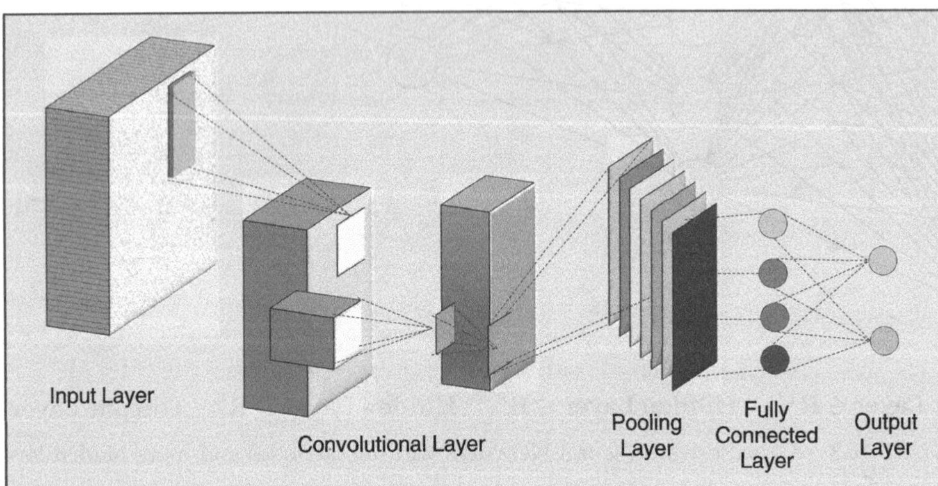

FIGURE 16.5 General Architecture of CNN Deep Learning Model (*See colour figure at the end of the book*).

Key terminology and important operations in CNN

Padding: The input image or data matrix is added with additional data (zeros) at the surrounding. Padding increases the size of the inputs and hence the size of the convolution. Additional rows and columns with the 0 values are added to the original data in padding. The padding operation is shown in Figure 16.6.

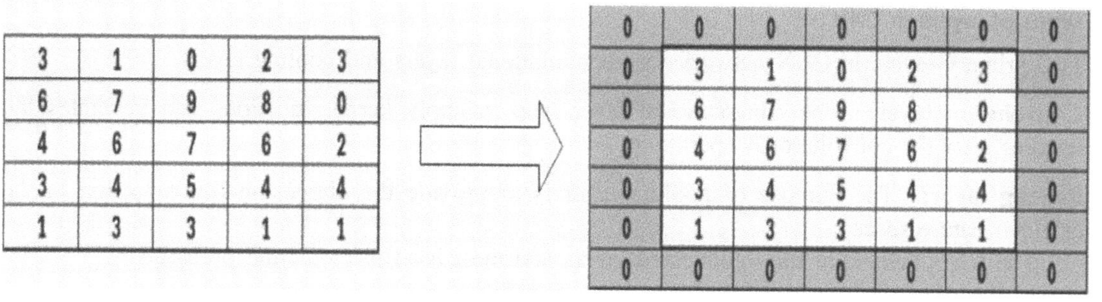

FIGURE 16.6 Graphical Representation of Padding Operation.

Stride: Striding is used for down-sampling in deep learning models. It decreases the results of convolution. The stride parameter indicates, how many cells can be shifted (number of rows and columns traversed per slide) at a time while performing polling operation in CNN deep learning networks. The stride operation is shown in Figure 16.7.

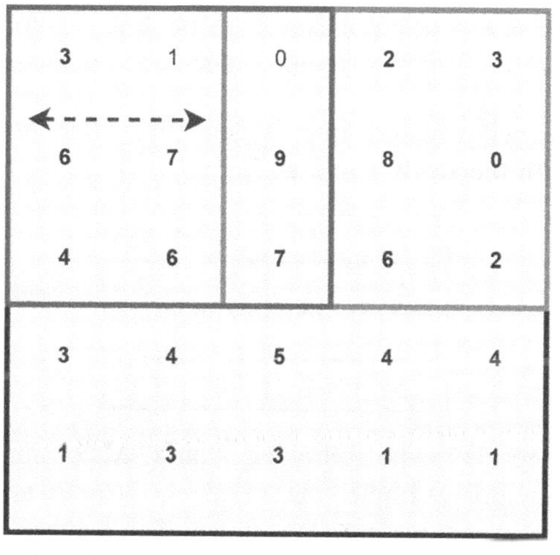

FIGURE 16.7 Graphical Representation of Stride Operation (stride=2).

The output dimensions or size of the output from a layer in CNN deep learning model is computed using the following equation:

$$n^{(l)} = \frac{n^{(l-1)} + 2p^{(l-1)} - f^{(l)}}{s^{(l)}} + 1$$

Where $n^{(l)}$ is the output of the lth layer, $n^{(l-1)}$ is the output of the previous layer, i.e., $(l-1)^{st}$ layer, p is the padding of the previous layer, s is the stride of the current layer, and $f^{(l)}$ is size of kernel.

Pooling: Pooling operation helps in dimensionality reduction and selecting the appropriate features from the original data.

Kernel: Kernel matrix is used for convolution operations. The size of kernel is selected as odd size so that exact centre can be identified easily from the kernel.

Types of layers in CNN

Two primary layers in CNN networks are convolutional layers and pooling layers.

Convolution layer: The convolutional layer help in apply kernel functions and generates the features after the convolutional operations.

Pooling layer: The purpose of pooling layer is to provide the dimensionality reduction in the original feature space.

The CNN layers are fully connected layers and most used in prediction problems.

Pooling layer and pooling operations

The objective of the pooling layer is to reduce the spatial dimensions of the input image in CNN model. It helps in controlling the overfitting and minimizing the number of parameters in CNN models. Pooling layers performs the pooling operation on the input data using a kernel matrix. The max (maximum) pooling and average pooling are the two major types of operations in pooling operations. In max pooling, maximum value is selected from feature map after pooling operation (most salient features are selected), whereas in average pooling, average values are computed for the features. Apart from the max pooling and average pooling, L_2-norm pooling is also available. In L_2-norm pooling, square root of sum of square values are calculated from the feature map.

Example: Suppose the following feature map is generated after the pooling operations. Feature map matrix size is 4 × 4 with the stride value as 2.

1	5	8	6
4	7	2	4
4	5	2	1
3	1	0	3

Then the max pooling will result in the following matrix. Maximum value is selected from the subspace of the feature map. For example, max(1, 5, 4, 7) = 7, and so on. Similarly, average pooling and L_2-norm pooling operations are also shown. The average pooling is calculated for the first subspace as $\frac{1+5+4+7}{4} \cong 4$. The L_2-norm pooling is calculated as $\sqrt{1^2+5^2+4^2+7^2} \cong 9$.

Max Pooling

7	8
5	3

Average Pooling

4	5
3	2

L_2-norm Pooling

9	11
7	4

16.5.3 Autoencoders

The autoencoder deep learning models learn itself for encoding of the information. The autoencoder networks are symmetrical structures, i.e., autoencoders has same number of inputs and outputs. The general architecture of autoencoders deep learning models have five layers, these layers are—input, encoder, latent, decoder, and output layers. The architectural diagram of autoencoder is presented in the Figure 16.8. The primary function of the encoder layer is to transform the input data into lower dimensional space. The latent or code layer captures the essential features from the lower dimensional data and provides the efficient representation. The decoder layer reconstructs the approximate original input samples.

Mean square function is the most commonly used loss function in autoencoders. The loss function measures the reconstruction error (the difference between the original sample and the sample generated by the generator). The autoencoders are the powerful tools for unsupervised learning. The primary applications of autoencoders are in dimensionality reduction, feature extraction, anomaly and fraud detection, and pretraining for the complex deep learning models.

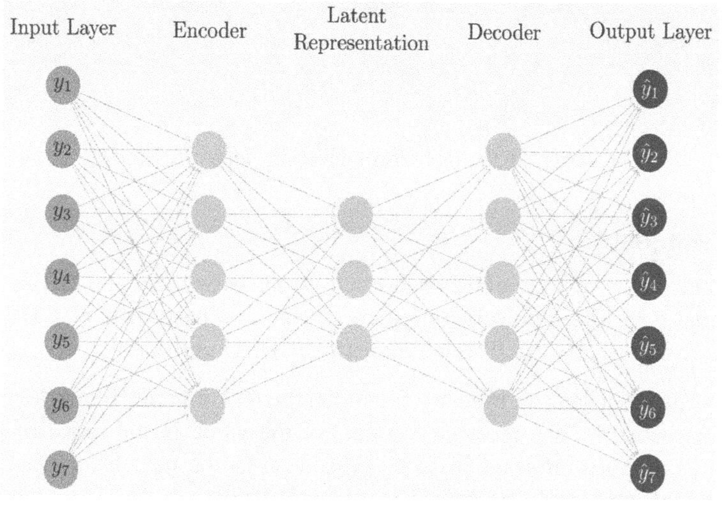

FIGURE 16.8 General Architecture of Autoencoder Deep Learning Model.

Variational autoencoders

The variational autoencoders are the extensions of the autoencoders deep learning models. The limitations of the Autoencoders networks are, it takes input data in a fixed point in latent space. Whereas the variational autoencoders takes the input in the multivariate normal distribution, so as a result it is capable of generating diverse and realistic outputs. It is primarily used for generative modelling because of regularized latent space. The main challenge with the variational autoencoder network is the computational complexity and performance issues. Although it generates more realistic outputs, but the complexity of the network will lead to compromise in the performance of these networks.

16.5.4 Recurrent Neural Networks (RNN)

RNN networks are useful for sequential data. A sequenced data is meaning ordering of data. The feedforward networks (FFNs) are not able to recognize the sequenced information and the parameters are not shared between the layers to discover the sequential patterns. So, in order to eliminate the issues with the FFNs, RNNs are introduced. The general recurrent operation in RNN network is presented in Figure 16.9.

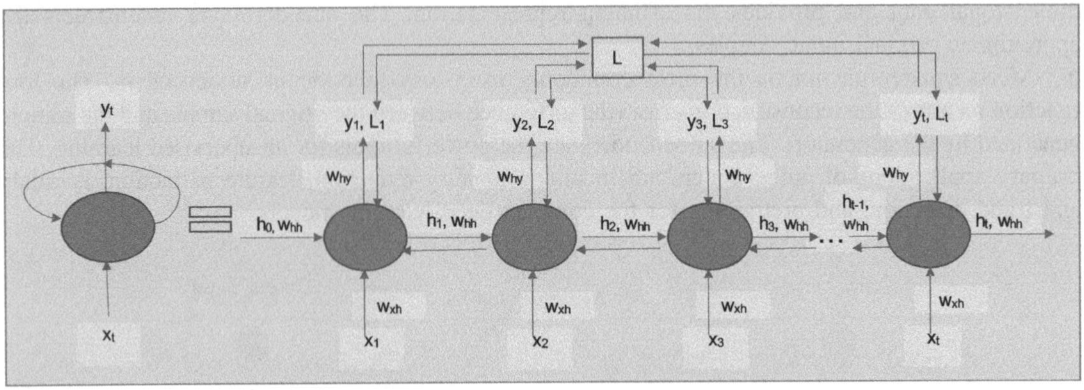

FIGURE 16.9 Recurrent Neural Network Model.

Gated recurrent unit (GRU)

The gated recurrent unit is a type of RNN deep learning networks. The GRUs are developed to processed sequential data like time series prediction, etc. The basic unit of a GRU network is the GRU cell (shown in Figure 16.10). The components of GRU cell are:

Reset gate (r_t): The reset gate is used by for indicating the amount be irrelevant information to be forgotten by the network. The reset gate generates the value in the range of [0...1]. The value near to 1 indicates the more information to be passed on to the next layer where value near to 0 indicates the lesser information to be passed to the next layer.

Update gate (z_t): The update gate decides about the amount of past information to be incorporated into the current information.

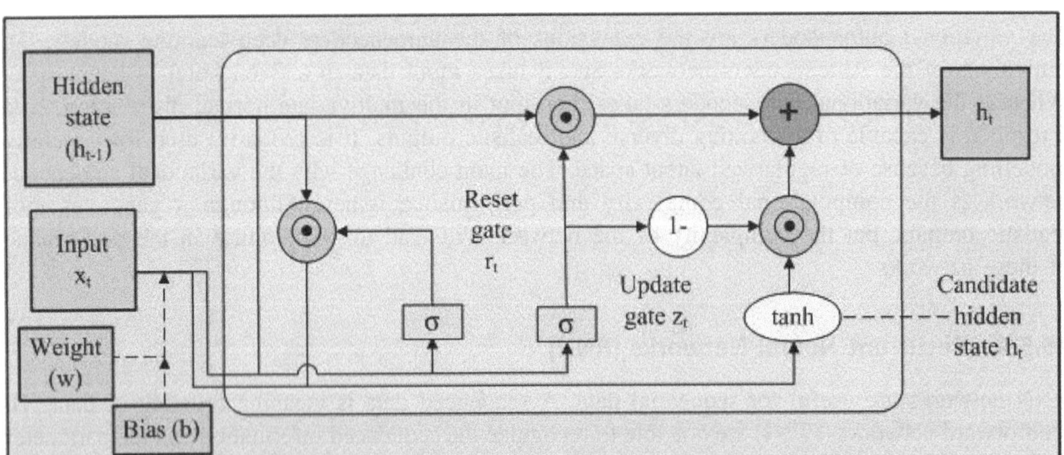

FIGURE 16.10 Cell Diagram of Gated Recurrent Units.

Following equations are used in the GRU cell operations:

$$z_t = \sigma\left(W_z \cdot \left[x_t, h_{t-1}\right] + b_z\right)$$

$$r_t = \sigma\left(W_r \cdot \left[x_t, h_{t-1}\right] + b_r\right)$$

$$\tilde{h}_t = tanh\left(W_n \cdot \left[x_t, r_t \odot h_{t-1}\right] + b_h\right)$$

$$h_t = \left(1 - z_t\right) \odot h_{t-1} + z_t \odot \tilde{h}_t$$

The symbols used in the equation of the GRU cell are presented in the table below.

Symbol	Description
z_t	Output of update gate at time t
r_t	Output of reset gate at time t
x_t	Input at time t
h_{t-1}	Previous hidden state at time t–1
$\tilde{h}_t$	Proposed new state at time t
h_t	Hidden state at time t
W_z, W_r, W_n	Weight matrices for different gates
b_z, b_r, b_h	Biases for different gates
$\cdot$	Dot product (inner product) operator
$\odot$	Sum of element-wise multiplication operator
σ	Sigmoid activation function
tanh	Tanh activation function

Long short-term memory (LSTM)

Both the GRU and LSTM are the types of RNN deep learning models and can handle the sequential data in a efficient manner. The purpose of both of these models is same but there are some technological differences between them. The GRU model is simpler as compared to the LSTM model. The LSTM model has additional memory cells to store the long-term and short-term memories. Due to the simplicity of GRU, it takes lesser amounts of computational resources whereas the LSTM requires the higher number of computational resources. Both of these technologies are suitable for handling of sequential data and choice of selecting one of these technologies depending on the nature of dataset, availability of computing resources, etc. **Bi-LSTM** (Bidirectional—Long Short-Term Memory) model is the extension of the LSTM model in which sequential data is allowed to flow in both directions, i.e., forward and backward directions.

The basic computing unit in LSTM model is LSTM cell shown in Figure 16.11. The LSTM cell is consisting of following components:

Cell state: The internal state of LSTM cell is maintained with the cell state. It is a basic memory unit for LSTM cell.

Hidden state: The hidden state presents the output of a cell state at given time.

LSTM uses three types of gates controlling the flow of information across the network:

Forget gate: The forget gate is used for determining the amount of information to be forgotten in the next cell. It has the value in the range of [0...1], value neat 1 indicates more information to be retained whereas value neat 0 indicates more information to be forgotten.

Input gate: The input gate controls the amount of information to be carried in the new state. The relevance and importance of new candidate is determined by the input gate.

Output gate: The output gate controls the amount of information to be taken as output from the current state based on the inputs and information present in the hidden state.

Cell state update: The cell state update, updates the value of the cell state using the value of the input gate and generates new candidate value.

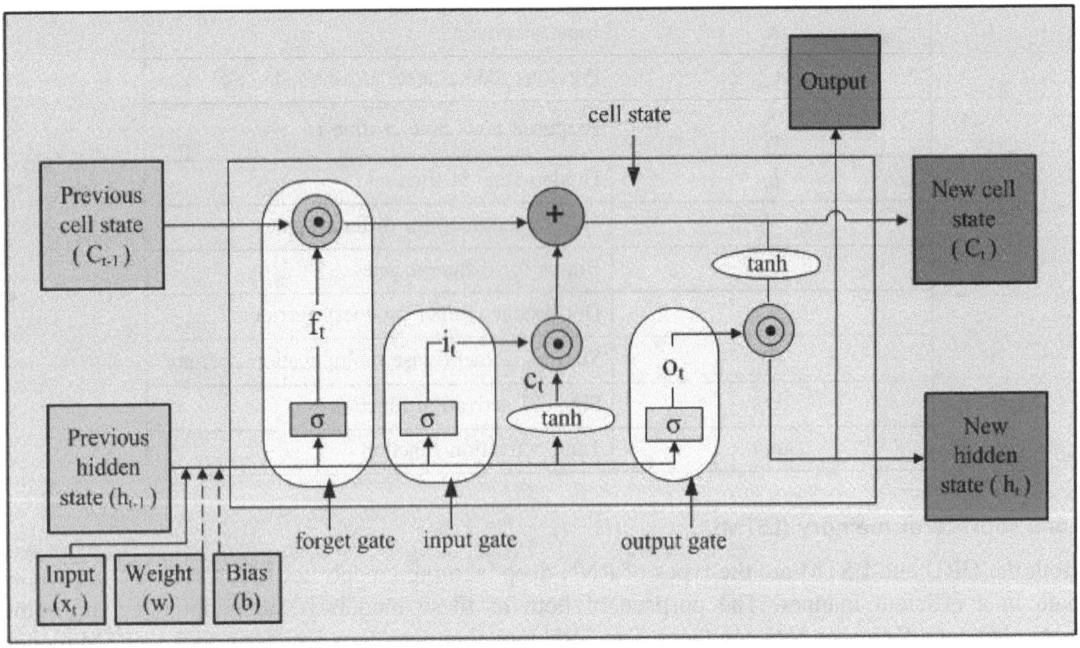

FIGURE 16.11 Cell Diagram of Long Short-Term Memory Model.

The mathematical expression for LSTM is presented by the following set of equations:

$$f_t = \sigma\left(W_f \cdot [x_t, h_{t-1}] + b_f\right)$$

$$i_t = \sigma\left(W_i \cdot [x_t, h_{t-1}] + b_i\right)$$

$$\tilde{C}_t = tanh\left(W_C[x_t, h_{t-1}] + b_C\right)$$

$$C_t = f_t \odot C_{t-1} + i_t \odot \tilde{C}_t$$

$$o_t = \sigma\left(W_o \cdot [x_t, h_{t-1}] + b_o\right)$$

$$h_t = o_t \odot tanh\left(C_t\right)$$

The symbols used in the equation of the LSTM cell are presented in the table below:

Symbol	Description
f_t	Output of forget gate at time t
i_t	Output of input gate at time t
x_t	Input at time t
h_{t-1}	Previous hidden state
C_t	Output of candidate cell state at time t
C_t	Output of cell state at time t
o_t	Output of output gate at time t
W_f, W_i, W_C, W_o	Weight matrices for different gates and states
b_f, b_i, b_C, b_o	Biases of different gates and states
$\cdot$	Dot product (inner product) operator
$\odot$	Sum of element-wise multiplication operator
σ	Sigmoid activation function
tanh	Tanh activation function

16.5.5 Generative Adversarial Networks (GAN)

GAN are the discriminative models and has two major components—generator and discriminator. The generator model generates the data and discriminator model calculates the difference between the original data and the data generated by the generator. The architectural diagram of GAN is presented in Figure 16.12. Both generators and discriminator components try to outperform with each other. GAN models are used for high resolution scaling, development of personal devices such as blood pressure devices, and are most commonly used for identification of deep fakes (the fake data generated by the AI models). The GANs are also used for style transfer in images.

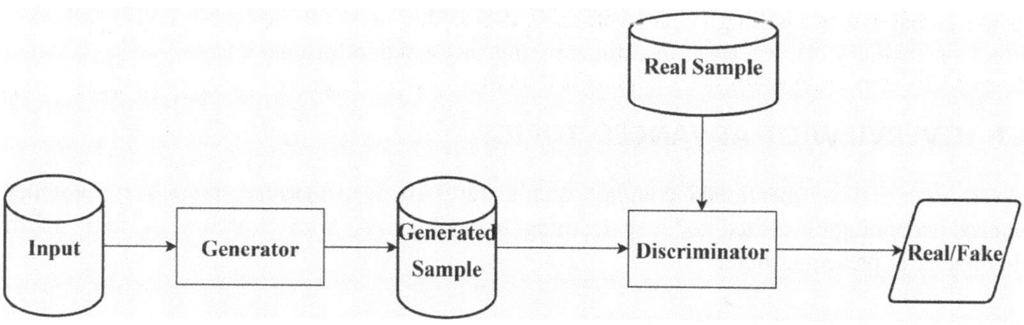

FIGURE 16.12 The General Architecture of GAN Network.

16.6 TRANSFER LEARNING

Transfer learning is a key technology in deep learning. With the help of transfer learning, high-performance data science applications can be developed without much worrying about the designing of the deep learning model. Transfer learning is the process of utilizing existing pretrained models for the new task.

In transfer learning the existing pretrained models are fine-tuned and configured for the newer analysis tasks. The transfer learning models are most useful for the problems of similar nature, e.g., a pretrained deep learning model of classification may be best suited to the classification of newer objects. Modern examples of transfer learning models include AlexNet, VGG, ResNet, and GoogleNet, etc. A brief description of some of the popular transfer learning models is presented in this section.

LeNet-5: LeNet is type of CNN deep learning network with the input size of 32 × 32 pixels. It has two convolutional layers with 60 thousand parameters. It is primarily developed for digit recognition for 10 classes.

AlexNet: It is a type of CNN network with 60 million parameters. It has the 224 × 224 pixels input size. Relu activation function is used for updating the weights. AlexNet uses batch normalization and dropout layers in the architecture. The architecture has 8 layers. AlexNet is used for classification task for classifying the objects into 1000 classes.

VGG-16: The VGG-16 model is developed by Visual Geometric Group. It is a type of CNN deep learning model with 138 million parameters and consists of 16 layers (13 CNN and 3 fully connected). It takes the input size of 224 × 224 pixels and uses Relu activation function. The VGG-16 model can classify up to 1000 classes.

ResNet (Residual Network): ResNet is another pretrained deep learning model, developed on the basis of skip connection concept. In skip connection concept, network may skip one/more layers during training process. The ResNet model is build using residual blocks. A residual block is consisting of 2 CNN, batch normalization using Relu activation function. ResNet is build using the deep stacking of residual blocks.

GoogleNet: GoogleNet deep learning model uses 9 inception modules for classification. In inception model, the network decides the best size for filters dynamically. The GoogleNet was developed using the first version of inception model namely Inception-V1. GoogleNet is capable of multi-scale feature extraction from the input data for improving the classification performance. GoogleNet uses the global average polling (GAP) before final SoftMax layer (at the output layer) and uses the concept of auxiliary classification to estimate vanishing gradient problem.

16.7 OVERVIEW OF ADVANCED TOPICS

Apart from the above-mentioned common architectures of deep learning, there are a number of advanced technologies related to deep learning technology. A brief overview of some of these technologies is presented here.

16.7.1 Style Transfer

Style transfer is applying the artistic content of one image to the other image. It is performed by creating a new image by combining the two images. CNN and GAN networks both typically used in style transfer. The style transfer process is consisting of six major steps.

1. *Pre-processing*: In the first step, the input image is pre-processed, and noise is eliminated.
2. *Feature extraction*: In the second step, content and information from image is captured.

3. *Style representation*: In the third step, style representation is performed by using gram matrix of feature maps.
4. *Content representation*: In this step, content captures are captured.
5. *Optimization*: The optimization step minimizes the difference between the contents.
6. *Post-processing*: In the last step, artifacts are removed for proving a natural look to the image.

Gram matrix (Gramian matrix) is a popular data structure in style transfer. It represents correlations between the feature maps from the images. The gram matrix is computed by dot product of each pair of feature map. Gram matrix is helpful in capturing the style information from images.

16.7.2 Transformer Network and Attention Mechanism

Transformer networks are the popular networks in the recent time. Due to its popularity in large language models (LLMs) such as ChatGPT, Google's Gemini, etc. transformers became popular in the recent time. Transformers networks works on the concept of self-attention. The attention mechanism allows a particular deep learning model to focus on the relevant information from the input data. In order to focus on some of the information, in attention mechanism weights are dynamically assigned to different components of model depending on the context. The attention mechanism most suited for sequence-to-sequence models such as machine translation, summarizing large text, and image captioning, etc.

Self-attention mechanism is a special type of attention mechanism in which the weights are decided and adjusted based on the current state of the model and as per the query (context). The input elements are filtered based on the keys (relevant information). The self-attention model is able to capture complex relationships between the context and input data and able to filter most appropriate information.

Advanced transformers models are designed based on multi-headed attention mechanism. In multi-headed attention mechanism, multiple parallel attention models are deployed for a task. The multi-headed mechanism is composed of positional encoding, feedforward neural networks, layer normalization, and encoder and decoder stacks for making the information filtering more relevant.

16.7.3 Generative AI

Generative AI is a powerful and popular AI technology. In generative AI, models are created that are capable of generating new content with the help of AI. Today, there are many applications present in the domain of generative AI. Different deep learning models are utilized for generating different types of content with the help of AI. Following table summarizes the major deep learning models utilized for different tasks under generative AI.

Content	Deep Learning Technology
Image generation	GANs, Autoencoders
Text generation	RNN
Music generation	RNN
LLMs like ChatGPT, Google's Gemini NLP, machine translation, text generation	RNN, Transformers

16.7.4 Explainable AI

The explainable AI systems are the emerging trends in the deep learning domain. Explainable AI models help in improving, understanding and interpretation of the developed deep learning models. Explainable AI system help in understanding the importance of relevant features in decision-making processes. The explainable AI system provides insight into the local explanation of the models, i.e., it is easier to interpret the model as a whole but a specific point of view how model behaves is explained with the help of explainable AI models. Two popular techniques for explainable AI models are—LIME (Local Interpretable Model Agnostic Explanations) and SHAP (SHapley Additive explanations) models. The LIME model can be utilized for both local and global explanations of the AI model whereas the SHAP model can be utilized for analysing the importance of a feature in the decision-making process. The explainable AI models also help in understanding the model transparency, and post-hoc explanation.

16.7.5 Responsible AI

Another set of AI models are developed in the domain of responsible AI in which deep learning models are developed in an ethical transparent and accountable systems manners. The responsible AI models focuses on fairness, explainability, privacy preserving, robustness and safety of the deep learning models. Responsible AI help in understanding unintended consequences of the AI models and algorithms.

16.7.6 Few Shots Learning (FSL)

Training of deep learning models requires a lot of training dataset for effective training of the model and to attain the desired level of performance. But sometimes, there are situations where the amount of training data is less than the desired amount, that can lead to compromising with the performance of deep learning models. To address this challenge, another set of technologies are invented, few shot learning (FSL) technologies are one of them. The FSL is applicable when small number of training samples are available for a deep learning model. The FSL allow learning of model by few samples only. Learning is feasible for any kind of model by few samples per class using FSL techniques.

The FSL techniques are based on transfer learning or meta learning, where models are trained (learned) on how to learn by itself. Two major components of FSL technology are support set and query. The support set indicates the small set having a smaller number of training samples, and query refers to the object to classify. The FSL techniques are also called as the k-way n-shot models, where k is number of classes and n is the number of samples per class. FSL techniques typically uses a triplet loss functions for measuring the performance of the models. The triplet loss function is calculated based on distances between anchor objects, positive samples, and negative samples. The anchor object is the object needs to be classified, positive and negative samples refer to the objects belongs to the same and different classes to the anchor object class respectively.

16.7.7 Word Embedding

Word Embedding is a representation of words (terms) from the collection of text documents where the words with the similar meanings are located nearby in the vector space. Word embeddings represent the semantic relationship between the words. Word embedding is a powerful tool for knowledge discovery in text and NLP related tasks.

Word2Vec

Word2Vec is the basic technique of word embedding. It has two models CBOW and Skip-gram models. Word2Vec embeds the words in lower-dimensional vector space.

Continuous Bag of Words (CBOW): CBOW model predicts middle word based on surrounding words.

Skip-gram: Skip-gram model predicts word before and after current word.

Glove

Glove (**Glo**bal **Ve**ctors for word embedding) is another word embedding model which is based on co-occurrence probability. Glove is developed by Stanford University. It minimizes the difference between dot product of word vector and logarithm of their co-occurrence by utilizing a least square objective function. In Glove embedding, in a fixed window size, occurrence of a word in context to occurrence of other words is calculated and semantic representation for the contextual correlated words is presented.

FastText

FastText is another word embedding technique in which embeddings are presented as a composition of n-gram characters. The sub-words are represented as n-gram characters. The FastText word embedding model is developed by Facebook's AI research (FAIR) laboratory. The FastText word embedding can capture morphological nuances and utilizes SoftMax and negative sampling technology for achieving the embeddings. FastText word embedding technique can handle unseen words or out-of-vocabulary words, which makes FastText word embedding technique a popular choice of word embeddings.

16.8 DEEP LEARNING FRAMEWORKS AND TOOLS

Deep learning is a very popular technology and have numerous applications in the recent time. Today, there are a lot of frameworks and tools which provides a set of application programming interfaces (API). The key tools and frameworks are summarized in the table below:

Framework	Description
TensorFlow	Developed by Google, popular API for machine learning and deep leaning, optimized for GPU and TPU, best suited for image recognition, natural language processing, and reinforcement learning.
PyTorch	Open-source platform developed by Facebook AI Research (FAIR), developed on the basis of dynamic computation graph, best suited for computer vision natural language processing, and reinforcement learning.
Keras	Python based open-source neural network library, high level API runs on top of other platforms, provides supports for neural network architectures—CNNs, RNNs, provides data pre processing, and visualization.
DeepLeaning4J	Java based open-source API for deep learning, provides architectures for CNN, RNN, LSTM.

(Contd.)

Framework	Description
Caffe	Deep leaning framework developed by University of California, Berkeley, written in C++ with python interface, faster API, can process over 60M images per day.
Theano	Open-source library in Python for numerical computation, developed by Montreal Institute for Learning Architecture (MILA) at the University of Montreal, training of deep learning networks, supports GPU acceleration.

16.9 APPLICATIONS

Deep learning is a most popular technology in data science and artificial intelligence domain. Deep learning has tremendous applications in variety of domains. Deep learning has applications in image classification and object detection, natural language processing, speech recognition, medical diagnosis, autonomous vehicles, finance and trading and so many other domains. The deep learning technology follows and implement ***universal approximation theorem*** and hence any kind of computable function can be implemented with the deep learning technology with the acceptable performance. The universal approximation theorem says that the neural network can approximate any kind of function, as the deep learning technology is the deeper neural network technology, so universal approximation theorem with best feasibility. In simple words, deep learning technology is a ***backbone technology for the artificial intelligence*** applications of the modern era.

EXERCISES

1. Compute the complete $I * K$ matrix for the given input and kernel matrix:

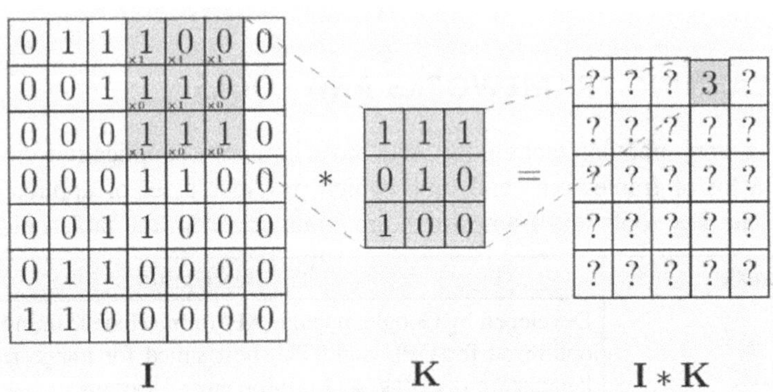

2. If the kernel matrix is given as under for the previous question, then what is the output:

0	0	0
1	0	1
0	1	1

3. What is the result after applying the Max pooling, Average pooling, and L_2-norm pooling in the following feature map with the stride value as 2.

1	1	2	1
2	3	2	3
4	0	3	0
3	2	0	4

4. List the major operations carried out by the LSTM networks by writing and explaining all the equations.

MULTIPLE CHOICE QUESTIONS

1. Low learning rate can lead to the problem of:
   (a) Vanishing Gradient (b) Exploding Gradient
   (c) Overfitting (d) Underfitting
2. High learning rate can lead to the problem of:
   (a) Vanishing Gradient (b) Exploding Gradient
   (c) Overfitting (d) Underfitting
3. Which of the following techniques can help in implementing regularization?
   (a) Applying Dropout Layers in the Deep Learning Models.
   (b) Applying Data Augmentation and Batch Training.
   (c) Applying L_1 and L_2 regularization.
   (d) All of these.
4. Regularization helps in:
   (a) Identifying most relevant features.
   (b) Improving performance of deep learning models.
   (c) Handling data imbalances.
   (d) Penalizing from memorizing or overfitting of deep learning models.
5. What is the purpose of convolutional operation in CNN algorithm?
   (a) Transform the input image to the higher-dimensional space using the kernel function.
   (b) Transform the input image to the lower-dimensional space using the kernel function.
   (c) Transform the input image to the most relevant features using the kernel function.
   (d) None of these.
6. What is the purpose of Stride operation in deep learning model?
   (a) Stride is used for data imbalance.
   (b) Stride is used for down sampling in deep learning models.
   (c) Stride is used for up sampling in deep learning models.
   (d) Stride is used for improving accuracy of the deep learning model.

For question no. 7 and 8, suppose the following feature map is generated after the pooling operations. Feature map matrix size is 4 × 4 with the stride value as 2.

5	3	7	6
4	5	2	4
1	5	2	5
3	4	2	7

7. The L_2-norm pooling will result in the following matrix?

(a)

5	7
5	7

(b)

3	2
1	2

(c)

4	5
3	4

(d)

9	10
7	9

8. The max pooling will result in which of the following matrix?

(a)

5	7
5	7

(b)

5	5
4	4

(c)

3	7
3	7

(d)

5	4
3	7

9. How variational autoencoder differ from the autoencoder technique?

(a) The variational autoencoders varies the autoencoder as per the variation in data.
(b) The variational autoencoders takes input data in a fixed point in latent space.
(c) The variational autoencoders takes the input in the multivariate normal distribution.
(d) None of these.

10. What is the purpose of Update gate in GRU deep learning model?

(a) The update gate controls the amount of information to be taken as output.
(b) The update gate decides about the amount of past information to be incorporated into the current information.
(c) The update gate is used by for indicating the amount be irrelevant information to be forgotten by the network.
(d) The update gate presents the output of a cell state at given time.

11. How GRU models are different from the LSTM model?

(a) The GRU model is simpler as compared to the LSTM model.
(b) The GRU takes lesser amounts of computational resources whereas the LSTM requires the higher number of computational resources.
(c) The LSTM model has additional memory cells to store the long-term and short-term memories.
(d) All of these.

12. What is the purpose of Cell State gate in LSTM deep learning model?

(a) The internal state of LSTM cell is maintained with the cell state.
(b) The cell state presents the output at given time.
(c) The cell state gate is used for determining the amount of information to be forgotten in the next cell.
(d) The cell state gate controls the amount of information to be carried in the new state.

13. For style transfer in image which of the deep learning model is most suitable?

(a) CNN (b) RNN
(c) GAN (d) LSTM

14. A residual block of ResNet algorithm is consisting of:

(a) A residual block is consisting of CNN, 2 batch normalization using SoftMax activation function.
(b) A residual block is consisting of 2 CNN, batch normalization using SoftMax activation function.
(c) A residual block is consisting of CNN, 2 batch normalization using Relu activation function.
(d) A residual block is consisting of 2 CNN, batch normalization using Relu activation function.

15. The GoogleNet uses which particular operation before the final SoftMax layer?

(a) GoogleNet uses the global average polling before final SoftMax layer
(b) GoogleNet uses the global maximum polling before final SoftMax layer

(c) GoogleNet uses the L_2-regularization before final SoftMax layer
(d) GoogleNet uses the batch normalization before final SoftMax layer.

16. What is the purpose of Gram Matrix in style transfer technique?
(a) It represents important features from the images.
(b) It represents correlations between the feature maps from the images.
(c) It represents most relevant features from the images.
(d) It transforms the feature from the images for better processing.

17. What is the objective of attention mechanism in transformers?
(a) The attention mechanism focuses on a particular layer in the deep learning model to process the information.
(b) The attention mechanism focuses on a particular output in the deep learning model to process the information.
(c) The attention mechanism allows a particular deep learning model to focus on the relevant information from the input data.
(d) None of these.

18. For which applications the attention networks is most suitable?
(a) Summarizing Large Text (b) Machine Translation
(c) Image Captioning (d) All of these

19. Responsible AI focuses on:
(a) Fairness (b) Privacy Preserving
(c) Robustness and Safety (d) All of these

20. What is the technical meaning of *k*-way *n*-shot learning?
(a) It is a scheme of few shots learning with *k* number of classes with *n* number of examples in each class.
(b) It is a scheme of few shots learning with *n* number of classes with *k* number of examples in each class.
(c) It is a scheme of few shots learning with *n* number of classifiers (classification models) with *k* number of runs.
(d) None of these.

21. What is the main difference between the Word2Vec and Glove word embedding techniques?
(a) The Word2Vec technique is based on contextual similar vectors, but Glove does not use the vectors.
(b) The Glove model does not use any specific word representation, but Word2Vec model uses the word to vector representation.
(c) The Word2Vec technique is based on the co-occurrence within the local context of the words whereas the Glove model is based on the word-to-word co-occurrence count.
(d) The Word2Vec technique is based on the word-to-word co-occurrence count whereas the Glove model is based on the co-occurrence within the local context of the words.

REFERENCES

[1] Shrestha, A., & Mahmood, A. (2019), Review of deep learning algorithms and architectures, *IEEE access*, 7, pp. 53040–53065.
[2] Mathew, A., Amudha, P., & Sivakumari, S. (2021), Deep learning techniques: An overview. Advanced Machine Learning Technologies and Applications: Proceedings of AMLTA 2020, pp. 599–608.
[3] Wang, Y., Yao, Q., Kwok, J-. T., & Ni, L. M. (2020), Generalizing from a few examples: A survey on few-shot learning, *ACM computing surveys (csur)*, 53(3), pp. 1–34.

ANSWER KEY

1. (a)	**2.** (b)	**3.** (d)	**4.** (d)	**5.** (b)	**6.** (b)	**7.** (d)	**8.** (a)	**9.** (c)	**10.** (b)
11. (d)	**12.** (a)	**13.** (c)	**14.** (d)	**15.** (a)	**16.** (b)	**17.** (c)	**18.** (d)	**19.** (d)	**20.** (a)
21. (d)									

17 Time Series Analysis

Introduction

A time series is a sequential series of data points varying over time. The values in a time series are shown for a time period. For example, hourly weather data represents the weather data for the period of an hour. The daily closing price for a stock in the stock market is capped at end of the day (hence the time period is 1 day for this series). The time series data for HDFC Bank stock is presented in Table 17.1. The volume data and closing price time series for the stock HDFC Bank is presented in Figure 17.1 and Figure 17.2 respectively.

TABLE 17.1 Stock Price of HDFC Bank on NSE for 20 Days

Date	Open	High	Low	Close	Volume
2/14/2024 15:30:00	1376	1391.5	1363.55	1384.05	45660405
2/15/2024 15:30:00	1385	1415.5	1384.35	1414.05	20792472
2/16/2024 15:30:00	1423.9	1427.7	1408.45	1419.9	16087871
2/19/2024 15:30:00	1429	1429	1415.2	1417.1	17225878
2/20/2024 15:30:00	1415	1457.25	1411.8	1454.3	28066754
2/21/2024 15:30:00	1464	1464	1435	1439.15	22946568
2/22/2024 15:30:00	1417.75	1428.8	1412.2	1419.55	25280441
2/23/2024 15:30:00	1422.55	1433.9	1418	1420.6	14916726
2/26/2024 15:30:00	1413.55	1434.85	1413.55	1422.3	11753435
2/27/2024 15:30:00	1413.55	1426.7	1413.05	1420.15	16043575
2/28/2024 15:30:00	1420.15	1424.2	1404	1409.4	12660993
2/29/2024 15:30:00	1402.1	1410.4	1397.3	1403.4	26647850
3/01/2024 15:30:00	1400	1432.75	1400	1430.75	17369449

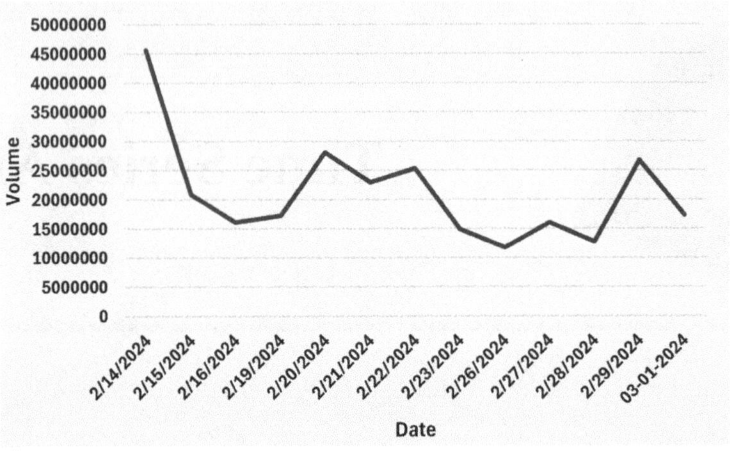

FIGURE 17.1 The number of shares traded (volume) of the HDFC Bank stock on NSE in 20 Days.

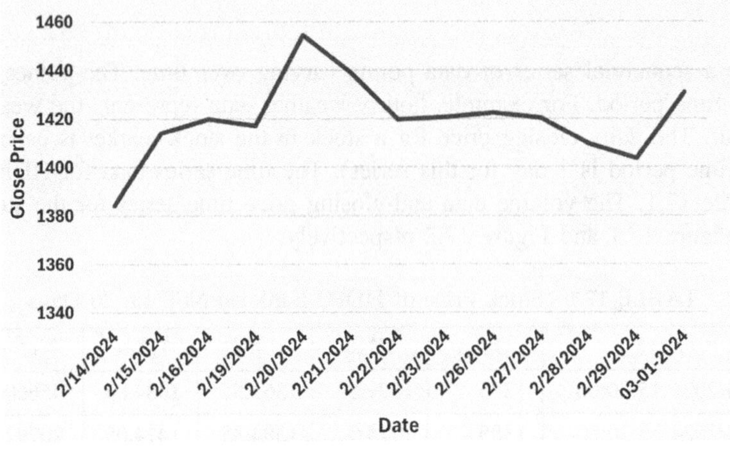

FIGURE 17.2 The closing price of HDFC Bank stock on NSE for 20 Days.

A time series is composed of several components. The four major components of a time series are cyclic, seasonality, irregularity, and trend. A time series, consisting of these components can be represented either by the additive or multiplicative models as described below.

Additive model of time series is expressed as per the equation given below:

$$Y = C + S + I + T$$

Multiplicative model of time series is expressed as per the equation given below:

$$Y = C \times S \times I \times T$$

Where C, S, I, and T represent the cyclic, seasonal, irregular and trend components of the time series. Y indicates the original value in the time series. Let's understand these terms in brief.

Cyclic: The cyclic component refers to the data values in a time series which repeats over a short period in a time series.

Seasonal: The seasonal components indicate that value changes (increase or decrease drastically) for a particular period of time.

Irregular: The irregular components refer to the random change in the time series at a particular time period or time interval.

Trend: Trend indicates continuous increase or decrease of the time series over the period of time.

17.1 TYPES OF TIME SERIES

Broadly time series are classified into two major categories namely, stationary and non-stationary. A stationary time series is one in which the mean and variance of the series are constant over time, whereas the non-stationary time series consists of varying mean and variance over time. The stationary time series is further classified into two subcategories namely, strong stationary and weak stationary time series. The primary difference between the strong and weak stationary time series is, in the weak stationary time series, the values in a time series fluctuates more around the mean as compared to the string stationary time series. Stationary time series does not only provide the constant mean and variance but also the higher order moments such as skewness and kurtosis, etc. Non-stationary series on the other hand indicates trends, seasonality and irregularity in the time series. Most of the time series analysis techniques require that the non-stationary time series should be first transformed to a stationary time series before applying the technique.

17.1.1 Non-Stationary Time Series to Stationary Time Series

Converting a non-stationary time series into the stationary time series requires certain steps to be followed. The entire process is illustrated using a simple numerical example. Let's assume that the 5 years (60 months) monthly sales data is recorded and stored as a time series as shown in the table below (Table 17.2). Table 17.2 is showing an upward trend as the sales figures are increasing over time. So clearly it is an example of the non-stationary time series.

TABLE 17.2 Sample non-stationary time series

Month	Sales
1	100
2	110
3	120
4	130
5	140
...	...
58	350
59	360
60	370

The process of converting the non-stationary time series to stationary time series consists of four basic steps. In the first step, the time series is checked for stationarity by applying certain statistical tests. If the statistical test gives the hint that the given time series is stationary then conversion is not required, otherwise a second step is followed. In the second step, some suitable transformation techniques are applied to the data values of the time series. In the third step, the transformed time series is evaluated. The transformed time series is checked again using some of the statistical tests, if the transformed time series is found stationary then no more operations are required otherwise another transformation technique is selected and applied over the data values for the time series to convert the given time series to stationary.

One of the common statistical tests for checking whether the given time series is stationary is Dickey-Fuller or DF test. In this test, the null hypothesis and alternate hypothesis are framed. The null hypothesis is that the given time series has a unit root (the time series is non-stationary) and the alternate hypothesis is that the time series has no unit root (i.e., the time series is stationary). The statistical values from the DF test are calculated and compared against the critical values. If the calculated statical value is less than the critical value, then the null hypothesis is rejected. The rejection of null hypothesis indicates that time series is stationary, otherwise the time series is non-stationary. The Augmented Dickey-Fuller (ADF) test is the extension of DF test in which more flexibility is provided in the models to verify the stationarity of a time series.

Two simple transformation techniques for converting the non-stationary time series to stationary time series are differencing and long transformation techniques.

Differencing: In this method the values are replaced with the consecutive difference between the values available in the time series. For example, the differenced sales are stored in place of sales value. The differenced value is calculated by taking the difference between the sales value for the time t and t–1. The differencing technique removes the trends from the time series data therefore it is also called as detrending technique.

$$\text{Differenced Sales} = \text{Sales}_t - \text{Sales}_{t-1}$$

Log Transformation: In the long transformation, the actual values of time series are replaced by the natural long transformed values in the time series.

$$\text{Log}(\text{Sales}) = \ln(\text{Sales})$$

Applying transformation to the time series data will update the values for the time series and it will make the time series approximately stationary. The transformed time series data is presented in Table 17.3.

TABLE 17.3 Transformed time series data

Month	Sales	Differenced Sales	Log(Sales)
1	100	–	4.605
2	110	10	4.7
3	120	10	4.795
4	130	10	4.882
5	140	10	4.968

It is clear that from the transformed time series data, the mean and variance are almost constant. So, the transformed time series is stationary now. As discussed earlier that most of the time series analysis techniques requires that the time series should be stationary so converting the non-stationary time series to stationary is a necessary step in time series analysis.

17.2 TIME SERIES ANALYSIS MODELS

In this section commonly used time series analysis techniques are covered in detail.

17.2.1 Autoregressive Models (AR)

The AR model is based on the correlation between the present value with the past values. In AR models the forecasting of the data value in a time series is performed by using the past values. The future predicted value is represented as a linear combination of the past values.

The autoregressive model of order p, $AR(p)$ is given by the equation below:

$$X_t = \sum_{i=1}^{p} \varphi_i X_{t-1} + \in_t$$

Where φ_i is the ith parameter of the model, X_t is the value of the time series at time t, and X_{t-1} is the value of time series at time $t - 1$, and $\in_t$ is the white noise in the time series.

Choosing appropriate value of order of AR model

The value of p (order) of the $AR(p)$ model is decided with the help of PACF (Partial Autocorrelation Function). In the partial autocorrelation function, when the order of the AR model is 1 (i.e., $p = 1$), then the model becomes:

$$X_t = \varphi_1 X_{t-1} + \in_t$$

So, the current value in the time series depends on the one previous value only.

Example 1: Let us understand the $AR(p)$ model with the help of a simple example. Suppose we have been given a monthly time series data consisting of the number of customers visiting a shopping mall in the city. Using AR model our task is to identify the visitors for the next upcoming month from this series.

TABLE 17.4 Monthly visitors data for a shopping mall

Month	Visitors
1	100
2	120
3	115
4	130
5	125
6	140
7	135
8	150
9	145
10	160
11	155
12	170

In order to predict the visitor for the next month using the *AR* model, certain steps are required to be followed. The ***first step*** is to check whether the given time series is stationary or not. From the manual observation we can see that there is a clear upward trend in the time series data. So, the given time series is not the stationary. In practice, the non-stationary time series should be converted to the stationary before applying any time series model, but for simplicity this step is skipped in this example. The ***second step*** is to select the appropriate *AR* model, i.e., identify suitable order for the *AR* model. Although there is a standard approach for estimating suitable order value for the *AR* model, let us assume that for simplicity the order of the *AR* model is 1. The order selection mechanism is discussed later in this chapter. So, p = 1, i.e., the number of visitors in the current month depends on the number of visitors of the previous month. The ***third step*** is to apply the *AR*(1) model on the given example time series and calculate the coefficient and intercept for the model. The ***next step*** is to apply the model using estimated values of the coefficient and intercept and forecast the value of visitors by considering the visitors of the previous month. Let us assume that the coefficient is $\varphi_1 = 0.7$, and intercept is $\in_t = 10$.

Then, the forecasted value for the number of visitors for the next month is:

$$\text{Visitors}_{\text{month}=13} = \varphi_1 \times \text{Visitors}_{\text{month}=12} + \in_t = 0.7 \times 170 + 10 = 129.$$

So, the number of visitors for the next months is 129. For simplicity, we have assumed that the order of AR model is 1, the coefficient is 0.7, and the intercept is 10, however, in real-world situations, using some special packages of time series analysis proper fitting of model is carried out and appropriate values are decided for the order, coefficients, and intercept.

Example 2: Let us assume that we have been given the month temperature (in °C) data for a city, and forecasting of temperature for the next month is required using AR model.

TABLE 17.5 Monthly temperature data for a city

Month	Temperature (°C)
1	15
2	16
3	18
4	20
5	22
6	25
7	28
8	29
9	27
10	24
11	20
12	18

For predicting the temperature for the next month, just like the previous example, similar steps are required to be followed. In the first step, time series is checked for stationarity. If the time series is non-stationary, then it should be converted to stationary. For simplicity it is assumed that the time series is stationary. In the second step, the order of the *AR* model is estimated, suppose the estimated order of the *AR* model for this example is 2 (p = 1). The *AR* model becomes as shown below:

$$AR(2) = X_t = \varphi_1 \, X_{t-1} + \varphi_2 \, X_{t-2} + \epsilon_t$$

In the third step, coefficients and intercept are estimated for the model and in the fourth step, the model is applied for forecasting of the temperature of the next month as given in the equation below:

$$\text{Temp}_{\text{month}=13} = \varphi_1 \times \text{Temp}_{\text{month}=12} + \varphi_2 \times \text{Temp}_{\text{month}=11} + \epsilon_t = 0.6 \times 18 + 0.3 \times 20 + 2 = 18.8$$

The estimated temperature for the next month is 18.8°C.

17.2.2 Moving Average (MA)

The MA model predicts the values by utilizing the past prediction errors. The value in a time series is represented as a linear combination of current prediction and past prediction errors. The moving average prediction technique is represented by using the following equation:

$$X_t = \mu + \epsilon_t + \theta_1 \epsilon_{t-1} + \ldots + \theta_q \epsilon_{t-q}$$

$$X_t = \mu + \sum_{i=1}^{q} \theta_i \epsilon_{t-i} + \epsilon_t$$

Where X_t is the data point of the time series at time t, θ_i is the coefficient of the moving average technique, ϵ_t is the error term for time t, and μ is the constant.

Example 3: A numerical example of moving average model is given below for better understanding. Suppose sales data for a supermarket is given below for a week. Suppose the prediction of next day is required from this time series. By using time series, the modelling can be done in the following steps for the prediction using moving average model.

TABLE 17.6 Sales data for a week for a supermarket

Day	Sales
1	20
2	30
3	25
4	40
5	35
6	28
7	32

The moving average (MA) model for prediction is prepared in the following steps. In the first step, window size is selected for calculating moving average. Suppose 3 days windows are selected for the model. Then in the second step, moving average values for the 3 days window is calculated as follows. For day 1, there is no previous data so no moving average value can be calculated. For the second day, the average of day 1 and day 2 is calculated as the moving average values as (20+30)/2 = 25. For the third day, the average of day 1, day 2, and day 3 is calculated as the moving average values (20 + 30 + 25)/3 = 25. Similarly, the moving average values can be calculated for the rest of the days. The moving average values are 25, 25, 31.67, 33.33, 34.33, 31.67. Once the moving average values are calculated then in the third step, coefficients for the moving average model are estimated and model is fitted for the data. Finally, in the last step, the developed model is used for forecasting the sales for the future days.

Example 4: Moving average (*MA*) model is explained using another simple working example. Let's assume that a sample time series for monthly rainfall in mm is given for 12 months (Table 17.7). The given task is to predict the rainfall for the next months using MA model.

TABLE 17.7 Sample time series for Moving Average model

Month	**Rainfall (mm)**
1	50
2	55
3	60
4	65
5	70
6	75
7	80
8	85
9	90
10	95
11	100
12	105

Let's assume that the moving average is required to be calculated for the 3 periods (3 months for this example). The calculation of moving average and forecasting error is shown in Table 17.8.

TABLE 17.8 Calculations of moving average and forecasting errors

Month	Rainfall (mm)	Moving Average	Error
1	50	–	
2	55	–	
3	60	–	
4	65	$\frac{50+55+60}{3} = 55$	10
5	70	$\frac{55+60+65}{3} = 60$	10
6	75	65	10
7	80	70	10
8	85	75	10

(Contd.)

Month	Rainfall (mm)	Moving Average	Error
9	90	80	10
10	95	85	10
11	100	90	10
12	105	95	10

For simplicity, let's create an MA(1) model, which means it depends only on the previous error term. The model can be represented as:

$$X_t = \mu + \theta_1 \in_{t-1} + \in_t$$

Let's assume that after the MA model fitting the values of the constant (μ), and coefficient (θ_1) are 95 and 0.5 respectively. Then the rainfall for the thirteenth month can be estimated using the following equation:

$$X_{13} = 95 + 0.5 \times \in_{12} + \in_{13}$$

$$X_{13} = 95 + 0.5 \times 10 + 10 = 110$$

Moving averaging techniques—SMA, WMA, EMA

In moving average model, averaging can be done in several ways. Three commonly used averaging techniques are Simple Moving Averaging (SMA), Weighted Moving Averaging (WMA), and Exponential Moving Averaging (EMA).

Simple Moving Average (SMA): In SMA technique, the moving average can simply be calculated using the simple mathematical average values of the previous values for a fixed period.

$$SMA(N) = \frac{Val_t + Val_{t-1} + \ldots + Val_{t-N+1}}{N}$$

Weighted Moving Average (WMA): In WMA moving average technique, different weights are assigned to different past values. Generally, most recent values are given higher weights as compared to the historical values.

$$WMA(N) = W_t \times Val_t + W_{t-1} \times Val_{t-1} + \ldots + W_{t-N+1} \times Val_{t-N+1}$$

Exponential Moving Average (EMA): In EMA moving average technique, the weights to the most recent values are assigned using a smoothing factor (α). The weights for the most recent values are exponentially higher than the previous values.

$$EMA(T) = \alpha \times Val_t + \left(EMA(T-1) \times (1-\alpha)\right)$$

Example: Let's assume that the following time series data is given for the three days for a stock price.

Day 1: ₹ 120

Day 2: ₹ 130

Day 3: ₹ 127

Then the moving average for the three different techniques can be calculated as follows:

***SMA*:** Three days MA can be calculated as

$$SMA(3) = \frac{120 + 130 + 127}{3} = 125.67$$

***WMA*:** Suppose for calculating 3 days–WMA the weights associated with the recent values are 0.5, 0.3, and 0.2 then the moving average can be calculated as:

$$WMA(3) = 0.5 \times 127 + 0.3 \times 130 + 0.2 \times 120 = 126.50$$

***EMA*:** Suppose the for EMA moving average the smoothing factor α = 0.5, then the moving average for 3 days–EMA can be calculated as:

Initially the first average is selected as ₹ 120 for the day one using simple moving average, so *EMA*(1) = 120. For the second day the average is calculated as

$$EMA(2) = 0.5 \times 130 + 120 \times (1 - 0.5) = 125$$

Similarly, for the third day exponential moving average can be calculated as:

$$EMA(3) = 0.5 \times 127 + 125 \times (1 - 0.5) = 126$$

17.2.3 ARMA

The *ARMA* (Auto-Regressive Moving-Average) model is the combination of the *AR* and *MA* models for forecasting the time series values. It utilizes the benefit of both *AR* and *MA* models to predict the values in a time series. The current value in the time series depends on the historical values and historical forecasting errors. The *ARMA* model is mathematically expressed as given below:

$$ARMA(p,q) = X_t = c + \sum_{i=1}^{p} \varphi_i X_{t-1} + \sum_{i=1}^{q} \theta_i \in_{t-i} + \in_t$$

In the above equation, p, and q are the orders for *AR* and *MA* models respectively. c is the constant and $\in_t$ is the forecasting error term at time t. The orders for *MA* and *AR* models are decided by the *ACF* (Autocorrelation Function) and *PACF* (Partial Autocorrelation Function) plots.

Autocorrelation function (ACF) and partial autocorrelation function (PACF)

The order of MA (Moving Average) time series model is decided by the ACF function by plotting the ACF values against the different time lags. Then a lag value is selected after which there is no significance in the ACF values for a given threshold value. This selected lag value indicates the order of the MA (Moving Average) model. Similarly, the partial autocorrelation values are calculated and plotted for the PACF function using different time lags. Then a suitable lag value is selected after which there is no significant change in partial correlation values. This selected lag value indicates the order of AR (Autoregressive) model. The ACF and PACF values range between –1 to +1. In case of ACF values for lag 0, the ACF value is always equal to 1, as the value is exactly correlated with itself. The dashed lines in the ACF and PACF plots represent the 95% confidence intervals.

For better understanding a synthetic time series is created in the R programming language with the code and ACF and PACF functions are plotted.

```
set.seed(123)
data <- arima.sim(list(order = c(1,0,0), ar = 0.7), n = 100)
acf(data, main="ACF Plot of Synthetic Time Series Data")
pacf(data, main="ACF Plot of Synthetic Time Series Data")
```

The above code will create a synthetic time series and the following ACF and PACF plots as shown in Figure 17.3 and Figure 17.4 respectively. The order of AR model is estimated from the PACF plot, whereas the order of MA model is estimated from the ACF plot. In both ACF and PACF plots, in the *x*-axis lag values are selected and, in the *y*-axis, autocorrelation and partial autocorrelation values are shown. In order to estimate the order of MA model from ACF the autocorrelation values are observed against the different lags. The point after which there is no significance of autocorrelation in the plot is selected as the order of the MA model. For example, in Figure 17.3, after lag 4 there is no significance of autocorrelation values in the plot so the order of MA is taken as 4, i.e., **MA(4)** is the most appropriate moving average model for forecasting in the time series. Similarly, in the PACF plot shown in Figure 17.4, there is no significance in partial autocorrelation values after lag 1, so the order of AR model is selected as 1 or in other words **AR(1)** is the most appropriate model for forecasting in the given time series. In other words, the current value of the time series just depends on previous value (the previous value is sufficient to make forecasting for the current value). The general characteristics of the PACF and ACF plots for deciding the orders for AR and MA models is summarized in the Table 17.9.

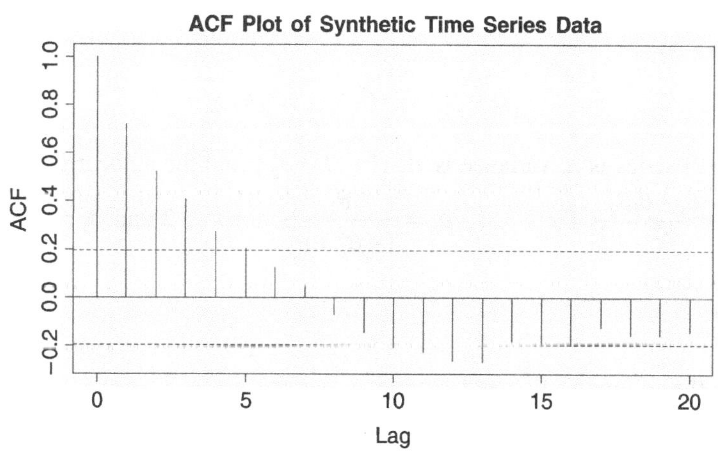

FIGURE 17.3 ACF plot for the synthetic time series.

TABLE 17.9 Choosing appropriate lags for *ARMA* model

Model	ACF	PACF
AR(p)	Dies down	Cuts off after lag p
MA(q)	Cuts off after lag q	Dies down
ARMA(p, q)	Dies down	Dies down

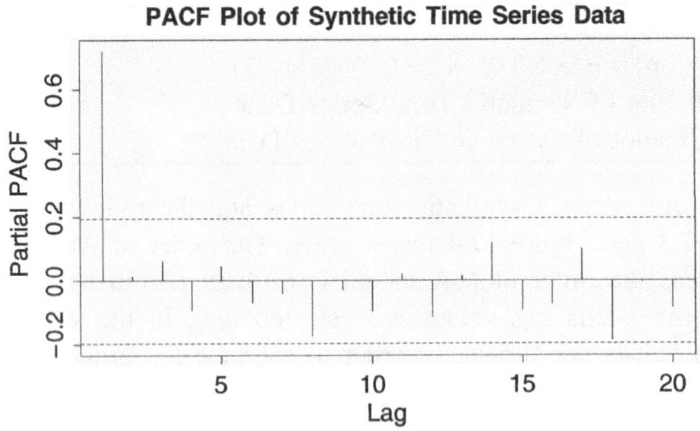

FIGURE 17.4 PACF plot for the synthetic time series.

Interpretation of the ACF plots for moving average (MA) models

MA(1)

$$X_t = \mu + \epsilon_t + \theta_1 \epsilon_{t-1}$$

Mean for the MA(1) series is μ, variance is $\sigma_\epsilon^2\left(1+\theta_1^2\right)$ and the autocorrelation function (ACF) is given by $\rho_k = \dfrac{\theta_1}{1+\theta_1^2}$ for $k = 1$, and $\rho_k = 0$ for $k \geq 2$, where k is the lag of time series.

MA(2)

$$X_t = \mu + \epsilon_t + \theta_1 \epsilon_{t-1} + \theta_2 \epsilon_{t-2}$$

Mean for the MA(2) series is μ, variance is $\sigma_\epsilon^2\left(1+\theta_1^2+\theta_2^2\right)$ and the autocorrelation function (ACF) is given by $\rho_k = \dfrac{\theta_1 + \theta_1\theta_2}{1+\theta_1^2+\theta_2^2}$ for $k = 1$, $\rho_k = \dfrac{\theta_2}{1+\theta_1^2+\theta_2^2}$ for $k = 2$ and $\rho_k = 0$ for $k \geq 3$, where k is the lag of time series.

Example:

MA(1)—Suppose the following first order moving average model is given, then the ACF function value for lag 1 is calculated as shown below.

$$X_t = 7 + \epsilon_t + 0.4 \times \epsilon_{t-1}$$

$\rho_1 = \dfrac{0.4}{1+0.4^2} = 0.34$, and $\rho_k = 0$ for $k \geq 2$.

MA(2)—Suppose the following second order moving average model is given, then the ACF functions for first and second legs will be calculated as shown below.

$$X_t = 7 + \epsilon_t + 0.6 \times \epsilon_{t-1} + 0.2 \times \epsilon_{t-2}$$

$\rho_1 = \dfrac{0.6 + 0.6 \times 0.2}{1+0.6^2+0.2^2} = 0.51$, $\rho_2 = \dfrac{0.2}{1+0.6^2+0.2^2} = 0.14$, and for $\rho_k = 0$ for $k \geq 3$.

17.2.4 ARIMA

The next important and popular time series model in time series analysis is ARIMA (Autoregressive Integrated Moving Average) model. The ARIMA model has three components and the mathematically ARIMA is expressed using the below equation. Where p, d, and q represent the order for AR, differencing, and moving average components.

$$\text{ARIMA}(p,d,q) = c + \sum_{i=1}^{p} \varphi_i X_{t-1} + \sum_{i=1}^{q} \theta_i \in_{t-i} + \in_t$$

Three components of ARIMA models are tabulated in the Table 17.10.

TABLE 17.10 Components of ARIMA model

Component	Description
AR(p)	The first component of ARIMA model is AR or autoregression with the order p.
I(d)	The second component is integrated and is consisting of order of differencing, handle non-stationarity, if time series data is having trends or seasonality then that is removed by differencing.
MA(q)	The third component is MA or moving average model with the order q.

Simple ARIMA Example: (Monthly Coffee Sales)—Let's imagine a small coffee shop tracks monthly coffee sales for a year (12 months). We want to forecast sales for the next 3 months using an ARIMA model.

TABLE 17.11 Monthly sales of coffee

Month	Sales
1	100
2	120
3	115
4	130
5	125
6	140
7	135
8	150
9	145
10	160
11	155
12	170

The first step is general and common for all the time series forecasting models, in which the given time series is checked for stationarity. If the given time series is non-stationary, then it should be converted to stationary first. For the given time series, it is manually observed that it is showing the upward trend in the sales data, so it is non-stationary. To make it stationary, differencing operation is performed on the sales data. The differencing will result in the following dataset;

TABLE 17.12 Updated time series after differencing

Month	Sales	Difference
1	100	–
2	120	20
3	115	–5
4	130	15
5	125	–5
6	140	15
7	135	–5
8	150	15
9	145	–5
10	160	15
11	155	–5
12	170	15

Now, the updated time series is nearly the stationary one. So now ARIMA components can be identified. The next step is to identify the appropriate ARIMA model for the given dataset. Suppose it is identified that ARIMA(1, 1, 1) best suited the given dataset, then the ARIMA equation for forecasting is represented as given below.

$$\Delta X_t = c + \varphi_1 \Delta X_{t-1} + \theta_1 \in_{t-1} + \in_t$$

Where ΔX_t is the differenced series at time t, c is the constant, φ_1 is the coefficient of autoregressive component, ΔX_{t-1} is the differenced series at time t–1, θ_1 is the coefficient of moving average component, $\in_{t-1}$, and $\in_t$ are the forecasting error terms at time t–1 and t respectively. In the next step, by training the model using the dataset, parameters c, φ_1, and θ_1 are estimated. After parameters estimation in the final step, the forecasting is performed by putting the historical values and error terms.

17.2.5 SARIMA

The SARIMA (Seasonal Autoregressive Integrated Moving Average) model is the combination of non-seasonal ARIMA model with the seasonal components.

$$\text{ARIMA}(p, d, q) \times (P, D, Q)_S$$

Where p, d, and q are the order of non-seasonal autoregressive, differencing, and moving average models. P, D, and Q are the order of seasonal autoregressive, differencing, and moving average models over a repeating seasonal period of S. The parameters P, D, and Q are estimated in the similar way by which the ARIMA parameters p, d, and q are estimated. The seasonal component requires the backshifts of the seasonal periods.

The general expression for the SARIMA $(p, d, q)(P, D, Q, s)$ model after removing the seasonality is given as below. The expression can be obtained by multiplying the ARIMA model with the differenced seasonal component of time series variable $\Delta_s^D X_t$.

$$\Theta(L)^p \theta(L^s)^P \Delta^d \Delta_s^D X_t = \Phi(L)^q \phi(L^s)^Q \Delta^d \Delta_s^D \epsilon_t$$

Because of the backshifts of seasonal periods, the SARIMA expression can be written in alternative formats also. For example, SARMIA (1, 1, 1) × (1, 1, 1)$_4$ with the repeating season of 4 can be written as:

$$(1-\varphi_1 B)(1-\Phi_1 B^4)(1-B)(1-B^4) = (1+\theta_1 B)(1+\Theta_1 B^4)\epsilon_t$$

Expressions for the special case: The Seasonal ARIMA (SARIMA) models for the special cases are explained in brief as an interesting fact.

Case 1: ARIMA(0, 0, 1) × (0, 0, 1)$_{12}$

This model has non-seasonal MA(1) and seasonal MA(1) components.

MA(1) non-seasonal component is $\theta(B) = 1 + \theta_1 B$.

MA(1) seasonal component is $\Theta(B^{12}) = 1 + \Theta B^{12}$.

The combined model is $(x_t - \mu) = \Theta(B^{12})\theta(B)w_t = (1+\Theta B^{12})(1+\theta_1 B)w_t$.

Case 2: ARIMA (1, 0, 0) × (1, 0, 0)$_{12}$

This model has non-seasonal AR(1) and AR(1) seasonal components.

AR(1) non-seasonal component expression is $\phi(B) = 1 - \phi_1 B$.

AR(1) seasonal component expression is $\Phi(B^{12}) = 1 - \Phi_1 B^{12}$.

The combined model is $(1-\phi_1 B)(1-\Phi_1 B^{12})(x_t - \mu) = w_t$.

The SARIMA time series forecasting model is explained using a simple conceptual working example. Suppose quarterly sales data for 4 years (total 16 quarters) is given for a shop, and sales forecast is required for the next 4 quarters. The given time series data have some seasonal components, i.e., the sales is higher during the winter quarters.

TABLE 17.13 Quarterly sales data for a shop

Quarter	Sales
1	100
2	115
3	130
4	140
5	125
6	110
7	105
8	120

(Contd.)

Quarter	Sales
9	145
10	160
11	135
12	120
13	110
14	130
15	150
16	145

The SARIMA model is applied in the following sequence of steps. In the first step, the time series checked for the stationarity. If the time series is non-stationary, then should be converted to stationary by differencing, etc. The present time series is showing upward and seasonal pattern, so it is not stationary. It should be converted to stationary first. The second step is to identify the seasonality in the time series. The quarterly time series is showing seasonality as during the winter seasons (e.g., quarter 9, 10) is showing seasonality. The next step is to identify and choose the suitable SARIMA model using ACF and PACF plots, etc. Let's assume that the SARIMA(1, 1, 1)(0, 1, 4) model is identified as the most appropriate one for this time series. The components of SARIMA(1, 1, 1)(0, 1, 4) model are tabulated in Table 17.14.

TABLE 17.14 Components of SARIMA(1, 1, 1)(0, 1, 4) model

Component	Description
AR(1)	Autoregressive model with order 1, i.e., the present quarter's sales depend on the previous quarter's sales value.
I(1)	The order of differencing is 1 to eliminate the trends in the time series.
MA(1)	Moving average model with the order 1, i.e., the present value depends on the forecasting error for the previous sales value.
(0, 1, 4)	Seasonality term, period of 4 and multiplicative term.

In the fourth step, the selected model is fitted by training with the time series values with the help of some statistical software. The fitting will provide the values of intercepts (constant terms) and coefficients for AR and MA models, and also for the seasonal terms. Finally, in the last step forecasting is carried out using the fitted SARIMA(1, 1, 1)(0, 1, 4) model.

ARIMAX

Autoregressive Integrated Moving Average with Exogenous Variables (ARIMAX) model is the extension of the ARIMA model, where exogeneous variables are additionally considered in the time series forecasting.

$$\text{ARIMAX}(p, d, q) = c + \sum_{i=1}^{p} \varphi_i X_{t-1} + \sum_{i=1}^{q} \theta_i \in_{t-i} + \sum_{i=1}^{m} \beta_m Z_{i,t} + \in_t .$$

Where c is the constant. β_i is the coefficient of the exogenous variable $Z_{i,t}$ at time t. Remaining variables and coefficients are similar to the ARIMA model (i.e., the AR and MA components of order p and q respectively. So ARIMAX model combines the autoregressive (AR), integrated (I), moving average (MA), and exogenous (X) components for forecasting in time series.

The exogenous parameters can affect the forecasting of time series values. For example, for profit and sales data predictions exogenous parameters such as labor cost, advertisement cost, seasonal factors can affect the sales and profit value for some organizations. So, such types of exogenous parameters should also be considered for improving the forecasting in a time series.

Example: Suppose monthly sales data for any organization along with the advertising expenses (exogenous variables) is given for two years (24 months) as shown in the Table 17.15.

TABLE 17.15 Monthly sales data along with the advertising expenses (exogenous variable)

Month	Sales	Advertising Expenses ($)
1	100	500
2	110	550
3	120	600
4	115	580
5	125	620
6	130	650
7	135	670
8	140	690
9	145	710
10	150	730
11	155	750
12	160	770
13	165	790
14	170	800
15	175	820
16	180	840
17	185	860
18	190	880
19	195	900
20	200	920
21	205	940
22	210	960
23	215	980
24	220	1000

Suppose the model **ARIMAX(1, 1, 1)** is best suited to the given time series with the exogenous variable. In this model the order for autoregressive, differencing, and moving average model is selected to be 1. The advertising expenses is used as an exogenous variable.

The **ARIMAX (1, 1, 1)** model can be represented as:

$$\text{ARIMAX}(p, d, q) = c + \sum_{i=1}^{p} \varphi_i X_{t-1} + \sum_{i=1}^{q} \theta_i \in_{t-i} + \sum_{i=1}^{m} \beta_m Z_{i,t} + \in_t$$

$$\Delta X_t = c + \varphi_1 \Delta X_{t-1} + \theta_1 \in_{t-1} + \beta_1 Z_{1,t} + \in_t$$

Where ΔX_t is the differenced series at time t, c is the constant term, φ_1 is the autoregressive coefficient, ΔX_{t-1} is the differenced series at time $t-1$, θ_1 is the coefficient of moving average component, $\in_{t-1}$ is the forecasting error term at time $t-1$, β_1 is the coefficient of exogenous variable, $Z_{1,t}$ is the exogenous variable at time t, and $\in_t$ is the forecasting error at time t.

The model is provided training with the time series values and coefficients and constant values are estimated. Let the parameters estimates are as follows, $c = 10$, $\varphi_1 = 0.5$, $\theta_1 = 0.3$, and $\beta_1 = 0.1$, then the equation will be rewritten as shown below.

$$\Delta X_t = 10 + 0.5 \times \Delta X_{t-1} + 0.3 \times \in_{t-1} + 0.1 \times Z_{1,t} + \in_t$$

The fitted model will then be utilized for forecasting of the monthly sales for the next upcoming months by putting the values of previous months and forecasting errors.

17.2.6 SARIMAX

The SARIMAX model (Seasonal Autoregressive Integrated Moving Average Model with Exogenous Variables) is the combination of SARIMA model (ARIMA with stationarity) and exogenous variables. SARIMAX model is represented by similar variables like SARIMA. Technically it is represented by $\text{SARIMAX}(p, q, d)(P, Q, D, s)$.

The $\text{ARIMAX}(p, d, q)$ with n exogenous variables can be expressed as given below.

$$\Theta(L)^p \Delta^d X_t = \Phi(L)^q \Delta^d \in_t + \sum_{i=1}^{n} \beta_i Z_t^i$$

Adding seasonality components in the $\text{ARIMAX}(p, d, q)$ will give us the expression for $\text{SARIMAX}(p, d, q)(P, D, Q, s)$ as shown below. The β_i is the coefficient of ith exogenous variable Z_t^i at time t.

$$\Theta(L)^p \theta(L^s)^P \Delta^d \Delta_s^D X_t = \Phi(L)^q \phi(L^s)^Q \Delta^d \Delta_s^D \in_t + \sum_{i=1}^{n} \beta_i Z_t^i$$

Example: A simple working example of the SARIMAX model is given for better understanding of the model. Suppose weekly customer visits for a supermarket are given over a period of one year (52 weeks) in the below tables with some exogenous variables such as weekend, holiday, and average temperature of the week. These exogenous variables can affect the number of visitors, for example, during weekends more visitors are expected to visit the supermarket with better weather conditions.

TABLE 17.16 Weekly customer counts for a supermarket over a year (52 weeks)

Week	Count	Weekend	Holiday	Temperature
1	100	FALSE	FALSE	20°C
2	120	FALSE	FALSE	18°C
3	115	FALSE	FALSE	15°C
4	130	TRUE	FALSE	22°C
5	145	FALSE	FALSE	25°C
6	125	FALSE	FALSE	23°C
7	105	TRUE	FALSE	18°C
8	120	FALSE	FALSE	15°C
9	145	FALSE	FALSE	20°C
10	160	TRUE	FALSE	25°C
...	...	...	...	...

The forecasting using SARIMAX model requires some steps to be followed just like the previous models. The first step is the common steps for all the models of time series forecasting. In this step, the given series is checked for stationarity. If the time series is non-stationary, then it should be converted to stationarity before applying the ARIMAX model. The second step in this model is identify the seasonality for the model. The time series data is weekly so a simple choice of seasonality could be 7, but it could be some higher value also depending on the nature of the data. For simplicity in this example let's assume that the seasonality is 7 days. In the third step, SARIMAX model is selected. Let's assume that the selected model is SARIMAX(1, 1, 1)(0, 1, 7) s(1,0,1,7). The actual value of order for SARIMAX depends on the ACF and PACF plots for the different lags. In the selected model, the components are consisting of AR model with order 1, I (differencing) with order 1, MA model with order 1, seasonality of the order (0, 1, 7). The model has two exogenous variables, first for the weekends (it's a binary variable 0 for weekdays and 1 for weekends) and temperature a linear exogenous variable. Once the model along with the exogenous variables are selected, then in the nest step, the model is fitted with the time series data using some statistical software and all the coefficients and intercepts (constant values) are estimated. Finally, in the last step, forecasting is carried out using the fitted SARIMAX model for future weeks.

17.3 MODEL SELECTION CRITERIA

There are various choices of selection of appropriate and best suited time series forecasting models. Selecting the best model is a complicated task and generally with the help of statistical software the best model is selected for forecasting in time series. The best model is selected using the two popular criteria in the time series forecasting. These criteria are Akaike Information Criterion (AIC), and Bayesian Information Criterion (BIC). Both of these criteria are explained in brief in this section.

17.3.1 Akaike Information Criterion (AIC)

The Akaike Information Criterion (AIC) indicates the goodness of fit for a time series model.

$$AIC = 2k - 2l$$

Where l is log-likelihood and k are the number of parameters in the time series model. A model which minimizes the AIC value is considered to be the best model in time series analysis. The log likelihood measures the variation in the data.

17.3.2 Bayesian Information Criterion (BIC)

$$BIC = -2l + k \times \log(N)$$

Where l is the log-likelihood and k are the number of parameters in the time series model. N is the number of samples selected in time series. BIC is also known as Schwarz Information Criterion (SIC) or Schwarz-Bayesian Criterion (SBC). The selection of best time series analysis model criteria is to minimize the BIC value. BIC criteria are similar to the AIC criteria but the primary difference between AIC and BIC is, the BIC model penalizes the model complexity higher than the AIC as it works on a sample size of N in a time series.

17.4 VOLATILITY IN TIME SERIES

Volatility is the measure of uncertainty in the time series. Volatility indicates the degree of variation of data values in a time series over a time period. A sudden and drastic change in data values causes volatility in a time series. The volatility evolves continuously and does not persist permanently (or not persist infinitely) For example, a sudden rise or decrease in the stock price due to some news about the company indicates volatility in the stock price time series. Handling volatility in a time series is a challenging issue, however there are certain techniques in the time series analysis which deal with handling of volatility in a time series. In this section, two popular techniques ARCH and GARCH are discussed in brief for handling of volatility in the time series.

17.4.1 ARCH and GARCH

ARCH (Autoregressive Conditionally Heteroscedastic) and GARCH (Generalized Autoregressive Conditionally Heteroscedastic) are two popular models for handling volatility in the time series. Volatile time series refers to a time series where variance of the time series is not stable (fluctuates over the period of time). The stock market data is said to be the highest volatile data as the data fluctuates very rapidly in any direction and thus prediction of stock prices is a complicated task. The ARCH and GARCH techniques help in understanding the volatility of the time series data. Both ARCH and GARCH models are developed on the basis of Heteroscedastic assumptions. The Heteroscedastic assumption states that the expected value of sum of squared error in the regression techniques is always the same. The first version of ARCH model was proposed by Eagle in 1981, is used to estimate the best suited weights for forecasting of the variance. The generalized version of ARCH was proposed in the year 1986 by Bollerslev in which the primary assumptions was in long run the variance may be best predicted using the average variance of the past long run values.

The ARCH(1) is given by the following expression:

$$Var(X_t|X_{t-1}) = \sigma_t^2 = \alpha_0 + \alpha_1 \epsilon_{t-1}^2$$

Higher order ARCH model with the order q, ARCH(q) is given by the following equation:

$$\sigma_t^2 = \alpha_0 + \alpha_1 \epsilon_{t-1}^2 + \alpha_2 \epsilon_{t-2}^2 + \ldots + \alpha_q \epsilon_{t-q}^2$$

The GARCH(1, 1) is given by the equation below:

$$\text{GARCH}(1,\ 1) = \sigma_t^2 = \alpha_0 + \alpha_1 y_{t-1}^2 + \beta_1 \sigma_{t-1}^2$$

Where y_{t-1} refers the previous value at time t–1, and σ_{t-1} is the variance at time t–1. α_0, α_1, and β_1 are the constants.

The higher order GARCH model is described as follows:

$$\text{GARCH}(p,q) = \sigma_t^2 = \alpha_0 + \alpha_1 \epsilon_{t-1}^2 + \alpha_2 \epsilon_{t-2}^2 + \ldots + \alpha_p \epsilon_{t-p}^2 + \beta_1 \sigma_{t-1}^2 + \beta_2 \sigma_{t-2}^2 + \ldots + \beta_q \sigma_{t-q}^2$$

The GARCH model works on the principle of volatility clustering. The high volatility is generally followed by high volatility and low volatility is generally followed by low volatility; this concept is known as volatility clustering. So, to capture the concept of volatility clustering, GARCH model includes the term for previous variation (or volatility) for a given time series.

17.4.2 ARCH Example

The ARCH model is explained using a simple working example for a given time series. Let's assume that a time series for the daily stock price (closing price) is given in the Table 17.17.

TABLE 17.17 Daily closing stock price for a company

Day	Price	Return
1	$100	0%
2	$102	2%
3	$98	–4%
4	$104	6.12%
5	$101	–2.88%
6	$106	4.95%
7	$103	–2.83%
8	$99	–4.02%
9	$105	6.06%
10	$102	–2.88%

The ARCH model is applied in the following steps. In the first step, the return square is calculated. The return square indicates the volatility of daily price change. In the second step, a suitable ARCH model is selected. For simplicity, let's assume that ARCH(1) is selected (the volatility depends on the precious day's squared volatility). Then using the training of the dataset, coefficient and constant variables are estimated. In the last step, the model is fitted with the estimated variables. Let's assume that coefficient is 0.5 and squared volatility is 0.0833%. The volatility is estimated using the below equation.

$$0.5 \times 0.0833\% + \text{constant}(\text{estimated})$$

TABLE 17.18 Calculation of returned squared for ARCH model

Day	Return Squared
1	0.00%
2	0.04%
3	0.16%
4	0.37%
5	0.08%
6	0.25%
7	0.08%
8	0.16%
9	0.37%
10	0.08%

The GARCH method is applied in a similar way to the ARCH model but in case of GARCH, previous terms volatility is also considered.

EXERCISES

1. Consider the following time series:

Time	1	2	3	4	5	6	7	8	9	10
Value	11	13	11	14	12	11	14	14	13	15

Calculate:
(a) Simple Moving Average SMA(4)
(b) Exponential Moving Average WMA(4) with $\alpha = 0.3$
(c) Weighted Moving Average WMA(4) with the weights associated with the recent values are 0.4, 0.3, 0.2 and 0.1

2. Consider the following second order moving average model MA(2), then calculate the ACF functions for first and second legs.

$$X_t = 12 + \epsilon_t + 0.3 \times \epsilon_{t-1} + 0.4 \times \epsilon_{t-2}$$

3. Transform the given time series using (a) differencing, and (b) log transformation,

Time	1	2	3	4	5	6	7	8	9	10
Value	101	112	104	108	105	111	106	112	107	115

MULTIPLE CHOICE QUESTIONS

1. A stationary time series indicate which of the following information?
(a) Constant Mean & Variance (b) Skewness
(c) Kurtosis (d) All of these

2. A non-stationary time series indicates which of the following information?
(a) Trend (b) Seasonality
(c) Irregularities (d) All of these

3. Which sentence is TRUE about the Dickey-Fuller (DF) Test?
   (a) It is statistical tests for checking whether the given time series is stationary.
   (b) In this test, the null hypothesis and alternate hypothesis are framed with the null hypothesis is that the given time series has a unit root.
   (c) The statistical values from the DF test are calculated and compared against the critical values.
   (d) All of these.

For question no. 4 to 6, the following time series is given:

Time period	Value
1	21
2	24
3	29
4	40

4. The calculate value of SMA (4) for the given time series:
   (a) 25 (b) 28.5
   (c) 29.0 (d) 32
5. The calculate value of WMA (4) for the given time series, if the weights to the recent elements of the time series are 0.5, 0.3, 0.1, and 0.1 respectively:
   (a) 23.5 (b) 24.1
   (c) 24.6 (d) 25.2
6. The calculate value of EMA (2) for the given time series with $\alpha = 0.7$:
   (a) 36.7 (b) 35.0
   (c) 34.2 (d) 33.0
7. The order of AR model is determined using the ACF and PACF plots by observing the which of the following?
   (a) The order of AR model is p, if the ACF plots dies down after p lags, and PACF cuts off after p lags.
   (b) The order of AR model is p, if the ACF cuts off after p lags, and PACF dies down after p lags.
   (c) The order of AR model is p, if both the ACF, and PACF dies down after p lags.
   (d) None of these.
8. The order of MA model is determined using the ACF and PACF plots by observing the which of the following?
   (a) The order of MA model is q, if both ACF, and PACF plots dies down after lag q.
   (b) The order of MA model is q, if the ACF plot dies down after lag q, and PACF cuts off after lag q.
   (c) The order of MA model is q, if the ACF plot cuts off after lag q, and PACF dies down after lag q.
   (d) The order of MA model is q, if both ACF, and PACF plots cuts off after lag q.
9. The value of ACF function for first leg for the given MA (1) series

$$X_t = 5 + \epsilon_t + 0.2 \times \epsilon_{t-1}$$

   is calculated as:
   (a) 0.06 (b) 0.11
   (c) 0.16 (d) 0.19
10. The value of ACF function for first and second leg for the given MA (2) series

$$X_t = 5 + \epsilon_t + 0.7 \times \epsilon_{t-1} + 0.1 \times \epsilon_{t-2}$$

   are calculated as:
   (a) 0.71, and 0.11 (b) 0.51, and 0.07
   (c) 0.71, and 0.07 (d) 0.51, and 0.17

11. Which statements about the SARIMA time series model is TRUE?

(a) Sarima model can handle seasonality
(b) It has 6 parameters
(c) It can detect complex recurring patterns
(d) All of these

12. Which statement is TRUE about the ARIMAX time series model?

(a) The ARIMAX model is designed particularly for the univariate time series analysis.
(b) The ARIMAX model degrades the accuracy of predictions in time series prediction as compared to ARIMA model.
(c) The ARIMAX model uses additional external variables for multivariate time series analysis
(d) The ARIMAX model can handle the missing values for the external variables utilized for time series analysis.

13. What is the primary difference between the Akaike Information Criterion (AIC), and Bayesian Information Criterion (BIC) models in time series analysis?

(a) The AIC is the probability-based model whereas BIC is not.
(b) The BIC model penalizes the model complexity higher than the AIC as it works on a sample size in a time series.
(c) The AIC model is used for assessment of performance whereas the BIC model is used for assessment of complexity of time series model.
(d) None of these.

14. What is the primary difference between the ARCH (Autoregressive Conditionally Heteroscedastic) and GARCH (Generalized Autoregressive Conditionally Heteroscedastic) models?

(a) The GARCH model works on the principle of volatility clustering.
(b) The GARCH model includes the term for previous variation (or volatility) for a given time series.
(c) Both a and b.
(d) None of these.

15. What is the first step in converting a non-stationary time series to a stationary one?

(a) Apply transformation techniques
(b) Check for stationarity using statistical tests
(c) Calculate the mean and variance
(d) Apply the Dickey-Fuller test.

16. Consider the following PACF values:

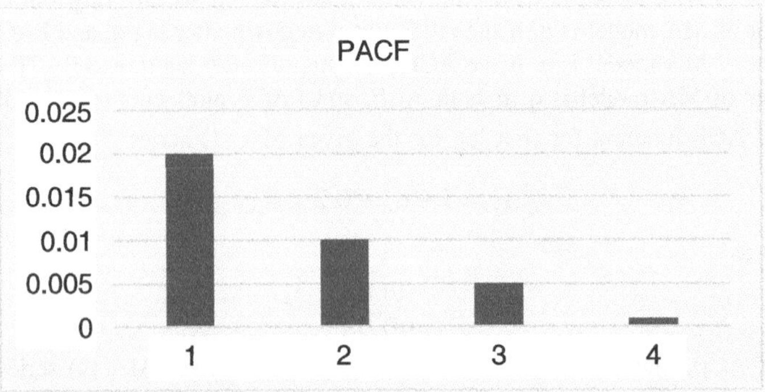

Determine the order of the autoregressive (AR) term.

(a) AR(1)
(b) AR(2)
(c) AR(3)
(d) AR(4)

17. What is the primary purpose of differencing in time series analysis?
(a) To remove seasonality
(b) To stabilize variance
(c) To make the series stationary
(d) To identify trends

18. Consider the following ACF plot:

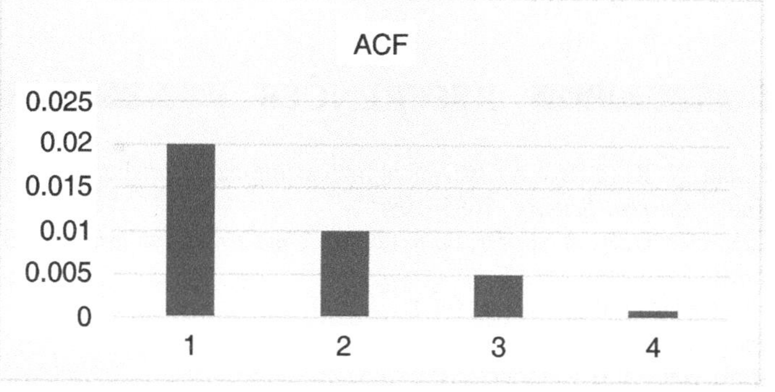

What can be inferred from this ACF plot?
(a) The series is non-stationary with a trend.
(b) The series has significant autocorrelation up to lag 2.
(c) The series has no significant autocorrelation.
(d) The series is seasonal with period 4.

19. Given the following ACF values:

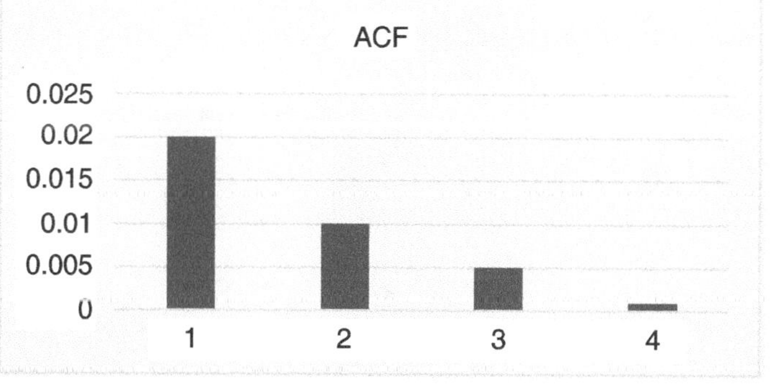

Determine the order of the autoregressive (AR) term.
(a) AR(1)
(b) AR(2)
(c) AR(3)
(d) AR(4)

20. Consider the following ACF plot for residuals:

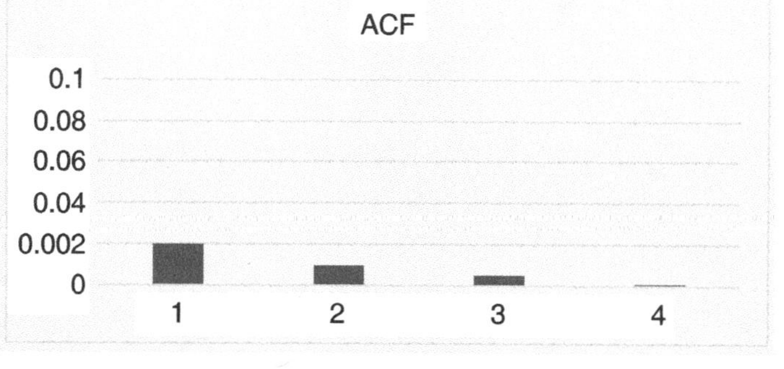

What does this ACF plot indicate?

(a) The residuals have significant autocorrelation.
(b) The residuals are non-random.
(c) The residuals are random and uncorrelated.
(d) The model is under-specified.

REFERENCES

[1] Sena, D., & Nagwani, N. K. (2016), A time-series forecasting-based prediction model to estimate groundwater levels in India, *Current Science*, 1083–1090.

[2] Shumway, R. H., Stoffer, D. S., & Stoffer, D. S. (2000), *Time series analysis and its applications* (Vol. 3), New York: Springer.

[3] https://online.stat.psu.edu/stat510/lesson/11/11.1

[4] https://otexts.com/fpp2/seasonal-arima.html

[5] https://online.stat.psu.edu/stat510/lesson/2/2.1

ANSWER KEY

1. (d)	**2.** (d)	**3.** (d)	**4.** (b)	**5.** (c)	**6.** (a)	**7.** (a)	**8.** (c)	**9.** (d)	**10.** (b)
11. (d)	**12.** (b)	**13.** (b)	**14.** (c)	**15.** (b)	**16.** (b)	**17.** (c)	**18.** (b)	**19.** (a)	**20.** (c)

18 Graph Data

Introduction

Graph data structure is an important technique for organizing the related data. It is one of the very efficient and powerful tools for representing the related data. In the recent times, there are a plenty of modern applications where related data is stored. For analysing such related data, graph representation is the most powerful tools used widely in most of the data analysis tasks. For example, the social network data, where one person is connected (or related) to other persons can be represented in an effective way using the graphs. Two basic entities of the graphs are vertices (or nodes), and edges (connectivity). There are a number of data analysis tasks which can be performed over the graph data. Analysing the graph data using data science techniques is called as graph mining. It is the knowledge discovery process from the data represented as graphs. This chapter provides an overview of major technologies related to the graph mining.

The graph mining technology have several important techniques which can be applied to numerous data analysis tasks, where data is collected and can be represented as a graph. The important graph mining tasks include link prediction, community detection, graph classification, graph clustering, and subgraph mining, etc. This chapter provides an overview of most of the important techniques of graph mining. A brief description of basic graph theory and graph terminology is also covered.

18.1 BASICS OF GRAPH THEORY

Some of the basic concepts and terminologies related to the graph data mining is presented in this section.

18.1.1 Nodes and Edges

A graph is mathematically defined as $\langle V, E\rangle$, where V is the set of vertices or nodes and E is the set of edges (or connections) between the vertices. A sample graph is presented in Figure 18.1.

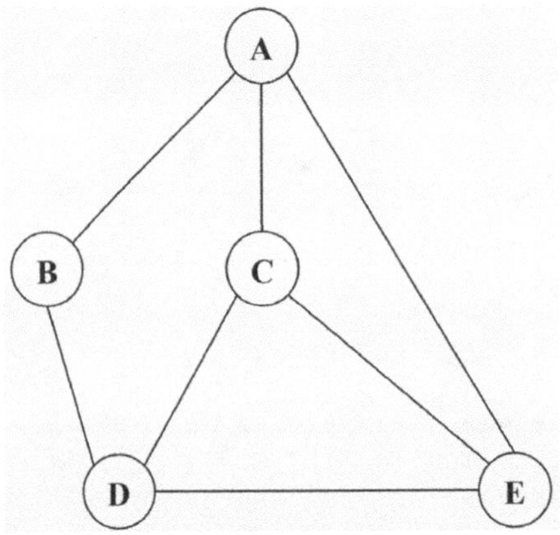

FIGURE 18.1 A Sample Graph.

In the example graph, the set of vertices $V = \{A, B, C, D, E\}$ and the set of edges E is the connection between $\{AB, AC, AE, BD, CD, CE, DE\}$.

18.1.2 Directed vs. Undirected Graphs

Graphs are broadly categorized into two types. The first category is directed graph, and the second category is undirected graph. In directed graphs the direction of connectivity is specified, whereas in the undirected graphs the direction of connection is not specified (hence the connection is equally important from both side).

***Undirected Graph Example*:** In a social media platform both A and B are friends of each other.

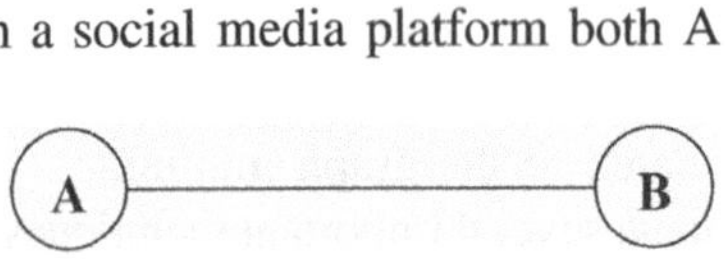

FIGURE 18.2 A Sample Graph.

***Directed Graph Example*:** A follows B in a social platform, but B does not follow A on the same platform.

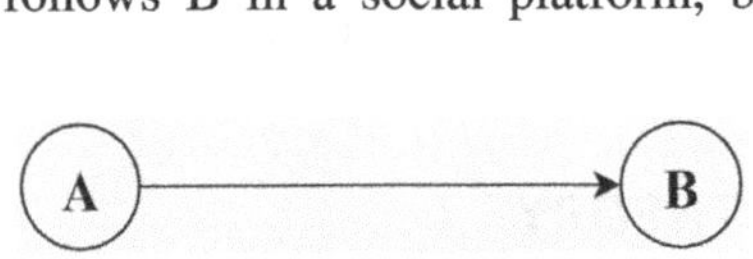

FIGURE 18.3 A Sample Graph.

18.1.3 Weighted Graphs

A weighted graph is a graph in which the weights are assigned to the edges. The weight may represent the importance of connection or some important information that how one node is connected with the others. In the following example weights are assigned to the edges of the graph, is an example of weighted graph. A weighted graph may be directed or undirected graph.

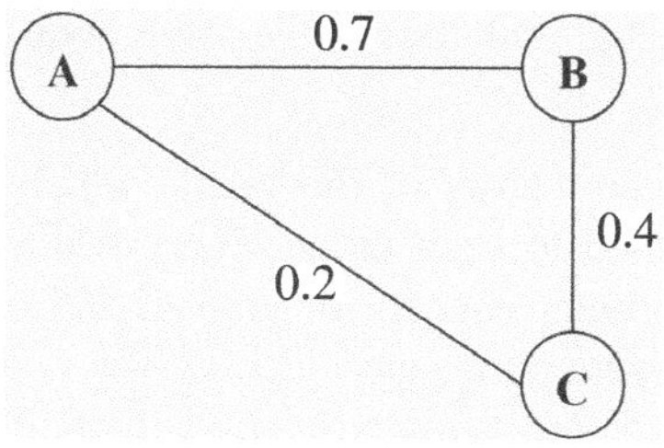

FIGURE 18.4 A Sample Graph.

18.1.4 Degree of a Node

The degree of a node in the undirected node is defined as the number of edges associated with that particular node. In the example graph of Figure 18.1, the degree of the nodes is given as follows: $D(A)=3, D(B)=2, D(C)=3, D(D)=3$, and $D(E)=3$. Where $D(N)$ refers to the degree of a node N.

The degree of the node for the directed graph is categorized into two major categories namely, in-degree, and out-degree. The in-degree of a node is defined as the edges reaching to a particular node, whereas the out-degree refers to the number of edges going out from a node. The in-degree and out-degree for the following graph is given as follows: $IN(A) = 0$, $OUT(A) = 3$, $IN(B) = 1$, $OUT(B) = 1$, $IN(C) = 1$, $OUT(C) = 2$, $IN(D) = 2$, $OUT(D) = 1$, $IN(E) = 3$ and $OUT(E) = 0$.

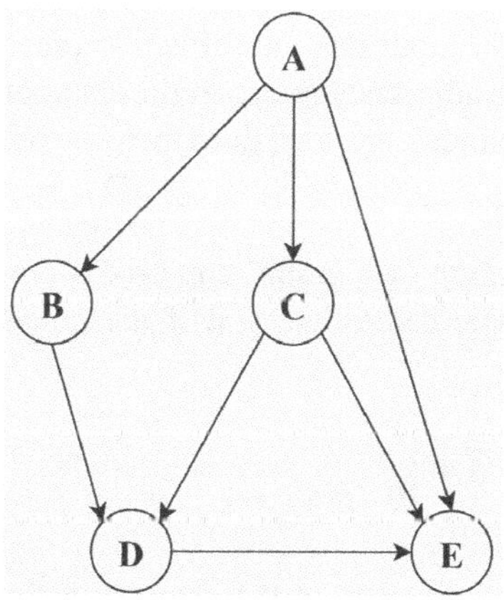

FIGURE 18.5 A Sample Weighted Graph.

18.1.5 Some Useful Graph Terminologies

Adjacent Node: A node B is called as adjacent node of node A, if B is connected with A (in other words, there is an edge between B and A).

Complete Graph: A graph is said to be complete, if all the nodes of the graph are connected with each other.

Path: A path in a graph is sequence of connected nodes. It is a sequence of nodes connected with each other. Mathematically the path is presented as $v_1, v_2, v_3, \ldots, v_K$, where v_i is the ith vertex.

Cycle: A cycle is a path which start and ends at the same node in the graph. If a graph has cycle, then it is called as cyclic graph.

Clique: A clique of a graph is the subset of the graph, which is complete, i.e., every vertex of the subset of the graph is connected to each other. Every two vertex of the subset is adjacent to each other. A clique is very important concept in graphs, and has plenty of applications such as finding communities is a social networking, etc.

Diameter of Graph: The number of nodes in a longest shortest path in a graph is called as diameter of a graph.

Subgraph: *A* graph *S* is called as the subset of a graph $G(S \subseteq G)$, if $V_S \subseteq V_G$, and $E_S \subseteq E_G$. Where V_S, and V_G are the set of vertices for the graphs *S* and *G*, and E_S, and E_G are the set of edges for the graphs *S* and *G* respectively.

Graph Isomorphism: Two graphs *G*, and *G′* are said to be isomorphic to each other, if the two pair of vertices v_i, and v_j are connected with each other in the graph *G*[i.e., $(v_i \to v_j) \in G$], then the equivalent of the pair of vertices v_i', v_j' are also connected in the graph *G′*[i.e., $(v_i' \to v_j') \in G'$]. The graph isomorphism is used to discover the identical graphs (similar graphs) and is used for many analytical works in graph mining such as graph clustering, and graph pattern mining.

18.1.6 Graph Representations

In order to process the graph as an input data, an effective presentation of graph is required. Two popular presentations of graphs are adjacency matrix representation and adjacency list representation. Both of these representation techniques are explained here in brief.

Adjacency Matrix Representation

In the adjacency matrix representation of a graph, a matrix is created with the following conditions for the cell entry in the matrix. The cell value is 1, if the nodes are connected otherwise the cell value is 0.

$$A = \begin{cases} 1 & \text{if } v_i \to v_j \\ 0 \ \text{ if } v_i \nrightarrow v_j & \text{or } i = j \end{cases}$$

If the graph is weighted graph, i.e., weights of the edges is defined then instead of 1 and 0, actual weight value of the edge is mentioned in the adjacency matrix. This is sometimes also called as weighted adjacency matrix.

The adjacency matrix for the sample graph presented in Figure 18.1 is given as follows:

$$\begin{array}{c} \\ \\ \\ A = \end{array} \begin{array}{c} \\ A \\ B \\ C \\ D \\ E \end{array} \begin{array}{c} \begin{matrix} A & B & C & D & E \end{matrix} \\ \begin{bmatrix} 0 & 1 & 1 & 0 & 1 \\ 1 & 0 & 0 & 1 & 0 \\ 1 & 0 & 0 & 1 & 1 \\ 0 & 1 & 1 & 0 & 1 \\ 1 & 0 & 1 & 1 & 0 \end{bmatrix} \end{array}$$

Incidence Matrix: In case of directed graph, the adjacency matrix is termed as incidence matrix and if vertex i connects to vertex j (i.e., $i \rightarrow j$) then the cell value of the matrix (i, j) is set to 1, otherwise the cell value is set to 0.

Adjacency List Representation

Another useful representation of the graph is called as adjacency list representation in which, the list of connected nodes to a node is maintained separately. An example of adjacency list representation for undirected and directed graph is presented in Figure 18.6, and Figure 18.7.

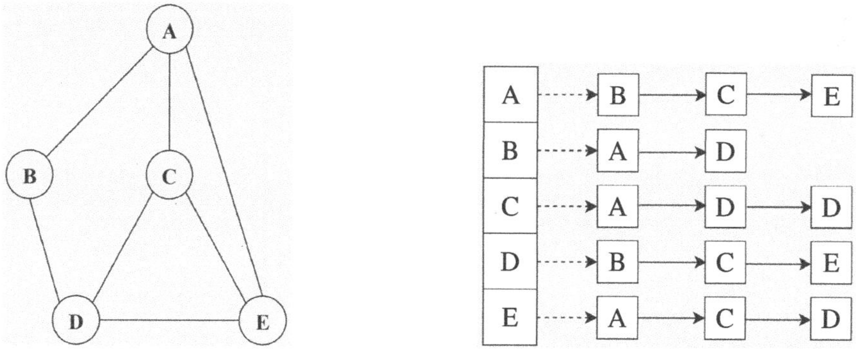

FIGURE 18.6 Example of Adjacency List Presentation of Undirected Graph.

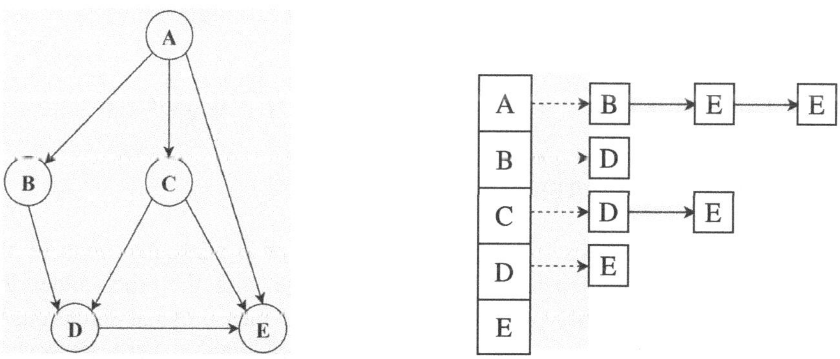

FIGURE 18.7 Example of Adjacency List Presentation of Directed Graph.

The choice of selecting adjacency matrix, or adjacency list representation is a subjective matter and depends on the type of algorithms, which takes matrix or list representation as an input. In general, both of these techniques are very popularly and widely used in most of the applications.

Graph Laplacian

Graph Laplacian is an important graph representation technique. The Laplacian of the graph is defined as follows:

$$\mathcal{L} = D - A$$

Where $\mathcal{L}$ is the graph Laplacian, D is the degree matrix, and A is the adjacency matrix.

The degree matrix for the sample graph shown in the Figure 18.1 is calculated as follows.

$$D = \begin{matrix} & A & B & C & D & E \\ A & 3 & 0 & 0 & 0 & 0 \\ B & 0 & 2 & 0 & 0 & 0 \\ C & 0 & 0 & 3 & 0 & 0 \\ D & 0 & 0 & 0 & 3 & 0 \\ E & 0 & 0 & 0 & 0 & 3 \end{matrix}$$

Then the Laplacian matrix is calculated as follows:

$$\mathcal{L} = \begin{matrix} & A & B & C & D & E \\ A & 3 & -1 & -1 & 0 & -1 \\ B & -1 & 2 & 0 & -1 & 0 \\ C & -1 & 0 & 3 & -1 & -1 \\ D & 0 & -1 & -1 & 3 & -1 \\ E & -1 & 0 & -1 & -1 & 3 \end{matrix}$$

The row sum of Laplacian matrix is always zero. A graph with K connected components can be expressed as a Laplacian matrix with K diagonal values represents the K Laplacian matrices. Laplacian provides a better way of one or higher dimensional embedding with the help of eigenvalues of the Laplacian matrix. The relation of embeddings is mathematically expressed as:

$$\mathcal{L}f = \lambda f$$

Where $\mathcal{L}$ is the Laplacian matrix, f is any given function, and λ is the eigenvalues.

18.2 CENTRALITY MEASURES

Graph centrality measures indicates importance or ranking of a particular node in the graph. It represents the weight of the relationship of a particular node with the other nodes in the graph. The most important nodes are highly ranked. Graph centrality measures has numerous applications particularly in finding the influential node in a social network graph. There are several measures for the graph centrality. Some of the popular and important centrality measures are discussed here in brief. Some of the commonly used centrality measures are discussed in this section with the help of numerical examples.

18.2.1 Degree Centrality

Degree Centrality is calculated based on degrees of nodes. The highest degree indicates the higher centrality. For directed graph, the degree centrality is calculated using the number of connected nodes, and for the unidirectional graph it is calculated using the number of in and out degrees. The equation for calculating degree centrality is shown below.

$$C_D = \frac{d(i)}{n-1}$$

Where C_D is the degree centrality, $d(i)$ is the degree of the ith node, and n is the number of nodes in the given graph G.

Example: The calculation of the degree centrality for the graph given in Figure 18.1, is shown in this example.

Degree of node A, B, C, D, and E are 3, 2, 3, 3, 3 respectively. The degree of all the nodes is highest except the node B, which indicates that all the nodes are more important than the node B. The degree centrality simply measures the degree of the node with higher degree indicates the importance of the node.

18.2.2 Centroid Centrality

In centroid centrality the sum of distances of a node from all the other nodes is calculated. The minimum distance value indicates that the node is the central node or important node in the graph. The minimum distance indicates the maximum centrality of a node.

18.2.3 Betweenness Centrality

Betweenness centrality is calculated based on how many times appears in the shortest paths between the nodes. Betweenness centrality is used in many applications particularly in telecommunication, e-commerce, and in recommender systems. The mathematical expression for calculating betweenness centrality is shown below.

$$C_B(i) = \sum_{j<k} \frac{sp_{jk}(i)}{sp_{jk}}$$

Where $C_B(i)$ is the betweenness centrality for the ith node, $sp_{jk}(i)$ is the shortest paths between j and k via node i, and sp_{jk} are all the shortest paths between nodes j and k.

Example: The betweenness centrality for the graph given in Figure 18.1, is calculated as shown below.

B(A) = 0
B(B) – 1 (AD via B)
B(C) = 1 (AD via C)
B(D) = 2 (BC via D, BE via D)
B(E) = 1 (AD via E)

The maximum betweenness centrality is for the node D.

18.2.4 Eigenvector Centrality

The eigenvector centrality is calculated as a function of neighbouring nodes. The basic concept behind the eigenvector centrality is a node linked surrounded by highly important node has a high eigenvector. The number of connected nodes and importance of connected nodes defines the centrality. Higher centrality value is assigned to higher central node connectivity.

Example: The eigenvector centrality for the graph given in Figure 18.1, is calculated as shown below.

The adjacency matrix for the above graph is:

$$A = \begin{bmatrix} 0 & 1 & 1 & 0 & 1 \\ 1 & 0 & 0 & 1 & 0 \\ 1 & 0 & 0 & 1 & 1 \\ 0 & 1 & 1 & 0 & 1 \\ 1 & 0 & 1 & 1 & 0 \end{bmatrix}$$

The eigenvalues of the adjacency matrix are calculated and then eigenvectors are calculated. Let's assume that the principal eigenvector is [0.93, 0.65, 1, 0.93, 1]

EV(A) = 0.93/(0.93 + 0.65 + 1 + 0.93 + 1) = 0.93/4.51 = 0.21
EV(B) = 0.65/(0.93 + 0.65 + 1 + 0.93 + 1) = 0.65/4.51 = 0.14
EV(C) = 1/(0.93 + 0.65 + 1 + 0.93 + 1) = 1/4.51 = 0.22
EV(D) = 0.93/(0.93 + 0.65 + 1 + 0.93 + 1) = 0.93/4.51 = 0.21
EV(E) = 1/(0.93 + 0.65 + 1 + 0.93 + 1) = 1/4.51 = 0.22

Nodes C and D have highest eigenvectors centrality in the given graph.

The eigenvector centrality gives priority to the connectivity to the highest influential nodes. More connectivity to the influential nodes will give more eigenvectors centrality score.

18.2.5 PageRank Centrality

The PageRank centrality is a types of eigenvectors centrality technique and is calculated based on Google's famous PageRank algorithm. It is typically applicable for unidirected (one-directional connected) graph. The mathematical expression for calculating PageRank centrality is shown below.

$$PR(i) = \sum_{(j,i)\in E} \frac{PR(j)}{O_j}$$

Where *PR*(*i*) is the page rank of ith node, *PR*(*j*) is the page rank of node *j* such that *i* is the landing node from node *j*, i.e., $j \rightarrow i$, and O_j is the number of out links from the node *j*.

Example: The PageRank centrality for the graph given in Figure 18.1, is calculated as shown below. PageRank centrality is suitable for the directed graphs and works on the basis of PageRank algorithm.

PR(A) = 1/5 = 0.2
PR(B) = 1/5 = 0.2
PR(C) = 1/5 = 0.2
PR(D) = 1/5 = 0.2
PR(E) = 1/5 = 0.2

Update the PageRank score based on the outgoing edges for each node.

$$PR(A) = 0.2 + \frac{PR(B)}{1} + \frac{PR(C)}{2} + \frac{PR(E)}{1} \cong 0.2 + 0.1 + 0.07 + 0.2 = 0.57$$

Similarly, update the PageRank for all the nodes and repeat these steps till the PageRank of the nodes converges. The highest value indicates the maximum value of PageRank centrality.

18.2.6 Closeness Centrality

The closeness centrality is calculated based on how node is close to other nodes. The closeness is measured using suitable geodesic distance (GD). The geodesic distance is the geometry-based distance function. The centrality is calculated using the sum of geodesic distances of all the other nodes. The closeness centrality is applied for various applications such as identifying the importance of words in given document.

$$C_C(i) = \frac{n-1}{\sum_{j=1}^{n} sp(i,j)}$$

Where $C_C(i)$ is the closeness centrality of the ith node, n is the total number of nodes in the graph, $sp(i, j)$ is the shortest path between node i and node j, the shortest path between the nodes is a type of geodesic distance between the nodes.

Example: The closeness centrality for the graph given in Figure 18.1, is calculated as shown below. The closeness centrality is measured as the inverse of sum of shortest paths from a node to the other nodes.

$$Closeness(A) = \frac{1}{sp(A,B)+sp(A,C)+sp(A,D)+sp(A,E)} = \frac{1}{1+1+2+1} = 0.2$$

$$Closeness(B) = \frac{1}{sp(B,A)+sp(B,C)+sp(B,D)+sp(B,E)} = \frac{1}{1+2+1+2} = 0.17$$

$$Closeness(C) = \frac{1}{sp(C,A)+sp(C,B)+sp(C,D)+sp(C,E)} = \frac{1}{1+2+1+1} = 0.2$$

$$Closeness(D) = \frac{1}{sp(D,A)+sp(D,B)+sp(D,C)+sp(D,E)} = \frac{1}{2+1+1+1} = 0.2$$

$$Closeness(E) = \frac{1}{sp(E,A)+sp(E,B)+sp(E,C)+sp(E,D)} = \frac{1}{1+2+1+1} = 0.2$$

All the nodes have highest closeness similarity except the node B.

The closeness centrality may be calculated by considering the weights between the pair of nodes if the graph is weighted graph.

18.2.7 Katz Centrality

The Katz centrality is like eigenvector centrality. The centrality using Katz centrality is decided by directions with neighbours, and number of direct connections. This is a weighted centrality measure in which the weights are exponentially decreased for the away located nodes.

Example: An illustrative example of calculating Katz centrality for the sample graph presented in Figure 18.1 is shown below. The Katz centrality is measured by sum of weighted paths from a node to the other nodes, the weights controlled by a factor α. The typical values for α is between 0.1 and 0.01.

$$Katz(A) = \alpha \times [sp(A,B) + sp(A,C) + sp(A,D) + sp(A,E)] + \alpha^2 \times [sp(A,B) + sp(A,C) + sp(A,D) + sp(A,E)] + \ldots$$

$$Katz(A) = 0.1 \times [1+1+2+1] + 0.1^2 \times [1+1+2+1] = 0.1 \times 5 + 0.01 \times 5 = 0.55$$

Similarly, the Katz is calculated for all the nodes. The value of the Katz centrality depends on the weight factor α. The highest value indicates the most influential node in the graph.

18.2.8 HITS Centrality

The HITS (Hyperlink-Induced Topic Selection) centrality is computed based on the HITS technique. The HITS algorithm is a popular algorithm in the web mining used to compute the Authority and Hub pages. The HITS centrality is computed based on authority and hub scores. In World Wide Web domain the authority pages are the primary source of information and considered to be most trustworthy pages for proving the information, whereas the hub pages are the pages which links to the authority pages. Similar concept is applied to the graphs. The HITS centrality is measured as a function of authority and hub nodes, where more weightage is given to the authority nodes and more centrality score is calculated for the more hub nodes connectivity.

18.2.9 Motifs Centrality

A motif is the small frequent patterns in graph. The motifs centrality is calculated using the feedforward loops in a graph to determine the most important and influential node in a graph. The motifs centrality is calculated based on the occurrence of a particular node in the feedforward path (motif). In motifs centrality, higher weightage is assigned to the subgraphs which are most frequent in the given graph G.

18.2.10 Harmonic Centrality

Harmonic centrality is a special type of closeness centrality. The centrality of a particular node is calculated by taking the harmonic mean of the distances of other nodes from a node.

Example: An illustrative example of harmonic centrality is shown below for the sample graph shown in Figure 18.1. The distance matrix between all pairs of nodes is calculated first for measuring harmonic centrality..

$$D = \begin{bmatrix} 0 & 1 & 1 & 2 & 1 \\ 1 & 0 & 2 & 1 & 2 \\ 1 & 2 & 0 & 1 & 1 \\ 2 & 1 & 1 & 0 & 1 \\ 1 & 2 & 1 & 1 & 0 \end{bmatrix}$$

$$H_{Mean}(A) = H_{Mean}(1,1,2,1) = \frac{4}{\frac{1}{1}+\frac{1}{1}+\frac{1}{2}+\frac{1}{1}} = \frac{4}{3.5} = 1.14$$

Similarly, harmonic means for all the nodes is calculated and highest value indicates the most influential node using harmonic centrality.

18.3 GRAPH KERNELS

The graph kernels techniques are used for finding similarities between the graphs. The commonly used kernels are discussed in this section. The kernels functions are used in various graph mining tasks but most widely used in graph clustering techniques. The other applications of graph kernels are in the area of graph classification, anomaly detection, link prediction, and searching subgraphs.

18.3.1 Vertex Histogram Kernel

In vertex histogram kernel the graph is first converted to a vector of vertices based on the frequency of vertices. Then similarity is measured by calculating the similarity between the pair of vectors. Mathematically, vertex histogram is represented as shown below.

$$K(G,G') = \langle f, f' \rangle$$

Where $K(G,G')$ is the kernel function between the two graphs G, and G'. f, and f' are the functions that transforms the graph into the vectors of the vertices.

18.3.2 Shortest Path Kernel

In shortest path kernel method, the shortest path between the pair of nodes is compared to calculate the similarity between the graphs. The shortest path kernels are most frequently used in the field of bioinformatics particularly in gene expression analysis to discover the similarity between the gene expressions. The sum of shortest paths is calculated as shown below.

$$K(S_i, S_j) = \sum_{e_i \in E_i} \sum_{e_j \in E_j} K_{walk}^{(1)}(e_i, e_j)$$

Where $K(S_i, S_j)$ is the kernel computed between two shortest paths S_i, and S_j. The sum of paths between is computed using the function $K_{walk}^{(1)}(e_i, e_j)$.

18.3.3 Graphlet Kernels

Graphlets are the basic entities of a graph which are the connected subgraphs of a graph. The Graphlet kernels works on the basis of graphlets. The graphlet kernels calculate the graph similarity in the following way. First, graphlet enumeration is performed from the given graph, then vector construction is performed which represents the feature vectors consisting of frequencies of graphlets. The graph similarity is calculated using the similarity between the vectors constructed. Mathematically graphlet kernels are represented as shown below.

$$K_g(G, G') = f_G \cdot f_{G'}$$

Where $K_g(G, G')$ is the graphlet kernel function between the graphs G, and G', f_G, and $f_{G'}$ are the functions that transforms the graphs into the vectors of the graphlets. The dot product of the vectors measures the similarity between the pair of graphs.

18.3.4 K-step Random Walk Kernel

The K-step random walk kernel measures the graph similarity using the random walks. Initially the random walks of length K are performed on the graphs and the random walk is repeated K number of times. For the random walks, walk encoding is performed where the walks (sequences of nodes are converted to the vectors). During walk encoding, the sequence of random walk is encoded. After encoding, the sequence of random paths, similarity techniques like cosine similarity are used to measure the similarities between the encoded paths (vectors) which represent the graph similarity between the graphs. Choosing suitable value of K (random walk parameter) is important in K-step random walk kernel function, experimentally best value of K is identified. The mathematical expression for K-step random walk kernel is given by the following equation.

$$K_K(G,G') = \sum_{p,q=1}^{|V_K|} \left[\sum_{l=0}^{K} \lambda^l \cdot M_l \right]$$

Where $K_K(G, G')$ is the K-step random walk kernel between the graphs G, and G', K is the length of the random walks, λ is the positive weight assigned, M is the walk encoding, and $|V_K|$ is the number of vertex sets for the product graphs G, and G'.

18.3.5 WL Kernel

The WL Kernel (Weisfeiler-Lehman Kernel) identifies the graph similarity using the node labelling techniques of graphs. The neighbourhood aggregation is performed for the neighbouring node labels and labels are refined over the iterations. This update process of label refinement is repeated a number of times to get the proper label distribution for the graphs. The similarity between the graphs is measured using the similarity between label distributions. The WL kernel is mathematically expressed as given below.

$$K_{WL}(G,G') = \sum_{i=0}^{h} \langle \phi_i(G), \phi_i(G') \rangle$$

Where $K_{WL}(G, G')$ is the WL kernel function between the graphs G, and G', $\phi_i(G)$, and $\phi_i(G')$ are the label encodings of the two graphs respectively, and h is the number of iterations (number of times update is carried out). The operator $\langle \cdot,\cdot \rangle$ represents the dot products.

18.4 LINK PREDICTION IN GRAPHS

Link prediction is a popular and common technique in the area of graph mining. Link prediction technique is used for prediction of possible new connections between the nodes based on the neighbouring node's information. It has plenty of applications in many real-world applications such as prediction of new possible connections in the social networking sites such as Facebook,

LinkedIn, etc. Another example of link prediction is in citation network is predicting co-authorship in a citation network. The link prediction technique is also used widely in the domain of developing recommender systems, and world wide web applications for prediction of new links in the web graphs. In summary, the problem of link prediction is to estimate the likelihood of a connection (link/edge) in the existing network. The link prediction problem is shown graphically in Figure 18.8, where the link between the nodes B and C is predicted by the link prediction technique.

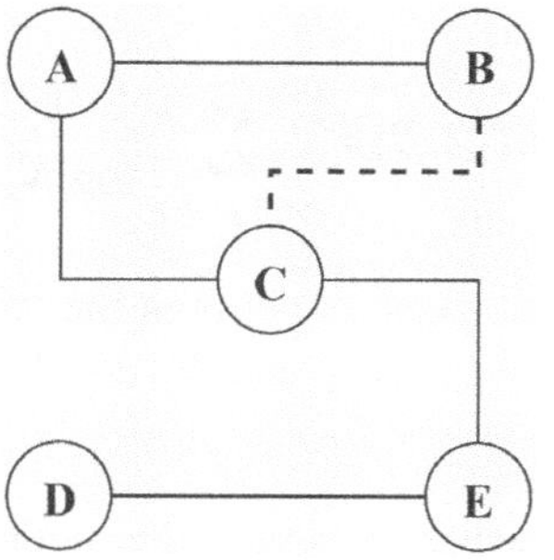

FIGURE 18.8 Link Prediction Problem in a Graph.

The link prediction techniques are broadly categorized into two categories namely, topology-based, and node-based link prediction techniques. The topology-based technique focuses on the topology of the graph and neighbouring node information, whereas the node-attribute-based method focuses on the properties (attributes) of the nodes present in the graph. A brief description of both of these techniques and major methods under these techniques is presented in this section.

18.4.1 Topology-based Link Prediction

The topology-based link prediction techniques consider the structure of the graphs to predict the possible missing links (edges between the nodes) for the given graphs. There are several topology-based link prediction techniques, some of the popular ones are discussed here.

Common Neighbours: This is the simplest technique of link prediction in which the link is predicted based on the neighbour's information. The link prediction is made using the parameter, number of common neighbours, i.e., nodes with the common neighbours can have a link. The number of common neighbours is mathematically expressed as $G_1 \cap G_2$. The greater number of common neighbourhoods indicates more chances of links between the nodes. The common neighbours link prediction technique works on the principle that, if two graphs have more common neighbours and if the nodes are connected in the first graph, then there is a high possibility of connection in the second graph also.

Jaccard Method: Jaccard method of link prediction is a type of common neighbour's link prediction technique which is designed based on Jaccard similarity. The Jaccard similarity between the two graphs is expressed as follows:

$$\frac{|G_1 \cap G_2|}{|G_1 \cup G_2|}$$

Where G_1, and G_2 are the two graphs. The Jaccard similarity is the ratio of common nodes in two graphs with the total number of nodes in two graphs.

If the two graphs have a higher Jaccard similarity then there is possibility of the common links in both graphs also, so if a link is present in the first graph and missing in the second graph then the missing link is predicted using the Jaccard method of link prediction technique.

Adamic-Adar Measure: The Adamic-Adar measure-based link prediction technique is designed based on number of common shared link between the nodes. The Adamic-Adar measure is the summation of the log of common neighbours of two nodes (two-hop similarities). The measure is calculated as shown below.

$$AA(A,B) = \sum_{K \in N_A \cap N_B} \frac{1}{\log|N_K|}$$

Where $AA(A,B)$ is the Adamic-Adar measure between the two nodes A, and B, K is the common nodes between the nodes A, and B, N_A, N_B, and N_K are the number of neighbours of A, B, and K respectively.

Example: The Adamic-Adar measure between the nodes B, and E for the below graph (Figure 18.9) is calculated as follows.

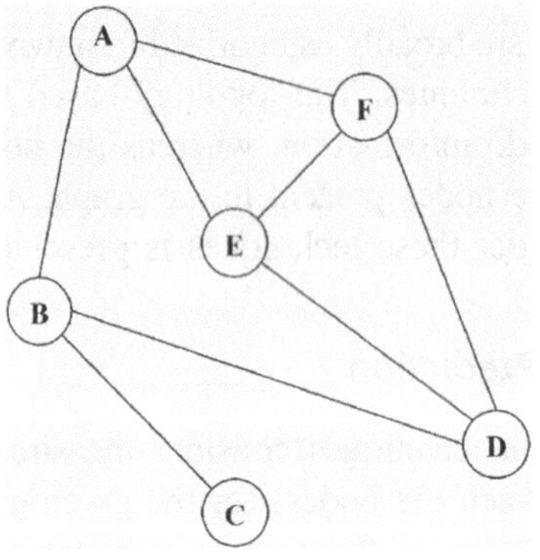

FIGURE 18.9 Example Graph for Adamic-Adar Measurement.

The common nodes between the nodes B, and E are $\{A, D\}$, so

$$AA(B,E) = \frac{1}{\log|N_B|} + \frac{1}{\log|N_E|}$$

The neighbours of B, and E both are 3, i.e., $|N_B| = 3$, and $|N_E| = 3$, so

$$AA(B,E) = \frac{1}{\log 3} + \frac{1}{\log 3} \cong 4.19$$

In this way, the similarity between the nodes is calculated using the Adamic-Adar method. Higher similarity between the nodes indicates that high chances of similar links (edges) connected with the nodes, and thus, link prediction is carried out using this similarity information.

Preferential Attachment: The preferential attachment (PA) technique of link prediction works on the principle of nodes with higher connectivity (higher degree of the nodes, or higher edges are connected with the node) are more likely to attract new links. The preferential attachment technique works in three steps–degree (similarity) calculation, score assignment, and link prediction. The similarity between the nodes using the preferential attachment is calculated as given below.

$$PA(i, j) = k_i \times k_j$$

Where $PA(i,j)$ is the preferential attachment similarity between the nodes i, and j, and k_i, and k_j are the degrees of both of nodes. So preferential attachment similarity between the nodes is simply the product of degrees.

The preferential attachment similarity for all the nodes are calculated as shown above in second step, and finally in the third step link prediction is performed by calculating the probability of the new possible links as shown below.

$$P(i \rightarrow j) = \frac{k_i \times k_j}{\sum_l k_l}$$

Where $P(i \rightarrow j)$ is the probability that nodes i, and j will be connected (linked) to each other, k_x represents the degree of the xth node. A higher probability indicates that more chance of new links.

Other Topological Approaches of Link Prediction

Few other approaches for link prediction are presented based on common neighbourhood and node similarity. One of the approaches for link prediction is weights of the common neighbours in which the inverse of the log of degrees is calculated for node similarity and then link prediction is carried out using the node similarity values. Various graph kernels and kernel measures discussed previously in this chapter are also utilized for the purpose of link prediction in the graphs. The similarity between the graphs and subgraphs are measured using kernel functions using which the link prediction can be made. The matrix factorization techniques can also be utilized for solving the link prediction problem. In matrix factorization approach, factors of adjacency matrix (latest features identification for link prediction) are calculated using which the link prediction can be carried out.

18.4.2 Node-Attribute based and Other Link Prediction Technique

Another set of link prediction techniques are designed based on the node-attribute information. The node-attribute can be represented and organized in a better way to measure the similarity between the nodes and predicts the link between the nodes. The node embedding techniques such Node2Vec, and machine and deep learning models can be utilized based on node-attributes to predict the missing links.

Node2Vec based Link Prediction: The Node2Vec provides a lower dimensional representation of a graph which captures the structural and relational properties between the nodes in a graph. The node similarity using Node2Vec, and other embedding models is calculated using the similarities between the vectors. The measures similarity can be utilized for prediction of new links in the graph. If the node similarity is higher then there are more chances of new links as per the neighbours of the similar nodes.

Machine-Learning and Deep-Learning based methods: There are various proven algorithms in the domain of machine and deep learning for performing a number of tasks. The problem of link prediction can also be solved with the help of these algorithms. The training dataset should be provided to these algorithms for prediction of missing links. The deep learning models have shown the higher rate of performance parameters such as accuracy for the prediction problems so the problem of link prediction of graph mining can also be solved in an efficient and effective way.

Mixed or Hybrid methods: Apart from the above discussed techniques for link prediction, hybrid methods can also be developed as per the requirements and availability of different techniques for the purpose of link prediction. In hybrid methods, multiple methods are combined together with the help of some mathematical models for prediction of the missing links in the graphs. Various mathematical models such as Markov logic networks, probabilistic relationship models (PRM), probabilistic soft logic (PSL), and other probabilistic models can be utilized for the purposes of link prediction in the graph mining domain.

18.5 COMMUNITY DETECTION IN GRAPHS

Community detection techniques helps in identify groups or communities based on some relations in the nodes in a graph. Community detection determines the more densely connected subgraph in a graph. Community detection techniques has plenty of applications in real world, for example, identification of persons with similar interest or common friends in social media, identification of similar protein function in DNA, development of recommender systems for recommending newer products to users, and identifying new topics and subcommunities in community question answering sites like Quora, etc.

The community detection techniques can be broadly classified into four categories:

(a) Node-centric community: The node-centric techniques focus on node attributes. The community assignment of nodes is carries out based on the properties satisfied by the nodes.
(b) Group-centric community: Community detection using group-centric techniques focuses on group properties. Groups with whole connections represent the communities in a graph.
(c) Network-centric community: The network (graph) is partitioned into disjoint sets in the network-centric community detection techniques.
(d) Hierarchy-centric community: The hierarchy-centric community detection techniques create the communities with hierarchies, just like the hierarchical clustering techniques. From the hierarchical representation communities are identified using some threshold values or criteria.

18.5.1 Modularity-based Community Detection Techniques

Louvain and Leiden Algorithms

The Louvain and Leiden both techniques are hierarchical and modularity-based techniques for community detection techniques in graph mining. The Louvain algorithm of community detection is a greedy optimization-based technique. The communities are identified using the maximum network modularity. Initially nodes are assigned to some random communities then the communities are updated with maximum gain information of nodes. The modularity is estimated by the modularity function Q. The mathematical expression for the modularity function is given by:

$$Q = \frac{1}{2^m} \sum_i \sum_j \left(A_{ij} - \frac{k_i k_j}{2^m} \right) \delta\left(c_i, c_j\right)$$

Where k_i is the degree of ith node, A_{ij} is weight, c_i and c_j are the ith and j^{th} communities, m is the sum of weights for all edges in G, δ is the Kronecker delta function the value of this function is 1, if $c_i = c_j$, 0 otherwise.

The modularity parameter Q is the ratio of density of links inside the community vs. density of links within communities. The range of modularity is between –1 to +1, and higher value is desired for better community identification. The modularity parameter considers in-degree and out-degree for the directed graphs.

Louvain vs. Leiden algorithms for community detection

Although both Louvain and Leiden algorithms are hierarchical community detection techniques, and working of both of these algorithms is almost similar to each other, still there are some minute differences between these algorithms.

Generally, Leiden algorithm gives more densely connected communities as compared to the Louvain algorithm. The Leiden algorithm is faster than the Louvain algorithm as the Leiden algorithm visit the nodes whose neighbourhood is changed or updated unlike the case with the Louvain algorithm which traverse through with all the nodes. In summary, the Leiden technique includes a refinement step in which the technique ensures that the communities are densely connected. The Leiden technique ensures high quality communities as compared to Louvain technique. The Leiden technique is faster and scalable as compared to Louvain technique.

Girvan-Newman Algorithm

The Girvan-Newman algorithm is a hierarchical technique of community detection. In this technique, edges from a graph are eliminated based on maximum betweenness centrality. Betweenness centrality is calculated based on how many times appears in the shortest paths between the nodes. The community detection is carried out in the following steps. First of all, the edge betweenness are calculated in the graph. Then edges with the maximum betweenness similarity is eliminated from the graph. After eliminating the edge, betweenness similarity is updated, and this process is repeated till the communities are identified from the graph. A dendrogram is generated in the process and then using suitable threshold communities are identified from the graph.

18.5.2 Label Propagation Algorithm

Using the label propagation algorithm (LPA), the node labels are initialized. Then node labels are updated based on the neighbourhood, this process is known as the label propagation. The labels are updated till the values of the node labels are converges. The process is semi-supervised that assigns labels to nodes iteratively and update label based on neighbourhood. The node with the same labels belongs to the same community. The communities are identified based on the similar node labels. Two popular techniques under the label propagation algorithm are Influence-based Label Propagation, and Fast Label Propagation Algorithm (FLPA). In the influence-based LPA, the communities are identified using node labels and link strengths of a node which indicates the influence of a node. The fast LPA technique on the other hand, updates and process the labels of the nodes in the queues manners and provides a faster computation for community identification.

18.5.3 Clustering-based Community Detection Techniques

Graph clustering techniques can also be used for community detection in the graphs. The purpose of graph clustering is to generate the groups of similar nodes. The generated groups can be treated as communities in the graph. Popular graph clustering techniques like K-Means, hierarchical clustering methods, and spectral clustering, etc. can be utilized for creating the graph clusters (groups of similar nodes in a graph) which can be mapped as communities in the graph.

18.5.4 Graph Clustering vs. Community Detection

The graph clustering is the process of creating clusters (groups of similar nodes) from a given graph G. The clusters are generated using the node similarity, and node connectivity information. Graph clustering is broadly categorized into two categories vertex clustering, and graph clustering.

The community detection on the other side focuses on the identification of unknown communities (groups of nodes under similar or common interest) and is closely related to the graph clustering. The community detection technique determines more close regions with dense connections of a graph. The communities are identified using the quality measures, modularity, number of links, etc. from a graph. Community detection generates the groups using higher internal connectivity using the node properties, and structures focuses on node properties.

18.6 SUBGRAPH MINING TECHNIQUES

The subgraph mining is the process of identifying the frequent graph pattern in a given graph. If the frequency of a subgraph is greater than some threshold value then it is called as a frequent subgraph, i.e., $freq(g) \geq \theta$, where θ is the threshold parameter. The parameter θ is also called as minimum support parameter and is presented as % (percentage) of graphs. The process of subgraph mining is summarized in Figure 18.10, the dotted regions on the output represents the subgraphs which are frequent (whose frequency is higher than the threshold value θ).

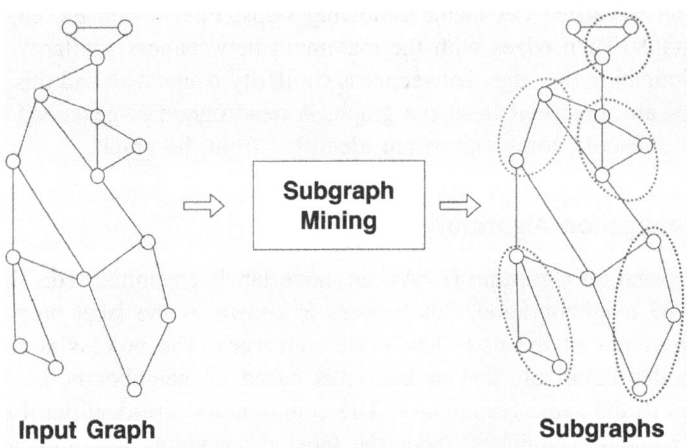

FIGURE 18.10 The process of Subgraph Mining.

Frequent subgraph mining is the process of discovering the most frequent subgraphs in a graph. If the frequency of the subgraph is greater than the specified threshold value, then those subgraphs are filtered as frequent subgraphs. The subgraph mining techniques are designed using the concept of frequent itemsets mining or association rule mining, where frequent itemsets are identified using some minimum support and confidence values. Accordingly, the first set of methods of subgraph mining are also taken from the association rule mining techniques. Two most common approaches for mining subgraphs from a graph are derived from the basic association rules mining techniques namely, Apriori algorithm and Frequent-Pattern algorithm.

The **Apriori algorithm** works on the basis of Apriori principle. The ***Apriori principle*** states that, subgraphs with k nodes are frequent then it will help in identifying the frequent subgraphs with $k + 1$ nodes. So starting from a single node, its frequency is counted, if the counted frequency is higher than the threshold value then it is taken for the next iteration. Then combinations of two nodes are selected and its frequency is counted, if the frequency is higher than the threshold value, it is taken into the next level. In this way, frequent subgraphs are identified using the Apriori algorithm. The **pattern-growth algorithm** uses the ***frequent-pattern tree*** (FP-Tree) data structure for maintaining the frequent nodes and subgraphs but takes lesser number of graph scans to identify the frequent subgraphs from the graph.

Apart from the above two techniques for subgraph mining, other popular techniques are closed and maximal subgraph mining, and subgraph enumeration techniques which are described here in brief.

Closed subgraph mining: The closed subgraph mining technique works on the principle that no super graph has the same frequency as the subgraph. Both frequent and closed subgraphs are identified in closed subgraph mining techniques. In this technique non closed subgraphs are pruned to reduce the searching space of finding frequent subgraphs. Two important algorithms in this category are gSpan (graph-based sub-structure pattern mining), cgSpan (Closed gSpan).

Maximal subgraph mining: In maximal subgraph mining there is no possibility of adding additional nodes in the subgraph which is already frequent (maximal subgraph is the largest subgraph which is frequent). Two important algorithms under the maximal subgraph mining techniques are RASMA (reverse search algorithm for mining maximal frequent subgraphs), and FLEXIS (FLEXible Frequent Subgraph Mining using Maximal Independent Sets).

Subgraph Enumeration: Subgraphs enumeration is another important technique for mining subgraphs from a graph. The subgraph enumeration method filters the subgraphs using some of the filtering criteria that makes this technique different from the other frequent subgraphs mining techniques.

18.7 GRAPH CLUSTERING

Graph clustering the process of creating the groups of similar nodes (or subgraphs). The outcome of any graph clustering technique is the set of subgraphs in which the nodes are similar to each other. The process of graph clustering is presented in Figure 18.11.

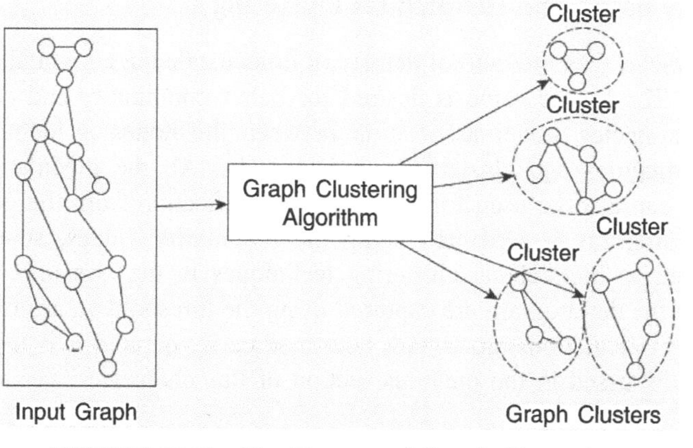

FIGURE 18.11 The Process of Graph Clustering.

Although there are many algorithms for graph clustering, and most of the community detection techniques can also be utilized for graph clustering (as there is some minor difference between community detection and graph clustering). Some of the commonly used techniques for graph clustering are discussed here in brief.

18.7.1 K-Means Clustering

The most popular partitioning-based K-Means clustering can also be applied to generate clusters from the given graph *G*. The prefix K in K-Means specifies the number of clusters. So, in K-Means, K number of initial means $\mu_1, \mu_2, \mu_3, \ldots, \mu_K$ are selected as the cluster centres. In case of graph clustering, K number of nodes are selected as cluster centres. The centres can also be selected using the node centrality measures. Then using the similarity approaches such as graph kernels, modularity, etc. the nodes are assigned to closet cluster (whose distance is closer to the centre). Then cluster centres are updated as per the latest assignment of the nodes to the clusters. The updation is done with minimizing the variation of clusters till the values of means unchanged. The means or centres are updated as per the below equation.

$$\mu_i = \frac{\sum_{j=1}^{n} \alpha_{ji} x_j}{\sum_{j=1}^{n} \alpha_{ji}}$$

Where μ_i is the mean or centre of the ith cluster, x_j is the jth node, α indicates an assignment of a data point (node here) to a cluster, and n is the total number of nodes in the graph.

18.7.2 Spectral Clustering

Partitions the graph based on spectral characteristics. It is also known as eigenvalue decomposition of a graph which is computed by calculating the Laplacian of a graph and then calculating the eigenvalue decomposition of the Laplacian matrix for a given graph. The graph partitioning problem is also known as the min-cut graph problem in which a given graph G is partitioned into k-sections using some criteria. The spectral clustering is used for many tasks in graph mining such as community detection, and dimensionality reduction.

18.7.3 Modularity-based and Hierarchical Clustering

The modularity parameter *Q* is the ratio of density of links inside the community vs. density of links within communities. The higher value is desired for better community and clusters identification. Using modularity parameter, better association between the nodes is identified which helps in identifying the communities and clusters from the graphs. All the modularity-based community detection techniques can also be used for the cluster identification from the graphs. A hierarchical structure called dendrogram is generated using the modularity values, so these techniques are sometimes also called as hierarchical clustering techniques in the domain of graph mining. The desired clusters from the dendrogram are captured using the threshold values of the modularity. The process of modularity calculations along with how modularity parameter is utilized for community detection is already discussed in the previous section of this chapter.

18.7.4 Node Embedding and Graph Neural Network-based Clustering

The node embedding techniques are used for creating the lower dimensional representation for the graphs. The node embedding techniques along with the graph neural networks (GNN) such as graph convolution networks, graph attention networks, graph recurrent networks, etc. can also be utilized for graph clustering. The GNN model along with the node embedding techniques provides better performance and accuracy for graph clustering. An overview of various node embedding techniques and graph neural networks is presented in the separate sections of this chapter.

18.7.5 Density-based Clustering

The density-based clustering techniques such as DBSCAN creates the clusters based on the dense regions of the data points. The density-based algorithms can also be modelled for the purpose of graph clustering. The dense regions with higher connectivity can be identified as the clusters from the graphs.

18.7.6 Community Detection Techniques for Graph Clustering

Community detection and graph clustering both are very closely related technologies in graph mining. The community detection techniques are used to discover the communities in the graphs. Communities are created based on the node similarities so these communities can also be treated as the graph clusters. All the community detection techniques discussed earlier like Louvain algorithm, Leiden algorithm, and Girvan-Newman algorithms can be utilized for graph clustering also. The key difference between the community detection and graph clustering approaches is already discussed in the previous section of this chapter.

18.8 GRAPH CLASSIFICATION

Graph classification is the process of categorizing the nodes, edges, and subgraphs. Graph classification has numerous applications in various domain like social network analysis, bioinformatics, recommender system development and so many others. The process of graph classification is presented in Figure 18.12. The input graph can be first converted into the adjacency matrix or lower-dimensional vector format using node embedding techniques before applying the suitable graph classification algorithm.

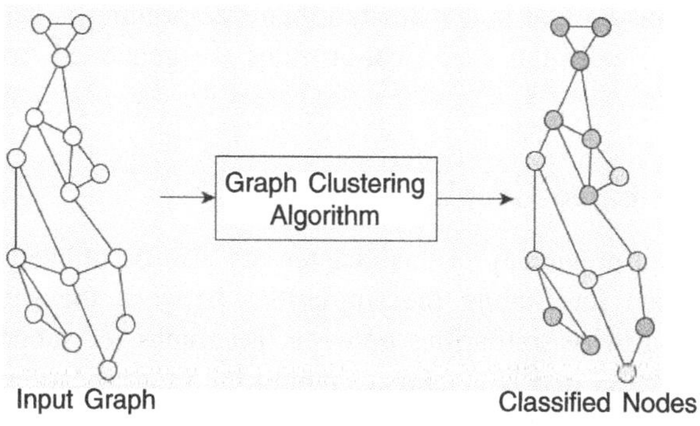

FIGURE 18.12 The process of Graph Classification.

After a suitable representation, classification algorithms are applied for categorization of the graph data, and classified nodes, edges, or subgraphs are generated as the output of the classification algorithm. The problem of graph classification can be broadly categorized into the three major categories namely, node classification, edge classification, and graph classification.

Node classification: The node classification techniques categorize the nodes based on the node attributes. Mathematically the problem of node classification is represented by $Y_i = f(v_i)$, where Y_i is the node label for the ith node, v_i.

Edge classification: The edge classification categorizes the edge of the graph using the connected pair of nodes. Mathematically, it is represented as $Y_{ij} = f\left(v_i, v_j, e_{ij}\right)$, where Y_{ij} is the label of the edge e_{ij}, connecting the nodes v_i, and v_j.

Graph classification: The graph classification problems deal with the classification of the entire graph (all the nodes and edges present in the graph). Mathematically it is expressed as $Y_G = f\left(\sum_i v_i\right)$, where Y_G represents the label of the entire graph computing using aggregation of the individual node v_i.

There are several algorithms for graph classification, and most of the machine and deep learning-based models can be utilized for achieving graph classification. A brief overview of decision-tree, kernel-based, and graph neural networks classifiers for graph classification is presented here.

18.8.1 Decision-Tree based Graph Classifiers

Decision-Tree classifiers are the most popular classification algorithms in machine learning domain, which can also be used for classification of the graphs. The decision-tree classifiers partition the datasets in different parts based on some attributes measures or criteria. Similarly, when utilized for the graph classification, the decision-tree classifier partition (split) the tree-based structure into two parts based on the criteria that one partition has a particular feature $\mathcal{g}$, whereas the other does not.

If graph has structure t then that is partitioned to first part, if not have the structure, then partitioned in the second part, mathematically expressed as:

$$h_{\langle t,y \rangle}(x) = \begin{cases} y & \text{if } t \subseteq x \\ -y & \text{otherwise} \end{cases}$$

This partition is continued till there is no more possibility of partitioning (or splitting) of the decision tree. Once the decision tree is constructed then tree-pruning is performed to eliminate the non-desired branches, and finally the classification rules are generated from the decision tree for classifying the graphs.

18.8.2 Graph Kernels-based Graph Classifiers

The graph kernels discussed previously in this chapter can also be utilized for graph classification. The graph kernels are used for finding the similarities between the subgraphs or graphs. The kernels can measure the pairwise similarities between the graphs (or subgraphs) and generates the similarity matrix. The similarity matrix is taken as input to the classification algorithm like decision-tree classifiers, support vector machines, regression-based classifiers, etc. to train the classification model. Once the model is trained with the training graphs similar matrix, then it can be utilized for classification of the graphs (or subgraphs).

18.8.3 Graph Neural Networks-based Graph Classifiers

Graph neural networks (GNNs) such as graph convolutional networks (GCN), graph attention networks (GATs), graph autoencoders (GAEs), and graph recurrent neural networks (GRNN), etc. can be modelled for performing the graph classification with accepted performance. Transfer learning-based models such as ResNet, VGGNet, GoogleNet, etc. can also be used for the purpose of graph classification tasks.

18.9 GRAPH EMBEDDING TECHNIQUES

The node embedding is the process of transforming the graph nodes into the vector space. The transformation is carried out in such a way that the similarity in embedding is nearly equal to similarity in the original graph G.

$$f : N \rightarrow \mathbb{R}^d$$

Where N is a node present in the graph, and $\mathbb{R}^d$ is the d-dimensional vector representation of the node. Graphically the node embedding process is shown in Figure 18.13.

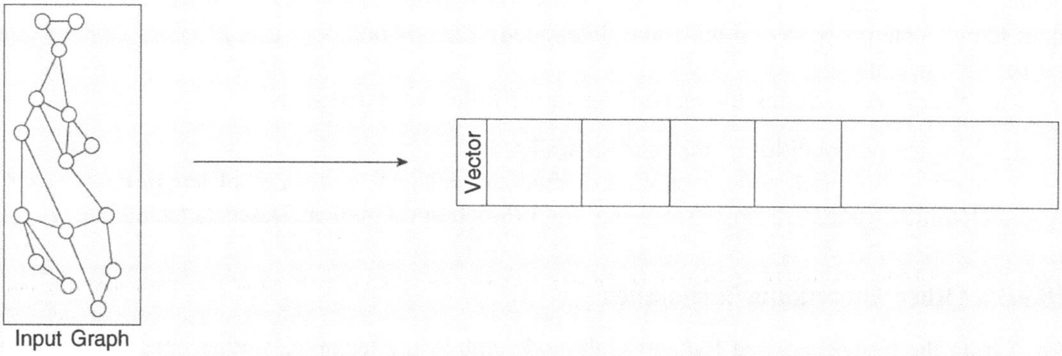

FIGURE 18.13 Node Embedding Representation.

The node embedding technique transforms the node in four major steps. The first step in encoding the node information. The second step is defining the node similarity function. The third step is to decode the node information and the last step is to optimize the encoder parameters for fine tuning of the node embeddings so that the similarity in the embeddings is nearly equal to the similarity in the original graph. There are several ways to define the node similarity, RandomWalk is one of such methods. Apart from the RandomWalk, Node2Vec is also a popular node embedding technique. An overview of the node embedding techniques and graph embedding is presented in this section.

18.9.1 RandomWalk

As the name suggests, the in the RandomWalk technique, a start from a node in a graph and then randomly proceed and move to the other node. The sequence of node in the random path indicates a random walk. Two nodes u and v are said to be similar to each other if both have the similar probabilities on a random walk in the given graph G. The nodes are similar to each other if the neighbourhoods of the nodes are same, and the sequence traversed in the RandomWalk is similar. The random walk is typically performed for fixed length (the number of nodes traversed are fixed in length). RandomWalk perform an unbiased walk on fixed length of nodes. In RandomWalk technique, depending upon the random walk strategy calculate the probability of transition from a single node to another node. Optimize the statics generated from the random walk to encode the random walk information.

DeepWalk node embedding technique is a special type of RandomWalk embedding technique which applied natural language processing (NLP) techniques over the random walk information to generate the embeddings. The DeepWalk technique, uses the word embedding methods such as Word2Vec to generate embeddings for a node.

18.9.2 Node2Vec

Node2Vec is a technique by which a node information of a graph is transformed into the vectors of numerical data. In the recent time, it has emerged as a very popular graph presentation technique. This technique is based on the random walk in a graph (which is translated into the vectors). Each node is treated as a word in the graph and each walk is identified as a sentence (sentence is formed by the words) as this technique is inspired and derived from the natural language processing technique. Probability calculations for edge transition is required for random walk. The Node2Vec embedding technique works on maximum likelihood of neighbourhood. It is 2nd order random walk for network neighbours.

The Node2Vec performs the embedding in the following three steps:

1. Compute probabilities of the random walks.
2. Starting from each node, *r* number of random walks are performed of length *r*.
3. Optimize Node2Vec objective using SGD (Stochastic Gradient Descent) technique.

18.9.3 Other Embedding Techniques

Apart from the Node2Vec, and RandomWalk node embedding techniques other important methods of node embedding are factorization based embedding, and deep learning-based embedding methods. Local Linear Embedding (LLE) is a factorization-based embedding technique which assumed that the nodes of a graph are linear combinations of the neighbouring nodes. The linear relationship is captured using the matrix factorization techniques (as the graph is transformed to the adjacency matrix in this technique). Another method is deep learning-based methods, which captures non-linear relationships between the node and its neighbours. The deep learning-based embedding methods also help in dimensionality reduction of the larger graphs. Deep learning techniques such as autoencoders are widely used for the node embedding in graph mining.

18.9.4 Embedding Entire Graph

The above discussed techniques are suitable for embedding of a particular node in the graph. There are certain situations where the embedding of entire graph is necessary. There are three common approaches for embedding of the entire graphs.

The first technique is suitable for embedding of entire graph or subgraph rather than a particular node of the graph. It is very simple approach of graph embedding in which the embedding of all the nodes is computed first and then in the second step the individual embeddings are aggregated using sum or average operator. The technique is presented mathematically as:

$$Z_G = \sum_{v \in G} Z_v$$

The above equation represents that the embedding of the entire graph Z_G is computed using aggregation of individual embedding of the node Z_v, all vertices v belongs to the Graph $G(v \in G)$.

The second technique is based on the concept of virtual node embedding. The virtual node will act as a subgraph and then apply graph embedding on it, that will represent the embedding of the entire graph.

The third technique is designed using the anonymous walk embedding. In this technique, m number of random walks are performed, and nodes are visited randomly. Then walk embedding is performed. In walk embedding, embedding starts with anonymous random walks, learn to predict walk. The walk embedding presents the embedding of the entire graph. Estimating the value of number of random walks (m) is a big issue in this technique.

Apart from the above three techniques, graph embedding is also performed using the graph neural networks such as graph convolution networks (GCNs), and graph attention networks (GATs).

18.10 OVERVIEW OF GRAPH NEURAL NETWORKS

Graph neural networks (GNNs) are the specialized types of artificial neural networks designed to deal with the graph data types. The GNNs can also address the problem of implementing node embedding, i.e., how the graph nodes are transformed (mapped) to the d-dimensional space. Just like the artificial neural, the graph neural network also deals with solving a large number of problems where the input data is provided as a graph. The major approaches of GNNs includes Message Passing Graph Neural Networks (MPGNNs), Graph Sampling and Aggregator (GraphSage), Graph Convolution Networks (GCNs), Graph Autoencoders (GAEs), Graph Recurrent Neural Networks (GRNNs), and Graph Attention Nctworks (GATs). An overview of all these architectures is presented in this section.

The architecture of GNNs is similar to the architecture of any deep learning model. The input layer deals with the input data, which is the input graph in case of GNNs, followed by multiple hidden layers with non-linear transformations of graphs, and finally an output layer. For different kinds of applications like node classification, link prediction, community detection/subgraph mining, networks similarity/graph clustering, etc., the hidden layers, and output layer may be designed differently.

The deep learning models designed for graphs (GNNs) takes the inputs from various information sources of graphs such as vertices, edges, adjacency matrix, node features, etc. depending upon the domain of graphs. For example, for social network graphs, user profiles and user connections as the primary source of information. The graph neural networks transform information collected from the neighbours of a node and combine layer-k embeddings to identify the useful patterns from the graph. Node similarity is calculated by various techniques such as random walks, matrix factorization, and proximity of node. Loss function depends on the type of patterns to be discovered and type of GNN models.

18.10.1 Message Passing Graph Neural Networks (MPGNNs)

The Message Passing Graph Neural Network (MPGNN) is a spatial network (topology based) and is applicable to many applications where geometric locations are important for analysis. The purpose of MPGNN is twofold, first is to predict graph label, and second is to predict node in a graph. The primary function of MPGNNs is to update the properties of a node based on its neighbourhood nodes. MPGNN is a type of spatial network. MPGNN allows the node representation updation based on the neighbourhood node information. The neighbourhood node information is aggregated using some aggregate function. The MPGNN works in three major phases. First to initialize the information of a node, then aggregate the information from the neighbouring nodes, and then transform and update the node. This process is performed in iterative manners. The node update process using MPGNN is shown in Figure 18.14, where for a given input graph, for a node A, how the information of the node is updated using the neighbouring nodes.

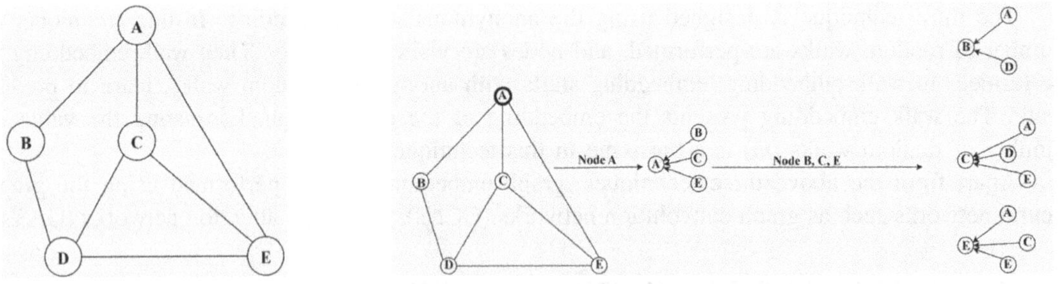

FIGURE 18.14 Node Update Process in MPGNNs.

The node update process is mathematically represented as:

$$m_{ij} = f\left(v_i, v_j, e_{ij}\right)$$

$$v_i = f\left(v_i, \sum_{j \in N_i} m_{ij}\right)$$

Where v_i, and v_j are the ith, and j^{th} nodes, e_{ij} is the edge between the nodes v_i, and v_j, m_{ij} is the node update function considering the edge e_{ij}.

MPGNNs have numerous applications in graph mining such as graph classification, graph generation, and analysis of chemical molecules etc. The MPGNNs are the building blocks for various graph mining technologies like GraphSage embedding technique, and Graph Attention Networks (GANs).

18.10.2 GraphSage Networks

The Graph Sample and Aggregation (GraphSage) networks are primarily used for sampling of the graphs. Sampling of a larger graphs is a very challenging problem in the domain of graph mining. A sample node selected from the graph does not only provides its information but also the information related to the neighbourhood's nodes in the graph, so selecting most appropriate samples from the graph is the key requirement for larger graphs for effective and efficient knowledge discovery.

The GraphSage algorithm works in three steps, in the first step, uniform samples from the neighbouring nodes are selected from a given graph, then in the second step, feature aggregation is performed for the selected nodes and neighbouring nodes, and finally in the third step, node or graph classification is performed using the aggregate information computed in the second step. The aggregate computation function is very important in GraphSage algorithm. There are three standard functions utilized for computing the aggregate information, these functions are using mean or average of the information, LSTM aggregator, and max-pooling aggregate functions.

18.10.3 Graph Convolutional Network (GCN)

The Graph Convolutional Network (GCN) architecture is taken from the Convolutional Neural Network (CNN) of the deep learning, the primary difference between the CNN and GCN is that in case of GCN networks the input is provided as a graph. The general architectural diagram for GCN is shown in Figure 18.15. The GCN architecture works mainly on the feature matrix which is generated from the adjacency matrix given as input to the GCN architecture. After input layer, a stack of GCN layers is deployed for performing convolutional operation on graph features. Pooling layer is used dimensionality reduction of the graph features. The last component of the GCN is the fully connected layer which is connected to the output layer. The final output is generated from the output layer.

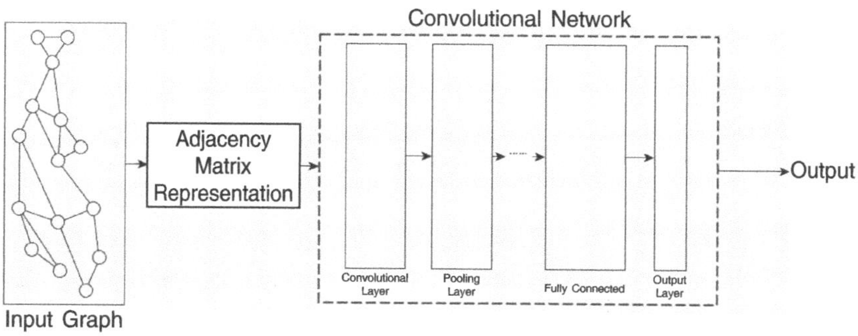

FIGURE 18.15 The Block Diagram of Graph Convolutional Network.

The GCN network also works in similar fashion like GAT but instead of updating the node by aggregating the neighbourhood nodes it performs the convolution operation on the neighbourhood node information. The first order approximation of spectral graph is calculated in convolution operation.

The equation for node updation in GCN model is shown below.

$$H^{(l+1)} = \sigma\left(\tilde{D}^{-\frac{1}{2}} \tilde{A} \tilde{D}^{-\frac{1}{2}} H^{(l)} W^{(l)}\right)$$

Where σ is the sigmoid activation function, $\tilde{D}$ is the row sum of the degree matrix, $\tilde{A}$ is the row sum of the adjacency matrix, $W^{(l)}$ is the weight matrix at layer l, and $H^{(l+1)}$ $H^{(l+1)}$, $H^{(l)}$ are the hidden layers at level $l + 1$, and l.

$$h_i^{(l)} = \sigma\left(\sum_{i \in N_j} c_{ij} W h_j\right)$$

Where $h_i^{(l)}$, is the node updation at l^{th} layer for the node h_i, W is the weight matrix, and c_{ij} is the coefficient of node updation and is calculated as shown below.

$$c_{ij} = \frac{1}{\sqrt{|N_i||N_j|}}$$

The coefficient c_{ij} is computed using N_i, and N_j, the number of neighbouring nodes for i^{th}, and j^{th} nodes.

18.10.4 Graph Autoencoder (GAE)

The primary purpose of the autoencoder is to generate the approximate output as much as similar to original input. The purpose of Graph Autoencoder (GAE) is also similar to the autoencoder model in which the input graph is approximately generated as the output of the model. The process of GAE is depicted in the Figure 18.13. The graph is provided as the input in the GAE architecture, the graph is first transformed into the adjacency matrix and then the autoencoder model is applied. The autoencoder model is consisting of three major components, encoder, latent-code, and decoder. Finally, the approximated adjacency matrix is generated by the GAE model. Using the generated adjacency matrix, the graphs (approximately similar to original graph) is generated.

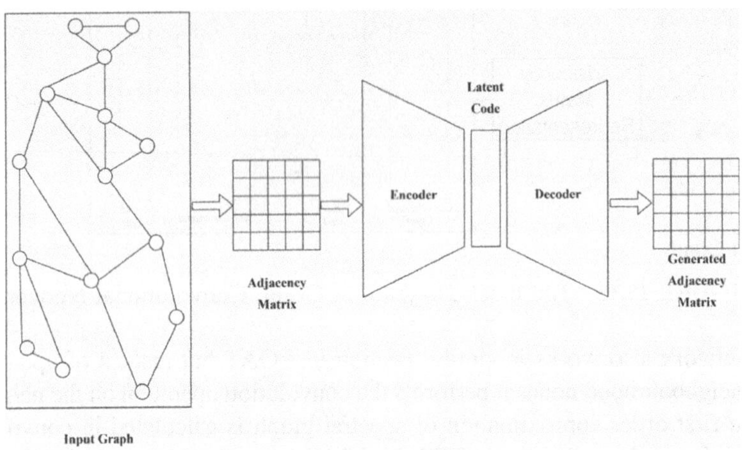

FIGURE 18.16 General Graph Autoencoder Architecture

18.10.5 GRNN (Graph Recurrent Neural Networks)

Graph recurrent neural networks (GRNNs) models the graph as a sequence of nodes or edges and then applies the RNN deep learning models on this sequence for making decisions. The GRNNs are categorized into two major types namely, node-level RNN, and edge-level RNN. The block diagram of GRNN network is presented in the Figure 18.16. Just like the other architectures, the GRNN start by taking the graph as input by transforming the graph into the adjacency matrix to the input layer. After input layer processes the input, then the stack of recurrent layers are applied and then finally in the output layer, output is generated.

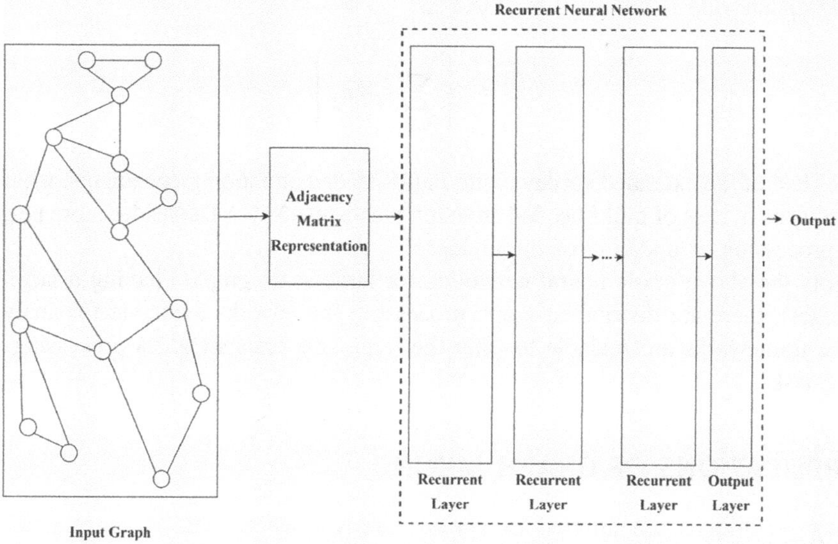

FIGURE 18.17 The Block Diagram of Graph Recurrent Neural Network.

The RNN layers can utilize the models like Gated Recurrent Units (GRUs), Long Short-Term Memory (LSTM), or Bidirectional Long Short-Term Memory (Bi-LSTM) to process the sequence of the graph data. For GRNN model, typically the binary cross entropy (BCE) loss function is used, which is given by:

$$\mathcal{L} = -\left[\hat{y}\log(y) + (1-\hat{y})\log(1-y)\right]$$

Where $\hat{y}$ is the output generated by the network, and y is the expected output.

18.10.6 Graph Attention Networks (GATs)

The Graph Attention Networks (GATs) utilizes the attention mechanism for processing of the graphs. Attention mechanism is very popular in the recent deep learning technologies like GPT (Generative Pre-trained Transformers) models, etc. The GAT utilizes the self-attention features, in which the weights of the features depend on neighbourhood data. In GAT, the node similarity is measured using the attention mechanism.

Technically the primary difference between the GCN, and GAT is that the coefficient for node updation (c_{ij}) for GCN is computed in the implicit manners, whereas the same coefficient for the node updation using GAT is computed using the attention mechanism which utilizes the node features.

$$a_{ij} = \text{attention}\left(h_i, h_j\right)$$

$$a_{ij} = \frac{\exp\left(a_{ij}\right)}{\sum_{k\in N_i}\exp\left(a_{ik}\right)}$$

Where $h_i^{(l)}$, is the node updation at l^{th} layer for the node h_i, W is the weight matrix, and a_{ij} is the coefficient of node updation computed using the node features.

The node update rule is modified for GAT as:

$$h_i^{(l)} = \sigma\left(\sum_{i \in N_j} a_{ij} W h_j\right)$$

GAT provides one of the extended variants with multi-headed attention mechanisms, which provide a higher scalability as in case of multi-headed attention mechanisms, GAT consider more neighbourhood features for processing or updating of the nodes.

Apart from the above graph neural networks, for large-scale graphs (having a large number of nodes and edges), there are distributed graph processing frameworks available for analysis of such graphs. These frameworks are scalable to cater the large size graphs and its processing for various graph mining tasks.

18.11 APPLICATIONS OF GRAPH MINING

Graph mining techniques are applied to various domain where data is correlated, and graph representation of data is possible. An overview of some of the popular applications in the domain of graph mining is presented in this section.

Chemical Compound Analysis: The graph mining techniques can be utilised efficiently for analysing the complex chemical compounds and structures. For example, the link prediction technique of graph mining can be utilised for identification of new possible links between the different chemical compounds that can be used for new drug discovery. The subgraph mining of graph mining techniques can be used for identification of finding frequent common structures inside a chemical compound. Graph classification techniques can be used for classification of different compounds of a chemical structure which can help to analyse and understand the complex chemical structures.

Program Flow: The program flow is one of the technical graphs indicating the flow of the logic of a software. By utilising the graph mining techniques on the program flow can help in identification of important pieces of code, dependency between the modules and so many other information available inside the software code that can be useful for software developers to optimise the code more efficiently.

Social Network Analysis: Graph mining techniques are more frequently utilised for analysing the social networks. Community identification in graph is one such popular example of craft mining in social network analysis. Link addiction techniques can also be utilised for identification of new possible collaborations between the users and other entities in a social network.

Protein Structure: Graph mining techniques are also replies for several important tasks in protein structure analysis. Some of the important tasks in protein structure analysis are, protein structure prediction, drug discovery and classification, prediction of protein structures interactions, and protein functions annotations. The complicated information available in proteins is modelled as a graph. Then why utilising the graph finding techniques knowledge discovery from complex protein structures is performed.

Recommender Systems: The problem of developing recommendation systems can be modelled as graph mining applications. The interactions between user, items and the attribute information of the product can be modelled as a graph. Once a graph is generated between the user's items and product attributes then by applying the suitable graph mining techniques recommendations can be made. Techniques like link prediction, subgraph mining, graph clustering, etc. can be utilised for development of recommended systems.

Fraud Detection and Anomaly Detection: The graph mining techniques are also applied for the purpose of anomaly detection and fraud detection in transactional data. The transactional data can be modelled as a graph where nodes representing different entities and edges represent the transactions between the entities. By applying graph clustering, link prediction, and other techniques of graph mining, abnormal transactions can be identified. Anomaly detection and fraud detection is performed based on identified abnormal transactions in the transactional data.

Transportation Networks: Transportation networks are important networks about the commute information of travellers by different ways of travelling like roadways railways and airways. Graph mining techniques can help in identification of important nodes (node represents the city in the transportation network), where maximum travelling is performed. Graph mining can also help in traffic prediction and route optimisation in transportation networks.

Citation Networks: Citation networks are the important networks in the research domain where one author cites the research papers and articles written by the other authors. By applying graph mining techniques my number of useful patterns can be identified from the citation network, for example, in future which research papers or articles may be sighted by a particular user. This type of operations may be performed with the help of link prediction techniques community detection techniques graph clustering techniques and other important techniques of graph mining. New research domains and amazing research fields can be identified with the help of community detection techniques of crop mining in citation networks.

EXERCISES

Consider the following graph for answering the questions:

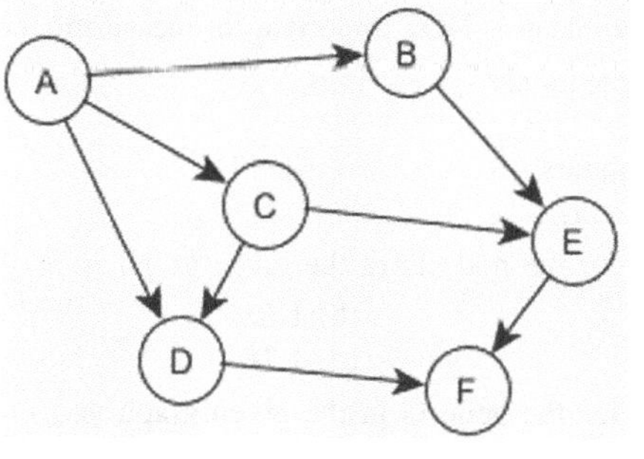

1. Compute the in-degree and out-degree of the given graph.
2. Compute the adjacency matrix for the graph.
3. Compute the Laplacian matrix for the graph.
4. Calculate the (a) Degree Centrality, and (b) Betweenness Centrality of all the nodes.

MULTIPLE CHOICE QUESTIONS

1. Which is true about the Graph Laplacian matrix?
   (a) The diagonal elements of the Laplacian matrix represent the eigenvalues of matrix.
   (b) The Laplacian matrix for the weighted graphs cannot be calculated.
   (c) The eigenvalues of the Laplacian matrix are always 0 or 1.
   (d) The row sum of the graph Laplacian matrix is always 0.

For question no. 2 to question no. 7, consider the following graph:

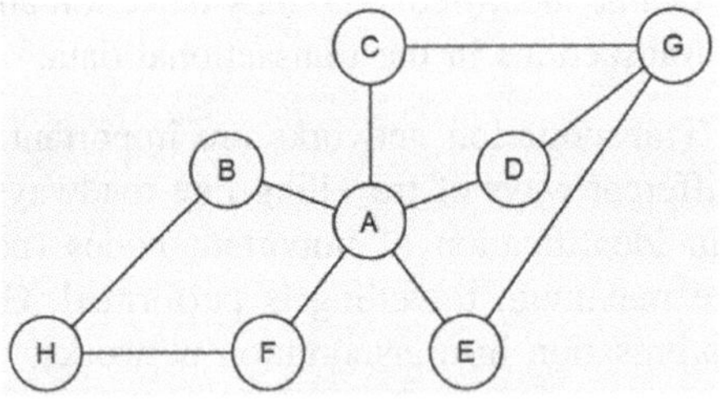

2. What is the maximum value present in the Graph Laplacian for the given graph?
   (a) 2 (b) 3
   (c) 4 (d) 5
3. What is the minimum value present in the Graph Laplacian for the given graph?
   (a) –2 (b) –1
   (c) 1 (d) 2
4. The degree similarity for the node G in the given graph is:
   (a) 0.25 (b) 0.30
   (c) 0.38 (d) 0.63
5. The betweenness similarity is calculated using which of the following parameter?
   (a) Eigenvalues of the nodes.
   (b) Degrees of the nodes.
   (c) Number of times a particular node appears in paths between the nodes.
   (d) Number of times a particular node appears in between of the shortest paths between the nodes.
6. Which of the following parameter is NOT important for measuring the Katz similarity for a given graph?
   (a) Number of direct connections.
   (b) Degree of the node.
   (c) Directions with neighbours.
   (d) Weights controller factor.
7. The Harmonic similarity for the node D in the given graph is:
   (a) 1.58 (b) 1.62
   (c) 1.72 (d) 1.78
8. The Harmonic similarity for the node G in the given graph is:
   (a) 1.58 (b) 1.62
   (c) 1.72 (d) 1.78
9. What is the key difference between the topology-based and node-based link prediction techniques?
   (a) The topology-based technique focuses on the properties (attributes) of the nodes in the graph, whereas the node-attribute-based method focuses on the topology of the graph and neighbouring node information.
   (b) The topology-based technique focuses only on the topology of the graph, whereas the node-attribute-based method focuses only on the properties (attributes) of the nodes in the graph.

(c) The topology-based technique focuses on the topology of the graph, whereas the node-attribute-based method focuses centrality of the nodes in the graph.

(d) The topology-based technique focuses on the topology of the graph and neighbouring node information, whereas the node-attribute-based method focuses on the properties (attributes) of the nodes in the graph.

10. The Adamic Adar measure between the nodes A and D for the following graph is:

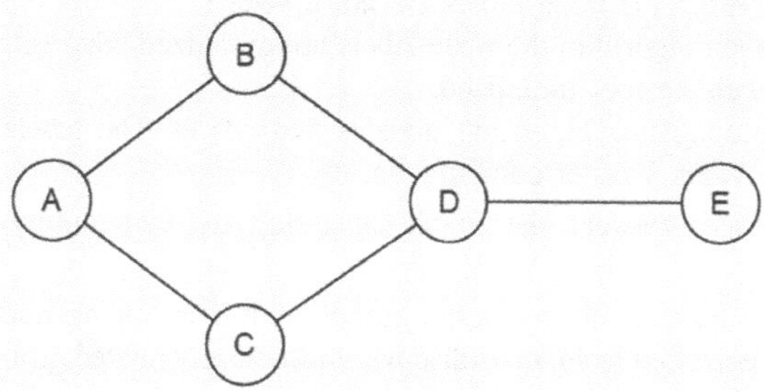

(a) 4.18 (b) 3.21
(c) 6.64 (d) 5.41

11. What is the approximate value of Katz centrality of node B for the following graph (given weights controlling factor $\alpha = 0.05$)?

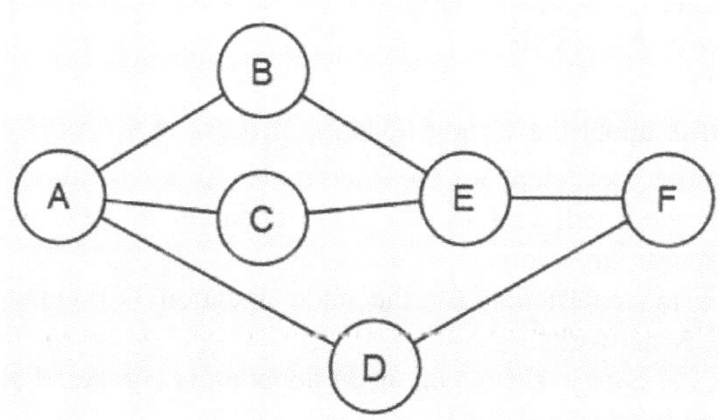

(a) 0.26 (b) 0.37
(c) 0.42 (d) 0.53

12. The Preferential Attachment technique of link prediction works on which of the following principles:

(a) Nodes with lower connectivity are more likely to attract new links.
(b) Nodes with higher centrality are more likely to attract new links.
(c) Nodes with higher connectivity are more likely to attract new links.
(d) None of these.

13. Which of the following is NOT a type of community detection technique?

(a) Node-centric community detection
(b) Attribute-centric community detection
(c) Network-centric community detection
(d) Group-centric community detection.

14. What is the primary difference between the Louvain and Leiden algorithms for community detection (multiple answers are correct?

(a) Leiden algorithm gives more densely connected communities as compared to the Louvain algorithm.
(b) The Leiden technique ensures high quality communities as compared to Louvain technique.
(c) The Louvain technique is scalable as compared to Leiden technique.
(d) The Leiden algorithm is faster than the Louvain algorithm.

15. The Girvan-Newman algorithm for community detection is based on which centrality measure?

(a) Degree Centrality (b) Katz Centrality
(c) Betweenness Centrality (d) Harmonic Centrality

16. What is the difference between the label propagation algorithm and fast label propagation algorithm?

(a) Both algorithms have different purpose.
(b) In label propagation algorithm the node labels are updated iteratively whereas for the fast label propagation algorithm the node labels are not updated.
(c) In label propagation algorithm the node labels are initialized whereas for the fast label propagation algorithm the labels are not initialized.
(d) The fast label propagation algorithm updates and process the labels of the nodes in the queues manners and provides a faster computation.

17. What are the differences between the Graph Clustering and Community Detection (multiple answers are correct)?

(a) The clustering techniques discovers the groups with overlapping nodes.
(b) The community detection techniques discover most closely related groups with overlapping of nodes.
(c) Both clustering and community detection creates the similar groups.
(d) The community detection techniques detect the communities which is the opposite process of graph clustering.

18. Which of the following techniques can be used for subgraph mining (multiple answers are correct)?

(a) Minimal Subgraph Mining
(b) Closed and Maximal Subgraph Mining
(c) Higher Connectivity Algorithm
(d) Apriori Algorithm.

19. Which statement is true about the weight updating process in GATs (Graph Attention Networks)?

(a) In GAT network the coefficient for the node updation is computed in the implicit manners.
(b) In GAT network the coefficient for the node updation is same as the mechanism of Message Passing Graph Neural Networks.
(c) In GAT network the coefficient for the node updation is computed in similar way and it is computed for GCN networks.
(d) In GAT network the coefficient for the node updation is computed using the attention mechanism by utilizing the node features.

20. What is the primary purpose of node and graph embedding techniques?

(a) The node and graph embedding techniques identifies the neighbourhood information.
(b) The structural information of graphs and nodes can be identified using node and graph embedding techniques.
(c) High dimensional node and graph information is transformed into the lower dimensional rector representation.
(d) The local and global structural information and the relationship between features can be identified using node and graph embedding techniques.

21. What is the primary purpose of update operation in Message Passing Graph Neural Networks (MPGNNs)?

(a) The update operation updates the neighbourhood and structural information for nodes in a graph.
(b) The update operation identifies the similar nodes in a graph.
(c) The update operation updates and pass the message to different communities in a graph
(d) The update operation processes and communicates messages between the neighbouring nodes.

22. How Graph Convolutional Network (GCN) is different from Convolutional Neural Network (CNN)?

(a) Both CNN and GCN are best suitable for image processing.
(b) The GCN network is best suitable for irregular structure data analysis where relationship between the feature is complex.

(c) The GCN network does not identifies neighbourhood information.
(d) The GCN network utilizes attention mechanism to update weights of neighbourhood nodes.

23. Which is TRUE about the Graph Attention Networks (GATs) (multiple answers are correct)?
(a) The GAT network dynamically adopts the weights of neighbouring nodes using the attention mechanism.
(b) The GAT network focuses more on structural information as compared to neighbourhood information.
(c) The GAT network transforms the node and graph information into the sequences of vectors.
(d) The GAT networks are the extensions of GCN networks with attention mechanism.

24. Which of the following statement is FALSE about the Node2Vec node embedding technique?
(a) It is based on random walk strategy.
(b) It applies skip-gram model
(c) It has a return parameter and also has an in-out parameter to control the embedding.
(d) None of these.

REFERENCES

[1] https://snap.stanford.edu/node2vec/

[2] Bhattacharya, R., Nagwani, N. K., & Tripathi, S. (2021), A Comparative Study of Graph Kernels and Clustering Algorithms, *International Journal of Multimedia Data Engineering and Management (IJM-DEM)*, *12*(1), pp. 33–48.

[3] Zhou, J., Cui, G., Hu, S., Zhang, Z., Yang, C., Liu, Z., Wang L., Li C., & Sun, M. (2020), Graph neural networks: A review of methods and applications, *AI open*, *1*, pp. 57–81.

[4] Khemani, B., Patil, S., Kotecha, K., & Tanwar, S. (2024), A review of graph neural networks: concepts, architectures, techniques, challenges, datasets, applications, and future directions, *Journal of Big Data*, *11*(1), p. 18.

[5] https://theaisummer.com/gnn-architectures/

ANSWER KEY

1. (d) **2.** (c) **3.** (b) **4.** (c) **5.** (d) **6.** (b) **7.** (b) **8.** (a) **9.** (d) **10.** (c)
11. (c) **12.** (c) **13.** (b) **14.** (a), (b) and (d) **15.** (c) **16.** (d) **17.** (b) **18.** (b) and (d)
19. (d) **20.** (c) **21.** (a) **22.** (b) **23.** (a) and (d) **24.** (d)

19 Natural Language Processing and Text Data

Introduction

With the advancement of web and mobile technologies a lot of applications are developed in various domains such as social media applications, healthcare applications, email, and messaging applications. The recent focus of data science is on the LLMs (Large Language Models), which is consist of plethora of text data. These applications are carrying a lot of text data and analysing these huge amount of text data is a challenging task. A large collection of unstructured text documents is technically named as text corpus. Pattern discovery from text corpus is always a challenging issue because text data is unstructured data, so processing of the text data needs a lot of processing before analysis.

Although pattern discovery and analysis of text data is a complicated process, there are some basic laws that help in understanding the basic information of the text data and opens the gateway for more detailed analysis of text data. Two distribution laws namely, Heap's Law and Zipf's Law help in basic understanding of the unstructured text data. Both of these laws are discussed here in brief.

Heap's Law

Heap's law is given by George Heap for showing the relationship between the size of the text corpus and vocabulary size in that corpus. The law states that, as size of the text corpus increases then vocabulary size also increases but at a decreasing rate. In other words, the vocabulary size is sublinear w.r.t. size of corpus. The large text corpora indicate greater variety of words, but the vocabulary growth slows down as corpus size increases. The Heap's law is mathematically expressed as:

$$M = kT^b$$

Where M is vocabulary size, T is the number of tokens, k, and b are the parameters. Typical values of k, and b are $30 \le k \le 100$ and $b = 0.49$.

Zipf's Law

Zipf's law states that the frequency of any word is inversely proportional to the rank of the word in the frequency table. In other words, Zipf's law states that only a set of words are used frequently, and a larger set of words are used infrequently.

$$cf_i \propto \frac{1}{i}$$

Where cf_i is the frequency of a particular word and i is the rank of the word.

19.1 BASIC TEXT PRE-PROCESSING TECHNIQUES

Text pre-processing is an important activity in analysing the text data. The primary pre-processing tasks includes tokenization, stopping, stemming, and lemmatization. A brief description of all of these techniques is presented in this section.

Tokenization: Tokenization is the process of generating tokens from the text documents. Tokens are the basic units of information in a text document. A token is a single word of the text document. A word is also known as term in the text document. The text document representation sometimes can be carried out by combining multiple terms such bi-grams (two terms combined), trigrams (combination of three terms), or *n*-grams (combination of *n* terms), etc.

Stopping: Stopping is the process of eliminating stop-words from the text data. There are many words in the text documents which are not relevant and important for data analysis, such words are called as stop words. Examples of stop words include the articles such as a, an, the, and other words such as is, am, are, etc. which do not provide the specific information for analysis of text data. These useless words are eliminated from the text documents for data analysis after tokenization process. A stop list is maintained by the user for performing stopping process. Most of the data science APIs (Application Programming Interfaces) provides some default stop list for implementation of stopping. The stop list can be updated as per the requirements of the data analysis task.

Stemming: Stemming is the processing of elimination of prefix and suffix from the word's root form. Stemming is performed with the help of stemmer algorithms. Porter's stemmer is one of the popular algorithms for stemming. Example of stemming is converting the words playing or plays into the root form of the word as play, so suffixes from the other format of the words plays and playing is eliminated.

Lemmatization: Lemmatization is the process of converting the words into their root forms (lemma's). Lemmas are the root words or basic dictionary words in which the words are transformed. Example of lemmatization includes the word ran will be converted to run, and the word best will be converted to the root form good.

Token Normalization: Token normalization is the process of transforming the words into their equivalence classes. The equivalence classes can be created by maintaining the list of synonyms, and equivalent words of a given word. For example, the word "e.g." refers to "for example" in the English vocabulary.

Case Folding: Case folding is the transformation technique in which the words written in the different cases are converted into the unique case. For example, capital letters can be converted to the small letters uniquely for the entire set of words after tokenization, stopping, stemming, and lemmatization.

19.2 TEXT REPRESENTATION

Text data is unstructured data and before applying any machine learning algorithm, it should be prepared and represented in such a manner that the machine learning algorithm can interpret the input text data. There are several standard text representation techniques, the most common techniques are bag-of-words (BoW), term-document matrix (TDM), and TF-IDF representation. Typically, the vector representation technique is very simple and frequently used text representation technique. In the vector representation technique, a text document is represented as the vector of word frequency in lexicographical order. Instead of the term frequency, TF-IDF measure is preferred in the vector representation as TF-IDF is the most effective way of indicating the relevance of a particular word in the text document. Before selecting any text representation technique, the text data is cleaned with the help of text pre-processing techniques.

TF-IDF

Term-Frequency–Inverse-Document-Frequency (TF-IDF) is a measure to indicate the relevance importance of a particular term in the text document collection. The term-frequency indicates the frequency (count) of a particular term in the text document. The inverse-domain-frequency indicates the inverse of the common terms appears in all the documents in the text document collection. The TF-IDF is calculated by multiplying the term-frequency with the inverse-document-frequency.

$$tf(t,d) = \frac{f_{t,d}}{\sum_{t' \in d} f_{t',d}}$$

$$idf(t,D) = \log\left(\frac{N}{|\{d : d \in D and t \in D\}| + 1}\right)$$

Where N is the number of documents in the text collection (i.e., $N = |D|$). One is added in the denominator to avoid divide by zero error (if the term does not appear in the document, then it will make the denominator part 0).

$$TF - IDF(t,d,D) = tf(t,d) \cdot idf(t,D)$$

Bag-of-words (BoW) model

The Bag-of-Word model is a popular data structure and important model for text data representation. In BoW model, a text document collection can be seen as a bag of words (the primary difference between a set and a bag is, in bag repetition of elements is permitted whereas in a set duplicate or repeated elements are not allowed). In BoW model, the word is listed along with its frequency in the text document collection. The word list is generated after performing the basic text pre-processing tasks such as stopping, stemming, lemmatization, case control, etc.

Term-document matrix

The TDM (Term-Document Matrix) is another popular text representation technique in which the text document is represented as a matrix of numbers (term frequency or TF-IDF measures). One of the cells represents the frequency of the word in a particular document. The words are presented in rows and documents are presented in the columns (both positions are interchangeable).

Example of text representation techniques

Suppose three sentences are given as the collection of text documents for which text presentation is required.

Sentence 1: Data science is the modern trending technology.
Sentence 2: Machine learning technology is the backbone of data science.
Sentence 3: Data science uses machine learning and deep learning technologies to develop modern applications.

After pre-processing a total of 12 tokens are generated—{application, backbone, data, deep, develop, learn, machine, modern, science, technology, trend, use}

The **VSM** representation is shown below.

Sentence 1: [0, 0, 1, 0, 0, 0, 0, 1, 1, 1, 1, 0]
Sentence 2: [0, 1, 1, 0, 0, 1, 1, 0, 1, 1, 0, 0]
Sentence 3: [1, 0, 1, 1, 1, 2, 1, 1, 1, 1, 0, 1]

The **bag of words** representation for the given example sentences is shown below.

BoW = {"application":1, "backbone":1, "data":3, "deep":1, "develop":1, "learn":3, "machine":2, "modern":2, "science":3, "technology":3, "trend":1, "use":1}

The **term-document matrix** is shown below.

$$
\begin{array}{c} \\ Application \\ backbone \\ data \\ deep \\ develop \\ learn \\ machine \\ modern \\ science \\ technology \\ trend \\ use \end{array}
\begin{array}{c} \begin{array}{ccc} s_1 & s_2 & s_3 \end{array} \\ \begin{bmatrix} 0 & 0 & 1 \\ 0 & 1 & 0 \\ 1 & 1 & 1 \\ 0 & 0 & 1 \\ 0 & 0 & 1 \\ 0 & 1 & 2 \\ 0 & 1 & 1 \\ 1 & 0 & 1 \\ 1 & 1 & 1 \\ 1 & 1 & 1 \\ 1 & 0 & 0 \\ 0 & 0 & 1 \end{bmatrix} \end{array}
$$

Apart from the above representations, the deep learning technology provides an advanced text representation technology called as word embedding. The word embedding technology provides the way of exploring the semantic relationships of the words in a vector space. The three popular word embedding techniques are Word2Vec, GloVe, and FastText embedding. The overview of these embedding techniques is presented in the chapter of Deep Learning.

19.3 PART-OF-SPEECH (POS) TAGGING

The Part-of-Speech (POS) tagging is an important activity in text mining in which tagging (labelling) is performed for the parts of the sentences (part of sentences may be specific words or sentences).

The POS tagging can be performed for any noun, verb, adjectives, etc. The POS tagging is useful for many purposes in text mining particularly in identifying the importance of a word. The POS tagging helps in improving the accuracy of any text mining operations as the importance of a particular word or term directly impacts the text mining task.

The POS tagging is performed in the following steps. Initially tokenization is performed from the text documents and pre-processing activities are performed to eliminate the stop words, etc. Then lexical look-up operation is performed to identify the terms associated with various tags. In the next step, disambiguation process is carried out to eliminate any type of confusion or ambiguity and in the final step POS tagging is performed with the unambiguous tags. The POS tagging techniques are broadly categorized into three major categories namely, rule-based POS tagging, stochastic POS tagging, and transformation-based POS tagging.

Rule-based POS tagging: Under this tagging technique, a set of rules are specified for POS tagging. The rules are framed by the syntactic rules, and grammatically positions of word. The rule-based POS tagging techniques are not able to handle out-of-vocabulary words (words that have not been seen by the model).

Stochastic POS tagging: The stochastic POS tagging technique is based on the probabilistic models, in which the probabilities are calculated for each term related to the different tags. The higher probability values indicate more related tags and selected as the final tags in POS tagging.

Transformation-based POS tagging: Transformation-based tagging systems are invented as part of deep learning technologies. As name indicates, it uses transformer architecture consisting of encoding and decoding mechanisms along with the attention mechanism. The attention mechanism allows more focus and relevancy of terms associated with different tags.

Apart from the above **HMM (Hidden Markov Models) technique**, and **dynamic programming techniques** are also utilized for implementing the POS tagging. **Viterbi algorithm** is also a popular algorithm for POS tagging. In the recent times, **machine learning algorithms** such as KNN, SVM, and decision tree-based classifiers are also applied for implementation of POS tagging.

Viterbi Algorithm

Viterbi algorithm is a dynamic programming algorithm used to find sequence of a hidden state. It calculates the probabilities of each state recursively. It finds the sequence of POS tagging by maximizing the probabilities of a word for the associated tag. It uses two matrices namely, Viterbi matrix, and back-pointer matrix. The Viterbi matrix maintains the transition probabilities, whereas the back-pointer matrix memorizes the previous state that achieves the maximum probability.

The Viterbi algorithm for POS tagging uses two types of probabilities, the transition probability, and the emission probability. The transition probability is based on the HMM (Hidden Markov Model) and indicates the probability of transition from previous state to the current state. The emission probability indicates how a particular word is related to the given tag.

Applications

The POS tagging is a building block for natural language processing and text mining and applied to various tasks of analysing text data. The POS tagging can also be used to identify the context in a sentence that can be utilized for improving the performance of any search engine also.

19.4 NAMED ENTITY RECOGNITION (NER)

The named entity refers to the information related to the people, location, date and time information, numerical values, or any specific piece of relevant and useful entity (words or information) in the collection of text. The named entity recognition (NER) is a problem which indicates the extraction of structural information (named entities) from the unstructured text data.

Example: Suppose the following sentence is given for NER recognition.

The Data Science Conference is scheduled at New Delhi on 01st August 2024.

Then, the NER tagging of the above sentence can be performed as shown below.

The Data Science **Subject** Conference **Event** is scheduled at New Delhi **Location** on 01st August 2024 **Time**

The named entity recognition (NER) task is performed in the following steps. Initially tokens are generated, and text pre-processing is performed for the given text documents. Then by applying POS tagging, tagging is performed for the different entities. Followed by this, the named entities are recognized using one of the standard NER techniques and finally the named entities are classified for better interpretation. The primary objective of NER is to detect the entity and recognize the entity (as shown in the previous example).

There are several techniques for implementing named entity recognition. The three major categories of NER techniques are—dictionary-based, rule-based, machine and deep learning-based techniques. A brief description of these NER techniques is presented below.

- Dictionary-based NER techniques—In dictionary-based NER techniques, dictionary data structure is used for implementing NER recognition. A dictionary is a mapping table where all the words are listed along with its named entities (person name, locations, date and time information, etc.). During the implementation, each term (token generated from the text document after pre-processing) is matched with the terms available in the dictionary and based on the matching, named entity is recognized.
- Rule-based NER techniques—In rule-based NER techniques, a set of predefined rules are framed to identify the named entities for the term present in the text document. The rules are framed by considering the lexical, contextual, syntactical, and morphological information for the given terms.
- Machine and deep learning-based NER techniques—NER can also be implemented using machine and deep learning techniques. Machine and deep learning models require the training dataset for training of the model for the NER recognition task. There are a variety of machine and deep learning models available for NER task. Some of the popular algorithms are support vector machines (SVM), random forest classifier (RF), recurrent neural networks (RNN), and convolution neural networks (CNN). Due to high accuracy of machine and deep learning algorithms, it provides an efficient way of implementing named entity recognition in a given collection of text documents.

Applications

The NER technique is useful for many applications. NER is very useful in information retrieval and improving search engines. If the search query is properly recognized by NER techniques, then it will generate more relevant and accurate results from the search engines. The NER can also be effective tool for summarizing the text documents. NER will identify most relevant terms to be included in the summary of the text documents. NER can also be very useful for automation of question answering systems, where based on the question, NER can identify the names entities to provide the most relevant and accurate answers.

19.5 SENTIMENT ANALYSIS

Sentiment analysis is an important technique in text data analytics. It helps in extracting and analysing sentiments associated with text information. Sentiments associated with the social media messages, customers review in e-commerce platforms, etc. can be extracted and analysed with the help of sentiment analysis. Since the sentiment analysis deals with identify the opinion of the users based on their reviews, etc., sometimes it is also called as opinion mining. The sentiment analysis classifies the sentiment associated with the text as positive sentiment, negative sentiment, and neutral. Sentiments associated with text is also called as the polarity of the text, for example, positive sentiments are called as sentences with positive polarities. The sentimental analysis approaches are broadly categorized into three categories namely, lexicon-based approaches, machine learning approaches, and hybrid approaches.

Lexicon-based approach

The lexicon-based approach focuses on identifying the word indicating the polarity of the sentences. For example, the word, "good" or "best" indicates the positive sentiments so it can infer the positive polarity. In lexicon-based approach the list of words (or terms) is identified for the different polarities (positive, negative, or neutral). For the given text document, after tokenization and pre-processing sentiment score is calculated based on the positive, negative, and neutral polarity terms and then using the final sentiment score, overall sentiment of the text document is decided.

Machine learning approach

In machine learning approach, first the training dataset for sentiment analysis is generated and then machine learning model is trained with positive, negative and neutral polarity data. The task of sentiment analysis is transformed as a classification task where for a given sentence, it is going to be classified as positive, negative or neutral sentiment sentence. All the popular classification algorithms such as SVM, RandomForest, XGBoost, decision-tree based classifiers, Naïve Bayes classifier, etc. may be utilized for the purpose of classifying the polarity of the sentence.

Hybrid approach

Hybrid approaches for sentiment analysis are the combination of lexicon-based approaches and machine learning-based approaches. Both of these approaches are combined together for optimizing and improving the performance of sentiment analysis approaches.

Sentiment analysis applications

The primary use of sentiment analysis techniques is in the analysing the reviews provided by the users in various e-commerce platforms to assess the quality of the products and getting the general idea about the products. This will help both the customers and manufacturers of the products. Customers will have information to decide about the best product to buy, whereas manufacturers can assess this information for improving their products for better profitability.

Another major application of sentiment analysis is in social media platforms. Based on the posts of a variety of users in the social media platforms, a number of decisions making, and fruitful knowledge can be discovered. For example, the sentiments generated by the YouTube video can help other users to decide whether they should watch the video or not. Similarly, the same information can be useful for the content creator to identify whether the uploaded video content is liked by the users or not, so that more improvements can be made in future. Sentiment analysis is also very popular in understanding sentiments of peoples for the political parties, and other organizations. Opinion mining provides a better insight into how peoples are thinking about something in a social media platform. Apart from the e-commerce sites and social media platforms, sentiment analysis is also useful and relevant technology for many different applications.

19.6 TEXT CLASSIFICATION

Text classification is the process of categorizing the text documents into the various predefined categories. The process of text classification is shown in Figure 19.1. The text document collection is provided as the input for which categorization is required to be performed. Then in the first step, pre-processing operations are performed on the input text data. The text data is cleaned and prepared for categorization. After cleaning the text data, features are extracted from the text documents using the text representation techniques such as TF-IDF, BoW, or word embedding models. In the next step, one of the classification algorithms is selected to categorize the text documents. Algorithms such as Naïve Bayes (NB), Support Vector Machine (SVM), decision trees-based classifiers, Random Forest, Gradient Boosting Machine (GBM), linear regression, neural networks such as Long Short-Term Memory (LSTM), KNN may be selected for categorization of the text documents. The output of the algorithm is evaluated using the performance parameters and validation is also performed using one of the standard validation techniques. For validation, typically cross validation or testing-training split models are used. For measurement of performance, confusion matrix is used to evaluate the performance of the text classifier. Parameters such as accuracy, precision, recall, and F-measure are derived from the confusion matrix. The final outcome of the process is the categorized text documents.

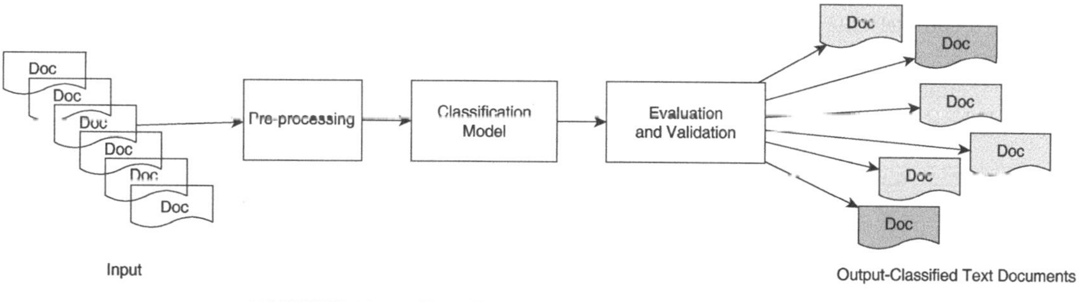

FIGURE 19.1 Text Document Classification Process.

Text document classification has numerous applications in various domains. Some of the highlighted applications are described here in brief.

- **Spam Detection:** Text classification help in determining the spams from the communications messages such email or SMS (short messaging service). The problem of spam detection is transformed as the binary classification task where the message is categorized in two major categories spam or non-spam. The message data is taken as the input and by following the text classification process spam messages are detected.

- **Sentiment Classification:** Text classification is very useful in sentiment classification also in which the reviews and feedback provided by various users (provided in textual formats) are analysed and categorized as positive sentiments, negative sentiments or natural sentence.
- **News Classification:** The text classification is also applied for classification of news contents and generating the appropriate topics from the news.
- **Product Classification in e-Commerce sites:** The text classification is also applied for classification of products in the e-commerce site. The product description is mentioned in the textual format so text classification can help in automating the classification of a large number of products sold in the e-commerce platforms.

19.7 DOCUMENT CLUSTERING

Text document clustering is the process of creating groups of similar text documents. The similarity between the text documents is measured by the similarity techniques such as cosine similarity function. The process of text document clustering is presented in Figure 19.2. Just like the text classification process the text document clustering process also starts with the pre-processing of the input text document collection. Pre-processing techniques such as stopping, stemming, lemmatization, etc. is applied on the input text data and the processed text data is presented using the appropriate text representation techniques such as TF-IDF, BoW, word embedding models, etc. Then suitable clustering algorithms like K-Means, Hierarchical clustering, DBSCAN, Topic Modelling-based algorithms such as LDA, etc. are applied for clustering of the text documents. The clustering model is evaluated using various performance metrics and validation of the model is carried out using one of the validation techniques such as cross-fold validation.

The details of clustering techniques and its performance parameters is discussed in the chapter of "Cluster Analysis". Apart from the other clustering techniques, topic modelling techniques such as LDA technique can also be utilized for document clustering purpose. In LDA-based document clustering approach, a document is represented as bag of words and clustering is performed on topics generated by LDA technique.

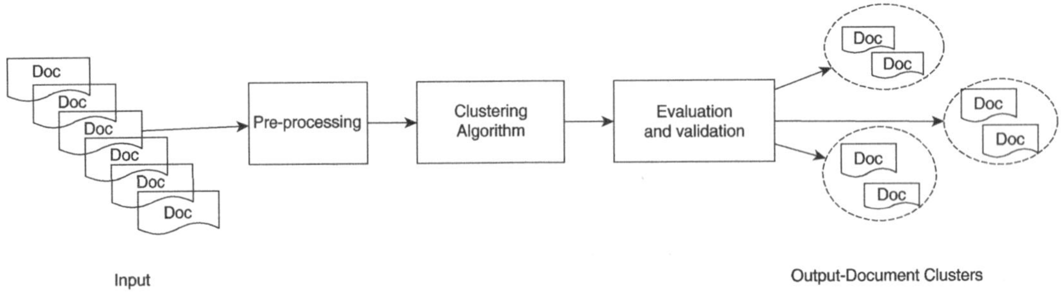

FIGURE 19.2 Text Document Clustering Process.

The clustering algorithm uses one of the similarity measurement techniques (or the distance measurement techniques) to identify the similar text documents. Cosine similarity technique is the popular technique utilized by most of the document clustering algorithms. A brief overview of cosine similarity technique is presented below.

Cosine similarity

Calculating the similarity between the text document is mostly carried out using the cosine similarity technique. Cosine similarity is calculated as shown below.

$$Cos(d_1, d_2) = \frac{\vec{d_1} . \vec{d_2}}{\|\vec{d_1}\| \times \|\vec{d_2}\|}$$

Where d_1, and d_2 are the two text documents represented in the word vector format. The similarity value ranges between 0 and 1. The cosine similarity technique is the most popular and standard technique for calculating the similarity between two objects and follows the basic similarity properties:

- *Non-negative*: The similarity value should be greater than or equal to 0.
- *Symmetric*: The similarity between A to B should be equal to similarity between B to A.
- *Reflexivity*: The similarity between and element with itself should be 1.
- *Triangular inequality*: The similarity between A to C should be greater than or equal to similarity between A to B, and similarity between B to C.

Example: Suppose the word vector of the two sentences are given as:

Sentence 1: [0, 0, 1, 0, 0, 0, 0, 1, 1, 1, 1, 0]
Sentence 2: [0, 1, 1, 0, 0, 1, 1, 0, 1, 1, 0, 0]

Then the cosine similarity between these two sentences is calculated as follows:

$$Cos(S_1, S_2) = \frac{0\times0+0\times1+1\times1+0\times0+0\times0+0\times1+0\times1+1\times0+1\times1+1\times1+1\times0+0\times0}{\sqrt{0^2+0^2+1^2+0^2+0^2+0^2+0^2+1^2+1^2+1^2+1^2+0^2} \times \sqrt{0^2+1^2+1^2+0^2+0^2+1^2+1^2+0^2+1^2+1^2+0^2+0^2}}$$

$$Cos(S_1, S_2) = \frac{3}{\sqrt{5} \times \sqrt{6}} \approx 0.55$$

Document clustering technique is also very useful for several applications. Some of the major applications of document clustering are discussed below.

- Information Management—The document clustering can solve the problem of managing a large collection of text documents such as e-books, digital magazines, newspapers, and a lot of other textual information available in digital media. The document clustering can identify the similarities between the text documents and create the groups of similar documents for better management of the textual information. The similar documents will be available within the same cluster, and it will provide ease in document searching, indexing, and other information management activities.
- Topic Modelling—Document clustering can also help in topic modelling. Similar documents are grouped together in document clustering so generating appropriate topics will be easier from the similar documents, as the relevant terms can be identified in a more accurate way.
- Text Summarization—Text summarization can also be done using the document clustering. Initially the summaries will be generated from the individual document cluster and then the similarities across the clusters are combined together to summarize the large text document collections. Again, the summary generated from a document cluster will be more relevant and appropriate as the relevant terms from the similar documents can be identified easily.

- Recommender Systems—Document clustering can also help in developing effective recommender systems dealing with the textual information. The group of similar documents will provide the best features and most appropriate terms to identify the user preferences and interests towards the products they wish to buy in future.

19.8 TOPIC MODELLING

The topic modelling is an important text mining activity. In topic modelling technique, for a given text document collection suitable and most appropriate topics are generated. The topics are identified based on the relevance of the terms present in the text document collection. For example, for a given collection of new snippets, topic modelling may generate the topics such as "Finance News", or "Political News", etc. Two popular techniques for topic modelling are Latent Dirichlet Allocation (LDA) and Non-negative Matrix Factorization (NMF). Both of these techniques are discussed briefly here.

19.8.1 Latent Dirichlet Allocation (LDA)

The latent Dirichlet allocation technique (LDA) works on the basis of probability distributions. LDA is the unsupervised leaning technique for guessing topics for the given text document collections. In LDA, a topic technically is seen as the distribution of the words. LDA takes the input parameter as K, i.e., the number of topics to be generated from the collection of text documents. Initially the topics are randomly selected, then in the subsequent steps the probability of the words is updated for making the topics more relevant. The probability of each topic with respect to the documents and probability of topics in context to words is updated for the entire set of documents to generate the final topics from the collection of text documents. The process of LDA technique is mathematically expressed as follows:

$$P(W,Z,\theta,\phi;\alpha,\beta)=\prod_{i=1}^{M}P(\theta_j;\alpha)\prod_{i=1}^{K}P(\phi;\beta)\prod_{t=1}^{N}P(Z_{j,t}\mid\theta_j)P(W_{j,t}\mid\phi_{j,t})$$

The above mathematical expression of LDA can be explained with the help of plate notation. The plate notation helps in understanding the working of LDA model graphically. The plate notation for the LDA model is presented in the Figure 19.3.

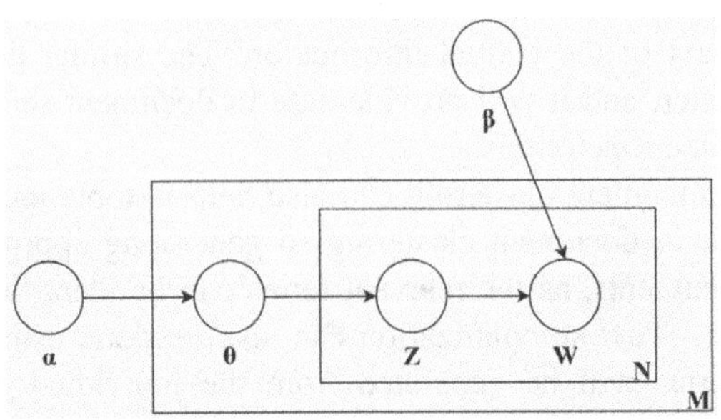

FIGURE 19.3 Plate Notation of Latent Dirichlet Allocation.

In the plate notation (and the mathematical expression), *M* indicates the number of documents in the text collection, *N* indicates the number of words in the document, α is the parameter of

Dirichlet prior on per document topic distribution, β is the parameter of Dirichlet prior on per topic word distribution, θ is the topic distribution of document, and Z is the topic for a document (topic for a particular word in document).

19.8.2 Non-negative Matrix Factorization (NMF)

The LDA technique is probability distribution technique whereas the non-negative matrix factorization (NMF) technique is matrix factorization (decomposition) technique. The NMF technique starts with the term-document matrix (TDM). In NMF matrix factorization method the original term-document matrix is decomposed into two non-negative (positive) matrices. The first decomposed matrix denotes the document-topic matrix, and second decomposed matrix denotes the topic-term matrix.

The NMF technique is mathematically expressed as:

$$V \cong WH$$

Where V is term-document matrix, W is the document-topic matrix, and H is topic-term matrix.

The term-document matrix is decomposed in non-negative matrices in the following steps. Initially the matrices W and H are initialized with the random positive numbers and then in the subsequent steps, the values are updated based on the reconstruction errors. The objective of NMF is to minimize the reconstruction error.

Evaluation of Topic Modelling technique

Evaluation of topic modelling technique is not a simple task. The topic modelling techniques can be evaluated using manual human inspection, where manually the topic relevance with the text document is analysed and decided whether the topics generated are appropriate or not. The other technique for topic modelling evaluation is observing the probabilities of the terms appears in topic with respect to the probabilities of terms in the text document. It is expected that the higher probability terms should appears in the topics generated. Apart from these two, two most important and popular evaluation techniques for evaluating the topic modelling techniques are coherence techniques, and perplexity measure.

Coherence

Coherence is calculated as the conditional likelihood of the co-occurrence of the terms. It is the measure of how the words are correlated with each other. The coherence score is calculated by using a reference text corpus. Two most popular ways of calculating coherence score are U-Mass and UCI coherence scores.

The U-Mass coherence score is calculated as shown below.

$$C_{UMass} = \log \frac{D\left(w_i, w_j\right) + \frac{1}{D}}{D\left(w_i\right)}$$

Where $D(w_i, w_j)$ is the function indicating how two words w_i, and w_j appears together, and $D(w_i)$ indicates how the word w_i appears individually in the document, and D is the number of documents in the text corpus.

The UCI coherence score is sliding window-based score, that is calculated on a fixed size window consisting of fixed number of words at a time. It is based on pointwise mutual information of the topic words with the text document. The UCI coherence score is calculated as follows:

$$C_{UCI} = \log \frac{P(w_i, w_j) + 1}{P(w_i) \cdot P(w_j)}$$

Where $P(w_i, w_j)$ is the probability that the word w_i, and w_j appears together in the sliding window, and $P(w_i)$, and $P(w_j)$ are the probabilities that word w_i, and w_j appears individually in the sliding windows respectively.

Higher value of coherence indicates that the topics are more correlated with the text documents and the topic modelling techniques is perfectly able to guess the appropriate topics for the given text documents.

Perplexity

Perplexity is another popular measure for evaluating the topic modelling techniques. The perplexity is calculated by log likelihood of the held out set of data (set of the data not taken as training data). The log-likelihood is calculated as shown below.

$$\mathcal{L}(w) = \log p(w \mid \Phi, \alpha) = \sum_d \log p(w_d \mid \Phi, \alpha)$$

$$perplexity(w_{test}) = e^{\left(-\frac{\mathcal{L}(w)}{token\_count}\right)}$$

Where w_d is the unseen documents, Φ are the topics, α is the hyperparameter for the topic distribution θ_d.

The perplexity is not able to depict the relationship between the terms of the topic and text document. However, perplexity focuses more on the unseen data which is not covered during the training phase of the topic modelling. Lower values of the perplexity indicates that the technique is best for predicting topics for the given text document collections.

Applications of Topic Modelling

The primary use of topic modelling technique is to generate appropriate and relevant topics for the given text document collections. There are several applications of topic modelling in data science. Topic modelling is most widely used in plastering of the text documents, summarisation of large text documents, and is also widely used in information retrieval particularly in searching of a document.

19.9 TEXT SUMMARIZATION

Text summarization techniques are broadly categorized into two categories namely, extractive summarization techniques and abstractive summarization techniques. In the extractive summarization technique, the most relevant sentences are filtered and kept in the generated summary in the original documents format, whereas in the abstractive summarization technique, the important terms are extracted, and its semantics are also captured, and summary is generated in the other sentences preserving the meaning of the original documents.

19.9.1 Extractive Methods for Text Summarization

Extractive text summarizes filters the most appropriate sentences for generating summaries. The appropriate sentences are identified with the help of some ranking scores of the sentences. There are a number of methods of extractive text summarization. Some of the important methods are discussed here in brief.

TextRank: TextRank is a graph-based ranking algorithm for ranking of relevant text. The summarization is performed in the following steps, initially the pre-processing is performed on the input text corpus. After pre-processing, a rank graph is created based on word relatedness (like co-occurrence, etc.). In the rank graph, the weights of edges are identified, and important nodes are determined iteratively by updating the weights of the edges. Then the sentence ranking is decided based on important nodes. Finally, the text summarization is performed based on the ranking of the sentences.

LexRank: LexRank is another graph-based ranking model like TextRank. In case of TextRank, the node in the graph represents sentence and edge represents similarity between the nodes. The primary difference between the TextRank and LexRank algorithms is, the TextRank algorithm works on the basis of words at node level whereas the LexRank algorithm works on the basis of sentences at the node level.

SumBasic: The SumBasic is a centroid-based multi-document summarization technique. In this technique, the word-frequency is computed, and sentence ranking is performed using the word-frequency. The sentence ranking is normalized in the next step, and sentence selection for summarization is performed based on the higher-ranking value for generating the summary.

Cluster-based: Document clustering is also utilized efficiently for generating the summaries from the text documents. Under this technique, pre-processing is performed first on the input text corpus. After pre-processing, clusters are created using some of the document clustering techniques like K-Means, or hierarchical clustering, or density-based clustering. The generated clusters are then summarized individually and finally cluster summaries are combined to generate the summary of the text corpus.

LSA (Latent Sematic Analysis): The latent semantic analysis (LSA) technique uses Term-Document Matrix (TDM) as input. The text corpus is first pre-processed and TDM is created. Once the TDM is created, then Singular Value Decomposition (SVD) is applied to the TDM, and matrix factorization is performed as follows:

$$A = U\Sigma V^T$$

Where U is the word-context distribution, Σ is the context association, and V is context-document distribution.

The LSA identifies semantic relation in unstructured text data. As the LSA technique utilizes the SVD decomposition, it also helps in dimensionality reduction of the large text corpus. In order to generate summary from the text corpus, LSA extracts the semantic representation from the output of SVD and then the sentence and document similarity scores are computed. Once the similarity scores are calculated then ranking is performed based on similarities values. Finally, the sentence selection is performed based on ranking of the sentences for generating the final summary.

Luhn-frequency based: The Luhn-frequency based summary technique is one of the oldest techniques of document summarization. The Luhn-frequency based technique generates summary in the four major steps. In the first step, text pre-processing is performed. In the second step, frequent keywords identified from the pre-processed text documents. In the third step, sentence scoring and normalization is performed and finally in the last step, sentence selection for summary is carried out to generate summary from the text corpus.

KL Sum: The KL-Sum summarization technique is based on the Kullback-Leibler divergence technique. It is a probability-based model for generating the summary from the text documents. It maximizes the similarity between the original document and generated summaries using probability distributions by applying KL divergence. It handles the redundancies (eliminate repeated sentences) in the generated summaries.

19.9.2 Abstractive Methods for Text Summarization

In abstractive text summarizers, the important and meaningful terms for summarizing the text documents are identified and then summary is created by framing the newer sentences using the identified terms rather than just filtering the important and relevant sentences in case of extractive summarization techniques. So, newer sentences are generated in the summary by utilizing the individual relevant and important terms present in the text corpus. Thus, the abstractive summarization techniques are slightly complicated than the extractive summarization techniques. Some of the important abstractive text summarization techniques are discussed here in brief.

Seq2Seq: The Seq2Seq is the deep learning model to handle the sequential data. The Seq2Seq model has the encoder and decoder layers which extracts the important text features and generates most relevant summary from the text document. The Seq2Seq model can be applied to the problem of text summarization in a efficient way as it gives a higher level of accuracy for the generated summaries.

PointerGenerator: The pointerGenerator networks are the extensions of the Seq2Seq models to handle and process the sequential data like text steams, so it is very much useful for summarization of the text data. The primary difference between the Seq2Seq model and the PointerGenerator model is, the Seq2Seq model is not capable of handling of out-of-vocabulary words whereas the PointerGenerator model can handle the out-of-vocabulary words. The PointerGenerator model has the pointer mechanisms, which allows copying of the original text data into the summary. It also has the attention mechanism that allows focusing on the relevant and important words of the text document. In this way PointerGenerator is one of the effective techniques for the text summarization.

Reinforcement Learning (RL): The RL-based text summarization allows the use of reinforcement leaning technologies for generating summaries from the text. The text summarization is performed in the Reinforcement Learning environment where text documents are taken as input. Then agent is defined for RL environments based the actions associated with the summarization. The reward, and policy is defined for the RL environment. Reward is awarded for the best summaries generated and penalties are assigned for the bas summaries. The policy is defined for making the strategy for deciding more relevant terms for the summaries.

Transformer-based Models: The transformer architecture is very popular for LLMs (Large Language Models) and are capable of handling of large text collections in an efficient manner. The transformer architecture utilizes the attention mechanism which provides the facilities on focusing on the specific context for generating the summaries. It uses the encoder-decoder framework to analyse the text properly and make the most perfect decisions from the text document collections. The popular transformer-based models are—T5 (Text-To-Text-Transfer-Transformer), BART (Bidirectional Encoder Representations from Transformers), and GPT (Generative Pre-trained Transformer) transformers. All these models can be effectively utilized for generating the summaries from the text documents with a high level of accuracy.

19.9.3 Hybrid Models for Text Summarization

Under the category of hybrid models, various models from both of the categories abstractive, and extractive are combined together for summarizing the text document collections. The hybrid model takes the advantage of both of the techniques to generate a real-world summary of the text documents.

19.9.4 Performance Evaluation of Text Summarizers

The performance evaluation of any text summarizer algorithm can be performed in many ways. The four major performance parameters frequently used to evaluation of the text summarization algorithms are compression ratio, retention ratio, rouge score, and pyramid score.

Compression ratio (CR)

The compression ratio (CR) is the ratio of length of the summary document to the length of the original document. Obviously, for the better summary lesser value of compression ratio is desired.

$$CR = \frac{\text{Length}(\text{Summary})}{\text{Length}(\text{Original Text})}$$

Retention ratio (RR)

Retention ratio (RR) is the ratio of valuable information contained in the summary document to the information contained in the original document. The information contained can be measured in several ways, one of which is the entropy measure. For a good summary, a higher value of retention ratio is desired.

$$RR = \frac{\text{Info}(\text{Summary})}{\text{Info}(\text{Original Text})}$$

Rouge score

The Rouge (Recall-oriented understudy for gisting evaluation) score is a popular metric for evaluating the text summarizers. Typically, the rouge score is calculated based on ratio of *n*-grams generated in summaries to the *n*-grams presented in the reference document. The *n*-gram indicates the combination of *n* words (or terms) as a single unit of processing in the text document. The expression of calculating the rouge score with *n*-grams is presented below, for a good summarizer a higher value of rouge score is expected.

$$Rouge-N = \frac{\sum_{Summaries}\sum_{n-grams} Count(gram_n)}{\sum_{References}\sum_{n-grams} Count(gram_n)}$$

N is the length of *n*-grams, $Count(gram_n)$ indicates the number of *n*-grams present in the summaries generated and the number of *n*-grams present in the reference document. The variations of Rouge-N scores are Rouge-LCS, and Rouge-S that considers the longest common sequence and skip bigrams instead of *n*-grams generated in the summary.

Pyramid score

The pyramid score is calculated based on the summary content units (SCU's). The SCU is the basic unit of the summary generated by the text summarizer. Each SCU is assigned weights depending on the importance of summary units. The pyramid score is defined as the ratio of sum of weights of the summary content units (SCU's) in summary and the sum of weights of the SCU's in the ideal summary. The ideal summary is the maximal informative summary of the text documents with the highest possible weights. The pyramid score is calculated as shown in the equation below.

$$Py(S) = \frac{\sum_{SCU \in Summary} W_i}{\sum_{SCU \in Ideal-Summary} W_k}$$

19.9.5 Applications of Text Summarization

The text summarization techniques are good tools to analyse and summarize large text documents. Since the summaries are generated by the relevance and importance of the sentences, the summaries generated can also be utilized for many knowledge discovery tasks such as dimensionality reduction of text data, clustering and classification of text documents, and many applications dealings with larger text documents such as medical research, legal documents analysis, customer feedback and services, etc.

19.10 INFORMATION RETRIEVAL AND TEXT SEARCH

Information retrieval is the process of extracting or retrieving most relevant information from the collection of large unstructured text data. The relevancy of information is decided by the search query (set of keywords). Search operation in the web-based search engines are the best example of information retrieval systems. The retrieved information from the collection of information is measured with the help of two popular performance metrics namely, precision, and recall. The precision indicates the fraction of relevant documents retrieved from the total retrieved documents during the information retrieval. The recall metrics is fraction of relevant documents retrieved from the total relevant documents available in the text collection. The F-measure combines both the precision and recall metrics.

$$precision = \frac{|\{Rel\} \cap \{Ret\}|}{|\{Ret\}|}$$

$$recall = \frac{|\{Rel\} \cap \{Ret\}|}{|\{REL\}|}$$

$$F = \frac{2 \times precision \times recall}{precision + recall}$$

Generally, the term-document matrix for large text collection is sparse (most of the entries in the TDM matrix are 0's). To handle this issue inverted index (or inverted files) data structure is used in most of information retrieval tasks. The inverted index is a special type of data structure useful for information retrieval and search engine operations. In inverted index data structure, each unique word is mapped to the set of relevant text documents. For a given search query, the tokens are generated from the search query and then for each token the set of documents are retrieved and provided as a search result.

19.10.1 Approaches for Information Retrieval

In a broader way there are two common approaches for the information retrieval namely, Boolean retrieval models and vector space models. This categorization is done based on the text information representation and the way the query is processed by the information retrieval engines. An overview of both of these approaches is presented below.

Boolean retrieval models

Boolean retrieval models are the ones in which the search query is presented in the Boolean expression model, e.g., search words are combined with keywords AND, OR, and NOT. In the Boolean model, the document is seen as the set of words and results are given in the Boolean format depending on the presence and absence of terms in a document. The advantage of Boolean retrieval models is that computationally it is simpler as compared to the vector space model.

Vector space model (VSM)

In vector space model, bag of words representation is used to represent the documents. The collection of documents is presented as numerical vectors. The search query is processed at the vector space and retrieval is performed by computing the similarities between the query vector and document vectors in the vector space model. Cosine similarity technique is one of the popular techniques for computing the similarities between the pair of documents in vector space. Since different terms can be assigned different weights (as per the relevance and importance) in the vector space model, it is more flexible approach as compared to the Boolean retrieval models.

19.10.2 Information Retrieval and Web Analytics

Information retrieval (IR) techniques are more relevant and applicable in web analytics domain particularly in the web-based search engines. IR techniques for the web analytics, including crawling, link-based algorithms, and metadata usage, etc. Web crawling and web harvesting includes extracting and getting more relevant information from web pages specified by the set of keywords. Document clustering and classification is closely related to the information related tasks as web pages classification and clustering techniques are similar to the text documents classification and clustering in NLP and text mining. Modern information retrieval applications utilize the traditional and machine learning-based ranking approaches for improving web analytics and other information retrieval tasks.

19.10.3 Term Weighting Schemes

Generally, for NLP and text mining tasks measures like TF-IDF are sufficient but when it comes to keywords (terms) sensitive operations such as web-based search engines, a proper term weighting scheme is required. The term weighting scheme assigns higher weights to the specific terms based on context and importance of information of the terms in a text document collection. There are so many terms weighting scheme available but BM25 weighting scheme is a proven popular scheme which can handle the document length normalization in an effective way.

Document length normalization is an important activity in information retrieval. It helps in adjusting the weights of various terms based on the length of the documents. The document length normalization technique helps in avoiding the biases of dominating terms (most frequent terms) appearing in the longer documents as compared to the shorter documents.

BM25 (best matching 25) scheme

BM25 weighting scheme a.k.a. Okapi weighting scheme is one of the popular term weighting schemes. The BM25 weighting scheme is a probabilistic model and is capable of providing document length normalization. The BM scheme calculates the score of the relevance for a given document using term frequency, TF-IDF, normalized document length, and average length of the documents. The mathematical expression for calculating the BM25 weighting scheme is given below.

$$B_{i,j} = \frac{(K_1 + i) f_{i,j}}{K_1 \left[(1-b) + b \frac{len(d_j)}{avg\_doclen} \right] + f_{i,j}}$$

$$sim_{B25}(d_j, q) \sim \sum_{K_i[q,d_j]} B_{i,j} \times \log\left(\frac{N - n_i + 0.5}{n_i + 0.5} \right)$$

Where K_1, and b are the empirical constants derived from probabilistic models.

A good term weighting should have the three basic properties. The first property is term frequency (TF), the second property is IDF (inverse domain frequency), and the third property is document length normalization. The BM25 satisfies all these properties, which makes it a popular weighting scheme in information retrieval domain. Most of the computational sensitive tasks in information retrieval domain prefers BM25 weighting scheme as compared to TF-IDF measure.

19.11 VISUALIZATION OF TEXT DATA

Text visualization is an important technique in text mining and natural language processing. It helps in visualizing the distribution and importance of terms in the document collections. In the recent times there are several advanced visualization techniques available for visualizing the text information. Word clouds and term distribution histograms are two basic and popular visualization techniques most widely used in the field of text mining and natural language processing. Both of these techniques are presented here in brief.

Word clouds

Word clouds represents the visualization of important terms present in the collection of text data. The importance of terms is decided based on the frequency of the terms in the document collection. The word cloud uses different font sizes, font colours, and sometimes different orientations (horizonal, vertical, or rotated) to present a cloud kind of image for displaying the key terms present in the collection of text data. The extensions of word cloud techniques provide many modern visualizations such as tag cloud, and tree cloud, etc. A sample word cloud is presented in the Figure 19.4.

Histograms

Histograms are another popular standard visualization technique for text information visualization. The frequency distribution information of the important terms and distribution of terms in the text documents can be visualized with the help of histograms. The frequency distribution information and distribution of terms across the document can help in understand the context and semantics from the collection of text document. A sample term frequency distribution using histogram is presented in Figure 19.5.

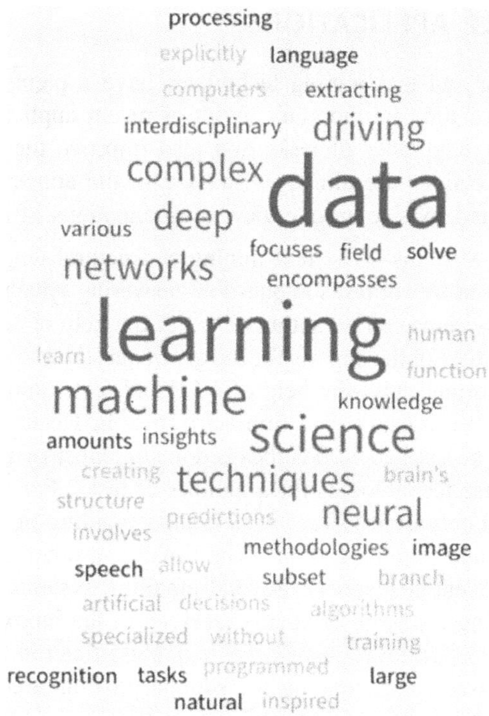

FIGURE 19.4 An Example Word Cloud for Text Visualization.

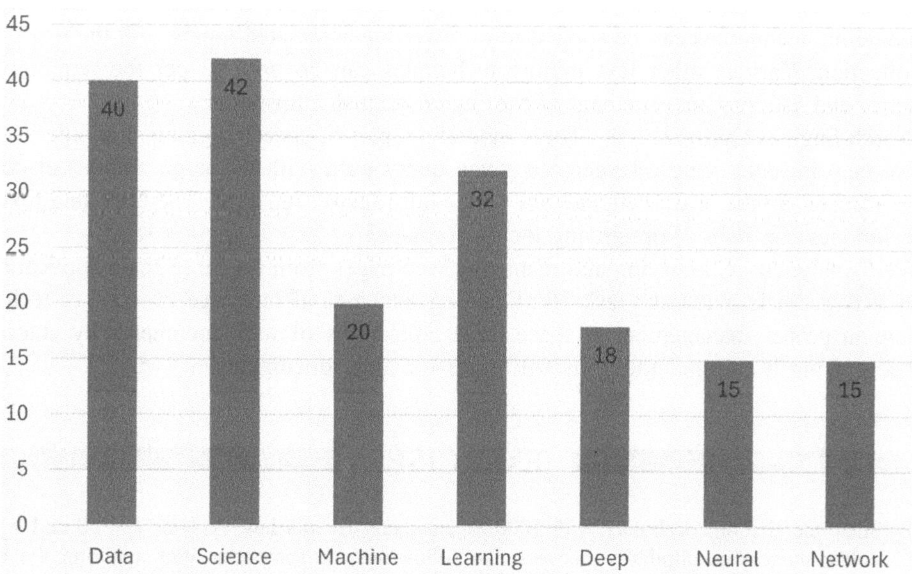

FIGURE 19.5 Term Frequency Histogram for the Text Documents.

19.12 ADVANCED NLP APPLICATIONS

Natural language processing and text mining techniques have a plenty of applications in various domains where textual information is important. A lot of recent applications utilized both of these technologies for automating a number of tasks and also improve their decision-making systems. Although some of the applications are already discussed in the above sections, some other major applications are also presented to give an overview of applications of these technologies.

- Question Answering Systems—The text mining and natural language processing techniques help in automating a number of tasks in question-answering systems. Question classification in question-answering systems can be automated with the help of text classification algorithms. Answer ranking, identifying the experts for the given question, identifying duplicate questions, etc. task can be performed with the help of NLP and text mining approaches.
- Medical Transcript Classification and Summarization in Healthcare—NLP and text mining approaches can also be applied in healthcare domain. Most of the healthcare systems these days are utilizing these technologies for a number of tasks. For example, medical transcripts can be classified and summarized for a quick understanding of the health records.
- Email Classification and Summarization—The Email and other digital communication media is increasing in exponential manners. Several emailing systems are providing certain ways of efficiently managing the large of emails received in the inbox. Spam detection and email categorization tasks is achieved using the text classification techniques. Summarization techniques are also used for generating the summary of large collection of emails.
- Digital Information Management—Digital information management is a challenging task in the recent time. The NLP and text mining can help in managing these vast information-like similar documents can be clustered together for better indexing and searching. Topic modelling techniques can be applied to discover the associated topics with the text document collection. Various other text mining techniques can be used as per the requirements for better and efficient management of the digital textual information.
- Search Engines Optimization—Topic modelling, part-of-speech tagging, and other techniques can help in identifying relevance of given query term with the large amount of content to be scanned by the search engines for better information retrieval. The NLP and text mining techniques can help in optimizing the performance of search engines results.
- Web Analytics—Classifying and managing web pages from the large-scale applications such as Wikipedia is a tedious task. Text mining and natural language processing technologies help in proper management of these large collections of web documents by automatically categorizing it and generating useful topics for these documents.

EXERCISES

1. Estimate the size of vocabulary with 1000 tokens using Heap's law. Assume $k = 50$ and $b = 0.49$.
2. Calculate the cosine similarity between the following two sentences after applying the necessary pre-processing steps such stopping and stemming:

   S_1: AI and Data Science are the trending technologies.

   S_2: Machine Learning is a key component of Data Science technologies.
3. Create the Term-Document matrix (TDM) representation for the following three sentence:

   S_1: AI and Data Science are the trending technologies.

   S_2: Machine Learning is a key component of Data Science technologies.

S_3: Deep Learning is an advanced Data Science technology.

S_4: Without Data Science it is impossible to imagine about AI.

4. In your opinion, which of the NER (Named Entity Recognition) technique is better? Explain the reason behind it.
5. How document clustering techniques can help in building a recommendation system?
6. How coherence and perplexity parameters evaluate the topic modelling models?

MULTIPLE CHOICE QUESTIONS

1. What is the difference between the stemming and lemmatization in term of text pre-processing?
   (a) Both stemming and lemmatization perform the same task.
   (b) Stemming removes the useless words whereas the lemmatization transforms the word into its root form.
   (c) Stemming transforms the text data into vector representation whereas lemmatization transforms the word into its root form.
   (d) Stemming removes the prefixes and suffixes from words and convert it to the raw form whereas the lemmatization transforms the word into its root form.
2. What does Heap's law states about the text corpus size in context to natural language processing and text data analysis?
   (a) It states that the size of vocabulary increases with a faster rate of increase of the text corpus.
   (b) It states that the size of vocabulary increases with a slower rate of increase of the text corpus.
   (c) It states that there is no relationship between the size of vocabulary and the size of the text corpus.
   (d) It states that the size of vocabulary is inversely proportionate to the size of the text corpus.
3. What is the difference between POS tagging and NER (named entity recognition) (multiple answers are correct)?
   (a) The POS tagging works at the word level whereas NER works at phrase level.
   (b) The POS tagging identifies the syntactic relationship whereas NER tagging identifies the entities related to semanticity.
   (c) The POS tagging identifies the most relevant part of the text for analysis whereas NER identifies the known entities like name or place, etc.
   (d) Both POS tagging and NER are essential operations for any kind of text analysis.
4. In which of the following NER techniques the predefined patterns, and regular expressions are used to identify named entities?
   (a) Machine Learning-based Techniques
   (b) Dictionary or Lookup-based Approaches
   (c) Rule-based Approaches
   (d) Transfer Learning-based Techniques
5. The Viterbi algorithm for POS tagging is based on which algorithm design approach?
   (a) Divide and Conquer (b) Dynamic Programming
   (c) Greedy Approach (d) Branch and Bound.
6. In which of the sentiment analysis approach focuses on identifying the word indicating the polarity of the sentences?
   (a) Machine Learning Approach (b) Deep Learning Approach
   (c) Lexicon-based Approach (d) Transfer Learning Approach.
7. The opinion mining technique is most closely related to which of the following technologies?
   (a) POS Tagging (b) Named Entity Recognition
   (c) Text Classification (d) Sentiment Analysis

8. What is the purpose of topic modeling in text data analysis?
   (a) To categorize the text documents.
   (b) To perform sentiment analysis.
   (c) To generate appropriate topics for the given text collection.
   (d) To summarize a text document.
9. The primary difference between the Latent Dirichlet Allocation (LDA) and Non-negative Matrix Factorization (NMF) techniques is:
   (a) The LDA technique is a matrix factorization technique whereas the NMF technique is probability distribution technique.
   (b) The LDA technique uses random sampling whereas the NMF technique uses Gibbs sampling.
   (c) The LDA technique indicates topic weights whereas the NMF technique does not indicate any topic weights.
   (d) The LDA technique is probability distribution technique whereas the NMF technique is matrix factorization technique.
10. Which of the following evaluation parameters of topic modeling focuses more on the unseen data which is not covered during the training phase?
    (a) U-Mass Coherence (b) Perplexity
    (c) UCI Coherence (d) Log Likelihood Coherence.
11. Which of the following is NOT a method of abstractive text summarization?
    (a) Latent Semantic Analysis
    (b) Seq2Seq
    (c) PointerGenerator
    (d) Reinforcement Learning-based Summarizer
12. Which of the following is NOT a method of extractive text summarization?
    (a) Latent Semantic Analysis (b) Seq2Seq
    (c) LexRank (d) Cluster-based summarization.

For questions 13 to 17, suppose the following text sentences are given:

S_1: I am reading a book on Data Science.
S_2: I like reading.
S_3: Data Science is a popular topic.

For answering the following questions, please apply standard text pre-processing techniques such as stopping, stemming, etc.

13. The total number of tokens generated for the above text collection of sentences is:
    (a) 5 (b) 6
    (c) 7 (d) 8
14. The vector representation for second sentence is:
    (a) 1100110 (b) 0010100
    (c) 0101011 (d) 0100010
15. The TF (Term Frequency) of term "read" in sentence S_2 is:
    (a) 0.33 (b) 0.50
    (c) 0.67 (d) 0.80
16. The TF-IDF (Term Frequency – Inverse Document Frequency) of term "science" for sentence S_3 is:
    (a) 0.58 (b) 0.145
    (c) 0.40 (d) 0.25

17. The cosine similarity between the sentences S_1, and S_3 is:

(a) 0.35 (b) 0.5
(c) 0.75 (d) 0

18. The Rouge score is the best evaluation parameter for text ____________, whereas Bleu score is best evaluation parameter for text ________.

(a) Translation, Summarization (b) Summarization, Classification
(c) Classification, Translation (d) Summarization, Translation

19. The BM25 similarity considers which of the following parameters to evaluate the similarity (multiple answers are correct)?

(a) Document Length Normalization (b) Inverse Document Frequency
(c) TF-IDF (d) Term Frequency

20. A word cloud does NOT provide the information about (multiple answers are correct):

(a) Context of a word in the document
(b) Frequency of a word in the document
(c) Relative importance of a word in the document
(d) The word with semantic similar with the words in the document

REFERENCES

[1] Nagwani, N. K. (2015), Summarizing large text collection using topic modelling and clustering based on MapReduce framework, *Journal of Big Data*, *2*(1), p. 6.
[2] http://web.stanford.edu/class/cs276/
[3] https://www.baeldung.com/cs/topic-modeling-coherence-score
[4] https://qpleple.com/perplexity-to-evaluate-topic-models/
[5] https://mimno.infosci.cornell.edu/nips2013ws/nips2013tm_submission_7.pdf

ANSWER KEY

1. (d) **2.** (b) **3.** (a) and (b) **4.** (c) **5.** (b) **6.** (c) **7.** (d) **8.** (c)
9. (d) **10.** (b) **11.** (a) **12.** (b) **13.** (c) **14.** (b) **15.** (b) **16.** (a) **17.** (b)
18. (d) **19.** (a) and (d) **20.** (a) and (d)

20 Stream Data

Introduction

A stream is the ordered (sequenced) tuple representing the continuous and rapid flow of the data over the period of time. A stream data can be mathematically represented as $s = \{x_1, x_2, x_3, \ldots, x_m\}$, where x_i indicates the element at i^{th} time and $\text{time}(x_i) < \text{time}(x_{i+1})$ or in other words x_{i+1} is the more recent data element as compared to x_i. The non-streamed (ordinary) data is generally available as whole for any kind of processing, whereas the streamed data is available as flow data over of the period of time. So, it is practically difficult for the computers to store the streamed data for processing as computers have limited storage. Moreover, the other major problem with the streamed data is, as one cannot store the data, all the processing and analysis can be carried out in the single pass only unlike the ordinary way of analysis where multiple pass of data is carried out. Hence, stream data analysis algorithms are generally single pass algorithms, where data scanning is carried out once for identifying any pattern from the data. The data from the streamed data is fetched as per the requirement of the analysis so most of the stream mining algorithms are ad-hoc queries driven, i.e., the way of accessing and processing the data is not always the same rather it is changed as per the requirement of the different kind of pattern to be mined. Example of streamed data includes Twitter likes, YouTube video data, share market data, and the data captured and transmitted by various sensors deployed for different purposes like weather forecasting, etc.

20.1 GENERAL STREAM PROCESSING MODEL

A general stream processing model is presented in Figure 20.1. As discussed, the stream is a continuous flow of data so it needs to be processed in the single pass and the working storage is limited (as the complete stream cannot be stored entirely). Important and fruitful information from stream is captured and stored in the limited working storage for analysis. The historical useful stream information is stored and kept in archival storage, whereas the unwanted (not relevant) information is discarded. Ad-hoc queries are applied on the limited working storage to extract the useful knowledge and patterns from the streams. Most of the stream algorithms are designed in such a way that only one scan of stream data is sufficient for discovery of knowledge and useful patterns from the stream data.

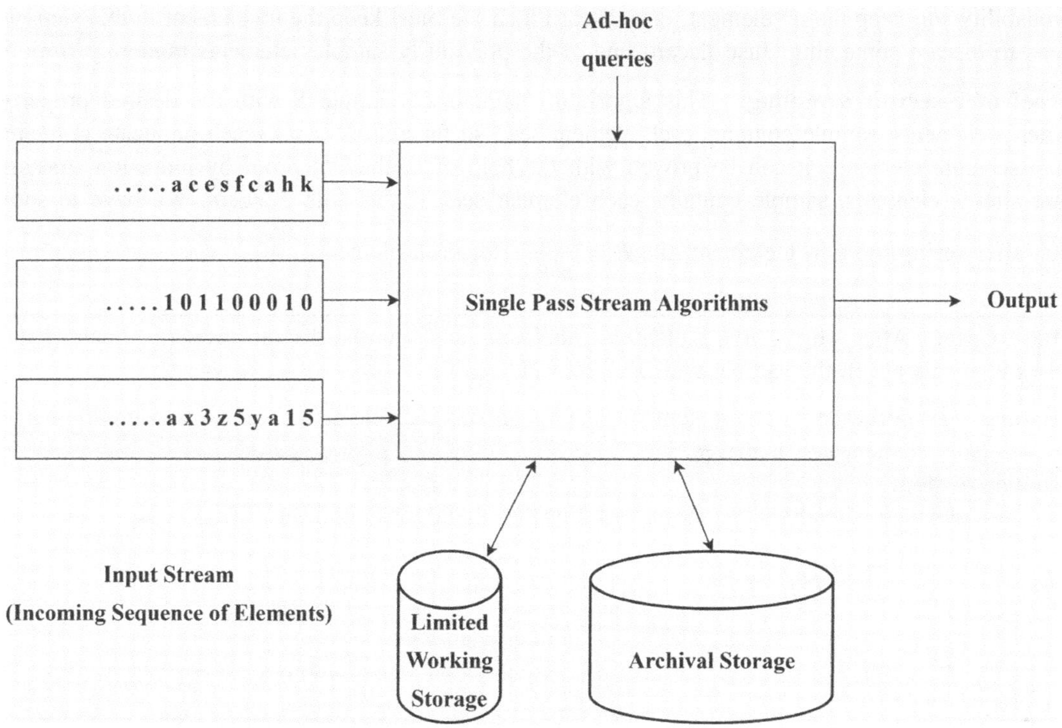

FIGURE 20.1 A General Stream Processing Model.

20.2 SAMPLING TECHNIQUES

As the volume of data for streamed data is very high, for effective time-bound analysis suitable data from the stream should be selected. Sampling techniques play an important role in choosing and selecting appropriate subsets of the data from the streamed data.

20.2.1 Reservoir Sampling

Reservoir sampling is a popular stream data sampling technique. It is a random sampling technique in which the samples from stream data are selected randomly. In reservoir sampling, a representative reservoir space is maintained for randomly selected samples from the stream. There are two variants of the reservoir sampling techniques in stream sampling:

(a) **Biased:** In biased reservoir sampling some data points are favoured for being selected as a sample. This biasedness is problem specific and for giving priority to some specific type of data from the pattern discovery point of view.
(b) **Unbiased:** The other very common variant of reservoir sampling technique is unbiased reservoir sampling in which selection of samples from all data points is considered with equal probability. Most of the common stream mining tasks utilize the unbiased variant of reservoir sampling for extracting useful patterns from the stream data.

The reservoir sampling technique works as follows. Initially, store all the first s elements of the stream to S. Suppose we have seen $n-1$ elements, and now the nth element arrives ($n > s$), with probability s/n, keep the nth element, else discard it. If we must keep the nth element in this step, we need to discard something. Just discard one of the previously samples elements randomly from S.

Proof of reservoir sampling: This algorithm maintains a sample S with the desired property: After n elements, sample contains each element seen so far with $P = s/n$ (each duplicate is treated as a separate element). It can be proved with the help of method of proof by induction. Assume that after n elements, sample contains each element seen so far with $P = s/n$. We have to show that after seeing the $n + 1$ element, the $P = \frac{s}{n+1}$ for each element.

Base Case: After we see $n = s$ elements, the sample S, has the desired property. Each of the $n=s$ elements are in the sample with $P = s/s = 1$

Inductive Hypothesis: After n elements, the S_n contains each element i seen so far with $P\left[i \in S_n\right]$ = s/n. Now element $n + 1$ arrives.

Inductive step:

For elements already in S_n, the probability that the algorithms keep it in S_{n+1} is:

$$P\left[i \in S_{n+1} | i \in S_n\right] = \left(1 - \frac{s}{n+1}\right) + \left(\frac{s}{n+1}\right)\left(\frac{s-1}{s}\right) = \frac{n}{n+1}$$

$$P\left[i \in S_{n+1}\right] = P\left[i \in S_n\right].P\left[i \in S_{n+1} | i \in S_n\right] = \frac{s}{n}.\frac{n}{n+1} = \frac{s}{n+1} \quad \{i \in S_{n+1}\} \subset \{i \in S_n\}$$

20.2.2 Sliding Window

A useful model of stream processing is that queries are about a ***window*** of length N—the N most recent elements received. The elements present in the window are selected as the stream samples for identification of patterns from the stream data. Sliding window sampling technique is useful in the case when patterns are expected to be identified in most recent items present in the stream.

Interesting case: N is so large that the data cannot be stored in memory, or even on disk or, there are so many streams that windows for all cannot be stored.

Example case study in e-commerce site: Suppose we wanted to keep track of sales of products in the e-commerce site like Amazon. In order to achieve this, for every product $\boldsymbol{X}$ we keep 0/1 stream of whether that product was sold in the $\boldsymbol{n}^{\text{th}}$ transaction. We want to answer queries, how many times have we sold $\boldsymbol{X}$ in the last $\boldsymbol{k}$ sales.

Given a stream of items/symbols, find the most frequent item in the sliding window. In the given example, $N = 5$ (the size of the window is 5).

d s f h s j l d g h j s [d g f a w] e u h f i w e y t w o u y p

d s f h s j l d g h j s d [g f a w e] u h f i w e y t w o u y p

d s f h s j l d g h j s d g [f a w e u] h f i w e y t w o u y p

d s f h s j l d g h j s d g f [a w e u h] f i w e y t w o u y p

← Previous Values Future Values →

Counting bits problem: Another common use of window sampling technique is counting the number of bits in the recent part of stream. Given a stream of **0**s and **1**s (for each item), suppose we wanted to estimate, how many 1's are in the last k bits? Where $\boldsymbol{k} \leq \boldsymbol{N}$.

0 1 0 0 1 1 1 0 0 1 0 1 0 1 0 0 0 1 1 | 0 1 1 1 0 |

← Previous Values Future Values →

One of the obvious solutions is to store the most recent N bits and when a new bit comes in, discard the $N + 1^{st}$ bit. For counting bits problems, the exact answer cannot be estimated without storing the entire window. The real problem is for stream data the storing of large numbers of bits is not affordable for example, when $N = 1$ billion. But an approximate answer is acceptable for the large size stream. So approximate numbers of 1's can be counted easily with the help of window-based sampling techniques.

20.2.3 Time Decayed Sampling

In time decayed sampling technique, higher priority is given to the most recent data as compared to the older data. This is suitable for the cases particularly when the importance of data reduces over time. Time decayed sampling focuses on the most up-to-date information for pattern identification. The probability function of selecting the samples is designed in such a way that for older data the probability decay is more. It is very adaptable for the changing trends in the streamed data where knowledge discovery is mainly focused on the recent data. The time decayed sampling is useful in many applications like stock market analysis, social media trend identification, etc.

20.2.4 Chain Sampling

Chain sampling is a special type of stream sampling technique, where a sequence or chains of the data items are sampled together unlike a single data point considered in the other sampling techniques. Consecutive data points in the same sequence of arrival in stream are selected as samples in this technique to preserve the order of arrival of the elements in the stream. The length of each chain is predetermined and kept constant in the sampling process. Chain sampling is useful in identifying local patterns and trends in the streamed data. Chain sampling provides reduced variability of data in a stream, which could be helpful for some of the specific applications in stream data analysis.

20.2.5 StreamSamp Sampling

StreamSamp is another type of reservoir sampling technique in which the samples are selected from the summary of the window (consisting of a fixed number of stream elements). This summary is generated from any suitable data summarization algorithm. The summarized data reduces the volume of stream data drastically for faster decision-making on-stream data. Summarized stream data may be useful in various applications such as, healthcare monitoring, network monitoring, financial data analysis, and Internet of Things (IoT)-based applications.

20.2.6 Histogram Sampling

In histogram sampling technique, a summary of distribution of stream elements are computed and stored in histograms. The computed histograms are selected as samples for analyzing the stream data. Histogram sampling is useful for the scenarios where the distribution of the stream data elements is sufficient to analyze the stream data. Binning techniques are utilized for computation of histograms from the stream data and the number of bins is kept constant during the analysis. A few common applications of histogram sampling techniques are financial data analysis, network traffic analysis, and resource management in cloud computing where the summary of data distribution is an important measure of data analysis.

20.2.7 Priority Sampling

It is a random sampling technique with weightage items. The total weight of the arbitrary items is calculated and then sum is calculated for selecting the samples from the streamed data. The maximum calculated weight is selected for taking the samples from the streamed data. The weight of different items is assigned using some criteria. The choice of criteria depends on the type of analysis task. Priority sampling is useful in many applications. For example, in environmental data analysis where data comes from various sensors deployed, the priority sampling technique focuses on the critical parameters affecting the environment. In social media analysis, priority sampling may focus on some specific trending topics or influential users for extracting trending knowledge. Another application is, in health care monitoring systems, critical health parameters may be prioritized for analysis as compared to the other parameters.

20.3 STREAM PROCESSING TECHNIQUES

There are several stream processing tasks which help in understanding and analyzing streamed data. Counting the frequency of the data elements and identification of concept drifts are two important operations in processing of the data. As most of the data analysis tasks require the counting of the individual elements present in the stream so frequency counting is an essential operation in stream processing. At the same time, concept drift detection techniques identify the changes in the sequence of streamed data so that helps in identifying the useful patterns from the stream. In this section both of these operations along with the supporting parameters of stream processing are discussed.

20.3.1 Important Properties

A stream is characterized using some basic properties. Some commonly used properties are length of the stream, frequency moments of the stream, and entropy.

Length of the stream: The length of the stream at any moment is calculated using the following equation:

$$L = \sum_{i=1}^{m} f_i$$

Estimating frequency moments: The frequency moments of the data stream is calculated using the following equation:

$$F_K = \sum_{i=1}^{m} f_i^K$$

Estimating entropy: Entropy refers to the amount of randomness in the collection of data. In the case of streamed data, it is measured using the following equation:

$$H = -\sum_{i=1}^{m} \frac{f_i}{L} \log_2 \left(\frac{f_i}{L} \right)$$

Where L indicates the length of the stream, and f_i indicates the frequency moment of the ith data element in the stream.

20.3.2 Counting Distinct Elements and Counting 1's in Stream

Counting distinct elements and counting 1's in stream are two important problems in stream processing which have a plethora of applications in analysis of streamed data. In this section, foundations, and common techniques of both of these problems are discussed and explained.

Counting distinct elements in stream: It is also known as cardinality estimation problem in a given stream. Suppose we have been given any stream $x_1, x_2, x_3, \ldots, x_K$ consisting of n-distinct elements $\left|\{x_1, x_2, x_3, \ldots, x_K\}\right| = \{e_1, e_2, e_3, \ldots, e_N\}$. Then N is the cardinality of the stream or in other words there are N distinct elements present in the stream. The counting distinct elements or cardinality estimation problem is defined as below:

$$D = \left|\{i \mid f_i \neq 0\}\right|$$

Where D indicates the cardinality of all the stream elements i, such that frequency of the element is not zero, i.e., $f_i \neq 0$.

Example: Let the stream is $x_1, x_2, x_1, x_3, x_4, x_2, x_4, x_1, x_3$ be the stream then $N = \{\left|\{x_1, x_2, x_3, x_4\}\right|\}$ – 4.

The variation of counting distinct element problem in stream is weighted count distinct problem, in which weights are assigned to each element of the stream. For example, in the below given stream weights are shown in the brackets for each element.

$$x_1(3), x_2(2), x_3(4), x_4(1), x_1(3), x_3(4), x_2(2), x_1(3)$$

$$e_1 = x_1, e_2 = x_2, e_3 = x_3, e_4 = x_4$$

$$w_1 = 3, w_2 = 2, w_3 = 4, w_4 = 1$$

The sum of weight in weighted count distinct problem is calculated as below:

$$\sum_{j=1}^{N} w_j = w_1 + w_2 + w_3 + w_4 = 3 + 2 + 4 + 1 = 10$$

There are two types of counting algorithms based on stream windows (stream samples are taken from windows sampling techniques). These techniques are:

1. Lossy counting—It identifies elements in a data stream whose frequency count exceeds a user given threshold.
2. Sticky sampling—It is technique for counting (probabilistic) the elements where higher weights are associated with some specific elements of stream. The weights may be assigned using some problem specific criteria.

Naïve approach to distinct counting—Suppose we need an approximate estimate of how many distinct users saw a news clip? In general, for solving this problem we write the database query as, "***select count(distinct user) from very_large_stream***". The execution (Naïve) way of doing this is, insert each user into a hash table and then compute the number of keys in the table. Cost estimation needs to be calculated as follows:

Cost:
- Let N = 1 million, 64 bits/user
- Hash table size per website/issue: 16 MB
- 100 websites/issues/day ⇒ 1.6 GB/day
- Over 1 month ⇒ 50 GB/month
- With dimension breakdowns (user demographics), much higher costs

Another concern for solving the problem of counting distinct problems is sometimes uniform sampling will be misleading, if some user watched it many times, then that will lead to wrong estimation. Another real challenge is, what if we do not have space to maintain the set of elements seen so far? In this scenario, estimate the count in an unbiased way (E[estimate]=actual) and accept that the count may have a little error, but limit the probability that the error is large. Most of the stream processing algorithms follows this concept.

20.3.3 DGIM Algorithm

DGIM algorithm is used to count approximate 1's in a given stream. DGIM algorithm is given by Datar, Gionis, Indyk, and Motwani and is used for counting ones in a window. Algorithm DGIM is also known as Data Generalized Inverted Indexing Method. The complexity of the algorithm is $O\left(\log^2 N\right)$ with error is not more than 50%. The DGIM algorithm divides the stream into buckets of different size (power of 2), and each bucket maintains a count the number of 1's in it. The DGIM algorithm follows the six basic rules in a given stream window for count 1's. The six rules are:

1. The right most side of the bucket should always be 1.
2. Every position with a 1 is in some bucket.
3. No position is in more than one bucket.
4. There should be a maximum of 2 buckets of the same size.
5. The size of the bucket should be the power of 2, i.e., 2^K.
6. The bucket size should not decrease while moving towards the left direction.

To estimate the number of 1's in the most recent N bits:

1. Sum the sizes of all the buckets but the last size, i.e., number of 1's in the bucket
2. Add half of the size of the last bucket.

Example: Let us assume that given stream of bits is:

. . . 1 0 1 0 1 1 1 0 0 0 1 0 1 0 1 1 . . .

Then, as per the DGIM algorithm the buckets will be created for different sizes. One such way of creation of buckets is:

1 0 1 0 1 1 1 0 0 0 1 0 1 0 1 1

The first bucket is created with one 1 in it, then second bucket is created using two 1's, third bucket is created using three 1's, now only three 1's are left so last bucket is also consisting of three 1's.

Estimating the number of 1's in the example stream is = size of all buckets except the last + half of the size of the last bucket.

So, the number of ones is = $1+2+3+\frac{3}{2}=7.5 \cong 8$ (approximately).

Another way by which the buckets can be created is:

1 0 1 0 1 1 1 0 0 0 1 0 1 0 1 1

The first and second bucket of only one 1 is created, then third and fourth bucket is consisting of two 1's and fifth bucket is consisting of three 1's.

So, the number of 1's using this bucketing is = $1+1+2+2+\frac{3}{2}=7.5 \cong 8$ (approximately)

Just like with the above two cases buckets can be created using the rules mentioned in the DGIM algorithm and then number of 1's are estimated for a given stream of bits. Whenever new data comes into the data stream the buckets are again rearranged as per the DGIM algorithm and estimation if updated. If the newly entered data in stream is 0 then there is no change, and no update is required in the buckets as the buckets are only driven by the 1's and not the 0's. When the new stream data arrives, and if the new stream data arrives as 1, and there is only one bucket with size 1, then we need to create another bucket for the newly arrived data 1. If two buckets exist with the size 1, then we need to look forward to the buckets having two 1's.

The DGIM algorithm offers a maximum of 50% error rate, let us see formal proof of this now.

Error Bound: Proof

1. Suppose the last bucket has size 2^r.
2. Then by assuming 2^{r-1} (i.e., half) of its **1s** are within the last bucket (but out of last-N bits), we make an error of at most $\pm 2^{r-1}-1$.
3. Since there is at least one bucket of each of the sizes less than 2^r, the true sum is at least $\mathbf{1 + 2 + 4 + ... + 2^{r-1} = 2^r - 1}$.

Thus, error at most **50%** $\mathbf{[= 2^{r-1}/2^r > (2^{r-1})/(2^r - 1)]}$

Further Reducing the Error: Is there any way of reducing the error rate to less than 50%? The answer to this question is Yes! By applying some logic, the error rate can be reduced. For example, instead of maintaining **1** or **2** of each size bucket, we allow either $\boldsymbol{r-1}$ or $\boldsymbol{r}$ buckets ($\boldsymbol{r > 2}$). Except for the largest size buckets, we can have any number between **1** and $\boldsymbol{r}$ of those. In this case, the **error is at most $\boldsymbol{O(1/r)}$.** By picking $\boldsymbol{r}$ appropriately, we can tradeoff between number of bits we store and the error.

The Extensions to general DGIM algorithm are counting 1's in Dynamic Window Size. This extension addresses the question, can we use the same trick to answer queries: **How many 1's in the last $\boldsymbol{k}$?** Where $\boldsymbol{k} < N$. For solving this problem, find earliest bucket **B** that at overlaps with $\boldsymbol{k}$, and number of **1s** is the **sum of sizes of more recent buckets + ½ size of B.** Another question arises is how can we handle the case where the stream is not bits, but integers, and we want the sum of the last k elements? This question is asked with another extension of DGIM algorithm namely,

sum of last *k* elements problem. In this problem, stream of positive integers is taken as input, and we want to estimate the sum of the last *k* elements. This problem has numerous applications, particularly in e-commerce for addressing queries like what is the average price of last ***k*** sales? The solution of sum of last *k* elements is shown below.

> ***Solution:***
>
> 1. **If you know all have at most *m* bits**
>   Treat ***m*** bits of each integer as a separate stream
>   Use DGIM to count **1s** in each integer/stream.
>
>   The sum is = $\sum_{i=0}^{m-1} c_i 2^i$
> 2. **Use buckets to keep partial sums**
>   Sum of elements in size *b* bucket is at most 2^b

20.3.4 Lossy Counting Algorithm

The Lossy Counting algorithm is used to estimate the approximate frequent items from a stream with controlled amount of error (ε). The algorithm estimates the approximate frequency of the data elements in a stream with user defined controlled amount of error (guarantee of the amount of error). The algorithm starts by defining the value of ε, i.e., the amount of error. Then by maintaining the counter the value of the counter is updated as per the presence of the elements in stream and frequency values of the elements is estimated. The Lossy Counting algorithm guarantees that the approximate value of the frequency of any element should not exceed the $\varepsilon \times N$, where N is the actual frequency of a data element in the stream.

20.3.5 A Hashing-based Approach

In Hashing-based approaches of estimating the number of distinct elements in a stream, hash functions are utilized to map the unique elements into the hash values. Then by utilizing the computed hash values and by performing logical operations, approximation of counting distinct values is carried out. There are three important algorithms under the category of hashing-based approaches for estimating the number of distinct elements in the stream. These algorithms are Bitmap algorithm, Flajolet Martin algorithm, and HyperLogLog algorithm. These algorithms are briefly discussed in this section.

Bitmap algorithm

In Bitmap algorithm, first we initialize a bitmap (array of bits) of size B with 0 at all the positions. Then by applying a suitable hash function map all the stream elements to the bitmap. For each value from stream data, apply the hash function and mark the calculated value as 1 in the bitmap. Count the number of 1's in the bitmap, store it in a variable *c*. Then estimate the number of distinct items using the formula $B \times \ln\left(\frac{B}{B-c}\right)$. An example of mapping the stream elements to hash values is shown in Figure 20.2.

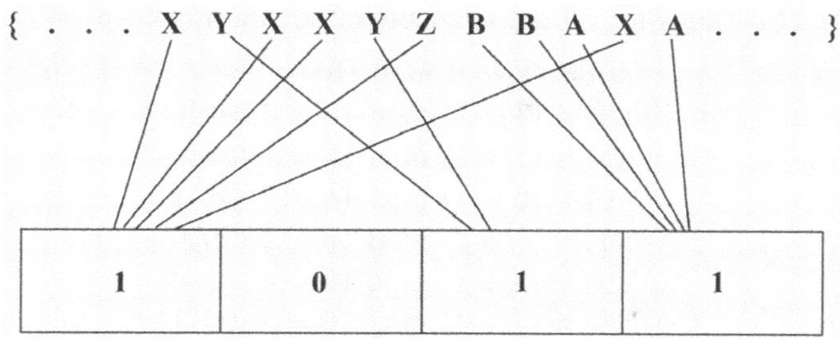

FIGURE 20.2 Mapping Stream Elements to Hash Values.

For the given example, the approximate number of distinct values are = $4 \times \ln\left(\frac{4}{1}\right) = 5.55 \approx 6.$

Flajolet martin algorithm

Flajolet Martin algorithm is another algorithm used for estimating the approximate number of unique elements in a large collection of data such as stream in single pass using small storage. The algorithm works as follows. Given hash function $hash(x) = \left[0; 2^L - 1\right]$, hash values are calculated for given input stream element x. The output generated from the hash function is the set of integers from 0 to $2^L - 1$. For generated output the equivalent binary string of length L is computed. The value of trailing zero is computed from the binary representation as $bit(y, k)$, k^{th} bit of binary representation of y. Out of all the trailing positions maximum value $\boldsymbol{R}$ is selected. The number of distinct elements is estimated as $\boldsymbol{2^R}$. In the original proposed algorithm, the estimated number of distinct elements are divided by a parameter $\varphi \approx 0.77351$, called the correction factor. For simpler calculations, this division is skipped sometimes.

Working of the algorithm:

1. Initialize a bit-vector *BITMAP* to length L contains all 0.
2. For each element x in M
   (a) Calculate the index $i = p(hash(x))$
   (b) Set $BITMAP[i] = 1$
3. Let R denote the smallest index i such that $BITMAP[i] = 0$
4. Estimate the cardinality of M as $2^R/\varphi$, where $\varphi \approx 0.77351$ is called the correction factor.

Applications: The Flajolet Martin algorithm is used for numerous applications of stream mining tasks such as Document comparison and clustering, Collaborative filtering, Spam detection, and Fraud detection.

Drawback: The main drawback of the algorithm is one random occurrence of high frequency 0 prefix from hashing function will result in bad estimation. To avoid this, use multiple hash functions, estimate, and average the results.

Example: Let's assume that the given stream of integer numbers is 3, 5, 6, 1, 3, 2, 1, 4, 6, 4 in which we have to count distinct elements. The given hash functions are (a) $h(x) = (x + 1) \bmod 16$, and (b) $h(x) = (2x + 5) \bmod 16$, then first of all we need to compute the hash values for all the elements of stream.

(a) compute the has values for all the elements of stream as:

$$h(x) = (x + 1) \bmod 16$$
$$h(3) = (3 + 1) \bmod 16 = 4\ (0100)$$
$$h(5) = (5 + 1) \bmod 16 = 5\ (0101)$$
$$h(6) = (6 + 1) \bmod 16 = 7\ (0111)$$
$$h(1) = (1 + 1) \bmod 16 = 2\ (0010)$$
$$h(3) = (3 + 1) \bmod 16 = 4\ (0100)$$
$$h(2) = (2 + 1) \bmod 16 = 3\ (0011)$$
$$h(1) = (1 + 1) \bmod 16 = 2\ (0010)$$
$$h(4) = (4 + 1) \bmod 16 = 5\ (0101)$$
$$h(6) = (6 + 1) \bmod 16 = 7\ (0111)$$
$$h(4) = (4 + 1) \bmod 16 = 5\ (0101)$$

The trailing zeros in the computed hash functions are {2, 0, 0, 1, 2, 0, 1, 0, 0, 0}
The maximum value is 2.

So, the number of distinct elements are $2^R = 2^2 = 4$.

(b) Solve part (b)

HyperLogLog algorithm

The HyperLogLog (HLL) algorithm also summarizes the multisets of items available in the streamed data to count the approximate unique elements from the stream. The HLL algorithm works in three steps. The first step is to initialize all the hash functions and outputs to 0. In the second step, a hash function is applied to each element. From the computed hash values, position of leading 0's are calculated for each element. After counting the number of leading 0's in hash binary representation, by applying the formula of HLL algorithm the cardinality is estimated. In HyperLogLog algorithm the margin of error is about 2%. The algorithm is based on counting the number of leading 0's in objects hash binary representation.

$$\text{The cardinality is estimating by } m \times \frac{\text{Harmonic Mean}\left(2^{L_i}\right)}{\varphi}$$

In the formula, φ is the correction factor and m are the number of hash functions/registers (or buckets). The HyperLogLog algorithm is the extension of LogLog algorithm. The LogLog algorithm is similar to the HyperLogLog algorithm but the formula for estimating the set cardinality of stream is different. The HyperLogLog function uses harmonic mean for estimating the set cardinality. The harmonic mean is calculated using the following formula:

$$\text{Harmonic Mean}(a, b, c\ldots) = \frac{n}{\frac{1}{a}+\frac{1}{b}+\frac{1}{c}+\ldots}$$

Example, harmonic mean of (1, 2, 4) is $= \dfrac{3}{\frac{1}{1}+\frac{1}{2}+\frac{1}{4}} = 1.714.$

Example of LogLog and HyperLogLog algorithm for estimating set cardinality

Suppose there are 4 buckets (or hash functions) so $m = 4$. These hash functions transform the input values and arrange the hash values in the binary bit representation as shown below.

Hash(N1) = 10|0101

2nd Bucket   1 Leading 0

Hash(N2) = 01|0011

Hash(N3) = 00|1111

Hash(N4) = 11|0101

$$\text{Average length of longest leading zero} = \frac{(L_1 + L_2 + \ldots + L_m)}{m} = \frac{0+2+1+1}{4} = 1$$

$$\text{The general estimation is given by} = m \times 2^{\frac{(L_1+L_2+\ldots+L_m)}{m}} = 4 \times 2^1 = 8$$

The cardinality estimation using the LogLog algorithm is given by:

$$\text{Cardinality}_{\text{LogLog}} = m \times \frac{2^{\frac{(L_1+L_2+\ldots+L_m)}{m}}}{\phi} = 4 \times \frac{2^1}{0.77} = 10.38 \approx 10$$

Where ϕ is correction factor $\phi \approx 0.77$.

The cardinality estimation using the HyperLogLog algorithm is given by:

$$m \times \frac{\text{Harmonic Mean}\left(2^{L_i}\right)}{\varphi}$$

$$\text{Harmonic Mean}\left(2^{L_i}\right) = \frac{4}{\frac{1}{2^0} + \frac{1}{2^2} + \frac{1}{2^1} + \frac{1}{2^1}} = 1.7778$$

$$\text{Cardinality}_{\text{HyperLogLog}} = 4 \times \frac{1.778}{0.77} = 9.236 \approx 9$$

So, there is a slight difference in estimating the set cardinalities using LogLog and HyperLogLog algorithms. In general, the HLL algorithm is popularly used as compared to the LogLog algorithm as it is an advanced version of LogLog algorithm only.

20.3.6 Sketch-based Algorithm

Sketch-based algorithms use the probabilistic data structures known as sketches for analyzing the streams. Three sketch-based algorithms namely, KMV (K Minimum Value), MG, and Count-Min sketch algorithms are discussed in this section for estimating the set cardinality (i.e., number of distinct elements) in a stream.

KMV (K Minimum Values) for set cardinality using KMV Sketch

The KVM algorithm is used for estimating set cardinality and the approximate k smallest values in a given stream. The summary of KVM algorithm is also used to identify the duplicate items from the streamed data. The KMV algorithm uses a suitable hash function. The output of the selected hash function is normalized in the range of 0 to 1, i.e., $[0\ldots1]$. In order to estimate the cardinality of the stream, average spacing in the computed hash space is calculated. From the hashing space itself, the k minimum values can be identified and separated from the stream data. The working of the KMV algorithm is summarized below.

Data (sequence of items): $x_1, x_2, x_3, \ldots, x_t$

Universal hash function '*h*': $x_i \rightarrow Z_i \sim \text{Uniform}(0, 1)$

- Results in ***N*** distinct values (e.g., 2^{32} or 2^{64})
- Distribution is known and depends only on the desired value N

Summary: Maintain k minimum values of $h(x_k)$;

$$Z_1 \leq Z_2 \leq Z_3 \ldots \leq Z_k$$

Estimate: $N_{hat} = \dfrac{k-1}{Z_k}$

Error: std dev $\sigma(N_{hat}) = \dfrac{N_{hat}}{\sqrt{k-2}}$

From the computed hash space, the minimum values are identified and separated as shown below in Figure 20.3.

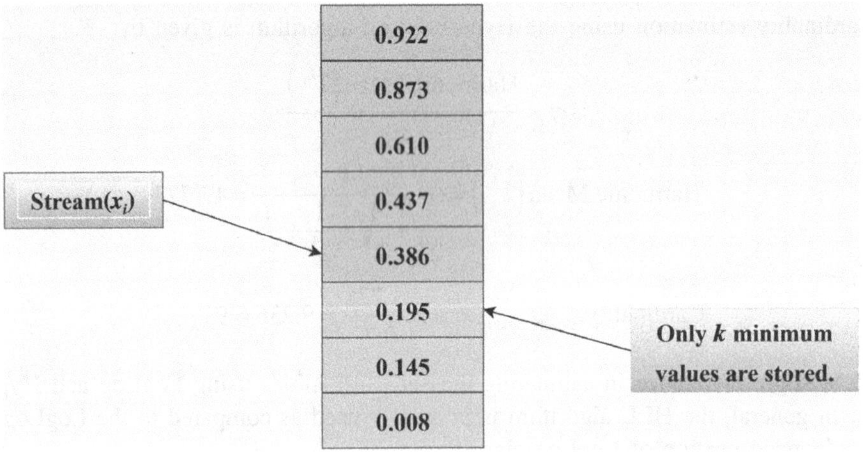

FIGURE 20.3 Working of KMV Sketch Algorithm.

Hash function maps the element to any of the n values with equal probability. After d items, the spacing between them is roughly $1/d$. The value of the minimum is close to $1/d$. Thus, estimate of $d = 1/(\text{min})$. But there may be a lot of variation in this. We may get a small value, which may disturb the estimate. One variation is to keep many values (k), and the estimate is $k/(k^{\text{th}}$ minimum). This can be useful because we have computed the minimum, hence lost one degree of freedom. Furthermore, to make it unbiased, we have to use $\dfrac{k-1}{Z_k}$ for calculating minimum.

Sometimes, we need an alternative approach for calculating set cardinality or getting the maximum frequent elements in a stream (rather than the case where we have calculated minimum using KMV). For instance, while developing applications like detection of DDoS attack in a network destination, we need to analyze the network traffic (packet streams) by considering the heaviest users, top websites, most-significant failure reasons, etc. So, out of the packet stream we need to discover the maximum frequent packet information rather than minimum. This leads to the set of problems where, given a stream of (key, increment) pairs, we need to find the keys with the largest total sums. In other words, we need to identify top K, or most frequent items in a given stream. For addressing these types of situations following alternative sketch algorithms are used:

- **MG and Space Saving techniques:** Maintain only fixed number of bins and delete infrequent items.
- **Count Min:** Hash into multiple bins and report the minimum value when queried.

Both of the above sketch algorithms are now discussed in brief.

MG Sketch/Misra and Gries algorithm

The Misra and Gries (MG) algorithm is used to identify the frequent items in a given stream. This algorithm uses a counter to count the frequency of each element present in the stream and based on some predefined threshold value filters the elements having higher frequency than the threshold value. The filtered set of elements presents the frequent items in a data stream. The algorithm works in three stages. In the first stage a counter is initialized with 0. In the second stage, for each element it increments the counter value as per the availability of the elements in the stream. In the third stage, using threshold value, all the elements whose frequency (counter value) is greater than the threshold value are selected as output. Thus, the algorithm filters the frequent elements from a stream for further analysis of the stream, so less frequent elements are not considered and eliminated from the stream. The algorithm guarantees that, given parameter $\in$, stores $\frac{1}{\in}$ items and count/weights, it returns the count/weights are within $\in$ of the total count/weight, C, over all items. The algorithm works in two steps. In the first step, an empty table T is created and initialized with space $k = \frac{1}{\in}$. The second step is the update step, in which the elements are inserted or removed from the table as shown below.

> **If** $i \in T$, $c_i = c_i + 1$ (increment count)
> **Else** $T = T \cup \{i\}$; $c_i = 1$ (insert into the Table)
>
> **If** Size (T) > k:
> $\forall\ i \in T$, $c_i = c_i - 1$ (decrement counts)
>   If $c_i = 0$, $T = T \backslash i$ (remove i from the table)

The proof of error bound is shown below.

Error bound proof sketch:

(a) We decrement counts only when the table is full
(b) A decrement operation reduces each of the k counts by 1
(c) There are C total elements seen in the stream
(d) Maximum number of decrement operations possible: C/k
(e) Maximum error in the estimate: $C/k = C\in$
(f) Works extremely well when the distribution is skewed (e.g., Words in English, Pop of city)

Count Min Sketch

The Count Min Sketch is a popular probabilistic data structure used for frequency table of events in a stream of data. It uses multiple hash functions to estimate the set cardinality in a stream. Because of its computational simplicity it is widely used in recommender systems where input data is streamed.

Count min sketch is a probabilistic data structure which stores the frequencies of the stream elements. Let us assume that there are N elements in the stream, the count min sketch requires K different hash functions to map the element to a hash value and this hash value is utilized for updating the frequencies of the elements.

	$F(e_1)$	$F(e_2)$	...	...	...	(e_N)
$H_1(x)$						
$H_1(x)$						
...						
$H_K(x)$						

For each element the K hash values are computed, and frequencies are updated in the frequency table. In order to get the frequency of any element, we need to select minimum of K hash values for any element. The minimum value will give the frequency of the element.

For example, 4 hash functions with 10 different outcomes has the size of 4×10. In general, it is an $M \times N$ integer matrix. For estimating the cardinality, it checks the index of corresponding column and selects the minimum value out of it. The selected value indicates the probability of "exact count" or "overestimation". This algorithm never provides under estimation for any element, i.e., the estimate values are always equal to or greater than the cardinality of the elements.

The algorithm sometimes suffers with the problem of hash collisions, where the frequency of the elements will count (updated) to higher values due to similar hash values. To avoid this issue, it is always recommended to use the random and unique hash functions so that the collisions may be minimized in the CM sketch.

Example: Let us assume that there is a stream of integer numbers $S = \{1, 3, 4, 2, 7, 5, 1, 2, 3, 3, 4, 2, 2, 5, 6, 2, 1, 7, 2, 1\}$. And we are using 3 different hash functions: $\text{Hash}_1(x) = x \bmod 3$, $\text{Hash}_2(x) = x + 1 \bmod 4$, and $\text{Hash}_3(x) = 2x + 1 \bmod 5$.

We can compute the hash values of all the elements from stream as shown below.

	$\text{Hash}_1(x)$	**$\text{Hash}_2(x)$**	**$\text{Hash}_3(x)$**
	x mod 3	**$x + 1$ mod 4**	**$2x + 1$ mod 5**
1	1	2	3
2	2	3	0
3	0	0	2
4	1	1	4
5	2	2	1
6	0	3	3
7	1	0	0

Now, for all the elements present in the stream, we take one element at a time and update the count min sketch. The count min sketch is initialized with 0 (empty) values for all the possible hash values. As there are 5 different hash values calculated from the hash functions, so the initial CM sketch will be:

	0	1	2	3	4
$Hash_1(x)$					
$Hash_2(x)$					
$Hash_3(x)$					

The first element in the stream is 1, and hash values for the input 1 for three hash functions are 1, 2, and 3 respectively. So, for the first element 1 of the stream the CM-Sketch will be updated as below.

	0	1	2	3	4
$Hash_1(x)$		1			
$Hash_2(x)$			1		
$Hash_3(x)$				1	

The second element in the stream is 3, and hash values for the input 3 for three hash functions are 0, 0, and 2 respectively. So, for the second element 3 of the stream the CM-Sketch will be updated as below.

	0	1	2	3	4
$Hash_1(x)$	1	1			
$Hash_2(x)$	1		1		
$Hash_3(x)$			1	1	

Just like the processing of the first and second elements of streams as shown above, CM-Sketch will be updated for the entire stream. The updated CM-Sketch for the given example stream is shown below.

	0	1	2	3	4
$Hash_1(x)$	4	8	8		
$Hash_2(x)$	5	2	6	7	
$Hash_3(x)$	8	2	3	5	2

The computed CM-Sketch is utilized for estimating the frequency of any element of the stream. For example, suppose we wanted to estimate the counting frequency of 1 then the hash values of 1 using different hash functions are $Hash_1(1) = 1$, $Hash_2(1) = 2$, and $Hash_3(1) = 3$. Then we need to get the values from computed CM-Sketch for 1, 2, and 3 for different hash functions. The values for column 1, 2, and 3 for the three hash functions are 8, 6, and 5 respectively. Out of these values we need to pick the minimum value, Min {8, 6, 5} = 5. So, the frequency estimation of element 1 in the given stream is 5. Similarly, the estimates of counting the frequency of element 5 is 2, and frequency of element 7 is 5.

CM-Sketch will always return exact or more frequency count. The best choice of hash function will lead to best possible values of the frequency (nearby exact frequency count).

3.3.7 Testing Element Membership in Stream

Sometimes it is important to check whether the given element is a member of stream or not. Bloom Filter addresses this problem. It verifies the presence of any element in the given stream.

Bloom Filter

Bloom filter is used to test whether any given element belongs to the stream. It is probabilistic data structure based on hashing. Used to add elements to a set and test if an element is in set. Bloom filter uses an array of bits of size N as shown below where all elements are initialized to 0.

0	0	0	0	...	0	0	0	0	0
0	1	2	3	...				N-2	N-1

Bloom filter uses K-hash functions simultaneously, and the output of the hash function indicates the position to set in the bit array. Deletion of elements is not allowed in Bloom filter.

Example: Suppose given a stream of integer numbers and two hash functions $H_1(x) = x \bmod 10$, and $H_2(x) = x \bmod 3$. Let the first number of the stream is 17, so we need to calculate the hash values using two functions as shown below:

$$H_1(17) = 17 \bmod 10 = 7, \text{ and } H_2(17) = 17 \bmod 3 = 2$$

The calculated values are 7 and 2, so the 7th and 2nd positions are set to 1 for element 17.

0	0	1	0	0	0	0	1	0	0
0	1	2	3	4	5	6	7	8	9

Let the second number of the stream is 13, the calculate hash values are:

$$H_1(13) = 13 \bmod 10 = 3, \text{ and } H_2(13) = 13 \bmod 3 = 1$$

So, the position of 3rd place, and 1st place is set to 1 for element 13 in the bloom filter.

0	1	1	1	0	0	0	1	0	0
0	1	2	3	4	5	6	7	8	9

To check whether 17 is already present in the set, calculate $H_1(17)$ and $H_2(17)$ and if the calculated value positions are all 1 in the updated bit array, then the number is already present.

One of the key challenges with the Bloom's filtering approach is that sometimes due to hash collision problems the bits may be set incorrectly due to the similar hash values, that will lead to provide false information about presence of any element in the stream. Therefore, hash functions should be selected carefully.

20.4 ESTIMATING MOMENTS

Moment provides the shape and characteristics of probability distribution of a given collection of data points (here the data points belong to a stream). The zeroth moment is the individual data point itself. The first moment is mean, 2nd moment is variance, 3rd moment is skewness, and 4th moment is kurtosis of the set of data points belonging to the stream. For better understanding of the stream data distribution, moment estimation is required. In this section some basic idea of moment of stream along with a popular algorithm namely, **Alon Matis Szegedy algorithm** is discussed for estimating the second moment of stream.

Consider a stream $S = \{a_1, a_2, \ldots, a_m\}$ with elements from a domain $D = \{v_1, v_2, \ldots, v_n\}$. Let m_i denote the frequency of value v_i, i.e., the number of times v_i appears in S. The kth frequency moment of stream is defined as:

$$F_K = \sum_{i=1}^{m} m_i^{K}$$

Alon Matis Szegedy algorithm approximates F_2. The 2nd order moment is also known as "**surprise number**". Let us assume that the length of stream S is known, and its value is n. Then sample K positions from the n. The algorithm works as follows, for each sample, maintain element and its count X.element and X.count, where X.element refers to the element of the stream and X.count refers to the count of the element in the stream. From the selected K sample, for each element perform the following operations:

X.element = element in that position, X.count $\leftarrow 1$
If X.element reoccurs again X.count $\leftarrow$ X.count + 1

Once all the selected elements are covered then estimate the second moments as $n \times (2\text{X.count} - 1)$. Calculate the second moments of all the elements and then find the average value to represent the second moments of the stream.

Example (Alon Matis Szegedy algorithm): Let the given stream of integer numbers is:

$$S = \{1, 3, 2, 3, 4, 1, 5, 3, 2, 1, 1, 3, 2, 1, 1, 3, 3, 4, 5, 5\}$$

Length of the stream S is $n = 20$. The frequencies of the elements are $m_1 = 6$, $m_2 = 3$, $m_3 = 6$, $m_4 = 2$, $m_5 = 3$.

Second moment = $6^2 + 3^2 + 6^2 + 2^2 + 3^2 = 94$

Suppose 3 samples are selected X1, X2, X3, with the Position at random selected is 5, 9, 11.

X1.element = 4, X2.element = 2, X3.element = 1

X1.count = 2, X2.count = 2, X3.count = 3

Estimate = $n \times$ (2X.count – 1)

First estimate = 20 × (4 – 1) = 60

Second estimate = 20 × (4 – 1) = 60

Third estimate = 20 × (6 – 1) = 100

Average of estimates = $\dfrac{60 + 60 + 100}{3} \cong 73$

Estimating higher order moments

Just like, the second order is estimated using **Alon Matis Szegedy** algorithm. The approximate moments are calculated as follows:

First order estimates v = X.count
Second order estimate = $n(2v - 1) = n((v)^2 - (v - 1)^2)$
Third order estimate = $n(3v^2 - 3v + 1) = n((v)^3 - (v - 1)^3)$
K^{th} order estimate = $n((v)^K - (v - 1)^K)$

These estimates are calculated for each element and then averaged for estimation of moments. For infinite stream, use a reservoir samplings or other suitable techniques to filter sample elements from the stream and then estimate the moments from these streams.

20.5 CONCEPT DRIFTS

Concept drift is an important topic in analyzing streamed data. Concept drifts help identify the statistical characteristics of stream data that starts changing over time. The changes in stream data are important to determine for proper assessment of dynamic and evolving streams, as knowledge patterns may vary over the period of time. There might be several reasons for change in the stream data, for example, if some new trending news is arriving in *X* (earlier twitter) then the flow of data from *X* will be drastically change and like and dislike will also be changed for the different topics. There are four major types of detection methods: Statistical, Statistical Process Control, Time Window Based, and Contextual Approaches. Some of the commonly used techniques for concept drift detection are covered in this section.

Statistical Test-based Methods: There are many statistical test-based methods to detect the concept drifts. In this category of techniques, a mathematical test is carried out to identify whether the data in the stream is coming from the same distribution or not. Two major tests under this category are the **Page-Hinkley method** and **Kolmogorov-Smirnov (KS) test.** In order to detect the change, a comparison is performed between sources of data and a decision is made whether the distribution is different. The mean and standard deviation from the different sources of data is observed and compared to decide whether it belongs to same distribution or not. Hypothetical tests are carried out on the distribution to make the decision. An example of drift detection under the statistical test is **Page-Hinkley method**. In this method, the initial means are calculated and keep updated as new data arrives. If the updated means at a given time is greater than threshold value (λ) then there is a drift. Another method is **Kolmogorov-Smirnov (KS) test**. The KS test is a non-parametric test compares two distributions, hypothesis is from to detect whether the data is from same distribution or not? If hypothesis is rejected, then there is a drift.

Population Stability Index

$$PSI = \Sigma\left(\left(\text{Actual }\% - \text{Expected }\%\right) \times \ln\left(\frac{\text{Actual }\%}{\text{Expected }\%}\right)\right)$$

Condition	Outcome
PSI ≤ 0.1	No change
PSI > 0.1 and PSI < 0.2	Alert
PSI ≥ 0.2	Drift Detected

Drift-Detection Method (DDM): DDM is proposed by Gama et al. In general, the error rate of any learning model decreases or becomes stable over the period of time. In DDM method this principle is utilized for detection of changes. Whenever there is some drastic change in the error rate, then change is detected. Let as assume that e_t is error rate at time *t*, and S_{min} is minimum standard deviation for the error rate: DDM algorithm initially gives warning when changes begin in the stream and finally it detects changes if changes continue. The two conditions for raising warning and detecting changes are (a) If $e_t + s_t \geq e_{min} + 2 \times S_{min}$ then warning is raised by the DDM algorithm, and (b) If $e_t + s_t \geq e_{min} + 3 \times S_{min}$ then change is detected by the DDM algorithm.

ADWIN (Adaptive Windowing): ADWIN (Adaptive Sliding Window) is a sliding window-based concept drift detection method. It tracks the average of stream bits or numbers in a variable length window. It is assumed that window has the maximal length statistically consistent. ADWIN works on the hypothesis that, "There has been no change in the average value inside the window". In order to determine changes in the stream it tests the consecutive windows over the period of time, i.e., W_t and W_{t+1}. If the difference between the consecutive windows is greater than the confidence value (δ), then change is detected in the stream.

EWMA (Exponentially Weighted Moving Average): The exponentially weightage moving average charts of error rates can also be used for detecting changes in the stream at a given time. It is a simple mathematical way by which sudden changes (in both side) can be observed from the exponential weighted moving average charts can be observed.

CDDM (Contextual Drift Detection Method): CDDM algorithm not only focuses on the change in the stream data but also monitors the external factors and additional context. The contest is characterized by various elements like time, demographics, users, external factors and events, etc.

HDDM (Histogram Drift Detection Method): Histogram represents the distribution of features of the stream elements. By comparing the histograms generated over the period of time, changes in the stream may be detected.

FHDDM (Frequent Histogram-based Drift Detection Method): FHDDM is another histogram–based technique in which the most frequent histograms are analyzed for finding the deviation in the streams.

20.6 IMPORTANT STREAM MINING OPERATIONS

Stream mining is defined as the process of discovering knowledge from stream data. Stream mining includes four major set of operations namely, mining frequent itemsets from stream, classification of stream elements, clustering, and summarizing the stream data. Although there are plenty algorithms for stream mining, some of the commonly used important techniques are highlighted in this section.

20.6.1 Mining Frequent Itemsets

Mining frequent elements in a stream includes extracting the most frequently occurring elements in a stream. There are plenty of applications of mining frequent elements from a stream. Algorithms for counting 1's in the streams and identifying set cardinalities for streams are utilized for mining of frequent itemsets in the stream. Examples of such algorithms include DGIM algorithm, Sketch-based algorithms (Count-Min, MG, etc.), Lossy Counting algorithm and many others. Some of the other popular algorithms for mining frequent itemsets on stream data are discussed here in brief.

Moment: It is a sliding window-based frequent itemset mining algorithm. A special data structure ***closed enumeration tree*** is used to store the frequent items. The algorithm moment uses a set of rules to add or remove the transactions from the tree to maintain the frequent itemsets in the tree.

FP-Stream: The algorithm FP-Stream uses FP Tree (Frequent Pattern Trees) as the data structure to hold the frequent itemsets. FP-Tree is created like FP-Growth algorithm for mining frequent itemsets with a smaller number of database scans. The FP-Stream algorithm maintains two FP-Trees, Global FP-Tree and Local FP-Tree. When new data elements arrive in the stream, FP-Stream computes the frequent itemsets and stores it to the local FP-Tree and using some of the threshold values it updates the Global FP-Tree by merging the frequent elements from local FP-Trees. The final frequent itemsets are extracted from the Global FP-Tree.

IncMine: Algorithm IncMine is the part of Massive Online Analysis framework for identifying frequent itemsets in big data. It is also applied on stream datasets to identify the frequent itemsets. In this algorithm a sliding window of most recent transactions is maintained then frequent closed itemsets are computed on it. On arrival of new transactions in streamed manners, the frequent itemsets are updated. Using the minimum support parameter the most frequent itemsets are filtered.

CM-SPADE (Counting-based Sequential Pattern Discovery from Data Streams): It is a sequential pattern mining algorithm derived from SPADE algorithm. SPADE stands for Sequential Pattern Discovery from Data Streams. The basic difference between SPADE and CM-SPADE is that CM-SPADE offers the functionality of co-occurrence pruning which makes the algorithm faster. The algorithm generates sequential frequent patterns from a given stream of data. Just like any frequent itemset mining, the frequent patterns are identified using a suitable value of the support. If the support value is greater than the minimum support count, then the patterns are called the frequent patterns.

FISH (Frequent Itemsets in Stream Mining using Concept Hierarchies): It is sliding window-based algorithm which combines concept hierarchies to discover frequent itemsets in the stream. It provides a threshold-based pruning methodologies by which appropriate frequent items can be filtered as the frequent. The algorithm dynamically adapts the parameters to find the frequent itemsets in a stream.

20.6.2 Classification

Classification is an important activity where data is classified in various predefined categories. As we know, stream data has a lot of limitations. One of the primary challenges is that in a single pass stream elements needs to be categorized, so general machine learning classification algorithms cannot apply directly to the streams, rather few specialized classification algorithms are required for categorizing stream data. In this section, some of the popular classification algorithms for stream data classification are discussed in brief.

20.6.3 VFDT (Very Fast Decision Tree)

VFDT (Very Fast Decision Tree) is a decision tree-based classifier for stream data classification. It uses a special type of decision tree called the Hoeffding Tree. The Hoeffding tree uses subsampling method to filter relevant information from the stream and provides higher scalability to accommodate a large number of stream data elements. Just like the ordinary splitting criteria in typical machine learning algorithms, like Gain, Gini index, etc. Hoeffding tree uses Hoeffding inequality as a measure of splitting. It is the fastest decision tree because it does not rely on the reuse of instances rather than it always prefers the new instances to update. The VFDT algorithm is an incremental classification algorithm which learns on the arrival of new instances. Initially the tree starts with an empty node (null node) as a root node of the tree and as per the arrival of new instances. Split the tree based on some splitting criteria and update the tree structure as per the available statistics of the tree.

Just like general decision trees, in Hoeffding tree also splitting criteria based on Gain which is derived from the entropy information. Based on the confidence interval for the estimation of entropy in the range [0...log n_c] for n_c class values. The Hoeffding bound chose a confidence interval for estimating entropy as given below.

$$\varepsilon = \sqrt{\frac{R^2 \ln \frac{1}{\delta}}{2n}}$$

where R is the range of the random variable, δ is the desired probability of estimation not being within $\in$, n is the number of examples collected. In Hoeffding tree gain G is computed for each attribute and splitting of the tree is performed as per the below mentioned splitting criteria.

$$G(\text{best attribute}) - G(\text{second best}) > \sqrt{\frac{R^2 \ln \frac{1}{\delta}}{2n}}$$

For efficient memory management, VFDT algorithm utilizes the concept of node deletion also, in which the non-meaningful nodes (based on some statistical measures) are deleted at runtime from the tree. CVFDT (Conceptual Very Fast Decision Tree) is the extension of VFDT classification algorithm which can handle the concept drifts in a sliding window-based model of stream processing.

20.6.4 Ensemble Algorithm for Stream Data

The primary challenge in the stream data classification is, it is difficult to store the entire stream data for processing and only pass is given to read the stream data. Stream-based ensemble learning algorithms utilize the parallel processing of stream batches in a single pass to classify the stream data. Most of the ensemble learning algorithms provide weighting schemes for assigning weights to the different classifiers considered for the ensemble learning model. In order to accommodate large data of stream, memory management features are also available in ensemble learning models for stream classification where the older items are discarded or deleted after it is decided by some statistical measures that it is not having any significant meaning in classification. Ensemble learning algorithms for stream data classification is available in two variants:

Incremental algorithms for stream data classification

Incremental or online algorithms updates on arrival of the new instances unlike with the traditional machine learning algorithms in which training is performed on the entire datasets. Two commonly used incremental algorithms for stream data classification are discussed in brief.

Incremental Naïve Bayes: Incremental Naïve Bayes is the incremental version of Naïve Bayes algorithm which is a probability-based classifier based on Bayes theorem. The algorithm starts with a single batch of stream data and calculates the probability of each class and then keeps updates on newly arrived batches of stream data. It is capable of handling concept drift and provides parallel way of computing probability values for the classes for stream data. Because of its simplicity (simple computation) it is a fast and efficient classification algorithm for streaming data.

Incremental Support Vector Machines (SVM): Just like the previously discussed incremental Naïve bayes algorithm for stream data classification, SVM algorithm is also utilized in incremental way for processing of stream data. There are several variants of incremental SVM classifiers for classification of stream data. One variant of incremental SVM classifiers is Online Passive-Aggressive SVM (PA-SVM) algorithm, in which the model updates itself on arrival of the new instances of stream batches.

Other variations of the incremental SVM algorithm include SMO (Sequential Mining Optimization)-based methods, Kernel approximation-based methods, and Working set methods. In Working set methods, a working set of current stream batch is maintained based on the importance of the data.

Combining-based models for classification

The other set of methods are designed by combining the multiple base classifiers for improving the performance of the classification of stream data. Just like the incremental algorithms, combined (ensemble) classifiers are also capable of handling concept drifts and are memory efficient.

Online Random Forests: Online random forests algorithm works parallelly on subsets of stream data for classification of stream data. In online random forest tree classification, a batch of data points of stream data are considered for categorization. The key important steps in online random forest algorithm are, starting with the empty tree, it selects one batch of stream data at a time and decide on whether new tree is to be created, it trains the newly created trees and adjust the weights of the trees and classification decisions are made with the help of majority voting. Adaptive Random Forests (ARF) is another variant of online random forest algorithms in which dynamic forest structures are used for creation of forest. The forest can grow or shrink using the dynamic forest structure. It also provides the capability to split the nodes and prune the nodes from a forest. The ARF algorithm provides a more sophisticated model for handling of concept drift as it is pluggable with the majority of the concept drift algorithms.

AdaBoost.MH: AdaBoost.MH is the stream data version of the AdaBoost machine learning algorithm in which multiple classifiers are trained for improving the accuracy of the classification process. AdaBoost.MH is abbreviated as Adaptive Boosting with ModHausdorff update. The weights of weak learners and data points are adjusted by ModHausdorff update rule in this technique. The ModHausdorff update rule uses the ModHausdorff distance function to calculate the proximity of the data points of the streams with the decision boundaries of the classes and adjust the weights according to the calculated proximity values.

20.7 CLUSTERING—STREAM, BIRCH, CLUSTREAM, COBWEB, DENSTREAM

Clustering is a type of unsupervised learning technique in which similar elements are grouped together based on the proximity (similarity) of the elements. Clustering techniques help in grouping of similar stream elements. This grouping helps in understanding the population density of the elements and general characteristics of the data. It might be useful for summarizing the nature of the stream also. Some popular stream clustering algorithms are discussed briefly in this section.

20.7.1 STREAM Algorithm

STREAM is a popular clustering algorithm for clustering stream data. It is an approximation algorithm. STREAM performs clustering of stream elements as mentioned in the below steps:

1. Input the first m points and reduce these to $O(k)$ points using randomized algorithm.
2. Repeat step 1 till $m^2/O(k)$ of the original data points are seen, then m intermediate medians are calculated.
3. Apply a local search algorithm, cluster m first level medians into $O(k)$ second level medians.
4. Maintain at most m level-i medians and generate $2k$ level if $i + 1$ medians with updated weights.
5. On processing of entire original data points, cluster all the intermediate medians into k final clusters.

The time complexity of STREAM clustering algorithm is $O(n^{1+e})$, and space complexity is (n^{ϵ}), where n is the number of points and $\in \leq \frac{1}{2}$.

20.7.2 BIRCH (Balanced Iterative and Clustering using Hierarchies)

The BIRCH clustering is an incremental clustering algorithm that uses hierarchical data structure to cluster incoming data points. Time complexity is $O(N)$, as it is a one pass algorithm. The algorithm works in four stages. It performs clustering of stream elements in the following steps:

1. Generate clustering features (CF)—a height balanced tree is created using clustering features defined as:
   Given a set of N d-dimensional data points CF = (N, LS, SS)
   Where $LS = \sum_{i=1}^{N} x_i$ and $SS = \sum_{i=1}^{N} x_i^2$
   Generate CF-Tree—a height balanced tree with two parameters branch factor B and T. Each leaf node contains at most B entries of the form $[Cf_i, Child_i]$, $Child_i$ is the pointer to the ith child node.
2. Generate smaller CF-Tree from the actual CF-Tree by removing outliers and grouping sub-clusters.
3. Existing clustering algorithms are applied for clustering all leaf nodes.
4. Optimize the clusters and remove outliers.

20.7.3 CluStream Algorithm

CluStream is an extension of the BIRCH clustering algorithm. It used the concept of Micro-clusters. A Micro-clusters stores summary of statics of data points considering the temporal component in a tuple $(CF_2X, CF_1X, CF_2T, CF_1T, N)$. The symbols of the tuples are explained with the help of an example. Suppose two micro-clusters (p_1, p_2) and (p_3, p_4) are given in time t_1 and t_2 then,

$$CF_2X = \{p_1^2 + p_3^2, p_2^2 + p_4^2\},\quad CF_1X = \{p_1 + p_3, p_2 + p_4\},\quad CF_2T - \{t_1^2 + t_2^2\},\quad CF_1T = \{t_1 + t_2\}$$

In the clustering features additional temporal features are added. The CluStream operated in offline and online phase. In the offline phase, K-means clustering is applied at the leaf node to cluster the lead node data. The online phase is similar to BIRCH clustering algorithm. The particular timestamp, a snapshot of the clustering is generated that is also called a pyramid time frame.

20.7.4 COBWEB Clustering Algorithm

COBWEB clustering algorithm is like BIRCH clustering algorithm and uses the concept of classification tree represents a class concept which summarizes the attribute value distribution. COBWEB supports the classification tree operations namely, merging two nodes, splitting a node, inserting a new node and posing down a node to the down in hierarchy. The new elements are inserted into the classification tree using the category utility function, which identifies importance of one of the stream elements in a particular category (cluster). The performance of COBWEB algorithm depends on the choice of suitable similarity function and similarity threshold criteria.

20.7.5 StreamKM++

StreamKM++ is a K-Means partitioning based clustering technique which utilizes the concept of coresets. A coreset represents a subset of the stream data which is processed at a time and approximates the solution of the clustering problem. The StreamKM++ algorithm is capable of handling concept drifts. The performance evaluation of the StreamKM++ algorithm for generated clusters is evaluated by the Silhouette index.

20.7.6 ClusTree

The ClusTree algorithm adjusts itself with the speed of the stream and generates cluster at any instance. The ClusTree algorithm uses a balanced tree structure, and each node of the structure consists of clustering features for a set of data points. On arrival of new stream elements, ClusTree algorithm updates or creates micro-clusters and updates the balanced tree structure by updating the clustering features. ClusTree algorithm is a hybrid approach based on hierarchical clustering algorithm and density-based clustering algorithm. The balanced tree (hierarchical tree) is updated based on the population density of the stream elements. ClusTree algorithm is also capable of handling concept drifts.

20.7.7 CURE

CURE (Clustering Using Representatives) is also a tree-based stream clustering algorithm, but it does not store the entire elements in the tree structure rather it stores the representative elements chosen from the streamed data. The representative elements are either selected on random basis or by using statistical measures. The CURE algorithm assigns each stream element to its nearest clustering representative using some appropriate distance functions such Euclidean distance function. It also detects and eliminates outlier elements during clustering. Concept drifts can be managed by periodic clustering of the stream elements in the CURE algorithm. It is capable of handling any shape and size of clusters.

20.7.8 DBStream and DenStream

DBStream (Density-Based Stream Clustering over evolving data with Micro-clusters) is a popular stream clustering algorithm and most suitable for continuous and rapid streams. It is a density-based clustering algorithm which focuses on population density of the stream elements. It incrementally updates itself and updates the micro-clusters from the stream data. DenStream (Density-Based Stream Clustering over Evolving Data with Noise) is another density-based clustering algorithm DBSCAN. Using a damped window model the stream data clustering is performed. DenStream is capable of handling noise in an effective manner. The outlier detection scheme in DenStream effectively eliminates noise from the streams. DBStream is a memory intensive clustering algorithm whereas DenStream is memory efficient method as it only stores the compact micro-clusters rather than storing all the elements of the stream. The DenStream algorithm has better capabilities of handling of concept drifts as compared to the DBStream clustering algorithm.

20.8 SUMMARIZATION

Summarization of stream data including generating summaries from a large stream. Summarization helps in understanding the nature of the data available in stream and basis characteristics of the data. It will further help in identifying suitable knowledge discovery processes for extracting useful patterns from the summary of the stream data. As the stream data is very large and practically it is not possible to store the entire stream data to the memory, so summarization is utilized as an effective tool for knowledge discovery from the streams. Using summarization, representative stream elements are selected which capture the statistical characteristics of the stream.

Reservoir Sampling: Sampling techniques like reservoir sampling techniques to select the random samples from the stream data. The selected random samples from the stream window at a particular time represent the summary of the data at a particular time.

Sketch Algorithms (e.g., Count-Min Sketch, HyperLogLog Sketch): Sketching algorithms like Count-Min, HyperLogLog, etc. are used for estimating the frequency of the elements in stream. Using the most frequent items present in the stream, stream data can be summarized.

Lossy Counting: Lossy counting algorithm gives frequent items (stream elements) whose frequency is greater than the a given threshold value. The higher frequency elements are streams that can be filtered to represent the summary of the stream.

Exponential Histograms: Histograms are the traditional state-of-the-art tools for summarizing big data. For stream data also, histograms can be utilized for summarizing the large stream data. There are various ways of creating the histograms but for the large stream data, exponential histograms are preferred, as the exponential weights gives a better understanding of data moment over a long period of time.

T-digest: The T-digest algorithm is an important probabilistic data structure. It is used for estimating quantiles from the given stream data. The T-digest algorithm groups similar elements into the weighted centroids. T-digest algorithm provides an accurate and efficient approximation of quantiles and other statistical measures which can be used as the representation of a given input stream. So instead of using the stream data (which is so large that can not be stored in the memory), representative points from T-digest algorithm are selected as a summary of the stream. In this way, the T-digest algorithm provides an effective way of summarizing the stream.

AMF (Adaptive Memory Factorization): AMF is a popular summarization algorithm in stream mining. It is widely used for dimensionality reduction and clustering of high dimensionality streams. It uses the matrix factorization technique to decompose the high dimensionality data into the low dimensionality data for a given stream. Whenever the new data point in stream arrives, the AMF algorithm first updates the representation of low-dimensionality representation using stochastic gradient descent technique. Then by utilizing the learning rate it updates the representation and validates the concept drift detection, at the same time it forgets the previously known data point to avoid influences. Finally, it clusters the data points based on their similarity values. The cluster presents the low dimensionality representation of the stream data points.

20.9 APPLICATIONS AND USE CASES

Today there are plenty of applications which generate data in the format of streams. From social media platforms (likes, comments, etc.) to industrial IoT-based applications (sensor data, etc.) generate a lot of streamed data. So far, we have discussed a number of stream processing techniques and stream mining techniques for streamed data. In this section, some of the important applications of stream processing and mining in recent years are discussed in brief.

20.9.1 Telecommunications Domain

Telecommunications industries are big sources of data generation particularly in the stream forms as telecommunication is the backbone of communication in today's world. Telephone call records are the primary source of the streamed data generated in the telecommunication domain. Stream mining in telecommunication domain provides applications like, real-time call rating, fraud detection and QoS monitoring from CDR (call detail record) and network performance analysis. Stream mining in telecommunications can also help in security intelligence for fraud detection and cybersecurity alerts. For example, detecting smart grid consumption issues, and SIM card misuse.

20.9.2 Financial Data Analysis

Stock markets and other financial instruments generally have a large amount of data. Particularly, the stock market data fluctuates rapidly over the period of time and generates a stream of stock prices. Stream processing and mining techniques help in understanding and analyzing such a vast amount of financial data. Many analytical activities like predicting stock prices, finding trending stocks, categorizing financial instruments, etc. can be carried out using the stream processing and stream mining operations.

20.9.3 Weather Forecasting and Analysis

Weather forecasting is performed by analyzing a number of parameters. These parameter values are generated by satellite image and a number of sensors deployed at various locations. The parameters of weather forecasting change every moment and therefore prediction of accurate weather is a complicated process. The data generated from the satellite images and sensors comes in streamed format, which can be analyzed using stream processing and stream mining techniques for effective and efficient weather forecasting systems.

20.9.4 Industrial Data Analysis Using IoT

With the invention of Internet of Things (IoT) devices, more smart devices are invented and deployed in a variety of industries for a large number of applications. Cloud infrastructure and web clickstream analysis on the other side for IT Operations in various organizations generate a lot of streamed data. The data generated from the Industrial automation, offering real-time analytics and predictive actions for patterns of manufacturing plant issues and quality problems.

For Smart Cities applications, stream mining can help in real-time traffic analytics, congestion prediction and travel time apps. In the oil and gas industry, stream mining can be utilized for real-time analytics and automated actions to avert potential equipment failures. Sensor network-based applications also generate huge, streamed data, e.g., million sensors sending 4 bytes every 0.1 sec, these data can also be processed and analyzed using stream mining techniques. Streamed data is also generated in the Image data format. Satellites images, surveillance cameras (city of London has six million cameras), etc. generate a large number of sequences of images over the period of time. These images can be analyzed for many applications. In IT companies for network security related issues, IP packets monitored are monitored at switch devices which gather information for optimal routing, detect denial-of-service attacks, etc.

20.9.5 Audio and Video Stream Analysis

There are several applications on the Internet which generate audio and video streams. Some of such important sources of streaming devices generating audio and video are YouTube, Netflix, and Spotify, etc. Other sources include video game consoles, drones, CCTV's, smartphones, video-conferencing systems, Microsoft Teams, Google Meet, and Zoom, etc. These vast amounts of data generated from the audio and video streams can be analyzed for content classification, moderation, recommendations, and personalization, etc. for effective management of the content on these applications using stream mining techniques.

20.9.6 Social Media Analysis

Social media is the primary source of data generated in the streamed format. Applications such Twitter (X), Facebook, Instagram, etc. generate a large volume of data based on the user's post, like, comments, etc. These click streams are used for advertising products and sentiment analysis, etc. by utilizing stream techniques. For example, Google wants to know what queries are more frequent today than yesterday (Google has several hundred million queries/day). Another example is Wikipedia wants to know which of its pages are getting an unusual number of hits in the past hour (billions of clicks/days). Apart from this, there are other plenty of analytical works that can be performed on the click stream data in the social networking sites. Mining social network-based news feeds, etc., can be analyzed for finding trending topics on Twitter, Facebook, and other social networking sites. Also, there might be several derived applications based on the analysis carried out from the click stream data such as an increase in queries for "sore throat" may help tracking of virus spread in some of the specific regions.

20.9.7 User Activity on e-Commerce Sites

E-commerce sites generate plenty of stream data. E-commerce sites contain user data like profile, navigation on the search sites, search patterns, product data information, and transaction data. This stream data can be analyzed for marketing and advertising products, offering combos, offering discounts, sentiment analysis, recommendations, fraud detection and a lot of other important analytical works for increasing the productivity of the e-commerce sites.

20.9.8 Event Drive Camera

Event driven cameras have enormous advantages like speed, low power consumption, low latency, performance, etc. Because of these advantages, event driven cameras are used in many modern industrial applications like automated vehicles, medical imaging, quality control in production units, environmental monitoring, surveillance, security, augmented and virtual reality-based applications. The event driven camera generates a lot of images and video and sends it to the servers. On the server side these cameras provide a continuous stream of image and video data. The processing of these vast amounts of stream data is carried out using stream processing and stream mining techniques. Stream processing and mining techniques are effective technologies in knowledge discovery and decision making on the data generated by the event driven cameras.

EXERCISES

1. Estimate the set cardinalities of the following streams using DGIM algorithm:
   (a) $S = \{a, a, a, c, c, c, d, d, b, b, b, e, e, e\}$
   (b) $S = \{1, 1, 1, 3, 2, 3, 3, 2, 2, 2, 3, 3, 3\}$
2. Estimate the set cardinalities of the following stream using Flajolet-Martin algorithm:
   (a) $S = \{1, 4, 5, 1, 3, 3, 2, 3, 1, 5, 3, 4, 2, 4\}$
3. Estimate the set cardinalities of the following stream using HyperLogLog and LogLog algorithms:
   (a) $S = \{a, e, f, c, g, c, d, d, b, e, b, g, f, e, c, d, d, b, e\}$
4. Given a stream of integer numbers $S = \{2, 7, 5, 1, 2, 1, 3, 1, 2, 3, 4, 2, 7, 5, 1, 2, 3, 3, 4, 2, 2, 5, 6, 2, 1, 7, 2, 1\}$ create a count-min sketch using 3 different hash functions: $\text{Hash}_1(x) = x \bmod 7$, $\text{Hash}_2(x) = x + 1 \bmod 3$, and $\text{Hash}_3(x) = 7x + 1 \bmod 5$. Sketch is calculated then, count the frequency of element 7.
5. Compute the surprise number (second moment) for the given stream of integer numbers 1, 5, 2, 3, 1, 2, 4, 2, 1, 3. Also calculate the third moment of this stream and compute the approximate higher order moments.

MULTIPLE CHOICE QUESTIONS

1. In which of the sampling techniques, higher priority is given to the most recent data as compared to the older data?
   (a) Sliding Windows Sampling (b) Time Decayed Sampling
   (c) Chain Sampling (d) Histogram Sampling
2. In which of the following sampling techniques, the samples are selected from the summary of the windows?
   (a) Sliding Windows Sampling (b) Time Decayed Sampling
   (c) Chain Sampling (d) StreamSamp Sampling.
3. What is the length and cardinality of the stream $x_1, x_2, x_1, x_3, x_4, x_2, x_4, x_1, x_3$?
   (a) Length: 4 Cardinality: 4
   (b) Length: 4 Cardinality: 9
   (c) Length: 9 Cardinality: 4
   (d) Length: 9 Cardinality: 9
4. Estimate the second order frequency moment for the stream $x_1, x_2, x_1, x_3, x_4, x_2, x_4, x_1, x_3$: :
   (a) 13 (b) 14
   (c) 16 (d) 18
5. For the given stream 1 0 0 1 1 1 0 1 0 1 1, the DGIM algorithm will estimate the number of 1's in the stream as:
   (a) 5 (b) 6
   (c) 8 (d) 9
6. Count the distinct elements in the given stream 2, 3, 5, 3, 2, 7, 4, 3, 5, 2, 3, 3 using the Flajolet Martin algorithm using the hash function $h(x) = x \bmod 3$.
   (a) 1 (b) 2
   (c) 3 (d) 4
7. Count the distinct elements in the given stream 2, 3, 5, 3, 2, 7, 4, 3, 5, 2, 3, 3 using the Flajolet Martin algorithm using the hash function $h(x) = (x + 4) \bmod 7$.
   (a) 2 (b) 3
   (c) 4 (d) 5

8. What is the purpose of HyperLogLog algorithm for the stream data?
   (a) It counts the number of 1's in the stream data.
   (b) It estimates the unique elements in the stream data.
   (c) It estimates the frequency moments in the stream data.
   (d) None of these.
9. What is the primary purpose of sketch-based algorithm in stream mining?
   (a) These algorithms use sampling techniques for counting 1's in the stream.
   (b) These algorithms use stream summaries for estimating unique elements.
   (c) These algorithms summarize the stream data.
   (d) These algorithms use probabilistic data structures for estimating the unique elements in the stream.
10. The primary difference between the KMV Sketch and MG Sketch algorithm is (multiple answers are correct):
   (a) The KMV Sketch algorithm is used to estimate the set cardinality whereas the MG Sketch algorithm is used to discover the frequent items in a stream.
   (b) The KMV Sketch algorithm is used to discover the frequent items whereas the MG Sketch algorithm is used to estimate the set cardinality in a stream.
   (c) The KMV Sketch algorithm does not uses hashing functions whereas the MG Sketch uses hashing functions to analyse the data stream.
   (d) The KMV Sketch algorithm stores *K* smallest elements whereas the MG Sketch algorithm uses fixed size counters.
11. Which of the following statement is FALSE regarding the Count-Min Sketch algorithm?
   (a) It is a probabilistic data structure.
   (b) It is computationally complex.
   (c) The algorithm sometimes suffers with the problem of hash collisions.
   (d) CM Sketch will always return exact or more frequency count.
12. Let the given stream of integer numbers is 1, 2, 4, 2 ,5, 1, 2, 3, 1, 1 and we have been given two hash functions $Hash_1(x) = x \bmod 3$, $Hash_2(x) = (x + 1) \bmod 3$ then the frequency of element 1 using Count-Min Sketch algorithm is:
   (a) 3 (b) 4
   (c) 5 (d) None of these
13. What is the purpose of Bloom filter algorithm in stream data analysis?
   (a) It is used to estimate the unique elements present in the stream.
   (b) It is used to estimate the approximate second order moment in the stream.
   (c) It is used to estimate the frequency of the elements in the stream.
   (d) It is used to test whether any given element belongs to the stream.
14. Using the Alon Matis Szegedy algorithm calculate the approximate value of second order moment for the stream 2, 3, 5, 3, $\underline{2}$, $\underline{7}$, 4, $\underline{3}$, $\underline{5}$, 2, 3, 3 (the underlined values indicate the location selected for the element of the stream).
   (a) 27 (b) 30
   (c) 36 (d) 44
15. Using the Alon Matis Szegedy algorithm calculate the approximate value of third order moment for the stream 2, 3, 5, 3, $\underline{2}$, $\underline{7}$, 4, $\underline{3}$, $\underline{5}$, 2, 3, 3 (the underlined values indicate the location selected for the element of the stream).
   (a) 62 (b) 78
   (c) 84 (d) 96
16. Which of the following concept drift detection technique also monitors the external factors and additional context along with the stream data to determine the concept drift?
   (a) CDDM (b) FHDDM
   (c) ADWIN (d) EWMA

17. In order to detect the concept drift what is the expected value of Population Stability Index (PSI)?

(a) PSI ≤ 0.1
(b) PSI > 0.1 and PSI < 0.2
(c) PSI ≥ 0.25
(d) PSI ≥ 0.2

18. Which of the following is NOT an algorithm for mining frequent itemsets from the stream data?

(a) CURE
(b) IncMine
(c) CM-SPADE
(d) FISH

19. Which of the following statement is FALSE about the VFDT (Very Fast Decision Tree) in stream classification?

(a) The VFDT algorithm is an incremental classification algorithm.
(b) It can handle the concept drifts in a sliding window-based model of stream processing.
(c) It is the fastest decision tree because it does not rely on the reuse of instances.
(d) It uses Hoeffding inequality as a measure of splitting.

20. The performance of COBWEB algorithm depends on the choice of (multiple answers are correct):

(a) Suitable similarity function
(b) Similarity threshold criteria
(c) Splitting of nodes
(d) Suitable category utility function

21. Which statement is FALSE about the T-Digest stream summarization algorithm?

(a) It is a probabilistic data structure.
(b) It uses the matrix factorization technique.
(c) It estimates quantiles from the given stream data.
(d) It groups similar elements into the weighted centroids.

22. Which of the following is NOT the application of stream data mining?

(a) Analysing the student's performance at the end of every semester.
(b) Analysing the user clicks in the social media such as "X" (earlier Twitter).
(c) Analysing the high-speed sensor data deployed in some industries.
(d) Analysing the stock price in the stock market.

REFERENCES

[1] https://www.cc.gatech.edu/classes/AY2009/cs7260_fall/lecture2.pdf

[2] Datar, M., Gionis, A., Indyk, P., & Motwani, R. (2002), Maintaining stream statistics over sliding windows, *SIAM journal on computing*, *31*(6), pp. 1794–1813.

[3] Flajolet, P., & Martin, G. N. (1985), Probabilistic counting algorithms for data base applications, *Journal of computer and system sciences*, *31*(2), pp. 182–209.

[4] https://en.wikipedia.org/wiki/Flajolet%E2%80%93Martin_algorithm

[5] Flajolet, P., Fusy, É., Gandouet, O., & Meunier, F. (2007, June), Hyperloglog: the analysis of a near-optimal cardinality estimation algorithm, In *Discrete Mathematics and Theoretical Computer Science* (pp. 137-156).

[6] https://en.wikipedia.org/wiki/HyperLogLog

[7] https://chatox.github.io/data-mining-course/theory/pdf/tt26_estimating_moments.pdf

[8] Alon, N., Matias, Y., & Szegedy, M. (1999), The space complexity of approximating the frequency moments, *Journal of Computer and system sciences*, 58(1), pp. 137–147.

[9] https://www.cms.waikato.ac.nz/~abifet/book/chapter_5.html (Bifet, A., Gavalda, R., Holmes, G., & Pfahringer, B. (2018), *Machine learning for data streams: with practical examples in MOA*, MIT press.)

[10] Aggarwal, C. C. (2018), A survey of stream clustering algorithms, In *Data Clustering* (pp. 231–258), Chapman and Hall/CRC

[11] Lahiri, B., Tirthapura, S. (2009), Stream Sampling, In: LIU, L., ÖZSU, M.T. (eds) Encyclopedia of Database Systems, Springer, Boston, MA. https://doi.org/10.1007/978-0-387-39940-9_372

[12] Nagwani, N. K. (2022), Stream Mining: Introduction, Tools & Techniques and Applications, *Data Mining and Machine Learning Applications*, pp. 99–124.
[13] https://www.cms.waikato.ac.nz/~abifet/book/chapter_6.html
[14] https://www.cms.waikato.ac.nz/~abifet/book/chapter_10.html
[15] https://www.philippe-fournier-viger.com/spmf/CM-SPADE.php
[16] https://www.cms.waikato.ac.nz/~abifet/book/chapter_9.html
[17] https://ocw.snu.ac.kr/sites/default/files/NOTE/L6-stream.pdf
[18] https://snap.stanford.edu/class/cs246-2015/slides/15-streams.pdf

ANSWER KEY

1. (b) **2.** (d) **3.** (c) **4.** (d) **5.** (b) **6.** (b) **7.** (c) **8.** (b) **9.** (d)
10. (a) and (d) **11.** (b) **12.** (c) **13.** (d) **14.** (b) **15.** (c) **16.** (a) **17.** (d)
18. (a) **19.** (b) **20.** (a) and (b) **21.** (b) **22.** (a)

21 Advanced Data Visualization Techniques

In this chapter, we will present some advanced techniques for data visualization. We will discuss visualization techniques for complex datasets such as time-series, graph data and text data. Finally, we will also discuss maps (cartographic visualizations) and how to set up dashboards for interactive data visualization.

21.1 TIME SERIES DATA VISUALIZATION

We have already studied time series data analysis in great detail in Chapter 17. Time series analysis involves understanding the underlying patterns, trends, and seasonal variations in the data to make informed decisions and predictions. Visualization of time series data can help identify long-term trends and patterns that are not immediately apparent in raw data. It highlights seasonal variations and cyclical patterns, which can be crucial for planning and forecasting. Visualization makes it easier to spot outliers and anomalies, which can indicate significant events or data quality issues. It also allows for comparison between different time periods or between different datasets to understand relative performance and changes over time.

Visualization of complex time-series datasets can be very difficult. For example, high-frequency time series data can become cluttered and difficult to interpret. In cases with multiple time series or dense data points, overplotting can obscure important details. One must apply proper scaling and normalization to avoid misleading trends or patterns that are not present. Finally, time series data often needs contextual information to be fully understood, such as economic events or seasonal factors, which might not be included in the visualization itself.

We now consider a dataset containing the daily closing prices of a stock over the past year. A well-crafted visualization can provide insights into the stock's performance, trends, and volatility.

21.1.1 Visualization Stock Prices Over Time

(1) Line Chart: A basic line chart can show the overall trend of the stock prices over time. Using different colors or styles for different segments (e.g., quarters) can enhance readability.

FIGURE 21.1 Line chart showing trend of the stock prices over time.

(2) Candlestick Chart: For more detailed analysis, a candlestick chart can display daily open, high, low, and close prices. This is particularly useful for financial data as it shows intra-day price movement.

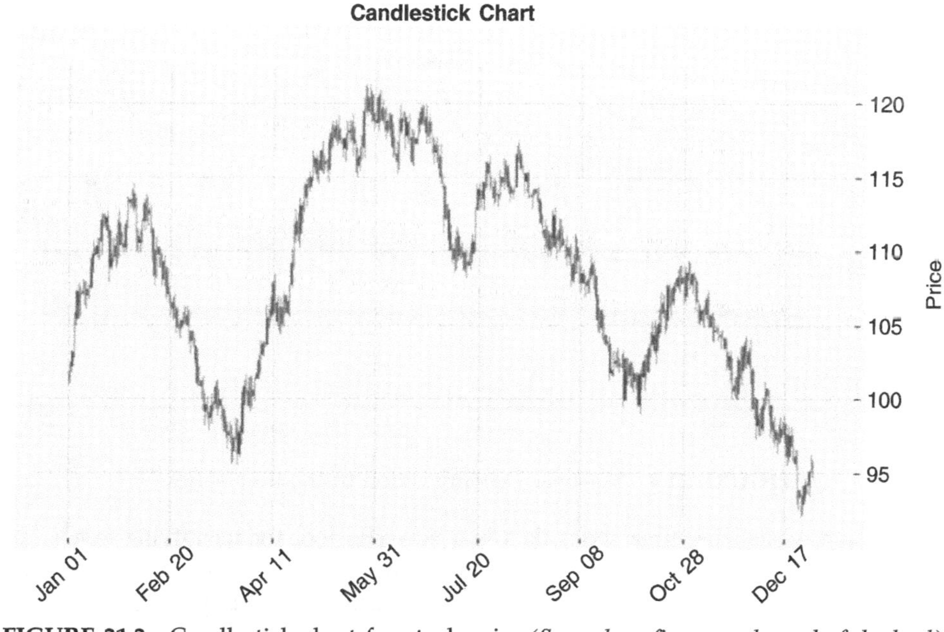

FIGURE 21.2 Candlestick chart for stock price (*See colour figure at the end of the book*).

(3) Moving Average Overlay: Adding moving averages (e.g., 30-day and 90-day) to the line chart can smooth out short-term fluctuations and highlight longer-term trends.

(4) Seasonal Decomposition: Decomposing the time series into trend, seasonal, and residual components can provide deeper insights into the data's structure.

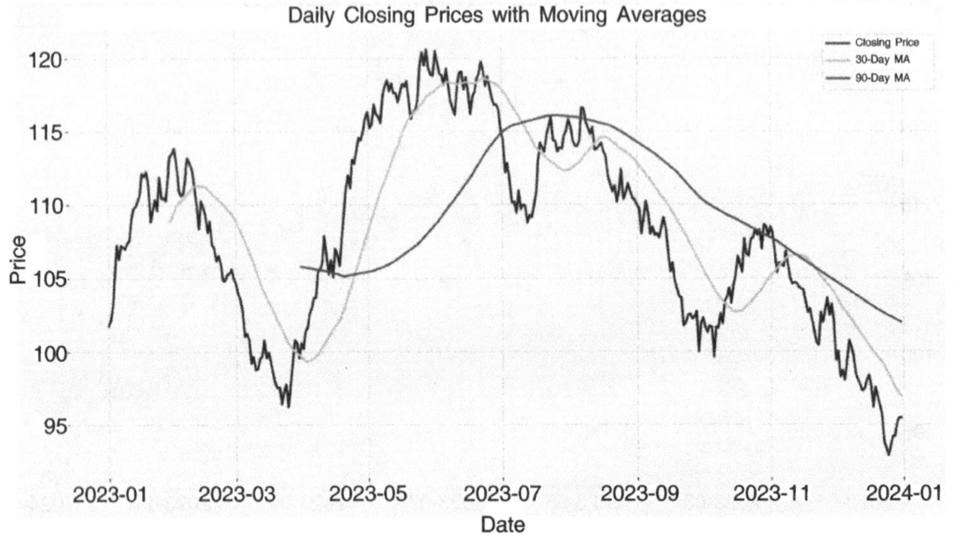

FIGURE 21.3 Moving Average chart for stock price (*See colour figure at the end of the book*).

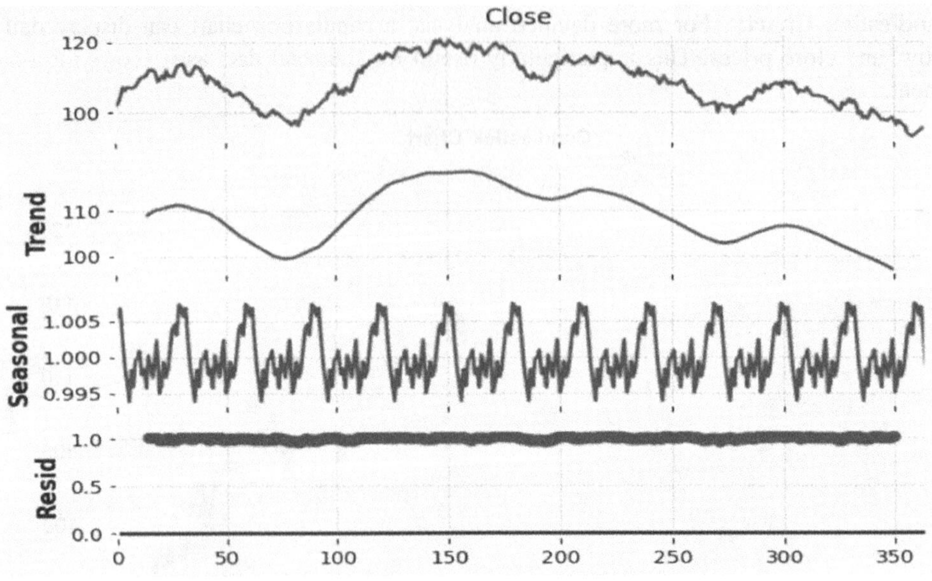

FIGURE 21.4 Seasonal Decomposition of the time series.

In conclusion, visualizing time series data is a powerful tool for identifying trends, detecting anomalies, and making predictions. By choosing the appropriate type of visualization and carefully considering the pros and cons, one can effectively communicate the underlying patterns and insights hidden in time series data.

21.2 GRAPH-RELATED VISUALIZATION

We now discuss some techniques for visualization of graph data. We have discussed graph data analysis in Chapter 18. It is crucial to understand the various methods available for representing and interpreting graph data. This section delves into three primary techniques: Force Directed Placement, Adjacency Matrix View, and Tree Map. Each method offers unique advantages and is suited for different types of graph data and analysis needs. We will explore each method with examples, diagrams, and a discussion of their pros and cons.

21.2.1 Force Directed Placement for Graph Visualization

Force Directed Placement is a method that visualizes graphs by treating nodes as repelling objects and edges as attractive forces, similar to springs. This results in a layout where nodes are distributed in a way that minimizes edge crossings and evenly spaces out the nodes.

Consider a social network graph where nodes represent individuals and edges represent relationships. The Force Directed Placement method can help visualize the clusters of friends and how they are interconnected.

Let's define three clusters of friends and some connections between these clusters:

1. **Cluster 1**:
   - Nodes: A, B, C, D
   - Edges: A-B, A-C, B-C, C-D
2. **Cluster 2**:
   - Nodes: E, F, G, H
   - Edges: E-F, E-G, F-G, G-H
3. **Cluster 3**:
   - Nodes: I, J, K, L
   - Edges: I-J, I-K, J-K, K-L
4. **Inter-cluster connections**:
   - Edges: D-E, H-I, B-K

Let's create the visualization with these clusters and connections.

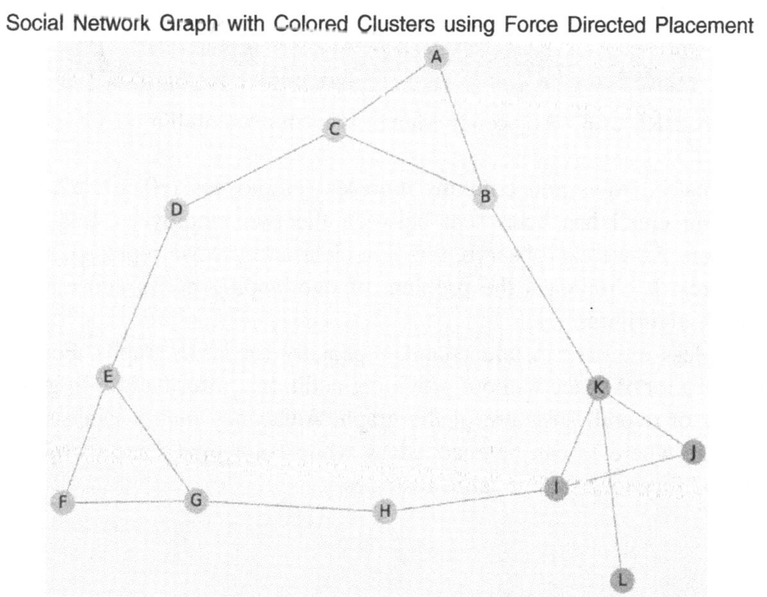

FIGURE 21.5 Graphical Visualization of Force Directed Placement.

The inter-cluster connections are clearly visible, and the different colors help to distinguish between the clusters, making the visualization more intuitive. The three important features of force directed placement are its intuitive layout, ability to reveal clusters and handling of dynamic changes to the graph such as adding or removing nodes/edges. However, it is computationally intensive and can be slow to compute and render. Dense graphs may result in overlapping nodes and edges, making the visualization cluttered. Finally, the layout can change with different runs, leading to inconsistent visualizations.

21.2.2 Adjacency Matrix View Graph Visualization

The Adjacency Matrix View represents a graph as a matrix. Each row and column correspond to a node, and the cell at the intersection indicates whether an edge exists between the nodes.

Consider a network graph of a company's email communication. Each node represents an employee, and an edge represents an email sent between them. The adjacency matrix shows the presence or absence of these communications.

Below is the adjacency matrix representing the presence (1) or absence (0) of email communications between employees:

	e0	e1	e2	e3	e4	e5	e6
e0	0	1	0	1	0	1	0
e1	1	0	1	0	1	0	0
e2	0	1	0	1	0	0	1
e3	1	0	1	0	1	1	0
e4	0	1	0	1	0	1	1
e5	1	0	0	1	1	0	1
e6	0	0	1	0	1	1	0

FIGURE 21.6 Adjacency Matrix View representation of Graph.

In the above matrix, rows and columns represent employees (e0, e1, e2, e3, e4, e5, e6). A "1" indicates that an email has been sent between the two employees, and a "0" indicates no email communication. As we can observe, this is a clear and precise representation of the presence and absence of edges. It eliminates the problem of overlapping nodes and edges. It is useful for implementing graph algorithms.

However, it is less intuitive to understand, especially for large graphs. For sparse graphs, the matrix can consume a lot of space without providing additional information. In general, it is difficult to visualize clusters or overall structure of the graph. Adjacency matrix can also be represented in the form of an image where 1s can be encoded by white color pixels and 0s by black color pixels. This increases the ability to visualize large matrices.

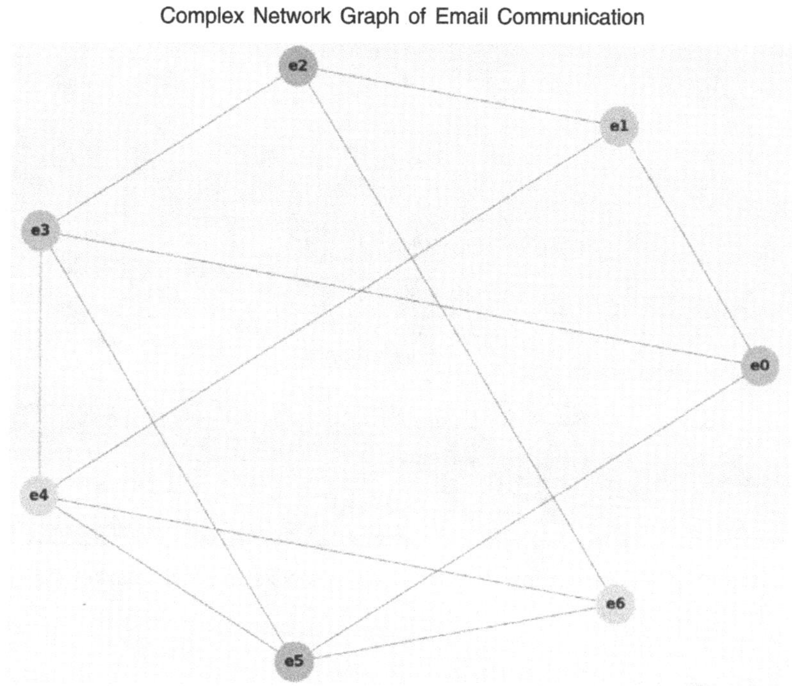

FIGURE 21.7 Network graph for the company's email communication.

21.2.3 Tree Map

Tree Maps are a method for displaying hierarchical data using nested rectangles. Each branch of the tree is represented as a rectangle, and its sub-branches are shown as smaller rectangles within it.

Consider a stock market system with different sectors. Each sector is represented as a rectangle, and stocks within that sector are represented as smaller rectangles within it. The size of each rectangle can represent the profit or loss.

Tree maps utilizes space efficiently to display a large amount of hierarchical data.

It makes it easy to compare the size of different nodes at the same level of the hierarchy. It can highlight the most significant nodes by size.

However tree maps are best suited for hierarchical data and not for general graph structures. It can become cluttered and hard to read if there are too many small rectangles. It is difficult to represent deeper hierarchical levels clearly.

Each of these methods—Force Directed Placement, Adjacency Matrix View, and Tree Map—offers unique ways to visualize graph data, each with its own strengths and weaknesses. The choice of method depends on the specific characteristics of the data and the goals of the visualization.

21.3 TEXT DATA VISUALIZATION IN NLP

Text data visualization involves transforming text data into visual formats that make it easier to understand patterns, trends, and insights. Leveraging NLP (Natural Language Processing) techniques allows for sophisticated analysis and visualization of text data. We will discuss two techniques here: Word Cloud and GloVe Embeddings.

FIGURE 21.8 Tree Map representation of profit-loss in stocks in stock market (*See colour figure at the end of the book*).

21.3.1 Word Cloud

A word cloud (or tag cloud) is a visual representation of text data where the size of each word indicates its frequency or importance. This technique is often used to quickly grasp the most prominent terms in a body of text.

It is intuitive and easy for viewers to quickly identify the most frequent terms. It is simple to create using various tools and libraries. It is attractive and engaging for presentations and reports. However, it does not convey the context or relationships between words. It can overemphasize common but less meaningful words. It is not suitable for in-depth analysis of text data.

Example: Imagine you have a dataset of customer reviews for a new smartphone. You want to visualize the most frequently mentioned terms to get an overview of common themes in the feedback.

Here is a simulation of a small dataset of customer reviews, performing text pre-processing, calculating word frequencies, and generating a word cloud.

Let's start with creating some sample customer reviews for a new smartphone:

1. "The battery life is amazing and the camera quality is fantastic!"
2. "I love the sleek design and the performance is top-notch."
3. "The screen resolution is great, but the battery life could be better."
4. "Very user-friendly interface and excellent customer support."
5. "The phone heats up quickly, and the battery life is disappointing."
6. "Great performance and camera, but the price is too high."

Step-by-Step Process:

1. **Data Collection:** Sample customer reviews as mentioned above.
2. Text Pre-processing:
    - Convert to lowercase
    - Remove punctuation

- Remove stopwords
- Perform stemming/lemmatization

3. **Word Frequency Calculation:** Calculate the frequency of each word in the preprocessed dataset.
4. **Generate Word Cloud:** Create the word cloud visualization using a Python library.

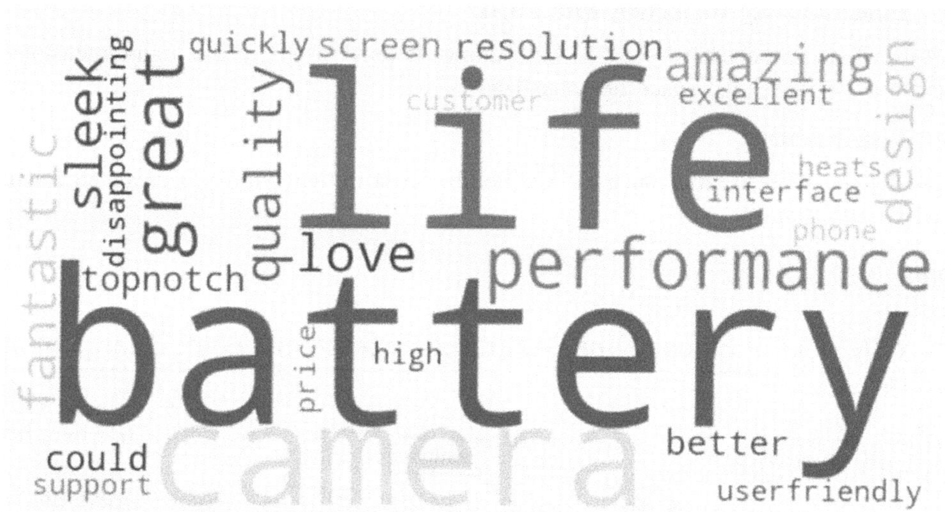

FIGURE 21.9 Word Cloud Visualization generated from the sample customer reviews (*See colour figure at the end of the book*).

21.3.2 GloVe Embeddings

GloVe (Global Vectors for Word Representation) is an unsupervised learning algorithm for obtaining vector representations for words. By mapping words into a high-dimensional space, GloVe captures semantic relationships between words. It effectively captures relationships and analogies between words. It is useful in various NLP tasks like clustering, classification, and similarity analysis. It provides a dense representation of words, encapsulating more information than simple frequency counts. However, they are more complex to implement and understand compared to simpler techniques like word clouds. It needs a large corpus of text data to generate meaningful embeddings. It can be resource-intensive to train and compute embeddings.

21.3.3 Visualization of Text Embeddings

t-SNE and PCA

To visualize GloVe embeddings, dimensionality reduction techniques like t-SNE (t-distributed Stochastic Neighbor Embedding) and PCA (Principal Component Analysis) are commonly used.

Example: Consider visualizing word vectors from a medical dataset. The dataset consists of medical and dermatological contexts to describe various conditions and characteristics of tissues or growths. By reducing the dimensions using t-SNE, we can create a 2D plot where similar words are clustered together, revealing insights into the relationships and groupings of words.

Step 1: Data Preparation

1. **Collecting Data:** Start with a dataset of news articles.
2. **Tokenization:** Tokenize the text into words.
3. **Word Embeddings:** Use a pretrained model like Word2Vec, GloVe, or FastText to convert words into vectors.

Step 2: Dimensionality Reduction with t-SNE

t-SNE (t-distributed Stochastic Neighbor Embedding) is used to reduce the high-dimensional word vectors into a 2-dimensional space for visualization.

Step 3: Visualization

We'll use Python with libraries such as Matplotlib, Seaborn, and Plotly to create interactive and advanced visualizations.

Diagram:

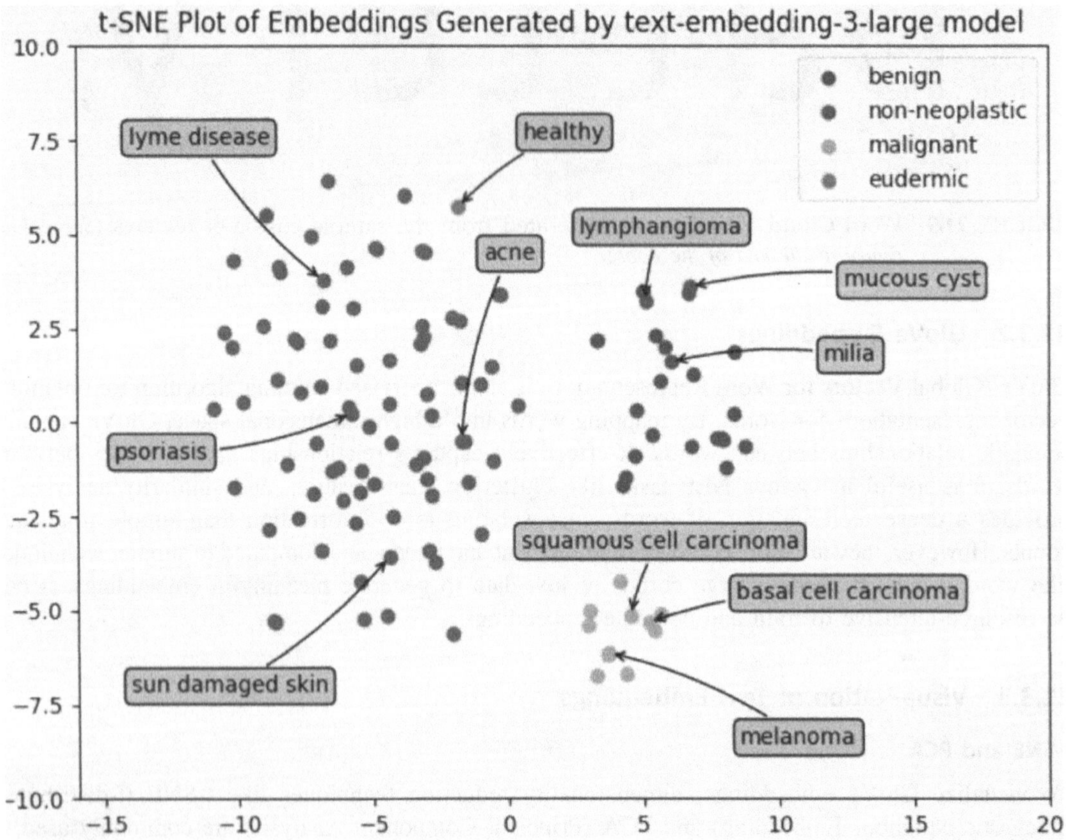

FIGURE 21.10 t-SNE plot of embeddings to showcase clustering of different skin conditions showing the relationships amongst them (*See colour figure at the end of the book*).

21.3.4 Conclusion

Both word clouds and GloVe embeddings offer unique ways to visualize text data, each with its strengths and limitations. Word clouds provide a quick and visually appealing overview of term frequency, while GloVe embeddings offer deeper insights into the semantic relationships between words. Combining these techniques can provide a comprehensive understanding of text data in NLP applications.

We now move on to the design of dashboards for real-time monitoring and interactive data visualization.

21.4 DASHBOARDS

Dashboards are powerful tools for data visualization, allowing users to monitor, analyze, and gain insights from data in real-time. They consolidate information from various sources into a single, easily accessible interface, making it possible to track key performance indicators (KPIs), metrics, and other important data points. Dashboards save time by presenting data in an easily digestible format, reducing the need for manual data analysis. They provide a clear and concise overview of important metrics, eliminating the clutter of raw data. Dashboards make data accessible to all stakeholders, regardless of their technical expertise. Interactive dashboards engage users, encouraging them to explore the data and uncover insights.

Key uses of dashboards are as follows:

1. **Real-time Data Monitoring:** Dashboards provide real-time updates, ensuring users have the most current information at their fingertips.
2. **Decision Making:** By presenting data visually, dashboards help users make informed decisions quickly.
3. **Performance Tracking:** They allow users to track the performance of different aspects of a business or project.
4. **Data Consolidation:** Dashboards bring together data from multiple sources, providing a comprehensive view of information.
5. **Trend Analysis:** Users can identify trends and patterns over time, aiding in forecasting and strategic planning.

Some of rules of thumb for creating effective dashboards are as follows:

1. **Define Clear Objectives:** Understand what the dashboard needs to achieve and who the audience is.
2. **Keep it Simple:** Avoid clutter by focusing on the most important metrics and using a clean design.
3. **Use Appropriate Visualizations:** Choose the right type of chart or graph for the data being presented. Use the guidelines given in Chapter 6 and 7 to design effective visualizations that help the users perform their tasks.
4. **Ensure Readability:** Use clear labels, legible fonts, and a logical layout.
5. **Make it Interactive:** Allow users to filter data, drill down into details, and customize their view.
6. **Regularly Update Data:** Ensure the dashboard reflects the most current information.
7. **Test and Iterate:** Gather feedback from users and make improvements as necessary.

21.4.1 Example Use Case: Sales Performance Dashboard

Let's illustrate these principles with a Sales Performance Dashboard example. We first decide on the important metrics and design the components of our dashboard.

21.4.2 Components of the Sales Performance Dashboard

1. **Overall Sales Summary Panel:**
   - **Metric:** Total Sales
   - **Visualization:** Large numeric display with comparison to the previous period
   - **Purpose:** Provides a quick snapshot of overall sales performance
2. **Sales by Region Panel:**
   - **Metric:** Sales broken down by geographic regions
   - **Visualization:** Choropleth map or bar chart
   - **Purpose:** Identifies regions with strong or weak sales performance
3. **Sales Trends Panel:**
   - **Metric:** Monthly or quarterly sales trends
   - **Visualization:** Line chart
   - **Purpose:** Shows sales performance over time and highlights trends
4. **Top Products Panel:**
   - **Metric:** Best-selling products
   - **Visualization:** Bar chart or pie chart
   - **Purpose:** Identifies which products are driving sales
5. **Sales by Channel Panel:**
   - **Metric:** Sales through different channels (e.g., online, in-store)
   - **Visualization:** Stacked bar chart
   - **Purpose:** Compares sales performance across different sales channels
6. **Customer Demographics Panel:**
   - **Metric:** Sales by customer demographics (age, gender, etc.)
   - **Visualization:** Pie chart or bar chart
   - **Purpose:** Understands the customer base and tailors marketi

Here is a visual representation of the Sales Performance Dashboard:

1. **Overall Sales Summary Panel:** Displays the total sales in a prominent and easy-to-read format.
2. **Sales by Region Panel:** Shows sales distribution across different regions using a bar chart.
3. **Sales Trends Panel:** Illustrates sales trends over several months with a line chart.
4. **Top Products Panel:** Highlights the top-selling products with a horizontal bar chart.
5. **Sales by Channel Panel:** Compares sales performance across online and in-store channels using a bar chart.
6. **Customer Demographics Panel:** Represents the sales distribution among different customer age groups with a pie chart.

This dashboard consolidates various aspects of sales performance, providing a comprehensive and clear overview for decision-makers.

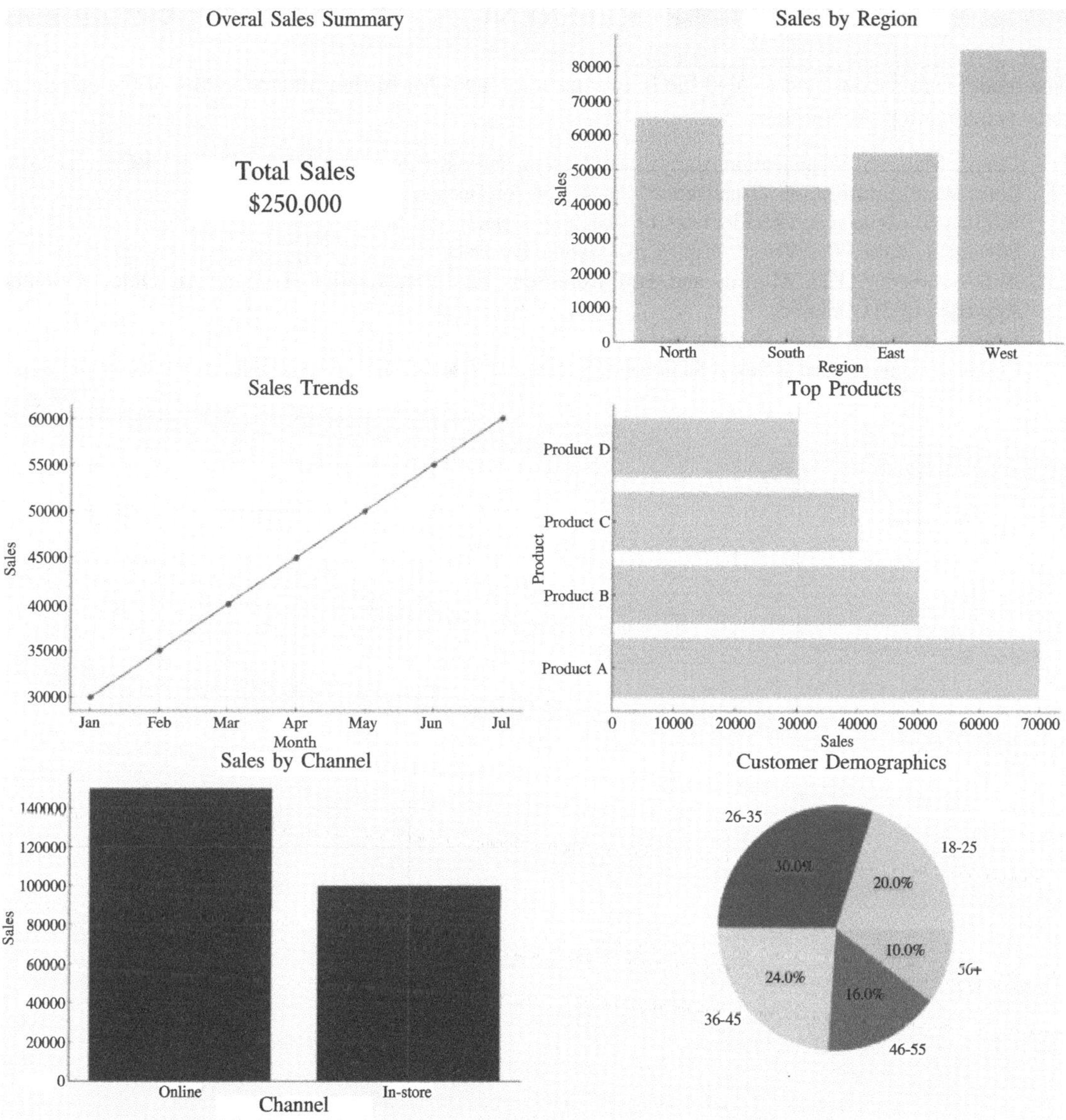

FIGURE 21.11 Sales Performance Dashboard (*See colour figure at the end of the book*).

21.5 CONCLUSION

In this chapter, we have studied various advanced techniques for visualization of complex datasets. As discussed in the book, data analysis is an iterative process and data visualization is essential to guide, interpret and disseminate the insights gained by data analysis.

REFERENCES

The readers are encouraged to read the following references for further understanding of the advanced data visualization techniques.

[1] Tamara Munzner, Visualization Analysis and Design, and AK Peters Visualization Series, CRC Press, 2014.
[2] Colin Ware, Information Visualization: Perception for Design.
[3] William S. Cleveland, The Elements of Graphing Data.
[4] Edward R. Tufte, The Visual Display of Quantitative Data.
[5] Will Schroeder, Ken Martin, and Bill Lorensen, The Visualization Toolkit: An Object-Oriented Approach to 3D Graphics.
[6] Edward R. Tufte, Visual Explanations.
[7] Christian Tominski and Heidrun Schumann, Interactive Visual Data Analysis, and AK Peters Visualization Series, CRC Press.

Index

I found this book to be very interesting and comprehensive. It covers both practical and theoretical aspects very well. It has several topics that one would not find in standard ML books, for example, data visualization and data streaming. Book also provides real life case studies which students will find quite useful.

Ashutosh Modi
Associate Professor
Department of Computer Science and Engineering
Indian Institute of Technology Kanpur (IITK)

Gagan is that rare teacher who understands what to teach and how to teach it. The book reflects his approach to knowledge, strong theoretical grounding but lucid commentary on how to put it to practice. This book is a must have for students looking to build a comprehensive understanding of Data Analytics and Visualization.

Prof Brejesh Lall
Former Head, Bharti School of
Telecommunication Technology and Management
Department of Electrical Engineering
Indian Institute of Technology Delhi (IITD)

Thank you for your good message with pages from your forthcoming new textbook. It is very good to see linear algebra as the foundation for data science (an important new topic). Best wishes for success!

Gilbert Strang
Professor Emeritus of Mathematics,
Massachusetts Institute of Technology (MIT)
Cambridge, USA

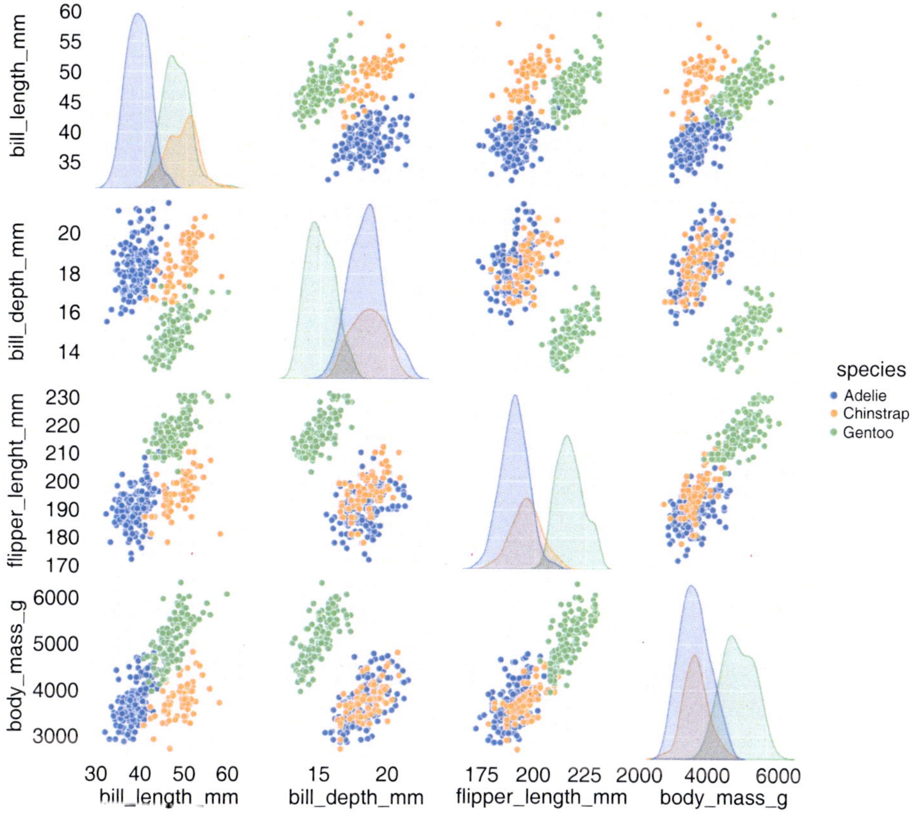

FIGURE 2.13 Pairplot of Penguin Dataset".

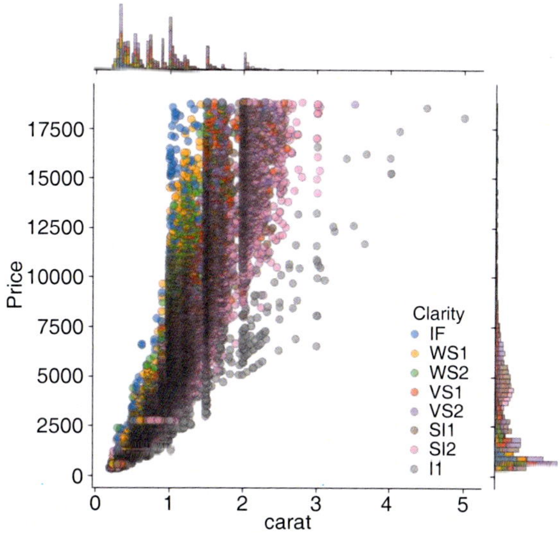

FIGURE 7.17 Scatter Plot of Diamond Price.

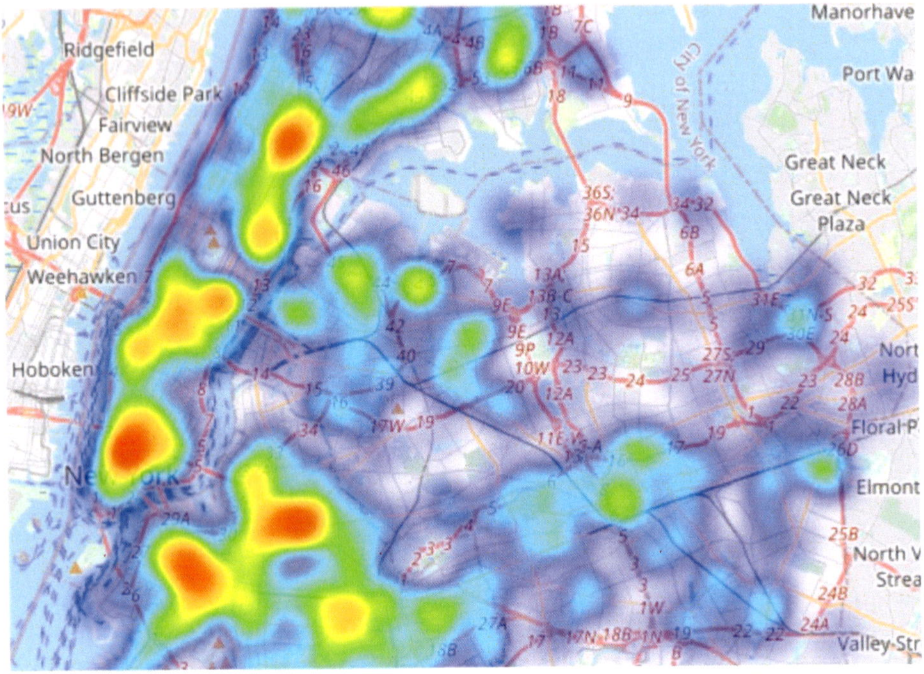

FIGURE 7.19 An example of Cartography showing information of fatal car accidents in New York City area.

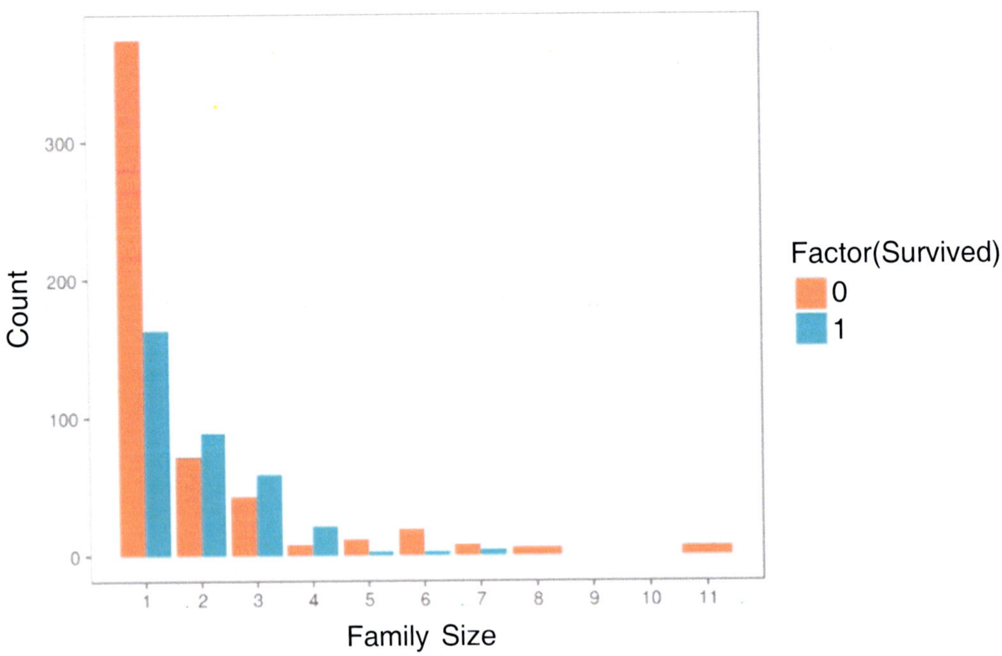

FIGURE 15.1 Bar plot showing how family size impacts survival.

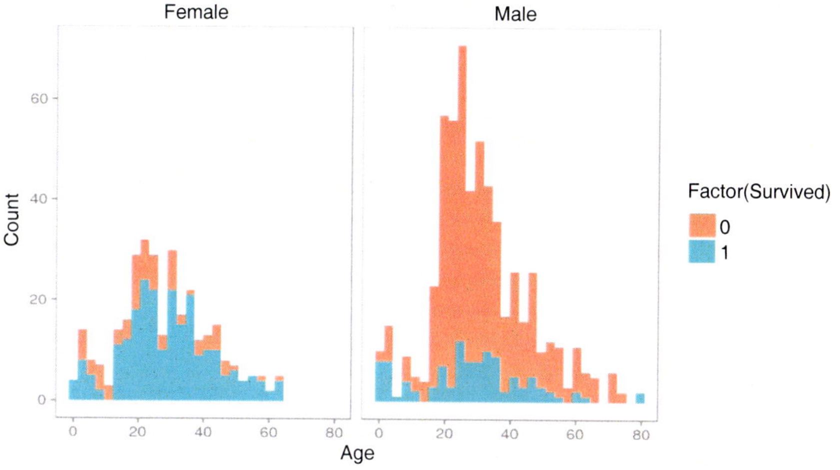

FIGURE 15.2 Titanic Survival by Gender and Age.

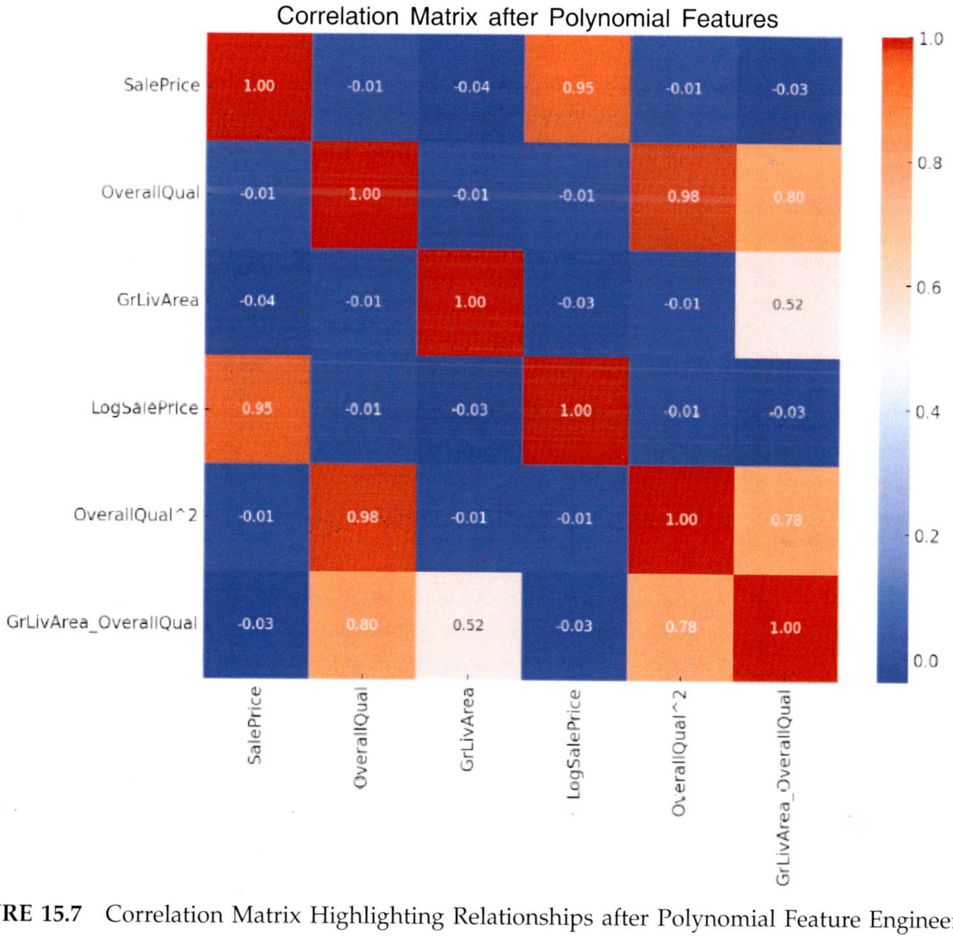

FIGURE 15.7 Correlation Matrix Highlighting Relationships after Polynomial Feature Engineering.

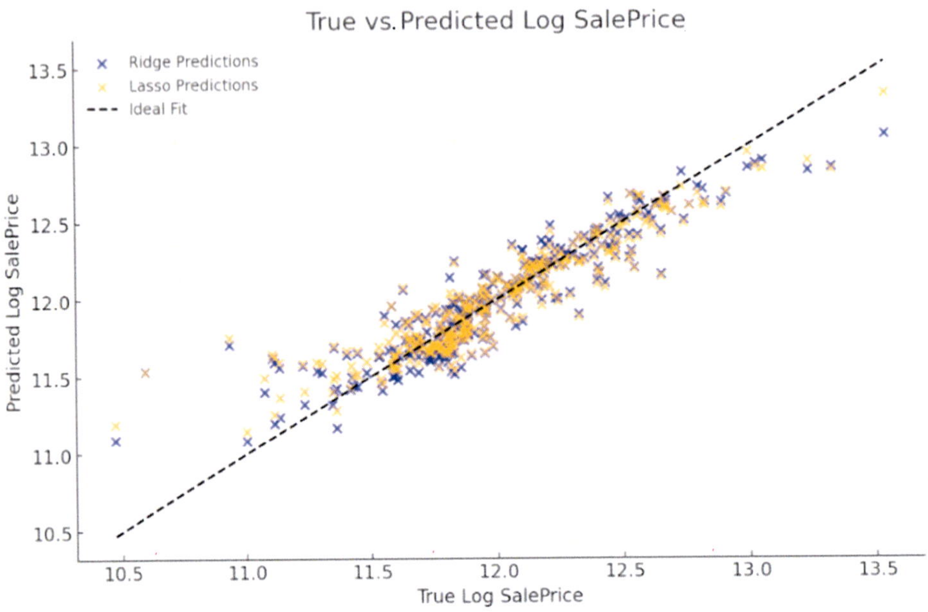

FIGURE 15.14 Actual vs Predicted Log Sale Price.

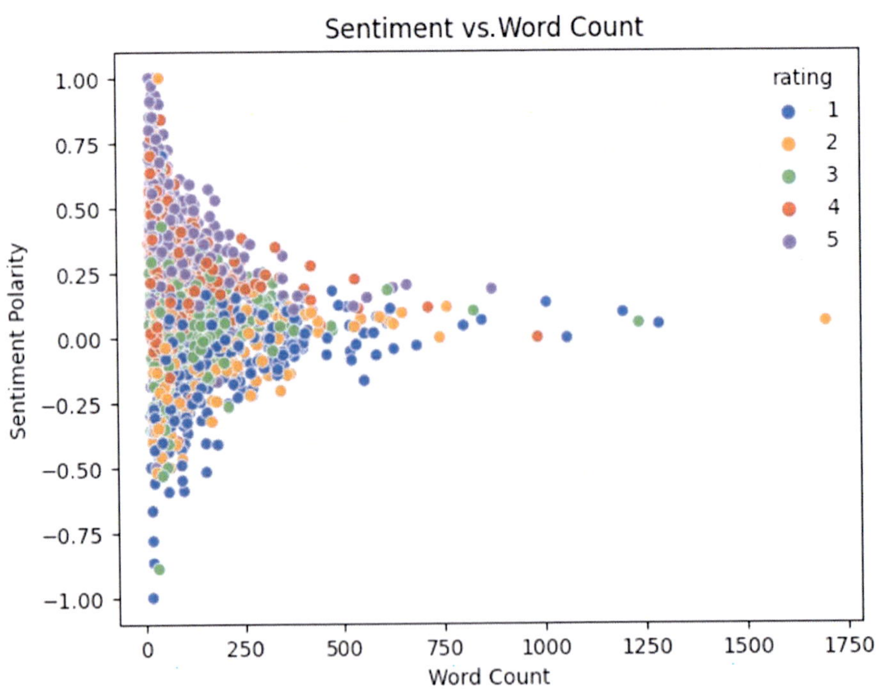

FIGURE 15.20 Sentiment Polarity vs Word Count in Airlines Dataset.

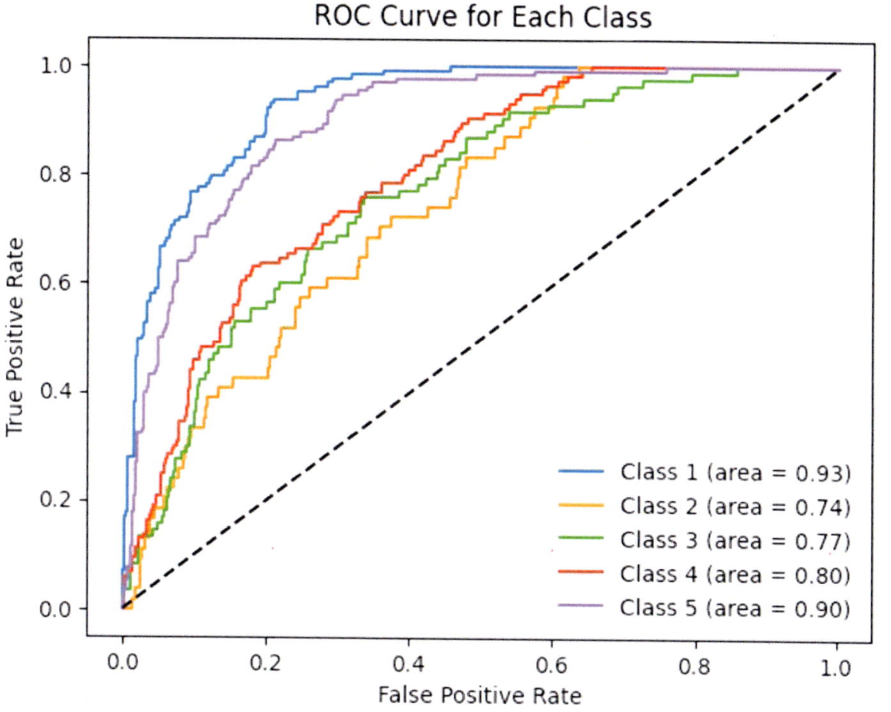

FIGURE 15.23 ROC Curve for Each Class.

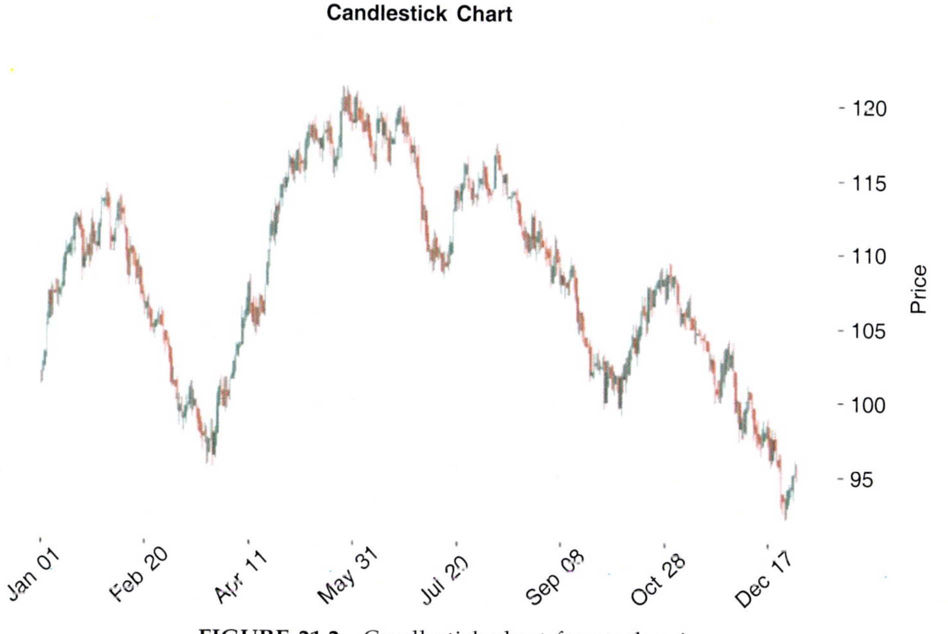

FIGURE 21.2 Candlestick chart for stock price.

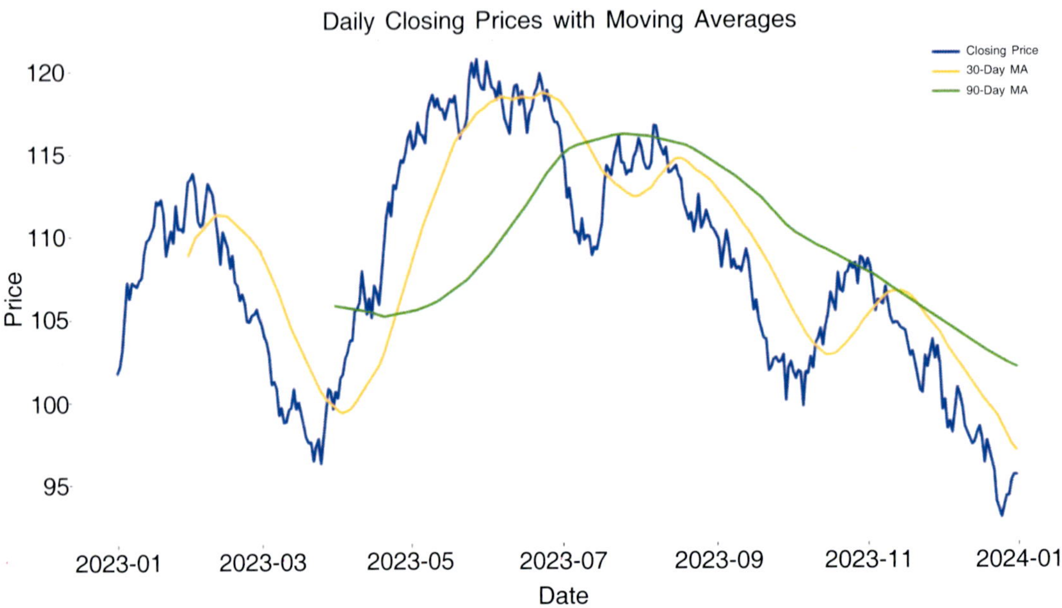

FIGURE 21.3 Moving Average chart for stock price.

FIGURE 21.8 Tree Map representation of profit-loss in stocks in stock market.

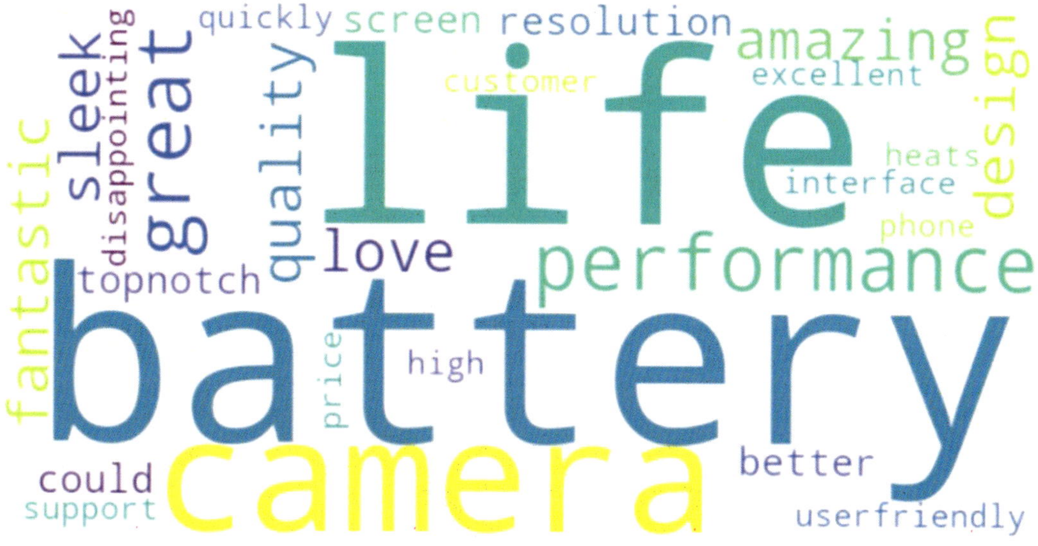

FIGURE 21.9 Word Cloud Visualization generated from the sample customer reviews.

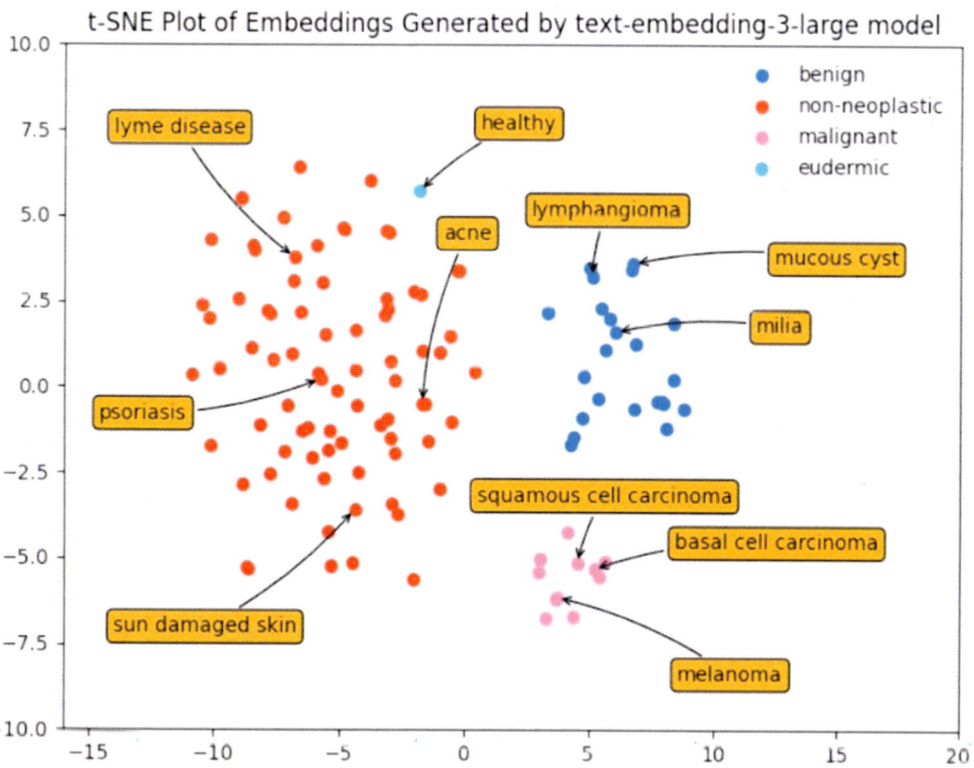

FIGURE 21.10 t-SNE plot of embeddings to showcase clustering of different skin conditions showing the relationships amongst them.

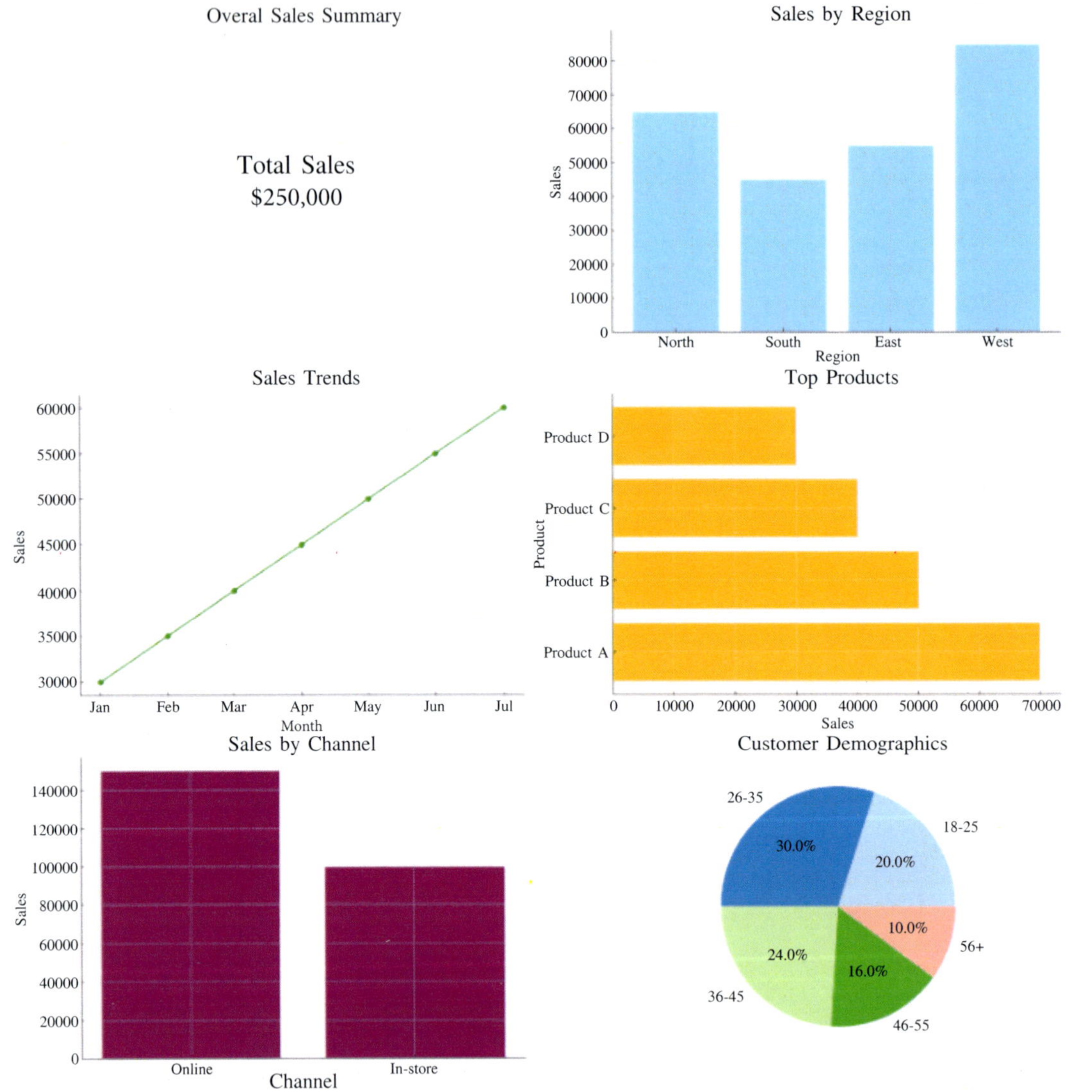

FIGURE 21.11 Sales Performance Dashboard.